lonely planet

Kenya

Northern
Kenya
p270

Masai Mara &
Western Kenya
p110

Central Highlands
& Laikipia
p148

Southern
Rift
Valley
p87

Nairobi
p54

Lamu &
the North Coast
p238

Southeastern
Kenya
p183

Mombasa & the
South Coast
p204

Anthony Ham,
Shawn Duthie, Anna Kaminski

Contents

PLAN YOUR TRIP

Welcome to Kenya 4
Kenya Map 6
Kenya's Top 18 8
Need to Know 18
If You Like 20
Month by Month 24
Itineraries 26
Safaris 31
Outdoor Activities 40
Travel with Children 46
Regions at a Glance 50

ALEKSANDAR TODOROVIC / SHUTTERSTOCK ©

NAIROBI P54

SARO17 / GETTY IMAGES ©

HELL'S GATE NATIONAL PARK P97

ON THE ROAD

NAIROBI 54
Ngong Hills 86

SOUTHERN RIFT VALLEY 87
Lake Magadi & Around 89
Longonot National Park 89
Naivasha 90
Lake Naivasha 92
Hell's Gate National Park 97
Lake Elmenteita & Around 98
Nakuru 100
Lake Nakuru National Park 102
Njoro 105
Lake Bogoria 107
Lake Baringo 108

MASAI MARA & WESTERN KENYA . . . 110
Narok 112
Masai Mara National Reserve 112
Maji Moto Group Ranch 120
Mara North Conservancy 121
Naboisho Conservancy 123
Olare-Orok Conservancy 124
Olderikesi Conservancy 125
Siana & the Southeastern Conservancies 126
Lake Victoria 127
Kisumu 127
Homa Bay 130
Ruma National Park 131

Mbita & Rusinga Island 132
Mfangano Island 133
Western Highlands 134
Kisii 134
Kericho 135
Kakamega 137
Kakamega Forest 137
Eldoret 140
Kitale 142
Mt Elgon National Park 144
Saiwa Swamp National Park 147

CENTRAL HIGHLANDS & LAIKIPIA 148
Aberdares 150
Nyeri 150
Aberdare National Park 152
Laikipia 154
Solio Game Reserve 154
Nyahururu (Thomson's Falls) 155
Nanyuki 156
Segera Ranch 160
Ol Pejeta Conservancy 160
Lewa Wildlife Conservancy 162
Il Ngwesi Group Ranch 165
Borana Conservancy 165
Lekurruki Community Ranch 166
Mt Kenya National Park 166
Naro Moru 173
Meru 176
Meru National Park 177
Chogoria 179
Embu 180

Contents

Ol Donyo Sabuk
National Park 181

SOUTHEASTERN
KENYA 183

South of Nairobi 185
Namanga 185
Southeast to Tsavo ... 185
Amboseli
National Park 185
Around Amboseli 188
Chyulu Hills
National Park 189
Tsavo West
National Park 190
Mbulia Conservancy 196
Tsavo East
National Park 197
Tsavo Conservancy 199
Voi 200
Taita Hills
Wildlife Sanctuary 201
Lumo Community
Wildlife Sanctuary 202
Wundanyi 203

MOMBASA & THE
SOUTH COAST 204

Mombasa 206
Shimba Hills
National Reserve 219
Tiwi Beach 220
Diani Beach 221
Gazi & Chale Island 228
Funzi Island 228
Shimoni &
Wasini Island 229
Lunga Lunga 231
Nyali 231
Bamburi 234
Shanzu Beach 236
Mtwapa 236

LAMU & THE
NORTH COAST 238

Kilifi 240
Watamu 242
Arabuko Sokoke
Forest Reserve 247
Mida Creek 247
Gede Ruins 250
Malindi 250
Lamu Archipelago 255
Lamu Island 255
Manda Island 266
Paté Island 266
Kiwayu Island 268

NORTHERN
KENYA 270

Isiolo 271
Archer's Post 274
Samburu, Buffalo
Springs & Shaba
National Reserves 275
Samburu Area
Conservancies 278
Matthews Range 279
Marsabit 279
Marsabit
National Park 281
Moyale 282
Maralal 284
Lesiolo 286
Baragoi 286
South Horr 287
North to
Lake Turkana 288
Loyangalani 288
North Horr 290
Kalacha 290
Marich to Lodwar 291
Lodwar 292
Eliye Springs 293
Ferguson's Gulf 294

UNDERSTAND

Kenya Today 296
History 298
Tribes of Kenya 310
Daily Life 315
The Arts 317
Kenyan Cuisine 321
Environment 351
National Parks
& Reserves 362

SURVIVAL
GUIDE

Directory A–Z 368
Transport 382
Health 392
Language 397
Glossary 402
Index 406

SPECIAL
FEATURES

Safaris 31
Tribes of Kenya 310
Kenyan Cuisine 321
Wildlife & Habitat
colour section 327
National Parks
& Reserves 362

Welcome to Kenya

Vast savannahs peppered with immense herds of wildlife. Snow-capped equatorial mountains. Traditional peoples who bring soul and colour to the earth. Welcome to Kenya.

Stirring Landscapes

When you think of Africa, you're probably thinking of Kenya. It's the lone acacia silhouetted on the savannah against a horizon stretching into eternity. It's the snow-capped mountain almost on the equator and within sight of harsh deserts. It's the lush, palm-fringed coastline of the Indian Ocean, it's the Great Rift Valley that once threatened to tear the continent asunder, and it's the dense forests reminiscent of the continent's heart. In short, Kenya is a country of epic landforms that stir our deepest longings for this very special continent.

Proud Peoples

Filling the country's landscape, adding depth and resonance to Kenya's age-old story, are some of Africa's best-known peoples. The Maasai, the Samburu, the Turkana, the Swahili, the Kikuyu: these are the peoples whose histories and daily struggles tell the story of a country and of a continent – the struggle to maintain traditions as the modern world crowds in, the daily fight for survival in some of the harshest environments on earth, the ancient tension between those who farm and those who roam. Drawing near to these cultures could just be a highlight of your visit.

Abundant Wildlife

Kenya is the land of the Masai Mara, of wildebeest and zebras migrating in their millions with the great predators of Africa following in their wake, of endangered species like black rhinos managing to maintain their precarious foothold. But Kenya is also home to the red elephants of Tsavo, to Amboseli elephant families in the shadow of Mt Kilimanjaro and to the massed millions of pink flamingos stepping daintily through lake shallows. Africa is the last great wilderness where these creatures survive. And Kenya is the perfect place to answer Africa's call of the wild.

Conservation's Home

The abundance of Kenya's wildlife owes everything to one of Africa's most innovative and successful conservation communities. Through some pretty tough love – Kenya pioneered using armed rangers to protect rhinos and elephants – Kenya stopped the emptying of its wilderness and brought its wildlife back from the brink after the poaching holocaust of the 1970s and 1980s. More than that, in places like Laikipia and the Masai Mara, private and community conservancies fuse tourism with community development and wildlife conservation to impressive effect. In other words, if you want your visit to make a difference, you've come to the right place.

Why I Love Kenya

By Anthony Ham, Writer

Kenya is where my love affair with Africa truly took hold. Wildlife (especially big cats) and wilderness rank among my life's grand passions and it was here that I saw my first lion on the march (in Amboseli), my first cheetah on the hunt (Tsavo East), my first leopard on a kill (Tsavo West), and where I came so close to elephants (Taita Hills) and black rhinos (Lewa) that I could have reached out to touch them. This is the home of Maasai and Samburu friends who give me hope that the old ways can survive.

For more about our writers, see p416

Above: A young Maasai woman

Kenya

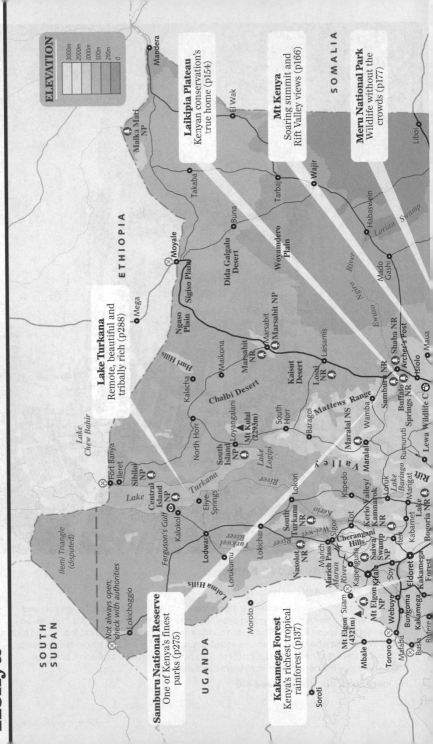

Lake Turkana
Remote, beautiful and tribally rich (p288)

Samburu National Reserve
One of Kenya's finest parks (p275)

Kakamega Forest
Kenya's richest tropical rainforest (p137)

Laikipia Plateau
Kenyan conservation's true home (p154)

Mt Kenya
Soaring summit and Rift Valley views (p166)

Meru National Park
Wildlife without the crowds (p177)

⊗ Not always open; check with authorities

ELEVATION

	3000m
	2000m
	1000m
	500m
	250m
	0

100 km
50 miles

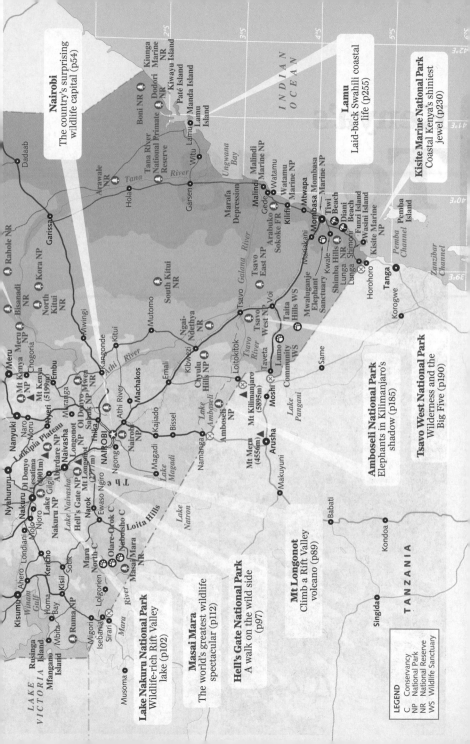

Nairobi
The country's surprising wildlife capital (p54)

Lamu
Laid-back Swahili coastal life (p255)

Kisite Marine National Park
Coastal Kenya's shiniest jewel (p230)

Lake Nakuru National Park
Wildlife-rich Rift Valley lake (p102)

Masai Mara
The world's greatest wildlife spectacular (p112)

Hell's Gate National Park
A walk on the wild side (p97)

Mt Longonot
Climb a Rift Valley volcano (p89)

Amboseli National Park
Elephants in Kilimanjaro's shadow (p185)

Tsavo West National Park
Wilderness and the Big Five (p190)

LEGEND
C   Conservancy
NP   National Park
NR   National Reserve
WS   Wildlife Sanctuary

Kenya's
Top 18

Wildlife Migration, Masai Mara

1 The Masai Mara (p112) is home to one of the highest concentrations of wildlife on the planet. Its rolling savannah studded with flat-top acacia trees is fantastic at any time but from July to October, the Mara's plains and rivers are flooded with wildebeest a million strong on their great migration, along with herds of zebras, elephants and giraffes. Trailing this walking buffet are lions, leopards, cheetahs, hyenas and crocs. If you only visit one place in Kenya, make it the Mara.

Elephants of Amboseli National Park

2 There's possibly no better place in the world to watch elephants than Amboseli National Park (p185) in the country's south. A big part of the appeal is the setting – Africa's highest mountain, the snow-capped Mt Kilimanjaro, is the backdrop for seemingly every picture you'll take here. Amboseli was spared the worst of Kenya's poaching crisis and these elephants are remarkably tolerant of humans (allowing you to get *really* close). And their tusks are among the biggest in Kenya. It's also an excellent place to see lions and cheetahs.

GAIL JOHNSON / SHUTTERSTOCK ©

KYSLYNSKYYHAL / SHUTTERSTOCK ©

NIGEL PAVITT / GETTY IMAGES ©

IHAB / GETTY IMAGES ©

Hiking Mt Kenya

3 Occupying the heart of the country and a special place in the hearts of the Kikuyu people, Mt Kenya (p166), the country's highest peak and the second highest on the continent, is not a mountain to be admired from afar. With four days, some determination and several layers of warm clothing, you could find yourself standing on the frozen summit of Point Lenana, mere minutes from the equator, but a whole world away from the other African experiences.

Lions at Tsavo National Park

4 Tsavo West National Park (p190) is a wilderness experience par excellence, a vast and dramatic landscape where wildlife lurks in the undergrowth. All of Africa's charismatic megafauna are present here, including rhinos, but it's the cats – leopards, lions and cheetahs – who bring this ecosystem to life. Against a backdrop of red soils, volcanic outcrops and sweeping savannah plains, these lions of legend (it was here that the legendary man-eaters of Tsavo once roamed) laze about in the shade, waiting for the right moment to pounce.

MICHELEB / SHUTTERSTOCK ©

TAMBAKO THE JAGUAR / GETTY IMAGES ©

Samburu National Reserve

5 Samburu (p275) does not enjoy the fame of other Kenyan parks, but that's just the way we like it. This stunning arid landscape of Kenya's soulful north is given life by the Ewaso Ngiro River, whose palm-fringed banks are as beautiful as any waterway in inland Kenya. Wildlife, too, is drawn to the river and its hinterland, the rugged terrain swarming with elephants, lions and leopards, but also some signature northern species, such as the blue-legged Somali ostrich and the endangered Grevy's zebra.

Mt Longonot

6 Mt Longonot (p89) not only has the near-perfect shape we imagine all volcanoes to have, it's also the most accessible of Kenya's Rift Valley climbs. Unlike the more famous Mt Kenya ascent, the climb to the crater rim is more of a strenuous 90-minute hike than a serious expedition; even the climb, circumnavigation and descent can be accomplished in four hours. The rewards are glorious Rift Valley views (including overlooking Hell's Gate National Park) and a bird's-eye view down to the lost forests of the crater floor.

MANOJ SHAH / GETTY IMAGES ©

VANESSA BURGER / AGE FOTOSTOCK ©

Laikipia Plateau

7 In the shadow of Mt Kenya, this plateau (p154) hosts a network of conservancies and private wildlife reserves – it's both beautiful and one of the most exciting stories in African conservation. At the forefront of efforts to save endangered species such as lions, African wild dogs, Grevy's zebras and black rhinos, the plateau's ranches offer an enticing combination of high-end lodge accommodation, big horizons and charismatic megafauna. Best of all, this is a more intimate experience than most national parks, with scarcely another vehicle in sight.
Top left: African wild dogs

Lake Turkana

8 Amid the deserts and horizonless tracts that characterise so much of Kenya's north, Lake Turkana glitters like a jade-and-turquoise mirage. Rising from its waters is Teleki, one of the world's most perfectly shaped volcanic cones, while the shores are dotted with dusty and utterly intriguing villages, such as Loyangalani (p288), that are home to the beguiling mix of traditional peoples – Turkana, Samburu, Gabbra, El-Molo – who call this isolated corner of Africa home. And there are crocodiles here. Lots of them.

Kakamega Forest

9 Paths lace the Kakamega Forest (p138) and offer a rare opportunity to ditch the safari 4WD and stretch your legs. This ancient forest is home to an astounding 330 bird species, 400 butterfly species and seven different primate species. Like all rainforests, though, the trees themselves are the chief attraction here, and in the forest gloom you'll stumble upon the botanical equivalent of beauty and the beast: delicate orchids and parasitic figs that strangle their hosts as they climb towards the light. Above: Great Blue Turaco

NIGEL PAVITT / GETTY IMAGES ©

JAVARMAN / SHUTTERSTOCK ©

Wandering the Streets of Lamu

10 Lamu (p255) is surely the most evocative destination on the Kenyan coast. With no cars around, the best way to get to know this graceful town is by wandering its backstreets, admiring the grand old Swahili doors, peeking into hidden courtyards bursting with unexpected colours, slipping into an easy chair and sipping on a fruit juice, and accepting all invitations to stop and shoot the breeze. Do all this and the backstreets of Lamu will become a place you'll dream of forever.

Lake Nakuru National Park

11 This world-class national park (p102) with strong echoes of *Out of Africa* is dominated by one of the Rift Valley's most beautiful lakes. The waters are lined on one side by an abrupt escarpment and the shoreline is at times given colour and texture by massed birdlife. But Lake Nakuru is also a wildlife haven for landborne mammals, home as it is to tree-climbing lions, leopards, the highly endangered Rothschild's giraffes, zebras, buffaloes, various primate species and some of Kenya's most easily spotted rhinos.

Kisite Marine National Park

12 Hiding away like a secret jewel is the laid-back isle of Wasini, close to the border of Tanzania. You can sail to it from Diani Beach or Shimoni like an Omani sultan in a magnificent dhow, and dive overboard to snorkel with fish big and small in the stunning Kisite Marine National Park (p230), which fringes the island. Or you can come under your own steam and walk the footpaths to the near-forgotten village of Mkwiro – the perfect spot to be engulfed by Swahili culture.

INGOLF POMPE / AGE FOTOSTOCK ©

12

Hell's Gate National Park

13 It's one thing to watch Africa's megafauna from the safety of your vehicle and quite another to do so on foot or on a bicycle. Hell's Gate National Park (p97) – a dramatic volcanic landscape of red cliffs, otherworldly rocky outcrops and deep canyons in Kenya's Rift Valley – may lack predators, but experiencing the African wild at close quarters certainly gives most people frisson. The landscape of Hell's Gate heightens the senses, bringing alive the African wild like no other national park in Kenya.

TONI TEJON / SHUTTERSTOCK ©

13

Nairobi National Park

14 No other city in the world can boast a national park (home to four of the Big Five) within sight of city sky-scrapers. The park (p61) may have its detractions – one of Africa's smallest parks, it's almost completely encircled by human settlements – but this is an important refuge for the endangered black rhino (more than 50), all three big cats and abundant birdlife. There's also an elephant orphanage, a nearby breeding centre for the Rothschild's giraffe, great restaurants and numerous opportunities to forget you're in Nairobi at all.

Mt Elgon National Park

15 Far enough from well-trammelled tourist trails to feel like an adventure. Mt Elgon (p144), with its five summits ranging from 4161m to 4321m, encompasses an astonishing range of landscapes. Hiking trails climb through rainforest to bamboo jungles before traversing alpine moorland with all its weird-and-wonderful flora. Rich birdlife, the odd primate species (black-and-white colobus and blue and de Brazza's monkeys), the opportunity to look out over two countries and the chance to climb without a guide are other selling points.

ITHITMHA / SHUTTERSTOCK ©

BYELIKOVA OKSANA / SHUTTERSTOCK ©

Aberdares

16 Rising up from the eastern edge of the Rift Valley like the spine of central Kenya, the verdant Aberdares (p150) don't feel like Kenya at all. Yes, there's wildlife, and some of it's pretty unusual, from high-altitude elephants and rhinos to rare mountain bongos and black leopards. But this is a place of sprawling farms, dense forests and walking trails that pass among flora that has no right residing this close to the equator. For mountain trekking, it's a fine alternative to the busier trails of nearby Mt Kenya. Above: Chania Falls

Watamu

17 Kenya's Indian Ocean coast is one of Africa's prettiest shores and Watamu (p242) is one of its prettiest beaches. Sitting roughly halfway between Mombasa and Lamu, it's a fine base for exploring the Kenyan coast with its long stretches of white sand, translucent waters and coves sheltered by palm trees. Plenty of water sports (from fishing to windsurfing), traces of the coast's African heritage and a healthy dose of *hakuna matata* add up to one of those places you'll never want to leave.

Meru National Park

18 One of Kenya's most underrated parks, Meru (p177) is a beguiling mix of iconic African landscapes (fertile hills, river forests, baobabs and doum palms) and a fine range of fauna (including black and white rhinos, elephants, lions and zebras). Meru is also where the lion legends of George Adamson's *Born Free* came into being. But above all else, Meru is the safari as it used to be, with unusually quiet trails and the thrill of stumbling upon wildlife when you least expect it. Above: Crowned crane

Need to Know

For more information, see Survival Guide (p367)

Currency
Kenyan shilling (KSh)

Language
English and Swahili; other tribal languages also spoken

Visas
Visas, needed by most foreign nationals, are straightforward. An e-visa scheme (www.evisa.go.ke) is the simplest way to apply, pay and receive a visa almost instantly.

Money
All banks change US dollars, euros and UK pounds into Kenyan shillings. ATMs found in medium-sized towns, so bring cash and debit or credit card.

Mobile Phones
Buy a SIM card from one of the Kenyan mobile-phone companies: Safaricom (www.safaricom.co.ke), Airtel (www.africa.airtel.com/kenya) or Telkom (www.telkom.co.ke). SIM cards cost about KSh100.

Time
East Africa Time (GMT/UTC plus three hours).

When to Go

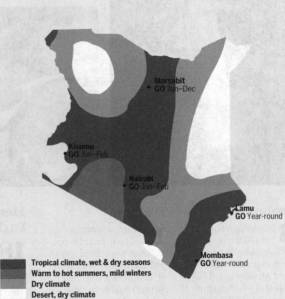

Marsabit
GO Jun–Dec

Kisumu
GO Jun–Feb

Nairobi
GO Jun–Feb

Lamu
GO Year-round

Mombasa
GO Year-round

Tropical climate, wet & dry seasons
Warm to hot summers, mild winters
Dry climate
Desert, dry climate

High Season
(Jun–Oct, Jan & Feb)

➡ Wildebeest in the Mara usually from mid-July to October.

➡ January and February offer hot, dry weather good for wildlife watching.

➡ Sky-high lodge prices, especially July to October.

Shoulder
(Nov & Dec)

➡ Short rains fall in October and November, but still an excellent time to visit.

➡ Prices drop from November, but advance reservations still a good idea.

➡ Excellent time for birdwatching as migrant species arrive.

Low Season
(Mar–May)

➡ Long rains mean accommodation is much quieter and prices can be a bargain.

➡ Wildlife is harder to spot and more dispersed, but fewer vehicles.

➡ Some tracks are impassable and mosquitoes are rife.

Useful Websites

Lonely Planet (www.lonely planet.com/kenya) Destination information, hotel bookings, traveller forum and more.

Kenya Wildlife Service (www. kws.org) News and information on national parks and reserves.

Safari Bookings (www. safaribookings.com) Invaluable resource for choosing safari operators and destinations.

Kenya Association of Tour Operators (www.katokenya. org) Full list of KATO-approved member companies.

Eco Tourism Kenya (www. ecotourismkenya.org) Excellent resource for gauging the sustainability of Kenyan tourism.

Important Numbers

Regional area codes must be dialled in full, followed by the number, if calling from within Kenya; the code '0' is dropped if calling from overseas.

International access code	☏000
Kenya's country code	☏254
Directory enquiries	☏991
Police, ambulance & fire	☏999
Tourist helpline (24 hours)	☏020-604767

Exchange Rates

Australia	A$1	KSh83
Canada	C$1	KSh83
Europe	€1	KSh127
Japan	¥100	KSh94
New Zealand	NZ$1	KSh75
UK	UK£1	KSh145
US	US$1	KSh103

For current exchange rates, see www.xe.com.

Daily Costs

Budget: Less than US$100

➡ Hostel or budget hotel: US$15–50

➡ Camping: from US$20

➡ Eat in local restaurants: US$2–5

➡ Travel by matatu (minibus): US$1–5

➡ Share wildlife drives with other travellers: US$20–40

Midrange: US$100–250

➡ Double room in midrange hotel: US$75–150

➡ Independent safari with car rental (two people): US$75–100 per day

➡ Full board in lodges: US$150–250

Top end: More than US$250

➡ Double room in top-end hotel: from US$200

➡ lunch and dinner in top-end restaurant: US$30–40

➡ No-expenses-spared safari in luxury tented camps: from US$600

Opening Hours

Hours vary throughout the year, particularly in tourist areas, less so in larger cities. We've provided high-season opening hours.

Banks 9am–3pm or 4pm Monday to Friday, 9am–noon Saturday

Post offices 8.30am–5pm Monday to Friday, 9am–noon Saturday

Restaurants 11.30am–2pm or 3pm and 5pm or 6pm–9pm

Shops 9am–5pm Monday to Friday, 9am–noon Saturday; some open later and open on Sundays

Supermarkets 8.30am–8.30pm Monday to Saturday, 10am–8pm Saturday

Arriving in Kenya

Jomo Kenyatta International Airport (Nairobi) Taxis cost KSh1800 to KSh3000. They take 30 minutes to one hour to the city centre, depending on traffic; book at the 'information' desk in the arrivals hall. There's a danger of theft on city bus 34 (one way KSh40) so it's best avoided. Taxis are the only option at night.

Wilson Airport (Nairobi) Take bus or matatu 15, 31, 34, 125 or 126 from Moi Ave (KSh50, 15 to 45 minutes depending on traffic). A taxi from the city centre will cost at least KSh1200.

Moi International Airport (Mombasa) There is no public transport. Taxis cost around KSh1500 and take 20 to 30 minutes into the city.

Getting Around

Getting around Kenya is relatively easy. Unless you're travelling on an organised safari, in which case your transport will be taken care of, there's a mix of bus, train, matatu and flights to choose from.

For much more on **getting around**, see p382

If You Like...

Big Cats

The sight of prowling predators is guaranteed to produce a frisson of excitement, and it's the big cats – lions, leopards and cheetahs – that most visitors come to see.

Masai Mara National Reserve The best place to spot all three cats, often on a kill from July to October. (p112)

Naboisho & Olare-Orok Conservancies Fabulous Mara conservancies with high big-cat densities. (p123)

Tsavo East National Park A good spot for relatively easy sightings of lions and cheetahs. (p197)

Amboseli National Park Good for lions and cheetahs in the dry season (May to October and January to March). (p185)

Ol Pejeta Conservancy Go lion-tracking after dark. (p160)

Lewa Wildlife Conservancy Good for all three big cats without the crowds. (p162)

Meru National Park Lions regularly sighted. (p177)

Lake Nakuru National Park Resident leopards and lions. (p102)

Nairobi National Park All three present within sight of the capital. (p61)

Elephants & Rhinos

The African elephant and the rhinoceros (black and white) are enduring icons of a continent. Both are in peril, but both are also relatively easy to track down in Kenya.

Lewa Wildlife Conservancy Get up close and personal with elephants and more than 100 rhinos. (p162)

Tsavo West National Park An important sanctuary for black rhinos; also 'red' elephants. (p190)

Aberdare National Park Elephants and black rhinos on the Central Highlands' forested slopes. (p152)

Ol Pejeta Conservancy East Africa's largest population of the endangered black rhino. (p160)

Lake Nakuru National Park One of the best places in Kenya to see the highly endangered black rhino. (p102)

Nairobi National Park Rhinos in abundance with skyscrapers nearby. (p61)

Amboseli National Park As close as you'll ever get to a big-tusked elephant with Mt Kilimanjaro in the background. (p185)

Samburu National Reserve Elephants set against one of Kenya's most beautiful regions. (p275)

Tsavo East National Park Kenya's largest elephant population of over 11,000 elephants. (p197)

Marsabit National Park Kenya's northernmost elephants. (p281)

Birdwatching

Kenya is one of Africa's premier destinations for bird watchers, with around 1100 bird species recorded. Northern migrant species escaping Europe's winter begin arriving to the country in November.

Lake Nakuru National Park Flamingos (maybe), pelicans and 400 other species. (p102)

Amboseli National Park Over 370 bird species, including raptors and the grey-crowned crane. (p185)

Lake Bogoria National Reserve A flamingo spectacular when conditions are right, with internationally recognised wetlands. (p107)

Kakamega Forest Reserve Rainforest habitat and over 330 recorded species. (p138)

Tsavo West National Park The Ngulia Hills are an important flyway for migratory species. (p190)

NIGEL PAVITT / GETTY IMAGES ©

Saiwa Swamp National Park Over 370 bird species in just over 15 sq km. (p147)

Arabuko Sokoke Forest Reserve Prolific birdlife in a wonderful stand of indigenous forest. (p247)

Lake Baringo Over one-third of Kenya's species have been recorded here. (p108)

Hiking

They may not let you get out of your vehicle in national parks, but Kenya is a fabulous hiking destination whether you're keen to climb a mountain or stay within sight of your lodge.

Mt Kenya Climb Africa's second-highest mountain and gaze out upon Kenya in all its glory. (p166)

Mt Elgon Uncrowded trails lead to the top of this stirring mountain on the cusp of Uganda. (p144)

Mt Longonot Accessible Rift Valley volcano with views down into the crater's lost world. (p89)

Hell's Gate National Park One of few national parks where you're encouraged to explore on foot. (p97)

Aberdare National Park Unusual alpine flora and fauna and quiet walking trails. (p152)

Mbulia Conservancy Hike through thick woodland to viewpoints out over the immensity of Tsavo. (p196)

Matthews Range Trek these spectacular highlands in the heart of Samburu country. (p279)

Loita Hills Hike across the remote south like a Maasai. (p121)

Top: Hiking towards Mt Kenya (p166)

Bottom: Rhino at Lewa Wildlife Conservancy (p162)

Beaches

Kenya's coastline is utterly gorgeous. It is home to some heaving resorts but also to many more quiet and idyllic beaches – the places you'll always remember as your own slice of paradise.

Shela Beach With 12km of white sand and one of Lamu's most beautiful beaches. (p263)

Watamu Enjoy 7km of unspoiled beach with a lovely fishing village nearby. (p244)

Manda Island The land time forgot, with sand dunes, mangroves and quiet beaches. (p266)

Tiwi Beach The alter ego to Diani Beach and its equal in beauty. (p220)

Diani Beach A crowded but still stunning beach. (p221)

Dhow Trips

Travelling the East African coast in a dhow (ancient Arab sailing vessel) carries echoes of ancient civilisations and trade winds past from the days of the spice trade. Their slow rhythm is perfectly suited to this tropical coast.

Mkwiro There's no other way to reach this quieter-than-quiet village. (p230)

Matondoni Watch dhows being built, then take to the water and sail around the Lamu archipelago for a day. (p265)

Lamu Find yourself a good captain and sail between Lamu and Manda Island for the day. (p256)

Takwa The pick of the Lamu archipelago trips. (p266)

Diving & Snorkelling

Reefs proliferate all along Kenya's coastline and the diving and snorkelling here rank among the best in East Africa. There are top-notch dive schools, or snorkel off the back of a dhow.

Malindi Marine National Park Excellent diving from July to February. (p250)

Manda Toto Island The snorkelling here is highly favoured among devotees of the Lamu archipelago. (p266)

Kisite Marine National Park Snorkel with the dolphins, with diving also possible. (p230)

Watamu Marine National Park Fabulous reefs, fish and sea turtles. (p243)

Diani Beach Professional dive schools and even a purpose-sunk shipwreck. (p221)

Luxury Lodges & Tented Camps

Kenya does luxury extremely well, and nothing quite beats the experience of returning from a day's safari to be pampered with luxury accommodation, spa and massage packages and impeccable standards of personal service.

Ol Donyo, **Around Amboseli** The sort of lodge and location that safari dreams are made of. (p188)

Segera Retreat, **Segera Ranch, Laikipia** Peerless cottages that take you back to *Out of Africa*. (p160)

Giraffe Manor, **Nairobi** Top-end luxury wedded to world-class service, and a Rothschild's giraffe looking in your window. (p72)

Sasaab Lodge, **Samburu** Northern Kenya's finest with river views near Samburu National Reserve. (p279)

Cottar's 1920s Camp, **Masai Mara** Safari nostalgia in overdrive with peerless levels of comfort. (p126)

Campi ya Kanzi, **Around Amboseli** Supremely comfortable tents, gorgeous setting and Kili views. (p188)

Finch Hatton's Safari Camp, **Tsavo West National Park** Dress for dinner and eat from bone china deep in the African wilds. (p195)

Mara Plains, **Masai Mara** Palatial tents with details no-one else has thought of. (p125)

Asilia Naboisho Camp, **Naboisho Conservancy** One of the best camps for big cats and guided walks in the Mara. (p124)

Elsa's Kopje, **Meru National Park** Stunning lodge and a real sense of oneness with the African wilderness. (p179)

Escaping the Crowds

The wildebeest migration is not the only mass migration in Kenya from July to October – visitors also arrive in the millions. Avoiding them is easier than you think.

Meru National Park A match for the more famous parks of Kenya's south, but without the crowds. (p177)

Shompole Conservancy One of Kenya's more remote tented camp experiences with good wildlife encounters and a chance to get to know the Maasai. (p90)

Sasaab Lodge (p279), Samburu

Segera Ranch One of Laikipia's premier properties with excellent wildlife viewing for an elite few. (p160)

Il Ngwesi Group Ranch Immerse yourself in the Maasai wilderness close to Lewa and Laikipia. (p165)

Ruma National Park You'll have wild Africa all to yourself, with rhinos and fascinating antelope species. (p131)

Loyangalani The essence of remote northern Kenya, with fascinating cultures and Lake Turkana. (p288)

Paté Island Leave the modern world behind on this enchanted island in the Lamu archipelago. (p266)

Olare-Orok Conservancy The Mara's high concentrations of predators, but just one tent for every 280 hectares. (p124)

Mfangano Island Blissfully quiet Lake Victoria islands with rock paintings. (p133)

Culture & Wildlife Immersion

Community-run projects now run hand in hand with conservation and can offer travellers opportunities that will live long in the memory.

Lewa Wildlife Conservancy Visit local schools and Maasai communities as part of the new conservation model. (p162)

Ewangan Catch a glimpse of Maasai life on relatively equal terms with the Masai Mara just outside your *manyatta*. (p119)

Campi ya Kanzi Explore Maasailand with the Maasai,

then visit a Maasai village. (p188)

Saruni Mara Experience local Maasai communities with market visits and other encounters in Mara North. (p121)

The Maa Trust Watch the Maasai benefit from the conservancy model in the Mara. (p126)

Kibera Explore a Nairobi shanty town with all its complications and dynamism. (p74)

Ol Pejeta Conservancy Track lions, pat a blind rhino and draw near to critically endangered wildlife. (p160)

David Sheldrick Wildlife Trust Encounter orphaned elephants en route to freedom. (p63)

Month by Month

January

A popular months for visiting. Animals congregate around waterholes and bird migration is underway. Days are warm and dry.

◉ Birds in Abundance

Migratory bird species have arrived in their millions, giving Kenya close to its full complement of more than 1100 bird species. Rift Valley lakes and other wetlands are a birdwatcher's paradise.

◉ Dry-season Gatherings

It can depend on the October/November rains, but perennial water sources have dried up, drawing predators and prey to the last remaining waterholes.

Wildlife watching at this time can be tense, exhilarating and very rewarding.

February

High season in Kenya. Days are hot and dry, accommodation is often full, there's excellent wildlife watching around waterholes and countless bird species on show.

March

In most years, Kenya's big annual rains begin, flooding much of the country and making wildlife viewing difficult. But prices are rock-bottom and the rains aren't always reliable.

🏃 Late-rains Safari

The cheapest time to visit Kenya – roads can be impassable, mosquitoes are everywhere and wildlife disperses. But if the rains are late, conditions couldn't be better, with wildlife desperate for a drink and most birds still around.

April

The inundation continues to batter Kenya if the rains arrive as they're supposed to. Getting around (and spotting wildlife) is difficult. Unless the rains have failed entirely, avoid visiting now. Easter can be a minipeak.

May

The rains usually continue into May. By late May, they should have subsided; when they stop and you can see the horizon, the country is wonderfully green, although wildlife can still be tough to spot.

June

Kenya emerges from the rains somewhat sodden but ready to make up for lost time. The annual migration of wildebeest and zebra in their millions sometimes begins midmonth, but doesn't really take hold until July.

🎎 Lake Turkana Cultural Festival

One of the country's biggest cultural events, this fascinating festival focuses on the numerous tribal groups that inhabit northern Kenya, among them the El-Molo, Samburu, Pokot and the Turkana.

✦ Rhino Charge

This charity cross-country rally (www.rhinocharge.co.ke) in aid of Rhino Ark and other worthy conservation causes challenges mad motorists to reach the finish in the straightest line possible, whatever the crazy obstacles. The location changes annually. (p357)

✦ Run with Lions

In late June or early July, Lewa Wildlife Conservancy hosts one of the world's more unusual marathons, with a winning combination of wildlife watching and serious fundraising. (p163)

July

The wildebeest and zebra migration is in full swing. So too is the annual migration of two-legged visitors who converge on the Mara. Weather is fine and warm, with steaming conditions on the coast.

◉ Return to Amboseli

When the rains begin in March, the herbivores of Amboseli (elephants, antelope, zebras...), followed by the predators, leave for grasslands outside the park. By July, they're on their way back within park confines.

◉ Annual Wildebeest Migration

Following the rains, wildebeest begin arriving in the Masai Mara National Reserve (the Mara) anywhere between late June and mid-July and stay around until October, with predators following in their wake. It's the greatest wildlife show on earth.

August

The mid-year high season continues; the Mara is still the focus, but other parks are also rewarding. Europeans on holiday flock to Kenya: prices go up, room availability goes down.

✦ International Camel Derby

Maralal's International Camel Derby offers serious camel racing and a chance to join the fun. (p284)

✦ Kenya Music Festival

Kenya's longest-running music festival is held over 10 days in Nairobi, drawing international acts along with its predominantly African cast of stars. (p69)

September

Crowds drop off ever so slightly, but the weather remains fine and the Mara is still filled to bursting with wildlife, so prices and visitor numbers remain high.

October

Wildebeest are usually around until mid-October and migratory birds begin arriving. The best season for diving and snorkelling begins.

◉ Here Come the Rains

Unlike the main rainy season from March to May, the short rains that usually begin in October and continue into November cause only minor disruptions to safaris.

✦ Tusker Safari Sevens

Nairobi hosts this international rugby tournament. Drawing world-class rugby-union players. (p69)

November

The short rains appear almost daily, but disruptions are minimal. Some animals range beyond the parks, birds arrive in numbers.

✦ East African Safari Rally

This classic-car rally is over 50 years old. The rally traverses Kenya, Tanzania and Uganda and is open to pre-1971 vehicles only.

✦ Maulid Festival

This annual celebration (commencing 20 November 2018, 9 November 2019 and 28 October 2020) of the Prophet Mohammed's birthday rouses Lamu from its slumber.

◉ Migratory Birds

Birdwatchers couldn't hope for a better time to visit, as millions of birds and hundreds of species arrive for their wintering grounds.

✦ Mombasa Carnival

Mombasa throws its biggest party of the year, with this carnival taking over the streets with music, dance and other events. (p213)

December

A reasonable time to visit, with lower prices and fine weather and plenty of migratory birds in residence.

Itineraries

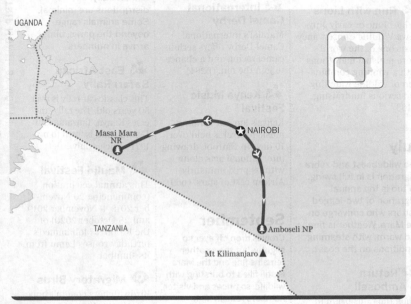

UGANDA

Masai Mara NR

NAIROBI

TANZANIA

Amboseli NP

Mt Kilimanjaro ▲

Safari Njema

1 WEEK

Ideal for those with limited time, this classic safari route brings you face to face with the continent's most charismatic creatures. To do it in a week, you'll need to fly between the three destinations. *Safari njema* – have a good trip!

Begin in **Nairobi**. Kenya's (in)famous capital is not without charm – track down endangered giraffes, orphaned elephants and four of the Big Five set against a backdrop of not-so-distant skyscrapers. Plan on one full day, then fly from the capital's Wilson Airport to the **Masai Mara National Reserve**. Between July and October, the Mara hosts the annual wildebeest migration, one of the greatest wildlife concentrations on earth, but it's worth visiting any time. Three days is a minimum; spend four if you can.

From Maasailand fly, possibly via Nairobi, to **Amboseli National Park**, where you can get closer to elephants than almost anywhere else in Africa. From here, the views of Mt Kilimanjaro, Africa's highest peak, are without rival. After two nights, you'll fly back to Nairobi, wondering why you're not staying longer.

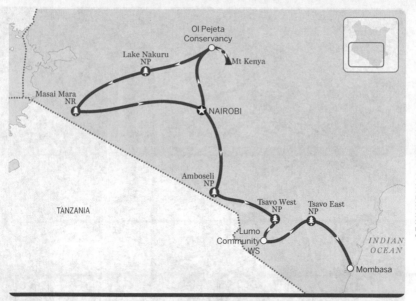

 Big Five & the Best of the Parks

4 WEEKS

Kenya has some of the best national parks and reserves in Africa and seeing the Big Five (elephant, lion, leopard, rhino and buffalo) is something of a mantra for many first-time visitors to Africa. With three weeks to cover all this territory, you could easily get around in your own rented vehicle.

Many Kenyan safaris begin in **Nairobi** and this one's no exception. You can see four of the Big Five in much-underrated Nairobi National Park, before heading north to **Ol Pejeta Conservancy**, up on Laikipia Plateau – it's the closest place to Nairobi where you can see the Big Five and, at last count, they had 111 black rhinos. Ol Pejeta has plenty of organised activities to get you lion-tracking, cycling within sight of rhinos or simply walking out into the wild. Stay at least three days to make the most of it.

Before leaving Kenya's Central Highlands, allocate a week for one of East Africa's most rewarding adventures – the trek to the summit of **Mt Kenya**, Africa's second-highest peak, will leave you gasping for both air and superlatives. A roughly southwesterly trajectory takes you down to **Lake Nakuru National Park**, one of Kenya's most compact and excellent parks for buffalo, lion, leopard and rhino.

A loop down to Kenya's far southwest takes you onto one of Africa's most celebrated terrains with the **Masai Mara National Reserve**. Allow at least three days to explore and consider a few extra days in a luxurious tented camp in one of the surrounding conservancies. It's a long day's drive back to Nairobi, with another half day to **Amboseli National Park**, home to lions, cheetahs and elephants in the shadow of Mt Kilimanjaro.

From Amboseli it's a short hop to wildlife- and wilderness-rich **Tsavo West National Park**, which is home to all the Big Five – see them in one day and you've hit the safari jackpot. Close to the southern fringes of Tsavo West, **Lumo Community Wildlife Sanctuary** is also good for the Big Five, before a visit to the outstanding **Tsavo East National Park**.

From here you can head down the highway to the ancient Swahili port of **Mombasa**, where you can either fly straight home, or start a whole new journey exploring the Kenyan coast.

Top: Gede ruins (p250)

Bottom: Zebras in Tsavo West National Park (p190)

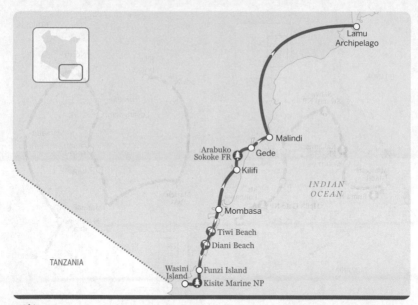

3 WEEKS Sun, Surf & Swahili

Whether you're interested in exploring the remaining vestiges of Swahili culture or simply kicking back on the beach for days on end, don't miss the chance to explore Kenya's sun-drenched coast. Three weeks is a minimum for this journey, which can be made on public transport. Check the security situation before setting out.

First explore the coastal gateway of **Mombasa**, one of the truly great port cities and the essence of East Africa. It gets steaming hot here, so after a few days your first stop heading south should be **Tiwi Beach**, a tranquil white-sand paradise popular with independent travellers. Just down the road, you can head on to the package-holiday destination of **Diani Beach** for a taste of the full-on resort experience with plenty of water sports thrown in.

Near the Tanzanian border, **Funzi** and **Wasini Islands** provide a dose of unspoilt coastal life; on the latter, Mkwiro is somewhere close to paradise. These islands also afford easy access to the excellent **Kisite Marine National Park**. Whether you spot crocodiles along the banks of mangrove-lined rivers or dolphins crashing through the surf, a visit to the marine park is a wonderful complement to Kenya's terrestrial wildlife destinations. Offshore, humpback whales are a possibility from August to October. A trip in a traditional dhow is also a must. Allow at least a week in this area.

Heading north back on the coastal trail, make a quick stop in the charming town of **Kilifi** before pressing on to **Arabuko Sokoke Forest Reserve**, one of the largest remaining tracts of indigenous coastal forest in East Africa. It has prolific birdlife, forest elephants and the golden-rumped elephant shrew.

Further north are the ruins of **Gede**, an ancient Swahili city dating back to the 13th century. Another historic destination along the Swahili coast is **Malindi**, a 14th-century trading post that's now one of the country's leading beach destinations for Italian holidaymakers. It has bucketloads of charm once you get beyond the beach.

This itinerary ends at the wonderful **Lamu Archipelago**, a veritable tropical paradise and Swahili heritage gem.

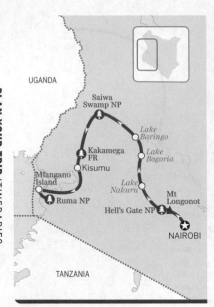

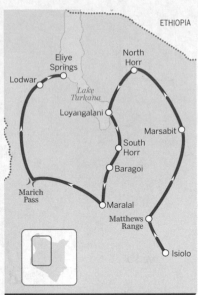

2 WEEKS — Rift Valley & Wetlands

Kenya's Rift Valley ranks among Africa's defining geological marvels. To complete this itinerary in two weeks, you'll need your own set of wheels. You're covering a lot of places, but many are quite close together.

Begin near **Nairobi** at the Olepolos Country Club, contemplating the Rift's glory while nursing a Tusker. Drive north to, and then climb, **Mt Longonot**, one of the Rift's prettiest vantage points, and walk amid the dramatic rock forms of **Hell's Gate National Park**. Allow a couple of days around here. Then it's an easy hop to Lakes **Nakuru**, **Bogoria** and **Baringo**; spend a further two days here.

Take the loop through the Cherangani Hills to the lovely **Saiwa Swamp National Park**, a real wetland treat.

Heading south, explore the lush **Kakamega Forest Reserve**, then pass through **Kisumu** on your way to **Mfangano Island**, arguably Lake Victoria's most rewarding island escape – plan on spending a couple of nights resting from life on the road. Finally, visit tiny **Ruma National Park**, a rarely visited gem. From here you can either make for the Masai Mara or head down into Tanzania.

3 WEEKS — Desert Frontiers

This adventurous trail winds through the barren but beguiling landscape around Lake Turkana. You could take forever exploring the area by public transport – rent a 4WD with a driver to get around.

The eastern gateway to this region is **Isiolo**. As you make your way north, the **Matthews Range** is great for walkers. Back on the road, **Marsabit** is a dusty tribal centre, home to a fine national park, and is a quintessentially northern Kenyan outpost.

Take the western loop to Turkana via **North Horr**, heading for the tiny lakeside settlement of **Loyangalani**, a base for trips into even more remote parts. From here the trail leads south again, passing all kinds of scenic zones and the stopover towns of **South Horr** and **Baragoi**. It's worth stopping for a couple of days in **Maralal** to replenish supplies and search for traces of Wilfred Thesiger.

If the remote north has you under its spell, head up to the other side of Turkana, passing through the lush western area around **Marich Pass** to reach sweltering **Lodwar** and the lovely lakeshore at **Eliye Springs**.

Plan Your Trip
Safaris

Safari (which means 'journey' in Kiswahili) must be one of the most evocative words ever to infiltrate the English language. From wildebeest fording raging rivers and lions stalking their prey through the savannah grass, to iridescent flamingos lining a salty shore at sunset, a safari is Africa at its finest.

Need to Know

Best Overall Wildlife Experience

Annual wildebeest migration at Masai Mara National Reserve (p112) from July to October.

Best for Big Cats

The community-run conservancies that surround the Mara, especially Naboisho (p123), Olare-Orok (p124) and Mara North (p121).

Best Wilderness Experience

Tsavo West National Park (p190) in the south, Lake Turkana (p288) in the north.

Best Times to Avoid

The rainy season (late March to May).

Best Safari Planning Resources

Try www.safaribookings.com, https://eco tourismkenya.org or www.responsibletravel. com.

Best Safari Circuits

The Mara Circuit and the Southern Circuit.

Best Specialist Safaris

For birdwatching Ben's Ecological Safaris (p37); for camel safaris Wild Frontiers (p292); for cultural insight IntoAfrica (p38); for cycling Bike Treks (p37); for DIY Adventure Upgrade Safaris (p389).

Planning a Safari

Booking

Many travellers prefer to get all the hard work done before arriving in Kenya by booking from home, either through travel agents or directly with safari companies. This ensures that you'll be able to secure a spot at the more famous lodges, especially during peak seasons when places start filling up months in advance. However, while most safari operators will take internet bookings, making arrangements with anyone other than a well-established midrange or top-end operator can be a

risky business. If you're going for a budget option, you should do your research both in advance and on the ground when you arrive.

If you want to book a safari once in Kenya, allow at least a day to shop around, don't rush into any deals and steer clear of any attempts of intimidation by touts or dodgy operators. The best way to ensure you get what you pay for is to decide exactly what you want, then visit the various companies in person and talk through the kind of package you're looking for. Budget travellers should also check out the various hostel choices around Nairobi, as most also organise safaris.

Costs

Compared to other countries on the continent, Kenya is not always the cheapest destination for safaris. That said, most safari operator quotes include just about everything, such as park entrance fees, the costs of accommodation or tent rental, transport costs from the starting base to the park, and the costs of fuel plus a driver/guide for wildlife drives. However, this varies enough that it's essential to clarify before paying. Drinks (whether alcoholic or not) are generally excluded, and budget camping safari prices usually exclude sleeping-bag hire. Prices quoted by agencies or operators usually assume shared (double) room/tent occupancy, with supplements for single occupancy ranging from an additional 20% to 50% of the shared-occupancy rate.

If you're dealing directly with lodges and tented camps rather than going through a safari operator, you may be quoted 'all-inclusive' prices. In addition to accommodation, full board and sometimes park fees, these usually include two 'activities' (usually wildlife drives, or sometimes one wildlife drive and one walk) per day, each lasting about two to three hours. They generally exclude transport costs to the park. Whenever accommodation-and-full-board-only prices apply, and unless you have your own vehicle, you'll need to pay extra to actually go out looking for wildlife, and costs can be considerable.

Budget Safaris

Most safaris at the lower end of the price range are camping safaris. In order to keep costs to a minimum, groups often camp outside national park areas (thereby saving camping fees) or stay in budget guesthouses outside the park. Budget operators also save costs by working with larger groups to minimise per-person transport costs, and by keeping to a no-frills set-up with basic meals and a minimum number of staff. For most safaris at the budget level, as well as for many midrange safaris, daily kilometre limits are placed on the vehicles.

For any budget safari, the bare minimum cost for a registered company is about US$75 to US$125 per person per day, which should include transport, food (three meals per day), park entry and camping fees, tents and cooking equipment. Sleeping-bag hire will cost you an additional US$10 to US$15 for the duration of the trip.

Midrange Safaris

Most midrange safaris use lodges, where you'll have a comfortable room and eat in a restaurant. Overall, safaris in this category are reliable and reasonably good value. A disadvantage is that they may have somewhat of a packaged-tour or production-line feel. This can be minimised by selecting a safari company and accommodation carefully, by giving attention to who and how many other people you travel with, and by avoiding the large, popular lodges during peak season.

In high season you're looking at US$150 to US$250 per person per night (usually full board) for staying in lodges or tented camps, though these prices do drop a bit in the low season.

Top-end Safaris

Private lodges, luxury tented camps and even private fly-in camps are used in top-end safaris, all with the aim of providing guests with as 'authentic' and personal a bush experience as possible without forgoing the creature comforts. For the price you pay (from US$250 up to US$600 or more per person per day), expect a full range of amenities, as well as top-quality guiding. Even in remote settings without running water you will be able to enjoy hot, bush-style showers, comfortable beds and fine dining. Also expect a high level of personalised attention and an intimate atmosphere – many places at this level have fewer than 20 beds.

Wildebeest migration, Masai Mara National Reserve (p112)

Tipping

Assuming service has been satisfactory, tipping is an important part of the safari experience, especially to the drivers/guides, cooks and others whose livelihoods depend on tips. Many operators have tipping guidelines, although in general you can expect to tip about US$5 to US$10 per staff member per day from each traveller. This value should increase substantially if you're on a top-end safari, part of a large group or if an especially good job has been done.

When to Go

Wildlife can be seen at all times of year, but the migration patterns of the big herbivores (which in turn attract the big predators) are likely to be a major factor in deciding when to go. From July to October, huge herds of wildebeest and zebras cross from the Serengeti in Tanzania to the Masai Mara. This is prime viewing time as the land is parched, the vegetation has died back and the animals are obliged to come to drink at the ever-shrinking waterholes. Not surprisingly, most safari companies increase their rates at this time.

Cheetah encounter, Masai Mara National Reserve (p112)

Birdwatching is especially good from October to March.

The long rains (from March to May) transform the national parks into a lush carpet of greenery. It's very scenic, but it does provide much more cover for the wildlife to hide behind, and the rain can turn the tracks into impassable mush. It does, of course, depend on the year – we've travelled in Kenya in April and enjoyed both clear skies and low prices. Safaris may be impossible in the lowland parks during this time. Such problems are also possible during the short rains (from October to November), although getting around is rarely a problem.

Itineraries

Most itineraries offered by safari companies fall into one of three loosely defined 'circuits', which can all be combined for longer trips. Treks up Mt Kenya are a fourth option, sold separately or as an add-on.

The Mara Circuit

The standard safari itinerary centres on the Masai Mara (p112). The shorter versions generally involve two nights in the park and two half-days travelling. Possible add-ons include Lake Nakuru National Park (p102) or Amboseli National Park (p185), but consider flying between them to maximise your time.

The Southern Circuit

Offered as the main alternative to the Mara, southern itineraries make a beeline for Amboseli National Park (p185) and its famous Kilimanjaro backdrop. Anything longer than a three-day trip here should allow you to also visit Tsavo West (p190) for a couple of nights, with a couple more days required for Tsavo East (p197) as well. Most companies will give you the option of being dropped in Mombasa at the end of this route rather than heading back to Nairobi.

The Northern Circuit

The focal point of any northern safari is Samburu National Reserve (p275), which you could also combine with one or more of the conservancies around Laikipia (p154). For Lake Turkana (p288), you'll need at least a week to visit due to the long distances involved.

Types of Safaris

Birdwatching Safaris

Many safari companies offer some kind of birdwatching safari, though the quality is not always up to par for serious birders – if you are one, quiz any prospective companies at length before making a booking. Origins Safaris (p38) is one reliable specialist.

Camel Safaris

A camel safari is a superb way of getting right off the beaten track and into areas where vehicle safaris don't or can't go. Most camel safaris go to the Samburu and Turkana tribal areas between Isiolo and Lake Turkana, where you'll experience nomadic life and mingle with tribal people. Wildlife may also be plentiful, although it's the journey itself that is the main attraction.

You have the choice of riding the camels or walking alongside them. Most caravans are led by experienced Samburu *moran* (warriors), and accompanied by English-speaking tribal guides who are well versed in bush lore, botany, ornithology and local customs. Most travelling is done as early as possible in the cool of the day, and a campsite is established around noon. Afternoons are time for relaxing, guided walks and showers before drinks and dinner around the campfire.

All companies provide a full range of camping equipment (generally including two-person tents) and ablution facilities. The typical distance covered each day is 15km to 18km so you don't have to be superfit to survive this style of safari.

The following companies offer camel safaris of varying lengths:

Bobong Campsite (☎0735243075; olmaisor@africaonline.co.ke; camping per person KSh500, 3-bed banda KSh5000)

Desert Rose (p287)

Wild Frontiers (p292)

Camping Safaris

Few things can match the thrill of waking up in the middle of the African bush with nothing between you and the animals except a sheet of canvas and the dying embers of last night's fire.

Camping safaris cater for budget travellers, the young (or young at heart) and those who are prepared to put up with a little discomfort to get the authentic bush experience. At the bottom of the price range, you'll have to forgo luxuries such as flush toilets, running water and cold drinks, and you'll have to chip in with chores like putting up the tents and helping prepare dinner. Showers are provided at some but not all campsites, although there's usually a tap where you can scrub

---

BEATING SAFARI SCAMS

Every year we get emails from readers complaining about bad experiences on safari, from dodging park fees and ignoring client requests, to pure rip-offs and outright criminal behaviour. For the most part, these incidents are perpetrated by Nairobi's budget companies, which shave every possible corner to keep their costs down.

A persistent feature of Kenya's safari scene are the street touts, who will approach you almost as soon as you step out of your hotel in the streets of Nairobi and Mombasa. They're not all bad guys, and the safari you end up with may be fine, but you'll pay a mark-up to cover their commission.

We can't stress enough how important it is to take your time with your booking. Talk to travellers, do as much research as possible, insist on setting out every detail of your trip in advance, don't be pressured into anything and don't pay any substantial amounts of cash up front. If in doubt, think seriously about stretching your budget to use a reputable midrange firm. And even though we recommend some operators, satisfaction is by no means guaranteed whoever you go with.

Of course, we receive plenty of positive feedback as well, so don't let potential problems put you off. Indeed, wildlife safaris can be utterly unforgettable experiences for all the right reasons, so it's certainly worth making the effort to book one – just keep your wits about you.

> ### DON'T HURRY
>
> When planning your safari, don't be tempted to try to fit too much into your itinerary. Distances in Kenya are long, and hopping too quickly from park to park is likely to end with you tired, unsatisfied and feeling that you haven't even scratched the surface. Try instead to plan longer periods at just one or two parks – exploring in depth what each has to offer and taking advantage of cultural and walking opportunities in park border areas.

down with cold water. The price of your safari will include three meals a day cooked by the camp cook(s), although food will be of the plain-but-plenty variety.

There are more comfortable camping options, where there are extra staff to do all the work, but they cost more. A number of companies have also set up permanent campsites where you can just drop into bed at the end of a dusty day's drive.

Cultural Safaris

With ecofriendly lodges now springing up all over Kenya, remote population groups are becoming increasingly involved in tourism. There is also a growing number of companies offering cultural safaris, allowing you to interact with locals in a far more personal way than the rushed souvenir stops that the mainstream tours make at Maasai villages. The best of these combine volunteer work with more conventional tour activities and provide accommodation in tents, ecolodges and village houses.

One company that receives consistently good reviews for its cultural safaris is IntoAfrica (p38).

Flying Safaris

These safaris essentially cater for the well-off who want to fly between remote airstrips in the various national parks and stay in luxury tented camps. If money is no object, you can get around by a mixture of charter and scheduled flights and stay in some of the finest camps in Kenya – arrangements can be made with any of the lodge and tented-camp safari operators.

Lodge & Tented-camp Safaris

Safari lodges make up the bulk of most safari experiences, ranging from five-star luxury to more simple affairs. In the lodges you can expect rooms with bathrooms or cottages with air-conditioning, international cuisine, a terrace bar beneath a huge *makuti* (palm-thatched) canopy with wonderful views, a swimming pool, wildlife videos and other entertainment, and plenty of staff on hand to cater for all your requirements. Almost all lodges have a waterhole and some have a hidden viewing tunnel that leads right to the waterside.

If you can't do without luxuries, there's a whole world of luxurious lodges with swimming pools and bars overlooking waterholes, and remote tented camps that recreate the way wealthy hunters travelled around Kenya a century ago. Some of the lodges are beautifully conceived and the locations are to die for, perched high above huge sweeps of savannah or waterholes teeming with African wildlife. Most are set deep within the national parks, so the safari drives offer maximum wildlife-viewing time.

The luxury tented camps tend to offer semipermanent tents with fitted bathrooms (hot showers are standard), beds with mosquito nets, proper furniture, fans and gourmet meals served al fresco in the bush. The really exclusive ones are even more luxurious than the lodges and tend to be *very* expensive.

Motorcycle Safaris

Operating out of Diani Beach, **Fredlink Tours** (☎0786556900; www.motorbike-safari. com; Diani Beach Rd, Diani Sea Resort) runs motorcycle safaris to the Taita Hills, Rift Valley, Tsavo West and the Kilimanjaro foothills.

Walking & Cycling Safaris

For the keen walker or cyclist, and those who don't want to spend all their time in a safari minibus, there are a number of options, from short rides to multiday expeditions. In major wildlife areas, the best walking options are in Hell's Gate National Park (p97) and the conservancies that surround the Masai Mara National Reserve (p112).

Booking a Safari

The service provided by even the best safari companies can vary, depending on the driver, the itinerary, the behaviour of the wildlife, flat tyres and breakdowns and, of course, the attitude of the passengers themselves. We try to recommend some of the better companies, but this shouldn't take the place of your own hands-on research.

When choosing a safari company, the Kenyan Association of Tour Operators (KATO) has a list of members. It may not be the most powerful regulatory body in the world, but most reputable safari companies subscribe, and going with a KATO member will give you some recourse in case of conflict.

Useful Resources

Kenyan Association of Tour Operators (Map p56; ☑020-713348, 020-271 3386; www.kato kenya.org; Longonot Rd, Upper Hill, Nairobi) Reputable safari companies will be registered members. While KATO is not the most powerful of entities, going on safari with one of its members (there is a member list on the website) will at least give you some recourse to appeal in case of conflict or problems. KATO is a good source of information on whether a company is reputable or not, and it can be worth checking in with them before finalising your plans.

Safari Bookings (www.safaribookings.com) is a fabulous online resource for comparing safari operators and destinations.

Kenya Professional Safari Guides Association (KPSGA; ☑020-2342426; www.safariguides.org) Your guide's accreditation by this body is a good indicator of quality and experience.

Ecotourism Kenya (www.ecotourismkenya.org) Maintains a list of member companies and lodges who subscribe to its code of conduct for responsible, sustainable safaris.

Safari Companies

The following list of companies is by no means exhaustive. We've chosen these places either because of first-hand experience, consistently positive reports from travellers, and/or the fact that they've been around for a while. Most are members of KATO. More recommended companies are found elsewhere in this chapter, as well as in the Outdoor Activities chapter (p40)

and the Overland Tours (p385) section of the Transport chapter.

Abercrombie & Kent (Map p62; ☑020-6950000; www.abercrombiekent.com; Abercrombie & Kent House, Mombasa Rd) Luxury-travel company with excellent safaris to match.

Basecamp Explorer (Map p62; ☑0733333909; www.basecampexplorer.com/kenya; Gold Rock Bldg) Scandinavian-owned ecotourism operator offering comprehensive and often luxurious camping itineraries with an environmentally sustainable focus. The office is off Mombasa Rd.

Ben's Ecological Safaris (Map p56; ☑0706324970, 0722861072; www.bens ecologicalsafaris.com; Muranga'a Rd) This outfit is a birdwatching specialist, but it's good for just about any natural-history or cultural safari across East Africa.

Bike Treks (☑020-4446371, 020-2141757; www.angelfire.com/sk/biketreks; Kabete Gardens, Westlands) Bike Treks offers specialised trips, with everything from quick three-day jaunts to full-on expeditions; it might even have you cycling through the Masai Mara...

Bushbuck Adventures (Map p56; ☑020-7121505, 0722356838; www.bushbuckadventures.com; 2nd fl, Bhavesh Centre, Ngara Rd) Small company specialising in personalised (including walking) safaris. It has a private semipermanent camp in the Masai Mara.

Eastern & Southern Safaris (Map p66; ☑020-2242828; www.essafari.co.ke; 6th fl, Finance House, Loita St) Classy and reliable outfit aiming at the midrange and upper end of the market, with standards to match. It does all the classic Kenyan trips.

Eco-Resorts (☑0733618183; www.eco-resorts.com) US-based company with a variety of activity-based volunteer and cultural packages and

PLAN YOUR TRIP SAFARIS

BUDGET SAFARIS

In addition to the larger safari companies, numerous budget accommodation options in Nairobi organise camping safaris for budget travellers. These include the following:

Milimani Backpackers & Safari Centre (p71)

Wildebeest Eco Camp (p71)

customised safaris around Kenya. A proportion of profits goes to community and conservation projects.

Gametrackers (Map p62; ☏020-2222703; www.gametrackersafaris.com; Masai Lodge Rd, Karen) Long-established and reliable company with a full range of camping and lodge safaris around Kenya; one of the best operators for Lake Turkana and the north. Located off Magadi Rd.

IntoAfrica (☏UK 0114-2555610; www.into africa.co.uk; 40 Huntingdon Cres, Sheffield, UK) One of the most highly praised safari companies in East Africa, IntoAfrica specialises in 'fair-trade' trips providing insights into African life and directly supporting local communities. Combining culture *and* wildlife viewing is a speciality.

Natural World Kenya Safaris (Map p66; ☏0720894288, 020-2216830, Mombasa 041-2226715; www.naturaltoursandsafaris.com; 1st fl, Pioneer House, Kenyatta Ave) Well-organised safaris visiting all the major parks.

Origins Safaris (Map p56; ☏020-2042695, 0724253861; www.originsafaris.info; 5th fl, Landmark Plaza, Argwings Kodhek Rd) Has a natural-history and cultural focus, with everything from expert birdwatching to traditional ceremonies, as well as other more mainstream safaris.

Pal-Davis Adventures (Map p56; ☏020-2522611, 0733919613; 1st fl, Bhavesh Business Centre, Ngara Rd) Small Kenyan company that gets excellent reports from travellers for its wide range of personalised safaris.

Parading Africa Safaris (☏020-2007378; www.paradingafricasafaris.com; Nyayo Stadium Complex, Block C) An excellent safari company with a full portfolio of Kenyan and wider East African safaris across a range of budgets.

Pollman's Tours & Safaris (Map p62; ☏020-3337234; www.pollmans.com; Pollman's House, Mombasa Rd) Kenyan-based operator that covers all the main national parks, with coastal and Tanzanian trips as well.

Private Safaris (Map p62; ☏020-3607000, Mombasa 0722203780; www.privatesafaris.co.ke; 2nd fl, OiLibya Plaza, Muthaiga) Offering trips that can be highly customised, Private Safaris can book tours throughout sub-Saharan Africa.

Safari Icon Travel (Map p66; ☏0724112227, 020-2242818; www.safariicon.com; 4th fl, Nacico Chambers, cnr Kenyatta & Moi Aves) Well-regarded local company that covers a wide range of safari options in Kenya, Tanzania and Uganda.

Safe Ride Tours & Safaris (Map p66; ☏0722496558, 020-2101162; www.saferide safaris.com; 2nd fl, Avenue House, Kenyatta Ave) A budget operator recommended for camping excursions around the country.

Sana Highlands Trekking Expeditions (Map p56; ☏0722243691; www.sanatrekking kenya.com; Gem Lane, Kileleshwa) Operates five-day all-inclusive treks on Mt Kenya's Sirimon, Naro Moru and Chogoria routes.

Samburu Trails Trekking Safaris (☏020-2631594; www.samburutrails.com) Small British specialist outfit offering a range of foot excursions in some less-visited parts of the Rift Valley.

Savage Wilderness Safaris (Map p56; ☏0737835963; www.savagewilderness.org; Sports Ave) Arguably Kenya's leading adventure-tourism operator, specialising in whitewater rafting, kayaking and rock climbing. Its main base is in Sagana, a few hours north of Nairobi.

Somak Travel (Map p62; ☏020-4971000; www.somak-nairobi.com; Somak House, Mombasa Rd) A Kenyan-based operator with more than 30 years of experience on the safari circuit, Somak is a home-grown favourite.

Southern Cross Safaris (Map p62; ☏020-2434600; www.southerncrosssafaris.com; Symbion House, Karen Rd) A professional Kenyan company, Southern Cross is a good choice for individually designed safaris.

Do-it-yourself Safaris

A DIY safari is a viable and enticing proposition in Kenya. Doing it yourself has several advantages over organised safaris: total flexibility, independence and ability to choose your travelling companions. However, as far as costs go, it's generally true to say that organising your own safari will cost at least as much, and usually more, than going on an organised safari to the same areas. And you will, of course, need to book your own accommodation well in advance (if you're staying in lodges or tented camps) or carry your own camping equipment.

DIY Safari Companies

We recommend all of the following local companies. Most are focused on renting vehicles, but they may be able to make some arrangements on your behalf and/or provide camping equipment for an additional cost.

Ewaso Ngiro River, Samburu National Reserve (p275)

Adventure Upgrade Safaris (p389)

Central Rent-a-Car (p389)

Market Car Hire (p389)

Pal-Davis Adventures (p38)

Tough Trucks Kenya (Map p66; ☎020-2228725; www.toughtruckskenya.com)

Private Drivers

Choosing a driver can almost be as important as choosing a safari company – they will, after all, be your constant companion throughout the trip – and there are some travellers who base their visit around the availability of certain drivers. In most cases, the drivers will make the necessary vehicle arrangements, and some will double as guides, fixers and interpreters.

Drivers we recommend include the following:

Peter Ndirangu (☎0721922594; peterwamae1@gmail.com)

Duncan Waikwa (☎0722305206; waikwabull@gmail.com)

John Chege (☎0787422845; chege.john@gmail.com)

Peter Chomba (☎0727739769; peddcho@yahoo.com)

Camping Equipment

Some companies offer camping equipment for rent. Expect to pay from KSh250 per day for a sleeping bag with liner, KSh550 for a two-person dome tent and KSh150 per day for a gas stove (gas canisters are extra). On most items there is a deposit of KSh2000 to KSh4000.

It's also possible to hire a vehicle and camping equipment as one package. Adventure Upgrade Safaris (p389) is one such operator.

Companies in Nairobi that rent out camping equipment include Atul's (p81) and **Extreme Outdoors Africa** (Map p72; ☎020-4448000, 0728406937; www.extremeoutdoorsafrica.com; Alliance Pl, Slip Rd, Waiyaki Way, Westlands).

Plan Your Trip

Outdoor Activities

Kenya is not just about seeing – there's also so much to do here, from walking up some of Africa's highest peaks to drifting over the Masai Mara in a balloon, from snorkelling the Indian Ocean to cycling within sight of wild rhinos. So get down from your vehicle and explore.

Top Activities

Best Ballooning
Head to the Masai Mara National Reserve (p112) in Western Kenya – the best season is July to October.

Best Mountaineering
Scale the heights in Mt Kenya National Park (p166) in the Central Highlands from June to October.

Best Diving & Snorkelling
The Lamu archipelago's Manda Toto Island (p266) is the best option, from October to March.

Best Mountain Trekking
Head for Mt Elgon (p144) in Western Kenya or the Rift Valley's Mt Longonot (p89). Best time to go is June to February.

Best Cultural Trekking
Hike with Maasai Trails (p121) in Loita Hills in the Masai Mara. The best time is from June to February.

Best Windsurfing
Try the Lamu and Manda Islands (p255) from December to March.

Best for Water Sports
Diani Beach (p221), south of Mombasa, is great year-round.

Planning Your Trip

When to Go

Kenya is a fantastic year-round activities destination, with one important exception: we generally recommend that you avoid the long rains, which run from sometime in March (or later) through to May. At this time trails (and access roads) can be impassable, and underwater visibility is generally poorer. The shorter rains in October and November tend to be more localised and heavy downpours rarely last longer than an hour or two. These 'short rains' (as they're known locally) will rarely disrupt your plans to get active.

What to Take

There are few requirements for most activities. Operators who organise whitewater rafting and other similar sports will provide the necessary equipment; bicycles and mountain bikes can be rented in Kenya, but serious cyclists and bikers may want to bring their own. Most hikers head out onto the trail under their own steam (good boots are a must), but even those who plan on joining an organised hike with a guide will usually be required to bring their own equipment.

Airborne Activities

Ballooning

A balloon trip in and around the Masai Mara is a superb way of seeing the savannah and its animals. The almost ghostly experience of floating silently above the plains with a 360-degree view of everything beneath you is incomparable, and it's definitely worth the considerable outlay; prices start at around US$400 per person.

The flights typically set off at dawn and go for about 1½ hours, after which you put down for a champagne breakfast. You will then be taken on a wildlife drive in a support vehicle and returned to your lodge.

The main operators are Hot Air Safaris (p116) and Governors' Balloon Safaris (p116).

Gliding & Flying

Flying lessons are easily arranged in Nairobi and are much more affordable than in Europe, the USA and Australasia. Scenic flights include trips on the plane that appeared in *Out of Africa* at Segera Retreat (p160), and flying safaris at Lewa Wildlife Conservancy (p162). Campi ya Kanzi (p188), between Amboseli and Tsavo in the southeast, can also arrange scenic flights and flying safaris.

Land Activities

Climbing & Mountaineering

Kenya isn't particularly well known for its rock climbing, but that's more to do with a lack of infrastructure than a lack of suitable places.

One useful resource is the Mountain Club of Kenya (p68) in Nairobi. Members have a huge pool of technical knowledge about climbing in Kenya. Savage Wilderness Safaris (p38) offers organised and customised walking, climbing and mountaineering trips, including climbs up Mt Kenya.

Where to Climb

➡ Mt Kenya (p166)

➡ Tsavo West National Park (p190)

➡ Hell's Gate National Park (p97)

Cycling & Mountain Biking

If you're just after a trundle rather than some serious cycling, many local companies and accommodation places around the country (particularly campgrounds) can arrange bicycle hire. Prices generally start at KSh500 to KSh1200 per day, but always check the quality of the bike as standards vary wildly. The only national park where you're allowed to cycle is Hell's Gate National Park (p97).

An increasing number of companies offer more serious cycling trips in Kenya – try Rift Valley Adventures (p161). Expect to pay around US$120 to US$150 per day.

Where to Cycle

➡ Ol Pejeta Conservancy (p160)

➡ Hell's Gate National Park (p97)

➡ Mt Kenya (p166)

Trekking

Kenya has some of the best trekking trails in East Africa, ranging from strenuous mountain ascents to rolling-hill country and forests. It is, of course, always worth checking out the prevailing security situation in the area you wish to trek, not to mention the prevalence of any wild animals you might encounter along the trail. In some instances, it may be advisable to take a local guide, either from the Kenya Wildlife Service (KWS) if they operate in the area, or a local village guide.

Where to Trek

The following places are all good for proper mountain trekking in varying degrees of difficulty:

➡ Mt Kenya (p166)

➡ Mt Elgon National Park (p144)

➡ Mt Longonot (p89)

➡ Cherangani Hills (p291)

➡ Loita Hills (p121)

➡ Aberdare National Park (p152)

➡ Ndoto Mountains (p279)

For forest hiking, we especially like the following:

➡ Kakamega Forest Reserve (p138)

➡ Matthews Range (p279)

➡ Arabuko Sokoke Forest Reserve (p247)

Useful Trekking Resources

For more trekking information, get hold of a copy of Lonely Planet's *Trekking in East Africa;* it may be out of print, but it remains the definitive guide to trekking the region.

Among the operators we recommend, consider Savage Wilderness Safaris (p38), which offers trekking around the country, Samburu Trails Trekking Safaris (p38) for the Rift Valley, and Maasai Trails (p121), which runs cultural trekking in the Masai Mara's Loita Hills.

RESPONSIBLE TREKKING & CLIMBING

Help preserve the ecology and beauty of Kenya by following responsible trekking best practice.

Rubbish

➡ Carry out all your rubbish.

➡ Never bury rubbish: digging disturbs soil and ground cover and encourages erosion. Buried rubbish will likely be dug up by animals, which may be injured or poisoned by it.

➡ Minimise waste by taking minimal packaging and no more food than you will need. Take reusable containers or stuff sacks.

➡ Sanitary napkins, tampons, condoms and toilet paper should be carried out despite the inconvenience. They burn and decompose poorly.

Human Waste Disposal

➡ Where there is a toilet, please use it. Where there is none, bury your waste. Dig a small hole 15cm deep and at least 100m from any watercourse. Cover the waste with soil and a rock.

Washing

➡ Don't use detergents or toothpaste in or near watercourses, even if they are biodegradable.

➡ For personal washing, use biodegradable soap and a water container at least 50m away from the watercourse. Disperse the waste water widely to allow the soil to filter it fully.

➡ Wash cooking utensils 50m from watercourses using a scourer, sand or snow instead of detergent.

Erosion

➡ Stick to existing tracks and avoid short cuts.

➡ If a well-used track passes through a mud patch, walk through the mud so as not to increase the size of the patch.

Fires & Low-impact Cooking

➡ Don't depend on open fires for cooking. Cook on a lightweight kerosene, alcohol or shellite (white gas) stove and avoid those powered by disposable butane-gas canisters.

➡ Ensure that you fully extinguish a fire after use.

Wildlife Conservation

➡ Place gear out of reach and tie packs to rafters or trees.

➡ Do not feed the wildlife as this can lead to animals becoming dependent on handouts.

Water Activities

Diving & Snorkelling

The Kenyan coast promises some of the best diving and snorkelling in Africa beyond the Red Sea. In addition to myriad fish species and colourful coral, charismatic marine mammals – including dolphins, sea turtles, whale sharks and humpback whales (August to October) – also frequent these waters.

There is a number of professional dive centres on the coast. If you aren't certified to dive, almost every hotel and resort can arrange an open-water diving course. They're not much cheaper (if at all) than anywhere else in the world – a five-day PADI certification course starts at around US$470. Two tank dives for certified divers go for around US$100, including equipment and transport.

When to Dive & Snorkel

There are distinct seasons for diving in Kenya. October to March is the best time to dive.

From June to August it's often impossible to dive due to the poor visibility caused by the heavy silt flow from some rivers. That said, some divers have taken the plunge in July and found visibility to be a very respectable 7m to 10m, although 4m is more common.

Where to Dive & Snorkel

There is a string of marine national parks spread out along the coast between Shimoni and Malindi. As a general rule, these are the best places to dive and snorkel, and the better marine parks are those further away from Mombasa.

➤ Malindi Marine National Park (p250)

➤ Manda Toto Island (p266)

➤ Kisite Marine National Park (p230)

➤ Diani Beach (p221)

➤ Wasini Island (p230)

➤ Watamu Marine National Park (p243)

Fishing

The Kenya Fisheries Department operates a number of fishing camps in various parts of the country and also issues mandatory

---

PERSONAL TREKKING EQUIPMENT CHECKLIST

➤ Sturdy hiking boots

➤ A good-quality sleeping bag – at high altitude (such as Mt Kenya), nights can be bitterly cold and the weather can turn nasty at short notice

➤ Warm clothing, including a jacket, jersey (sweater) or anorak (windbreaker) that can be added or removed

➤ A sleeping sheet and a warm but lightweight sleeping bag

➤ A sturdy but lightweight tent

➤ Mosquito repellent

➤ A lightweight stove

➤ Trousers for walking, preferably made from breathing, waterproof (and windproof) material such as Gore-Tex

➤ Air-filled sleeping pad

➤ Swiss Army knife

➤ Torch (flashlight) or headlamp with extra batteries

---

fishing licences. Ask your accommodation or safari operator to help you make the arrangements.

Where to Fish

For freshwater fishing, there are huge Nile perch as big as a person in Lake Victoria and Lake Turkana. Some of the trout fishing around Mt Kenya (p166) and the Aberdares (p152) is exceptional.

The deep-sea fishing on the coast is some of the best in the world, and various private companies and resorts in the following places can arrange fishing trips. Boats cost US$250 to US$500 and can usually fit four or five anglers. The season runs from August to April.

➤ Diani Beach (p221)

➤ Watamu (p242)

➤ Malindi (p250)

➤ Shimoni (p229)

➤ Mtwapa (p236)

FERNANDOQUEVEDO / GETTY IMAGES ©

JOHN SEATON CALLAHAN / GETTY IMAGES ©

Top: Ballooning in
Masai Mara National
Reserve (p116)

Bottom: Dhow trip,
Lamu (p262)

Sailing

Kilifi, Mtwapa and Mombasa all have sailing clubs, and smaller freshwater clubs can also be found at Lake Naivasha and Lake Victoria, which both have excellent windsurfing and sailing. If you're experienced, you may pick up some crewing at the yacht clubs; you'll need to become a temporary member.

While rarely hands-on, a traditional dhow trip out of Lamu is an unforgettable sailing experience.

Windsurfing & Kitesurfing

Conditions on Kenya's coast are ideal for windsurfing – the country's offshore reefs protect the waters, and the winds are usually reasonably strong and constant. Most resort hotels south and north of Mombasa have sailboards for hire. Further north, the sheltered channel between Lamu and Manda Islands is one of the best places for windsurfing on the coast.

Kitesurfing is also possible at Diani Beach and Malindi.

Where to Windsurf

➡ Lamu and Manda Islands (p255)

➡ Watamu (p242)

➡ Malindi (p250)

➡ Diani Beach (p222)

Whitewater Rafting

The most exciting times for a whitewater rafting trip are from late October to mid-January and from early April to late July, when water levels are highest.

Where to Go Rafting

The Athi/Galana River (p197) has substantial rapids, chutes and waterfalls and there are also possibilities on the Tana River and Ewaso Ngiro River near Isiolo.

Plan Your Trip
Travel with Children

Kenya is a wonderful destination for families. Everyone will need vaccinations and Africa can seem like a daunting place for kids, but if you're prepared to spend a little extra and take comfort over adventure for the core of the trip, you might just have the holiday of a lifetime.

Best Regions for Kids

Masai Mara & Western Kenya
A safari in the Masai Mara, particularly during the extraordinary spectacle of the massed wildebeest migration (July to October), is surely one of the most memorable experiences your child will ever have in nature. If you take your kids to one wildlife reserve, make it the Masai Mara.

Southern Rift Valley
Shorter distances, better roads, scenic variety, child-friendly parks and great big lakes make the Rift Valley the best overall part of inland Kenya for little people.

Lamu & Diani Beach
You could go anywhere along Kenya's coast and find your family's own little slice of paradise. But there's something about the languid pace of life in and around Lamu that seems perfectly suited to a family holiday. On the south coast Diani Beach has loads to offer younger travellers.

Kenya for Kids

Families travelling with kids have long been an established part of Kenyan travel and most Kenyans will go out of their way to make your children feel welcome.

Beach Holidays

Beach holidays are a sure-fire way to keep the kids happy, and factoring in some beach time to go with the safari can be a good idea. Kenya's beaches alone should be sufficient, but some of the water sports on offer, such as snorkelling, may be suitable for children, depending on their age. And packing a picnic lunch and sailing out to sea on a dhow (a traditional old sailing boat) is a fine way to spend some fun family time.

Safaris

The safari could have been custom-built for children. Driving up almost to within touching distance of elephants, watching lion cubs gambolling across the plains or holding their breath as a cheetah accelerates across the savannah – these are experiences that will stay with your kids for a lifetime.

Nairobi for Kids

For the most part, Nairobi is not the most child friendly of cities. Crowded or poorly maintained pavements in the city centre will be a challenge for those with prams, while high chairs and baby-changing facilities are non-existent. The horrendous traffic, too, can be an endurance challenge for children and adults alike. Playgrounds are extremely rare and most are in poor condition.

That said, most supermarkets stock nappies and baby formula at prices comparable to those you may be used to back home, although don't count on finding your favourite brand. There are also fabulous, family-friendly attractions that should appeal to kids of all ages. Those with a wildlife focus include Nairobi National Park (p61), Nairobi Safari Walk (p61), David Sheldrick Wildlife Trust (p63) and the Giraffe Centre (p61), while the National Museum (p59), Karen Blixen's House & Museum (p64) and Bomas of Kenya (p65) could all maintain the interest of older kids for an hour or two. The Kazuri Beads & Pottery Centre (p65) is another possibility.

Many midrange and top-end hotels have swimming pools.

Children's Highlights

National Parks & Reserves

Masai Mara National Reserve Africa's charismatic megafauna in abundance. (p112)

Lake Nakuru National Park Lions, leopards and playful monkeys with easy access. (p102)

Nairobi National Park A kid-sized park with no time for interest levels to flag. (p61)

Shimba Hills National Reserve A quick half-day safari from the coast with good roads all the way. (p219)

Hell's Gate National Park Walk and cycle with megafauna. (p97)

Activities

Ballooning Ride high over the Masai Mara in a balloon (p116).

WHAT TO PACK

While supplies of the following are available in most large supermarkets, they can be expensive and may not be the brands you're used to back home. Bring as much as possible from home:

➡ canned baby foods

➡ child-friendly insect repellent (not available in Kenya)

➡ child seat if you're hiring a car or going on safari

➡ disposable nappies

➡ powdered milk

Dolphin watching Swim with the dolphins at Kisite Marine National Park (p230).

Snorkelling Snorkel at Manda Toto Island to discover a whole new underwater world. (p266)

Sailing Take a dhow trip from Lamu for a picnic lunch on the beach. (p262)

Elephant feeding Feed the elephant orphans at Nairobi's David Sheldrick Wildlife Trust (p63).

Planning

Local attitudes towards children vary in Kenya just as they do in the West, but kids will generally be welcomed anywhere that's not an exclusively male preserve, especially by women with families of their own.

Accommodation

Safari lodges can handle most practicalities with aplomb, whether it's an extra bed or cot, or buffet meals that will have something even the fussiest of eaters will try. Some lodges have children's playgrounds and almost all have swimming pools. In non-lodge accommodation, your chances of finding what you need (such as cots) increase the more you're willing to pay.

Budget hotels are probably best avoided for hygiene reasons. Most midrange accommodation should be acceptable, though it's usually only top-end places that cater specifically for families. Camping can be exciting for the little ones, but you'll need to be extra careful that your

DESIGN PICS / KEITH LEVIT / GETTY IMAGES ©

NIGEL PAVITT / GETTY IMAGES ©

Top: Giraffe Centre, Nairobi (p61)

Bottom: David Sheldrick Wildlife Trust (p63), Nairobi National Park

kids aren't able to wander off unsupervised into the bush.

Most hotels will not charge for children under two years of age. Children between two and 12 years who share their parents' room are usually charged 50% of the adult rate; you'll also get a cot thrown in for this price. Large family rooms are sometimes available, and some places also have adjoining rooms with connecting doors.

Be warned that some exclusive lodges, especially those aimed at a honeymoon or similar market, impose a minimum age limit for children. Others are more welcoming and lay on child-friendly activities.

Eating

Kenyans are family-friendly and dining out with children is no problem. Hotel restaurants occasionally have high chairs, and while special children's meals aren't common, it's easy enough to find items that are suitable for young diners.

Supermarkets stock boxes of fresh juice, and fresh fruit (tangerines, bananas and more) is widely available.

Health

Consult your doctor well in advance of travel as some vaccinations or medications (including some for preventing malaria) are not suitable for children under 12 years.

Transport

Safari vehicles are usually child friendly, but travelling between towns in Kenya on public transport is not always easy with children. Car sickness is one problem, and young children tend to be seen as wriggling luggage, so you'll often have them on your lap. Functional seatbelts are rare even in taxis and accidents are common – a child seat brought from home is a good idea if you're hiring a car or going on safari. You might also want to consider flying some parts of the journey in order to avoid long road trips.

Regions at a Glance

Nairobi

Wildlife
Museums & Culture
Food

City-fringe Wildlife
Track down the Big Five against an unlikely backdrop of not-so-distant skyscrapers in Nairobi National Park. With an orphanage for elephants and a nearby giraffe-breeding centre, Nairobi ranks among Kenya's most surprising wildlife-watching experiences.

Past & Present
Kenya's National Museum is one of Africa's best, an august colonial-era institution that tells Kenya's story exceptionally well, while the Karen Blixen Museum returns you to the realm of *Out of Africa* nostalgia. For something completely different, tour Kibera, Nairobi's pulsating heart.

Kenya's Table
Nairobi's culinary variety far surpasses anything you'll find elsewhere in the country. Here there's everything from fast and furious local places to upmarket options that evoke Nairobi's colonial past. And then there's Carnivore, one of Africa's most celebrated restaurants.

p53

Southern Rift Valley

Landscape
Wildlife
Activities

The Rift Fracture
The drama of Kenya's Rift Valley is one of natural Africa's grand epics, with astonishing rock formations and expansive lakes that are the aesthetic antidote to the horizonless world of the Masai Mara savannah.

Flamingo & Rhino
The Rift Valley lakes are rare natural phenomena that draw strange bedfellows to cohabit here. Delicate flamingos (when the mood takes them) and prehistoric rhinos are the headline acts among many, with fantastic birdlife (over one-third of Kenya's species) guaranteed.

Hike the Rift
While Mts Kenya and Kilimanjaro get all the attention, discerning hikers look to the relatively untrampled summits of Mt Longonot and Mt Susua. And there's nothing like a foot safari through Hell's Gate National Park for heightening the senses.

p87

Masai Mara & Western Kenya

Wildlife
Landscape
Birdwatching

Great Migrations

Western Kenya's Masai Mara, together with Tanzania's Serengeti, is home to the greatest wildlife show on earth. The great predators – lions, leopards, cheetahs, hyenas and crocs – share the plains with vast congregations of zebras and wildebeest, while elephants and giraffes look on.

Africa in Microcosm

The vast savannah plains of the Masai Mara may grab the headlines, but Western Kenya also boasts Lake Victoria, one of Kenya's most underrated natural wonders, as well as soaring mountains and Kakamega Forest that evokes the endless stands of green in central Africa.

Birders' Paradise

From graceful secretary birds on the plains of the Mara, to bumbling bright turacos in the jungles of Kakamega, the west flutters with birdlife. Other top spots include Saiwa Swamp and the islands of Lake Victoria.

p110

Central Highlands & Laikipia

Wildlife
Activities
Landscape

Beyond the Parks

With not a national park to be seen, Laikipia is nonetheless one of the best places in Kenya to see wildlife, from lions and African wild dogs to black and white rhinos. The focus for all this abundance are the cattle-ranches-turned-conservancies that are home to much cutting-edge conservation.

Stairway to Heaven

Walk or climb Mt Kenya, Africa's second-highest peak and you'll never forget the incongruity of snows this close to the equator or the sweeping views that extend across the continent.

The Aberdares

Africa's highest-dwelling elephant herd and all manner of weird and wonderful plants and animals inhabit this forested realm that's utterly unlike the Africa of popular imagination.

p148

Southeastern Kenya

Wildlife
Landscape & Culture
Activities

World-class Parks

From the elephant-and-Kili views of Amboseli to the vast, rugged beauty of the Tsavo parks with their history of man-eating lions and rescued rhino, southeastern Kenya is the scene of some of Kenya's most soulful wildlife experiences.

The Maasai Heartland

The Maasai presence here lends personality to a thinly populated landscape of sweeping savannah plains, volcanic cinder cones and jagged peaks. The ranches around Amboseli and the western foothills of the Chyulu Hills in particular are where the two come together most memorably.

Caves & Climbing

Spelunkers will relish the prospect of the world's longest lava tube in the Chyulu Hills National Park. Climbing is also possible in Tsavo West, as is hiking along the western fringe of the Chyulu Hills.

p183

Mombasa & the South Coast

Beaches
Wildlife
Culture

Sun, Sand & Sea

Despite the occasional rash of package-tourism development, some of East Africa's finest beaches are found on Kenya's south coast. Away from sands that sparkle like crystals, there are islands galore and world-class diving.

Beach & Safari

From elephants, buffaloes and giraffes in the inland reserves to whale sharks and dolphins by the dozen in the oceans, there's a lot of wildlife to be tracked down around here, but it's the profusion of birds that really stands out.

City & Coastal Vibes

Choose from the big-city attractions of Mombasa, with its ancient fort, twisting streets and bubbling contemporary character, or the quiet life found in fishing villages up and down the coast – getting wrapped up in the coast's Swahili culture couldn't be easier.

p204

Lamu & the North Coast

Beaches
Wildlife
Culture

Beach & Islands

If the security situation allows, pack a bucket and spade and struggle to choose between the lively beach at Malindi, the mellow vibes of Watamu or, maybe best of all, an island-hopping trip by dhow around the sublime sands of the Lamu archipelago.

Birds, Butterflies & Elephant Shrews

For most wildlife watchers the north coast is all about the birds. Everywhere you go around here you'll be accompanied by the sing-song notes of hundreds of different birds, but look a bit harder and you'll find elephant shrews, thousands of butterflies and fish in a plethora of colours.

Live Like a Swahili

Put simply, Lamu is the ultimate immersion in all things Swahili. This gorgeous town of narrow streets and *bui-bui*-clad women is the oldest in Kenya and the most complete Swahili settlement in existence.

p238

Northern Kenya

Adventure
Wildlife
Culture

The Road Less Travelled

These remote frontier lands where Kenya, Ethiopia, South Sudan and Somalia collide are only just starting to register with foreign tourists, thus giving wannabe explorers a genuine opportunity to go where few have trodden before. You're almost guaranteed, too, to stumble upon large mammals outside of protected areas.

Wild Lands

Deserts where the horizons never seem to end and one of Africa's most beautiful lakes, Lake Turkana, more than compensate for the long days in the saddle on rough tracks needed to get here.

A Tribal Heartland

From butterfly-bright Samburu warriors, to the dramatically pierced Turkana women and the elegant Gabbra peoples who wander the burning deserts with their camels, northern Kenya is arguably the tribal heartland of Kenya.

p270

On the
Road

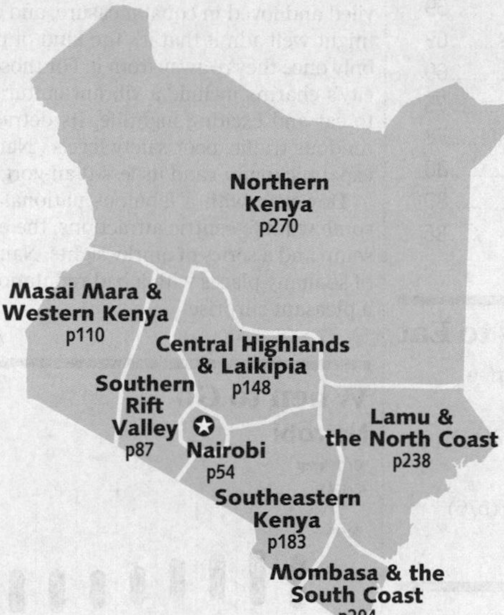

**Northern
Kenya**
p270

**Masai Mara &
Western Kenya**
p110

**Central Highlands
& Laikipia**
p148

**Southern
Rift
Valley**
p87

**Lamu &
the North Coast**
p238

✪ **Nairobi**
p54

**Southeastern
Kenya**
p183

**Mombasa & the
South Coast**
p204

Nairobi

📖 020 / POP 3.915 MILLION / ELEV 1661M

Includes ➡

History 55
Sights 59
Activities 68
Courses 69
Tours 69
Festivals & Events 69
Sleeping 69
Eating 75
Drinking & Nightlife 78
Entertainment 80
Shopping 80
Around Nairobi 86

Best Places to Eat

➡ Karen Blixen Coffee Garden (p78)

➡ Mama Oliech (p75)

➡ Talisman (p77)

➡ Roadhouse Grill (p76)

➡ Al-Yusra (p75)

Best Places to Stay

➡ Giraffe Manor (p72)

➡ Emakoko (p73)

➡ Acacia Tree Lodge (p72)

➡ Wildebeest Eco Camp (p71)

➡ King Post (p71)

Why Go?

East Africa's most cosmopolitan city, Nairobi is Kenya's beating heart, an exciting, maddening concrete jungle that jarringly counterpoints the untrammelled natural beauty to be found elsewhere in the country.

Nairobi's polarising character ensures that the city is reviled and loved in equal measure, and even those who love it might well admit that it's the kind of place many rave about only once they're away from it. For those who call it home, the city's charms include a vibrant cultural life, fabulous places to eat and exciting nightlife. Its detractors point to its horrendous traffic, poor safety levels ('Nairobbery' is a common expat nickname) and its less-than-gorgeous appearance.

However, with a fabulous national park on its doorstep, some wildlife-centric attractions, the excellent National Museum and a series of quirky sights, Nairobi's reality – like that of so many places with a bad reputation – will often come as a pleasant surprise.

When to Go
Nairobi

Jan, Feb & Jun–Sep The driest months; Nairobi National Park is at its best.

Oct–Dec The rain cools things off without causing more than the usual traffic jams.

Mar–May There are fewer tourists around, but it's the rainy season, which *can* be miserable.

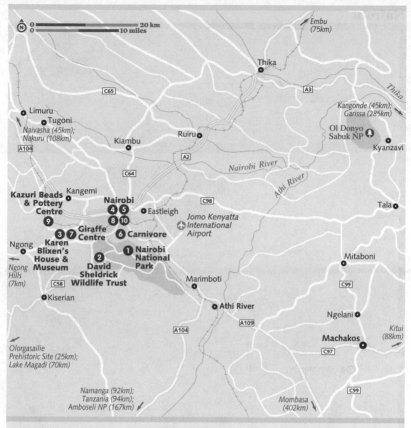

Nairobi Highlights

❶ Nairobi National Park (p61) Searching for wild lions and rhinos within sight of skyscrapers.

❷ David Sheldrick Wildlife Trust (p63) Bottle-feeding a group of orphaned baby elephants.

❸ Karen Blixen's House & Museum (p64) Reliving *Out of Africa* nostalgia.

❹ National Museum (p59) Deepening your understanding of all things Kenyan.

❺ Kibera (p74) Learning how much of Nairobi lives by taking a tour through one of Africa's largest and most vibrant shanty towns.

❻ Carnivore (p77) Indulging your inner predator at this legendary culinary pilgrimage.

❼ Giraffe Centre (p61) Tangling tongues with an endangered Rothschild's giraffe.

❽ Lord Delamere Terrace & Bar (p78) Listening for the echoes of tall tales told by colonial types.

❾ Kazuri Beads & Pottery Centre (p65) Learning all about beads and supporting a fabulous project at the same time.

❿ Kenyatta International Conference Centre (p59) Looking out on Nairobi in all its sprawling, chaotic glory.

History

Nairobi is a completely modern creation, and everything here has been built since the city was founded in 1899. As the tracks of the East African Railway were laid down between Mombasa and Kampala, a depot was established at a small stream known to the Maasai as *uaso nairobi* (cold water). The

Nairobi

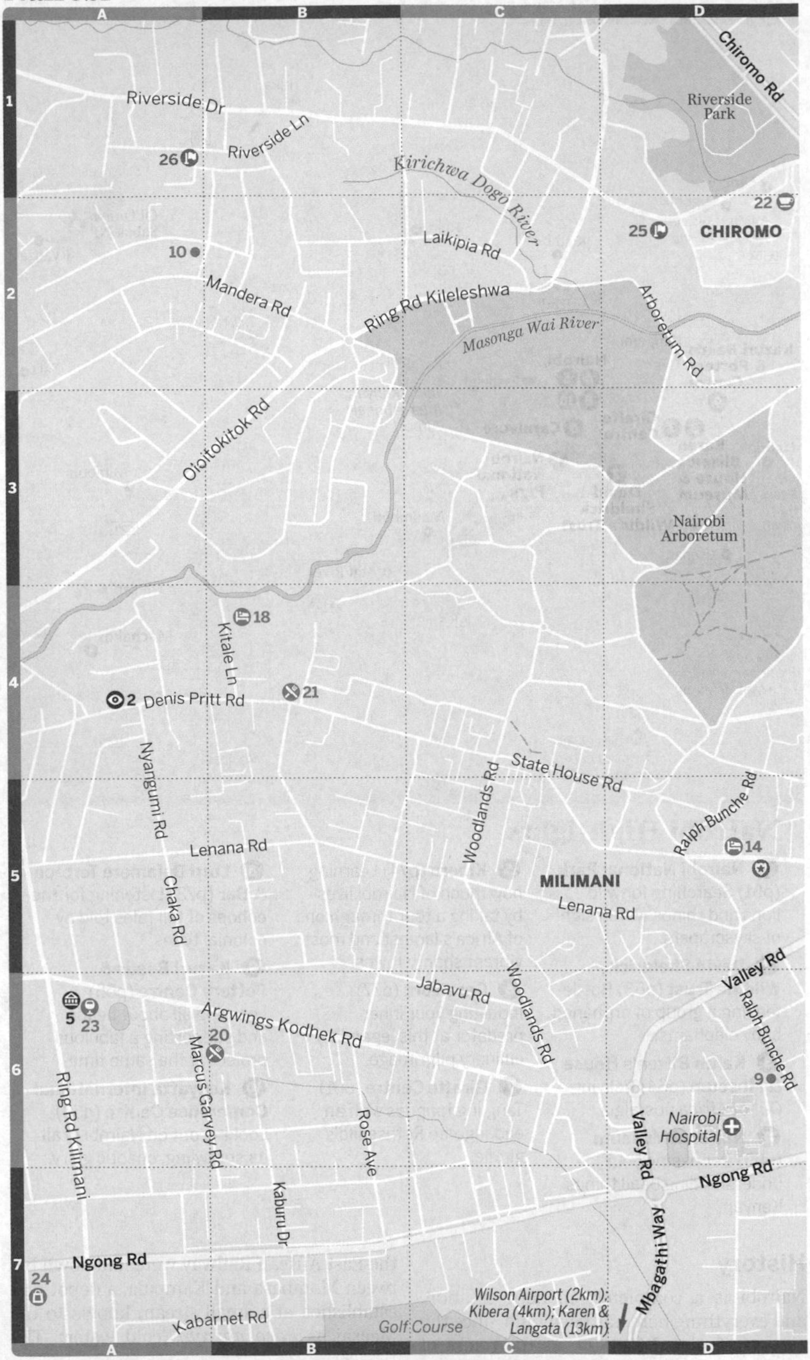

Chiromo Rd

Riverside Park

Riverside Dr

26

Riverside Ln

Kirichwa Dogo River

22

Laikipia Rd

25 **CHIROMO**

10

Mandera Rd

Ring Rd Kileleshwa

Arboretum Rd

Masonga Wai River

Oioitokitok Rd

Nairobi
Arboretum

Kitale Ln

18

2 Denis Pritt Rd

21

Nyangumi Rd

State House Rd

Woodlands Rd

Ralph Bunche Rd

Lenana Rd

14

Chaka Rd

MILIMANI

Lenana Rd

Jabavu Rd

Woodlands Rd

Valley Rd

5 23

Argwings Kodhek Rd

Ralph Bunche Rd

Marcus Garvey Rd

20

9

Ring Rd Kilimani

Rose Ave

Valley Rd

Nairobi
Hospital

Kaburu Dr

Ngong Rd

24

Ngong Rd

Wilson Airport (2km);
Kibera (4km); Karen &
Langata (13km)

Mbagathi Way

Kabarnet Rd

Golf Course

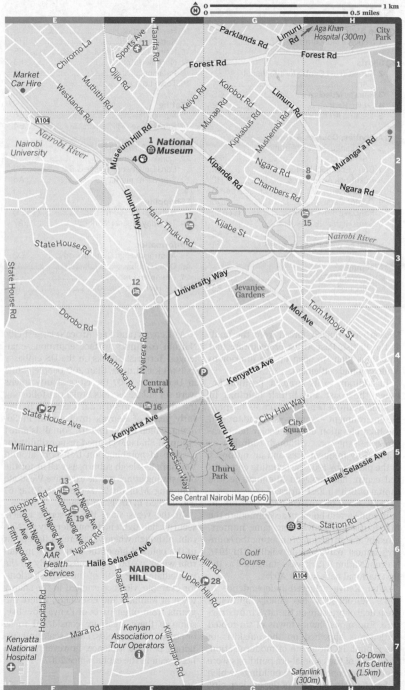

0   1 km
0   0.5 miles

Aga Khan
Hospital (300m)

City
Park

Parklands Rd
Limuru Rd
Forest Rd

Sports Ave
Taarita Rd
Forest Rd

Chiromo La
Muthithi Rd
Oljio Rd
Keiyo Rd
Kolobot Rd
Limuru Rd

Market
Car Hire

Westlands Rd

Munae Rd
Kipkabus Rd
Mushembi Rd

A104

Nairobi River

Museum Hill Rd

1 National
Museum

4

Kipande Rd

Ngara Rd

Muranga'a Rd

7

Nairobi
University

Uhuru Hwy

Chambers Rd

8

Ngara Rd

Harry Thuku Rd

17

Kijabe St

15

Nairobi River

State House Rd

University Way

Jevanjee
Gardens

Moi Ave

Tom Mboya St

State House Rd

12

Dorobo Rd

Mamlaka Rd

Nyerere Rd

P

Kenyatta Ave

City Hall Way

27

State House Ave

Central
Park

16

City
Square

Kenyatta Ave

Uhuru Hwy

Haile Selassie Ave

Milimani Rd

13

6

Bishops Rd
Fourth Ngong Ave
Third Ngong Ave
Second Ngong Ave
First Ngong Ave

19

Ngong Rd

Procession Way

Uhuru
Park

See Central Nairobi Map (p66)

3

Station Rd

Fifth Ngong Ave

AAR
Health
Services

Haile Selassie Ave

NAIROBI
HILL

Lower Hill Rd

Golf
Course

A104

Hospital Rd

Ragati Rd

Upper Hill Rd

28

Mara Rd

Kenyan
Association of
Tour Operators

Kilimanjaro Rd

Kenyatta
National
Hospital

Safarilink
(300m)

Go-Down
Arts Centre
(1.5km)

Nairobi

◎ **Top Sights**
1 National Museum.....................................F2

◎ **Sights**
2 Kuona Trust Centre for the Visual
   Arts...A4
3 Railway Museum.....................................G6
4 Snake Park...F2
5 Tazama Art Gallery.................................A6

⊕ **Activities, Courses & Tours**
6 ACK Language & Orientation
   School..F5
7 Ben's Ecological Safaris.........................H2
8 Bushbuck Adventures............................H2
   Nature Kenya...................................(see 1)
9 Origins Safaris...D6
   Pal-Davis Adventures.....................(see 8)
10 Sana Highlands Trekking
   Expeditions..A2
11 Savage Wilderness Safaris....................F1

⊜ **Sleeping**
12 Central YMCA..F3
13 Fairview Hotel...E5

14 Heron Portico Hotel................................D5
15 Kahama Hotel..H3
16 Nairobi Serena Hotel...............................F5
17 Norfolk Hotel...F3
18 Palacina..B4
19 Town Lodge..E6

⊗ **Eating**
20 Mama Oliech...B6
21 Roadhouse Grill.......................................B4

⊜ **Drinking & Nightlife**
22 Connect Coffee..D2
   Lord Delamere Terrace & Bar......(see 17)
23 Sierra Premium.......................................A6

⊜ **Shopping**
   National Museum Shop...................(see 1)
24 Tuesday Maasai Market.........................A7

ⓘ **Information**
25 Australian High Commission................D2
26 Dutch Embassy...A1
27 Ethiopian Embassy..................................E5
28 UK High Commission..............................G6

Maasai were quickly forced from the land, as the British East Africa protectorate had ambitious plans to open up the interior to white colonial settlement.

In addition to its strategic position between the coast and British holdings in Uganda, Nairobi benefited from its hospitable environment – water was abundant and the high elevation enjoyed cooler temperatures than the coast. Although Nairobi was blighted by frequent fires and an outbreak of the plague, by 1907 the booming commercial centre had replaced Mombasa as the capital of British East Africa.

Quite early on, the colonial government built some grand hotels to accommodate the first tourists to Kenya – big-game hunters, lured by the attraction of shooting the country's almost naively tame wildlife. In 1946 Nairobi National Park was established as the first national park in East Africa.

After Kenya achieved independence in 1963, Nairobi grew too rapidly, putting a great deal of pressure on the city's infrastructure. Enormous shanty towns of tin-roofed settlements appeared on the outskirts of the capital. In the name of modernisation, almost all of the colonial-era buildings were replaced by concrete office buildings, which today characterise much of the modern city.

As Kenya's (and East Africa's) largest city, Nairobi continues to face enormous challenges. Terrorist attacks on the US embassy in 1998 killed more than 200 people, while in December 2007 the city's shanty towns were set ablaze as riots broke out following the disputed presidential election. In the early years of Kenya's involvement in Somalia, which began in 2011, Somali Islamist group Al-Shabaab claimed responsibility for a spate of bombings on transport around Nairobi's Eastleigh suburb, as well as for the devastating attack on the exclusive Westgate Shopping Mall on 21 September 2013; 67 people died in the latter assault.

In the years since the Westgate attack, security has tightened considerably in Nairobi, although whenever there's a flashpoint in the political life of the nation, it's in Nairobi where it's often felt most keenly. In the immediate aftermath of the 2017 elections, for example, violence erupted in the shanty town of Mathare and elsewhere, where migrants from other parts of Kenya now live; some of these areas are considered to be opposition strongholds. Large-scale and sustained political violence, however, has not been seen in the capital since 2007.

⊙ Sights

⊙ City Centre

★ National Museum   MUSEUM
(Map p56; ☑ 020-8164134; www.museums.
or.ke; Museum Hill Rd; adult/child KSh1200/600,
combined ticket with Snake Park KSh1500/1000;
⊙8.30am-5.30pm) Kenya's wonderful National Museum, housed in an imposing building amid lush, leafy grounds just outside the centre, has a good range of cultural and natural-history exhibits. Aside from the exhibits, check out the life-size fibreglass model of pachyderm celebrity Ahmed, the massive elephant that became a symbol of Kenya at the height of the 1980s poaching crisis. He was placed under 24-hour guard by President Jomo Kenyatta; he's in the inner courtyard next to the shop.

The museum's permanent collection is entered via the Hall of Kenya, with some ethnological exhibits such as the extraordinary Kalenjin cloak made from the skins of Sykes' monkeys and a mosaic map of Kenya made from the country's butterflies. But this is a mere prelude. In a room off this hall is the Birds of East Africa exhibit, a huge gallery of at least 900 stuffed specimens. In an adjacent room is the Great Hall of Mammals, with dozens of stuffed specimens. Off the mammals room is the Cradle of Humankind exhibition, the highlight of which is the Hominid Skull Room – an extraordinary collection of skulls that describes itself as 'the single most important collection of early human fossils in the world'.

Upstairs, the Historia Ya Kenya display is an engaging journey through Kenyan and East African history. Well presented and well documented, it offers a refreshingly Kenyan counterpoint to colonial historiographies. Also on the 1st floor, the Cycles of Life room is rich in ethnological artefacts from Kenya's various tribes and ethnic groups, while at the time of writing there was also an exhibition (which may become permanent) of Joy Adamson's paintings covering Kenya's tribes.

If you're keen to really get under the skin of the collection (or the adjoining Snake Park), consider a tour with one of the volunteer guides who linger close to the entrance of both the National Museum and the Snake Park. Tours are available in English, French and possibly other languages. There's no charge for guide services, but a tip is appropriate.

Snake Park   ZOO
(Map p56; www.museums.or.ke; Museum Hill Rd; adult/child KSh1200/600, combined ticket with National Museum KSh1500/1000; ⊙8.30am-5.30pm) In the grounds of the National Museum, the Snake Park has some impressive snake species, including the puff adder, black mamba, Egyptian cobra, African rock python and Gaboon viper (with 4cm-long fangs, the longest in the world). There are also local fish species, lizards, turtles and some sad-looking crocodiles. Watch for the elephant fossil on the way down from the museum.

Kenyatta International Conference Centre   VIEWPOINT
(Map p66; Harambee Ave; viewing platform adult/child KSh500/250; ⊙viewing platform 9am-6pm) Nairobi's signature building was designed as

---

WHERE TO RELIVE *OUT OF AFRICA* IN KENYA

It was the film that made an entire generation long for East Africa. If you ever dreamed of following in the footsteps of Meryl Streep and Robert Redford, this list may just guide your path around Kenya.

Karen Blixen's House & Museum, Nairobi (p64) Where the real-life Karen Blixen actually lived (but not where the film was shot).

Railway Museum, Nairobi (p60) Board the steam train used in the movie.

Grave of Denys Finch Hatton, Ngong Hills (p86) Disappointingly unkempt for the last resting place of Blixen's celebrated lover.

Segera Retreat, Laikipia (p160) See (and perhaps even go for a ride in) the very plane in which Meryl Streep and Robert Redford flew out across the savannah.

Shaba National Reserve Many of the outdoor scenes were filmed here; it's northeast of Isiolo.

Out of Africa Lookout, Lake Nakuru National Park (p102) The birds-eye view of the flamingo-filled lake was filmed here.

NAIROBI ART GALLERIES

Go-Down Arts Centre (Map p62; ☑0726992200; www.thegodownartscentre.com; Dunga Rd; ⊙9am-5pm Mon-Fri) The Go-Down Arts Centre, a converted warehouse in Industrial Area, contains 10 separate studios and is a hub for Nairobi's burgeoning arts scene, bringing together visual and performing arts with regular exhibitions, shows, workshops and open cultural nights.

Circle Art Gallery (Map p62; ☑0790289991; www.circleartagency.com; 910 James Gichuru Rd; ⊙10am-5pm Mon-Fri, noon-5pm Sat) One of Nairobi's better exhibition spaces for contemporary art, Circle Art Gallery is more a gallery aimed at serious collectors than a shop aimed at a mass market. Its properly curated exhibitions feature paintings by predominantly local artists alongside works from elsewhere in East Africa.

Kuona Trust Centre for the Visual Arts (Map p56; ☑0733742752; www.facebook.com/Kuonatrustartcentre; Denis Pritt Rd; ⊙9am-5pm Mon-Fri) As much a studio for artists as a place for visitors to see art, this dynamic space hosts temporary exhibitions, artist workshops and seminars.

Tazama Art Gallery (Map p56; ☑020-3861750; Yaya Centre, Gigiri Lane; ⊙8am-8pm Mon-Sat, 10am-6pm Sun) Works by Kenyan artists are on display in a shopping-centre venue.

a fusion of modern and traditional African styles, though the distinctive saucer tower looks a little dated next to some of the city's newer and flashier glass edifices. Take the lift up to the 27th floor, then climb the remaining two floors to the **viewing platform** and (if it's open) helipad on the roof for marabou-stork's-eye views over Nairobi in all its wonderfully tangled madness.

The sight line goes all the way to the suburbs, and on clear days you can even see Mt Kenya. You're allowed to take photographs from the viewing level but not elsewhere in the building. You'll need to leave your passport with security at the building's entrance, then pay the admission fee at reception inside on the ground floor.

American Embassy Memorial Garden
GARDENS

(Map p66; Moi Ave; KSh30; ⊙6am-6pm) This well-tended walled garden occupies the former site of the American embassy, which was destroyed by terrorist bombings on 7 August 1998. It's a lovely spot, despite being right between busy Moi and Haile Selassie Aves. A short film describing the horrific events of the attack can also be viewed – ask the security guard if you'd like to see it.

Railway Museum
MUSEUM

(Map p56; ☑0724380975; www.facebook.com/nrailwaymuseum; Station Rd; adult/child KSh600/150; ⊙8am-5pm) The main collection here is housed in an old railway building and consists of relics from the East African Railway. There are train and ship models, photographs, tableware and oddities from the history of the railway, such as the engine seat that allowed visiting dignitaries like Theodore Roosevelt to take pot shots at unsuspecting wildlife from the front of the train.

In the grounds are dozens of fading locomotives in various states of disrepair, dating from the steam days to independence. You can walk around the carriages at your leisure. At the back of the compound is the steam train used in the movie *Out of Africa*. It's a fascinating introduction to this important piece of colonial history.

The museum is reached by a long lane beside the old train station.

Uhuru Park
PARK

(Map p66) FREE An expanse of manicured green on the fringe of the central city, this attractive park is a popular respite from the downtown noise and bustle. It owes its existence to Wangari Maathai, a Kenyan Nobel Peace Prize winner. In the late 1980s, she fought to save the park from the bulldozers of the former Moi government. Upon her death in late 2011, her funeral was held in the park and attended by thousands of mourners.

During the day, the park attracts picnicking families, business people stepping out of the office and anyone in need of a little communion with nature. It's not safe after dark.

Parliament House
NOTABLE BUILDING

(Map p66; ☑020-2221291; www.parliament.go.ke; Parliament Rd; ⊙8am-6.30pm Mon-Fri) If you fancy a look at how democracy works in Kenya, it's possible to obtain a free permit for the public gallery at Parliament House when parliament is in session. Visit the gate office to obtain a permit, and remember that applause is strictly forbidden. If parliament is out of session, you can tour the buildings by arrangement with the sergeant-at-arms; agree on any fee before you begin – start at KSh200 and see where it gets you.

Jamia Mosque   MOSQUE
(Map p66; Banda St) Amid the clutter of downtown, Nairobi's main mosque is a lovely building in typical Arab-Muslim style, with all the domes, marble and Quranic inscriptions you'd expect from an important Islamic site, plus the traditional row of shops down one side to provide rental income for its upkeep. Non-Muslims are very rarely allowed to enter, but the appealing exterior is visible from the street.

⦿ Karen & Langata

★ Nairobi National Park   NATIONAL PARK
(Map p62; ✆020-2423423; www.kws.go.ke/parks/nairobi-national-park; adult/child US$43/22; ☻6am-6pm) Welcome to Kenya's most accessible yet incongruous safari experience. Set on the city's southern outskirts, Nairobi National Park (at 117 sq km, one of Africa's smallest) has abundant wildlife that can, in places, be viewed against a backdrop of city skyscrapers and planes coming in to land – it's one of the only national parks on earth bordering a capital city. Remarkably, the animals seem utterly unperturbed by it all.

The park has acquired the nickname 'Kifaru Ark', a testament to its success as a rhinoceros (*kifaru* in Kiswahili) sanctuary. The park is home to the world's densest concentration of black rhinos (more than 50), though even the park's strong antipoaching measures couldn't prevent poachers from killing one of the rhinos in August 2013 and then again in January 2014. They were the first such attacks in six years, and reflect the current sky-high Asian black-market price for rhino horn.

Lions and hyenas are also commonly sighted within the park; rangers at the entrance usually have updates on lion movements. You'll need a bit of patience and a lot of luck to spot the park's resident cheetahs and leopards. Other regularly spotted species include gazelles, warthogs, zebras, giraffes, ostriches and buffaloes.

The park's wetland areas sustain approximately 400 bird species, which is more than in the whole of the UK.

Matatus 125 and 126 (KSh50, 30 to 45 minutes) pass by the main park entrance from the train station. You can also go by private vehicle. Nairobi tour companies offer half-day safaris (from US$75 per person).

Apart from the main entrance, which lies 7km from the city centre, there are other gates on Magadi Rd and the Athi River Gate; the latter is handy if you're continuing on to Mombasa, Amboseli or the Tanzanian border. The roads in the park are passable with 2WDs, but travelling in a 4WD is never a bad idea, especially if the rains have been heavy.

Unless you already have your own vehicle, the cheapest way to see the park is on the shuttle, a big KWS bus that leaves the main gate at 2pm on Sunday for a 2½-hour tour. You need to book in person at the main gate by 1.30pm, but do call ahead if you want to do the tour, as times can change.

Ivory-burning Site   MONUMENT
(Map p62; Nairobi National Park) This is one the most important landmarks in the annals of conservation: it was here that Kenyan president Daniel arap Moi made a dramatic statement to poachers by setting fire to 11 tonnes of seized ivory in 1989. The event improved Kenya's conservation image at a time when East African wildlife was being decimated by relentless poaching, and it's widely credited as playing a role in turning the tide against poaching in Kenya.

In 2016, President Uhuru Kenyatta oversaw the burning of 100 tonnes of ivory at the same site, amounting to the tusks from 6000 elephants, or 5% of global ivory stocks.

The site is just inside Nairobi National Park's main Langata Rd Gate.

Nairobi Safari Walk   ZOO
(Map p62; ✆020-2587435; www.kws.go.ke/content/nairobi-safari-walk; adult/child US$22/13; ☻9am-5.30pm) Just outside the main entrance to Nairobi National Park, off Langata Rd, this safari walk is a sort of zoo-meets-nature-boardwalk, with lots of birds as well as other wildlife, including a pygmy hippo, a bongo, an albino zebra and a white rhino, as well as primates and big cats. Children in particular love the chance to get closer to the animals than they're likely to be able to do in a national park.

★ Giraffe Centre   WILDLIFE RESERVE
(Map p62; ✆020-8070804; www.giraffecenter.org; Koitobos Rd; adult/child KSh1000/500; ☻9am-5pm) This centre, which protects

Nairobi National Park

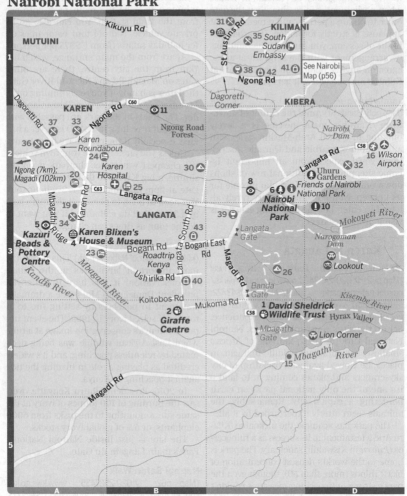

the highly endangered Rothschild's giraffe, combines serious conservation with enjoyable activities. You can observe, hand-feed or even kiss one of the giraffes from a raised wooden structure, which is quite an experience. You may also spot warthogs snuffling about in the mud, and there's an interesting self-guided forest walk through the adjacent Gogo River Bird Sanctuary.

This is one of Kenya's good-news conservation stories. In 1979 Jock Leslie-Melville (the Kenyan grandson of a Scottish earl) and his wife, Betty, began raising a baby giraffe in their Langata home. At the time, when

their African Fund for Endangered Wildlife (AFEW) was just getting off the ground, there were no more than 120 Rothschild's giraffes (which differ from other giraffe subspecies in that there is no patterning below the knee) in the wild. The Rothschild's giraffe had been pushed to the brink of extinction by severe habitat loss in western Kenya.

Today the population numbers more than 300, and the centre has successfully released these charismatic creatures into Lake Nakuru National Park (home to around 45 giraffes), Mwea National Reserve, Ruma National Park and Nasalot National Reserve.

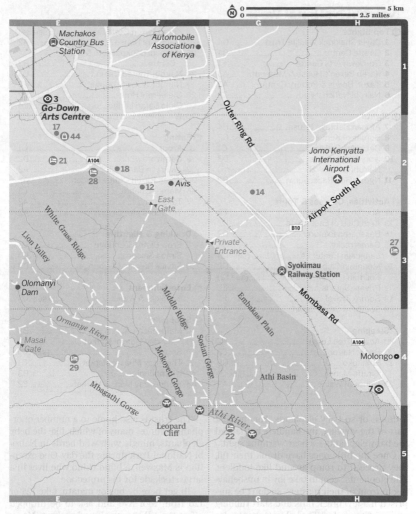

To get here from central Nairobi by public transport, take matatu 24 via Kenyatta Ave to the Hardy shops and walk from there. Alternatively, take matatu 26 to Magadi Rd, and walk through from Mukoma Rd. A taxi from the city centre should cost around KSh1500.

★ David Sheldrick
Wildlife Trust   WILDLIFE RESERVE
(Map p62; 📞 020-2301396; www.sheldrick wildlifetrust.org; Nairobi National Park; KSh500; ⏰ 11am-noon) Occupying a plot within Nairobi National Park, this non-profit trust was established in 1977, shortly after the death of David Sheldrick, who served as the antipoaching warden of Tsavo National Park. Together with his wife, Daphne, David pioneered techniques for raising orphaned black rhinos and elephants and reintroducing them into the wild, and the trust retains close links with Tsavo for these and other projects. The centre is one of Nairobi's most popular attractions, and deservedly so.

After entering at 11am, visitors are escorted to a small viewing area centred on a muddy watering hole. A few moments later, much like a sports team marching out onto the field, the animal handlers come in alongside

NAIROBI SIGHTS

Nairobi National Park

⊙ Top Sights
1 David Sheldrick Wildlife Trust C4
2 Giraffe Centre B4
3 Go-Down Arts Centre E1
4 Karen Blixen's House & Museum..........A3
5 Kazuri Beads & Pottery Centre A3
6 Nairobi National Park C2

⊙ Sights
7 African Heritage House H4
8 Bomas of Kenya C2
9 Circle Art Gallery C1
10 Ivory-burning Site D3
Nairobi Safari Walk .... (see 6)
11 Ngong Hills Racecourse B2

⊙ Activities, Courses & Tours
12 Abercrombie & Kent................................. F2
13 Aero Club of East Africa D2
14 Basecamp Explorer G2
15 Gametrackers...C4
Language Center Ltd .... (see 42)
16 Mountain Club of Kenya D2
Pollman's Tours & Safaris.............(see 12)
17 Private Safaris E2
18 Somak Travel.. F2
19 Southern Cross Safaris A3

⊖ Sleeping
20 Acacia Tree Lodge A2
21 Boma Nairobi.. E2
22 Emakoko...G5
Giraffe Manor.................................. (see 2)
23 House of Waine A3

Karen Blixen Cottages ....(see 34)
24 Margarita House A2
25 Milimani Backpackers & Safari
Centre... B2
26 Nairobi Tented Camp C3
27 Nairobi Transit Lounge H3
28 Ole Sereni Hotel..E2
29 Ololo Safari Lodge E4
30 Wildebeest Eco Camp B2

⊗ Eating
31 Arbor C1
32 Carnivore D2
33 J's Fresh Bar & Kitchen..........................A2
34 Karen Blixen Coffee Garden.................A3
35 Mama Ashanti C1
36 Talisman A2
37 Tin Roof Cafe A2

⊖ Drinking & Nightlife
38 Brew Bistro & Lounge C1
Simba Saloon ....(see 32)
39 Sirville Brewery & Lounge C3

⊛ Entertainment
Blankets & Wine............................(see 32)

⊕ Shopping
40 Matbronze B3
41 Saturday Maasai Market C1
Souk...(see 37)
42 Thursday Maasai Market........................C1
43 Utamaduni..B3
44 Wednesday Maasai Market...................E2

a dozen or so baby elephants. For the first part of the viewing, the handlers bottle-feed the baby elephants – a heartwarming sight.

Once the little ones have drunk their fill, they proceed to romp around like toddlers. The elephants seem to take joy in misbehaving in front of their masters, so don't be surprised if a few break rank and start rubbing up against your leg! The baby elephants also use this designated time slot for their daily mud bath; keep your guard up, as they've been known to spray a tourist or two with a trunkful of mud.

While the elephants gambol, the keepers talk about the individual orphans and their stories. Explanations are also given about the broader picture of the orphans project and some of the other projects in which the trust is involved. There's also the opportunity to 'adopt' one of the elephants. For those who do, there's a chance to visit when your elephant returns to the stockades around 5pm every evening – advance bookings essential.

The trust is also home to a number of orphaned rhinos, many of which, like the baby elephants, mingle with wild herds in Nairobi National Park during the day. One exception is Maxwell, a blind rhino who lives in a large stockade for his protection.

To get here by bus or matatu, take 125 or 126 from Moi Ave and ask to be dropped off at the KWS central workshop on Magadi Rd (KSh80, 50 minutes). It's about 1km from the workshop gate to the Sheldrick centre – it's signposted and KWS staff can give you directions. Be advised that at this point you'll be walking in the national park, which does contain predators, so stick to the paths. A taxi from the city centre should cost between KSh1500 and KSh2000.

★ **Karen Blixen's House & Museum**   HISTORIC BUILDING
(Map p62; ☏020-8002139; www.museums.or.ke/karen-blixen; Karen Rd; adult/child KSh1200/600; ⊙8.30am-6pm) If you loved *Out of Africa*, you'll love this museum in the farmhouse

where author Karen Blixen lived between 1914 and 1931. She left after a series of personal tragedies, but the lovely colonial house has been preserved as a museum. Set in expansive gardens, the museum is an interesting place to wander around, but the movie was actually shot at a nearby location, so don't be surprised if things don't look entirely as you expect!

Guides (nonmandatory but useful) are included in the admission fee, but they do expect a tip.

The museum is about 2km from Langata Rd. The easiest way to get here by public transport is by matatu 24 via Kenyatta Ave, which passes right by the entrance. A taxi from the city centre should cost KSh1500 to KSh2000.

★ Kazuri Beads
& Pottery Centre   ARTS CENTRE
(Map p62; ☏020-2328905; www.kazuri.com; Mbagathi Ridge; ⊙shop 8.30am-6pm Mon-Sat, 9am-5pm Sun, factory 8am-4.30pm Mon-Fri, to 1pm Sat) FREE An interesting diversion in Karen, this craft centre was started by an English expat in 1975 as a place where single mothers could learn a marketable skill and achieve self-sufficiency. From humble beginnings, the workforce has grown to over 100. A free tour takes you into the various factory buildings, where you can observe the process from the moulding of raw clay to the glazing of the finished products. There's also a gift shop with fixed prices.

Bomas of Kenya   CULTURAL CENTRE
(Map p62; ☏020-8068400; www.bomasofkenya. co.ke; Langata Rd; adult/child KSh800/400; ⊙performances 2.30-4pm Mon-Fri, 3.30-5.15pm Sat & Sun, villages 10am-6pm) The talented resident artists at this cultural centre perform traditional dances and songs taken from the country's various tribal groups, including Arabic-influenced Swahili *taarab* music, Kalenjin warrior dances, Embu drumming and Kikuyu circumcision ceremonies. It's touristy, of course, but still a spectacular afternoon out. The complex consists of a number of *bomas* (villages), each constructed in the architectural style of Kenya's major ethnic groups.

The centre has such a high profile that the first meeting of the National Constitutional Conference was held here in 2003, producing the Bomas Draft of the new constitution.

It's located at Langata, near the main gate of Nairobi National Park (p61). Bus or matatu 125 and 126 run here from Nairobi train station (KSh80, 30 minutes). Get off at Magadi Rd, from where it's about a 1km walk, clearly signposted on the right-hand side of the road. A taxi should cost KSh1500 to KSh2000. Note that if you bring a video camera there's an extra admission charge.

African Heritage House   NOTABLE BUILDING
(Map p62; ☏0721518389; www.africanheritage book.com; group of 4 KSh4000) Designed by Alan Donovan, an African-heritage expert and gallery owner, this stunning exhibition house overlooking Nairobi National Park can be visited by prior arrangement only. The mud architecture combines a range of traditional styles from across Africa, and the interior is furnished exclusively with tribal artefacts and artworks. For those with a bit of cash to spare, it's possible to negotiate overnight stays, formal meals and luxurious transfers by steam train or helicopter. The house is off Mombasa Rd.

NAIROBI NATIONAL PARK'S TOP FIVE

Nairobi National Park may be much maligned and fears remain over its future, but the park is one of Africa's most accessible and it has the potential to provide some signature safari experiences:

➡ *that* photo of a lion or rhino with skyscrapers looming in the background;

➡ spotting black rhinos from the world's densest population of the species;

➡ seeing a host of plains wildlife (giraffes, impalas, zebras) and four of the Big Five (lions, leopards, rhinos and buffaloes) before your safari has really begun;

➡ epic birdwatching: 400 species have been recorded here; look for the threatened Madagascar squacco heron, corncrake, lesser kestrel, red-throated tit and Jackson's widowbird – the latter featured in the BBC's *Planet Earth 2* series in 2017;

➡ sponsoring an orphaned baby elephant at David Sheldrick Wildlife Trust.

Central Nairobi

Harry Thuku Rd

Slip Rd

University Way

Monrovia La

Monrovia St

Jevanjee Gardens

Muranga'a Rd

Tom Mboya St

Kitome Rd

River Rd

Government La

Moi Ave

38

45

Moktar Daddah St

Muindi Mbingu St

Koinange St

Njugu La 20

Biashara St

25 🏦

Tubman Rd

Kigali Rd

Jamia Mosque

Kimathi La

13 ❌

Kimathi St

7

10 ❌

8

21 🔒

Loita St

Market St

Banda St

23 ✚

9 🏨

47

5

6

Kenyatta Ave

19 35 32 🏦

41

Standard St

Wabera St

16 ❌

Kaunda St

22 🔒

17

Uhuru Hwy

Central Park

P

39 🏧

Main Post Office
✉
29 ✉

Koinange St

11 ❌

46

30 🏦

Mama Ngina St

Kaunda St

Kenyatta Ave

Nairobi Immigration Office

Posta Rd

City Hall Way

City Square

Parliament Rd

4 ♣

3 ◉

Processional Way

Uhuru Hwy

Uhuru Park

County La

33 ✚

County Rd

Haile Selassie La

Parliament La

Haile Selassie Ave

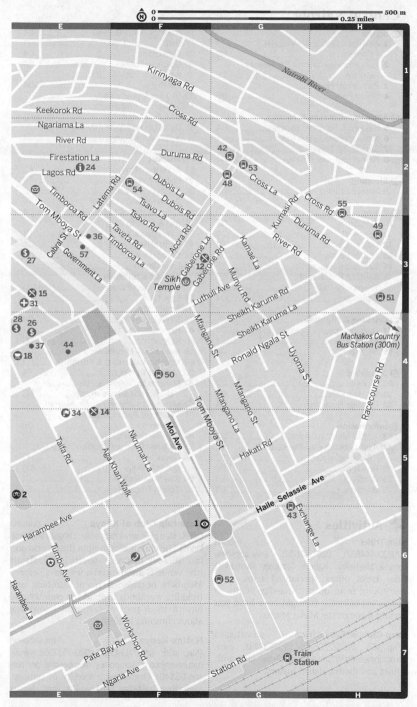

Central Nairobi

◉ Sights
1 American Embassy Memorial
   Garden F6
2 Kenyatta International Conference
   Centre E5
3 Parliament House C6
4 Uhuru Park B6

✪ Activities, Courses & Tours
5 Eastern & Southern Safaris B4
6 Natural World Kenya Safaris C4
7 Safari Icon Travel D3
8 Safe Ride Tours & Safaris D3

⬛ Sleeping
9 Sarova Stanley Hotel D3

✕ Eating
10 Al-Yusra D3
11 Beneve Coffee House C4
12 Malindi Dishes F3
13 Ranalo Foods D3
14 Seasons Restaurant E5
15 Seasons Restaurant E3
   Thorn Tree Café .... (see 9)
16 Trattoria D4

◉ Drinking & Nightlife
17 Dancing Spoon D4
18 Java House E4
19 Simmers C4

⬟ Shopping
20 Atul's C2
21 City Market C3
22 Prestige Bookshop D4

❶ Information
23 Acacia Medical Centre C3
24 Association for the Physically
   Disabled of Kenya E2
25 Barclays B2
26 Barclays E4
27 Barclays E3
28 Cosmos Forex Bureau E4
   DHL .... (see 37)
29 EMS Office C4
30 Goldfield Forex C4
31 KAM Pharmacy E3
32 Postbank D4
33 St John Ambulance C7
34 Tanzanian Embassy E5
   UAE Exchange .... (see 31)
35 Ugandan High Commission
   (Consular Section) C4

❶ Transport
36 Adventure Upgrade Safaris E3
37 British Airways E4
38 Budget A2
39 Bus & Matatu Stop (for
   Hurlingham & Milimani) B4
40 Bus & Matatu Stop (for
   Westlands) C1
41 Central Rent-a-Car C4
42 Dream Line C2
43 Easy Coach G6
   Easy Coach Terminal
   (Matatus to Eldoret) .... (see 43)
44 Egypt Air E4
45 Emirates A2
46 Ethiopian Airlines C4
47 Kenya Airways B3
   KLM .... (see 47)
48 Main Bus & Matatu Area G2
49 Matatus to Kericho & Kisumu H3
50 Matatus to Kibera F4
51 Matatus to Naivasha, Nakuru,
   Nyahururu & Namanga H3
52 Matatus to Wilson Airport, Nairobi
   National Park, Langata &
   Karen G6
53 Modern Coast Express G2
54 Mololine Prestige Shuttle F2
55 Narok Line H2
   Qatar Airways .... (see 47)
56 Riverside Shuttle C1
57 Tough Trucks Kenya E3

🏃 Activities

Bike Treks   CYCLING
(☑020-4446371, 020-2141757; www.angelfire.com/sk/biketreks; Kabete Gardens, Westlands) Bike Treks offers specialised trips, with everything from quick three-day jaunts to full-on expeditions; it might even have you cycling through the Masai Mara...

Aero Club of East Africa   SCENIC FLIGHTS
(Map p62; ☑0722205936, 0733832488; www.aeroclubea.com; Wilson Airport) Flying club with a long and distinguished history.

Mountain Club of Kenya   CLIMBING
(MCK; Map p62; www.mck.or.ke; Langata Rd, Westlands) The club meets at 8pm the second and last Tuesday of every month in Westlands (the venue is announced a few days before). Members organise frequent climbing and trekking weekends around the country and have a huge pool of technical knowledge about climbing in Kenya.

Nature Kenya   BIRDWATCHING
(Map p56; ☑0771343138, 020-3537568; www.naturekenya.org; temporary membership per person US$40) Organises a variety of outings, including half-day bird walks that depart

from the National Museum (p59). Contact the outfit for more information.

🐟 Courses

ACK Language & Orientation School
LANGUAGE

(Map p56; ☑ 0718233085, 020-2721893; www. acklanguageschool.org; Bishops Rd, Upper Hill) The Anglican Church runs full-time Swahili courses of varying levels lasting 14 weeks and taking up to five hours a day. Private tuition is available on a flexible part-time schedule.

Language Center Ltd
LANGUAGE

(Map p62; ☑ 020-3870610, 0721495774; www. language-cntr.com/welcome.shtml; Ndemi Close) A good Swahili centre offering a variety of study options ranging from private hourly lessons to daily group courses. Located off Ngong Rd.

🧭 Tours

★ Kibera Tours
TOURS

(☑ 0721391630, 0723669218; www.kiberatours. com; per person KSh2500) This well-regarded tour of the shanty town by two Kibera residents takes you to Toi Market, an orphanage, a bead factory, a local home as well as a lookout point.

★ Explore Kibera
TOURS

(☑ 072700517; www.explorekibera.com; per person US$29; ⊗ 9am & 2pm daily) Running since 2009, these three-hour tours take you deep into the Kibera shanty town, from the famous railway tracks to markets to local beadmakers and other artisans.

People to People Tourism
TOURS

(☑ 0722750073, 0734559710; www.peopletopeople tourism.com) This company does city tours and can take you further afield, with an emphasis on cultural encounters. Ask whether it's still running its introduction to the world of *jua kali*, Kenya's open-air manufacturing industry; it sometimes combines tours of the usual tourist sights with visits to *jua kali* workshops producing crafts and other goods.

🎊 Festivals & Events

Kenya Fashion Week
FAIR

(☑ 0736779259; www.kenyaworldwidefashionweek. com; Sarit Centre, Westlands) An expo-style event held in June, July or August, bringing together designers and manufacturers from all over the country.

Tusker Safari Sevens
SPORTS

(www.kru.co.ke/safari7s; ⊗ Oct & Nov) A high-profile, international seven-a-side rugby tournament, although poor governance issues in recent years have seen its prestige slip a little. Even so, it's always hotly contested and the Kenyan team has a strong record in the tournament, winning most recently in 2013 and 2016. It usually takes place at the Moi International Sport Centre.

Kenya Music Festival
MUSIC

(☑ 020-2712964; Kenyatta International Conference Centre; ⊗ Aug) Kenya's longest-running music festival was established almost 80 years ago by the colonial regime. African music now predominates, but Western and expat musicians still take part. It's held over 10 days in August.

🛏 Sleeping

Nairobi has Kenya's widest selection of places to stay, with particularly good midrange and top-end choices. You can expect to pay a bit more here than you would elsewhere in Kenya (excluding, of course, the exclusive lodges of the national parks). However, in a city where safety can be an issue, it's worth paying more for secure surroundings. Most midrange and top-end places also throw in a hearty buffet breakfast.

🛌 City Centre

★ Sarova Stanley Hotel
HOTEL $$

(Map p66; ☑ 0719048000; www.sarovahotels. com/stanley-nairobi; cnr Kimathi St & Kenyatta Ave; s/d from US$116/135; P ✴ 🛜 🏊) A Nairobi classic. The original Stanley Hotel was established in 1902 – past guests include Ernest Hemingway, Clark Gable, Ava Gardner and Gregory Peck. The latest version boasts large and luxurious rooms and a timeless lobby characterised by plush green leather banquettes, opulent chandeliers and lots of dark-wood trimmings. Rates drop slightly from Friday to Sunday.

★ **Kahama Hotel**   HOTEL **$$**
(Map p56; ☑ 0731430444, 0712379780; www.
kahamahotels.co.ke; Murang'a Rd; s/d from
US$45/55; [P][📶]) Almost equidistant between
the city centre and the National Museum
(p59), this place is a terrific budget choice.
Billing itself 'economy with style', it provides
just that, with pleasant rooms and comfy
beds. The only downside? The new highway
passes by the front door – ask for a room at
the back.

Norfolk Hotel   HOTEL **$$$**
(Map p56; ☑ 020-2265000; www.fairmont.com/
norfolkhotel; Harry Thuku Rd; r from US$180;
[P][✳][📶][🏊]) Built in 1904 but overhauled
many times since, Nairobi's oldest hotel was
the place to stay in colonial times. It remains
the traditional starting point for elite safaris, and Lord Delamere Terrace is still Nairobi's most famous meeting place. The hotel's
leafy grounds give it an almost rustic feel,
although the recently renovated rooms have
lost some of that classic Norfolk look.

Nairobi Serena Hotel   HOTEL **$$$**
(Map p56; ☑ 020-2822000; www.serenahotels.
com; Procession Way, Central Park; s weekday/
weekend US$215/175, d US$294/225; [P][✳][@]
[📶][🏊]) This member of the top-notch Serena
chain has a fine sense of individuality, with
its international-class facilities displaying a
touch of safari style. Of particular note is the
on-site Maisha health spa. Opt for one of the
amazing garden suites, where you can take
advantage of your own private patio, com-
plete with minipergola.

As the hotel is right opposite Uhuru Park,
avoid walking anywhere from here at night.

🛏 Milimani & Upper Hill

Central YMCA   HOSTEL **$**
(Map p56; ☑ 020-2724116; www.facebook.com/
ymcastatehsrd; State House Rd; dm/s/d from
KSh1100/1500/2300; [P]) While it might not
inspire the Village People to dedicate a song
to it, this central spot has a decent range of
passable rooms. You don't need to be a man
or a Christian to stay here, though you'll be
in the majority if you're either; lone women
should look elsewhere. Breakfast is available
for KSh500, other meals for KSh750.

Heron Portico Hotel   HOTEL **$$**
(Map p56; ☑ 020-2720740; www.theheron
portico.com; Milimani Rd, Milimani; s/d US$135/155;
[P][📶][🏊]) It's hard to see why anyone would
pay top-end prices when places like the Heron are around. Rooms are modern, extremely comfortable and well appointed, while
the staff are attentive and professional. The
location is quiet and there's not the merest
trace of Buffalo Bill's, a notorious brothel
that once occupied the site. This is highly
recommended.

★ **Palacina**   BOUTIQUE HOTEL **$$$**
(Map p56; ☑ 020-2715517; www.palacina.com;
Kitale Lane; 1/2-person ste US$250/350, pent-
houses US$550; [P][📶][🏊]) The fabulous collec-
tion of stylish suites – at what was one of
the first genuine boutique hotels in Kenya –
is perfect for well-heeled sophisticates

WHERE TO STAY IN NAIROBI
....

The heart and soul of Nairobi is the **city centre**, so if you want to go to bed and wake up
amid it all, look no further. The main budget area is between Tom Mboya St and River Rd,
where you'll find dozens of small hotels and guesthouses. Staying in this area is some-
thing of a budget travellers' tradition, but remember that these are some of Nairobi's
meanest streets. The area west of Moi Ave is generally fine and has a range of options,
although it empties after dark and at weekends.

The eastern districts of **Nairobi Hill** and **Milimani** host a clutch of reliable business
hotels and upmarket lodges, as well as some backpacker spots, all pleasantly removed
from the congestion of the city centre. If you want to be a bit further out, there's expat-
friendly **Westlands** and **Parklands**.

For a decidedly different take on Nairobi, consider heading right out into leafy **Karen**,
Langata and **Nairobi National Park**, which puts you pretty far from the city centre,
though that's precisely the point, offering as they do welcome respite from the grit of the
centre. For the most part, accommodation out here is at the top end, though the charm
exuded by many of these properties is worth every shilling and you're within striking
distance of some of Nairobi's top tourist attractions. If that's out of your price range,
however, there are a couple of campsites and other options worth checking out.

who still like the personal touch. Intimate rooms are awash with calming tones, boldly accented by rich teak woods, lavish furniture and private Jacuzzis. Cheaper monthly rates are also available. It's off Dennis Pritt Rd.

Town Lodge HOTEL $$$
(Map p56; ☑020-2881600; www.clhg.com; Second Ngong Ave, Milimani; s/d from KSh12,450/16,900; P@🖭) The focus here is on affordable comfort for business travellers, with attractive if somewhat sterile rooms. With a small gym and excellent breakfasts, it's one of the best-value options in Nairobi. You can also take advantage of the bars and restaurants at the Fairview next door.

Fairview Hotel HOTEL $$$
(Map p56; ☑020-2711321; www.fairviewkenya. com; Bishops Rd, Milimani; s/d/ste from KSh18,000/20,160/25,980; ✳🖭🖭) An excellent choice that puts many of the more prestigious and pricier places in town to shame. The Fairview is nicely removed from the central hubbub and defined by its winding paths and greenery-filled grounds. It all creates a refined atmosphere, especially around the charming courtyard restaurant.

🛏 Westlands

King Post HOTEL $$
(☑0722261182, 0734261182; www.gablesgroup. co.ke/properties/the-king-post-2; Rhapta Rd, Westlands; r from US$140; P✳🖭🖭) Brimful of personality and styled to resemble a traditional Swahili village, this original place has appealing rooms with whitewashed walls, lovely little niches and alcoves, intricately carved mahogany and oak furnishings, and a real sense of comfort wedded to the style.

Nelson's Court Seviced Apartments APARTMENT $$
(Map p72; ☑0773320392; www.nelsonscourt. com; Ring Rd, Parklands; studios/apt from US$105/124) The attractive modern apartments here, close to Westlands, are classy and contemporary without going over the top, and have fully-equipped kitchens and private balconies. The location is good and the sense of light and space and the comforts of home make a lovely alternative to the anonymity of a hotel. There are studios and attic apartments to choose from.

Lotos Inn & Suites HOTEL, SUITES $$
(Map p72; ☑0727168169; www.lotos.co.ke; 19 Mpaka Rd, Westlands; s/d from KSh11,500/13,000; 🖭) Despite the bizarre spelling of its name (the hotel logo is a lotus), this fantastic addition to Nairobi's hotel scene offers spacious, great-value and super-comfortable rooms within easy walking distance of Westlands' dining and nightlife. There's a great breakfast buffet in the top-floor restaurant and friendly staff. The only negative is the lack of mosquito nets or suitable prophylaxis – bring your own.

Concord Hotel HOTEL $$$
(☑0711111333, 0709466000; www.theconcord hotels.com; Wangapala Rd, Parklands; s/d from US$172/178; P🖭🖭) With well-sized rooms, a quiet location close to Westlands, a gym, a swimming pool and a collection of good onsite restaurants, the Concord is an excellent choice in the city's north. Some south-facing rooms partly overlook a shanty town, but otherwise there's a real sense of professionalism and style that makes it a good business option.

🛏 Karen & Langata

⭐**Wildebeest Eco Camp** TENTED CAMP $
(Map p62; ☑0734770733; www.wildebeesteco camp.com; 151 Mokoyeti Rd West, Langata; camping from KSh1250, dm tents KSh1750, garden tents s/d from KSh4000/6000, luxury safari tents s/d/ tr KSh10,800/13,500/16,000; 🖭🖭) This fabulous place is arguably Nairobi's outstanding budget option. The atmosphere is relaxed yet switched on, and the accommodation is spotless and great value, however much you're paying. The deluxe garden tents are as good as those at many exclusive safari places – for a fraction of the price, although the absence of mosquito nets is an issue. A great Nairobi base.

⭐**Milimani Backpackers & Safari Centre** HOSTEL $
(Map p62; ☑0722347616, 0718919020; www. milimanibackpackers.com; 57 St Helens Lane, Karen; camping KSh1000, dm KSh1500, cabins s/d KSh3000/3500; @🖭) This terrific place within a very secure gated community is one of the friendliest accommodation options in town, and whether you camp out back, cosy up in the dorms or splurge on your own cabin, you'll end up huddled around the fire at night, swapping travel stories and dining on home-cooked meals (from KSh500) with fellow travellers.

Westlands

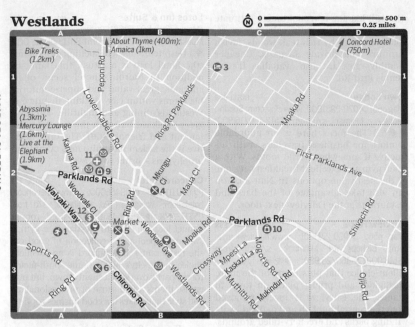

About Thyme (400m); Amaica (1km)

Bike Treks (1.2km)

Concord Hotel (750m)

Abyssinia (1.3km); Mercury Lounge (1.6km); Live at the Elephant (1.9km)

Parklands Rd

Waijaki Way

Parklands Rd

Westlands

● Activities, Courses & Tours
1 Extreme Outdoors Africa......................A3

▲ Sleeping
2 Lotos Inn & Suites................................C2
3 Nelson's Court Seviced Apartments...................................C1

✖ Eating
4 Mama Rocks at the Alchemist Bar.......B2
5 Open House..B3
6 Urban Eatery.......................................A3

◉ Drinking & Nightlife
Alchemist Bar.................................. (see 4)

7 Gipsy's Bar...A3
8 Havana Bar...B3
K1 Klub House ....(see 10)

◎ Shopping
9 Banana Box..A2
10 K1 Flea Market....................................C3

ⓘ Information
11 AAR Health Services Clinic...................A2
12 Barclays..A2
Barclays.......................................(see 11)
13 Travellers Forex Bureau B3

It's off Langata Rd. To get here, take matatu 126 (to Galeria) or 111 (Karen Shopping Centre), then change to a Karen matatu and ask to be let off at St Helen's Lane.

★ **Acacia Tree Lodge**　　　　LODGE **$$**
(Map p62; ☏ 0702460460; www.acaciatree lodgekenya.com; Marula Lane, Karen; s/d US$80/120; 𝐏 𝟮) Stylish decor, attention to detail in everything from the mattresses to the pillows, and a commitment to donating its profits to worthy causes, Acacia Tree Lodge ticks many boxes. The quiet Karen location is another winner. Exceptional value.

Margarita House　　　　GUESTHOUSE **$$**
(Map p62; ☏ 020-2018421, 0711424357; www.the margaritahouse.com; 53 Lower Plains Rd, Karen; s/d from US$80/112; 𝐏 𝟮 𝟮) Tucked away on a quiet street, this tranquil guesthouse offers large, comfortable rooms with contemporary artworks on the walls and plenty of stylish furnishings throughout. The roads can be a little confusing around here – check the detailed directions on the website.

★ **Giraffe Manor**　　　　HISTORIC HOTEL **$$$**
(Map p62; ☏ 0725675830, 020-8891078; www. thesafaricollection.com; Mukoma Rd, Karen; per

person with full board from US$550; P) Built in 1932 in typical English style, this elegant manor is situated on 56 hectares, much of which is given over to the adjacent Giraffe Centre (p61). As a result, you may find a Rothschild's giraffe peering through your bedroom window first thing in the morning. Yet the real appeal here is that you're treated as a personal guest of the owners.

★Emakoko   LODGE $$$
(Map p62; ☑0724156044, 0787331632; www.emakoko.com; Uhuru Gardens; s/d with full board US$620/960; P @ 🛜 ⚊) This stunning, artfully designed lodge inhabits a rise overlooking Nairobi National Park from its southern boundary and the Mbagathi River. It's a wonderful way to begin or end your Kenyan safari by bypassing the hassles of Nairobi altogether, and the rooms and public areas are exquisite. Rooms look out over the park.

★House of Waine   BOUTIQUE HOTEL $$$
(Map p62; ☑0734699973, 020-2601455; www.houseofwaine.com; Masai Lane, Karen; s/d from US$385/580; P ✴ @ 🛜 ⚊) Sophistication and style are the hallmarks of this stunning boutique offering. Every room is different according to its theme – the slate-grey colour scheme in the Tembo room is a standout – and the atmosphere is one of soothing, perfectly conceived spaces. The garden is a real oasis. It's little wonder that this has fast become one of Nairobi's premier addresses.

Karen Blixen Cottages   BOUTIQUE HOTEL $$$
(Map p62; ☑020-882138, 0733616206; www.karenblixencoffeegarden.com; 336 Karen Rd, Karen; s/d US$350/575; P 🛜 ⚊) Located near Karen Blixen's House & Museum (p64), this gorgeous clutch of spacious cottages is centred on a formal garden and adjacent to a small coffee plantation and a fine garden restaurant. It's sophisticated and supremely comfortable. If you're keen on having an *Out of Africa* experience, look no further.

Ololo Safari Lodge   LODGE $$$
(Map p62; ☑020-2177507, 0708844818; www.ololo lodge.com; Nairobi National Park; r US$486-886; P @ 🛜 ⚊) Built as a family home overlooking the southern boundary of Nairobi National Park (p61), popular Ololo feels every bit the luxury safari lodge despite its proximity to one of Africa's busiest cities. Rooms in the main building are stately and sophisticated, the tower room is high on novelty, and the safari tents (a mix of canvas and stone walls) are rather lovely.

Nairobi Tented Camp   TENTED CAMP $$$
(Map p62; ☑0774136524; www.nairobitented camp.com; Nairobi National Park; s/d incl breakfast US$193/260; P) 🌿 Staying at this luxury tented camp inside Nairobi National Park helps you forget that one of Africa's largest cities is just a few kilometres away. The camp offers the full-on safari experience: the eight tents are like those you'll find in Kenya's better-known parks, and there's a real (and somewhat incongruous) sense of solitude. Park entrance fees are not included.

Airport transfers are possible, or staff can meet you at the park gate.

🛏 Mombasa Road

Nairobi Transit Lounge   GUESTHOUSE $
(Map p62; ☑0732908174; www.nairobitransit lounge.co.ke; Ulinzi Ct, Kiungani Rd, Syokimau; r from US$29, with shared bathroom from US$24) Handy for Jomo Kenyatta International

---

YOU KNOW YOU'RE IN NAIROBI WHEN...

➡ The main topic of conversation is the terrible traffic, followed by an experience/discussion/argument on/with/against a Ma-3 (matatu – because *tatu* means 'three' in Swahili...)

➡ You hear people talking in *sheng*, a street slang that mixes English with Swahili

➡ Ghetto FM (*sheng* radio station) or Radio Jambo with Mbusi ('Goat' – a popular presenter) is playing on the radio

➡ Your plans for the weekend are plans for 'Sato' (Saturday)

➡ You spot the marabou storks near Nyayo Stadium Roundabout

➡ You see a Maasai warrior walking down the road chatting on a mobile (cell) phone

➡ You find yourself caught in rush-hour traffic going *out* of the city at 9am on Friday morning

➡ Did we mention the traffic?

KIBERA

Kibera (which is derived from a Nubian word, *kibra*, meaning forest) is a sprawling urban jungle of shanty-town housing. Home to as many as a million residents, Kibera is the world's second-largest shanty town (after Soweto in Johannesburg, South Africa). Although it covers 2.5 sq km in area, it's home to somewhere between a quarter and a third of Nairobi's population, and has a density of an estimated 300,000 people per square kilometre. The neighbourhood was thrust into the Western imagination when it featured prominently in the Fernando Meirelles film *The Constant Gardener*, which is based on the book of the same name by John le Carré. With the area heavily polluted by open sewers, and lacking even the most basic infrastructure, residents of Kibera suffer from disease and poor nutrition, not to mention violent crime.

Although it's virtually impossible to collect accurate statistics on shanty towns, as the demographics change almost daily, the rough estimates for Kibera are shocking enough. According to local aid workers, Kibera has one pit toilet for every 100 people; the shanty town's inhabitants suffer from an HIV/AIDS infection rate of more than 20%; and four out of every five people living here are unemployed.

History

The British established Kibera in 1918 for Nubian soldiers as a reward for service in WWI. However, following Kenyan independence in 1963, housing in Kibera was rendered illegal by the government. But this new legislation inadvertently allowed the Nubians to rent out their property to a greater number of tenants than legally permitted and, for poorer tenants, Kibera was perceived as affordable despite the questionable legalities. Since the mid-1970s, though, control of Kibera has been firmly in Kikuyu hands; the Kikuyu now comprise the bulk of the population.

Orientation

Kibera is located southwest of central Nairobi. The railway line heading to Kisumu intersects Kibera, though the shanty town doesn't actually have a station. However, this railway line does serve as the main thoroughfare through Kibera, and you'll find shops selling basic provisions along the tracks.

Visiting the Shanty Town

A visit to Kibera is one way to look behind the headlines and, albeit briefly, touch on the daily struggles and triumphs of life in the town; there's nothing quite like the enjoyment of playing a bit of footy with street children aspiring to be the next Didier Drogba. Although you could visit on your own, security is an issue and such visits aren't always appreciated by residents. The best way to visit is on a tour. Two recommended companies are Explore Kibera (p69) and Kibera Tours (p69).

Getting There & Away

You can get to Kibera by taking bus 32 or matatu 32c from the Kencom building along Moi Ave. Be advised that this route is notorious for petty theft, so be extremely vigilant and pay attention to your surroundings.

Airport (6km away) and/or Syokimau railway station, this fine little townhouse has tidy, simple rooms that are outstanding value, even more so once you throw in the friendly and knowledgeable staff.

Boma Nairobi HOTEL $$$
(Map p62; ☑ 0719050000, 020-3904000; www.the boma.co.ke; Red Cross Rd, Bellevue; s/d US$255/280; P❋@🛜🏊) Owned by the Red Cross, this smart hotel is popular with NGOs and businesspeople alike for its quiet location

– equally handy for (if not especially close to) the centre, Nairobi National Park and the airport – its excellent and well-equipped, large and colourful rooms, and professional service. Its neighbouring property, Boma Inn, has altogether simpler rooms (US$130).

Ole Sereni Hotel HOTEL $$$
(Map p62; ☑ 020-3901000; www.ole-sereni.com; cnr Mombasa Rd & Southern Bypass; r from US$195; P❋@🛜) Ole Sereni is as close as Nairobi comes to having an airport hotel (it's 12km

from Jomo Kenyatta International Airport), and some rooms (small but stylish) overlook Nairobi National Park (p61). The terrific restaurant has a terrace overlooking the park and there are shops, bars, a swimming pool, and a real buzz when things get busy. The professional service is another plus.

✕ Eating

The sheer breadth of flavours from across Kenya, the continent and beyond make Nairobi one of Africa's culinary capitals. Cool cafes are now a fundamental part of local and expat life, and downtown has dozens of old-style Kenyan canteens. Lovely garden settings also help to make eating out a pleasure. For upmarket choices, try Westlands or Karen.

✕ City Centre

Ranalo Foods   AFRICAN $
(Map p66; ☑0770785897; Kimathi St; mains KSh450-800; ⊙8am-11pm) There's nothing all that special going on here, but that's partly the point. It's all about good, honest local cooking, with dishes like fried tilapia – fish is the speciality here, true to the restaurant's Luo roots in western Kenya. The coconut fish stew with ugali or rice is a popular choice.

Malindi Dishes   KENYAN $
(Map p66; Gaberone Rd; mains KSh150-400; ⊙8am-10pm Sat-Thu, 3-10pm Fri) This small Swahili canteen serves great food from the coast, including pilau (curried rice with meat), *birianis* (spicy rice casseroles) and coconut fish, with side dishes such as ugali, naan and rice. You'll get a grand halal feed here, but, true to its Muslim roots, it's closed for prayer at lunchtime on Friday.

Seasons Restaurant   KENYAN, INTERNATIONAL $
(Map p66; Mutual Bldg, Kimathi St; mains KSh400-620, buffet KSh600; ⊙6.30am-11pm) The cafeteria vats here always brim with Kenyan and Western favourites, which is probably why this local chain has a strong following. The buffet is small but (unusually for those who've been staying in safari lodges) entirely African in orientation. You can bring in your own booze, food or *miraa* (twigs and shoots chewed as a stimulant) for a 'corkage' fee.

The Nairobi Cinema **outlet** (Map p66; ☑0708345602; Uchumi House, Aga Khan Walk; mains KSh400-620, buffet KSh600; ⊙6.30am-11pm) has a popular bar and beer garden,

where you can bring your own alcoholic beverage and pay a small corkage fee.

Beneve Coffee House   CAFE $
(Map p66; ☑020-217959; cnr Standard & Koinange Sts; mains KSh150-400; ⊙7am-4pm Mon-Fri) This small self-service cafe has locals queuing outside in the mornings waiting for it to open. Food ranges from African- and Indian-influenced stews to curries, fish and chips, samosas, pasties, and a host of other choices, all at low, low prices.

★Al-Yusra   SOMALI, KENYAN $$
(Map p66; ☑0712012012; www.alyusrakenya.com; Banda St; mains KSh220-550; ⊙7am-9pm) Roast camel, fried goat and plenty of pilau rice dishes just like Somalis and like-minded Kenyans love them make this busy 1st-floor place a hit, especially at lunchtime. The food is excellent (and halal) and also includes steaks, coconut rice with stew, Swahili fish curry and Ethiopian *injera* bread. Around since 2005, it's already a Nairobi institution.

Trattoria   ITALIAN $$
(Map p66; ☑020-3340855; www.trattoria.co.ke; cnr Wabera & Kaunda Sts; mains KSh650-2200; ⊙7am-midnight) Some things just don't change (this place has been around since 1981) and thank heavens for that! This classy Italian restaurant, swathed in trellises and plants, offers excellent pizzas, homemade pasta, risottos, varied mains (try the slow-braised lamb shanks) and a whole page of desserts. The atmosphere and food are excellent. It's packed every night and for lunch, especially on the balcony.

Thorn Tree Café   INTERNATIONAL $$$
(Map p66; ☑0719048000; www.sarovahotels.com; Sarova Stanley Hotel, cnr Kimathi St & Kenyatta Ave; mains KSh1000-2400; ⊙6am-9.30pm) The Stanley Hotel's legendary pavement cafe is still a traveller favourite, and it caters to most tastes with a good mix of food. The original thorn-tree noticeboard in the courtyard gave rise to the general expression and inspired Lonely Planet's own online Thorn Tree travel forum. The cafe's menu ranges from linguine with crab meat and ginger to Kenyan-style chicken stew.

✕ Milimani & Upper Hill

★Mama Oliech   KENYAN $$
(Map p56; ☑0723925604; Marcus Garvey Rd; mains KSh700-1350; ⊙11am-11.30pm) Fish dominates the menu here: the whole fried

tilapia from Lake Nakuru is the signature dish, especially when ordered with ugali and *kachumbari* (tomato-and-onion salsa). Wildly popular, the restaurant is considered one of Nairobi's best – the sort of place that locals take first-time visitors to the city (like Facebook founder Mark Zuckerberg in 2016).

★ **Roadhouse Grill** BARBECUE **$$**
(Map p56; ✆0720768663; www.facebook.com/RoadhouseGrillNairobi; Dennis Pritt Rd, Hurlingham; mains from KSh600; ⊙11am-6am Mon-Sat, to midnight Sun) Out beyond Milimani in the west, Roadhouse Grill is widely touted by locals as the best place for *nyama choma*. The meat (choose the goat) is prepared just as it should be: medium rare and perfectly tender. Order a side of ugali and some *kachumbari* (tomato-and-onion salsa), and you're halfway towards being Kenyan.

✗ Westlands

**Mama Rocks
at the Alchemist Bar** FOOD TRUCK **$$**
(Map p72; ✆0705801230; www.mamarocksburgers.com; Parklands Rd, Westlands; mains KSh750; ⊙6-11pm Tue, noon-3pm & 6-11pm Wed & Thu, noon-2am Fri & Sat, 1-10pm Sun) Nairobi's first and best food truck is very cool. With an African take on burgers and a location primed and ready for Westlands' night-time crowd, Mama Rocks' highlight is the Mango Masai Mama, a burger topped

NYAMA CHOMA AT THE RIFT

If you have your own wheels and a taste for barbecued meat, take the road southwest out of Nairobi, past Kiserian on the road to Lake Magadi, to Corner Baridi, where simple little **Olepolos Country Club** (✆0714032122; www.facebook.com/pg/olepolosnyama/about; C58, Corner Baridi; meals from KSh850; ⊙10am-5.30pm Mon-Thu, to 8pm Fri, 9am-midnight Sat & Sun) serves up roasted meat and roast chicken. Wash it down with cold Tuskers as you gaze over the Rift Valley and you'll be close to heaven.

It's around 34km southwest of downtown Nairobi near the town of Kisamis. If you don't have your own transport, take matatu 126 as far as Kiserian and then hire a taxi.

with mango, chilli-mango sauce and sweet roasted bell peppers. Samantha and Natalie keep things ticking over.

Urban Eatery INTERNATIONAL **$$**
(Map p72; ✆0709815000; www.urbaneatery.co.ke; PWC Tower, Waiyaki Way, Westlands; mains KSh650-1500; ⊙7am-11pm Mon-Thu, to 1am Fri & Sat, 8am-10pm Sun; ☏) This smart and upmarket place has a huge menu that takes in everything from pizza to sushi, including great salads, sandwiches, burgers and meat grills. Service is attentive and polite, and kids are welcome – there's even a bouncy castle outside.

Mama Ashanti AFRICAN **$$**
(Map p62; ✆0736222324; Muthangari Gardens Rd; mains KSh500-1300; ⊙11.30am-midnight) Pan-African cuisine can be surprisingly difficult to find in Nairobi, which is one of many reasons to make the pilgrimage out to Mama Ashanti. Here, the dishes are Ghanaian in inspiration and spicy as a basic starting point; the *pepe* (fiery goat stew) is a dish you're unlikely to forget for all the right reasons. The charcoal-grilled tilapia is also outstanding.

Arbor ASIAN, INTERNATIONAL **$$**
(Map p62; ✆0729400291; www.thearbor.wixsite.com/thearborcafe; 904 James Gicheru Rd, Maziwa; mains KSh500-950; ⊙10am-5pm Tue-Sun) So many cool Nairobi venues and cafes are set in a garden, and The Arbor knows the formula well. The Southeast Asian cooking (think curries and laksas) is assured, while the manicure-pedicure salon on site allows you to indulge yourself in more than just a culinary sense. It also serves up sandwiches, burgers and a handful of international dishes.

Abyssinia ETHIOPIAN **$$**
(✆0725151515; Brookside Grove, Westlands; mains KSh500-850; ⊙11am-11pm) Consistently good reviews from expats, locals and travellers alike make this an excellent choice for high-quality Ethiopian cooking. Aside from the rich tastes of the varied main dishes, the *injera* (Ethiopian crêpe-like bread) is perfectly light, just as it should be. It's worth coming here just for the coffee ceremony.

Open House INDIAN **$$**
(Map p72; ✆0727726345; www.openhouserestaurant.co.ke; Ring Rd, Westlands; mains KSh880-1220) Ask any long-term resident of Nairobi to nominate their favourite

FOR THE LOVE OF MEAT

Love it or hate it, **Carnivore** (Map p62; ☑ 020-5141300, 0733611608; www.tamarind.co.ke/carnivore; Langata Rd, Langata; buffet from KSh4000; ☺ 11.30am-11pm; P) serves up Kenya's most famous *nyama choma* (barbecued meat) – it's been an icon for tourists, expats and wealthier locals for over 25 years. At the entrance is a huge barbecue pit laden with real swords of beef, pork, lamb, chicken and farmed game meats such as crocodile and ostrich. It's a memorable night out.

UK magazine *Restaurant* named Carnivore one of the 50 best restaurants in the world in 2002 and 2003, when you could dine here on exotic game meats. Its legend seemed assured. In recent years, however, strict new hunting laws mean that zebra, hartebeest, kudu and the like are now off the menu, and you have to be content with camel, ostrich and crocodile in addition to more standard offerings. You also get soup, salads and sauces to go with the meats.

The experience works on a simple all-you-can-eat basis: as long as the paper flag on your table is flying, beautifully attired waiters will keep bringing the meat, which is carved right at the table. If you're in need of a breather, you can tip the flag over temporarily before eventually admitting defeat.

At lunchtime you can get to Carnivore by matatu 126 from the city centre – the turn-off is signposted just past Wilson Airport, and from the stop it's a 1km walk. At night it's best to hire a taxi, which should cost about KSh1000 each way, depending on your bargaining skills.

Indian restaurant and a fair few of them will plump for Open House. The service is friendly and the food is outstanding, from the signature chilli paneer or butter chicken to the *divine* ginger mushrooms. The number of Indians eating here seals the deal.

About Thyme   INTERNATIONAL **$$$**
(☑ 0721850026; www.about-thyme.com; cnr Peponi & Eldama Ravine Rds, Westlands; mains KSh1200-2500, lunch mains KSh1000; ☺ noon-10pm Tue-Sat, 10am-2.30pm Sun) In a welcoming garden setting in the city's north, About Thyme does some fine international dishes such as pumpkin-and-amaretti tortellini or battered red snapper in tamarind sauce. There's also a quick lunch menu, a creative cocktail menu (try the chilli-mango caipirinha) and a popular Sunday brunch (10am to 1pm). After your meal, sit back and smoke a sheesha (water pipe).

Amaica   KENYAN **$$$**
(☑ 0716687248; www.amaica.co.ke; Getathuru Garden, Peponi Rd, Westlands; mains KSh1000-2500; ☺ 10am-11pm; ☎) Dining at this wonderful place magically takes you out of the city for an hour or two, with views into the lush Karura Forest from the open terrace. The cooking also takes you on a journey through Kenya with its stellar menu of indigenous Kenyan cooking from all parts of the country. Don't miss the peanut soup!

🍴 Karen & Langata

Tin Roof Cafe   INTERNATIONAL **$$**
(Map p62; ☑ 0706348215; www.facebook.com/TinRoofCafe; Dagoretti Rd, Karen; mains KSh950-1100; ☺ 8.30am-5.30pm; ☎) This place has all the ingredients to be a Nairobi favourite: a quiet garden setting in Karen, great coffee, amazing juices, an Ottolenghi salad bar and a commitment to healthy eating. Despite the cafe vibe, full meals are possible and there's a set lunch for KSh750. The only complaint? It doesn't open for dinner.

Souk (p80), a fabulous shopping experience, is on the same property, which makes this an obvious place to combine lunch and shopping.

J's Fresh Bar & Kitchen   INTERNATIONAL **$$**
(Map p62; ☑ 0718607197; www.jsfreshbarandkitchen.com; Ngong Rd, Karen; mains KSh750-2100; ☺ noon-midnight) As good for a night out as for a great meal, J's is one of Karen's most popular venues. The food that emerges from the open kitchen is excellent, from creamy risotto with beetroot, ginger and veggies to burgers and traditional fish and chips. The wine list is one of Karen's most extensive, with choices from South Africa, France and Australia.

★ Talisman   INTERNATIONAL **$$$**
(Map p62; ☑ 0705999997; www.thetalismanrestaurant.com; 320 Ngong Rd, Karen; mains KSh1400-2350; ☺ 8am-midnight Tue-Sun; ☎) This classy cafe-bar-restaurant remains

KAREN BLIXEN

The suburb of Karen takes its name from Karen Blixen, aka Isak Dinesen, a Danish coffee planter and aristocrat who went on to become one of Europe's most famous writers on Africa. Although she lived in genteel luxury on the edge of the Ngong Hills, her personal life was full of heartbreak. After her first marriage broke down, she began a love affair with the British playboy Denys Finch Hatton, who subsequently died in a plane crash during one of his frequent flying visits to Tsavo National Park.

After the farm came close to bankruptcy, Blixen returned to Denmark, where she began her famous memoir *Out of Africa*. The book is one of the definitive tales of European endeavour in Africa, but Blixen was passed over for the 1954 Nobel Prize for Literature in favour of Ernest Hemingway. She died from malnutrition at her family estate in Denmark in 1962.

In 1985 *Out of Africa* was made into a movie starring Meryl Streep, Robert Redford and one of the retired trains from Nairobi's Railway Museum. The final production was terrific from a Hollywood perspective, but it left out enough of the colonial history to irk historians and Kenyan nationalists alike.

fashionable with the Karen in-crowd, and it rivals any of Kenya's top eateries for imaginative international food. The comfortable lounge-like rooms mix modern African and European styles, the courtyard provides some welcome air, and classics such as feta and coriander samosas and twice-cooked pork belly perk up the palate no end.

★ **Karen Blixen**

Coffee Garden INTERNATIONAL, KENYAN $$$

(Tamambo; Map p62; ☑ 0719346349; www.karenblixencoffeegarden.com; Karen Rd, Karen; mains KSh990-2290; ☺ 7am-10pm) The Coffee Garden offers diners five areas in which to enjoy its varied menu, including the plush L'Amour dining room, the historic 1901 Swedo House and the recommended main section, a casual restaurant set in a veritable English country garden. Dishes range from gourmet burgers to Swahili curries from the coast. The Sunday lunch buffet (KSh1800) is popular and excellent value.

🍷 Drinking & Nightlife

Locals love Nairobi's nightlife and you probably will, too, once you escape the clutches of the ubiquitous sports bars. Such a massive city naturally has plentiful opportunities for hedonistic nights out, and Westlands is generally the best neighbourhood for having a good time. If you take a taxi door to door, security is less likely to be an issue.

🍸 City Centre

★ **Simmers** BAR

(Map p66; ☑ 020-2217632; cnr Kenyatta Ave & Muindi Mbingu St; ☺ 8am-1am) If you're tired of having your bum pinched to the strains of limp R&B in darkened discos, Simmers could be your place. The atmosphere at this open-air bar-restaurant is amazing, with enthusiastic crowds turning out to grind the night away to parades of bands playing anything from Congolese rumba to Kenyan benga (contemporary dance).

★ **Lord Delamere Terrace & Bar** BAR

(Map p56; ☑ 020-2265000; www.fairmont.com/NorfolkHotel; Norfolk Hotel, Harry Thuku Rd; ☺ noon-3.30pm & 6.30-11pm) Once one of Africa's classic bars, the Lord Delamere Terrace was the starting point of many epic colonial safaris, and the scene of tall tales told by the likes of Ernest Hemingway and the Great White Hunters of the early 20th century. Not much of the former atmosphere remains, but come here as a pilgrimage to the Africa of old.

Java House CAFE

(Map p66; ☑ 0721494049; www.javahouseafrica.com; Mama Ngina St; ☺ 6.30am-10pm Mon-Fri, 7am- 9pm Sat, 8am-8pm Sun) This fantastic coffeehouse is rapidly turning itself into a major brand with cafes all over town, and you may see its logo on T-shirts as far afield as London and beyond. Aficionados say the coffee's some of the best in Kenya, and there are plenty of cakes and other sweet and savoury treats (even New York cheesecake).

Dancing Spoon WINE BAR

(Map p66; ☑ 0715336281; www.thewinebar.co.ke; 1st fl, 20th Century Bldg, Mama Ngina St; ☺ 10am-11pm) The Dancing Spoon is a good place to start the night before making for Westlands. With an impressive cellar of international wines and an equally good selection of whiskies, it has a classier atmosphere than that at many other central Nairobi drinking establishments. The attached restaurant does excellent pork ribs.

⚲ Westlands & Parklands

★ Connect Coffee   CAFE
(Map p56; ☑ 0708790480; www.connectcoffee. net; Prof David Wasawo Dr, Riverfront; ⊙ 8am-6pm Mon-Fri, 9am-6pm Sat & Sun) One of Nairobi's best and coolest cafes, Connect brings coffee sourced directly from farmers in Kenya, Ethiopia and Uganda to your table, and the barista-prepared offerings range from pour-over filter coffee to a popular cold brew or simply a long black. It's worth asking what's good on the day and then pondering your choices on the rather long menu.

★ J's Fresh Bar & Kitchen   BAR, CLUB
(☑ 0707612585; www.jsfreshbarandkitchen.com; Muthangari Dr, Westlands; ⊙ 9am-11pm) Building on the winning formula of its sister property (p77) in Karen, J's takes its DJs seriously enough to give them a permanent booth, and the food is so good that you could easily spend a whole night here. Each night's different, but Tuesday is hip hop laced with R&B, while Thursday Night Live is a good way to catch local bands.

★ Alchemist Bar   BAR
(The Yard; Map p72; ☑ 0727591116; www. alchemist.bar; Parklands Rd, Westlands; ⊙ noon-11pm Tue & Wed, to 2am Thu, to 5am Fri-Sun) One of Westlands' best nights out, Alchemist is an all-encompassing take on the Nairobi night, with the city's best DJs, terrific food (and a food truck outside) and bar staff (mixologists...) adept at creating perfect cocktails. There's an outdoor lounge area for when the dancing gets too hot and sweaty. Check the website for theme nights and events.

★ Havana Bar   BAR
(Map p72; ☑ 0723265941, 020-4450653; Woodvale Grove, Westlands; ⊙ noon-3am) In the heart of the Westlands nightlife district, the small Havana Bar packs them in tightly over two floors and is an enduring Nairobi favourite, drawing a broad cross-section of night owls, prostitutes among them. Latin tunes often morph into DJ-spun house, and you can drink Kenyan coffee, South African wines, middle-shelf international spirits or a rather fine mojito.

Champagne & Fishbowls   COCKTAIL BAR
(☑ 0737776677; www.experienceseven.com; Seven Seafood & Grill, ABC Pl, Waiyaki Way; ⊙ noon-11pm) This slick champagne bar in the Seven Seafood & Grill restaurant has fish tanks in abundance and has been endorsed by none other than Veuve Clicquot. There's an upmarket atmosphere (dress nicely) and there are fine champagnes and other cocktails to lubricate conversation. Happy hour runs from 5pm to 7pm on weekdays.

K1 Klub House   BAR
(Map p72; ☑ 0714579265; www.klubhouse.co.ke; Parklands Rd, Westlands; ⊙ 24hr) At the western end of Westlands, Klub House is a long-time local favourite. The spacious bar has plenty of pool tables and excellent DJs spinning reggae, dancehall, hip hop and R&B until late. There are live bands on Saturday night, while Monday is '80s night. Big sports events are shown here, but there's enough space to escape them if you prefer.

Gipsy's Bar   BAR
(Map p72; Woodvale Grove, Westlands; ⊙ 6pm-4am) This is one of the more popular bars in Westlands, pulling in a large, mixed crowd of Kenyans, expats and prostitutes, although the buzz has shifted elsewhere in recent years. Snacks are available and there's decent Western and African music, with parties frequently spilling out onto the pavement.

Mercury Lounge   COCKTAIL BAR
(www.mercurylounge.co.ke; ABC Pl, Waiyaki Way, Westlands; ⊙ 4pm-1am Sun-Thu, to 3am Fri & Sat) This sophisticated cocktail bar is smooth as silk,

---

WHERE TO DRINK
....

There are plenty of cheap but very rough-and-ready bars around Latema Rd and River Rd, although these places aren't recommended for female travellers; even male drinkers should watch themselves. There are some safer watering holes around Tom Mboya St and Moi Ave, and some restaurants and hotels are fine places for a drink.

Out in Westlands and Karen, the drinking scene brings in a lot more expats. Dress smart casual here. Wherever you go, foreign women without a man in tow will draw attention. Due to the high number of female prostitutes, men will generally get the bulk of the hassle.

with vaguely retro curves in the decor and a fine list of cocktails to keep the well-to-do crowd happy. It kicks off the week in suitably sedate fashion with 'Monday Blues', then Tuesday is 'Wine & Jazz', Thursday is all about salsa and Friday is nostalgia all the way.

🍸 Milimani

Sierra Premium
BAR

(Map p56; ☏0733505152; www.sierrapremium. com; 3rd fl, Yaya Centre, Argwings Kodhek Rd, Hurlingham; ⊙noon-11pm) At Sierra Premium, which claims to be Kenya's first boutique brewery, beer is brewed according to the 1516 German Purity Law, using just hops, malt, yeast and water. The 3rd-floor gastropub and brasserie is the perfect place to try the lagers and stouts.

🍸 Karen & Langata

Simba Saloon
CLUB

(Map p62; ☏020-501706; www.tamarind.co.ke/ simba-saloon; KSh300-500; ⊙5pm-late Wed-Sun) Next door to Carnivore (p77) on the road to Karen, this large, open-air bar-club pulls in a huge crowd. There are video screens, several bars, a bonfire, and a mix of Western and contemporary African music on the dance floor, although you might get the occasional African superstar playing live – Manu Dibango, Salif Keita and Ismaël Lô have all played here.

It's usually crammed with wealthy Kenyans, expat teenagers, travellers and NGO staff, plus a fair sprinkling of sex workers.

To get here, take matatu 126 from the town centre in daylight hours and walk from the main road. At all other times, take a taxi.

Sirville Brewery & Lounge
LOUNGE

(Map p62; ☏0713805380; www.sirvillebrewery. com; Galleria Mall, Langata Rd, Karen; ⊙noon-midnight) Upstairs in the Galleria Shopping Mall, Sirville is a popular Karen watering hole serving craft beers with names like Mara Pils, Tsavo Lager, Amboseli Ale and Aberdare Bitter Ale. The lounge is modern and its decor a little sterile, but the beers are a nice break from Tusker.

🍸 Beyond the Centre

★Brew Bistro & Lounge
MICROBREWERY, BAR

(Map p62; ☏0719648138; www.thebigfive breweries.com; Piedmont Plaza, Ngong Rd, West Nairobi; ⊙11am-1am Sun-Wed, to 2am Thu, to 4am Fri & Sat) Craft beers have been slow to take off in Nairobi, but Brew is a lesson in how to do things. The rooftop bar is a beacon of the Nairobi night for its heady mix of German beers, salsa dancing and live music. With five beers emerging from its brewery, great views and good snacks, it's a favourite to head to after dark.

It also does a fine Sunday brunch (11am to 4pm) to help you nurse that hangover.

☆ Entertainment

★Live at the Elephant
LIVE MUSIC

(☏0721946710; www.facebook.com/LiveAtThe Elephant; Gate 3, Kanjata Rd, Lavington; ⊙from 8pm Fri) This may just be the most appealing live-music venue in town. It draws a trendy, upmarket crowd with its fair share of Nairobi hipsters for the regular programme of up-and-coming artists (mostly Kenyan with some from further afield in Africa). Check out the Facebook page to see what's coming up.

★Blankets & Wine
LIVE MUSIC

(Map p62; ☏0736801333, 0720721761; www. blanketsandwine.com; tickets KSh2000-3000; ⊙1st Sun of month) This monthly picnic-concert is one of the best-loved features on Nairobi's live-music circuit. Musicians vary, but the underlying principle is to support local and East African acts, from singer-songwriter and acoustic to rock and roots. Families are welcome. The site is off Langata Rd.

🛍 Shopping

★Matbronze
ARTS & CRAFTS

(Map p62; ☏0721762855, 0733969165; www.mat bronze.com; Kifaru Lane, Karen; ⊙8am-5pm Mon-Thu, to 8pm Fri, to 5.30pm Sat, 9.30am-5.30pm Sun) More than 600 wildlife bronzes by Denis Mathews (from jewellery and small lion-cub-footprint dishes to much larger pieces running into thousands of dollars) make this one of the most appealing places to shop in Kenya. It's all produced at the on-site foundry and every piece is a work of art. There's also a small cafe serving light meals.

★Souk
ARTS & CRAFTS

(Map p62; ☏0706348215; www.thesoukkenya. com; Dagoretti Rd, Karen; ⊙9.30am-5.30pm Mon-Sat) Some of Kenya's more creative artists, photographers, leatherworkers and other high-quality artisans and artists have come together under one roof – the result is one of Kenya's most discerning shopping experiences. It shares premises with the equally excellent Tin Roof Cafe (p77).

★**Utamaduni** ARTS & CRAFTS

(Map p62; ☑0722205028; http://utamadunishops.com; Bogani East Rd, Karen; ⊗9am-6pm) Utamaduni is a large crafts emporium and easily one of the best places to souvenir shop in Nairobi, with more than a dozen shops selling all kinds of excellent African artworks and souvenirs. Prices start relatively high, but there's *none* of the hard sell you'd get in town. A portion of all proceeds goes to local conservation and other charitable projects.

K1 Flea Market MARKET

(Map p72; ☑0714579265; www.klubhouse.co.ke; Parklands Rd, Westlands; ⊗10am-6pm) This small flea market at the K1 Klub House (p79) is a terrific way to spend a morning. The shopping experience is limited to a few stalls, but the brunch is excellent and the atmosphere casual and cool.

Prestige Bookshop BOOKS

(Map p66; ☑0707660164; www.prestigebookshop.com; Mama Ngina St; ⊗9am-6pm Mon-Fri, to 3pm Sat) If you're looking for books on Kenya and Africa in the downtown area, this small bookshop is a terrific resource.

National Museum Shop BOOKS

(Map p56; National Museum, Museum Hill Rd; ⊗8.30am-5pm) Apart from a small and largely unimaginative collection of curios, Kenya's museum shop has one of the country's best selections of books about Kenya and surrounding places. You can enter without paying the museum (p59) admission fee.

Banana Box ARTS & CRAFTS

(Map p72; ☑0722746686, 020-3743390; www.bananabox.co.ke; Sarit Centre, Westlands; ⊗9.30am-6pm Mon-Sat, 10am-2pm Sun) Amid the rather-less-altruistic commercialism of the Sarit Centre, Banana Box works in conjunction with community projects and refugee groups and offers modern uses for traditional objects. It's one of the better handicrafts stores around town, with an upmarket feel but reasonable prices.

City Market MARKET

(Map p66; Muindi Mbingu St; ⊗9am-5pm Mon-Fri, to noon Sat) One of the city's main souvenir businesses is concentrated in this covered market, which has dozens of stalls selling woodcarvings, drums, spears, shields, soapstone, Maasai jewellery and clothing. It's a hectic place and you'll have to bargain hard (and that means *hard*), but there's plenty of good stuff on offer.

> **LOCAL KNOWLEDGE**
>
> ### FINDING OUT WHAT'S ON
>
> For information on entertainment in Nairobi and for big music venues in the rest of the country, get hold of the *Saturday Nation*, which lists everything from cinema releases to live-music venues. There are also plenty of suggestions in the magazine *Going Out*. Wh@t's On Nairobi (www.whats-on-nairobi.com) is another good resource.

Tuesday Maasai Market MARKET

(Map p56; ☑0701314575; www.facebook.com/MaasaiMarketNairobi; ⊗8am-6pm) Busy, popular Maasai markets move around the city according to the day of the week and are excellent shopping experiences. Sites change regularly. At the time of research, markets were held every Tuesday at the Prestige Plaza on Ngong Rd, with other locations on **Wednesday** (Map p62; Capital Centre, Mombasa Rd; ⊗8am-6pm), **Thursday** (Map p62; Junction Mall, Ngong Rd, West Nairobi; ⊗8am-6pm), **Friday** (upper car park, Village Market, Limuru Rd, Gigiri; ⊗8am-6pm) and **Saturday** (Map p62; High Court Parking, Ngong Rd; ⊗8am-6pm). Wares include beaded jewellery, gourds, baskets and other Maasai crafts.

Spinners Web ARTS & CRAFTS

(☑0731168996; 020-2072629; www.spinnerswebkenya.com; Kitisuru Rd, Kitisuru; ⊗9.30am-6.30pm Mon-Fri, to 5.30pm Sat & Sun) This place collaborates with workshops and self-help groups around the country. It's a bit like a handicrafts version of IKEA, with goods displayed the way they might look in a Western living room. There are some appealing items, including carpets, wall hangings, ceramics, baskets, clothing and wooden bowls.

ℹ️ Information

CAMPING EQUIPMENT

Atul's (Map p66; ☑020-2225935; Biashara St; ⊗9am-1pm & 2-5pm Mon-Fri, 9am-4pm Sat) hires out everything from sleeping bags to folding toilet seats.

DANGERS & ANNOYANCES

First-time visitors to Nairobi are understandably daunted by the city's reputation. However, don't let fear exile you to your hotel room: the majority of visitors never experience any problems.
➡ Always hand over valuables if confronted by a thief.

➡ Be confident and don't wear anything flashy.

➡ Be wary, polite but firm with safari touts and other scammers.

➡ Always take a taxi from door to door after dark.

➡ Take particular care with your bags in the streets east of Moi Ave and at bus stations.

➡ There's a free helpline (📞 020-604767; ⏱ 24hr) for tourists in trouble.

Theft & Mugging

The most common annoyance for travellers is petty theft, which is most likely to occur at budget hotels and campsites. Take advantage of your hotel's safe and never leave your valuables out in the open. While you're walking around town, don't carry anything that you wouldn't want to lose. As an extra precaution, it's best to only carry money in your wallet, hiding your credit cards and bank cards elsewhere.

In the event that you are mugged, never, ever resist – simply give up your valuables and, more often than not, your assailant will flee the scene rapidly. Remember that a petty thief and a violent aggressor are very different kinds of people, so don't give your assailant any reason to do something rash.

Scams

Nairobi's handful of active confidence tricksters seem to have relied on the same old stories for years, and it's generally easy to spot the spiels once you've heard them a couple of times.

Always exercise caution while talking to anyone on the streets. While there are genuinely good people out there, the reality is that foreign tourists are an easy target for scamming.

Trouble Spots

Compared to Johannesburg and Lagos – where armed guards, razor-wired compounds and patrol vehicles are the norm – Nairobi's Central Business District (CBD, bounded by Kenyatta Ave, Moi Ave, Haile Selassie Ave and Uhuru Hwy) is quite relaxed and hassle free. Walking around this area by day is rarely a problem. There are also plenty of askaris (security guards) about in case you need assistance.

Once the shops in the CBD have shut, the streets empty rapidly and the whole city centre takes on a deserted and slightly sinister air. After sunset, mugging is a risk anywhere on the streets and you should always take a taxi, even if you're only going a few blocks. This will also keep you safe from the attentions of Nairobi's street prostitutes, who flood into town in force after dark. Uhuru Park is a very pleasant place during daylight hours, but it accumulates all kinds of dodgy characters at night.

There are a few other places where you do need to employ a slightly stronger self-preservation instinct. Potential danger zones include the area around Latema and River Rds (east of Moi Ave),

which is a hotspot for petty theft. This area is home to the city's bus terminals, so keep an eye on your bags and personal belongings at all times if passing through here.

Terrorism

International terrorism first reared its head in modern Nairobi in August 1998 when Al Qaeda operatives bombed the US embassy, killing more than 200 people. Kenya's high-profile military presence in neighbouring Somalia since 2011 has increased the risk of terrorist reprisals. The most serious attack was on the Westgate Shopping Mall on 21 September 2013, with 67 people killed, while bombings on buses and matatus, primarily in the Eastleigh area of the capital, have also claimed a number of lives. Since then, tightened security across the city and a crackdown on suspected terrorists has kept things in check and the risk of terrorism appears to have fallen as a result.

Be vigilant. Avoid Eastleigh. Otherwise, go about your daily business and remember that, while terrorism can happen anywhere, your chances of being caught up in such an incident are extremely low.

Police Stations

Nairobi has police stations scattered across the city centre, including on **Harry Thuku Rd** (Map p66; 📞 020-240000, emergency 999; Harry Thuku Rd; ⏱ 24hr) and **off Haile Selassie Ave** (Map p66; 📞 emergency 999; Tumbo Ave; ⏱ 24hr), as well as in **Karen** (Map p62; 📞 020-3882538, emergency 999; Ngong Rd; ⏱ 24hr) and the **Milimani area** (Map p56; 📞 emergency 999; Milimani Rd; ⏱ 24hr).

There's also a **tourist helpline** (📞 020-604767; ⏱ 24hr), a free service for tourists in trouble. It has a good nationwide network and works closely with the police and local authorities.

EMERGENCY NUMBERS	
Emergency services	📞 999
Police (less-urgent calls)	📞 020-240000
St John Ambulance	📞 2210000
Tourist Helpline	📞 020-604767

INTERNET ACCESS

If you've been travelling elsewhere in East Africa, Nairobi's wireless speeds will seem like a dream. Pick up a local SIM card; 3G can be had all over the city and data use is cheap.

MEDICAL SERVICES

Nairobi has plenty of health-care facilities that are used to dealing with travellers and expats, which is a good thing. Avoid **Kenyatta National Hospital** (Map p56; 📞 0729406939; www.knh. or.ke; Hospital Rd; ⏱ 24hr) – although it's free, its resources are stretched.

AAR Health Services (Map p56; ☑0734225 225, 0725225225; www.aar-healthcare.com/ke; Williamson House, Fourth Ngong Ave; ⊘24hr) Probably the best of the private ambulance and emergency air-evacuation companies. It also runs private clinics at various locations around Nairobi, including in **Westlands** (Map p72; ☑0725225225, 0734225225; 4th fl, Sarit Centre Mall, Westlands; ⊘8am-7pm Mon-Fri, to 4pm Sat, 10am-4pm Sun).

Acacia Medical Centre (Map p66; ☑020-2212200; info@acaciamed.co.ke; ICEA Bldg, Kenyatta Ave; ⊘7am-8pm Mon-Fri, to 5pm Sat, 8am-5pm Sun) Privately-run clinic in the city centre.

Aga Khan Hospital (☑020-3662020; www.agakhanhospitals.org/Nairobi; Third Parklands Ave; ⊘24hr) A reliable hospital with 24-hour emergency services.

KAM Pharmacy (Map p66; ☑020-2227195; www.kampharmacy.com; Executive Tower, IPS Bldg, Kimathi St; ⊘8.30am-6pm Mon-Fri, 9am-2pm Sat) A one-stop shop for medical treatment, with pharmacy, doctor's surgery and laboratory.

Karen Hospital (Map p62; ☑0702222222, 020-6613000; www.karenhospital.org; Langata Rd; ⊘24hr) One of Kenya's best private hospitals.

Nairobi Hospital (Map p56; ☑0702200200, 020-2846000; www.nairobihospital.org; ⊘24hr) One of the city's largest hospitals. It's off Argwings Kodhek Rd.

St John Ambulance (Map p66; ☑020-2210000, 020-340262; www.stjohnkenya.org; County Lane; ⊘24hr) Ambulance services.

MONEY

Money is easily available throughout the city from guarded ATMs accepting international credit and debit cards. There is also no shortage of money-changing offices.

Banks & ATMs

Virtually all banks in Nairobi have guarded ATMs. Barclays has the most reliable machines for international withdrawals, with a large network of ATMs across the city. They support Mastercard, Visa, Plus and Cirrus international networks. Standard Chartered and Kenya Commercial Bank ATMs are also generally reliable, but some still only accept Visa cards. **Postbank** (Map p66; ☑020-2803000; www.postbank. co.ke; 13 Kenyatta Ave; ⊘8.30am-4.30pm Mon-Fri) is the local Western Union agent.

Barclays (Map p66; Muindi Mbingu St; ⊘9am-4pm Mon-Fri, to noon Sat)

Barclays (Map p66; Mama Ngina St; ⊘9am-4pm Mon-Fri, to noon Sat)

Barclays (Map p66; cnr Kenyatta & Moi Aves; ⊘9am-4pm Mon-Fri, to noon Sat)

Barclays (Jomo Kenyatta International Airport; ⊘24hr)

Barclays (Map p72; Woodvale Grove; ⊘9am-4pm Mon-Fri, to noon Sat)

Barclays (Map p72; Sarit Centre, Parklands Rd, Westlands; ⊘9am-4pm Mon-Fri, to noon Sat)

Moneychangers

Nairobi's private exchange offices offer slightly longer hours and shorter queues than the banks.

Cosmos Forex Bureau (Map p66; ☑0722525733; Kaunda St; ⊘8am-6pm Mon-Fri, to 5pm Sat, 9am-3pm Sun)

Goldfield Forex (Map p66; ☑020-2244554; EcoBank Towers, Kaunda St; ⊘9am-5pm Mon-Thu, 9am-12.30pm & 2-5pm Fri, 9am-1pm Sat)

Travellers Forex Bureau (Map p72; ☑0722386990; Mall Shopping Centre, Westlands; ⊘8am-5pm Mon-Sat)

UAE Exchange (Map p66; ☑0738200101; www.uaeexchange.com/ken; Kimathi St; ⊘9am-4.30pm Mon-Fri, to 2pm Sat)

POST

Main Post Office (Map p66; ☑0719072600, 020-243434; Kenyatta Ave; ⊘8am-6pm Mon-Fri, 9am-noon Sat)

Haile Selassie Ave (Map p66; ⊘8.30am-5pm Mon-Fri, 9am-noon Sat)

Tom Mboya St (Map p66; ⊘8.30am-5pm Mon-Fri, 9am-noon Sat)

Sarit Centre (Map p72; Parklands Rd, Westlands; ⊘8.30am-5pm Mon-Fri, 9am-noon Sat)

Mpaka Rd (Map p72; Westlands; ⊘8.30am-5pm Mon-Fri, 9am-noon Sat)

Courier Services

The **EMS office** (Map p66; ⊘8am-8pm Mon-Fri, 9am-12.30pm Sat) handles courier deliveries. It's around the back of the main post office building.

DHL has offices in the **city centre** (Map p66; ☑020-6925135; www.dhl.co.ke; International House, Mama Ngina St) and **Westlands** (Map p72; ☑0711017131; www.dhl.co.ke; Sarit Centre, Westlands).

TELEPHONE

Many stands downtown sell **Telkom Kenya** (Map p66; ☑020-232000; www.telkom.co.ke; Haile Selassie Ave; ⊘8am-6pm Mon-Fri, 9am-noon Sat) phonecards and top-up cards for prepaid mobiles. Alternatively, there are numerous private agencies in the centre of town offering international telephone services.

TOILETS

Nairobi now has a handful of staffed public toilets around downtown offering flush toilets with a basic level of cleanliness. Signs will indicate if you need to pay (about KSh10). Some central shopping centres, such as Kenya Cinema Plaza, have free public conveniences.

ℹ Getting There & Away

AIR
Airports

Nairobi has two airports:

Jomo Kenyatta International Airport (p382) Most international flights to Nairobi arrive at this airport, 15km southeast of the city. There are two international terminals and a smaller domestic terminal; you can easily walk between the terminals.

Wilson Airport (p382) Located 6km south of Nairobi's city centre on Langata Rd. It has some flights between Nairobi and Kilimanjaro International Airport or Mwanza in Tanzania, as well as scheduled and charter domestic flights. Check-in time for domestic flights is one to two hours before departure. Also be aware that the baggage allowance is only 15kg, as there isn't much space on the small turboprop aircraft.

Airlines

Major international airlines connect Nairobi with destinations in the region and further afield.

The following airlines connect Nairobi with regional Kenyan towns and airstrips:

African Express Airways (www.african express.co.ke)

Airkenya (www.airkenya.com)

Fly540 (www.fly540.com)

Jambo Jet (www.jambojet.com)

Kenya Airways (Map p66; www.kenya-airways. com)

Mombasa Air Safari (www.mombasaairsafari. com)

BUS

Most long-distance bus-company offices are in the River Rd area, clustered around Accra Rd and the surrounding streets, although some also have offices on Monrovia St for their international services. Always make your reservation at least 24 hours in advance and double-check the departure point for the bus.

The **Machakos Country Bus Station** (Map p62; Landhies Rd) is a hectic, disorganised place with buses heading all over the country; it serves companies without their own departure point. However, if you can avoid coming here, do so as theft is rampant.

Bus Companies

Dream Line (Map p66; www.facebook.com/ DreamlineExpress) A reliable company connecting Nairobi to Mombasa and Malindi.

Easy Coach (p384) Long-standing company serving western Kenyan destinations as well as running international buses to Uganda.

Modern Coast Express (p384) With a good safety record, these reliable and slightly more expensive buses link Nairobi to Mombasa, Malindi and Kisumu. There are also international links, including Mombasa–Dar es Salaam and Nairobi–Kampala.

Riverside Shuttle (p384) Mostly international services to Arusha, Moshi and Kilimanjaro International Airport (Tanzania).

ℹ **DEPARTURE TIMES**

Most long-distance bus services (to Mombasa or Kisumu, for example), leave in the early morning or late evening. If you have a choice, choose the former, as travelling after dark on Kenya's roads increases the chances of being involved in an accident.

MAJOR MATATU ROUTES

DESTINATION	FARE (KSH)	TIME (HR)	DEPARTURE POINT
Eldoret	800	6	Easy Coach Terminal (Map p66)
Kericho	750	3	Cross Rd (Map p66)
Kisumu	700-1000	5	Cross Rd
Meru	750	4	Main Bus & Matatu Area (Map p66; Accra Rd)
Naivasha	400	2	cnr River Rd & Ronald Ngala St (Map p66)
Nakuru	250-400	3	cnr River Rd & Ronald Ngala St
Namanga	500	2	cnr River Rd & Ronald Ngala St
Nanyuki	500	3	Main Bus & Matatu Area
Narok	500	3	Cross Rd (Narok Line; Map p66; ☏ 020-2212437)
Nyahururu	500	3½	cnr River Rd & Ronald Ngala St
Nyeri	500	2½	Main Bus & Matatu Area

BUSES FROM NAIROBI

DESTINATION	FARE (KSH)	TIME (HR)	COMPANY
Eldoret	1250	7-8	Easy Coach
Kakamega	1450	7½	Easy Coach
Kisumu	1400	7	Easy Coach, Modern Coast Express
Malaba	1400	9-12	Easy Coach
Malindi	1100-2200	10-13	Dream Line, Modern Coast Express
Mombasa	500-2200	6-10	Modern Coast Express, Dream Line

MATATU

Most matatus leave from the chaotic Latema, Accra, River and Cross Rds, and fares are similar to those for buses. Most companies are pretty much the same, although some aim for higher standards than others. **Mololine Prestige Shuttle** (Map p66; ☑ 0711558891; Latema Rd), which operates along the Nairobi–Naivasha–Nakuru–Eldoret route, is one such company.

TRAIN

A brand-new high-speed Nairobi–Mombasa railway line costing US$13.8 billion opened in 2017 and it has begun to revolutionise travel in Kenya, cutting the exhausting journey between Kenya's two biggest cities from 18 hours to just 4½. The line – operated by **Kenya Railways** (☑ 0728603581, 0709907000; www.krc.co.ke) – will eventually extend to Naivasha as well, and then on to Kampala in Uganda, if all goes to plan.

Services on the *Madaraka Express* are expected to increase over the coming years, but there's currently one 9am departure in each direction every day. In Nairobi, trains depart from and arrive at **Syokimau Railway Station** (Mombasa Rd), 19km southeast of the city centre, and stop at Mtito Andei (one way 2nd/1st class KSh360/1490, 2¼ hours) and Voi (KSh510/2130, 3½ hours) en route to Mombasa (KSh900/3000, 4½ hours). Over time, scheduled stops will also include Emali.

ℹ Getting Around

ARRIVING IN NAIROBI

Jomo Kenyatta International Airport Some hotels and most safari companies offer a free airport pick-up service. If not, before leaving the arrivals hall, pay for a pre-booked taxi service (KSh1800 to KSh3000, depending on the time of day and where you're going).

Wilson Airport A taxi to the centre of town will cost at least KSh1200. Alternatively, take bus or matatu 15, 31, 34, 125 or 126 to Moi Ave (KSh50, 15 to 45 minutes depending on traffic).

Syokimau Railway Station Semiregular morning trains (per person KSh120) connect Syokimau with Nairobi's old railway station. A matatu will cost around KSh500 to most

points around town, while a taxi could cost up to KSh1500.

CAR

If you're driving, beware of wheel-clampers: parking in the centre is by permit only (KSH200), available from the parking attendants who roam the streets in bright-yellow jackets. If you park overnight in the street in front of your hotel, the guard will often keep an eye on your vehicle for a small consideration.

Car-rental companies:

Adventure Upgrade Safaris (p389) An excellent local company with a good range of vehicles and drivers.

Avis (p389)

Budget (p389)

Central Rent-a-Car (p389) This longstanding car-rental agency has a number of 4WDs, SUVs and standard cars for hire at competitive rates. The owner knows the roads of Kenya well and can offer very helpful route tips.

Market Car Hire (p389) Local car-hire firm with a solid reputation.

Roadtrip Kenya (p389) A new arrival in Nairobi, this longstanding Dutch-run agency has nevertheless been working in Uganda and Tanzania for years and offers excellent value, local knowledge and support.

MATATU

Nairobi's horde of matatus follows the same routes as buses and displays the same route numbers. For Westlands you can pick up 23 on **Moi Ave** (Map p66) or Latema Rd. Matatu 46 to the Yaya Centre stops in front of the main post office, and 125 and 126 to **Langata** (Map p66) leave from in front of the train station. Buses and matatus for **Milimani** (Map p66) leave from Kenyatta Ave, close to the corner with Posta Rd. There's a central **stop** (Map p66; Moi Ave) for matatu to Kibera. You should keep an eye on your valuables while on all matatus.

TAXI

As people are compelled to use them due to Nairobi's endemic street crime, taxis here are overpriced and undermaintained, but you've little choice, particularly at night. Taxis don't

WORTH A TRIP

KIAMBETHU TEA FARM

A visit to **Kiambethu Tea Farm** (☑ 0729290894, Nairobi 020-2012542; www.kiambethufarm.com; guided tour & lunch per person KSh3300) is a wonderful chance to get an insight into Kenya's tea plantations (Kenya is the world's largest exporter of black tea), as well as being an immensely enjoyable excursion from the city. The guided tour takes you through the history of Kenyan tea growing, visits the lovely colonial-era farmhouse and can also encompass a nearby stand of primary forest.

Advance bookings are essential and some Nairobi tour companies can make the necessary arrangements, including transport. If you're coming in your own vehicle, print out the detailed directions from its website. The farm is around 25km northwest of central Nairobi.

cruise for passengers, but you'll find them on every other street corner in the centre – at night they'll be outside restaurants, bars and nightclubs.

Fares are negotiable but end up pretty standard. Any journey within the city-centre area costs KSh500, from downtown to Milimani Rd costs KSh600, and for longer journeys such as Westlands or the Yaya Centre fares range from KSh750 to KSh1000. From the city centre to Karen and Langata is around KSh1200 one way. It can be cheaper to hire a taxi for the day if you plan to do a lot of moving around town. Ask at your hotel or simply negotiate with a taxi driver.

AROUND NAIROBI

Ngong Hills

Immortalised in the opening lines from Karen Blixen's classic, *Out of Africa*, the green and fertile Ngong Hills have a certain mythical quality about them. The best views are from the road which climbs up and over the hills to Lake Magadi, or to put them in their most evocative historical context, from Karen Blixen's House & Museum (p64). Sadly, large swathes of the hills are in danger of being swallowed up by Nairobi's urban sprawl.

The Ngong Hills are still something of an expat enclave, and you may stumble upon perfect reproductions of English farmhouses with country gardens full of flowering trees – only the acacias remind you that you aren't rambling around the home counties of England. You can also try to track down the dishevelled last resting place of Denys Finch Hatton, but you'll need a guide.

⊙ Sights

Grave of Denys Finch Hatton   HISTORIC SITE
(☑ 0723758639) Close to Pt Lamwia, the summit of the range, is the grave of Denys Finch Hatton, the famous playboy and lover of Karen Blixen. The site, on private land, is almost completely overgrown and is difficult to find 4km up the hill from Kiserian; ask someone to show you the way from Kiserian and expect to pay a minimum KSh300 tip.

A large obelisk marks his grave, inscribed with a line from 'The Rime of the Ancient Mariner', one of his favourite poems. The inscription reads 'He prayeth well, who loveth well/Both man and bird and beast'. There are legends about a lion and lioness standing guard at Finch Hatton's graveside, but these days they'd have trouble getting past the padlocked gate. Call ahead to make sure the custodian of the key is nearby.

Ngong Hills Racecourse   STADIUM
(Map p62; ☑ 0722414598, 0733777417; www.jockey clubofkenya.com; Ngong Rd) Several Sundays a month, hundreds of Nairobi residents flee the noise and bustle of the city for the genteel surroundings of the Ngong Hills Racecourse, one of Nairobi's oldest colonial institutions. The public enclosure is free to enter; entry to the grandstand is KSh200. There are usually three races every month during the October–July season. It's just east of Karen and you can get here on the Metro Shuttle bus (KSh75, 30 minutes) and matatus 24 or 111 (KSh40) from Haile Selassie Ave.

In the past, races had to be cancelled because of rogue rhinos on the track, but the biggest danger these days is stray balls from the golf course in the middle!

❶ Getting There & Away

Ngong, the nondescript gateway town to the hills, lies 9km west of Karen; from Ngong it's a further 7km to the hills proper. Semi-regular matatu 111 (KSh60) heads out here from Nairobi.

Southern Rift Valley

Includes ➡

Longonot National Park	89
Naivasha	90
Lake Naivasha	92
Hell's Gate National Park	97
Nakuru	100
Lake Nakuru National Park	102
Lake Bogoria	107
Lake Baringo	108

Best Places to Eat

➡ Ranch House Bistro (p96)

➡ Club House (p96)

➡ Kikopey Nyama Choma Centre (p96)

➡ Island Camp Restaurant (p109)

➡ Thirsty Goat (p109)

Best Places to Stay

➡ Olerai House (p94)

➡ Dea's Gardens (p94)

➡ Island Camp (p109)

➡ Shompole Wilderness (p90)

➡ Lake Nakuru Sopa Lodge (p104)

Why Go?

It's difficult to believe that the geological force that almost broke Africa in two instead created such serene landscapes. But this slice of Africa's Great Rift Valley is, for the most part, cool and calm, swathed in forest and watered by moody mineral lakes that blanch and blush with the movement of pelicans and flamingos. Pretty Naivasha and Elmenteita with its forest halo are the most popular and greenest of the lakes. The altitude peaks and dips all the way from Nairobi to Nakuru, home to one of Kenya's premier wildlife parks, and ensuring pleasant weather almost year-round. Lake Baringo, with its hippos, crocodiles and fish eagles, is a place apart, while Lake Magadi, parched and salty, and its surrounds give strong hints of the drama that created this extraordinary corner of the continent.

When to Go
Nakuru

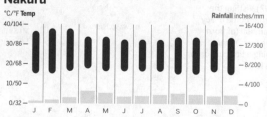

Nov–Mar Migratory bird species abound; weather is clear, dry and hot after November rains.

Jun–Oct Generally fine weather, no rains until October; good for climbing Mt Longonot.

Apr & May Avoid as rains drench the valley, mosquitoes proliferate and some roads are impassable.

Southern Rift Valley Highlights

1 **Lake Nakuru National Park** (p102) Looking for rhinos and tree-climbing lions in one of Kenya's most rewarding parks.

2 **Lake Baringo** (p108) Watching hippos shuffle into the spume and enjoying some of Kenya's best birdwatching.

3 **Hell's Gate National Park** (p97) Feeling like part of the food chain by walking through the wildlife-rich, red-cliffed gorges.

4 **Kembu Farm** (p106) Spotting pea-green chameleons beneath a disco-ball sky at Njoro.

5 **Mt Longonot** (p89) Scaling the volcanic rim for a kestrel's-eye view of the dramatic Great Rift Valley.

6 **Shompole Conservancy** (p90) Dropping off the map into the wild volcanic lands beyond Lake Magadi.

7 **Lake Naivasha** (p92) Visiting the former home of Joy Adamson (of *Born Free* fame) then taking a boat out onto the lake.

Lake Magadi & Around

The most mineral-rich of the Rift Valley's soda lakes is Lake Magadi, southwest of Nairobi. It is almost entirely covered by a thick encrustation of soda that supports small colonies of flamingos and gives the landscape a bizarre lunar appearance. It makes an interesting day trip from Nairobi, especially if you have your own transport and enough time to visit Olorgesailie Prehistoric Site en route. It can also be a launching pad for the remote, rarely visited Shompole Conservancy (p90), close to the Tanzanian border.

◉ Sights

To travel beyond the southern end of the town of Magadi (which is accessed along the main road from Nairobi), a checkpoint charges KSh300. It's worth it, for the causeway leads across the most visually dramatic part of this strange landscape to a viewpoint on the western shore; you'll need a 4WD. Otherwise you can head to the **hot springs** further south. The springs aren't particularly dramatic, but you can take a dip in the deeper pools and there are large numbers of fish that have adapted to the hot water.

Olorgesailie Prehistoric Site ARCHAEOLOGICAL SITE
(www.museums.or.ke/olorgesailie; adult/child KSh500/250; ⊘8am-6pm) Travelling between Lake Magadi and Nairobi, take the turn-off for the Olorgesailie Prehistoric Site. Several important archaeological finds were made by the Leakeys in the 1940s at this site, 40km north of Magadi, including hundreds of hand axes and stone tools thought to have been made by *Homo erectus* about half a million years ago. Fossils have also been discovered and some are still there, protected from the elements by shade roofs. Free guided tours are compulsory, although a tip is expected.

🏃 Activities

Ask at the Lake Magadi Tented Camp & Sports Club about hiking, swimming, birdwatching and cultural activities run by the local Maasai. For groups, they can also arrange a three-hour train safari between Magadi and Kajiado.

🛏 Sleeping

Olorgesailie Campsite CAMPGROUND $
(Hwy C58; camping KSh300, d new/old bandas KSh1800/2000; �ⓟ) This campsite, at the gate

of the Olorgesailie Prehistoric Site, is your only option out here. It's fairly basic (you'll need to bring your own food, bedding and drinking water), but you'll feel like you're properly in the bush.

Lake Magadi Tented Camp & Sports Club TENTED CAMP $$
(☑0727075986, 0717999228; www.lakemagadi adventures.com; s/d full board KSh7000/13,000; ⓟ🖭) In the town of Magadi, on a rise up from the lakeshore, these simple but appealing safari tents inhabit neat rows amid manicured lawns. It's not a wilderness experience, but it is an excellent base for exploring this little-visited corner of the country. There's a decent on-site restaurant.

ℹ Getting There & Away

Magadi is 105km southwest of Nairobi. The C58 road from Nairobi sees little traffic, but potholes remain a problem. There's usually one matatu a day to Nairobi (KSh350), leaving in the morning and returning to Magadi in the evening.

Longonot National Park

One of the shapeliest peaks in all the Rift Valley, Mt Longonot (2776m) and its serrated crater rim offer fabulous views. The dormant volcano rises 1000m above the baking-hot valley floor and was formed 400,000 years ago; it last erupted in the 1860s. The **park** (☑050-50255; www.kws.go.ke/content/mount-longonot-national-park; adult/child US$26/17; ⊘6am-6pm) itself covers only 52 sq km, and was set up to protect the volcano's

---

CLIMBING MT LONGONOT

The one- to 1½-hour hike from the park gate up to the crater rim (2545m) is strenuous but, without question, worth the considerable effort. There are two steep stretches that will challenge those not used to hiking. Your reward is to emerge at the lip of the crater rim for superb views of the 2km- to 3km-wide crater – a little lost world hosting an entirely different forest ecosystem.

It takes between 1½ and 2½ hours to circumnavigate the crater; watch for occasional steam vents rising from the crater floor. A guide to the crater rim and back is KSh1500 (KSh2500 including the summit).

ecosystem and little else. The name 'Longonot' comes from the Maasai name Olo Nongot, which means 'Mountain of Many Summits'.

The trail to the crater rim is clear and easy to follow, and taking along a ranger is not necessary, although a good one will certainly enhance your trek; rangers can be arranged at the main gate as you enter.

🛏 Sleeping

Most people stay in Lake Naivasha, a 30-minute drive away, although there is a **campsite** (camping US$20) – ideal for those who want to get an early start.

❶ Getting There & Away

If you're driving, Mt Longonot is 75km northwest of Nairobi on the Old Naivasha Rd. If you're without a vehicle, take a matatu from Naivasha to Longonot village, from where there's a path (ask locals) to the park's access road.

Naivasha

⏺ 050 / POP 182,000

Even though this small country town is the gateway to Lake Naivasha, it picks up few crumbs from the passing tourist trade. Most travellers only venture here on their way elsewhere, or to use an ATM or fill the fuel tank. Otherwise, it's a busy little place with a varied multiethnic population – it's home to many migrant workers from all across Kenya who come to work at the Lake Naivasha flower farms (p95).

🛏 Sleeping

Very few travellers overnight in Naivasha – the lake, with its much better sleeping options and far prettier outlook, is a mere 18km away. If you do find yourself stuck here, choices are limited to a handful of uninspiring choices.

La Belle Inn HOTEL $
(Map p91; ⏺ 050-3510404, 0722683218; Moi Ave; s/d KSh3500/4500; 🕸) This shabby but charming colonial hotel was built in 1922 and is a delight as long as you don't expect too much from your room. Set around an inner courtyard, the rooms are comfortable but elderly, infused with a certain grandmotherly charm. Anyone can take tea (or meals) on the verandah, which is complete with 1970s-era table numbers, bow-tied waiters and old-fashioned tablecloths.

Eseriani Hotel HOTEL $$
(Map p93; ⏺ 0727841680, Nairobi 020-2355095; www.eserianihotels.co.ke; Moi Ave; r from US$110; 🅿🕸) Probably the best of Naivasha's in-town options, Eseriani styles itself

---

WORTH A TRIP

SHOMPOLE CONSERVANCY

In a wild and remote corner of the country, between the Rift Valley lakes of Magadi (in Kenya) and Natron (Tanzania), **Shompole** is one of southern Kenya's most rewarding wilderness experiences. Isolated Maasai villages, dramatic escarpment views all along the Western Rift Valley wall and some surprisingly good wildlife watching more than compensate for the difficulty of getting here. And with much of the conservancy having only recently reopened, there's a chance you may be the only ones here.

The birdwatching is excellent with species you're more likely to see across the border in Tanzania's Crater Highlands than elsewhere in Kenya, while elephants, lions and other large mammals are all possible.

Sleeping

The classy **Shompole Wilderness** (⏺ 0716511162, 0722460958; www.shompolewilderness.com; s/d all inclusive US$750/1000) tented camp is the ideal place to rest in this remote corner of Africa with luxury, riverside safari tents that let you hear the night sounds of Africa. In addition to wildlife drives, go tubing down the croc-free Ewaso Ngiro River, or take a walk with baboons or the Maasai and their cattle.

Getting There & Away

There are a few small air strips in the area for those with access to a plane. Otherwise, Shompole Wilderness is around a 90-minute (4WD) drive beyond Magadi – check the website or contact Shompole Wilderness for detailed driving directions.

as a boutique hotel, which may be over-stating things a little, but the rooms are still attractive and contemporary. It's a bit out on a limb and close to the main road, but that's what you get for not staying out at Lake Naivasha...

✕ Eating

Tuskys Supermarket SUPERMARKET
(Map p93; www.tuskys.com; Buffalo Mall, off Moi Ave; ⊙8.30am-8.30pm Mon-Fri, 9am-7.45pm Sat & Sun) Out in Buffalo Mall where Moi Ave meets the Nakuru–Nairobi road, Tuskys is a well-stocked supermarket; their beef samosas (available from the bakery deli) are a terrific snack.

Smiles Café KENYAN $
(Map p91; ☎0714928777; Kariuki Chotara Rd; mains KSh100-270; ⊙6am-midnight) As basic as they come, this little green-and-white treasure offers cholesterol-filled fried breakfasts and hearty stews with a focus on dishes locals love.

🍷 Drinking & Nightlife

Java House CAFE
(Map p93; ☎0708406005; www.javahouseafrica.com; Buffalo Mall, off Moi Ave; ⊙7am-8pm Mon-Sat, 8am-8pm Sun; 🛜) This place is Kenya's version of Starbucks and locals love it. It's all there, from creative coffees, milkshakes and pastries to free wi-fi, and all served in a could-be-anywhere-shopping-mall setting. Even so, it's the classiest cafe in town with Naivasha's best coffees.

Naivasha Coffee House CAFE
(Map p93; Naivasha-Nakuru Hwy; ⊙6am-9pm) This sleek hole-in-the-wall coffee stop serves herbal teas, hot chocolate, frappuccinos and caramel concoctions, as well as – obviously – decent coffee. Find it opposite the petrol station at the Delamere Service Station, but head out back for the garden tables. Next door, there's a fruit shop selling freshly squeezed passionfruit and beetroot juices, among others.

🛈 Information

Most banks are along Moi Ave, just north of Station Lane and La Belle Inn.

Barclays (Map p91; Moi Ave; ⊙9am-4pm Mon-Fri, to noon Sat) Internationally enabled ATM and a foreign exchange desk for cash transactions.

KCB (Map p91; Moi Ave; ⊙9am-4pm Mon-Fri, to noon Sat) Foreign exchange desk, but

Naivasha

SOUTHERN RIFT VALLEY NAIVASHA

queues can be long as you're in line with local market traders cashing their earnings and grandmothers counting out their coins.

🛈 Getting There & Away

BUS & MATATU

The main **bus and matatu stand** (Map p91; off Mbaria Kaniu Rd) is close to the municipal market. Frequent buses and matatus leave for Nakuru (KSh200, 1¼ hours) and Nairobi (KSh400, two hours).

Frequent matatus run around the south side of the lake to Kongoni (KSh120) and Fisherman's Camp area (KSh150, 45 minutes). They depart from the bus station and from **Kenyatta Ave** (Map p91).

As an alternative to taking your chances at the main bus and matatu stand, there's the **Nairobi Matatu Booking Office** (Map p91) from where you can also catch local matatus around town.

CAR & MOTORCYCLE

Naivasha's petrol stations are in the town centre along Moi Ave. A couple of petrol stations were also under construction out along the southern shore of the lake.

OiLibya (Map p91; Moi Ave; ⊙24hr)
Shell (Map p91; Moi Ave; ⊙24hr)
Total (Map p91; Moi Ave; ⊙24hr)

WORTH A TRIP

MT SUSUA

With a crater that's even more of a lost world than that on nearby Mt Longonot, the unique **Mt Susua** (admission per person/car US$30/KSh500, camping KSh500) volcano is well worth the considerable effort of visiting. The steep outer crater protects a second inner crater, whose rim peaks at 2357m and begs to be trekked. There's also a network of unexplored lava caves on the mountain's east side, some of which are home to baboons. For an excellent local guide, contact Daniel (☑ 0722966302, 0721357415; www.daniel mountsuswa.wordpress.com), a local Maasai guide and wonderful companion and guide, for visiting Susua.

There's no designated route and all land is owned by local Maasai, so you'll have to find someone from the nearby villages that dot the B3 Nairobi–Narok road to guide you. It's a 90-minute drive from Nairobi to the point where you leave the tarmac road, with a sign indicating **Mt Suswa Conservancy**, whereafter it's a further 2½ hours to the crater's outer rim. It takes about eight hours to circumnavigate the outer crater. Two local councils were in dispute about where and to whom you had to pay the conservancy fees – ask your guide in advance for the latest situation.

If you do the trek, you'll need to camp overnight (and be completely self-sufficient in food and water); campsites in the conservancy are little more than cleared patches of grass under the trees, but wonderfully quiet. Is it worth it? Absolutely, not least because you and the Maasai will have it all to yourselves. For a fabulous insight into Susua's charms, watch the BBC's 2010 documentary, *The Great Rift Valley*.

Lake Naivasha

☑ 050

Hugged by grassy banks and shingled with cacti and sand olive trees, the Rift Valley's highest lake (at 1884m above sea level) extends like a vast, sunlit sea. But there's more to this spot than the lovely blue lake. You can ride among giraffes and zebras, sip on a glass of Rift Valley red, look for hippos on the lake and relax in the garden at Elsamere, the former home of late *Born Free* personality Joy Adamson. Although it's just a short drive from Nairobi, Lake Naivasha is a world away from the capital's choked arteries, although it can get overrun with visitors from the capital on weekends.

◉ Sights & Activities

Most of the camps and lodges along Lake Naivasha's southern shore rent out boats (per boat per hour from KSh3000); most boats have seven seats and come with pilot and lifejackets. Places where nonguests can organise a boat rental include **Fisherman's Camp** (Map p93; ☑ 0718880634, 0726870590, Nairobi 020-2139922; www.fishermanscamp.com; Moi South Lake Rd; bandas per person KSh1000-2000, camping KSh700; P) and Elsamere (p95).

★**Elsamere**   MUSEUM
(Map p93; ☑ 0726443151, 050-2021247; www.elsamere.com; KSh1050; ⊘9am-6pm; P) Stippled with sisal, yellow fever trees and candelabra euphorbia, this is the former home of the late Joy Adamson of *Born Free* fame. She bought the house in 1967 with her husband George and did much of her painting, writing and conservation work here until her murder in 1980. Guests can attend regular screenings of a flickering 1970s film about Joy's life and her myriad love affairs, notably with Elsa the lioness.

There's also a fascinating museum housed in the couple's former master bedroom, brimming with cloth-bound animal-behaviour manuals, dusty typewriters, photographs and Joy's art. In the yard, the vehicle in which George was shot dead sits empty.

Entry includes high tea (with cakes) on the peaceful lawn, and front-row seats to study the resident black-and-white colobus monkeys. You can also visit the conservation centre in the grounds, or even stay here in one of the lovely garden rooms (p95).

★**Crescent Island**   WILDLIFE RESERVE
(Map p93; www.crescentisland.co; adult/student US$30/20; ⊘8am-6pm) This private island sanctuary can be reached by boat, or by driving across the narrow, swampy causeway from Sanctuary Farm. Crescent Island

Lake Naivasha

Lake Naivasha

◎ Top Sights
1	Crescent Island	C3
2	Elsamere	B4

◎ Sights
3	Crater Lake Game Sanctuary	A3
4	Lake Oloiden	A4

🛏 Sleeping
5	Camp Carnelley's	B4
	Crater Lake Camp	(see 3)
6	Crayfish Camp	C4
7	Crescent Camp	D3
8	Dea's Gardens	D3
	Elsamere Lodge	(see 2)
9	Enashipai	D3
10	Eseriani Hotel	D2
11	Fisherman's Camp	B4
12	Hippo Point	A4

13	Kiangazi House	A4
14	Olerai House	A2
15	Sanctuary Farm	D3

✴ Eating
	Club House	(see 15)
16	Lake Naivasha Country Club	D3
	Lazybones	(see 5)
17	Ranch House Bistro	A4
	Tuskys Supermarket	(see 10)

◗ Drinking & Nightlife
	Java House	(see 10)
18	Naivasha Coffee House	D1

🛍 Shopping
19	Elmenteita Weavers	D3
	Farm Shop	(see 19)
	Fired Earth	(see 19)

is one of the few places in the Rift Valley where you can walk among giraffes, zebras, waterbucks, impalas and countless bird species. If you're very lucky, you might even spot a leopard, but don't count on it. Island walks, led by a guide, last between 90 minutes and three hours. It's also a good spot for a picnic lunch.

Lake Oloiden
LAKE

(Map p93; boat safaris per 30/60min KSh2250/4500) Lake Naivasha may be a freshwater lake, but it is the alkaline waters of its near neighbour Lake Oloiden that draw small but impressive flocks of flamingos. Boat safaris are available. Apart from anything else, the real appeal here is that it's one of the few stretches of public land in the area where you can walk near to the lakeshore.

Crater Lake Game Sanctuary
WILDLIFE RESERVE

(Map p93; per person US$25, plus car KSh200) Surrounding a beautiful volcanic crater lake fringed with acacias, this small sanctuary has many trails, including one for hikers along the steep but diminutive crater rim. The jade-green crater lake is held in high regard by the local Maasai, who believe its alkaline waters help soothe ailing cattle. As well as the impressive 150 bird species recorded here, giraffes, zebras and other plains wildlife are also regular residents on the more-open plains surrounding the crater.

🛏 Sleeping

★ Camp Carnelley's
CAMPGROUND, BANDAS $

(Map p93; ☑050-50004, 0722260749; www.campcarnelleys.com; Moi South Lake Rd; camping KSh800-1000, dm KSh1000, r from KSh3000, bandas KSh8000-16,000; P) 🍽 Right on the shoreline, this gorgeous budget spot has comfortable *bandas* (thatched huts), simple twin rooms with woolly blankets and one of the cleanest and most attractive campsites in Kenya. Come evening, head to the fantastic wooden-beamed bar and restaurant with its hip couches, roaring fireplace and creative menu – another highlight.

Crayfish Camp
CAMPGROUND $

(Map p93; ☑0720226829; www.crayfishcamp naivasha.com; Moi South Lake Rd; camping per tent KSh2300, s/d KSh4950/7500, fantasy r per person KSh2200; P🛜🍽) Fancy sleeping in a converted boat with leopard-print curtains? How about a romantic night crammed into a broken-down bus or a toy-sized 4WD? There are 82 rooms ranging from vanilla doubles to fantasy options, plus a theme pub, a kids' play area and a restaurant serving milkshakes. Still, it does feel a bit like a 1980s holiday camp.

★ Dea's Gardens
GUESTHOUSE $$

(Map p93; ☑0734453761, 0733747433; www.deas gardens.com; off Moi South Lake Rd; half board per person KSh9500; 🛜🍽) This charming guesthouse is run by the charismatic and elegant Dea. The main house has three guest rooms and is a gorgeous chalet of Swiss inspiration, while the cottages in the lush grounds are large and comfortable. Meals are served family style with Dea as your host; it's hard to imagine a warmer welcome.

★ Sanctuary Farm
BOUTIQUE HOTEL $$

(Map p93; ☑0722761940; www.sanctuary farmkenya.com; off Moi South Lake Rd; s/d KSh15,000/20,000, camping KSh6000; P🛜) 🍽 Within a private 400-acre conservancy and dairy farm, this beautiful place makes the perfect weekend escape from Nairobi. The rooms are stylish, high-quality and elegant, and there's access to a cosy wi-fi lounge/library. You can also go horse riding among giraffes and zebras. Lovely breakfasts, good wines and delicious, healthy mains are on offer at the farm-to-table restaurant (p96).

★ Olerai House
GUESTHOUSE $$$

(Map p93; ☑Nairobi 020-8048602; www.elephant watchportfolio.com/oleraihouse; Moi North Lake Rd; s/d full board US$495/800) Hidden under a blanket of tropical flowers, this beautiful house is like something straight out of a fairytale, where petals dust the beds and floors, zebras and vervet monkeys hang out with pet dogs, and the rooms are a delight. Perhaps best of all, the camp is owned by renowned elephant conservationists Iain and Oria Douglas-Hamilton – if they're at home, there are few more fascinating hosts in Kenya.

Hippo Point
LODGE $$$

(Map p93; ☑0733993713; www.hippopoint kenya.com; off Moi South Lake Rd; s/d full board US$950/1000) One of the most warmly eclectic places to stay anywhere in the Rift Valley, Hippo Point occupies a 1932 manor house on expansive, wildlife-rich grounds between Lake Oloiden and Lake Naivasha. The atmosphere is classy and colonial and a wonderful sense of peace pervades the whole place – walking the halls here makes one want to whisper.

The extraordinary 37m-high Dodo Tower is one of Kenya's most unusual architectural treasures and an extraordinary place to stay. It's all very gracious and supremely comfortable.

LAKE NAIVASHA FLOWERS

Depending on who you talk to, Lake Naivasha's blooming flower industry is either a blessing or a curse. The lake's freshwater bestows it with a unique ecosystem (many other Rift Valley lakes are highly alkaline), which means it can also be used for irrigation purposes.

Roses are the main export and, astoundingly, flowers picked here in the early morning can be at Europe's flower auctions the same day. In 2016, the industry generated US$141 million in revenues for the country, making it one of Kenya's most important foreign exchange earners. The industry attracts migrant workers from all over Kenya and there are more than 60 flower farms in the Lake Naivasha area, together employing 50,000 workers. So successful is the industry that an estimated 70% of the roses sold in the UK come from here.

But such success comes at a price. A decade ago, an international NGO called Women Working Worldwide (www.women-ww.org) exposed appalling conditions on many of the farms. Tighter regulations have generally led to improved working conditions – with the women making up the majority of the workforce, some farms now offer maternity leave and childcare facilities. There remain concerns, however, that not all farms have improved conditions for their workers, with low salaries, long hours and limited protection from harmful chemicals among the major concerns.

There are also environmental concerns. The cut-flower industry, especially roses, requires massive amounts of irrigation, raising concerns about water scarcity in an area where local subsistence farmers may not always get their share. The influx of workers has seen the population of the wider Lake Naivasha Basin swell from 300,000 in the mid-1990s to a projected population of more than one million by 2019, with all the concomitant strain that puts on already stretched resources. Increasing pollution in the lake and deforestation are just two of the growing environmental concerns.

It's a delicate balancing act between what is a hugely important local industry and the environment that sustains it. If you want to find out more, some of the better factories offer tours for visitors. Ask at your guesthouse or campsite for information.

Kiangazi House
LODGE **$$$**
(Map p93; ☑0722200596; www.oserengoni wildlife.com/category/kiangazi-house; off Moi South Lake Rd; per person full board from US$800; **P 🛜 ≋**) This stunning property off the southernmost tip of Lake Oloiden has fine views and captures that old-style feel that so defined the Lake Naivasha region in colonial times. The rooms are arrayed around the main building or in cottages around the gardens. The meals here are also a highlight.

Crescent Camp
TENTED CAMP **$$$**
(Map p93; ☑0715286001; www.crescentcamp. com; off Moi South Lake Rd; s/d full board US$270/360, Apr-Jun US$200/280; **P 🛜 ≋**) 🍃 There are 20 luxury safari tents set in landscaped surrounds here, plus a simple restaurant and a cute jungle-themed bar. Three of the tents are wheelchair-accessible.

Enashipai
HOTEL **$$$**
(Map p93; ☑051-2130000, 0713254035; www.enashipai.com; Moi South Lake Rd; s/d KSh19,500/27,000; **P @ 🛜 ≋**) By far the sleekest of the resorts along the lakeshore,

Enashipai comes from the Maasai name meaning 'state of happiness', and it's no misnomer. If you like your resorts polished and luxurious, with a private, gated-community feel, you're at the right place. Warm staff, a good restaurant and an ultra-chic spa make it easy to unwind here.

Elsamere Lodge
HOTEL **$$$**
(Map p93; ☑050-2021055; www.elsamere.com; Moi South Lake Rd; s/d full board US$150/245; **P 🛜**) 🍃 The conservation centre at the very lovely former home of Joy Adamson (p92) also doubles as a lodge with high novelty value. You can stay here in one of the 10 pleasant rooms dotted through the pretty garden where wild colobus monkeys roam, and enjoy high tea in Adamson's dining room.

Crater Lake Camp
TENTED CAMP **$$$**
(Map p93; ☑050-2020613; www.craterlake camp.com; off Moi South Lake Rd; s/d full board US$206/308) This tented camp inside the private Crater Lake Game Sanctuary nestles among trees and overlooks the tiny

KIKOPEY NYAMA CHOMA CENTRE

It's not often we give a cluster of restaurants their own coverage, but this agglomeration of roadside barbecued-meat stalls 31km north of Naivasha is famous throughout Kenya. Kikopey is a major truck stop and it's no surprise why. These places don't survive long if their meat isn't perfectly cooked. The restaurants closest to the road hassle new arrivals and try to draw you in. We keep returning to **Acacia Restaurant** (Nairobi-Nakuru Rd; meals per person KSh750; ◷10am-10pm), a little back from the main road, and find it outstanding. For those who think presidential power and culinary discernment go hand in hand, President Uhuru Kenyatta and his team stopped at **Kahatia Restaurant** (Nairobi-Nakuru Rd; meal per person KSh750; ◷10am-10pm) while campaigning in May 2017. At any of these places, you'll pay around KSh1300 for a well-provisioned goat leg.

jade-green crater lake. The tents aren't exactly luxurious, but they are extremely comfortable, and the honeymoon tent contains a whirlpool bath and other romantic essentials. Nature walks and night safaris are included in the price.

✕ Eating

Almost all of the campsites and guesthouses have their own restaurants, so there's little in the way of independent dining, though most accommodation places happily welcome nonguests to their restaurants.

★**Ranch House Bistro** INTERNATIONAL **$$**
(Map p93; ☎0722200596, 0700488475; www. oserengoniwildlife.com/category/ranch-house-bistro; Moi South Lake Rd; mains from KSh700; ◷10am-10pm) Opened in 2014, Ranch House Bistro is easily the best of the lakeside eating options. The food is expertly prepared and ranges across pizzas from the clay oven to pulled-pork varieties and exquisite desserts. The setting is superb with tables spread across the lawn, but you'll need to book ahead for their Sunday lunch buffet (KSh1300 per person).

★**Club House** RESTAURANT **$$**
(Map p93; ☎0722761940; www.sanctuaryfarm kenya.com/index.php/kitchen; Sanctuary Farm; lunch KSh3000, dinner KSh3500) ✿ Farm-to-table sustainable cuisine is more exciting when there are giraffes and hippos to spy on in the distance. The signature eatery at Sanctuary Farm (p94) is relaxed but stylish, with tables strewn over a wooden verandah. Inside, there are framed black-and-white posters and Rift Valley wines. Expect dishes such as beetroot salad, red-pepper chicken, home-baked focaccia and baklava with pineapple sorbet. Reservations only.

★**Lazybones** INDIAN **$$**
(Map p93; ☎050-50004; www.campcarnelleys. com/bar-and-restaurant; Camp Carnelley's, Moi South Lake Rd; mains from KSh500) Camp Carnelley's hip restaurant is popular with NGO workers and other Nairobians at weekends. Grab one of the gorgeous low-slung sofas, or pull up a chair around the roaring fireplace. Co-owner Chrisi's creative menu includes Indian fusion dishes, great salads, fresh fish and even breakfast smoothies. There's also a selection of wines, beers and spirits. Out back, you'll find a pool table.

Lake Naivasha Country Club BUFFET **$$$**
(Map p93; ☎0703048200; Moi South Lake Rd; buffet KSh2500; ☎) The country club is a bit of an institution in these parts, and is *the* place to be seen having lunch. The daily buffet here is very good, served inside the somewhat stiff dining room or outside on the lush green lawn. There's everything from a salad bar to a chicken grill, and a very tempting dessert counter. The stately hotel wing is adjacent.

🔒 Shopping

Farm Shop FOOD
(Map p93; ☎0733237813; off Moi South Lake Rd; ◷9.30am-5pm) This is the place to come for locally produced foods, from home-made jams and Longonot honey to delights such as chilli chocolate cashew butter. Although it's aimed mostly at expats with room in their larder, it's a wonderful place to stock up for a lakeside picnic.

Fired Earth ARTS & CRAFTS
(Map p93; ☎0710827632; pottersceramic@yahoo. com; off Moi South Lake Rd; ◷8am-6pm Mon-Fri, to 5pm Sat, 9am-5pm Sun) You'll be welcomed by Obadiah and other male potters at this simple, friendly workshop. Watch the spinning

kiln and browse the small store, where there's a range of lamps, bowls, cups and mosaic coasters for sale. Pottery classes are possible by appointment.

Elmenteita Weavers ARTS & CRAFTS
(Map p93; ☑ 0733603652; www.elmenteita weavers.com; off Moi South Lake Rd; ⊙ 8am-5pm) This tiny cooperative turns out beautiful rugs, throws and bags, and does a nice line in wooden souvenirs – including cute salt and pepper pots. Most things in the store are handmade by the two friendly weavers on the loom in the back.

ℹ Information

Hippos often wander on to the road at night, so take care when driving after dark. A greater threat is the traffic during the day, which loops around the road at speed: take care when out walking. Crime can also be an issue – never leave the property you're staying at to wander along the after sunset.

ℹ Getting There & Away

Frequent matatus (KSh100, one hour) run along Moi South Lake Rd between Naivasha town and Kongoni on the lake's western side, passing the turn-offs to Hell's Gate National Park and Fisherman's Camp (KSh70). Taxis charge upwards of KSh2000 for the hop from Naivasha. Contact **Nickson Gatimu** (☑ 0726797750) if you'd like to arrange a pick-up.

ℹ Getting Around

Most lodges and camps hire mountain bikes if you're heading for Hell's Gate National Park; costs start from KSh750 per day. Check the bikes carefully before paying.

Matatu hops around the lakeshore cost upwards of KSh80, depending on distance. The drivers know most of the lodges and campsites and can drop you close by.

Hell's Gate National Park

Dry, dusty and dramatic but infinitely peaceful, **Hell's Gate** (☑ 0726610508, Nairobi 020-2379467; www.kws.org; adult/child US$26/17, bike hire KSh500, car entry KSh300; ⊙ 6am-6pm; P) is that rare thing: an adventurous Kenyan park with large animals that's safe to explore by bicycle or on foot. Large carnivores are very rare, so you can cycle to your heart's content past grazing zebras, giraffes, impalas and buffaloes, spot rock hyraxes as they clamber up inclines and chase dust clouds as they swirl in the wind. And if the pedalling isn't enough exercise, hike the gorge or climb Fischer's Tower.

◉ Sights

Obsidian Cave CAVE
Close to the Elsa Gate end of the Buffalo Circuit, a side track leads for 2km to the Obsidian Cave, where you'll find moderately interesting examples of the glassy black rock so characteristic of Rift Valley lava flows.

Lower Gorge CANYON
(Ol Njorowa; guide per hour KSh500) Rising from the main gorge's southern end is the large **Central Tower**, an unusual volcanic plug. A picnic site and ranger's post are close by, from where a walk descends into the Lower Gorge (Ol Njorowa). In some places the riverbed is dry; in others you'll find yourself scrambling down a steep and slippery

Hell's Gate National Park

descent. Some steps have been cut into the rock and some parts may be perilous. We recommend taking a guide.

We also recommend that you don't make the descent during the rainy season, even if it's not raining at the time. In April 2012, seven members of a church group drowned here during a flash flood that swept down Lower Gorge after heavy rains fell in neighbouring areas.

Hell's Gate Gorge
CANYON

The gorge that runs through the heart of the park is a wide, deep valley hemmed in by sheer, rusty-hued rock walls. Marking its eastern entrance is **Fischer's Tower**, a 25m-high volcanic column which can be climbed with a guide. The tower was named after Gustav Fischer, a German explorer who reached the gorge in 1882. Commissioned to find a route from Mombasa to Lake Victoria, Fischer was stopped by territorial Maasai, who slaughtered almost his entire party.

🏃 Activities

Elsa Gate Bike Hire
CYCLING

(per day from KSh500) Mountain bikes are the best way to see the park and can be rented at Elsa Gate, but test them out rigorously before handing over the money – dodgy brakes and gears are common problems, although rangers are on hand to assist.

James Maina
CLIMBING

(📞 0727039388) James works as a climbing instructor and guide on weekends and also has some basic equipment. He offers relatively easy 10- to 15-minute climbs of Fischer's Tower (US$10 to US$20) and

> ### ⓘ HELL'S GATE NATIONAL PARK
> ·····································
>
> **Why Go** Dramatic volcanic scenery; a chance to walk or cycle through wildlife areas. Rock-climbing is another Hell's Gate highlight.
>
> **When to Go** June to February.
>
> **Practicalities** There's a small Information Centre at Elsa Gate.
>
> **Budget Tips** Get any matatu circling Lake Naivasha to drop you at the junction to Elsa Gate, where you can hire a bike for the 2km to the gate itself. Bike rental here runs cheaper than at the Information Centre.

more challenging routes on the gorge's sheer red walls (US$100). If he's not in his usual place at the base of Fischer's Tower, give him a call or check at the park gate before you enter.

🛏 Sleeping

Naiburta Public Campsite
CAMPGROUND $

(camping US$20) 🏕 Naiburta, sitting on a gentle rise on the northern side of the Hell's Gate Gorge and commanding fine views west past Fischer's Tower, is the most scenic site in the area. It has basic toilets, an open *banda* for cooking and freshwater taps.

Ol Dubai Public Campsite
CAMPGROUND $

(camping US$20) 🏕 Resting on Hell's Gate Gorge's southern side and accessible from the Buffalo Circuit track, Ol Dubai has basic toilets, a cooking *banda* and freshwater. It offers views west to the orange bluffs, and of the puffs of steam from the geothermal power station at the far end of the park.

ⓘ Information

Park information is available at the information centre next to the main gate.

ⓘ Getting There & Away

The usual access point to the park is through the main Elsa Gate, 2km from Moi South Lake Rd. Frequent matatus (KSh100) run along Moi South Lake Rd between Naivasha town and Kongoni on the lake's western side, passing the turn-offs to the park. Taxis charge around KSh2000 for the trip from Naivasha.

Lake Elmenteita & Around

Serene and framed by shaggy hills, **Elmenteita** (adult/child KSh500/200, car KSh200, guide KSh300) is quieter and prettier than the lakes to its south, although due to its relatively open surrounds it lacks the drama or mystique that you find elsewhere. Squint and, depending on the season and time of day, you could be in Arizona or the Scottish Highlands; euphorbia, cacti and rocks stipple the higher ground, while cattle graze along the green soda shoreline. The lake is famous for its flamingos and pelicans and birdwatching in general; more than 450 species have been recorded around the lake and its hinterland. If you're lucky, you might also spot zebras and antelope grazing on the edges.

👁 Sights

Soysambu Conservancy WILDLIFE RESERVE
(📞0711235039; www.soysambuconservancy.org;
adult/child US$47/24) This private conservan-
cy offers quite extensive wildlife viewing, as
well as camping. It is home to colobus monkeys, Rothschild's giraffes and about 450
species of birdlife.

Kariandusi ARCHAEOLOGICAL SITE
(www.museums.or.ke/kariandusi; adult/child
KSh500/250; ⊙8.30am-6pm) Kariandusi is
signposted off the A104 Hwy near Lake Elmenteita. It was here in the 1920s that the
Leakeys (a family of renowned archaeologists) discovered numerous obsidian and
lava tools made by early humans between
1.4 million and 200,000 years ago. Two excavation sites are preserved and the smallish
museum has two galleries with a brief overview of the region's geological and human
history.

🛏 Sleeping

Lake Elmenteita is a popular weekend escape from Nairobi and it draws a predominantly local clientele. As such, the lakeshore
has more accommodation than most other
Rift Valley lakes.

★Lake Elmenteita

Serena Camp TENTED CAMP $$$
(📞0732123333, Nairobi 020-2842400; www.
serenahotels.com; s/d full board Jul-Oct
US$496/641, rates vary rest of year; 🅿@🛜🌊)
🏝 A relatively recent addition to the Ser-
ena Hotel chain's fine portfolio, this clas-
sically styled tented camp at the northern
end of the lake has beautifully manicured
grounds and tented rooms with hardwood
floors. The decor is steeped in safari mem-
orabilia, such as four-poster beds and an-
tique chests.

★Sleeping Warrior LODGE $$$
(📞0735408698,0727067418;www.sleepingwarrior
kenya.com; Soysambu Conservancy, Lake Elmenteita; per person full board US$220-460; ❄🛜🌊)
🏝 Inside the private Soysambu Conservancy and named for the shape of the mountain formation that cradles it, the Sleeping
Warrior is exquisitely remote – it took us
90 minutes to reach it from the main road.
You'll be richly rewarded for doing so; its
stark beauty is softened by luxurious, arty
lodges with sleek balconies and plunge
pools; there's an attached tented camp.

WORTH A TRIP

BUFFALO CIRCUIT
····························

A well-signposted track loops away to
the south from close to the main Elsa
gate, climbing up and over the hills before rejoining the main valley after 14km.
En route, you'll have some outstanding
views of Mt Longonot, and there's
generally more wildlife here, including
giraffes, various antelope species and
the odd buffalo or two. The Buffalo Circuit would be a fairly strenuous walk or
cycle, but it's accessible by 2WD vehicle,
except after heavy rain.

 Close to the Elsa Gate end of the trail,
a side track leads for 2km to the
Obsidian Cave (p97), where you'll find
moderately interesting examples of the
glassy black rock so characteristic of
Rift Valley lava flows.

Kigio Wildlife Camp TENTED CAMP $$$
(📞Nairobi 020-2842400; www.africanspice
safaris.com; s/d full board Jul-Oct US$262/420,
rates vary rest of year) On the 14-sq-km Ki-
gio Wildlife Conservancy (conservancy fee
US$25 per person) east of the Naivasha–
Nakuru road and south of Lake Elmenteita,
Kigio Wildlife Camp makes a quiet alterna-
tive to the busier accommodation options
around Lakes Naivasha or Elmenteita.
Tented rooms are large (some would say
cavernous) and there's some decent wildlife
watching on your doorstep.

Sunbird Lodge LODGE $$$
(📞0733555777, 0715555777; www.sunbirdkenya.
com; off Naivasha-Nakuru hwy; d full board from
US$350; 🅿🛜🌊) 🏝 With a gorgeous view
of the lake and beautiful rooms tumbling
down the hillside, Sunbird really gets it
right. The rooms are stylish but not preten-
tious, the decor is lovely with attention to
detail, there's a curved pool, hyraxes hopping between rocks and lots of sundowner
nooks. Even if you're not staying here, stop
by for lunch and enjoy the warm welcome.

Oasis Eco Camp ECOLODGE $$$
(📞0729940165, 0729910410; www.oasis.co.ke;
camping US$10, s/d full board US$135/180; 🅿)
🏝 Homely and peaceful, Oasis is nestled at
the foot of the lake. The *bandas* combine
hip duplex balconies with simple, grand-
motherly decor. There's lakeshore camp-
ing and the freshly prepared breakfast is
served picnic-style, right by the lake.

ⓘ Getting There & Away

The route between Nakuru and Nairobi is one of the busiest stretches of road in the country – finding public transport here is easy and the highway passes within sight of the lake.

Nakuru

📞 051 / POP 308,000

Nakuru is changing fast and, in the process, transforming into one of Kenya's more agreeable towns, gentrifying around the edges and adopting some of the better aspects of Nairobi – minus the stress and the crime. Most travellers speed through the town on their way to the lakes and if that's all you do, you might wonder why anyone would choose to stay here – at first glance, Kenya's fourth-largest city can appear grim and provincial, without much to offer besides a convenient refuel. But stick around longer and we bet you'll start to like it.

If you don't want to fork out to overnight at Lake Nakuru, the city makes a good base for exploring the park and surrounds.

◎ Sights

Hyrax Hill
Prehistoric Site   ARCHAEOLOGICAL SITE
(Map p103; www.museums.or.ke/hyrax-hill; adult/child KSh500/250; ◷9am-6pm) This archaeological site, 4km outside Nakuru, is a great spot for a peaceful amble away from the rhinos and tourists. It contains a museum and the remains of three settlements excavated between 1937 and the late 1980s, the oldest

---

RIFT VALLEY RESOURCES

➡ *The Great Rift Valley: Being the Narrative of a Journey to Mount Kenya and Lake Baringo* (1896), JW Gregory

➡ *Africa's Rift Valley* (1974), Colin Willock

➡ *The Great Rift: Africa's Changing Valley* (1989), Anthony Smith

➡ *The Great Rift Valley of East Africa* (2001), Anup Shah & Manoj Shah

➡ *Tribes of the Great Rift Valley* (2007) Elizabeth L Gilbert

➡ *The Great Rift* (DVD; 2010) BBC

➡ *Birds of Kenya's Rift Valley* (2014) Adam Scott Kennedy

---

being possibly 3000 years old, the most recent 200 to 300 years old. You're free to wander the site, but it's rather cryptic and a guide is useful – a tip of KSh200 is plenty.

Murals   GALLERY
(Map p103; Flamingo Rd) Lining the western side of the road on the approach to Lake Nakuru if you're coming from town, these eye-catching murals depict everyone from George and Joy Adamson and Jomo Kenyatta to Kenya's Nobel Peace Prize winner, the late Wangari Maathai.

☞ Tours

Pega Tours   SAFARI
(Map p101; ☎0722776094, 0722743440; www.pegatours.co.ke; Utalii Arcade, Kenyatta Ave) Good budget tour company that organises reasonably priced trips to Lake Nakuru and beyond, with knowledgeable guides. Homestays can also be arranged from KSh1500.

🛏 Sleeping

★Milimani Guest House   GUESTHOUSE $$
(Map p103; ☎0753616263; Maragoli Ave; s/d KSh5500/6600; ℗🕸) Perched above the town with soaring views towards the lake, this well-run, stylish place is a tranquil escape from the traffic below. Rooms wrap around a living room furnished with sofas and a fireplace, and breakfast is served in the pretty garden. The rooms are bright and clean with hip touches, and the welcome is warm.

Kivu Resort   HOTEL $$
(Map p103; ☎0726026894; www.kivuresort.co.ke; off Flamingo Rd; r from US$50; ℗🕸🏊) This simple, U-shaped resort sits just 1.5km from Lake Nakuru's main gate. Rooms come without fanfare or pretension but do sport mosquito nets; the price and location are both winners. Residents' rates are cheaper, if you fancy bargaining. There's a tuk-tuk stage 100m away.

🍴 Eating

Hygienic Butchery   KENYAN $
(Map p101; Tom Mboya Rd; mains KSh180-270; ◷8am-10pm) Great name, great place. The Kenyan tradition of *nyama choma* is alive and well here. Sidle up to the counter, try a piece of tender mutton or beef and order half a kilo (per person) of whichever takes your fancy, along with chapatis or ugali (no sauce!).

Nakuru

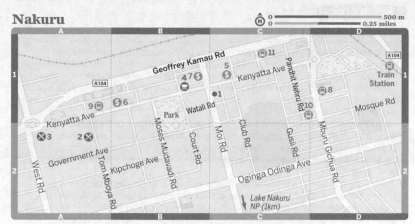

The meat will then be carved up and brought to your table; you dig in with your hands. Bliss! It also serves stews, barbecued chicken and other dishes.

Java House CAFE $$
(Map p101; www.javahouseafrica.com; Westside Mall, Kenyatta Ave; mains from KSh600; ⊗7am-9pm Mon-Fri, to 10pm Sat & Sun; ✳🛜) Located on the ground-floor terrace of Westside Mall, the Nakuru branch of the popular Java House coffee chain is probably the best place to eat in town, with a large menu of Tex-Mex, burgers, curries, wraps and grilled meats to choose from. There's also good coffee and plenty of pastries.

🍷 Drinking & Nightlife

Moca Loca CAFE
(Map p101; ☎0708084839; Kenyatta Ave; ⊗10am-10pm) Nakuru loves its coffee and Moca Loca is the new caffeinated kid in town. Located on the 2nd floor of a corner building, this is something of a stylish spot for people-watching; Parisian-style window boxes frame the booths. Besides coffee, there are pancake breakfasts, sandwiches, salads and burgers.

ℹ️ Information

Changing cash in Nakuru is easy, with numerous banks and foreign exchange bureaus.

KCB (Map p101; Kenyatta Ave; ⊗9am-4pm Mon-Fri, to noon Sat) ATM and foreign exchange bureau.

Barclays (Map p101; Kenyatta Ave; ⊗8am-6pm Mon-Fri, to 2pm Sat) Nakuru's most reliable ATM. Also has a foreign exchange desk.

Nakuru

🏃 Activities, Courses & Tours
1 Pega Tours..C1

🍴 Eating
2 Hygienic Butchery.................................... A2
3 Java House... A2

🍷 Drinking & Nightlife
4 Moca Loca..B1

ℹ️ Information
5 Barclays..C1
6 KCB B1
7 Standard Chartered Bank...................B1

🚍 Transport
8 Bus & Matatu Station...........................D1
9 Easy Coach..A1
10 Matatus to Kampi ya Samaki
& Marigat...C1
11 Molo Line..C1

Standard Chartered Bank (Map p101; Moi Rd; ⊗9am-5pm Mon-Fri, to 1pm Sat) Bureau de change and an ATM.

ℹ️ Getting There & Away

BUS

Easy Coach (Map p101; www.easycoach.co.ke; Kenyatta Ave) One of several bus companies offering services to Nairobi (KSh500, three hours), Eldoret (KSh650, 2¾ hours) and Kisumu (KSh750, 3½ hours).

MATATU

Ordinary matatus leave from the chaotic **bus and matatu station** (Map p101; Mburu Gichua Rd) next to the market. Services include Naivasha (KSh200,

WORTH A TRIP

MENENGAI CRATER

With transport and 15 minutes to play with, you can be out of the grimy streets of Nakuru and standing on the rim of **Menengai Crater** (adult/child KSh600/200, guides KSh1000; ⊙7am-5pm) , a 485m-high natural cauldron and local beauty spot. Outside of weekends, it's a peaceful place that affords striking views down below onto a cushion of lush vegetation. The crater was formed over one million years ago and the last eruption was about 350 years ago.

Geothermal excavation is now taking place on the crater floor, so it's hard to tell if those plumes of steam rising from the bottom are indeed the souls – as the story goes – of defeated Maasai warriors, or swirling clouds of dust. On the crater's western side is the **Mau Mau Cave**, where guerrillas hid from British colonial forces during the Mau Mau uprising.

If you want to take on the Menengai Crater on foot, we recommend taking a guide. **James Maina** (☑0723031150; jamesmaina11@yahoo.com) is a good local guide and can take you down into the crater and back up again (a four-hour round trip) or to the Mau Mau Cave. It's an isolated 6km walk from the main gate; hikers should never make the climb alone.

You can, at least in theory, camp atop the crater for KSh700 per person. There's a small group of *dukas* (shops) at the main viewpoint selling drinks and trinkets.

A motorbike taxi from town to the top of the crater should cost around KSh800.

1¼ hours), Eldoret (from KSh350, 2¾ hours), Nairobi (KSh250 to KSh400, three hours) and Kisumu (KSh600, 3½ hours).

Matatus for Lake Baringo (Kampi ya Samaki; KSh250, 2½ hours) or Marigat (for Lake Bogoria; KSh150, two hours) leave from the **stand** (Map p101) at the southern end of Pandhit Nehru Rd. **Molo Line** (Map p101; ☑0722761512; www.mololineprestige.com; Geoffrey Kamau Rd) is the most reputable of the matatu companies, running services to Nairobi that leave when full from opposite the old Odeon cinema; the first departures of the day are from 4.30am. There are 10 seats, usually with belts, and drivers tend to stick to the speed limit. This prestige shuttle service goes to Nairobi (KSh400), Eldoret (KSh400) and Kisumu (KSh600).

Lake Nakuru National Park

Lake Nakuru (Map p103; ☑0728355267, 0728355207; www.kws.go.ke; adult/child US$60/35; ⊙6.30am-6.30pm) is among Kenya's finest national parks. Flanked by rocky escarpments, pockets of acacia forest and at least one waterfall, the park is gorgeous year-round and is home to both black and white rhinos, lions, leopards, hippos and endangered Rothschild's giraffes. Rising water levels in 2014 forced the park's famous flamingos to flee (although a small number had returned at the time of research), and the lake is now hauntingly surrounded by drowned trees.

The southern end of the lake is the best place to see wildlife. The forested area below Flamingo Hill is a favourite lion-spotting point – lionesses love to sleep in the trees – while leopards frequent the same area, and are also sometimes seen around the Makalia camp.

⊙ Sights

Out of Africa Lookout   VIEWPOINT
(Map p103) To get the best view that takes in much of the park, head up to the rocky Out of Africa Lookout. Less frequented by tour groups than the lower Baboon Cliff, the incline is steeper but it offers sweeping views out over the lake and fond memories for fans of the film – parts of the movie were filmed in the park, with some shots taken from here.

Baboon Cliffs   VIEWPOINT
(Map p103) This popular viewpoint and one-time lunch spot has superlative views out over the lake, with some fine aerial vistas down onto the flooded lake shore. Baboons, however, are a problem and don't mind raiding vehicles, whether you're inside or not, for food scraps. Visit in the early morning before they've taken over for the day.

🛏 Sleeping & Eating

If you're camping, you'll have to bring your own food or eat in the pricey lodges, most of which welcome nonguests for meals if you

Lake Nakuru National Park

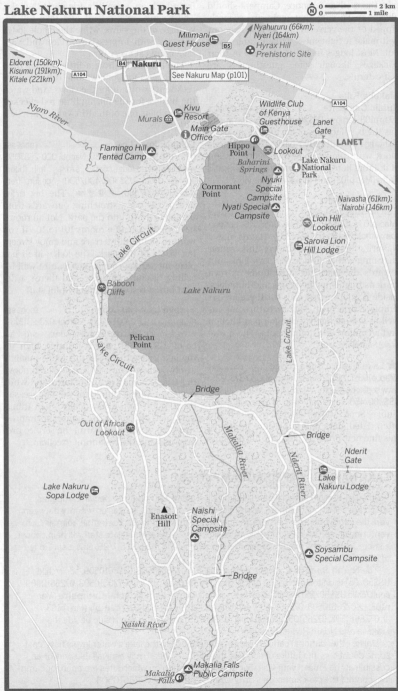

give them advance notice. Campers should always make sure that tents are securely zipped or the vervet monkeys and baboons will make a right mess while cleaning you out. Most lodges include full board in their packages, though some guesthouses are self-catering.

Makalia Falls
Public Campsite CAMPGROUND $
(Map p103; camping US$30; P) 🖋 This campsite has the best facilities of any inside the park, although it's still rather basic – an ablutions block with cold running water is the extent of it. From here you can walk to the **Makalia Falls** (Map p103) and check out the view.

Wildlife Club of
Kenya Guesthouse HOSTEL $
(Map p103; ☑ 0723760970, 0720456546; per person without bathroom KSh1250) Hands down Nakuru's best budget choice, this rather charming cottage inside the park looks out towards the lake and often finds its own gardens frequented by zebras and buffaloes. Inside it's nothing special, but there are six simple rooms with shared bathrooms, as well as a moderately well-equipped kitchen and a comfortable dining room. The hostel is self-catering only.

★ **Lake Nakuru Sopa Lodge** LODGE $$$
(Map p103; ☑ 072220632, Nairobi 020-3750235; www.sopalodges.com; s/d full board Jul-Oct US$300/450, rates vary rest of year; P🛜☰) Unlike Sopa Lodges elsewhere which are often dated, dark and in obscure locations, this fine new property has light-filled rooms from high on a perch overlooking the lake. The rooms are excellent and take full advantage of the views, while the whole lodge sparkles with impressive service and vantage points at every turn.

You'll need to drive a little further than other places for your wildlife drive, but we reckon it's worth it for the views. And watch the bushes for the flitting little red-cheeked cordon bleu, one of the Rift Valley's loveliest little birds.

Lake Nakuru Lodge LODGE $$$
(Map p103; ☑ 0720404480, Nairobi 020-2687056; www.lakenakurulodge.com; s/d/tr full board Jul-Mar from US$300/400/500, Apr-Jun from US$200/300/380; P@🛜☰) The big draw here is the view, stretching outwards from the lodge down into the park. Not all rooms have views – snaffle rooms 101 to 103 if you want to sit on your terrace and enjoy sweeping vistas of the park. The lodge itself has pleasant garden rooms that feature wall-to-ceiling balcony windows, and there's a decent buffet restaurant and helpful staff.

Sarova Lion Hill Lodge LODGE $$$
(Map p103; ☑ 0709111000, Nairobi 020-2315139; www.sarovahotels.com/lionhill-nakuru; s/d full board US$300/381; P🛜☰) Sitting high up the lake's eastern slopes, this lodge inhabits lovely, leafy grounds in a valley high above the lake. Rooms are understated and while some are a little simple for the high-season price, rates drop dramatically when things are quiet; the suites are large and impressive. The welcome is warm, the service professional and the restaurant excellent.

LAKE NAKURU'S SPECIAL CAMPSITES

As in other Kenyan national parks, Lake Nakuru has a number of 'special' campsites, which are essentially intimate, wild spaces with no facilities, fences or security between you, the carnivores and the stars. Rangers will light night fires to deter the animals from venturing close. But think romance; attacks are very rare. Main gate staff will help choose a spot. Costs for the special campsites per adult/child are US$50/25, plus a set-up fee of KSh7500.

The **Nyuki Special Campsite** (Map p103; ☑ 0726610508, 0726610509; adult/child US$50/25) is on the north side of the lake, **Nyati** (Map p103; ☑ 0726610508, 0726610509; adult/child US$50/25) is a little further south, while **Naishi Special Campsite** (Map p103; ☑ 0726610508, 0726610509; adult/child US$50/25) and **Soysambu** (Map p103; ☑ 0726610508, 0726610509; adult/child US$50/25) are on the south side beside the Makalia and Nderit Rivers respectively.

Unlike other national parks, however, fluctuations in the lake's water levels have cast some doubt over the future of some of the sites, so not all may be available and/or accessible at the time of your visit. For more information on which sites are open for camping, contact the park authorities on ☑ 0726610509 or ☑ 0726610508.

ℹ️ LAKE NAKURU NATIONAL PARK

Why Go One of Kenya's best national parks is an easy two-hour drive from Nairobi. You might see tree-climbing lions, flamingos and black and white rhinos.

When to Go Animal viewing is generally good year-round, but avoid the peak of the rainy season, from March to May.

Gateway Town Nakuru

Practicalities Park tickets are valid for 24 hours exactly (or 48 hours, 72 hours etc), so if you enter at 6.30am and plan to sleep in the park, you must leave by the same time the following day. The park's main gate was forced to move back up the hill during the 2014 floods.

Budget Tips Stay outside the park and you'll pay far less for accommodation, and won't risk needing a permit for longer than 24 hours. Pega Tours (p100) offers cheap vehicle hire with guides for those without vehicles.

Flamingo Hill Tented Camp   TENTED CAMP $$$
(Map p103; ☑️0727525279; www.flamingohill camp.com; full board per person from US$110; 🅿️🛜❄️) ✏️ Flamingo Hill strikes a balance between accessible and wild, and offers a good deal. There's a smart wooden communal area, 30 comfortable tents (which are a little dark), a spa and pool. The camp is just a short drive from the main gate, so you'll need to drive deeper into the park for the best wildlife viewing.

ℹ️ Information

There's limited park information at the **main gate office** (Map p103); at the time of research, plans were underway for the creation of an information centre.

ℹ️ Getting There & Away

Lake Nakuru National Park begins on the outskirts of Nakuru (p100), the main gateway town for the park. It is worth noting that there is no public transport from the town into the park – contact your accommodation for a transfer (which may or may not be free of charge) from the town, or rent a vehicle in Nakuru.

ℹ️ Getting Around

The park is accessible in a 2WD, though most visitors stay in the park and take hotel-run safaris. You'll need to pay KSh350 per car to bring your own vehicle into the park. It is possible for you to explore the park alone, but guides are available for KSh2500 per four hours. If you don't have your own wheels, Pega Tours (p100) in Nakuru is a good bet. Its daily hire rates include a pop-top minibus and a knowledgeable driver/guide from KSh2500 per person (based on four guests).

Njoro

☑️ 051 / POP 60,000

Karen Blixen, of *Out of Africa* fame, once described dusty little Njoro as one of her favourite places. And we think she might have been right; there's the climate, for starters, plus acres and acres of fertile farmland and a history worthy of novels.

In a fertile strip up above the lip of Lake Nakuru, Njoro was once slated as the potential capital of British East Africa by the influential British settler Lord Delamere. Delamere's close friend Beryl Markham, the first woman to fly westbound solo across the Atlantic, grew up nearby. Although the big dreams for Njoro never materialised, we think it's all the better for it because Njoro retains a dose of magic. It also makes a good base for exploring Lake Nakuru to the south, and Bogoria and Baringo to the north.

👁️ Sights

Kenana Knitters   WORKSHOP
(☑️0715262303; www.kenanaknitters.wordpress. com; Kenana Farm, off C56; ⏱️8.30am-5pm Mon-Fri) 🆓 What began as a hobby for three ladies knitting under a tree now employs more than 1200 local people and exports all over the world. The knitters use plant and flower dyes – including beetroot and dahlia – and sustainable wool and cotton in their cute, quirky designs. You can tour the innovative natural workshop, hear the story of how this became one of the most impressive non-profit initiatives in the region, and make a stop in the lovely shop.

LAKE NAKURU TROUBLES

Lake Nakuru is a park under pressure. For a start, there aren't many places in the park where you can't see or hear the clamour of Kenya's fourth-largest city just beyond the fence. But beyond such longer-lasting concerns, the park authorities just can't take a trick.

In 2002, two park rangers were killed by lions within weeks of each other – both were walking from the old park gate to a nearby building. In response, the park authorities killed 10 lions – it was impossible to identify the culprit and no-one wanted a man-eater roaming the park or surrounding area.

Then, in 2014, the lake levels rose, as they did across Kenya's Rift Valley lakes. Apart from considerably reducing the land surface area of the park, the waters forced the authorities to abandon the old main park entrance (as you enter from downtown Nakuru), which was moved to higher ground a couple of kilometres away. The waters have receded a little, but the old gate remains one of the park's more haunting spectacles, and many lakeside access roads remain submerged and, of course, impassable.

In 2015, more than 300 buffaloes (out of a total park population of 4500) and a smaller number of other herbivore species died in an anthrax outbreak.

As if such misfortunes weren't sufficient, six rhinos were poached from within the park's boundaries in 2014; while in January 2017, reports emerged that a rhino had been poached within the park, although the Kenya Wildlife Service (KWS) later reported that a poacher (and no rhinos) had been killed. If the KWS report is true, it would be rare piece of good news for the park authorities.

Egerton Castle CASTLE
(Njoro; US$12; ⊘ 9am-5pm Mon-Fri, 10am-2pm Sat & Sun) If you want to muse on lost love and where it goes, visit Egerton Castle on the outskirts of Njoro. A replica of Tatton Hall in England, the castle was constructed between 1938 and 1954 by Lord Maurice Egerton – who also set up the agricultural training college that would later become Egerton University. With cared-for gardens and a small petting zoo that includes llamas and tortoises, it makes a pleasant afternoon picnic spot.

🛏 Sleeping & Eating

★ Kembu Cottages COTTAGE $$
(☑ 0722355705, 0722361102; www.kembufarm.com; off C56; camping KSh650, r KSh5000-16,000; P) 🍴 Green and peaceful, Kembu Farm has nine cosy cottages set in beautiful gardens on the edge of Njoro. Each cottage tells a story; you can sleep in the restored childhood home of aviator Beryl Markham, in a vintage 1920s railway carriage, or in a hip treehouse. The food is home-cooked and delicious, the welcome is warm and there's real attention to detail, including working fireplaces.

Ziwa Bush Lodge LODGE $$$
(☑ 0707698822; www.ziwalodge.com; off Njoro Rd; s/d full board from KSh14,200/19,500; P 🛜) With fresh, sleek rooms set in spacious, manicured grounds, this small resort marries safari chic with the peace and quiet of the Njoro countryside. It's owned by an Australian family and visits to a nearby supported orphanage can be arranged. It's near the Rift Valley Institute of Science & Technology. Rooms are extremely tasteful and the family and executive rooms are particularly lovely.

Ribs Butchery GRILL $
(Main Rd (C56); mains from KSh200; ⊘ 7am-8pm) Brightly painted Ribs Butchery does all the usual *nyama choma* options and is the pick of numerous such places along the main road.

🍷 Drinking & Nightlife

Njoro Country Club SPORTS BAR
(off C57, Golf Course Rd; ⊘ noon-10pm) It's worth stopping by to see who's propping up the bar at this old-fashioned country club. There's an ancient pool table, a piano, television, outdoor tables and a golf course. Simple meals are on offer and it's generally a real White Highlands institution.

ⓘ Getting There & Away

Regular matatus connect Njoro with Nakuru (KSh80, 30 minutes) throughout the day.

Lake Bogoria

Lake Bogoria (🖰 Nairobi 020-6000800; www.
kws.org; adult/child US$25/15) is backed by the
bleak Siracho Escarpment, and moss-green
waves roll down its rocky, barren shores. A
road that becomes a rough track (and then
peters out entirely) runs along the lake's
western shore, which is where flamingos
gather. About halfway along the lake, **hot
springs and geysers** spew boiling fluids
from the earth's insides. If you're here early
in the morning, you may have the place to
yourself.

While the isolated wooded area at the
lake's southern end is home to rarely seen
leopards, klipspringers, gazelles, caracals
and buffaloes, an increase in human activity
means that the extravagantly horned greater
kudu is increasingly elusive. You can explore
on foot or bicycle. If you'd like a guide, enquire at Loboi Gate.

🏃 Activities

Kesubo Swamp   BIRDWATCHING
Just outside Lake Bogoria National Reserve's
northern boundary and just off the road in
from the main B4, Kesubo Swamp is a birdwatcher's paradise: more than 200 species
have been recorded and one lucky person
spotted 96 species in one hour – a Kenyan
record. You'll need to park your car close to
Lake Bogoria Spa Resort and walk around
the perimeter.

🛏 Sleeping

Fig Tree Campsite   CAMPGROUND $
(🖰 0723370114; camping US$20) Easily the pick
of Lake Bogoria's camping areas, remote Fig
Tree is a wonderfully shady lakeshore spot
with a small stream nearby and a small ablutions block. Mosquitoes and baboons are
the main drawback.

Acacia Camp   CAMPGROUND $
(🖰 0723370114; camping US$20) On the lake's
southwestern shore, this acacia-shaded site
has an ablutions block and (cold) running
water. It's a pretty spot and the busiest of the
reserve's campsites, although it's all relative
out here in this quiet place.

Lake Bogoria Spa Resort   HOTEL $$
(🖰 0710445627, Nairobi 020-2249055; www.
lakebogoria-hotel.com; camping KSh5065, s/d full
board KSh11,340/17,500; 🅿 🛜 ⛲) Set in lovely
grounds, the biggest draw here is the pool,
which is fed by a nearby hot spring. Other-
wise, the rooms (which do have mosquito
nets) don't quite live up to expectation, but
they are perfectly comfortable and will do
you just fine for a night or two. The resort
has an on-site restaurant, as well as a mas-
sage and spa centre based around the hot
springs.

ℹ Information

Limited information on the reserve is available at
the **Reserve HQ** (E461).

ℹ Getting There & Away

Entrances are at Loboi (north), Emsos (south)
and Maji Moto (west); only Loboi is accessible
by 2WD vehicle. The nearest petrol is available
in Marigat.

Matatus run to Loboi Gate from Marigat
(KSh120, 30 minutes). Regular matatus serve
Marigat from Nakuru (KSh275, two hours) and
Kabarnet (KSh180, 1¼ hours).

FLAMINGOS & THE ART OF STANDING ON ONE LEG

From Lake Bogoria in Kenya to Lake Natron in northern Tanzania, it's the classic Rift
Valley image: the flamingo, or, rather, the massed ranks of flamingos standing complete-
ly still on one leg. Why they do so has baffled scientists for decades.

Finally, a 2017 study found that this pose has a very strong scientific reason: flamingos, it
seems, expend less energy by standing on one leg than they do standing on two. More spe-
cifically, flamingos do not actively use their muscles in any way in this one-legged position.
Which is, of course, why flamingos can actually sleep while standing in this position. So easy
and perfectly balanced is this pose that the scientists who carried out the study discovered
that even dead flamingos could remain in this position on one leg (but not two legs) without
any means of upright support!

Closer examination of the position reveals that the standing foot sits directly beneath
the body, meaning that the leg angles inwards, thereby enabling the birds to assume the
position and remain almost entirely motionless for significant periods.

Lake Baringo

📷 051

Wild and beautiful Lake Baringo is the most remote of the Rift Valley lakes. Steeped in stories, its harsh climate and rocky islets give it a faraway feel; on a hot day, this freshwater lake has more in common with northern Kenya than the rest of the Rift Valley. Birdwatching in Kenya rarely gets better than this, with over 460 species including owls, nightjars, Goliath herons and rare Hemprich's hornbills. Crocs and hippos are also present.

The small village of **Kampi ya Samaki**, on Lake Baringo's shore, is the gateway to the lake. Lake Baringo is not a fee-paying park, but the community charges a toll (KSh200) to access the lake; keep your receipt.

🏃 Activities

Boat Rides

A boat ride, naturally, is by far the best way to experience the lake. A speciality is a trip to see fish eagles feeding; the birds dive for fish at a whistle.

Trips generally cost around KSh3000 per hour and the most reliable ones are organised by **Lake Baringo Boats & Excursions** (📞0721548657; boatexcursions@lake-baringo. com; Kampi ya Samaki; per boat per hour KSh3000), Island Camp and Roberts Camp.

Bird & Nature Walks

Even the most cynical are easily won over by Baringo's birdlife and it can be hard to resist setting off on a dawn walk – this is when the birds are most active and twitchers will be in their element. Roberts Camp leads excellent one- to three-hour walks for between KSh400 and KSh600 per person; night-time bird walks (great for owls and nightjars) can also be arranged.

Village Tours

Roberts Camp and Island Camp both offer tours (from KSh1200 per person) to Pokot and Njemps villages close to the lake, where you can eat at a *manyatta* (traditional village) and feel seriously drab in comparison in the style stakes.

Trips to visit bush clinics – where snake bites are treated using natural remedies – can also be arranged from Roberts Camp (from KSh350 per person).

Lake Baringo & Lake Bogoria National Reserve

🛏 Sleeping

★ **Roberts Camp** CAMPGROUND $
(📞0717176656; www.robertscamp.com; Kampi ya Samaki; bandas for 2/4 people KSh6000/12,000,

RISING WATERS

Like most Rift Valley Lakes, Baringo experienced a sudden and still largely unexplained rise in water levels in mid-2014. It was an extraordinary and extremely worrying time for the peoples of the area, with houses, lakeside businesses and other buildings and properties suddenly submerged without warning. From a traveller perspective, the most obvious signpost to the change was the once-unimaginable sight of the lake's waters lapping at the doorstep of the **Thirsty Goat**, which had previously stood high on a hill well above the lake's surface. By one estimate, Lake Baringo doubled in size as a result of the rising waters.

The most plausible explanation for the phenomenon is the movement of subterranean tectonic plates which impacted upon the flow of water in the area after heavy rains. Waters have since receded slightly, but there remains uncertainty as to what the future holds for lakeshore communities.

d tents KSh2500-4500, camping KSh800; ℗) 🍴
A legend in its own right, this atmospheric camp sits right on the lakeshore, wherever that shore may be...The *bandas* are nicely decorated, with eco loos, and there's ample space for camping, plus the Thirsty Goat bar-restaurant. The helpful staff can organise boat rides and scorpion- or bird-spotting nature walks. After dark, keep your eyes peeled for hippos, fireflies and the ghosts of old adventurers.

⭐ **Island Camp**　　　TENTED CAMP $$$
(📞0724874661, 0728478638; www.islandcamp. com; Lake Baringo; room/cottage full board incl boat transfers from US$550/740; 🛜🍴) 🍴 Stylish but relaxed, this gorgeous tented camp covers the tip of an island in the middle of Lake Baringo. The lovely tents are a mixture of thatch and canvas, while the superior rooms have private plunge pools and Kenyan art. There's an atmospheric bar, community initiatives, wild gardens made for birdwatching, and a spa tent. Day visitors are welcomed for lunch.

Samatian Island Lodge　　　VILLA $$$
(📞0712579999, Nairobi 020-2115453; www. samatianisland.com; Lake Baringo; lodge from US$1000; 🍴) 🍴 Set on a private island, this intimate luxury spot can only be rented in its entirety. There's room for 12 in beautiful thatched *bandas*, and plenty going on in terms of nature and activities, including jetski hire. The food is good, healthy and served by candlelight.

✖ Eating

Thirsty Goat　　　INTERNATIONAL $$
(📞0717176656; www.robertscamp.com; Roberts Camp, Kampi ya Samaki; mains from KSh750; ⏰7am-10pm) Even if you're not staying at Roberts Camp, the Thirsty Goat is an institution worth visiting. Sip sundowners, listen to snorting hippos, grab a book from the small library or entertain the bar with your travel banter. The menu includes tilapia fish and chips or traditional goat curry, as well as pizzas, vegetable stir fry and toasted sandwiches.

⭐ **Island Camp Restaurant**　　　BUFFET $$$
(📞0728478638, 0724874661; www.islandcamp. com; Island Camp, Lake Baringo; buffet KSh2500; ⏰lunch; 🍴🛥) 🍴 A popular weekend activity, if you can call it that, is to charter a boat and hop across to Island Camp's sleek restaurant for lunch. The buffet includes a mix of cold dishes such as gazpacho, Indian mains, salads and lovely desserts, served overlooking the lapping water. Make sure you call ahead of time in order to secure a table.

ℹ Getting There & Away

Lake access is easiest from Kampi ya Samaki on the lake's western shore, some 15km north of Marigat on a rough road.

A 25-seater bus leaves for Nakuru each morning (KSh400) between 6.30am and 9.30am (it departs when full).

Slightly more regular pick-up trucks head to Marigat (KSh120, 30 minutes) and you can catch more frequent matatus from there to Nakuru (KSh340, two hours) or Kabarnet (KSh230, 1¼ hours).

Masai Mara & Western Kenya

Includes ➡

Narok 112

Masai Mara
National Reserve 112

Kisumu. 127

Ruma National Park. . 131

Mbita & Rusinga
Island 132

Kisii 134

Kericho. 135

Kakamega Forest 137

Mt Elgon
National Park 144

Best Places to Eat

➡ Lakeshore tin-shack restaurants, Kisumu (p129)

➡ Mara Plains (p125)

➡ Cottar's 1920s Camp (p126)

➡ Green Garden Restaurant (p129)

➡ Sunjeel Palace (p142)

Best Places to Stay

➡ Mara Plains (p125)

➡ Kicheche Bush Camp (p125)

➡ Asilia Naboisho (p124)

➡ Saruni Mara (p121)

Why Go?

For many travellers, the magic of western Kenya is summed up in two poetic words: Masai Mara. Few places on earth support such high concentrations of animals, and the Mara's wildebeest-spotted savannahs, where drama unfolds on a daily basis, are undeniably the region's star attraction. The Maasai bring cachet to their lands and your encounters with this ancient people are likely to be the soulful highlight of your journey.

But there's much more to western Kenya than these plains of herbivores and carnivores. The dense forests of Kakamega are buzzing with weird and wonderful creatures, the rain-soaked hills of Kericho and their verdant tea gardens bring new meaning to the word 'green', and amid the boat-speckled waters of Lake Victoria lies a smattering of seldom-visited islands crying out for exploration.

When to Go
Kisumu

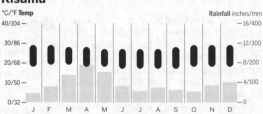

Mar–May The 'heavy rains' *usually* fall, particularly in the cooler Western Highlands.

Jul–Oct Arrival of the wildebeest migration; the Masai Mara groans with herbivores.

Nov–Dec The 'lesser rains' appear briefly before things dry out in January.

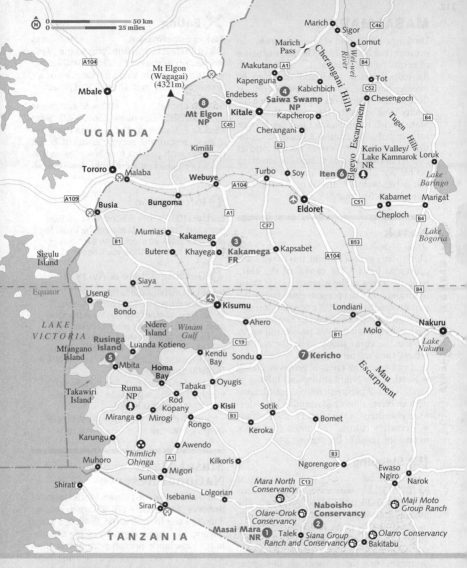

Masai Mara & Western Kenya Highlights

① **Masai Mara National Reserve** (p112) Watching one of the greatest wildlife shows on Earth.

② **Naboisho Conservancy** (p123) Enjoying one of East Africa's finest wildlife territories.

③ **Kakamega Forest Reserve** (p138) Looking for birds and primates in Kenya's last true rainforest.

④ **Saiwa Swamp National Park** (p147) Wading through the backwaters in search of paddling antelope.

⑤ **Rusinga Island** (p132) Throwing away your watch and planning to stay forever on Lake Victoria's idyllic islands.

⑥ **High Altitude Training Centre, Iten** (p139) Running on the trails that have created so many long-distance legends.

⑦ **Kericho** (p135) Learning how to brew a proper cuppa in Africa's tea capital.

⑧ **Mt Elgon National Park** (p144) Climbing to the summit of Kenya's second-highest peak.

MASAI MARA

Dream of Africa and chances are that you dream of the Masai Mara. This huge expanse of gently rolling grassland – specked with flat-topped acacia trees and trampled by massive herds of zebras and wildebeest – is the ultimate African cliché. But for once the reality lives up to the image and the Masai Mara, which comprises not just the famous reserve but also around a dozen community conservancies, several group ranches and numerous Maasai villages, is for many people not just the highlight of their Kenyan adventure but the very reason they came in the first place.

Narok

📍 050 / POP 40,000

Three hours west of Nairobi, this ramshackle provincial town – the capital of the Mara region – serves as the gateway to the Masai Mara and is the last proper centre before the vast savannahs begin. It's a friendly and surprisingly hassle-free place, but few travellers have reason to stop. Most people roll on in, browse the curio shops while their driver refuels, then roll on out again.

If you stay long enough, however, Narok is worth a few hours sitting and talking to locals – it's a predominantly Maasai town with an increasingly high number of settlers from elsewhere in the country. The result is a fascinating cultural mix and a good place to take the pulse of the region.

🛏 Sleeping

Seasons Hotel　　　　　　　HOTEL **$$**
(📞 0718323213; www.seasonshotelskenya.com; B3; s US$60-110, d US$100-140; [P][🛜][♨]) The largest and most popular place to stop in town, the Seasons Hotel has tired but large, adequate rooms with mosquito nets; the swimming pool is a bonus. If staying overnight, ask for a room on the upper floors at the back to combat street noise. Some of the ground-floor rooms are a little claustrophobic.

Lexingtone Hotel　　　　　　HOTEL **$$**
(📞 0705699417; www.lexingtonehotel.com; C57; s/d from US$60/70) Just north of town and therefore quieter than most, the Lexingtone has tidy, if fairly standard, midrange rooms with mosquito nets and colourful walls to brighten things up a little.

 ## Eating

Tuskys Supermarket　　SUPERMARKET **$**
(B3, 1st fl, Oltalet Mall; ⊘ 8am-8pm) A large, well-stocked supermarket in Oltalet Mall on the way through town. Good for supplies or for takeaway meals from the deli and bakery.

Seasons Hotel　　KENYAN, INTERNATIONAL **$$**
(📞 0718323213; B3; mains KSh400-700, buffet KSh800; ⊘ 11am-9pm) The Seasons Hotel has a good restaurant serving a lunch buffet (popular with passing tour buses) as well as spicy beef, chicken stew and a few vegetarian options.

ℹ Information

Barclays (B3; ⊘ 9am-3.30pm Mon-Fri, 9am-noon Sat) The only ATM around the Masai Mara is at Talek Gate, so stock up on cash here – take more than you think you'll need.

ℹ Getting There & Away

Narok Line matatus run to Nairobi (KSh500, three hours) from the Shell petrol station on the B6 Hwy. All other matatus leave from the main matatu stand just around the corner in the centre of town. Destinations include Naivasha (KSh350, 2½ hours), Kisii (KSh500, three hours), Kericho (KSh500, 2½ hours) and Nakuru (KSh500, two hours).

Matatus and share taxis also leave from the matatu stand to Sekenani and Talek gates (matatu/taxi KSh500/700).

It's much cheaper to fill up with petrol here than in the reserve.

Masai Mara National Reserve

The world-renowned **Masai Mara National Reserve** (adult/child US$80/45, subsequent days if staying inside the reserve US$70/40; ⊘ 6.30am-6.30pm) is a huge expanse of tawny, sun-burnt grasslands pocked with acacia trees and river woodlands, and heaving with animals great and small. Impressive at any time of year, it's at its best between July and October when a million migrating wildebeest and tens of thousands of topis, zebras and other animals pour into the reserve from Tanzania in search of fresh grass. It is, arguably, the most spectacular wildlife show on the planet and the one thing that no visitor to Kenya should consider missing.

Reliable rains and plentiful vegetation underpin this extraordinary ecosystem and the millions of herbivores it supports. Wildebeest, zebras, impalas, elands, reedbucks, waterbucks, black rhinos, elephants, Masai giraffes and several species of gazelle all call the Mara home. Predators here include cheetahs, leopards, spotted hyenas, black-backed jackals, bat-eared foxes, caracals and the highest lion density in the world.

Sights

Central Plains

The southeast area of the park, bordered by the Mara and Sand Rivers, is characterised by rolling grasslands and low, isolated hills. With the arrival of the migration, enormous herds of wildebeest and zebras, as well as other plains wildlife, graze here. The riverine forests that border the Mara and Talek Rivers are great places to spot elephants, buffaloes and bushbucks. Leopards are sometimes seen near the Talek and Sand Rivers and around the Keekorok valleys.

Rhino Ridge & Paradise Plains

Rhino Ridge is a good place to see black-backed jackals, as they're known to use the old termitaria here for den sites. Lookout Hill is worth a detour as it offers phenomenal views over the seasonal Olpunyaia Swamp. You may also get lucky and spot one of the few black rhinos that inhabit the reserve anywhere between Lookout Hill and Rhino Ridge and in the vicinity of Roan Hill.

To see lions, the Marsh Pride near Musiara Swamp and the Ridge Pride near Rhino Ridge both starred in the BBC's *Big Cat Diary* so they (as celebrities) are fairly easy to find.

Cheetahs are far more elusive, but are sometimes found hunting gazelles on the Paradise Plains.

Mara River

Pods of hippos can be found in any of the major rivers, with the largest and most permanent concentrations occurring in the

---

THE 'WHEN' OF THE MARA MIGRATION

While it is easy to make *fairly* reliable predictions about when the migration will arrive in Kenya, there are no guarantees where the herds will be at the time of your visit. As a general rule...

Mid-July–August By the second half of July, the herds are in the northern Serengeti (Tanzania) and heading into the Masai Mara. It is during this stage of the migration that you're most likely to encounter the incredible river crossings of the Mara River.

September–October By early September, the last stragglers should have left the Serengeti and most will remain in the Masai Mara throughout October. It's a time of massive numbers, although river crossings become less common as the year progresses and the wildebeest enjoy the grassy plains they came so far to feed on.

November With the arrival (or in anticipation) of the short rains in November, the herds usually begin to leave the Mara and cross back into Tanzania.

This is what usually happens. But, of course, it doesn't always work out this way. In November 2013, for example, it began raining in the Masai Mara when the herds had already crossed into Tanzania, prompting the wildebeest to return en masse to the Mara. They stayed there for three weeks before resuming their southwards push.

In June 2014, unseasonal rains in the southern Serengeti prompted the herd to split in two – most continued north as usual but a significant number of zebras and wildebeest occupied the plains south of Seronera until well into July, and didn't arrive in Kenya until a month or two later.

In June 2017, the herd again split (which is, according to scientists with whom we spoke, an increasingly common phenomena) and an advance herd crossed the Sand River and into the Masai Mara almost six weeks earlier than usual. The remainder of the herd headed to the Serengeti's western corridor but then moved swiftly north and began crossing into Kenya in early July.

Masai Mara National Reserve

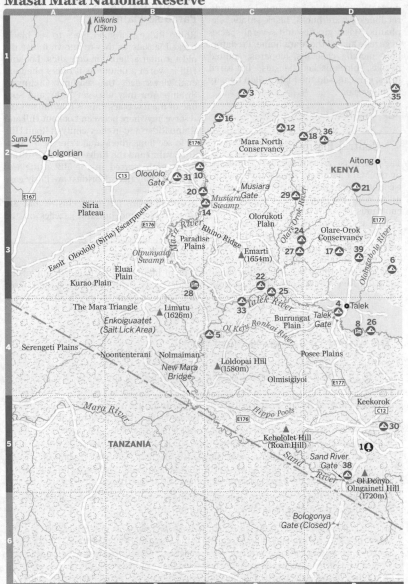

Mara River. The river is also home to huge Nile crocodiles and is the scene where wildebeest make their fateful crossings during the migration. The New Mara Bridge in the south is the only all-weather crossing point and another great place to see hippos.

◉ Mara Triangle & Esoit Olololo (Siria) Escarpment

Unlike the rest of the park, which is under the control of the Narok County Council, the northwest sector of the reserve is managed

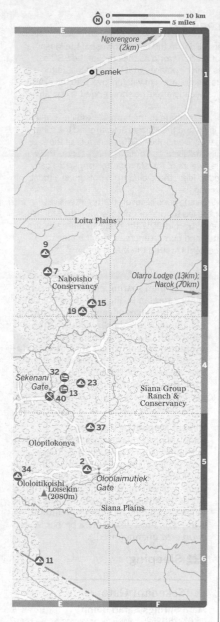

Masai Mara National Reserve

◎ Sights
1	Masai Mara National Reserve.............D5

✦ Activities, Courses & Tours
	Governors' Balloon Safaris........(see 14)
	Hot Air Safaris..........................(see 40)
	Semadep.....................................(see 13)

🛌 Sleeping
2	Acacia Camp...E5
3	Alex Walker's Serian.............................C1
4	Aruba Mara Camp...................................D4
5	Ashnil Mara...C4
6	Asilia Naboisho Camp..........................D3
7	Basecamp Eagle View.........................E3
8	Basecamp Masai Mara.........................D4
9	Basecamp Wilderness..........................E3
10	Bateleur Camp.......................................B2
11	Cottar's 1920s Camp........................... E6
	Crocodile Camp Masai Mara.......(see 4)
12	Elephant Pepper....................................C2
13	Ewangan..E4
	Fig Tree Camp..............................(see 4)
14	Governors' Camp....................................C3
15	Hemingways Ol Seki Mara....................E3
16	Karen Blixen Camp...............................C2
17	Kicheche Bush..D3
18	Kicheche Mara..D2
19	Kicheche Valley Camp..........................E3
	Kichwa Tembo Camp..................(see 10)
20	Little Governors' Camp........................B2
21	Mahali Mzuri Camp................................D2
	Manyatta Camp............................(see 2)
22	Mara Bush Camp....................................C3
23	Mara Bushtops.......................................E4
24	Mara Expedition Camp.........................C3
	Mara Explorers Camp.................(see 13)
25	Mara Intrepids.......................................C3
26	Mara Leisure Camp...............................D4
27	Mara Plains...C3
28	Mara Serena Safari Lodge..................B3
	Mara Springs Safari Camp........(see 13)
29	Off Beat Mara..C2
30	Ol Moran Tented Camp........................D5
	Oldarpoi Maasai Safari Camp....(see 13)
31	Public Campsite.....................................B2
32	Real Maasai Experience.......................E4
33	Rekero Camp..C4
34	Sala's Camp...E5
35	Saruni Mara...D1
36	Saruni Wild..D2
37	Sekenani Camp.......................................E5
38	Special Campsite...................................D5
39	Speke's Camp...D3

✖ Eating
40	Rex Restaurant......................................E4

ⓘ Information
	Kenya Commercial Bank..............(see 4)

by the non-profit Mara Conservancy. The only way to reach this part of the park is from either the Oloololo Gate or via the New Mara Bridge. Consequently, this area is less visited than elsewhere, despite having high concentrations of wildlife.

WHAT HAPPENED TO THE MARSH PRIDE?

From 1996 until 2008, the lions from the Marsh Pride in the far northwest of the Masai Mara National Reserve were the celebrities of the lion world as the stars of the BBC's wildly popular series *Big Cat Diary*. Such was their popularity that Bibi, Notch and the rest of the pride became household names to a generation of wildlife lovers, to the extent that tracking down the Marsh Pride remains, a decade after the show ended, a popular safari request for visitors to the Masai Mara.

But even lion celebrities such as these are not immune to the human–wildlife conflict that is increasingly complicating the lives of lions and the Maasai alike around the fringes of parks and reserves like the Masai Mara. In early December 2015, members of the pride killed cattle belonging to a Maasai family that lived just outside the reserve. Knowing that the lions would return to their kill, the owners of the slain cattle sprinkled a carcass with pesticide. When eight lions returned to feed, three died from poisoning almost immediately. Seventeen-year-old Bibi was among them.

The perpetrators were arrested and the remaining lions recovered after intensive treatment from the reserve's vets. But the stress led to further damage, with the Marsh Pride splitting into a number of groups. However, by mid-2017 the pride appeared to be once again together, though the issues of cattle and human encroachment on the reserve and the impact of growing human settlements around the Mara remain.

The Oloololo Escarpment, which forms the northwest boundary of the park, was once wooded, but fire and elephant damage mean that it's now mostly grasslands. Rock hyraxes and klipspringers can be readily seen here.

🏃 Activities

Wildlife Drives

Virtually all lodges organise wildlife drives through the park. At some cheaper places it will be in a battered old Land Rover or similar, while in the more expensive places safaris will be conducted in 'pop-top' mini-vans with other guests. The super-exclusive lodges will use state-of-the-art customised vehicles with open sides. Self-drive safaris in your own vehicle are also perfectly possible.

Guided Nature Walks

One of the best ways to experience the African bush is on foot. You'll learn all about the medicinal properties of various plants, see the telltale signs of passing animals and have some thrilling encounters with wildlife. As it's forbidden to walk within the reserve due to predators, guided walks generally take place in the company of a Maasai *moran* (warrior) outside the park itself, but in the nonetheless wildlife-rich conservancies that surround the reserve to the north and east.

Balloon Safaris

Several companies operate dawn balloon safaris and there's no better way to start your day than soaring majestically over the rolling grasslands. Flights can be booked at most of the lodges or campsites and include a champagne breakfast, wildlife drive and transport to and from the launch point. Two recommended companies are **Hot Air Safaris** (📞0733300302; www.maraballooning.com; Sekenani; per person US$400-500) and **Governors' Balloon Safaris** (📞0733616204; www.governorsballoonsafaris.com; Governors' Camp; per person US$400-500).

Maasai Manyatta Visits

Some Maasai *manyattas* (villages) now welcome visitors (around US$20 per person). Village visits can be organised through any lodge or camp or, if travelling under your own steam, you can just turn up at any of the villages (look for the signs saying something along the lines of 'cultural village' – don't just stroll into a proper Maasai *manyatta* unannounced!).

🛏 Sleeping

🛏 Sekenani Gate

Mara Springs Safari Camp TENTED CAMP $
(📞0722511252; www.mountainrockkenya.com/marasprings; camping per tent KSh1000, safari tent full board per person KSh4500-5000) The simple safari tents here come in two categories, with the cheaper tents being a little darker and smaller than the pricier ones. All have private bathrooms, cloth

wardrobes, firm beds and share the same pretty woodland glade around 3km from the Sekenani Gate.

Oldarpoi Maasai Safari Camp
TENTED CAMP $$

(☑ 0721731927; www.oldarpoimaracamp.com; camping per person US$10, camping full board US$65, per person full board US$80-100) ⓟ Set on a hill of dry acacia woodland about 3km back from Sekenani Gate, this Maasai-run place offers fairly hot and simple safari tents, but the welcome is equally warm. With 40% of profits being ploughed into local community projects, staying here means your money goes into the pockets of locals.

Mara Explorers Camp
TENTED CAMP $$

(www.maraexplorers.com; camping KSh1500, per person full board in budget dome tent/cottage/safari tent KSh5000/7000/8000) Just outside Sekenani Gate, Mara Explorers Camp is a fine budget option, with dome tents or camping up to en-suite tents and cottages. The accommodation is simple by Mara standards, but the price is about right and it's a traveller-savvy and a good place to meet other travellers.

🛏 Talek Gate

★ Crocodile Camp Masai Mara
TENTED CAMP $$

(☑ 0772397597, 0721975456; www.crocodilecamp-masaimara.com; camping per person US$6, tent & bedding rental US$15, per person safari tent room only/full board US$40/75; 🕿) Whether you're camping or looking for a little more comfort in one of their simple safari tents, Crocodile Camp, close to Talek Gate, is an excellent place to stay. With wi-fi in the evenings, a decent bar-restaurant, hot showers and an active safari programme geared towards budget and midrange travellers, it's a good all-round package.

Aruba Mara Camp
TENTED CAMP $$

(☑ 0723997524; www.aruba-safaris.com; Talek Gate; camping KSh820, bush tent without bathroom per person KSh2700, safari tent full board per person KSh9200; 🕿) ⓟ Set alongside a narrow river where animals often come to drink, this is arguably the Mara's best-value camp, and one of few aimed at budget and midrange travellers. There are three categories of wonderfully plush tents with good self-contained bathrooms as well as several small, but comfortable, tents (meals not included) that share bathrooms.

★ Mara Expedition Camp
TENTED CAMP $$$

(☑ Nairobi 020-6000457; www.greatplainsconservation.com; s/d full board US$1290/1720; ⊙ closed Apr–mid-Jun; 🕿) ⓟ A tiny camp that's so well hidden under the riverside trees it's impossible to see until you're pretty much in it. Yet again, Great Plains Conservation has produced a winner that combines clever conservation work with five tents that are the epitome of refined-safari style with leather armchairs, old travellers' trunks and brass bucket showers.

Basecamp Masai Mara
LODGE $$$

(☑ 0733333909; www.basecampexplorer.com/kenya/hotels/basecamp-masai-mara/; tent s/d full board from US$380/600; 🕿) ⓟ This upmarket lodge has 16 extremely comfortable tents with large wooden verandahs and smart bathrooms. The camp is very serious about sustainability and recycling, and enjoys a gold eco rating from Ecotourism Kenya. It also has huge grounds and overlooks the river and the Mara beyond. Don't miss the trees planted by the Obama family on their stay here.

Mara Leisure Camp
TENTED CAMP $$$

(☑ 0737799990, 020-2101333; www.maraleisurecamp.co.ke; s/d full board Jul-Oct US$292/390, rates vary rest of year) Extremely attractive, light-filled safari tents just outside Talek Gate overlook the river and have a star quality lacking in many of the older Mara camps. The price is exceptionally good value for these parts.

Speke's Camp
TENTED CAMP $$$

(☑ 0733637966, 0717793424, Nairobi 020-2663397; www.maasaitrails.com; per person full board using own/camp safari vehicle US$292/396) This tented camp sits between Naboisho and Olare-Orok Conservancies and is run by Maasai Trails (p121), one of the best hiking operators in western Kenya. It's a good base for visiting the Masai Mara National Reserve, or as a waystation on your way through the area. It can also organise walking safaris with fly camps along the way.

Fig Tree Camp
TENTED CAMP, LODGE $$$

(☑ 0722202563, Nairobi 020-605328; www.madahotels.com; s/d full board Jul-Oct from US$485/580, rates vary rest of year; 🕿🏊) Vegetate on your tent's verandah, watching the Talek River gently flow past this appealing camp with a colonial-days feel. The gardens are about the most luxurious you'll ever see, and the bathrooms about the biggest you'll find under canvas.

Oloolaimutiek Gate

Acacia Camp
TENTED CAMP $

(☎0733601441; mara@acaciacamp.com; Oloolaimutiek Gate; camping US$10, tent without breakfast s/d US$28/42) A little tricky to find, Acacia is 2.5km over sand roads from Oloolaimutiek Gate, just outside the park. Here you'll find thatched roofs sheltering simple tents in a pleasant garden against a beautiful backdrop of bougainvillea. There's a kitchen, bar and a campfire, as well as a canteen providing meals at US$10 a pop. The bathrooms have evening hot water.

Manyatta Camp
TENTED CAMP $

(☎072059252547; Oloolaimutiek Gate; full board per person KSh4500) This is an excellent-value choice just moments from the park gates. The large camp has 40 tents spread out in its rather chaotically tended gardens, all of which have their own bathrooms with hot water and thatch shelter. There is none of the sheen of the pricier camps, but it's cheap and cheerful.

Mara Intrepids
TENTED CAMP $$$

(☎0727523734, Nairobi 0722205894; www.heritage-eastafrica.com; s/d all inclusive Jul-Oct US$835/1114, rates vary rest of year; P🛜💺) Nestled nicely in the centre of the reserve and overlooking the Talek River, Mara Intrepids has excellent safari tents that blend safari nostalgia with smart modern throws and soothing earth tones to create something close to your ideal safari tent. There are fabulous views from various points around the property, both along the river and out onto the vast plains.

Ol Moran Tented Camp
TENTED CAMP $$$

(☎Nairobi 020-882923; www.olmorantentedcamp.com; tent s/d/tr full board from US$195/254/371; P) The safari tents here come in two flavours: the 'superior' are large with a wooden deck and a private bathroom, while the 14 'standard' tents are smaller and simpler, but entirely presentable. Walk-in rates are frequently considerably lower then the official rates.

Musiara & Oloololo Gates

Kichwa Tembo Camp
TENTED CAMP $$$

(☎Nairobi 020-3688620; www.andbeyond.com; per person full board Jul-Oct US$450-625, rates vary rest of year; 💺) Just outside the northern boundary of the reserve, Kichwa has been recently renovated and has permanent tents with grass-mat floors, stone bathrooms and tasteful furnishings. Hop in a hammock and take in spectacular savannah views. The camp has an excellent reputation for its food and is well positioned for the migration river-crossing points.

Bateleur Camp
TENTED CAMP $$$

(www.andbeyond.com; per person per night all inclusive Jun-Oct US$1235, rest of year US$680-790; P🛜💺) As we've come to expect from &Beyond's wonderful portfolio of camps, Bateleur combines a contemporary design look with the old-school necessities of a safari experience – they understand, for example, that sometimes it's necessary to see the Mara's sweeping plains without even getting out of bed.

Governors' Camp
TENTED CAMP $$$

(☎0733616204, Nairobi 020-2734000; www.governorscamp.com; s/d full board US$686/1098; 💺) This camp (and the Little Governors' Camp) is widely regarded as the most magisterial camp in the reserve itself. It offers great service, a pleasing riverside location and activities aplenty.

Little Governors' Camp
TENTED CAMP $$$

(☎0733616204, Nairobi 020-2734000; www.governorscamp.com; tent s/d full board US$826/1320; 💺) 🍃 Surrounding a waterhole, the 17 tents here are crammed with memories of colonial times and offer some of the reserve's most memorable nights under canvas. Stepping out onto the tents' wooden platform is like announcing your arrival on the plains – watch every animal head turn.

Inside the Reserve

There are luxury lodges and tented camps scattered across the reserve. It's only possible to camp within the reserve in its Mara Triangle sector, in either the **public campsite** (camping per person US$20) or **special campsites** (☎020-2379409; per person US$30) that can be reserved. If camping, you will need to be totally self-sufficient, to the point of bringing your own firewood (using the dead wood within the park is prohibited).

★ Rekero Camp
TENTED CAMP $$$

(☎0736500515; www.asiliaafrica.com; per person all-inclusive Jul-Oct US$930, rest of year US$615-870) We're big fans of Asilia Africa's properties, and Rekero is no exception. On a bend in the Talek River in the heart of the Masai Mara, Rekero is ideally placed for reaching all corners of the reserve. Its tents are the perfect mix of uncluttered safari simplicity, muted khaki tones that blend with the surrounds and a supremely comfortable set-up.

★ Sala's Camp TENTED CAMP $$$

(☑0725675830; www.thesafaricollection.com/ properties/salas-camp/; safari tent all-inclusive US$1700-2500, family tent US$4000-5400; P🔌🛜❄) 🌊 So far south in the Masai Mara that you're almost in Tanzania, Sala's Camp is a real find. Away from the busier central and northern areas of the reserve, you'll feel like you're in your own private corner of the Mara. That does mean you'll need to drive further to explore, but the remoteness and wonderful tents more than compensate.

Ashnil Mara TENTED CAMP $$$

(☑0717612499; www.ashnilhotels.com/ashnil -mara; s/d all-inclusive Jul-Oct US$694/1226, rates vary rest of year; P🔌❄) This highly recommended safari camp is the jewel in the Ashnil crown, overlooking a bend in the Mara River and with fabulous wildlife watching close by. The tents are large and

light-filled, service is professional and the camp is laid out so that it doesn't feel as large as it is (40 tents). There's a wellness and massage centre.

Mara Serena Safari Lodge LODGE $$$

(☑0732123333; www.serenahotels.com; s/d full board Jul-Oct US$424/638, rates vary rest of year; 🛜❄) This large, resort-style lodge, with a pool complex and even a gym, would fit better in a city rather than a supposed wilderness, although the views from the property are wonderful. Of all the park lodges, it has the best view. Built on a small hill, most of its rooms have commanding views over not one, but two, migration crossing points.

Mara Bush Camp TENTED CAMP $$$

(☑0722525400; www.marabushcamp.com; s/d all inclusive Jul-Oct US$478/790, rates vary rest of year; 🛜) Flying a little under the radar compared to the Mara's better-known camps, Mara Bush Camp combines simplicity with classic East African safari features – the wooden chest, the writing desk, the gnarled wood furnishings. You're also in the heart of the park and with a fine vantage point

---

MAASAI VILLAGE HOME STAYS

Some years ago James Ole Lesaloi, a young Maasai man from the Sekenani area, got fed up with the lack of development and opportunities for the Maasai living around the reserve and set up **Semadep** (Sekenani Maasai Development Project; ☑0721817757; www. semadepngo.com; Sekenani; 7-day camping & itinerary US$1100), with the aim to change the lives of the local Maasai. Fast forward a few years and the project, with little publicity or outside help, has been remarkably successful and includes a school, clinic, water projects, orphan projects and a media centre on its list of credits. But for tourists, what is perhaps most interesting is the opportunity it offers to stay in a genuine Maasai *manyatta* and get a real understanding of Maasai life and culture – and the issues they face.

One such place, run by James himself, is **Ewangan** (☑0721817757; www.maasaimara village.com; Sekenani Gate; camping US$20, full board per person US$70, children free) 🌊, a traditional Maasai *manyatta* 2km north of Sekenani Gate, offering a homestay with the Maasai. During your stay you'll help with daily chores such as milking the cows and goats, learn skills such as jewellery making and enjoy nature walks with a Maasai guide. At least 25% of your money goes to help support local community projects. Accommodation is very basic, but it's all very cosy and the food is excellent. It's a particularly fun experience for children (we've stayed there with a four-year-old and an 18-month-old and they much preferred this to the fancy lodges and wildlife drives). For the few people who've stayed so far, almost all come away saying it was the highlight of their Kenyan travels.

It's hoped that as the idea gains more popularity, other *manyattas* under Semadep guidance will also allow homestays (though to really work, no *manyatta* could host more than one small group at a time). **Real Maasai Experience** (Nkoiroro Cultural Village; ☑0728517355; peternarok@yahoo.com; Sekenani-Narok Rd; per person full board US$70) is one that has started up nearby.

from among the trees next to the Olare-Orok River.

✕ Eating

Rex Restaurant KENYAN $
(☑ 0723555576; Sekenani-Narok Rd; mains KSh200-300; ⊙ 8am-11pm) Just 400m from the Sekenani Gate, this casual roadside shack has a few tables out the back where they serve up breakfasts, home-baked bread, vegetables with rice or ugali and goat stew.

ℹ Information

MONEY
The only ATM in the area is **KCB** (Main Rd, Talek; ⊙ 8.30am-4pm Mon-Fri, 8.30am-noon Sat) in Talek village (KCB ATMs can be temperamental with foreign cards), so come prepared with cash.

TOURIST INFORMATION
For more on the Masai Mara and surrounding conservancies, see the independent website www.maasaimara.com.

ℹ Getting There & Away

AIR
Airkenya (p385), Mombasa Air Safari (p385), Safarilink (p385) and Fly540 (p385) each have daily (or more frequent) flights to any of the eight airstrips in and around the Masai Mara.

MATATU, CAR & 4WD
If you're driving to the Mara, be sure to fill up on petrol in Narok, the last chance to fill your vehicle at normal prices on the road from Nairobi. Expensive petrol is available at Mara Sarova, Mara Serena and Keekorok Lodges, as well as in Talek village.

The first 50km or so west of Narok on the B3 and C12 are smooth enough, but after the bitumen runs out you'll find yourself on one of Kenya's most notorious roads – a bone-shaking dirt road that many drivers simply dread. Most people drive in the sandy verges of the road, which makes for a far smoother experience, but either way the road is a pain and you might well wonder why you didn't fly. The road is slowly being upgraded: so slowly, in fact, that when they finish they might have to turn around and start again.

That said, having your own wheels in the Mara is a wonderful thing. Even if most safari drives will be done with a guide in their own vehicle, it still means you're free to self-drive through the reserve, which is a huge pleasure in itself, although getting lost is always a slight risk. It's possible to access Talek and Sekenani gates from Narok by matatu (KSh600), after which you'll need to arrange pick-ups from a lodge.

ℹ Getting Around

For independent travellers staying outside the reserve, count on paying around US$150 to US$200 per day for a 4WD with a driver-guide and (usually) a picnic lunch. This fee can, of course, be split between as many people as can be comfortably squeezed into the vehicle. There's no public transport within the park.

Maji Moto Group Ranch

Closer to Narok town than the reserve itself, Maji Moto (which translates as hot water and, true enough, there are some hot springs here) is a blissfully tourist-free, 600-sq-km group ranch. Its distance from the main Mara ecosystem and the abundance of Maasai communities in the area mean that wildlife numbers are far lower than in other conservancies, but this is a different type of conservancy, where the emphasis is as much on enjoying and learning about Maasai culture as it is on spotting animals. If you want a totally different kind of 'safari' experience, this could be the place.

🛏 Sleeping

★ **Maji Moto Eco Camp** TENTED CAMP $$
(☑ 716430722, 041-2006479; www.majimotocamp.com; per person full board US$100) 🌿 On a hillside among granite rocks contorted into fantastical shapes, Maji Moto is around 60km north of the reserve proper. The camp is fairly simple but beautifully conceived, where guests sleep in large dome tents with mattresses on the floor. The highlight here is more cultural than wildlife – there are animals on the nearby plains but predators are rarely sighted.

It's a brilliant camp for families, with warrior training, dances, village visits, bush walks, full-day safaris to the Mara and soaks in the hot springs all on offer. Multi-day walking safaris to the Masai Mara can be organised and your stay genuinely helps the locals.

★ **Maji Moto Maasai Cultural Camp** TENTED CAMP $$$
(☑ 0717699676, 0721778424; www.majimotomaasaicamp.com; camping US$45, r full board US$175-225) At the base of the Loita Hills, this fine Maasai camp offers simple accommodation, from camping to huts and tents. It's a rustic experience in the best sense – there is patchy solar power and luxuries are few, but the warmth of the welcome and the

MASAI MARA & WESTERN KENYA MAJI MOTO GROUP RANCH

THE LOITA HILLS

To the northeast of the Masai Mara National Reserve are the little-known and spellbindingly beautiful Loita Hills. When accessing them from the Mara area, the hills start out dry and unimpressive, but if you bounce along for enough hours (and we mean hours and hours – the roads here are some of the worst in Kenya), things start to change. The vegetation becomes greener and much more luxuriant, eventually turning into a tangled jungle. The mountains also grow ever bigger, peaking at a respectable 2150m.

This is the most traditional corner of Maasai land and change, though it's coming, is way behind many other parts of the country. Despite the number of Maasai living here, it's also an area of unexpected wildlife – colobus monkeys swing through the trees, turacos light the skies with colour and huge numbers of buffaloes, forest pigs and bushbucks move through the shadows. What makes this area so extraordinary is that it's not covered by any official protection and yet the forests remain fairly untouched. The reason is that there are many places in the forests sacred to the Maasai and the elders tightly control the felling of trees and grazing of cattle. It's a brilliant example of how traditional cultures can thrive alongside wildlife without outside aid.

For the most part, accommodation out here is restricted to a few basic boardings and lodgings in some villages. But there are exceptions. Based in the beautiful and low-key **Jan's Camp** (☑ 0718139359; www.maasaitrails.com; s/d 3-night accommodation, hiking & full board package US$2308/4092) ✐, **Maasai Trails** (☑ 0717793424, 0718139359; www. maasaitrails.com) organises hiking trips that take you out into some of the more remote reaches of Maasailand where few travellers ever reach, from day hikes out of Jan's Camp to the 12-day Great Maasailand Trail. The longer options take you completely across and over the Loita Hills and down into the Rift Valley near Lake Magadi.

Prices for walks depend on the number of people and length of hike. Stays at Jan's Camp are normally included in the walking package rates.

wide range of activities that offer an insight into Maasai life more than compensate.

It's especially good for families, and the camp's head, Salaton Ole Ntutu, is a marvellous host with a wealth of stories about the traditional Maasai world.

❶ Getting There & Away

There is no public transport to the group ranch. If driving, take the road from Narok to Sekenani Gate and ring ahead to your camp for detailed directions and/or an escort from the turn-off.

Mara North Conservancy

Established in 2009, the 300-sq-km Mara North Conservancy (www.maranorth. com) is one of our favourite conservancies in the Mara, ticking all the right boxes for wildlife, classic Mara landscapes and community engagement. Mara North, which abuts the northwestern edge of the Masai Mara National Reserve, is an absolute cliché of what East Africa is supposed to look like: the flat-topped acacias, the long golden grass and animals everywhere. Leopard sightings are common and there are lots of

very large lions, as well as some cheetahs and masses of plains wildlife. In fact, during the migration the horizon can be utterly covered in the black dots of wildebeest and seeing lions on a kill is very common.

🛏 Sleeping & Eating

★ **Alex Walker's Serian**　　TENTED CAMP $$$
(☑ 0718139359, Nairobi 020-2663397; www. serian.com; safari tents US$670-1400; ☎) Some of Mara North's most beautiful lodgings, Serian (which means 'serene' in the Maa language) overlooks the Mara River with the Oloololo Escarpment as a backdrop. The tents here, a winning mix of thatch, wood and canvas, are luxurious and they revel in the mystique and nostalgia of the East African safari. The guides here are excellent.

★ **Saruni Mara**　　TENTED CAMP $$$
(☑ 0735950903, Nairobi 020-2180497; www. saruni.com; s/d all-inclusive Jul-Sep US$930/1560, rest of year s US$560-750, d US$920-1260; ☎) ✐ Way to the north of any of the other camps, and virtually on the border of the conservancy, this breathtaking camp has around a dozen tents dusted with antique furnishings and colonial bric-a-brac. Some even

TROUBLE IN EDEN

In many ways the Masai Mara National Reserve is the epitome of the African dream. Its golden, bleached savannah is covered with unparalleled densities of animals, great and small, and the vast majority of it is untouched by the destructive hand of man. Visitors can't help but be bowled over by its natural riches.

The reality, however, is that not everyone is happy with this wildlife haven. Many local Maasai living in the immediate vicinity of the reserve feel they gain nothing from its presence, despite the sacrifices and hardships they face because of it. The issues they raise include things like:

➡ Not being allowed to graze their cattle inside the reserve, which many of them consider to be 'their' land.

➡ Insufficient and poorly organised compensation when animals kill their cattle outside of the reserve.

➡ Neglected needs of the Maasai communities. Many communities don't have sufficient access to clean, safe water sources and education and health facilities. Many lodges and camps in and around the reserve advertise their community development projects, but many Maasai dispute that all of this money actually goes to such projects.

Ironically, another problem the reserve faces comes from safari tourism itself. Sightings of big cats tend to attract large numbers of vehicles, and when the lion, cheetah or leopard eventually moves away, many guides (under pressure because their clients want to see such animals up close) break park rules by following the animals off the designated tracks. Such constant attention has caused some animals to change their patterns of behaviour – for instance, cheetahs now frequently attempt to hunt under the midday sun, when most tourists are having lunch in their camp (unfortunately, it's also a time when the chance of a successful kill is radically reduced). Some cheetahs have also been known to use safari vehicles as cover for stalking their prey. Reports are now showing that many animals are spending less time in the reserve itself, choosing to roam in the surrounding conservancies where there are fewer safari vehicles (and, incidentally, where local communities also gain more from tourism).

have open log fires and the decoration in each follows a theme of writer's, photographer's or artist's studio. The setting is in animal-packed, forested hills.

★ Kicheche Mara   TENTED CAMP $$$
(✆ Nairobi 020-2493569; www.kicheche.com; s/d all-inclusive Aug-Oct US$925/1580, per person rest of year US$625-665; ☎) ❀ Stunningly sited in a lush, intimate valley along a hippo-inhabited stream lined with acacias, Kicheche is a lovely property. The large tents with bucket showers have fine views and are wonderfully strung out along the valley, and there's a lovely mess area with free wi-fi. The safari vehicles have, like all at Kicheche camps, beanbags for photographers – a detail we always appreciate.

Saruni Wild   TENTED CAMP $$$
(✆ 0735950903, 020-2180497; www.saruniwild. com; s/d all-inclusive Jul-Sep US$930/1560, rest of year s US$560-750, d US$920-1260) Protected from view by a stand of riverine woodland and looking out across the plains of the northern Mara, Saruni Wild sits in the heart of some of Mara North's best wildlife country. The three tents are beautifully spaced, giving a wonderfully intimate in-camp experience, and the sundowner table feels like it's on infinity's edge.

Off Beat Mara   TENTED CAMP $$$
(✆ 0704909355; www.offbeatsafaris.com; s/d all-inclusive US$740/1480; ⊘ closed Apr, May & Nov; ☎) ❀ With just six tents on the bend of a tree-lined river, this is one of the smallest and most personable of the Mara North camps, with bush-chic tents filled with heavy wooden furnishings exuding an authentic old-African-safari feel. Wildlife abounds around the camp and this is one place where they've resisted the temptation to manicure the lawn – it *feels* wild.

The camp has a charming young staff who produce a nicely informal atmosphere, and excellent guides, including a specialist walking guide who takes guests on long bush walks. The newly built terrace at the back of the mess tent is a lovely breakfast spot to be serenaded by birdsong.

The wildlife in the vicinity rarely disappoints, with elephants, leopards, cheetahs and two lion prides (the Acacia pride and the 30-strong Offbeat pride) – we saw more lions in a single day here than we did anywhere else in the Mara, and you're always a chance to see all big cats before breakfast. The sundowner spots here are particularly well chosen.

Elephant Pepper TENTED CAMP $$$
(📞 0730127000; www.elephantpeppercamp.com; s/d full board US$952/1588; 🛜) This intimate camp has eight tents that are luxurious without being over the top and food that is of a genuinely high standard. But what really makes Elephant Pepper stand out is its setting, under a dense thicket of trees with views over rolling grasslands that, at times, can be a seething mass of grunting, growling and trumpeting megafauna.

Karen Blixen Camp TENTED CAMP $$$
(www.karenblixencamp.com; s/d all inclusive Jul-Oct US$687/1082, rest of year s US$495-611, d US$732-958; 🛜🏊) Overlooking the Mara River with its hippos and crocs and well placed to take advantage of Mara North's prolific wildlife, Karen Blixen Camp has 22 tents that are luxurious and large. There's also a wellness centre, public areas are adorned with numerous Maasai motifs and the camp supports a number of projects in local Maasai communities.

ℹ Getting There & Away

It takes about two hours to drive from Narok to the heart of the conservancy, although it depends where you're going. Self-driving is only permitted in Mara North if driving to/from your camp. Most visitors fly into one of the conservancy's airstrips, where vehicles from the various camps pick up guests.

Naboisho Conservancy

Created in 2011, the 222-sq-km Naboisho Conservancy is one of the Mara's youngest. It's also one of the best, with excellent camps, fabulous predator and other wildlife viewing, as well as picturesque, classic Mara landscapes of whistling thorn, open grasslands, rolling hill country and riverine acacia woodlands. Little wonder, then, that Naboisho won the prestigious Overall Winner of the African Responsible Tourism Awards in 2016, as well as sharing the Wildlife Conservation Prize with Ol Pejeta Conservancy. If you were looking to choose one place for your safari of a lifetime, Naboisho would have to be on the shortlist.

🏃 Activities

Most camps offer both wildlife drives and walking safaris – given the number of big cats that call Naboisho home, the latter is guaranteed to get the heart racing.

THE MASAI MARA AREA CONSERVANCIES

Changing the face of conservation and tourism in Kenya are the private and community conservancies, many of which now border the Masai Mara National Reserve. Each conservancy operates in a slightly different manner, but the general idea is to make tourism, conservation and the rights of local peoples work hand in hand to the mutual benefit of all. Most conservancies involve the local Maasai landowners leasing their communal lands for an average of 15 years at a time to several high-end lodges. The Maasai are still allowed to graze their cattle in the conservancies and receive a guaranteed income from each camp. In addition, all camps have to contribute to community-development projects.

In return the wildlife is allowed to live in peace and the lodges can offer their clients an exclusive kind of safari with minimal other visitors, as those not staying in the conservancies are not allowed to enter. Visitors also get the opportunity to partake in activities not allowed in the reserve itself, such as walking safaris and night drives.

Entry fees to the conservancies are covered in the nightly cost of accommodation. The costs and the necessity of keeping things quiet and exclusive preclude the availability of budget accommodation. However, prices include all meals, drinks, safaris, guides and other activities – things not always included with top-end places in the reserve proper.

Wildlife Watching

When it comes to wildlife watching, there are plenty of elephants as well as all the usual plains species. When we last visited, there was one family of five cheetahs and another of three, and the conservancy was home to 60 adult lions spread across three prides. The camps have agreed on a policy of just four vehicles at any viewing – while it can be frustrating waiting if you're in the fifth vehicle on the scene, it's policies like these that help make Naboisho so special and keep its wildlife from being overwhelmed by vehicles.

🛏 Sleeping

★ Asilia Naboisho Camp   TENTED CAMP $$$
(🖉 Nairobi 020-2324904; www.asiliaafrica.com; per person all-inclusive Jul-Oct US$895, per person rest of year US$300-635; 🛜) ✐ So what if the tents, with their huge beds and indoor and outdoor showers, are among the most extravagant around. Why people really stay here is the opportunity to walk over animal-crammed savannah with an expert guide. If that wasn't enough, the wildlife viewing right outside the tents is superb, with big cats frequently passing in front of the camp.

There are nine tents here, wonderfully spread out across the gentle slope – some are so nicely submerged in the bush that getting there can be a walking safari in its own right. The decor in the tents and public areas is stylish and contemporary, and the atmosphere warm and relaxed thanks to Della and Rich, the engaging camp hosts. The tents also get the right mix between luxury and comfort and a sense of being open to the elements. A coveted Gold Eco Rated award issued by Ecotourism Kenya is another selling point.

Activities include walking safaris, night drives, horse riding, fly camping and visits to local villages and community projects.

★ Kicheche Valley Camp   TENTED CAMP $$$
(🖉 Nairobi 020-2493569; www.kicheche.com; Naboisho; s/d all-inclusive Aug-Oct US$925/1580, per person rest of year US$625-665; ⊘ closed Apr-May) ✐ High in a valley that looks down into the heart of the conservancy – there is not a single light in view at night – Kicheche Valley is a terrific property. Top-level guides, a Gold Eco rating for sustainability and original safari tents with wonderful light floors made from recycled tetrapak, which

give them a refreshingly contemporary look, are huge selling points.

Hemingways Ol Seki Mara   TENTED CAMP $$$
(🖉 0718669856; www.hemingways-collection. com/mara; s/d all-inclusive Jul-Sep US$790/1360, s/d rest of year US$620/1080; 🛜) The name gives things away a little: the look here is classic safari decor, but panoramic views and use of light linens give the whole place a lighter feel than you might expect. Rooms are suitably luxurious and nights here are blissfully quiet. Activities include all the usual night and day wildlife drives, walking safaris and cultural visits to nearby communities.

Basecamp Eagle View   TENTED CAMP $$$
(🖉 0733333909; www.basecampexplorer.com/kenya/; s/d all-inclusive Jul-Oct US$580/1050, rates vary rest of year; 🛜) ✐ The most upmarket of the three Basecamp offerings around the Mara. The six tents here are stretched along a ridge with mind-boggling views over a salt lick and miles of savannah. Despite the undisputed luxury, Eagle View still follows the company ethos of uncompromising sustainability. Excellent walking safaris are a highlight of a stay here.

Basecamp Wilderness   TENTED CAMP $$$
(🖉 0733333909; www.basecampkenya.com; s/d all-inclusive Jul-Oct US$450/790, rates vary rest of year) ✐ Of all the camps in the Mara conservancies, Wilderness is probably the most authentically 'safari'. There are five simple, but very comfortable, tents with hot bucket showers and good beds set in a hidden valley that's home to a resident leopard and lots of other animals.

❶ Getting There & Away

Like other Mara conservancies, Naboisho is not open to private vehicles, although you'll generally be allowed to proceed if you're driving directly to/from your lodging – wildlife drives are only possible in vehicles belonging to the conservancy's camps. Most visitors arrive on an air transfer.

Olare-Orok Conservancy

Established in 2006 (as Olare Motorogi), this is now one of the longest established and most successful of the conservancies. It also has one of the highest concentrations of animals, including loads of predators (it has one of the highest lion densities in East

Africa) and the lowest densities of tourists – just one tent for every 280 hectares. If you're looking for a Mara conservancy success story, this, along with neighbouring Naboisho, is probably our pick.

🛏 Sleeping

★ Mara Plains   TENTED CAMP $$$

(www.greatplainsconservation.com; s/d all-inclusive mid-Jun–Oct US$2700/3600, per person US$920-1315; 🕾) 🍃 This utterly captivating camp has a dozen tents with beds and showers carved from old wooden railway sleepers and quality rugs lazing across the floors. The highlight for most, though, are the big, free-standing brass bathtubs overlooking a river of wallowing hippos. In keeping with Great Plains philosophy, the camp's footprint is minimal and could be removed without a trace.

It's the details here that people remember – the footbridge approach across the river, the perfectly sited acacia tree in your line of sight and the furniture built from coastal wood. The food is some of the best of any of the camps and the manager-hosts are charmers. As an added bonus, each tent is supplied with a box of high-quality Canon camera equipment and binoculars to borrow.

★ Kicheche Bush   TENTED CAMP $$$

(📱 Nairobi 020-2493569; www.kicheche.com; s/d all-inclusive Aug-Oct US$925/1580, per person rest of year US$625-665; 🅿🕾) 🍃 Considered one of the premier camps in the area, and run with the kind of casual efficiency that brings guests back, Kicheche Bush has

well-spaced, enormous tents set within a light fringe of trees, beyond which stretches some of the most reliably impressive wildlife countryside in the whole Mara region. Two resident leopards are sometimes seen close to camp.

Mahali Mzuri Camp   TENTED CAMP $$$

(www.virginlimitededition.com/en/mahali-mzuri; s/d all-inclusive mid-Jun–mid-Oct US$1620/2400, rest of year US$1100/1660; 🕾) Part of Richard Branson's portfolio of exclusive holiday destinations around the world, Mahali Mzuri has large and lovely tents that look out over the plains from an elevated hillside. Rooms are a mix of safari nostalgia (heavy leather sofas and dark-wood furnishings) with contemporary colour splashes and everything designed to maximise the views.

ℹ Getting There & Away

Olare-Orok inhabits a triangle between Aitong (in Mara North Conservancy) and the Masai Mara's Talek and Sekenani gates. While many arrive here by chartered air transfer as part of their accommodation package, those coming in their own vehicles should be aware that private vehicles are not allowed in the conservancy, although you should be allowed to continue if driving directly to your camp.

Olderikesi Conservancy

In the far southeast of the Mara region, on the border with Tanzania and the famous Serengeti, the Olderikesi Conservancy covers around 80 sq km. One of the most exclusive of the Mara conservancies, it's also one

---

THE NORTHERN MIGRATION

The Loita Hills are important for what's known as the northern migration, a smaller version of the mass migration of wildebeest from the Serengeti to the Masai Mara. During the northern migration, as many as 250,000 wildebeest and zebras migrate down onto the Mara plains from the Loita Hills, bringing prey in abundance into Mara North, Olare-Orok, Naboisho and the other conservancies, as well as the northern reaches of the reserve itself. The northern migration usually begins with the first rains in March, although in some years these rains – and the migration itself – may not begin until May. The herds generally remain until rains fall in the Loita Hills, which could be in November, but also as late as the following March.

There are concerns that growing human populations in the Loita Hills area and the growing number of fences will seriously threaten the migration's future. The northern version may also lack the drama of the main migration, due to the absence of significant river crossings. But as long as it continues, it can still be quite the spectacle during months otherwise known as the low season.

of the richest in wildlife, including large numbers of lions.

⊨ Sleeping

★ **Cottar's 1920s Camp**   TENTED CAMP $$$
(☑ 0700122122, 0733773378; www.cottars.com; s/d all-inclusive Jul-Oct US$1243/2072, rest of year s US$719-1008, d US$1200-1680; ☒) One of the most storied camps in the Mara region, Cottar's, owned by a legendary safari family, induces a misty-eyed sense of longing from those lucky enough to have visited. As the name suggests, the enormous, stunning tents are dressed up like a well-to-do 1920s gentleman's lodging, with all manner of colonial and safari memorabilia.

But there's more to Cottar's than just elegant style. There's some of the best food of any camp, a beautiful pool and a host of activities for children. Get the guides or hosts talking about the camp and family history and you'll spend one of your most memorable evenings out on safari. Guides here are among the best in Kenya.

ⓘ Getting There & Away

Although you can drive into the conservancy (contact Cottar's in advance for directions), most visitors arrive by air, flying into the airstrip, then exploring in the camp's safari vehicles.

THE MAA TRUST

The conservation model behind the Mara conservancies is based on the assumption that wildlife conservation and community development and protection go hand in hand. Working along the border between the Naboisho and Olare-Orok conservancies, The Maa Trust (www.themaatrust.org) is a not-for-profit NGO that seeks to ensure that local Maasai communities benefit from tourism in the area. Their projects include education, clean water and public health initiatives, while local honey production, bead making and the sale of handicrafts help bring in revenue in addition to the conservancy proceeds. Visits to the trust can be arranged by a number of camps in the area – Asilia Naboisho Camp (p124) is one with a particularly close relationship with the trust.

Siana & the Southeastern Conservancies

Away to the east and southeast of the Greater Mara region, a collection of group ranches – Siana, Isaaten and Leleshwa-Olarro – offer a more remote experience than is the case elsewhere. Encompassing a huge array of habitats, this vast area includes heavily forested mountain slopes, swamps and open grasslands, which means there's plenty of wildlife to be found. These conservancies have generally taken longer to work out lasting management plans with the local Maasai, but the feeling in these parts is that things are finally starting to bed down and the future is rosy.

⊨ Sleeping

Mara Bushtops   TENTED CAMP $$$
(☑ 020-2137862; www.bushtopscamps.com/mara; s/d all-inclusive Jul-Oct US$1280/1980, rest of year s US$760-1350, d US$1520-2080; ☎☒) Mara Bushtops is close enough to Sekenani Gate to allow easy excursions into the reserve, yet is set on its own conservancy that's a worthy destination in its own right. Each of the 12 tents come with expansive 100-sq-m private terraces, telescopes, private hot tubs and views that seem to go on forever, plus supremely comfortable beds and elegant furnishings.

Olarro Lodge   LODGE $$$
(☑ 0737463731, Dubai +971-43253322; www.olarro kenya.com; Olarro; s/d all-inclusive US$490/840; ☎☒) This sublime lodge on the Leleshwa-Olarro Conservancy sits halfway up a lightly forested hill. The cottages have a warm and inviting feel to them, with curved spaces, canopied ceilings and everything designed to take advantage of the sweeping views. Remember, however, that this is a lodge, not a tented camp, so it lacks the close-to-nature feel of the camps.

Sekenani Camp   TENTED CAMP $$$
(☑ Nairobi 020-891169; www.sekenani-camp.com; Siana; s/d all-inclusive from US$315/490; ☎☒)
🍃 Set within a jungly tangle of trees and waterways in a beautiful bird-filled valley, this discreet and memorable camp has a unique raised treetop walkway leading from the pool and bar-restaurant area to the tents, which are large and comfy without being over the top.

ℹ Getting There & Away

Unless you're flying in on an air charter arranged through your accommodation, you'll need your own vehicle. Some of the camps are signposted off the Sekenani–Narok road, but you'll need to contact your camp ahead of time to get detailed directions and/or arrange an escort.

LAKE VICTORIA

Spread over 68,000 sq km, yet never more than 80m deep, Lake Victoria, one of the key water sources of the White Nile, ranks among East Africa's most important geographical features, but is seen by surprisingly few visitors. This is a shame, as its humid shores hide some of the most beautiful and rewarding parts of western Kenya – from untouched national parks to lively cities and tranquil islands.

Kisumu

☑ 057 / POP 410,000

Set on the sloping shore of Lake Victoria's Winam Gulf, Kisumu might be the third-largest city in Kenya, but its relaxed atmosphere is a world away from that of Nairobi and Mombasa. Until 1977 the port was one of the busiest in Kenya, but decline set in with the collapse of the East African Community (EAC; the common market between Kenya, Tanzania and Uganda) and the port sat virtually idle for two decades. Since the revival of the EAC in 2000, Kisumu has begun to thrive again, and though it was declared a city during its centenary celebrations in 2001, it still doesn't feel like one and remains a pleasant and laid-back place with a number of interesting sights and activities nearby.

◉ Sights

★ **Kisumu Main Market**   MARKET
(off Jomo Kenyatta Hwy; ⊙7am-3pm) Kisumu's main market is one of Kenya's most animated markets and certainly one of its largest – it spills out onto the surrounding roads. If you're curious, or just looking for essentials such as suits or wigs, it's worth a stroll around.

Ndere Island National Park   NATIONAL PARK
(www.kws.go.ke/content/ndere-island-national-park; adult/child US$25/15; ⊙6am-6pm)

Gazetted as a national park in 1986, this 4.2-sq-km island has never seen tourism take off. It is forested and very beautiful, housing a variety of bird species, plus occasionally sighted hippos, impalas (introduced) and spotted crocodiles, a lesser-known cousin of the larger Nile crocodiles.

⚑ Activities

Hippo Point Boat Trips   BOATING
Hippo Point, sticking into Lake Victoria at Dunga, about 3km south of town, is a beautiful spot at which you're highly unlikely to see any hippos. It is, though, the launch point for pleasant boat rides around the lake. Prices vary among the boats, but expect to pay KSh700 per person, per hour in a group of five.

☞ Tours

Ibrahim Tours Kisumu   TOURS
(☑0723083045; www.ibrahimtours.weebly.com) A well-known and trusted tour guide to the many sights and sounds of the Kisumu region. Ibrahim Nandi can arrange boat trips, birdwatching tours, nature walks and excursions to Ndere Island National Park. He can be contacted directly, or through the **New Victoria Hotel** (☑057-2021067; Gor Mahia Rd; s without bathroom KSh1250, s/d/tr KSh1900/2700/3800).

Zaira Tours & Travel   SAFARI
(☑0722788879; Ogada St) The best safari operator in town, with pop-top minivans and 4WDs. They also handle airline tickets.

Integri Tours   TOURS
(☑0700517969; www.integritour.com; Duke of Breeze, off Jomo Kenyatta Hwy) Professional operator with some excellent day-trip itineraries.

⌂ Sleeping

New East View Hotel   HOTEL $
(☑0711183017; Omolo Agar Rd; s KSh2000-2750, d KSh2800-3500; P ⊛) The town's standout budget option is one of many family homes in the area that have been converted into small hotels. Splashed in bright colours, the rooms have a homely, preloved feel and the welcome is, even for Kenya, unusually warm. Good hot showers with decent water pressure are another plus. Security is also tight.

Kisumu

Kisumu

⊙ Top Sights
1 Kisumu Main Market............................C2

⊕ Activities, Courses & Tours
   Ibrahim Tours Kisumu ....(see 6)
2 Integri Tours C2
3 Zaira Tours & Travel B2

⊜ Sleeping
4 Imperial Hotel Express B2
5 New East View Hotel............................C2
6 New Victoria Hotel B1
7 Sooper Guest House.............................B1

⊗ Eating
8 Green Garden Restaurant.......................B1
9 The Laughing Buddha B3

⊖ Drinking & Nightlife
10 Juiz Parlour......................................A2
11 Social Centre....................................D2

ⓘ Information
12 Aga Khan Hospital C1
13 Barclays B2
14 Kenya Commercial Bank B3
15 Kisumu Immigration Office B3
   Shiva Travels ....(see 4)

ⓘ Transport
16 Bus & Matatu Station...........................D2
17 Easy Coach.......................................D1
18 Kenya Airways...................................B3

Sooper Guest House HOSTEL $

(☏ 0725281733; www.sooperguesthouse. com; Oginga Odinga Rd; s/tw/d excl breakfast KSh1400/1800/2300; ☂) Sooper has become the de facto backpackers in town and you have a good chance of meeting other travellers here. The rooms, which come in a dizzying array of styles, are immaculately well kept and have hot showers, though those facing the road are very noisy. It has helpful staff and good security. Breakfast is not included in the price.

★ Vittoria Suites APARTMENT $$

(☏ 0791574747; www.vittoriasuites.com/; Ring Rd, off Tom Mboya Rd; s/d US$65/85; ⓟ❄☂) It may be a touch removed from the centre, but this wonderful place has appealing, brightly painted rooms that are among the best in urban western Kenya. Some have balconies, all have flat-screen TVs and there's a really professional air to the whole place – it wouldn't look out of place in Nairobi.

Imperial Hotel Express
HOTEL $$
(☎0713555365; www.imperialexpress.com; Oginga Odinga Rd; s/d from KSh5900/6900; ❉☎) Minimalist decor, flat-screen TVs and an overall cool and contemporary look – we very much hope that the Imperial Hotel Express, which opened in 2015, catches on and causes a revolution in urban Kenyan hotels. Pitched at the lower midrange market but with standards that put to shame many much pricier establishments, it's as popular with tourists as with business travellers.

Le Savanna Country Lodge & Hotel
HOTEL $$
(☎0714995510, 057-2021159; www.lesavanna countrylodge.com; off Nyerere Rd; r US$83; P❉☎) This delightfully calm place is where everyone who's anyone likes to stay when in town. The large, well-dressed rooms have good bathrooms, fast in-room wi-fi and no exterior noise or disturbance. There's also a reasonable in-house restaurant and a quiet bar.

★Kiboko Bay Resort
RESORT $$$
(☎0711905540; www.kibokobay.com; Dunga Beach; s/d/tr US$140/170/200) At last, a top-end hotel with Lake Victoria frontage. Rooms here have some lovely hardwood furnishings in the safari tents, while the artful use of driftwood brings personality to the deluxe rooms. There's a well-stocked bar (even a sommelier for wine buffs) where you can watch the sunset, a fine restaurant and a classy and sophisticated atmosphere.

✖ Eating

As you'd expect from a town on Lake Victoria, fish is abundant on the menus of Kisumu. If you want an authentic local fish fry, there are no better places than the dozens of smoky tin-shack restaurants sitting on the lake's shore at Railway Beach at the end of Oginga Odinga Rd.

★Green Garden Restaurant
INTERNATIONAL $
(Odera St; mains KSh380-500; ☺8am-11pm) Surrounded by colourful murals and potted palms, the Green Garden is an oasis of culinary delight set in an Italian-themed courtyard. As you would expect, it's an expat hotspot and the word is that the tilapia in spinach and coconut sauce is the way to go. Be prepared to wait a long time for your meal.

The Laughing Buddha
INTERNATIONAL $
(Swan Centre, Accra St; mains KSh350-600; ☺10.30am-11pm Tue-Thu, 11am-6am Fri & Sat, noon-midnight Sun; ✍) The Laughing Buddha has a limited menu (made even more so by the fact that half the items probably won't be available) of pastas, pizzas and chips in dozens of different flavours, which will likely come as a surprise to anyone who grew up thinking chips were just chips! The street-side tables earn it big points.

☙ Drinking & Nightlife

Kisumu's nightlife has a reputation for being even livelier than Nairobi's. Check flyers and ask locals who are plugged into the scene. Be careful when leaving venues as muggings and worse have occurred; don't go out alone. Clubs are liveliest on Friday and Saturdays. The Laughing Buddha may be better known as a restaurant, but DJs reign Fridays and Saturdays.

LAKE VICTORIA'S UNWELCOME GUESTS

Lake Victoria's 'evolving' ecosystem has proved to be both a boon and a bane for those living along its shores. For starters, its waters are a haven for mosquitoes and snails, making malaria and bilharzia (schistosomiasis) all too common here. Then there are the Nile perch, introduced 50 years ago to combat mosquitoes, but which eventually thrived, growing to over 200kg in weight and becoming every fishing-boat captain's dream. The ravenous perch have wiped out more than 300 species of smaller tropical fish unique to the lake.

Last but not least is the ornamental water hyacinth. First reported in 1986, this exotic pond plant had no natural predators here and has quickly reached plague proportions, even managing to shut down much of the lake's shipping industry. Millions of dollars have been ploughed into solving the problem, with controversial programmes such as mechanical removal and the introduction of weed-eating weevils. The investment seemed to be paying off at first, with hyacinth cover shrinking for the first time in years, but the project has since halted over fears that the weevils were invading nearby agricultural fields. Scientists are still desperately looking for a solution as the hyacinth continues its relentless sprawl.

Social Centre BAR
(off Omino Cres; KSh100) Tucked behind the main matatu stage, this club is big on *ohangla* (Luo traditional music) with the odd Kiswahili hip-hop tune thrown in for good measure.

Juiz Parlour CAFE
(off Station Rd; juice from KSh70; ⊘ 7.30am-8pm) You name it and they'll stick it in a blender and pulverise the bejesus out of it. The pumpkin-and-beetroot juice looked foul so we shared a very special moment with a mango-and-pineapple combo instead.

☆ Entertainment

Oasis LIVE MUSIC
(Kondele, Jomo Kenyatta Hwy; KSh150-200) With live music most nights, this is the place to see Lingala music performed by Congolese bands. Be prepared for mellifluous rhythms and a fair bit of gyrating, shaking and sweating.

🛍 Shopping

Kibuye Market MARKET
(Jomo Kenyatta Hwy; ⊘ 7am-3pm Sun) Come past the huge Kibuye Market on any quiet weekday and you'll find it as empty as a hyena's heart, but visit on a Sunday and it transforms into a blossoming spring flower of colour and scents.

ⓘ Information

MEDICAL SERVICES

Aga Khan Hospital (☏ 057-2020005; Otiena Oyoo St) is a large hospital with modern facilities and 24-hour emergency room.

MONEY

Barclays (Kampala St; ⊘ 9am-3pm Mon-Fri, 9am-noon Sat) With ATM.
Kenya Commercial Bank (Jomo Kenyatta Hwy; ⊘ 8am-5pm Mon-Fri, 8am-noon Sat) With ATM (Visa only).

VISA EXTENSIONS

Kisumu Immigration Office (p380) provides visa extensions.

ⓘ Getting There & Away

AIR

Fly540 (www.fly540.com), Jambo Jet (www.jambojet.com) and Kenya Airways (www.kenya-airways.com) offer daily flights to Nairobi (50 minutes). Fly540 also flies to Eldoret.

Shiva Travels (☏ 057-2022320, 0733635200; Oginga Odinga Rd) and Zaira Tours & Travel (p127) are good for airline ticketing and hotel reservations.

BUS & MATATU

Buses, matatus and Peugeots (shared taxis) to numerous destinations within Kenya battle it out at the large bus and matatu station just north of the main market. Peugeots cost about 25% more than matatus.

Easy Coach offers the smartest buses out of town. Its booking office and departure point are in the car park just behind (and accessed through) Tusky's Shopping Centre. It has daily buses to Nairobi (KSh1400, seven hours, every couple of hours), Nakuru (KSh800, 4½ hours, every couple of hours) and Kampala (KSh1500, seven hours, 1.30pm, 1.30am and 10.30pm).

ⓘ Getting Around

BODA-BODA & TUK-TUK

Both *boda-bodas* and tuk-tuks (motorised mini-taxis) have proliferated and they are a great way to get around Kisumu. A trip to Hippo Point should be no more than KSh60/180 for a *boda-boda*/tuk-tuk.

MATATU

Matatus 7 and 9, which travel along Oginga Odinga Rd and Jomo Kenyatta Hwy, are handy to reach the main matatu station, main market and Kibuye Market – just wave and hop on anywhere you see one.

TAXI

A taxi around town costs between KSh150 and KSh250, while trips to Dunga range from KSh300 to KSh450, with heavy bargaining.

Homa Bay

☏ 059 / POP 60,000

Stretched out across the plains between Mt Homa and Winam Gulf on Lake Victoria, the predominantly Luo town of Homa Bay has a slow, tropical, almost central-African vibe. Not many tourists make it out here – it's a noticeably friendly place, getting about its business without worrying too much about chasing the tourist dollar.

In the town itself, there's little to do beyond wandering the dusty, music-filled streets or strolllng down to the lake edge to watch the marabou storks pick through the rubbish as they wait for the fishermen and their morning catch. But there are some interesting walls in the neighbouring hills – the easiest summit to bag is the unmistakable conical mound of **Asego Hill**, which is just beyond the town and takes about an hour to clamber up – and the town makes a great base from which to visit Ruma National Park and Thimlich Ohinga.

🛏 Sleeping & Eating

Twin Towers Hotel HOTEL $
(☏0704164539, 0775612195; Off C19; s/d from KSh2500/3000; 🛜) In the town centre, Twin Towers (slightly unfortunate name, that) is a solid choice if all you require is a comfy bed and a bathroom that doesn't need a biohazard suit to enter. It can suffer quite badly from street noise, though – the market is just around the corner. The restaurant here offers decent, if unimaginative, mains for around KSh350.

Homa Bay Tourist Hotel HOTEL $$
(☏0727112615; s/d from US$62/72; 🅿🛜) This lakeside 'resort' is the town's original hotel and though the rooms are rather faded they also have character and catch a lake breeze in the evening. The expansive lawns running down to the water's edge are home to many a colourful songbird and there's an outdoor bar with live music on Saturdays (so avoid rooms at the front).

ℹ Information

MONEY

Barclays (Off C19; ⊙9am-4pm Mon-Fri, 9am-noon Sat) With ATM.

TOURIST INFORMATION

KWS Warden's Office (⊙9am-4pm Mon-Fri, 10am-2pm Sat) In the district commissioner's compound, it's the place for information on Ruma National Park.

ℹ Getting There & Away

The Easy Coach office (www.easycoach.co.ke) is just down the hill from the bus station, in the Total petrol station compound. It has buses to Nairobi (KSh950, eight hours) at 8.45am and 8.45pm. Several other companies and matatus (operating from the neighbouring bus station) ply the routes to Mbita (KSh250, 1½ hours), Kisii (KSh250, 1½ hours) and Kisumu (KSh300, three hours).

Ruma National Park

Bordered by the dramatic **Kanyamaa Escarpment**, and home to Kenya's only population of roans (one of Africa's rarest and largest antelope) is the seldom-visited, 120-sq-km **Ruma National Park** (☏0717176709, 020-35291129; www.kws.go.ke/content/ruma-national-park; adult/child US$25/15, vehicle from KSh300; ⊙6am-6pm). Besides roans, other rarities such as Bohor's reedbucks, Jackson's hartebeests, the tiny oribi antelope and Kenya's largest concentration of endangered Rothschild's giraffes can also be seen here. The most treasured residents are some (very hard to see) rhinos, both black and white, that have been translocated from other parks. Birdlife is also prolific, with 145 different species present, including the migratory blue swallow that arrives between June and August.

You wouldn't make this your first African safari, but it's a chance to track down some species you may not see elsewhere. The park also has an oasis feel to it, so intense is the human settlement and cultivation in this part of the country and surrounding the park.

⊙ Sights & Activities

Although dense bush in parts of the park makes wildlife-watching difficult, there's plenty to see in the open savannah areas. In just a short visit you can expect to see masses of giraffes as well as impalas, waterbucks and zebras. The area around the airstrip is particularly rewarding.

Thimlich Ohinga Archaeological Site ARCHAEOLOGICAL SITE
(☏0710236164, Nairobi 020-8164134; www.museums.or.ke/thimlich-ohinga/; KSh1000; ⊙sunrise-sunset) South of Ruma National Park, this is one of East Africa's most important archaeological sites. It holds the remains of a dry-stone enclosure, 150m in diameter and containing another five smaller enclosures, thought to date back as far as the 15th century. Its name translates in Luo as 'frightening dense forest'.

🛏 Sleeping

Oribi Guesthouse COTTAGE $$
(☏0717176709; www.kws.go.ke; cottage excl breakfast US$100; 🅿) This KWS-run guesthouse, near the park headquarters at Kamato Gate, is extortionate if there are only two of you, but quite good value for groups. It has dramatic views over the Lambwe Valley and is well equipped with solar power, hot showers and a fully functioning kitchen, but bring your own food.

ℹ️ RUMA NATIONAL PARK

Why Go A surprising range of wildlife (roan antelopes and Rothschild's giraffes are the pick) and very few visitors.

When to Go Best in the dry season of June to October. During the rains, tracks can become impassable.

Practicalities Easily accessible from Homa Bay, but to be there at dawn when animals are most visible, stay in the park.

Budget Tips The park is set up for those with vehicles, but if you don't have your own wheels, contact the KWS Warden's Office (p131) in Homa Bay, who may be able to arrange a jeep for you.

ℹ️ Getting There & Away

In your own vehicle, head a couple of kilometres south from Homa Bay and turn right onto the Mbita road. After about 12km you'll come to the main access road, which is signed just as Kenya Wildlife Service (coming from Homa Bay, you might not see the sign as it faces the other way). From there it's another 11km to the park entrance. The park's roads are in decent shape, but require a strong, high-clearance 4WD in the rainy season.

Mbita & Rusinga Island

POP 30,000

Mbita and Rusinga Island (connected by a causeway) are delightful and great places to draw near to Lake Victoria. Tiny, languid and rarely visited, they offer a glimpse of an older Africa – an Africa that moves to the gentle sway of the seasons rather than the ticking of a clock. This is the sort of place where schoolchildren abandon their classes to watch you pass by and old women burst into song at your arrival.

👁️ Sights

Tom Mboya's Mausoleum   HISTORIC SITE

(Kasawanga Village, Rusinga; donation; ⏰ 6am-6pm Mon-Sat) A child of Rusinga, Mboya was one of the few Luo people to achieve political success. He held a huge amount of influence as Jomo Kenyatta's right-hand man and was widely tipped to become Kenya's second president before he was assassinated in 1969. His tomb and a small museum dedicated to his life are on the island's north side. The inscription on his tombstone begins 'Go and fight like this man...'

Mbasa Island   WILDLIFE RESERVE

Also known as Bird Island, Mbasa is home to a wide variety of wetland birds, including long-tailed cormorants (which have a breeding colony here), fish eagles, marsh harriers and little white egrets. Bird concentrations are thickest at sunset, when birds return to roost. To get here you'll need to arrange a boat with a local fisherman or ask at the Wayando Beach Club Eco Lodge; expect to pay between KSh4000 and KSh7500 per boat.

🛏️ Sleeping

⭐ **Wayando Beach Club Eco Lodge**   BANDA, CAMPGROUND $

(☎ 0723773571,   0708593513;   www.wayando beachclub.com; Rusinga; camping KSh950, camping incl breakfast & using lodge tents KSh1500, banda per person incl breakfast KSh4484; 🅿️ 🛜) 🏄 Four kilometres from the causeway (turn right at the junction) is this large American-owned grassy compound with easy lake access, loads of birds in the gardens, campsites under the acacia trees and a couple of very comfortable and colourful stone *bandas*. There's also a cool bar-restaurant (dinner KSh850).

Rusinga Guesthouse   GUESTHOUSE $

(☎ 0705146134;   www.rusingaguesthouse.com; Rusinga; s KSh1500-1800, d KSh2000-5000; 🅿️ 🛜) Far enough from the bars to offer a quiet night's sleep, this guesthouse sets a bar of its own in terms of value for money. The rooms are clean and the mosquito nets are yet to acquire holes. Members of staff are endearingly shy and the restaurant can sort you out with standard chicken or fish options (mains KSh250 to KSh300).

⭐ **Rusinga Island Lodge**   LODGE $$$

(☎ 0716055924; Rusinga; s/d full board from US$500/700; 🌐 🛜 🏊) One of the finest places to stay in Kenya's corner of Lake Victoria, Rusinga Island is an exclusive lakeside lodge with its own private air strip. The seven thatched-roof bungalows have their own private terraces overlooking the lake and the atmosphere is one of a quiet, high-end retreat. Birdwatching is a highlight, with 369 species recorded on the property.

ℹ️ Getting There & Away

The best way of getting from Mbita to Kisumu is to take the ferry (foot passenger KSh150, vehicle from KSh900, one hour) to Luanda Kotieno on the northern shore of the narrow Winam Gulf and catch a connecting matatu (KSh300, two hours). Boats leave Mbita at 7am, 10am, 2pm and 5pm. Coming from the other direction, boats depart Luanda Kotieno at 8am, 10am, noon, 3pm and 5.30pm.

The road between Mbita and Homa Bay has been upgraded and is now surfaced for all but a small section. Matatus (KSh250, 1½ hours) frequently pass between the two or there are a few normal buses (KSh200) as well as a daily bus to Kisumu (KSh450). To get around the island, you might find a taxi in Mbita for a half-day loop, stopping at sites of interest for around KSh1000; a *boda-boda* (known as a *piki-piki* here) will do the same for about half that price.

Mfangano Island

POP 22,000

If you want to fall totally off the radar but still be in Kenya, then Mfangano Island, sitting out in the placid lake waters, is an idyllic place to get lost. Home to many a monitor lizard, inquisitive locals, intriguing rock paintings and the imposing but assailable Mt Kwitutu (1694m), Mfangano Island is well worth a day or two. In some ways, it's the quintessential Lake Victoria experience for those looking to catch the essence of lakeshore life.

Sights

Rock Paintings　　　　ARCHAEOLOGICAL SITE
(KSh500) These rock paintings, often featuring sun motifs, are both revered and feared by locals (which has hindered vandalism) and are thought to be the handiwork of the island's earliest inhabitants, Bantu Pygmies from Uganda. The entry fee is used to help fund some very needy children at the local orphanage. The orphanage and the rock paintings are found near the settlement of Kakiimba, a 3km (KSh150) *boda-boda*

(motorcycle taxi) ride from Sena, the island's 'capital'.

Tours

George Ooko Oyuko　　　　TOURS
(☑ 0716537317; per day KSh700) Local George Ooko Oyuko can act as a guide to the rock paintings and other sites, as well as help organise ascents of Mt Kwitutu. He can also arrange homestays (KSh400), though be prepared for some extremely basic conditions, a humbling experience and a warm reception.

Sleeping

Joyland Hotel　　　　HOTEL $
(☑ 0720768968; Sena; s/tw with shared bathroom excl breakfast KSh500/1000) Although the basic rooms are essentially clean, those with delicate sensibilities might find the shared toilets a bit grim. Food is available in the attached (and only) restaurant in Sena.

★ **Mfangano Island Camp**　　　　RESORT $$$
(☑ Nairobi 020-2734000; www.governorscamp.com; Mfangano Island; s/d full board US$650/1100; ☉ closed Apr & May; ⚹⚹) Nestled into the banks of beautifully maintained gardens alive with monitor lizards and birdlife, these stone-and-thatch cottages, 6km north of Sena, are the smartest digs on Lake Victoria and have a real desert-island, end-of-the-road feel to them. The camp, formerly a fishing resort, now offers a number of other water sports, all included in the tariff.

ℹ Getting There & Away

Boats ply the lake waves between Mbita and Mfangano Island daily (foot passenger KSh250, car KSh900, 1½ hours). In theory they leave at 10am and 5pm, returning at 8am and 2pm.

MASAI MARA & WESTERN KENYA MFANGANO ISLAND

ROAN ANTELOPE

The roan antelope, which goes by the Harry Potter-esque scientific name of *Hippotragus equinus*, is found in small populations and geographic pockets across sub-Saharan Africa. One of the largest species of antelope in Africa (males can weigh up to 300kg), the roan is often mistaken for the sable antelope, which is darker in colour; like the sable, the roan has a shaggy neck and an oryx-like face. They are found in open savannah and light woodlands throughout their range, where a single male will lord it over between five and 15 females; males often clash over territory and control of the harem.

According to the International Union for the Conservation of Nature (IUCN), which gives the roan 'Least Concern' status, there are an estimated 76,000 roan across Africa, but the species nonetheless remains at risk of decline due to habitat loss. Unusually the roan is doing well in west and central Africa, but is in decline in east and southern Africa. Although the species is doing reasonably well in Tanzania, its last foothold in Kenya is believed to be Ruma National Park. A small population may still survive in the Shimba Hills, southwest of Mombasa.

In practice they go only when full and they're almost always dangerously overloaded. Usually they call at Takawiri Island en route, stop at Mfangano's 'capital', Sena, and then carry on around the island, stopping at most villages on the way.

Private boats for a full-day trip from Rusinga can be arranged through Wayando Beach Club Eco Lodge (p132) for between KSh8000 and KSh16,000, depending on boat type.

WESTERN HIGHLANDS

Despite media impressions depicting a land of undulating savannah stretching to the horizon, the real heart and soul of Kenya, and the area where most people live, are the luminous green highlands. Benefiting from reliable rainfall and fertile soil, the Western Highlands are the agricultural powerhouse of the country; the south is cash-crop country, with vast patchworks of tea plantations covering the region around Kisii and Kericho; while further north, near Kitale and Eldoret, dense cultivation takes over.

The settlements here are predominantly agricultural service towns, with little of interest unless you need a chainsaw or water barrel. For visitors, the real attractions lie outside these places – the rolling tea fields around Kericho, the tropical beauty of Kakamega Forest, trekking on Mt Elgon, the prolific birdlife in Saiwa Swamp National Park and exploring the dramatic Cherangani Hills.

Kisii

📞 058 / POP 120,000

Kisii is an important transit town for western Kenya and there's a good chance you'll pass through at some point in your explorations here. Some travellers also use it as an access point to the region's renowned soapstone carvings in nearby Tabaka. Important as it may be, Kisii wouldn't win a beauty contest. Actually, that's being kind. Kisii is a noisy, polluted and congested mess and most people (quite sensibly) roll right on through without even stopping.

🛏 Sleeping & Eating

St Vincent Guesthouse GUESTHOUSE $
(📞0733650702; s/d/tw KSh1700/2200/2700; 🅿) This Catholic-run guesthouse off the Moi Hwy isn't the place for a party, but it's hands down the best place to stay in Kisii. Rooms are very clean and cosy, it's quiet and security is good. No alcohol allowed.

Nile Hotel HOTEL $
(📞0786706089; Hospital Rd; r KSh1000-1600, tw KSh2000) Clean, cheap rooms and a central location make the Nile the best deal in the town centre, although their claim to four stars is, shall we say, aspirational rather than descriptive. The 2nd-floor restaurant (mains KSh250 to KSh400) has a commanding view of the chaos below.

🛈 Getting There & Away

The congested matatu terminal in the centre of town is a chaos of loud and often somewhat drunk people trying to bundle you onto the nearest matatu, whether or not you want to go where it's going. If you do manage to pick your own matatu, you'll find regular departures to Homa Bay (KSh250, 1½ hours), Kisumu (KSh300, 2½ hours), Kericho (KSh500, two hours) and Isebania (KSh300, 1¾ hours) on the Tanzanian border.

Tabaka matatus (KSh100, 45 minutes) leave from Cemetery Rd. Returning, it is sometimes easier to catch a *boda-boda* (KSh100) to the 'Tabaka junction' and pick up a Kisii-bound matatu there.

Easy Coach (www.easycoach.co.ke; Moi Hwy) has twice-daily departures to Nairobi (KSh900, eight hours, 10am and 9.30pm). It also has a bus to Narok (KSh500, four hours, 1pm), which is handy for the Mara.

Kisii 🗺 0 / 500 m / 0.25 miles

Kisii

🛌 **Sleeping**
1 Nile Hotel...B2
2 St Vincent Guesthouse.........................A1

🛈 **Transport**
3 Easy Coach...B2
4 Matatus...B2
5 Matatus to Tabaka...............................B1

Kericho

♫ 052 / POP 180,000

Kericho is a haven of tranquillity and one of Kenya's most agreeable towns. Its surrounds are blanketed by a thick patchwork of manicured tea plantations, each seemingly hemmed in by distant stands of evergreens, and even the town centre seems as orderly as the tea gardens. With a pleasant climate and a number of things to see and do, Kericho makes for a very calming couple of days.

◉ Sights

Arboretum GARDENS

(B4 Hwy; ☺ 8am-8pm, closed when raining) Eight kilometres east of town, this tropical park is popular with weekend picnickers and colobus, vervet and red-tailed monkeys (best seen in the early morning). The main attraction is the shade afforded by the tropical trees planted by estate owner Tom Grumbley in the 1940s. The nearby Chagaik Dam is responsible for the lovely lily-covered pond.

🏃 Activities

Kericho is the centre of Africa's most important tea gardens and the countryside surrounding the town is one of interlocking tea estates mixed with patches of forest. You might expect tea-plantation tours to be touted left, right and centre, but they are surprisingly few and far between. If you just want to take a stroll in the fields, the easiest plantations to get to are those behind the Tea Hotel.

If you want something more organised, ask at the Tea Hotel or contact Harman Kirui who organises fun and informative tea-estate and factory tours. Most tours involve walking around the fields and watching the picking (note that the pickers don't work on Sunday). If you want to actually see the process through to the end by visiting a factory, you should book at least four days in advance through the Tea Hotel or by emailing Harman directly.

Harman Kirui TOUR

(📞 0721843980; kmtharman@yahoo.com; per person KSh200) Mr Harman Kirui organises fun and informative tea estate and factory tours. Most tours involve walking around the fields and watching the picking (note that the pickers don't work on Sunday). If you want to actually see the process through to the end and visit a factory, you

KISII SOAPSTONE

While the feted Kisii soapstone obviously comes from this area, it's not on sale here. Quarrying and carving take place in the Gusii village of **Tabaka**, 23km northwest of Kisii. Soapstone is relatively soft and pliable (as far as rocks go) and with simple hand tools and scraps of sandpaper the sculptors carve chess sets, bowls, animals and the unmistakable abstract figures of embracing couples. Each artisan specialises in one design before passing it on to someone else to be smoothed with wet sandpaper and polished with wax. Most pieces are destined for the curio shops of Nairobi and Mombasa and trade-aid shops around the world. As you would expect, prices are cheaper here than elsewhere. If you're undaunted by adding a few heavy rocks to your backpack, you can save a considerable sum by buying close to the source.

should book at least four days in advance by emailing Harman directly.

Momul Tea Factory TOUR

(KSh500; ☺ Mon-Sat) The factory most often visited around Kericho is the Momul Tea Factory, 28km from the town. The factory has 64 collection sites servicing the area's small-scale farmers; it processes a staggering 15 million kilos of green leaf a year. Note: no processing takes place on Mondays.

🛏 Sleeping & Eating

New Sunshine Hotel HOTEL $

(📞 052-2030037, 0725146601; Tengecha Rd; s/d/tr KSh2300/3000/3500; 🛜) Without doubt the best budget hotel in town (not that the competition is especially stiff). The rooms, while not large, are spotless and the showers are actually hot rather than lukewarm. The attached restaurant (meals KSh350 to KSh550) does a roaring trade.

Tea Hotel HOTEL $$

(📞 0714510824; Moi Hwy; camping KSh700, s/d US$70/95; 🅿🛜🏊) This grand property was built in the 1950s by the Brooke Bond company and still has a lot of (very faded) period charm. The hotel's most notable features are the vast hallways and dining rooms full of mounted animal heads, and its beautiful gardens with their tea-bush

Kericho

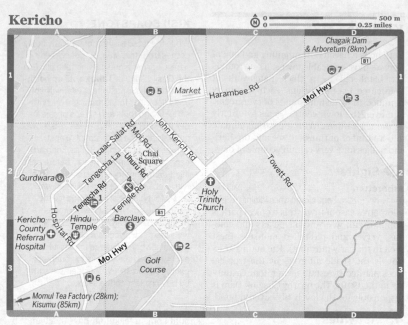

Kericho

😴 Sleeping
1 New Sunshine Hotel A2
2 Sunshine Upper Hill Hotel.................. B3
3 Tea Hotel D1

🍴 Eating
4 Litny's Restaurant............................... B2

ℹ️ Transport
5 Bus & Matatu Stand............................ B1
6 Buses to Kisumu, Kisii & Homa
　Bay A3
7 Easy Coach D1

backdrops. Many of the rooms, though, are literally falling to pieces.

Sunshine Upper Hill Hotel　　HOTEL **$$**
(📞 0721700358, 0052-2021285; www.sunshine hotel.co.ke; off Moi Hwy; s/d from US$70/81; P 📶) This large hotel block, consisting of new, modern rooms overlooking the town park, is where business types settle in to do important stuff in Kericho. The rooms have comfortable beds, vast bathrooms and in-room wi-fi.

Litny's Restaurant　　KENYAN **$**
(Temple Rd; mains KSh250-500; ⏱ 6am-8pm) Along with New Sunshine Hotel (p135), this is regarded as one of the better restaurants

in town, though in truth the fried chicken and chips here were no different to the fried chicken and chips we ate elsewhere.

ℹ️ Information

Barclays (Moi Hwy; ⏱ 9am-4pm Mon-Fri, 9am-noon Sat) Has an ATM that accepts Visa and Mastercard.

Kericho County Referral Hospital
(📞 0780174556; Hospital Rd)

ℹ️ Getting There & Away

Most buses and matatus operate from the **main stand** (John Kerich Rd) in the town's northwest corner, while those heading south and west (such as to Kisii and Kisumu) leave from the **Total petrol station** (Moi Hwy).

Matatus to Kisumu (KSh300, 1½ hours), Kisii (KSh300, two hours), Eldoret (KSh400, three hours) and Nakuru (KSh300, two hours) are frequent. The odd Peugeot also serves these destinations, but costs about 25% more.

Easy Coach (www.easycoach.co.ke; Moi Hwy) offers the best buses, but its office, and departure point, is inconveniently located out of town, opposite the Tea Hotel and inside the Libya petrol station. It has buses to Nairobi (KSh1100) throughout the day, as well as frequent buses to Nakuru (KSh550) and Kisumu (KSh500).

Kakamega

📞 056 / POP 100,000

This agricultural town can be a convenient stopover if you arrive late in the day and can't stock up on supplies before heading to nearby Kakamega Forest Reserve. Otherwise, there is no real reason to stay.

👁 Sights

Crying Stone of Ilesi   LANDMARK
The Crying Stone of Ilesi is a local curiosity perched on a ridge 3km south of town. The formation, looking like a solemn head resting on weary shoulders, consists of a large boulder balanced atop a huge column of rock, down which 'tears' flow.

🛏 Sleeping & Eating

Kakamega Guesthouse   GUESTHOUSE $
(📞 0710548388; www.facebook.com/kakamega guesthouse/; off A1; s/d incl breakfast KSh1600/2600) This well-priced if rather unexciting place in the town centre aims primarily at the local business market. The rooms are fine for the price and the downstairs restaurant (mains from KSh350) is one of the better places to eat in town. It's opposite the well-signed Ambwere Complex, next to the petrol station and close to the market.

Kakamega Golf Hotel   HOTEL $$
(📞 056-31713; www.golfhotelkakamega.com; Kenyatta Ave; s/d incl breakfast US$100/126; P 🛜 🏊) Easily Kakamega's best place to stay, Kakamega Golf Hotel has tidy if somewhat overpriced rooms, a swimming pool and (sometimes) vultures on the lawn.

Tuskys   SUPERMARKET $
(📞 056-31760; www.tuskys.com; A1; ⏱ 7.30am-9pm) Kakamega's best supermarket has plenty of supplies as well as ready-made foods (including yummy samosas) in the deli and bakery.

ℹ Information

MONEY
Barclays (A1 Hwy; ⏱ 9am-4pm Mon-Fri, 9am-noon Sat) With ATM.

TOURIST INFORMATION
KWS Area Headquarters (A1) Kakamega Forest information, located 1.5km from the town centre.

ℹ Getting There & Away

Easy Coach (www.easycoach.co.ke; off Mumias Rd) has buses to Nairobi (KSh1450; seven to nine hours) at 8.30am and 8pm. Services to Nakuru leave at midday and midnight in Nakuru (three to four hours) and will cost you KSh800.

Matatus, which leave from behind the market, will whizz you to Kitale (KSh300, three hours) and Eldoret (KSh300, two hours). To get to Kakamega Forest Reserve, take a matatu to Khayega (KSh50, 30 minutes), followed by a *boda-boda* to the reserve (KSh200, 45 minutes). Matatus for Kisumu (KSh200, 1¾ hours) can be found near the Total petrol station on the northern edge of town.

Kakamega Forest

📞 056

Kakamega Forest, surrounding the town of Kakamega, is like nowhere in Kenya. Indeed, beneath Kakamega's dense, dark canopy – when the monkeys caterwaul through the treetops and birdsong filters

---

ℹ KAKAMEGA FOREST

Why Go This unique rainforest ecosystem has more than 330 species of birds, 400 species of butterflies and seven different primate species, including the rare de Brazza's monkey.

When to Go The best viewing months are June, August and October, when many migrant bird species arrive. October also sees many wildflowers bloom, while December to March are the driest months.

Practicalities As the northern section of the forest is managed by KWS and the southern section by the Kenyan Forest Department, it is not possible to visit the whole park without paying both sets of admission charges. Both areas have their pros and cons.

Budget Tips Entry fees to the southern Kakamega Forest Reserve are lower, and accommodation generally cheaper, than in the northern Kakamega Forest National Reserve, so it makes sense for budget travellers to base themselves there.

Kakamega Forest

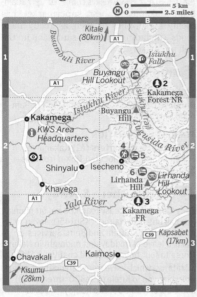

Kakamega Forest

◉ Sights
1 Crying Stone of Ilesi..............................A2
2 Kakamega Forest National Reserve...B1
3 Kakamega Forest Reserve.................B3

◉ Activities, Courses & Tours
  Kafkogoa ....(see 4)
4 Kakamega Rainforest Tour Guides....B2
  KEEP ....(see 4)

◉ Sleeping
5 Forest Rest House B2
  Isikuti Guesthouse ....(see 7)
6 Rondo Retreat B2
7 Udo's Bandas & Campsite..................B1

through the foliage like sunlight – you'll feel as if the last 200 years never happened. That's because not so long ago, much of western Kenya was hidden under a dark veil of jungle and formed part of the mighty Guineo-Congolian forest ecosystem. With customary colonial disregard for long-term environmental perils, the British turned much of that virgin forest into tea estates.

As Kenya's last stand of tropical rainforest, **Kakamega Forest National Reserve** (www.kws.go.ke; adult/child US$25/15, vehicles KSh300) is especially good for birders, with 330 species recorded, including turacos, African grey parrots and hornbills that sound like helicopters when flying overhead. Kakamega is also home to several primates, including de Brazza's, colobus, black-cheeked-white-nosed, and Sykes' monkeys. During darkness, hammer-headed fruit bats take to the air.

◉ Sights

Kakamega Forest Reserve   PARK
(adult/child KSh600/150) Kakamega Forest Reserve is the more degraded area of the forest, yet it's the more popular area with tourists. The five-hour return hike to Lirhanda Hill for sunrise or sunset is highly recommended. An interesting short walk (2.6km) to a 35m-high watchtower affords views over the forest canopy and small grassland.

Lirhanda Hill Lookout   VIEWPOINT
Depending on where you're staying, it can be about a five-hour return hike to Lirhanda Hill. Being there for sunrise or sunset is highly recommended.

Buyangu Hill Lookout   VIEWPOINT
It's a 4km drive or walk from the park entrance to Buyangu Hill, from where there are uninterrupted views east to the Nandi Escarpment.

◉ Activities

The best way – indeed the only real way – to appreciate the forest is to walk. While guides are not compulsory, they are well worth the extra expense. Not only do they prevent you from getting lost, but most are walking encyclopaedias and will reel off both the Latin and common names of almost any plant or insect you care to point out, along with any of its medicinal properties.

There are two main patches of forest; confusingly, they often use the same name. The northern Kakamega Forest National Reserve (also known as the Buyangu area) has a variety of habitats, but is generally very dense with considerable areas of primary forest and regenerating secondary forest. The forest here is managed by the Kenya Wildlife Service (KWS). There's a total ban on grazing, wood collection and cultivation in this zone. The southern section (known as Isecheno) forms the Kakamega Forest Reserve. Predominantly forested, this region supports several communities and

ITEN & THE HIGH-ALTITUDE TRAINING CENTRE

As a source of world-class athletes, the town of Iten, 36km northeast of Eldoret, has few peers. Over the past three decades, it (and the St Patrick's High School in particular) has produced a staggering number of world champions and Olympic medalists, among them Peter Rono (1988 Olympics), Matthew Birir (1992), Wilson Boit Kipketer (2000) and David Rudisha (2012).

Partly the success has to do with altitude: Iten sits at 2400m above sea level, which is ideal training conditions (thanks to the thinness of the oxygen in the air) for marathon and other long-distance runners seeking to build up their endurance. Another factor has been the presence of world-class coaches – Brother Colm O'Connell of Ireland arrived here in 1976 and has coached world champions ever since; O'Connell has been credited with helping to bring Kenya's female athletes to the world's attention, including some-time Iten residents Edna Kiplagat, Florence Kiplagat, Lornah Kiplagat, Linet Masai, Mary Keitany, Sally Barsosio and Rose Cheruiyot.

And then there's the **High Altitude Training Centre** (HATC; ☑0772700701; www. hatc-iten.com; Eldoret Rd, Iten; ⊙8am-8pm), which attracts well-known runners on a pilgrimage to one of the world's best-known mother lodes of athletic talent. Founded in 1999 by four-time world champion Lornah Kiplagat, the centre has a swimming pool, gym and, of course, running tracks. They welcome everyone from world-class athletes to recreational runners, and they've coaches to suit all levels. Contact the centre to ask about the numerous packages on offer.

The book *More Fire: How to Run the Kenyan Way* (Toby Tanser; 2008) was written in and about Iten, as was *Running with the Kenyans* (Adharanand Finn; 2012).

If you don't have your own wheels, matatus (KSh120, one hour) connect Iten with Eldoret's Sergoit Rd.

is under considerable pressure from both farming and illegal logging, but entry fees are lower and it has better accommodation.

☞ Tours

Kakamega Rainforest Tour Guides   WALKING
(☑0726951764; short/long walk per person KSh600/1200) Next to the forest reserve office, KRTG supplies knowledgeable guides to the forest for a variety of walks, including recommended night walks (KSh1500 per person) and sunrise/sunset walks (KSh1000 per person). These are some of the best-value nature walks you'll find in Kenya, with lots of wildlife to spot.

KEEP   WALKING
(☑0704851701) The Kakamega Environmental Education Programme (KEEP) is a locally established initiative that aims to educate the local community and visitors on the wonders of the Kakamega Forest and the threats it's under. The organisation also runs various community and conservation programmes and has been credited with much of the success in slowing the pace of destruction of the forest.

Kafkogoa   TOUR
(☑0724143064) Guides from this association cost KSh2000 for up to three hours and can be arranged at the park gates.

🛏 Sleeping

Forest Rest House   GUESTHOUSE $
(camping KSh650, r per person KSh500) The four rooms of this wooden house, perched on stilts 2m above the ground and with views straight onto a mass of jungle, might be very basic (no electricity, no bedding and cold-water baths that look like they'd crash through the floorboards if you used one), but they'll bring out the inner Tarzan in even the most obstinate city slicker.

Udo's Bandas & Campsite   BANDAS $
(☑Nairobi 020-2654658; www.kws.go.ke; camping adult/child US$20/15, bandas per person US$40) Named after Udo Savalli, a well-known ornithologist, this lovely KWS site is tidy, well maintained and has seven simple thatched *bandas*. Nets are provided, but you will need your own sleeping bag and other supplies. There are long-drop toilets, bucket showers and a communal cooking and dining shelter.

Isikuti Guesthouse
GUESTHOUSE **$$**

(✒ Nairobi 020-2654658; www.kws.go.ke; cottage US$60) Hidden in a pretty forest glade close to Udo's is the KWS Isikuti cottage, which has equipped kitchen and bathroom and an idyllic setting. It can sleep up to four people.

★ Rondo Retreat
GUESTHOUSE **$$$**

(✒ 056-2030268, 0733299149; www.rondoretreat. com; s/d half board US$200/275; P) To arrive at Rondo Retreat is to be whisked back to 1922 and the height of British rule. Consisting of a series of wooden bungalows filled with a family's clutter, this gorgeous and eccentric place is a wonderful retreat from modern Kenya. The gardens are absolutely stunning and worth visiting even if you're not staying.

ⓘ Getting There & Away

BUYANGU AREA

Matatus heading north towards Kitale can drop you at the access road, about 18km north of Kakamega town (KSh100). It's a well-signposted 2km walk from there to the park office and Udo's (p139).

ISECHENO AREA

Regular matatus link Kakamega with Shinyalu (KSh90), but few go on to Isecheno. Shinyalu is also accessed by a rare matatu service from Khayega. From Shinyalu you will probably need to take a boda-boda to Isecheno (KSh100).

The improved roads are still treacherous after rain and you may prefer to walk once you've seen the trouble vehicles can have. Shinyalu is about 7km from Khayega and 10km from Kakamega. From Shinyalu it's 5km to Isecheno.

The dirt road from Isecheno continues east to Kapsabet, but transport is rare.

Eldoret

✒ 053 / POP 335,000

The Maasai originally referred to this area as *eldore* (stony river) after the nearby Sosiani River. Today, Eldoret is a thriving service town straddling the Kenya–Uganda highway. It's the principal economic hub of western Kenya, but for the traveller there is little to see and less to do. The highlight is a visit to the **Doinyo Lessos Creameries Cheese Factory** (✒ 0726600204, 020-2115300; www. doinyolessos.com; Kenyatta St; ⊙ 8am-6pm) to stock up on any one of 20 different varieties of cheese. It's also a gateway to Iten, the home of long-distance Kenyan running.

Eldoret is a Kalenjin stronghold (the tribe of former president Daniel arap Moi and controversial vice-president William Ruto) and something of a bellweather for the political health of the nation. In 2008, it achieved notoriety when 35 people (mostly Kikuyus) were burnt alive in a church on the outskirts of town. This incident was the largest single loss of life during the 2007 post-election violence.

🛏 Sleeping

Keellu Resort Centre
HOTEL **$**

(✒ Nairobi 020-2601258; www.keelluresort.com; Iten Kapkoi Rd; s/d from KSh2500/4000; P 🛜) Around 36km northeast of Eldoret in high-altitude Iten, Keellu Resort Centre was

---

WHERE BOYS BECOME MEN

The Bungoma/Trans-Nzoia district goes wild in August with the sights and sounds of the Bukusu Circumcision Festival, an annual jamboree dedicated to the initiation of local boys into manhood.

The tradition was apparently passed to the Bukusu by the Sabaot tribe in the 19th century, when a young hunter cut the head off a troublesome serpent to earn the coveted operation.

The evening before the ceremony is devoted to substance abuse and sex. In the morning the youngsters are trimmed with a traditional knife in front of their entire village.

Unsurprisingly, this practice has attracted a certain amount of controversy in recent years. Health concerns are prevalent, as the same knife can be used for up to 10 boys, posing a risk of HIV/AIDS and other infections. The associated debauchery also brings a seasonal rush of underage pregnancies and family rifts that seriously affect local communities.

Education and experience now mean that fewer boys undergo the old method, preferring to take the safe option at local hospitals. However, those wielding the knife are less likely to let go of their heritage. To quote one prominent circumciser: 'Every year at this time it's like a fever grips me, and I can't rest until I've cut a boy.'

Eldoret

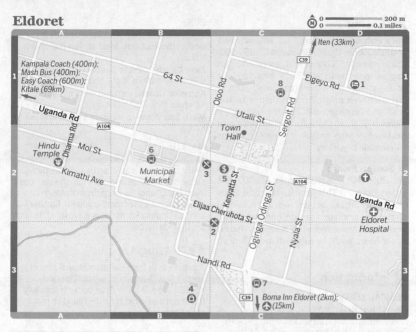

Kampala Coach (400m);
Mash Bus (400m);
Easy Coach (600m);
Kitale (69km)

Iten (33km)

Eldoret

🛏 Sleeping
1 White Highlands Inn.............................D1

🍴 Eating
2 Sunjeel Palace C3
3 Will's Pub & Restaurant.....................B2

🛍 Shopping
4 Doinyo Lessos Creameries Cheese
Factory..B3

ℹ Information
5 Barclays...C2

🚌 Transport
6 Bus & Matatu Stand............................B2
7 Local Matatus C3
8 Matatus to Iten & Kabarnet C1

founded in 2012 by world-renowned athlete Wilson Kipsang. It's a decent base if you're here to visit or train at the High Altitude Training Centre (p139). Rooms are tidy rather than exciting, but come with mosquito nets. The restaurant serves Kenyan, Chinese and Indian dishes.

White Highlands Inn HOTEL $
(☎0734818955; Elgeyo St; s/d KSh2250/2800; P) In a quiet corner on the edge of town,

this place offers good value. Its spacious rooms were so spotless that we actually lay in the bathtub instead of just looking at it wistfully. The whole complex is a bit rambling, but retains a certain old-fashioned charm and has a popular bar and less-popular restaurant.

★ Boma Inn Eldoret HOTEL $$$
(☎0719025000; www.theboma.co.ke/boma-inn-eldoret/; Ramogi Dr, off Elgon Rd; s/d/ste from US$165/198/330; P🖐🗺🏊) 🍃 This swish business-class hotel, 2km from the city centre, is hands down the best place to stay in Eldoret. The large rooms are smart and stylishly decorated, and they have comfortable beds, big desks to work at and piping-hot showers. There's a decent in-house restaurant as well as a pool and gym. All profits go to the Kenyan Red Cross.

Poa Place Resort HOTEL $$$
(☎0703129990; www.poaplace.co.ke; off B54; safari tent/cottage US$144/206; P🖐) The safari tents on manicured lawns and between high hedgerows are a little incongruous, but the quality of both the tents and lovely cottages is unimpeachable. Colourful furnishings, four-poster beds and hardwood floors make staying here a real pleasure.

✕ Eating

Will's Pub & Restaurant   INTERNATIONAL $
(☑0703730666; Uganda Rd; mains KSh150-500; ⊙6pm-midnight) Looks and feels like an English pub, with similarly heavyweight food – steak and fried breakfasts – but it also produces a few African dishes of the ugali and beef-stew ilk. The big-screen TV makes it a great place for a cold beer and the low-key vibe makes it a safe spot for solo female travellers.

★Sunjeel Palace   INDIAN $$
(☑0720554747; Kenyatta St; mains KSh400-650; ⊙11am-11pm; ☑) This formal, dark and spicy Indian restaurant serves superb, real-deal curries. Portion sizes are decent and if you mop up all the gravy with a freshly baked butter naan, you'll be as satisfied as Ganesh himself.

❶ Information

MEDICAL SERVICES

Eldoret Hospital (☑053-2062000; www. eldorethospital.com; Makasembo Rd; ⊙24hr) One of Kenya's best hospitals, with a 24-hour emergency unit. It's off Uganda Rd.

MONEY

Barclays (Uganda Rd; ⊙9am-4pm Mon-Fri, 9am-noon Sat) With ATM.

❶ Getting There & Away

AIR

Fly540 (p385) has flights that connect Eldoret with Nairobi and (less frequently) Lodwar.

Jambo Jet (p385) This Kenya Airways subsidiary flies to/from Nairobi.

BUS

A string of bus companies lines Uganda Rd west of the Postbank. Most service Nairobi via Nakuru.

Easy Coach Buses to Nairobi (KSh1250, 9.30am and 10pm, eight hours).

Kampala Coach Noon and midnight buses to Kampala (KSh2000, six hours).

Mash Bus Buses to numerous cities across Kenya.

MATATU

The main **matatu stand** is in the centre of town by the municipal market on Uganda Rd, though some local matatus and more Kericho services leave from Nandi Rd. Irregular matatus to Iten and Kabarnet leave from Sergoit Rd. Further west on Uganda Rd, matatus leave for Malaba on the Uganda border.

❶ Getting Around

A matatu to or from the international airport costs KSh100, and a taxi will cost around KSh1000 to KSh1500. *Boda-bodas* (especially the motorised variety) can be found on most street corners.

Kitale

☑054 / POP 120,000

Agricultural Kitale is a friendly market town with a couple of interesting museums and a bustling market. But we like it best as the gateway to some of the more rewarding excursions in this part of the country. It makes a fine waystation en route to explorations of Mt Elgon and Saiwa Swamp national parks. It also serves as the take-off point for a trip up to the western side of Lake Turkana.

MATATUS FROM ELDORET

DESTINATION	FARE	DURATION
Iten	KSh120	1 hr
Kabarnet	KSh350	2 hr
Kakamega	KSh300	2 hr
Kericho	KSh400	3 hr
Kisumu	KSh500	3 hr
Kitale	KSh250	1¼ hr
Nairobi	KSh800	6 hr
Nakuru	KSh350	2¾ hr
Nyahururu	KSh600	3½ hr

Kitale

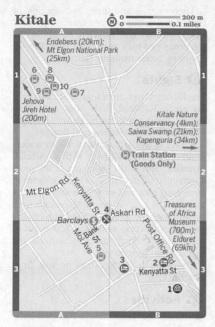

and Turkana peoples. There are also any number of stuffed dead things shot by various colonial types, including a hedgehog and a cheetah with a lopsided face.

Treasures of Africa Museum MUSEUM
(☑0722547765; A1 Hwy; KSh500; ⊙9am-12.30pm & 2-5pm Mon-Sat) This private museum is the personal collection of Mr Wilson, a former colonial officer in Uganda and quite a character. Based mainly on his experiences with the Karamojong people of northern Uganda, Mr Wilson's small museum illustrates his theory that a universal worldwide agricultural culture existed as far back as the last ice age.

🛏 Sleeping

Iroko Twigs Hotel HOTEL $
(☑0773475884; Kenyatta St; s/d KSh3200/3800; ☎) If you can overlook a few missing bathroom tiles and a little wear and tear, this is far and away the smartest hotel in town, although that's not saying a whole lot. The rooms (doubles more than singles) are pleasingly decorated with polished wood and art and there are coffee- and tea-making facilities and even dressing gowns in the wardrobes.

Alakara Hotel HOTEL $
(☑072280023; Kenyatta St; s/d KSh1600/2200, without bathroom KSh1200/1350; ℗) The most inviting super cheapie in town is safe, friendly, clean and has comfortable beds and reliable(ish) hot water. It also has a good bar, restaurant and TV room. Or to put it another way: this is as good as it gets.

Jehova Jireh Hotel HOTEL $
(☑0716805512; Laini Moja St; s/d from KSh1500/2800) A solid choice that boasts spacious, quiet and clean rooms with exceptionally helpful management. It's not quite as God-fearing as it sounds. There's an excellent downstairs restaurant that serves food later than most.

🍴 Eating

Iroko Boulevard Restaurant KENYAN $
(Askari Rd; mains KSh150-300; ⊙6.30am-6.30pm) It's got style, it's got glamour, it's got big-city aspirations and it's totally unexpected in Kitale. With cheap dishes and an old Morris car hanging from the ceiling, this is the most popular place to eat in town.

Kitale

◉ Sights
1 Kitale Museum................................B3

🛏 Sleeping
2 Alakara Hotel................................B3
3 Iroko Twigs Hotel..........................B3

🍴 Eating
4 Iroko Boulevard Restaurant.............A2

ℹ Transport
5 Easy Coach..................................A3
6 Main Bus & Matatu Park.................A1
7 Matatus to Eldoret & Nairobi...........A1
8 Matatus to Kapenguria...................A1
9 Matatus to Kisumu & Kakamega.......A1
10 Matatus to Marich Pass.................A1

◉ Sights

Kitale Museum MUSEUM
(☑054-30996, Nairobi 020-3742741; www.museums.or.ke/81-2/; A1 Hwy; adult/child KSh500/250; ⊙9.30am-6pm) Founded on the collection of butterflies, birds and ethnographic memorabilia left to the nation in 1967 by the late Lieutenant Colonel Stoneham, this museum has an interesting range of ethnographic displays of the Pokot, Akamba, Marakwet

The food is reliably good with a few international dishes to vary things a little.

ℹ️ Information

Barclays (Bank St; ⊘9am-4pm Mon-Fri, 9am-noon Sat) With ATM. Other banks are next door.

ℹ️ Getting There & Away

Matatus, buses and Peugeots are grouped by destination, and spread in and around the main bus and matatu park. Matatus run from different points in the scrum. Those to Eldoret and Nairobi leave from the other side of the main road, the departure points for Kapenguria and Marich Pass are right next to each other, while those to Kisumu and Kakamega are a further block west.

Regular matatus run to Endebess (KSh100, 45 minutes, change here for Mt Elgon National Park), Kapenguria (KSh150, 45 minutes, change here to continue north to Marich), Eldoret (KSh250, 1¼ hours), Kakamega (KSh250 to KSh300, 2½ hours) and Kisumu (KSh500, four hours).

Most bus companies have offices around the bus station and serve Eldoret (KSh250, one hour), Nakuru (KSh750, 3½ hours), Nairobi (KSh1000, seven hours) and Lodwar (KSh1600, 8½ hours) each day.

Easy Coach (www.easycoach.co.ke; Moi Ave) runs to Nairobi (KSh1350, seven hours) via Nakuru (KSh850, six hours) at 8.30am and 8pm.

Mt Elgon National Park

Straddling the Ugandan border and peaking with Koitoboss (4187m), Kenya's third-highest peak, and Uganda's Wagagai (4321m), the slopes of **Mt Elgon** (☑Nairobi 020-3539903; www.kws.go.ke/content/mount-elgon-national-park; park entrance adult/child US$26/17, vehicles from KSh300; ⊘6am-6pm) are a sight indeed – or at least they would be if they weren't buried under a blanket of mist and drizzle most of the time.

With rainforest at the base, the vegetation ascends through bamboo jungle to alpine moorland featuring giant groundsel and giant lobelia plants.

Common animals include buffaloes, bushbucks (both of which are usually grazing on the airstrip near Cholim Gate), olive baboons, giant forest hogs and duikers. The lower forests are the habitat of black-and-white colobus monkeys and blue and de Brazza's monkeys.

There are more than 240 species of birds here, including red-fronted parrots, Ross's turacos and casqued hornbills. On the peaks you may even see a lammergeier dropping bones from the thin air.

⊙ Sights

The Elkony Caves are a highlight of visiting Mt Elgon National Park. Four main lava tubes (caves) are open to visitors: **Kitum**, **Chepnyalil**, **Mackingeny** and **Rongai**.

Kitum extends more than 200m underground, while Mackingeny, with a waterfall cascading across the entrance, is the most spectacular of the caves and has colonies of large fruit bats and smaller horseshoe bats towards the rear. If you plan on entering, be sure to bring whatever kind of footwear you feel will cope well with 100 years of accumulated, dusty bat shit and all the roaches that feed off it.

The caves are a 6km drive or walk from Chorlim Gate.

🏃 Activities

★**Koitoboss Trek**   HIKING

The climb up Koitoboss is one of the best Mt Elgon treks. Allow at least four days for any round-trip hikes, and two or three days for any direct ascent of Koitoboss from Chorlim Gate. Once you reach the summit, there are a number of interesting options for the descent, including descending

---

ℹ️ **MT ELGON NATIONAL PARK**

Why Go Some superb overnight treks along with some interesting half-day options to caves occasionally visited by salt-loving elephants.

When to Go It's extremely wet most of the year. Serious trekkers should visit between December and February when it's at its driest.

Practicalities Waterproof gear and warm clothing are essential, as the area is as chilly as it is wet. Altitude may also be a problem for some people.

Budget Tips The easiest section of the park to visit is the area accessed through Chorlim Gate, from where you can walk to the caves and surrounding forest.

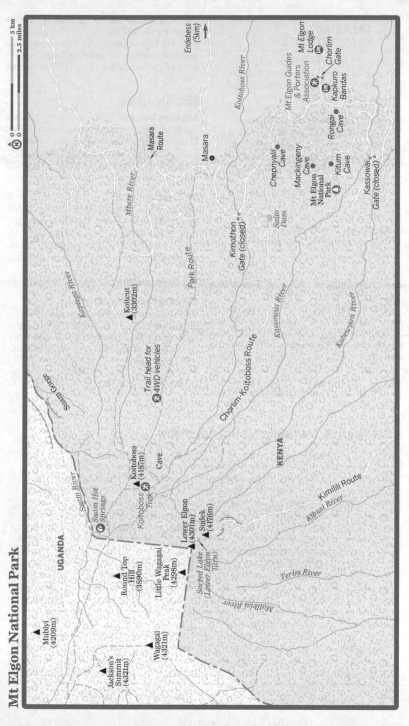

Mt Elgon National Park

TREKKING PRACTICALITIES

Unusually for a Kenyan national park, it is possible to walk unescorted, but due to the odd elephant and buffalo you will need to sign a waiver to do so.

We strongly recommend taking a guide. **Mt Elgon Guides & Porters Association** (☎0733919347) is a cooperative of guides and porters based at the KWS headquarters. Their services (per day guide/porter KSh3500/1200) can be booked through KWS.

If you're trekking, your only option is to camp (US$20). The fee is the same whether you drop tent in the official campsites (Chorlim, Nyati, Saito and Rongai) or on any old flat spot during your trek.

northwest into the crater to **Suam Hot Springs**.

Alternatively you could go east around the crater rim and descend the Masara Route, which leads to the small village of Masara on the eastern slopes of the mountain (about 25km) and then returns to Endebess. Or you can head southwest around the rim of the crater (some very hard walking) to **Lower Elgon Tarn**, where

you can camp before ascending **Lower Elgon Peak** (4301m).

If all this sounds too tiring, you'll be pleased to know it's possible to get within 4km of the summit with a 4WD in decent weather.

🛏 Sleeping

Kapkuro Bandas   BANDAS $
(☎020-3539903; www.kws.go.ke; banda US$40) These decent stone *bandas* (thatched-roof huts) can sleep three people in two beds. They have simple bathrooms and small, fully equipped kitchen areas.

Mt Elgon Lodge   LODGE $$
(☎0722875768; s/d/tr US$45/70/110) A few hundred metres before the main gate, this very faded lodge is set in grassy grounds with views down to the lowlands. Rooms are plain but clean and meals are available.

ℹ Information

ENTRY & EXIT FORMALITIES

With prior arrangement through the KWS it's theoretically possible to walk into Uganda and back again without needing to go through immigration procedures, or to cross into Uganda and complete formalities in the nearest town. Note: these are quite recent developments and we're yet to hear from anyone who's actually done it.

ELEPHANTS, MARBURG & KING SOLOMON

The Elkony Caves have some remarkable stories attached to them.

For a start, elephants love them and, while rarely seen, are known to 'mine' for salt from the walls of the caves. This process has been captured in BBC footage that has appeared in a number of natural history series, including *Elephant Cave* (2008). Kitum cave holds your best hope of glimpsing them, but sadly the number of these saline-loving creatures has declined over the years. Nonetheless, a torchlight inspection will soon reveal their handiwork in the form of tusking – the grooves made by their tusks during the digging process. Other animals are also known to enter the caves to lick salt from the walls, including hyenas, leopards and buffaloes.

Far more worryingly, in 1980 and in 1987 visitors to Kitum contracted the Marburg virus, a frightening illness closely tied to the much-better-known Ebola virus. The outbreak was attributed to the bats that inhabit the cave and their dung – to learn more about the outbreaks and the cave as a repository of the virus, read *The Hot Zone* (Richard Preston; 1994). It is worth noting that despite such sensational accounts, thousands of people visit Kitum every year with no ill effects.

As if all of this wasn't enough, the caves have a distinguished literary heritage. They were mentioned in the account of the first colonial journey across Masaailand, *Through Maasailand* (Joseph Thomson; 1885), while some historians have claimed that the caves (and perhaps Thomson's account) were the inspiration for the 1885 bestselling classic *King Solomon's Mines* by H Rider Haggard.

ℹ️ SAIWA SWAMP NATIONAL PARK

Why Go Kenya's smallest national park has great appeal for ornithologists, thanks to its prolific birdlife. It's also the most reliable place to see the semiaquatic sitatunga antelope.

When to Go The park can be visited at any time, though access roads become very slippery after rain.

Practicalities This is an easy and cheap park for independent travellers to visit. The park is only accessible on foot and walking trails skirt the swamp. Duckboards go right across it, and there are some rickety observation towers. Guides are not compulsory, though your experience will be greatly enhanced by taking one.

Budget Tips Stay in Kitale and catch a matatu to the junction for the park. Walk to the gates and explore the park without the aid of a guide.

MAPS

KWS produces a 1:35,000 map (KSh450) of the park as well as a guidebook (KSh750), both of which are sold at Chorlim Gate.

ℹ️ Getting There & Away

From Kitale, catch an Endebess-bound matatu to the park junction (KSh100, 45 minutes), from where it's a 15-minute motorbike taxi ride (KSh100 to KSh150) to the park gate. Be sure to grab your driver's phone number so you can contact him for a ride back to Endebess.

Saiwa Swamp National Park

North of Kitale, the small, rarely visited **Saiwa Swamp National Park** (☑ 0789312901; www.kws.go.ke/content/saiwa-swamp-national-park; adult/child US$22/13; ⏱ 6am-6pm) is a real treat – as long as you're not here for the Big Five, this is a chance to tick off some real safari highlights. Originally set up to preserve the habitat of Kenya's only population of sitatunga antelope, the 15.5-sq-km reserve is also home to blue, vervet and de Brazza's monkeys and some 370 species of birds. The fluffy black-and-white colobus and the impressive crowned crane are both present, and you may see Cape clawless and spot-throated otters (watchtower 4 is the best place from which to look for these).

☞ Tours

Maurice Sinyereri TOURS
(☑ 0728272339; ornithological day tour KSh2500) Expert bird guide Maurice has been involved with Saiwa since its earliest days and is a highly regarded guide to the park. Ask him about his bird-collecting past.

🛏️ Sleeping

Sitatunga Public Campsite CAMPGROUND $
(☑ 0789312901; www.kws.go.ke/content/saiwa-swamp-national-park; camping US$20; 🅿) A lovely site with flush toilets, showers, two covered cooking *bandas* and colobus in the trees above. It's close to the park entrance from where it's signposted, and adjacent to Sitatunga Treetop House.

★ Sirikwa Safaris GUESTHOUSE $$
(Barnley's Guesthouse; ☑ 0723917953; www.sirikwasafaris.com; camping KSh700, tents excl breakfast s/d KSh2500/3000, s/d with shared bathroom excl breakfast KSh3500/6000) Owned and run by the family that started Saiwa, this beautiful old farmhouse is 11km from the swamp. You can choose between camping in the grounds, sleeping in a well-appointed safari tent or, best of all, opting for one of the two bedrooms full of *National Geographic* magazines, old ornaments and antique sinks.

Sitatunga Treetop House HUT $$
(☑ 0789312901; www.kws.go.ke; tree house US$50; 🅿) Perched on stilts overlooking the Saiwa swamp, this KWS tree house can sleep three (there's a double and single bed). It has electricity, bedding and mosquito nets. There are no cooking facilities, but you can use those at the campsite next door.

ℹ️ Getting There & Away

The park is 18km northeast of Kitale. Take a matatu towards Kapenguria and get out at the second signposted turn-off (KSh90, 15 minutes), from where it's a 5km walk or KSh100 *moto-taxi* ride.

Central Highlands & Laikipia

Includes ➜

Aberdare
National Park 152

Solio Game
Reserve 154

Nanyuki 156

Ol Pejeta
Conservancy 160

Lewa Wildlife
Conservancy 162

Mt Kenya
National Park 166

Meru National Park . . 177

Chogoria 179

Ol Donyo Sabuk
National Park 181

Best Places to Eat

➜ Trout Tree Restaurant (p175)

➜ Le Rustique (p158)

➜ Tusks Restaurant (p159)

Best Places to Stay

➜ Lewa Safari Camp (p163)

➜ Elsa's Kopje (p179)

➜ iKweta Safari Camp (p178)

➜ Segera Retreat (p160)

➜ Treetops (p154)

Why Go?

The Central Highlands are the spiritual heartland of Kenya's largest tribe, the Kikuyu. This is the land the Mau Mau fought for, that the colonists coveted and whose natural, cyclical patterns define the lives of the country's largest rural population. These highlands form one of the most evocative sections of Africa's Great Rift Valley. It is here that Mt Kenya, Africa's second-highest mountain, rises into the clouds – climbing it is one of the great rites of passage of African travel.

In its shadow lie two of Kenya's most intriguing national parks: rhino- and lion-rich Meru National Park, and Aberdare National Park, home to some of the oldest mountains on the continent. Finally there's Laikipia, fount of so much that's good about modern conservation. It's also the scene for some of the best wildlife watching anywhere in Kenya.

When to Go
Nanyuki

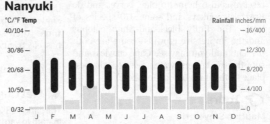

Mid-Jan–Feb & mid-Jul–Aug Your best chance of favourable weather to bag Mt Kenya.

Mar–early Jun The long rains fall everywhere.

Oct & Nov The short rains make a brief appearance.

History

The first *wazungu* (white) settlers arrived in the Central Highlands in the 19th century. At the height of white settlement, as many as 10,000 settlers lived here; many were granted 999-year leases over the land. It mattered little to the colonial authorities, of course, that Africans, especially the Kikuyu, were here before them: from as early as the 1880s, the authorities displaced the Kikuyu from their homes to make way for white agriculture and the Mombasa–Uganda railway.

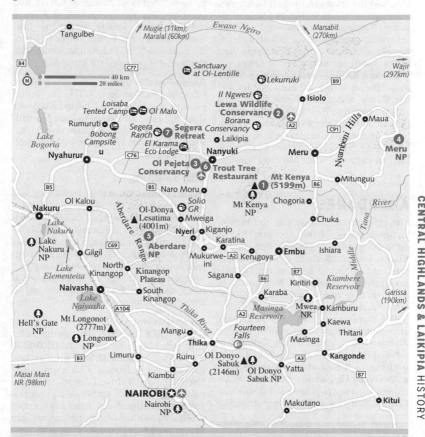

Central Highlands & Laikipia Highlights

1 Mt Kenya (p166) Holding a frozen Kenyan flag in your frozen hands atop the frozen summit of Point Lenana, 16km from the equator.

2 Lewa Wildlife Conservancy (p162) Doing a David Attenborough with an orphaned rhino then getting up close and personal with its wild cousins.

3 Ol Pejeta Conservancy (p160) Spending an evening here learning how to track lions.

4 Meru National Park (p177) Communing with the ancestors of some of Africa's most famous lions on safari at this national park.

5 Aberdare National Park (p152) Trekking through the otherworldly forests where elephants and bongo lurk.

6 Trout Tree Restaurant (p175) Fishing for your supper then climbing a tree at one of Kenya's most original restaurants.

7 Segera Retreat (p160) Indulging in *Out of Africa* nostalgia alongside contemporary art at this sublime lodge.

It was perhaps no surprise that, having borne the brunt of colonialism's abuses, the Kikuyu shouldered much of the burden of nationalism's struggle and formed the core of the Mau Mau rebellion in the 1950s. That struggle was largely fought in highland valleys, and the abuses of the anti-insurgency campaign were largely felt by highland civilians. The movement, combined with the general dismantling of the British Empire, forced colonial authorities to reassess their position and eventually abandon Kenya.

It was a Kikuyu, Jomo Kenyatta, who assumed the presidency of the new country, and the Kikuyu who assumed control over the nation's economy. They also reclaimed their rich fields in the Central Highlands, although many *wazungu* farmers remain, and their huge plots can be seen stretching all along the highways between Timau, Meru and Nanyuki.

ABERDARES

The cloud-kissed contours of the brown-and-grey slopes of the Aberdare Range, dubbed Nyandarua (Drying Hide) by the Kikuyu, stretch 160km from South Kinangop, east of Naivasha, up to the Laikipia Escarpment northwest of Nyahururu. In doing so, they form the solid spine of western Central Province.

But there's more to this soulful range of mountains than its geography, and the Aberdares still evoke strong feelings. In colonial times, this was a bastion of white settlement – the area was often referred to as the White Highlands – and later the Aberdares became a popular base for Mau Mau fighters during the independence struggle.

Nyeri

061 / POP 225,357

Nyeri is a welcoming and bustling Kikuyu market town. It's as busy as the Central Highlands get, but unless you have a thing for chaotic open-air bazaars and the restless energy of Kikuyu and white Kenyans selling maize, bananas, arrowroot, coffee and macadamia nuts, there's no real reason to linger for longer than it takes to plot your onward journey.

○ Sights

Baden-Powell Museum　　　　　　MUSEUM
(KSh500; ⊙opened on request) Lord Baden-Powell, the founder of the Boy Scout Association, spent his last three years at Paxtu cottage in the Outspan Hotel (p151), where this museum is located. The ultimate scoutmaster's retirement was somewhat poetic: to 'outspan' is to unhook your oxen at the end of a long journey. Paxtu is now filled with scouting scarfs and paraphernalia.

Baden-Powell clearly loved his final home: he once wrote 'the nearer to Nyeri, the nearer to bliss'. Famed tiger-hunter Jim Corbett later occupied the grounds.

Baden-Powell's Grave　　　　　　CEMETERY
(B5 Hwy; ⊙8.30am-5pm) FREE The scoutmaster's grave is tucked behind St Peter's Church, facing Mt Kenya and marked with the Scouts trail sign for 'I have gone home'. His more famous Westminster Abbey tomb is, in fact, empty.

🛏 Sleeping

**Nyama Choma Village
Accommodation**　　　　　　HOTEL $
(📋0788174384; Gakere Rd; r KSh1200; 🕸) With its light-blue walls and blue-linoleum showers, Nyama Choma is as colourful as it is cheap. Meat-eaters will love the large restaurant downstairs (*nyama choma* means 'barbecued meat'), though the smell of cooked meat does tend to permeate the rooms. Breakfast is not included.

Green Hills Hotel　　　　　　HOTEL $$
(📋0716431988, 061-2030604; www.greenhills.co.ke; Bishop Gatimu Rd; s/d from KSh6000/8100, s/d ste KSh23,000/28,000; P🕸🏊) The best deal in town is actually a little way out of Nyeri. The small drive is worth it for the palm-lined, poolside ambience and general sense of serenity. A few questionable style choices notwithstanding, the rooms are nicely turned out, comfortable and have mosquito nets.

White Rhino Hotel　　　　　　HOTEL $$
(📋0726967315; www.whiterhinohotel.com; Kanisa Rd; s/d US$105/130; P@🕸) This hotel boasts smart rooms that are polished to within an inch of their lives, and swanky, tiled bathrooms. With three bars and two restaurants, it's the top hotel in the city centre.

★ Sandai Farm　　　　　　GUESTHOUSE $$$
(📋0721656699; www.africanfootprints.de; camping KSh500, s/d full board US$145/250, cottages from US$80; P@) Fourteen kilometres northwest of town (ask locals for directions),

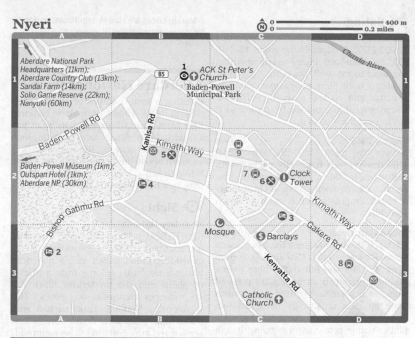

Nyeri

◎ Sights
1 Baden-Powell's Grave B1

⬚ Sleeping
2 Green Hills Hotel A3
3 Nyama Choma Village
   Accommodation...................................C2
4 White Rhino Hotel B2

✗ Eating
   Green Hills Hotel............................(see 2)
5 Raybells..B2
6 Rayjo's Café..C2

ⓘ Transport
7 Local Matatus...C2
8 Lower Bus Stand......................................D3
9 Upper Bus Stand C2

Sandai is run by the effervescent Petra Allmendinger, whose enthusiasm and warm welcome make this a great escape for those looking for something a little more personal than what's on offer elsewhere. Accommodation is either in the extremely cosy lodge or in self-contained cottages that can accommodate up to six.

Outspan Hotel HOTEL **$$$**
(☎ 0722207761, Nairobi 020-4452095; www.aberdaresafarihotels.com; s/d from US$189/276; ⓟ 🛜 🏊) This atmospheric lodge was last decorated in the 1950s, when wood panelling was the height of interior design, and some of the plumbing seems to date from then as well... Nineteen of the 34 standard rooms have cosy fireplaces, and all have a whiff of history that won't necessarily be to everyone's taste.

The dining room is a cross between the Hogwarts School hall and a colonial retreat, though dinner is best enjoyed outside on the patio.

Aberdare Country Club HOTEL **$$$**
(☎ 0737799990; www.aberdarecountryclub.com; s/d/tr full board US$180/305/434, day entry adult/child KSh1000/500; ⓟ 🛜 🏊) This stately stone club will transport you back to colonial days. For those without their own vehicle, it also acts as the staging post for the Ark (p154) in Aberdare National Park (p152). Rooms are enjoyably old world, with wooden furnishings, parquetry floors and even fireplaces in some rooms.

Eating

Raybells INTERNATIONAL $
(☑ 020-2370035; Kimathi Way; mains KSh150-500; ⊙6.30am-8pm) Pretty much anything you want to eat (well, anything Kenyan or Western) from pizza to *nyama choma* is available and cooked passably well here. You may want to avoid the fresh juice as it has tap water added to it.

Rayjo's Café KENYAN $
(Kimathi Way; meals KSh50-150; ⊙6am-8pm) This tiny canteen is usually packed with customers, including bus and matatu drivers, notoriously good judges of cheap places to eat. Emphasis on fish (mostly tilapia) and chips.

Green Hills Hotel INTERNATIONAL $$
(☑ 061-2030604; www.greenhills.co.ke; Bishop Gatimu Rd; mains/buffets KSh750/1650; ⊙6am-11pm; P🛜🐾) The full buffet here (when numbers permit) is an impressive piece of work, with some tasty mixed-grill options done up in a satisfyingly fancy fashion. Steaks are tender and come sizzling on a platter with a good mix of veggies, though the star dish is the *kuku wa kupaka* (chicken in spicy coconut milk).

ℹ Information

MONEY
Barclays (Kenyatta Rd; ⊙9am-4pm Mon-Fri, to noon Sat) One of several banks around town with an ATM; will exchange cash.

POST
Main Post Office (Kanisa Rd; ⊙7.45am-6pm Mon-Fri, 9am-1pm Sat) Send home postcards as well as larger items with the EMS courier service.
Post Office (Gakere Rd; ⊙7.45am-6pm Mon-Fri, 9am-1pm Sat) Good for stamps; near the lower bus stand.

ℹ Getting There & Away

The **Upper Bus Stand** deals with sporadic buses and a plethora of matatus to destinations north and west of Nyeri including Nanyuki (KSh250, one hour), Nyahururu (KSh350, 1¼ hours) and Nakuru (KSh550, 2½ hours).

From the **Lower Bus Stand**, matatus head in all directions south and east including Thika (KSh300, two hours) and Nairobi (KSh500, 2½ hours).

If you are without transport and want to explore the area surrounding Nyeri, head to the **local matatu** stand.

Matatu prices are always negotiable, so don't be afraid to shop around if you are on a tight budget.

Aberdare National Park

Boasting a large number of elephants as well as black rhinos, Aberdare National Park lures those who want more than just a safari. With dense forests, 300m-high waterfalls and amazing hikes, this park is as much about the flora as it is the fauna. While trekking, keep an eye open for bush pigs, rare black leopards and buffaloes.

⊙ Sights

Aberdare National Park NATIONAL PARK
(☑0772171247, Nairobi 020-2379407; www.kws.org; adult/child US$52/26; ⊙6am-6pm) Herds of wildlife thunder over an open African horizon, elephants emerge from a thicket of plants and the mysterious black rhino munches tranquilly on leaves. This is Aberdare National Park, packed with 300m-high waterfalls, dense forests and serious trekking potential. Also commonly seen here are buffaloes, black rhinos, spotted hyenas, bush pigs, black servals and rare black leopards.

Aberdare can claim some of Kenya's most dramatic up-country scenery. The fuzzy moors, in particular, possess a stark, wind-carved beauty, wholly unexpected after driving up from the richly cultivated plots of the eastern Aberdares. The park has two major environments: an eastern hedge of thick rainforest and waterfall-studded hills known as the Salient; and the Kinangop plateau, an open tableland of coarse moors that huddles under cold mountain breezes.

Karura Falls Lookout VIEWPOINT
The lookout gives a breathtaking view of the 50m waterfall dropping down through the forest. If you are short on time, enter via the Mutubio West Gate, which is roughly 8km from the lookout. It's a fairly easy 20-minute hike through the forest to view the falls.

🛏 Sleeping

Reedbuck Campsite CAMPGROUND $
(☑0774160327; www.kws.go.ke; camping per adult/child US$20/15; P) Reedbuck is one of Aberdare's public campsites. Located

Aberdare National Park

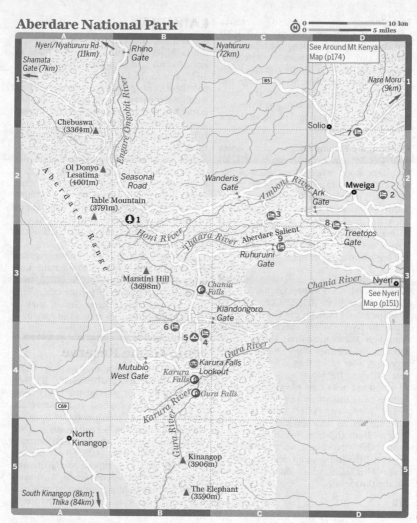

roughly 2.5km from the Kiandongoro Gate, the campsite has kitchen and ablution facilities for campers.

Sapper Hut   BANDAS **$**
(☎ 0774160327; www.kws.go.ke; bandas US$45)
A simple two-room cabin with an open fire, two beds and a hot-water boiler, overlooking a lovely waterfall on the Upper Magura River. It's best to bring your own gear and to use a 4WD vehicle to access the cabin, especially during the rainy season.

Aberdare National Park

⊙ **Sights**
1 Aberdare National Park B2

🛏 **Sleeping**
2 Aberdare Country Club D2
3 Ark C2
4 Kiandongoro Fishing Lodge B4
5 Reedbuck Campsite B4
6 Sapper Hut B4
7 Solio Game Reserve Lodge D2
8 Treetops D2
9 Tusk Camp C3

Tusk Camp
CABIN $$

(☑0774160327; www.kws.go.ke; cottages US$120) The Tusk Camp was undergoing minor renovations at the time of research, but we were assured that the cosy alpine cottage, located near Ruhuruini Gate, won't change too much. Comfortably sleeping six, the cabin has a comfy lounge area with great views (if the fog hasn't rolled in) and plenty of rhinos around if you're lucky.

Kiandongoro Fishing Lodge
CABIN $$

(☑0774160327; www.kws.go.ke; cottages US$210) Two large stone houses sleep seven people each and command a good view of the moors that sweep into the Gura River. There are two bathrooms in each house. All utensils and linens are provided, along with gas-powered kitchens, paraffin cookers and fireplaces. Four-wheel-drive vehicles are recommended and are essential in the rainy season.

★ Treetops
HISTORIC HOTEL $$$

(☑0722207761; www.treetops.co.ke; s/d US$234/360, s/d ste US$259/385; P@🖤) Treetops is sold through the Outspan Hotel (p151) in Nyeri, where check-in happens. From here guests must drive themselves to Treetops, where they dine, sleep and have breakfast, after which they leave at their leisure. Although the rooms are small, they are all kitted out with dark-wood floors, ochre feature walls and attractive prints.

The suites are better value than the standard rooms and you can request the Queen Elizabeth 'suite' (for the same price as the other two suites), where in 1952 the current British monarch learned of the death of her father, which led to her ascending the throne.

Ark
HOTEL $$$

(☑0737799990; www.thearkkenya.com; s/d US$195/315) The Ark dates from the 1960s, and has petite rooms and a lounge that overlooks a waterhole. An excellent walkway leads over a particularly dense stretch of the Salient, and from here and the waterhole lounge you can spot elephants, rhinos, buffaloes and hyenas.

❶ Getting There & Away

The best option is to drive or take a bus/matatu to Nyeri from Nairobi (KSh500, 2½ hours), which can be used as your staging point for the park. Most of the resorts inside the park can arrange transport, though it is easiest if you have your own wheels. It's a three-hour drive along the A2 from Nairobi to Nyeri.

LAIKIPIA

Set against the backdrop of Mt Kenya, the Laikipia Plateau extends over 9500 sq km of semi-arid plains, dramatic gouges and acacia-thicket-covered hills. This patchwork of privately owned ranches, wildlife conservancies and small-scale farms has become one of the most important areas for biodiversity in the country. It boasts wildlife densities second only to those found in the Masai Mara, is the last refuge of Kenya's African wild dogs and it's here that some of the most effective conservation work in the country is being done. Indeed, these vast plains are home to some of Kenya's highest populations of endangered species, including half of the country's black rhinos and half of the world's Grevy's zebras.

For more information on the region's ecosystems and wildlife, contact the **Laikipia Wildlife Forum** (☑0726500260; www.laikipia.org) and pick up a copy of *Laikipia – A Natural History Guide,* sold at many lodge gift shops across the region.

Solio Game Reserve

The family-run, private 71-sq-km **Solio Game Reserve** (☑0725786450; B5 Hwy; US$80, car KSh500), part of the larger Solio Ranch, is Kenya's oldest rhino sanctuary and an important breeding centre for black rhinos; many of the horned beasts you see wandering national parks were actually born here. Day visitors (US$80 per person) and lodge guests can experience the dramatic clumps of yellow-fever acacia, wide skies and wild marsh, plus an abundance of rhinos as well as oryxes, gazelles, hartebeests, giraffes, lions, hyenas and buffaloes.

🏃 Activities

Self-drive safaris are permitted and, while not necessary, it is helpful to be accompanied by a Solio guide (KSh500). Horse riding, mountain biking and helicopter trips are also part of the mix.

🛏 Sleeping

Solio Game Reserve Lodge
LODGE $$$

(☑Nairobi 020-5020888; www.thesafaricollection.com; s/d ste full board US$1368/1824; P🖤) Built in 2010, this upmarket lodge forsakes the classic look of so much safari accommodation and goes instead for a refreshing contemporary look – slick curves, white-washed walls and colourful prints. The suites are enormous and utterly gorgeous.

ⓘ Getting There & Away

The reserve is 22km north of Nyeri. If you do not have your own vehicle, you can fly into Nanyuki or Solio's private airstrip and the lodge can arrange a car and driver for you (at an extra charge).

Nyahururu (Thomson's Falls)

📞 065 / POP 36,450 / ELEV 2360M

This unexpectedly attractive town leaps out of the northwest corner of the highlands and makes a decent base for exploring the western edge of the Aberdares. Its former namesake, Thomson's Falls, are beautiful in their own right with great trekking potential when the security situation permits.

◎ Sights

Thomson's Falls WATERFALL
(adult/child KSh200/50; ⊙7am-6pm) Set back in an evergreen river valley and studded with sharp rocks and screaming baboons, the white cataracts plummet over 74m. The dramatic experience of looking up at the falls as baboons pad over the surrounding cliffs is worth the drenching you get from the falls' spray. While the vicinity of the falls is generally safe (minus several overbearing vendors), there have been incidents of serious assaults, particularly of women, on the nearby treks.

🛏 Sleeping

Safari Lodge HOTEL $
(📞065-2022334; Go Down Rd; s/d KSh800/1000; 🅿) Clean toilets with *seats;* big, soft beds with couches in the rooms; a nice balcony; TV and a place to charge your phone – what did we do to deserve this luxury? Especially at this price, which makes Safari one of the best budget deals around. Breakfast not included.

Thomson's Falls Lodge HOTEL $$
(📞065-2022006; www.thomsonsfallslodge.org; off B5 Hwy; camping KSh1200, s/d/tr US$80/100/140; 🅿🛜) While in need of a makeover, the lodge sits right above the falls and does a great job of instilling that good old 'I'm a colonial aristocrat on a hill-country holiday'

vibe. Rooms are spacious but cosy, thanks in no small part to the log fireplaces.

Panari Resort HOTEL $$$
(📞0709070000; www.panariresort.com; off B5 Hwy; s/d/tr KSh15,300/17,100/18,900, cottage s/d/tr KSh17,000/19,000/21,000; 🅿❄🛜🏊) Opened in March 2016, this is the most luxurious spot in Nyahururu. With sprawling grounds, plush grass and loads of activities for the family, this is the place to splurge. The rooms are large, though minimal, with a big fireplace for winter nights. Some cottage rooms have direct views of the falls.

🍴 Eating

Club Comfort KENYAN $
(📞065-2022326; mains KSh150-600; ⊙6am-midnight) To eat with the locals, head here and unleash your inner carnivore as you chow down a 1kg plate of *nyama choma.* The food isn't the quickest, so bring a book or brush up on your Swahili with the local crowd.

Thomson's Falls Lodge BUFFET $$
(📞065-2022006; www.thomsonsfallslodge.co.ke; breakfast/lunch/dinner buffet KSh1250/1500/1500; ⊙6am-9pm) The lodge's restaurant offers a set buffet for each of the day's three meals, and while they're pricey for this area, you'll

Nyahururu

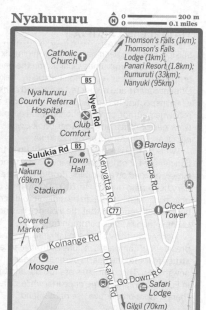

walk away well stuffed and satisfied. You can also bring your own picnic and sit outside on a lush lawn overlooking Thomson's Falls (p155).

Panari Resort
BUFFET $$$

(☑ 0709070000; www.thepanariresort.com; off B5 Hwy; mains KSh600-1700, breakfast/lunch/dinner buffet KSh2000/3000/3000; ⊘ 7am-10pm; P ⛱) The most upscale restaurant in Nyahururu; you can order off the menu though everything is also offered at the buffet. While there is no mistaking that the cold and impersonal restaurant is inside a hotel (p155), the food is tasty and you won't leave hungry.

ⓘ Information

MEDICAL SERVICES

Nyahururu County Referral Hospital (B5 Hwy, opposite police station; ⊘ 24hr) The hospital provides a variety of services, from X-rays to vaccinations, though expect a long wait to be seen by a doctor.

MONEY

Barclays (cnr Sulukia & Sharpe Rds; ⊘ 9am-4pm Mon-Fri, to noon Sat) Full-service bank with 24-hour ATM.

POLICE STATIONS

Nyahururu Police Station (B5 Hwy, opposite hospital; ⊘ 24hr) The police station is often busy, but the officers are friendly and ready to help if you meet some bad luck. It is located directly opposite Nyahururu County Referral Hospital.

ⓘ Getting There & Away

There are numerous matatus that run from the **Bus & Matatu Station** (Ol Kalou Rd) to Nakuru (KSh220, 1¼ hours) and Nyeri (KSh350, 1¾ hours) until late afternoon. Less plentiful are services to Naivasha (KSh400, two hours), Nanyuki (KSh420, three hours) and Nairobi (KSh500, 3½ hours). The occasional morning matatu reaches Maralal (KSh600, four hours).

Several early-morning buses also serve Nairobi (KSh450, three hours).

Don't be afraid to haggle or shop around for the best-priced matatu.

Nanyuki

☑ 062 / POP 49,233

Nanyuki serves as a gateway to the Laikipia Plateau, one of Africa's most important wildlife conservation areas. Despite being a market town, it is probably the most cosmopolitan city in the area outside of Nairobi, with its share of international tourists (here to climb Mt Kenya or to visit the myriad safari parks), British Army soldiers (there is a training facility nearby) and Kenyan Air

TROUBLE IN LAIKIPIA

Laikipia has long been held up as a shining example of a partnership between conservation and local communities, balancing the needs of local livestock herders with wildlife protection. But this reputation has been shaken recently. In March 2017, founder of Offbeat Safaris and respected guide and conservationist Tristan Voorspuy was killed while inspecting his Sosian Lodge in Laikipia after an arson attack. The following month, renowned author, conservationist and Laikipia resident Kuki Gallmann, who wrote I Dreamed of Africa among other books, was shot and critically injured while patrolling her Ol Ari Nyiro ranch, also in Laikipia.

While no tourists have been caught up in the violence, the developments are deeply concerning for other ranches and conservancies in the region. The violence has been largely blamed on a crippling drought that has prompted armed cattle rustlers and ordinary herders to drive up to 200,000 head of livestock onto the Laikipia Plateau in search of grazing. Although it can be difficult to disentangle the various parties involved, it has been widely reported that the violence has been led more by armed gangs from beyond Laikipia than by local communities.

Worryingly, the violence in Laikipia became a political football during the August 2017 presidential campaign. In June of that year, leading opposition candidate Raila Odinga struck fear into the hearts of ranch owners in the area when he told the London Times newspaper, 'These ranches are too big and the people don't even live there; they live in Europe and only come once in a while... There's a need for rationalisation to ensure there's more productive use of that land.'

MUGIE CONSERVANCY

At the very western edge of the Laikipia Plateau, the **Mugie Conservancy** (☑0722385727; www.mugie.org; adult day visitor US$50) is a 200-sq-km private wildlife reserve. It's crawling with heavyweight animals – almost half of the ranch is given over to the 89-sq-km **Mugie Sanctuary** with big cats, elephants, Grevy's zebras and endangered Jackson's hartebeests. Even if you are not staying overnight, you can still enter the park as a day visitor.

Sadly there are no longer any rhinos – poaching forced the ranch to move the remaining 25 rhinos in 2012 to other sites around the country.

High on an escarpment overlooking Mugie Conservancy, **Mutamaiyu House** (☑0722385727; www.mugie.org; s/d full board US$470/860; ☒) has six attractive cottages, each with big glass windows to take advantage of the views.

At the time of research, there was an increase in the number of cattle-rustler incidents (people either wanting land for their own cattle or to steal cattle) on the ranch, so all extra activities, such as golf and horse riding, were put on hold, though wildlife-watching drives were still functioning.

Force pilots (this is the site of the country's main air-force base).

◉ Sights & Activities

Nanyuki is a popular base for launching expeditions to climb Mt Kenya's Sirimon or Burguret routes. Otherwise, you should stroll 3km south to the **equator** (there's a sign) and get a lesson from the men who make a living giving demonstrations of the Coriolis effect.

Mt Kenya Wildlife Conservancy Animal Orphanage ZOO
(☑Nairobi 020-2330079; www.animalorphanagekenya.org; Mt Kenya Safari Club; per person KSh1500; ☉10am-5pm; ☒) It may come off a little zoo-like at first but this orphanage is one of the few places in the world to have successfully bred the rare mountain bongo. Its success is such that there are now plans to release some of the captive-bred antelope into the Mt Kenya forests to bolster the current population of around 70. Children, and anyone who wants to have a baby monkey scramble over their head, will love this place.

☞ Tours

Montana Trek & Information Centre TREKKING
(☑062-2037231; www.montanatrekks.com; Lumumba Rd; 4-day trip per person US$750-810) This community-based association has friendly and knowledgeable guides. The centre is particularly useful for Sirimon trekkers.

🛏 Sleeping

Acacia Apartments & Villas APARTMENT $
(☑0713906349, 0722312300; nanyukiacacia@gmail.com; off the A2 Nyeri–Nanyuki Hwy; r from KSh2000; ℗☎) Located slightly out of town on the way to Mt Kenya Safari Club (p158), this is the best budget option in the area. Each apartment has two en-suite bedrooms, a full kitchen with microwave and stove, and a lounge with couches and TV. There is also a balcony attached to each room, as well as the lounge.

Kirimara Springs Hotel HOTEL $
(☑0726370191; www.kirimarapringshotel.com; Kenyatta Ave; s/d/tw KSh2500/3200/4500; ℗☎) While Kirimara isn't going to win any architecture awards, and its website's claim that the rooms are comfortable and luxuriously furnished is absurd, the spacious, bright rooms are cleaner and cheaper than others in this price bracket. Rooms on the western side of the building catch less traffic noise, while those on the east get Mt Kenya glimpses. Friendly staff.

Nanyuki River Camel Camp HUT $
(☑0722361642; www.fieldoutdoor.com; camping KSh1250, huts with shared bathroom KSh5000) The most innovative sleep in town (well, 4km outside of it, off the C76 Hwy) is this ecocamp, set in a dry swab of scrub. The camp offers lodging in genuine Somali grass-and-camelskin huts imported from Mandera; they have been relocated to sit close to the Nanyuki River.

Nanyuki

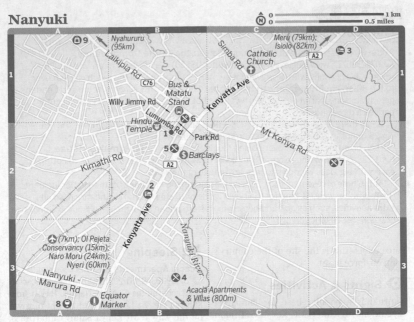

Nanyuki map. Scale: 0 — 1 km / 0 — 0.5 miles. N

Labels visible on map: Nyahururu (95km), Laikipia Rd, C76, Willy Jimmy Rd, Bus & Matatu Stand, Hindu Temple, Lumumba Rd, Park Rd, Kimathi Rd, A2, Barclays, Kenyatta Ave, Simba Rd, Catholic Church, Meru (79km); Isiolo (82km), A2, Mt Kenya Rd, Kenyatta Ave, Nanyuki River, (7km); Ol Pejeta Conservancy (15km); Naro Moru (24km); Nyeri (60km), Nanyuki - Marura Rd, Equator Marker, Acacia Apartments & Villas (800m)

Nanyuki

🟢 Activities, Courses & Tours
1 Montana Trek & Information
   Centre B2

🛏 Sleeping
2 Kirimara Springs Hotel B2
3 Kongoni Camp D1

✴ Eating
4 Cape Chestnut B3
5 Coffee Shack B2
  Kongoni Camp .... (see 3)
6 Kungu Maitu Hotel & Butchery B1
7 Le Rustique D2

🟢 Drinking & Nightlife
8 Painted Dog A3

🟢 Shopping
9 Nanyuki Spinners & Weavers A1

Best known for its camel treks, it's a good idea to give staff at least 48 hours advance notice as the camels are often grazed many kilometres away. Somali food such as *nyiri nyiri* (fried camel jerky with cardamom) is a house speciality but also requires advance notice.

★ Kongoni Camp   BANDAS $$
(📞0702868888, 062-2031225; www.kongoni camp.com; s/d KSh6700/12,500; 🅿@🛜) Founded by a friendly local-turned-Londoner-turned-local-again, Kongoni has five, concrete circular *bandas* as well as some newer rooms that are simple but designed with a touch of safari flair. It's one of the few genuinely midrange options around town and there's a large restaurant-cum-bar with a varied menu.

★ Mt Kenya Safari Club   HOTEL $$$
(📞Nairobi 020-2265555; www.fairmont.com; d from US$533; 🅿@🛜🏊) This is the kind of place that makes you want to grow a moustache, kick back and smoke a pipe. The rooms have a luxurious, classic look to them and are decorated to a sumptuous standard, all with their own open fires and exquisite bathrooms. The whole shebang overlooks the Mt Kenya Wildlife Conservancy (p157).

🍴 Eating

Kungu Maitu Hotel & Butchery   KENYAN $
(off Laikipia Rd; meals KSh200; ⊙8am-10pm) Friendly and utterly local, this simple place serves up Nanyuki's best barbecued meats. Choose your cuts of meat, order a chapati or

samosa to go with them and wait for it all to appear at your table. We found the toilets to be bearable only if you hold your breath and close your eyes – if you can wait, do so.

★ **Le Rustique** INTERNATIONAL $$
(📞0721609601; www.lerustique.co.ke; Mt Kenya Rd; mains KSh700-1500; ⏰8am-10pm; 🛜🚻) This one-time Nairobi favourite has upped sticks and headed north to Nanyuki. The fare, overseen to every last detail by owner Maike Potgieter, is superb, with pizzas, crêpes and an excellent wine list. But the atmosphere is as much of a drawcard, with an open fireplace for those cold Laikipia evenings or the quiet garden for warmer days.

Kongoni Camp INDIAN, INTERNATIONAL $$
(📞0702868888; www.kongonicamp.com; mains KSh800-1900; ⏰6am-10pm; 🛜🚻) One of the top restaurants in Nanyuki with a large variety of international dishes – hamburgers, steak, pizza – though its speciality is Indian food. With a proper tandoor oven, this place can cure any naan bread and chicken tikka masala cravings you may have! Ask about its 'top shelf' whisky collection for an after-dinner treat.

Barney's Bar & Restaurant INTERNATIONAL $$
(📞0723310064; mains KSh950-1190; ⏰7am-6pm; 🅿🛜🚻) If you are a plane enthusiast, then this is the place for you. Located inside the Nanyuki Airport, next to the runway, you can enjoy a pizza from the wood-fired oven or a plate of ribs while you wait for your flight.

Coffee Shack CAFE $$
(📞0702689163; Kenyatta Ave; mains KSh700-900; ⏰7.30am-6pm Mon-Sat) This family-run hip and artsy place across from Barclays offers a large variety of milkshakes and smoothies, along with the essential burgers and Kenyan cuisine.

Cape Chestnut INTERNATIONAL $$
(📞0705250650; www.capechestnut.com; mains from KSh700; ⏰8.30am-5pm Sat-Thu, to 11.30pm Fri; 🛜) This coffee garden is a terrific place to come to eat, a little removed from the Nanyuki scrum. The menu is always changing so check the board when you arrive. The atmosphere is relaxed and popular with local expats. Friday is tapas night. It's off Kenyatta Ave, 1km south of town.

Tusks Restaurant INTERNATIONAL, BUFFET $$$
(Mt Kenya Safari Club; lunch buffet KSh3500, dinner 4-course set menu KSh3500;

⏰12.30-2.30pm & 6.30-9.30pm) If you are looking to splurge then this place at the Mt Kenya Safari Club (p158) is the place to do so. Sink back into a sofa in the drawing room or saunter over to the pool and take in the vista. The buffet lunch is varied and outstanding, while the dinner set menu is equally memorable.

Cocktails in the adjacent ZeBar include a gemstone martini (with blue topaz, for example) – just be sure you don't accidentally swallow it (the gemstone that is...).

🍷 Drinking & Nightlife

Painted Dog BAR
(📞0799899970; mains Ksh800; ⏰11am-11pm) In the space where Lily Pond Arts Centre used to be, the Painted Dog is now a full-on expat bar, complete with happy-hour specials (5pm to 7pm), movie night (Tuesday) and chicken wings. The outside patio overlooks the river and is a nice place for a beer during the day.

🛍 Shopping

Nanyuki Spinners & Weavers CLOTHING
(📞0720220899; http://nanyukispinnersand weavers.org; C76 Hwy; ⏰hours vary) Started in 1977 and now providing employment to 107 women, this craft cooperative specialises in high-quality woven woollen goods. The women will show you the process of spinning, cleaning and dyeing the wool before you browse the selection of rugs and shawls. The store is a short walk past the main market on Laikipia Rd.

ℹ Information

Barclays (Kenyatta Ave; ⏰9am-4pm Mon-Fri, to noon Sat) Reliable ATMs.

ℹ Getting There & Away

Nanyuki is well connected to all points north and south as well as most major Rift Valley towns from the bus and matatu stand. Sample matatu fares include Nyeri (KSh250, one hour), Isiolo (KSh280, 1½ hours), Meru (KSh250, 1½ hours), Nakuru (KSh650, three hours) and Nairobi (KSh500, three hours).

Airkenya (p385) and Safarilink (p385) both connect Nairobi's Wilson Airport and Nanyuki (one way adult/child US$190/150). **Tropic Air** (📞071-5018740; www.tropicairkenya.com; Nanyuki Airport; flights US$470-6000) offers charter-helicopter and light-aircraft services from **Nanyuki Airport** (📞0722714000; off A2 Hwy).

Segera Ranch

North of Ol Pejeta Conservancy in southern Laikipia, this 202-sq-km ranch is a perfect example of how Laikipia works. It's a model cattle ranch, but wildlife is also prolific here, including the three big cats, elephants, buffaloes and endangered species such as Grevy's zebra (15 of them at last count), Patas monkey (a small troop lives along the ranch's eastern border) and the reticulated giraffe. The landscape here is classic Laikipia terrain – seemingly endless savannah country cut through with rocky river valleys and riverine woodland.

The ranch is owned by philanthropist Jochen Zeitz, whose **Zeitz Foundation** (www.zeitzfoundation.org) is active in local community projects with local schools, women's groups and the Samuel Eto'o Soccer Academy for budding football stars. The foundation's philosophy is based on the 'Four Cs' – conservation, community, culture and commerce.

🛌 Sleeping

★ Segera Retreat   LODGE $$$

(www.segera.com; s/d all-inclusive US$1190/2100, villas from US$1400; P ❄ 🛜 🏊) We can be difficult to impress, but this place left us speechless. Six villas and a couple of houses inhabit an oasis in the heart of the ranch, looking out onto the savannah, yet enclosed within their own natural compound that keeps dangerous animals out. The villas are utterly magnificent – spacious, luxurious in every way and steeped in safari tradition.

It's no coincidence that the villas capture perfectly that *Out of Africa* longing that caused a generation of would-be travellers to fall in love with the continent – one of the bar areas is strewn with original letters and personal effects of Karen Blixen, and the retreat even has the plane that was used in the movie (flights can be arranged). The food, too, is memorable, and there's a wine list to match. There's a spa, hi-tech gym, sculpture garden and thought-provoking installations of African contemporary art that fill the ranch's artfully converted stables.

❶ Getting There & Away

Segera is roughly 50km from Nanyuki, off the C76 Hwy. Segera Retreat can organise a car and driver for you if you do not have your own wheels.

Ol Pejeta Conservancy

Once one of the largest cattle ranches in Kenya, **Ol Pejeta Conservancy** (✆0707187141, 0735801101; www.olpejetaconservancy.org; adult/child/student US$85/42/21, vehicle from KSh400; ⊗7am-7pm) is now a 365-sq-km, privately owned wildlife reserve. It markets itself as the closest place to Nairobi where you can see the Big Five and possesses a full palette of African plains wildlife. It's also one of the few private conservancies in the region that is geared towards day visitors.

It's the rhinos that form the centrepiece of the conservancy effort here – its (at last count) 111 black rhinos form the largest population in East Africa. However, Ol Pejeta's role in the wider ecosystem extends beyond its boundaries thanks to its partner agreements and wildlife corridors with other Laikipia ranches. Ol Pejeta is also extremely active in local community projects including school infrastructure, health care and the provision of clean water.

◉ Sights

★ Endangered Species Enclosure   ZOO

(adult/child US$40/20) This 283-hectare drive-through enclosure next to the Morani Information Centre is home to the last three remaining northern white rhinos (one male and two females), an ever-so-close-to-being-extinct subspecies. The rhinos were brought here from the Dvur Kralove Zoo in the Czech Republic in 2009, but have not yet bred successfully. Also in the enclosure are the endangered Grevy's zebra and Jackson's hartebeest.

Chimpanzee Sanctuary   ZOO

(⊗10am-4.30pm) FREE Home to 39 profoundly damaged chimpanzees rescued from captivity across Africa and further afield, Ol Pejeta's Chimp Sanctuary encompasses two large enclosures cut in two by the Ewaso Ngiro River. There's an elevated observation post and keepers are usually on hand to explain a little about each chimp's backstory; note the tiny replica cage in which one of the chimps was chained for years on end prior to being brought to the sanctuary.

Morani Information Centre   MUSEUM

(⊗7am-6.30pm) FREE Part education or interpretation centre, part museum, this three-roomed structure is appealingly interactive and comes with instructions to 'please touch' the leopard skin, antelope horns and other similar objects. You'll also find displays and information on Ol Pejeta's predator-proof *bomas* (cattle enclosures designed to keep predators out) and the history of the conservancy's rhino conservation work.

🏃 Activities

The conservancy has many activities, such as **bird walks**, **guided bush walks**, **night wildlife viewing** and **dog tracking**, which you can arrange at the park gate or through your accommodation; each costs US$40/20 per adult/child.

The conservancy is now cashless. You can pre-pay online or via card or bank transfer.

★ Lion-tracking   WILDLIFE
(adult/child US$40/20) Easily our pick of the activities on offer, this nightly excursion trains you in the art of identifying individual lions and takes you out to find them using radio receivers. The data you gather forms part of the conservancy's database on Ol Pejeta's estimated 65 to 70 resident lions. The rangers will collect you from your accommodation.

Hippo Hide Walk   WALKING
(⏰7am-6.30pm) **FREE** This 20-minute meander along the riverbank happens in the company of a knowledgeable local ranger – hopefully you'll see hippos but it's worth doing even if you don't. Open to day visitors, there is no set schedule for the walks, but you can request one of the standby rangers to take you.

☞ Tours

Rift Valley Adventures   CYCLING, ADVENTURE
(📞0707734776; www.riftvalleyadventures.com; half-/full-day cycling tour from US$70/120) This highly recommended operator runs cycling tours through Ol Pejeta, as well as trekking, climbing, canyoning and whitewater rafting in the Mt Kenya area.

🛏 Sleeping

Ol Lerai Campsite   CAMPGROUND $
(📞0707187141; info@olpejetaconservancy.org; camping adult/child KSh1000/500) This attractive campsite on the Ewaso Ngiro River is right in the conservancy's centre and you're likely to be visited by elephants and other wildlife.

Ewaso Campsite   CAMPGROUND $
(📞0707187141; www.olpejetaconservancy.org; camping adult/child KSh1000/500) Protected by dense foliage but with good river views, this is probably the pick of the sites in the park centre.

Ngobit Campsite   CAMPGROUND $
(📞0707187141; info@olpejetaconservancy.org; camping adult/child KSh1000/500) Along the Ngobit River in the conservancy's far south, this is the quietest of Ol Pejeta's campsites.

★ Sweetwaters
Serena Camp   TENTED CAMP $$$
(📞0732123333; www.serenahotels.com; s/d full board from US$373/506; P 🛜 🌊) The 56 large and beautifully appointed en-suite tents by the reliable Serena chain are high-end but with prices that are more accessible than those of other properties. The central location is a plus (handy for most of the conservancy) and a minus (things can get busy around here), depending on your perspective.

★ Kicheche Laikipia   TENTED CAMP $$$
(📞Nairobi 020-2493569; www.kicheche.com; s/d all-inclusive US$700/1400; P) Close to the geographical centre of the park and overlooking a waterhole, this excellent tented camp has six stylishly furnished tents, an overall air of sophistication and impeccable service. It's Ol Pejeta's most exclusive accommodation.

Porini Rhino Camp   TENTED CAMP $$$
(📞0774136523; www.porini.com; r from US$445; ⏰closed mid-Apr–May; P) 🌿 Out in the far east of Ol Pejeta, Porini Rhino Camp overlooks a small stream, nicely removed

---

ⓘ OL PEJETA CONSERVANCY

Why Go East Africa's largest black-rhino population; excellent wildlife viewing and activities; most accessible of the Laikipia conservancies.

When to Go Year-round, although you'll need a 4WD from late March to late May.

Practicalities Only the Serat Gate and main Rongai Gate (both in the conservancy's east) are open to visitors.

Budget Tips Rent a matatu for the day with other travellers in Nanyuki; if staying overnight, stay at one of the campsites.

from the crowds of day trippers that visit the conservancy. The tents themselves are comfortable rather than luxurious, service is friendly, the food is excellent and, as with most Porini properties, the camp supports local conservation projects. Keep an eye out for rhinos.

Ol Pejeta House
LODGE $$$

(Nairobi 020-2842333; www.serenahotels.com; s/d full board US$373/506; P 🛜 🌊) As you'd expect from the former home of multi-billionaire Adnan Khashoggi, this imposing lodge has over-the-top decor and high levels of comfort. Avoid coming here on weekends, when it tends to fill up with a Nairobi crowd that likes to party. Rates tend to fluctuate; check the website for specials.

✖️ Eating

Safari Diner
FAST FOOD $

(0706160114; www.olpejetaconservancy.org; mains KSh200-800; ⏰ 8am-5pm) Located next to Morani's Restaurant, this small diner has a patio where you can grab a quick bite to eat before heading to the Endangered Species Enclosure (p160) or back out into the park. If there is a school group here when you arrive, it might actually be quicker, and more peaceful, to head to the restaurant.

Morani's Restaurant
CAFE $$

(0706160114; www.moranisrestaurant.com; mains KSh750-1000; ⏰ 8am-5pm) Next to the Morani Information Centre (p160), this terrific little cafe with outdoor tables serves up excellent dishes that range from the Morani burger made from prime Ol Pejeta beef to Kenyan beef stew or a Mediterranean wrap. Fresh juices, fine smoothies and Kenyan coffee round out an excellent package.

ℹ️ Information

MAPS
Pick up a copy of the *Ol Pejeta Conservancy* map (KSh700) from the entrance gate or download it for free from the website (www.olpejetaconservancy.org).

TOURIST INFORMATION
Useful (and free) resources include the *Mammal Checklist, Bird Checklist* and *Chimpanzee Factfile*, which are available at the entrance gate or your accommodation.

ℹ️ Getting There & Away
Ol Pejeta is 15km southwest of Nanyuki, which also has the nearest airport (p159). It's well signposted. The last 9km is a gravel road, but more than passable without a 4WD.

Lewa Wildlife Conservancy

Although technically not a part of Laikipia, **Lewa Wildlife Conservancy** (LWC; 064-3131405, 0722203562; www.lewa.org; conservation fee per adult/child per night US$105/53), a vast region of open savannah grasslands that falls away from the Mt Kenya highlands, is very much a part of Laikipia's story. It was at Lewa that the conservancy idea was pioneered and it remains a leader in all of the elements – serious wildlife protection wedded to innovative community engagement – that have come to define the private conservancies of Laikipia and elsewhere.

Apart from anything else, Lewa ranks among the premier wildlife-watching territories anywhere in Kenya. And unlike in Kenya's national parks, where off-road driving is prohibited, Lewa's guides delight in taking visitors to almost within touching distance of rhinos, elephants and other species.

🏃 Activities
Day and night wildlife drives are included with accommodation, though numerous other activities are available, such as

---

ℹ️ LEWA WILDLIFE CONSERVANCY

Why Go For some of the finest wildlife viewing in Kenya; almost guaranteed sightings of all the Big Five; walking safaris and night safaris. No minibus circus.

When to Go Year-round, but the dry season (June to October) is best.

Practicalities Lewa is closed to casual visitors: you must be staying at one of the (very expensive) lodges in order to enter. Most visitors fly in from Nairobi but road access is easy from Isiolo or the Central Highlands.

Budget Tips Not suitable for budget travellers.

THE LEWA STORY

Like so many Laikipia properties that later became wildlife conservancies, Lewa Downs was an expansive cattle ranch owned since colonial times by white settlers. In 1983, the owners, the Craig family, along with pioneering rhino conservationist Anna Merz, set aside 20 sq km of Lewa as the Ngare Sergoi Rhino Sanctuary. They received their first rhino a year later, and the numbers grew to 16 in 1988. The Craigs doubled the sanctuary's size, and by 1994 the entire cattle ranch (along with the adjacent Ngare Ndare Forest Reserve) was enclosed within an electric fence to create a 251-sq-km rhino sanctuary. The Lewa Wildlife Conservancy in its current form was formed in 1995.

True to its origins as a sanctuary to save Kenya's rhinos, Lewa's primary conservation focus continues to be rhinos. Lewa suffered not a single poaching event between 1983 and 2009 – the joke doing the rounds of the conservation community for much of this time was that Lewa was 'State House' (Kenya's presidential palace) for rhinos. Sadly, poaching has been on the rise ever since, with six of Lewa's rhinos killed in 2013, prompting a massive investment in anti-poaching operations. Since the start of these operations, Lewa has not had a single incident of rhino poaching.

At last count, Lewa was home to 83 black rhinos and 74 white rhinos (that's around 15% of the Kenyan total). And despite the poaching, the conservancy is close to its carrying capacity for rhinos. In 2014, the fence that separated Lewa from the 142-sq-km Borana Conservancy (p165) to the west was torn down, effectively increasing the size of the rhino sanctuary by 25%.

Rhinos aside, Lewa's conservation effort has been astounding and 20% of the world's Grevy's zebras call the reserve home.

Central to the Lewa model is a serious commitment to community development, fuelled by a recognition that local people are far more likely to protect wildlife if they have a stake (financial or otherwise) in its survival. Lewa Wildlife Conservancy is a non-profit organisation that invests around 70% of its annual US$2.5-million-plus budget into health care, education and various community projects for surrounding villages.

In 2013, Lewa Wildlife Conservancy was inscribed on Unesco's World Heritage list as an extension to the existing Mt Kenya National Park/Natural Forest site.

excursions to Il Ngwesi, walking safaris, quad biking, horseback riding and scenic flights.

The following activities (with sample per-person prices) can be booked through your accommodation.

➨ Il Ngwesi Excursions: US$40, half-day

➨ Tour of Lewa Wildlife Conservancy's HQ: Free (US$10 if you visit the tracker dogs), one to two hours

➨ Orphan Rhino Project: US$15, 30 minutes (this was where the moving final scene in Sir David Attenborough's Africa series was filmed)

➨ Visit to local school: US$50 donation

➨ Horse-riding safari: US$55, one hour

➨ Walking safari in Ngare Ndare Forest: US$30 conservation fee, one to three hours

➨ Quad bike/buggy safari: Price on application

➨ Flying safari: Price on application

☆☆ Festivals & Events

Lewa Safaricom Marathon   SPORTS
(www.safaricom.co.ke/safaricommarathon; adult/child KSh15,000/3000; ☉ late Jun/early Jul) It's one thing to run a marathon to the encouraging screams of people, but it's entirely another to run it sharing the course with elephants, rhinos and the odd lion! Established in 2000 to raise funds for wildlife conservation and community development, the Safaricom Marathon, run within the Lewa Wildlife Conservancy (p162), is renowned as one of the planet's toughest marathons.

🛏 Sleeping

★**Lewa Safari Camp**   TENTED CAMP $$$
(☎ 0730127000; www.lewasafaricamp.com; s/d all-inclusive US$921/1228; ☎ ☎) This impressive property lies in the northwest corner of the conservancy, about an hour's drive from the main Matunda Gate. Its safari tents are large and have that whole chic-bush-living thing down to a tee; they're arrayed around

a shallow valley and large wildlife is kept out so you can walk around freely (although you'll be given an escort at night).

Kifaru
LODGE $$$

(☏ Nairobi 020-2127844; www.kifaruhouse.com; per person all-inclusive US$1250; ☏ ✉) Luxury hilltop *bandas* with no expense spared, not to mention fine views over the plains and an air of exclusivity with no more than 12 guests in camp at any one time.

Lewa House
COTTAGE $$$

(☏ 0710781303; www.lewahouse.com; r & earth pod from US$1060, cottage from US$1800, all-inclusive; ☏ ✉) Close to the centre of the park. Apart from the main house, try the daringly designed 'earth pods' with curved walls, earth tones and superior levels of comfort.

Lewa Wilderness
COTTAGE $$$

(☏ 0796035177; www.lewawilderness.com; s/d full board from US$1060/1800; ☏ ✉) Nine cottages owned and run by the Craig family in Lewa's east. Rooms are classic safari in style and faultlessly luxurious.

Sirikoi
LODGE $$$

(☏ 0727232445; www.sirikoi.com; s/d tents all-inclusive US$1175/1970, 4-bed cottage US$4665, 6-person house US$7000; ☏ ✉) Stunning rooms in luxury tents, cottages and in the main house in the heart of the conservancy.

🛈 Getting There & Away

The turn-off to Lewa Wildlife Conservancy is only 12km south of Isiolo (the entrance gate is another 5km on) and is well signposted on the A2 Hwy.

LAIKIPIA LODGES

Virtually all of Laikipia's lodges and camps (now numbering close to 50) fall squarely into the luxurious bracket and cater to the well-heeled who visit as part of prepackaged tours. The vast majority of the parks do not allow camping, though there are cheaper hotels available in the nearby towns.

Sanctuary at Ol-Lentille (☏ 079-5440411; www.ol-lentille.com; s/d all-inclusive US$920/1540, conservation fee per person per night US$80; @ ☏ ✉) Utter exclusivity is the aim at this 97-sq-km conservancy sporting a series of opulent digs with names like 'The Sultan's House' and 'The Chief's House'; each comes with a private butler service. It's in the northwestern reaches of Laikipia and wildlife in the area includes elephants, Grevy's zebras, lions, leopards, giraffes and African wild dogs.

El Karama Eco Lodge (☏ WhatsApp 070-2996902; www.elkaramalodge.com; off C76 Hwy; adult/child full board US$400/200, conservation fee per adult/child per night US$70/35; P @ ✉) One of the most affordable places in the region. There are luxury tents where you can laze in your hammock overlooking the Ewaso Ngiro River, or if you're on a budget, opt for the basic (but still comfortable) tent with a bucket shower (full board US$300). Alternatively, try the campsite (KSh10,000 for up to five people, KSh2500 per extra person).

Children will love the wide variety of activities available, especially the wildlife tracking where they can make clay moulds of different animal tracks. Day visitors are welcome and the package (KSh4500 plus conservation fee) includes lunch, drinks and pool access. If you want to make use of the lodge's vehicle for wildlife viewing, it will cost an extra US$75.

Loisaba Tented Camp (☏ 071-2042982, Nairobi 073-0127000; www.loisaba.com; s/d all-inclusive US$975/1300; P ☏ ✉) Refined accommodation (including four-poster beds under the stars) on a 247-sq-km ranch in northern Laikipia plus activities that range from walking safaris and wildlife viewing to fishing, horse riding and camel safaris (the latter two activities are not included in quoted rates).

Ol Malo (☏ 0721630686, Nairobi 020-6000457; www.olmalo.com; s/d all-inclusive US$1115/1900, conservation fee per person per night US$80; ☺ closed Apr-May & Nov; ✉) Posh rock and olive-wood cottages in a stunning setting close to the Ewaso Ngiro River make this a fine choice. The surrounding conservancy is quite small, but that's not how it feels from the infinity swimming pool with views to the very distant horizon. The rooms have soaring thatched ceilings, stone-tiled floors and earth tones throughout. It's in northwestern Laikipia.

Private vehicles are not generally allowed into Lewa. Those arriving by private vehicle will have to leave their car at the entrance gate and change to a lodge-provided jeep.

Airkenya (p385) and Safarilink (p385) provide daily flights between Lewa and Nairobi's Wilson Airport (adult one way US$250), sometimes via Nanyuki.

Il Ngwesi Group Ranch

Il Ngwesi is a fine example of a private conservation project linking wildlife conservation and community development, albeit on a smaller scale than seen elsewhere. The Maasai of Il Ngwesi (the name Il Ngwesi translates as 'people of wildlife'), with help from the neighbouring Lewa Wildlife Conservancy (p162), have transformed this undeveloped land, previously used for subsistence pastoralism, into a prime wildlife conservation area hosting white and black rhinos, waterbucks, giraffes and other plains animals.

The south is quite steeply contoured in places, but the highest point (Sanga, at 1907m) lies on Il Ngwesi's western boundary. The northern lowlands mostly consist of light woodland. Just outside the eastern border of Il Ngwesi, Maasai, Turkana and Samburu villages line the trackside.

🛏 Sleeping

Il Ngwesi Eco Lodge   LODGE $$$
(☑0741770540, Nairobi 020-2033122; www.ilngwesi.com; s/d all-inclusive US$500/850; 🕮)
🌿 Il Ngwesi community supplements its herding income with tourist dollars gained from this award winning ecolodge. The divine open-fronted thatched cottages here boast views over the dramatic escarpment, and at night the beds in some rooms can be pulled out onto the private 'terraces', allowing you to snooze under the Milky Way. Profits go straight to the Maasai community.

ℹ Getting There & Away

Il Ngwesi is north of Lewa and accessed off the main Isiolo to Nairobi Rd. **Lewa Safari Camp** (p163) organises half-day visits to Il Ngwesi from Lewa, which include visits to a Maasai *manyatta* (village), nature walks and explanations of Maasai tradition.

Borana Conservancy

One of the longest-standing conservancies in the area, the Borana cattle ranch (now

---

the **Borana Conservancy** (☑0727735578; www.borana.co.ke)), owned by the Dyer family for three generations, turned its focus onto wildlife and community projects in 1992. This beautiful 142-sq-km conservancy suddenly became a whole lot more attractive in 2013, when rhinos from Lewa Wildlife Conservancy (p162) were translocated here. The following year the fence between Borana and Lewa was torn down. What that means is that Borana is now an integral part of one of Kenya's most important rhino sanctuaries. It's perfect rhino habitat (14 rhinos were born on the conservancy in 2016) and seeing African wild dogs (as well as, at last count, 18 lions and other plains species) is also a possibility here.

As it is something of a Laikipia trademark, Borana ploughs its money into antipoaching operations, community development and grasslands habitat management.

🛏 Sleeping

Borana Lodge   LODGE $$$
(☑0721702770, 0727735578; www.borana.co.ke; s/d all-inclusive US$736/1240, conservation fee per adult/child US$105/53; 🕮🕮) On a hill and overlooking a waterhole, this appealing, family-run lodge manages a perfect balance between rustic and luxury. The eight thatched cottages have stone floors and walls, and look down over the waterhole where wildlife is common. The main building is wonderfully colonial from its fireplace to its stiff drinks.

ℹ Getting There & Away

Located northeast of Nanyuki, the lodge is a 4½-hour drive from Nairobi along the A2 and a 4WD is not necessary. There is also an airstrip for those with larger wallets and less time. Note that you have to be staying at Borana Lodge in order to access the conservancy.

Lekurruki Community Ranch

Ranged across almost 120 sq km north of Il Ngwesi and northwest of Lewa Wildlife Conservancy (p162), this community ranch is the homeland of the Mukogodo Maasai. With a good mix of habitats – the bordering Mukogodo Forest is partially on the ranch and is often said to be one of the largest indigenous forests in East Africa, while the remainder of the ranch is made up of open savannah – the ranch has a rich variety of both flora and fauna. Of the latter, you'll find predators and buffalo here, but elephants are the main drawcard with one herd almost 500-strong. More than 200 bird species and over 100 butterfly species have been recorded on the ranch.

🛏 Sleeping

Tassia Lodge   LODGE $$$
(📞 0790486298; www.tassiasafaris.com; s/d all-inclusive US$810/1180, conservation fee per person per night US$60; 🏊) The immensity of African landscapes and the intimacy of the community lodge experience are perfectly combined at Tassia Lodge, high on a rocky bluff on Lekurruki Community Ranch. Rooms are open sided and have an original handmade look with natural wood and stone used throughout. Views are splendid and activities include walking safaris and botanical walks.

ℹ MT KENYA NATIONAL PARK

Why Go Awe-inspiring views from Africa's second-highest mountain; unlike Mt Kilimanjaro, it's possible to take different routes up and down, with arguably better scenery.

When to Go Climb during the driest months: mid-January to late February and late August to September.

Practicalities Don't underestimate the difficulty of this trek. You'd be flirting with death by not taking a guide.

Budget Tips Don't skimp on safety and length of acclimatisation; carry your own gear and cook your own meals; camp instead of staying in the huts.

ℹ Getting There & Away

Lekurruki Community Ranch is located north of Il Ngwesi and northwest of Lewa Wildlife Conservancy. You cannot self-drive to Tassia Lodge, but transfers can be arranged from Nanyuki (US$250 per six-seater vehicle, 2½ hours) or the Lewa airstrip (US$250 per six-seater vehicle, two hours). You can also organise a charter flight to the Tassia airstrip from Nairobi, Nanyuki or Gilgil.

MT KENYA NATIONAL PARK

Africa's second-highest mountain might just be its most beautiful. Here, mere minutes from the equator, glaciers carve out the throne of Ngai, the old high god of the Kikuyu. To this day the tribe keeps its doors open to the face of the sacred mountain, and some still come to its lower slopes to offer prayers. Besides being venerated by the Kikuyu, Mt Kenya and **Mt Kenya National Park** (📞 0712294084, Nairobi 020-3568763; www.kws.go.ke; adult/child US$52/26) have the rare honour of being both a Unesco World Heritage Site and a Unesco Biosphere Reserve.

The highest peaks of Batian (5199m) and Nelion (5188m) can only be reached by mountaineers with technical skills, but Point Lenana (4985m), the third-highest peak, can be reached by trekkers and is the usual goal for most mortals. When the clouds part, the views are simply magnificent.

Environment

There are ecosystems on the slopes of Mt Kenya that cannot be found anywhere else in the country.

This extinct volcano hosts, at various elevations, upland forest, bamboo forest (2500m), high-altitude equatorial heath (3000m to 3500m) and lower alpine moorland (3400m to 3800m), which includes several species of bright everlasting flowers. Some truly surreal plant life grows in the Afro-alpine zone (above 3500m) and the upper alpine zone (3800m to 4500m), including hairy carpets of tussock grass, the brushlike giant lobelias, or rosette plants, and the sci-fi-worthy *Senecio brassica*, or giant groundsel, which looks like a cross between an aloe, a cactus and a dwarf. At the summit it's all rock and ice.

Mt Kenya National Park

Map labels (clockwise): Old Moses Hut (3km); Sirimon Gate (9km); Sirimon Bandas (18km); Ontulili River; Liki North River; Liki North Valley; Sirimon Route; The Barrow (4192m); Kazita East River; Timau Route; Mutonga River; Mackinder's Valley; Liki River; Liki North Hut (3993m); Nanyuki North River; Terere (4714m); Sendeo (4704m); Hinde Valley; Lake Ellis; Nanyuki River; Hausberg Valley; Shipton's Caves; Shipton's Camp (4200m); The Hat; Chogoria Route; Meru; Mt Kenya Lodge (5km); Kampi Ya Machengeni (11km); Highland Castle; Burguret Route; See Mt Kenya Summit Map (p170); Lake Michaelson; Gorges Valley; Nittii Falls; Teleki Valley; Met Station Hut (3.5km); Batian Guest House (16km); Batian (5199m); Delamere Peak; Macmillan Peak; Northern Naro Moru River; Tilman Peak; Corydon Peak; Enchanted Lake; Ruguti North River; Naro Moru Route; Mackinder's Camp (4200m); Grigg Peak; Picnic Rocks; Somerfelt Peak; Hobley Valley; Carr Lakes; Nairobi River; Hohnel Valley; Castle Hill; Lake Hohnel; Hidden Tarn

Unfortunately, there's more rock than ice these days. Warmer weather has led to disappearing glaciers, and ice climbing in Mt Kenya is largely finished. The impact of reduced snow melt upon the region's rivers – Mt Kenya is the country's most important permanent watershed – is already being felt.

Wildlife

While you generally don't come to Mt Kenya for the wildlife, there are some unique life forms that cling to the mountain slopes.

At lower elevations large wildlife are around; you may need to clap and hoot as you trudge to stave off elephants and buffaloes. Rock hyraxes are common, as are, rather annoyingly, bees. There are also Sykes' monkeys, Mackinder's eagle owls, waterbucks and (very rarely spotted) leopards, hyenas and servals; these animals tend to stay hidden in the thick brush of the lower forests.

At around the 3000m-above-sea-level mark, watch for the side-striped chameleon, one of the world's highest-altitude reptiles. Whenever the sun breaks through, watch for it sunning itself on a branch at right angles to the sun, its scales dark like a solar panel. Once warm, it turns a vivid green colour.

Higher up the mountain watch for the distinctive ostrich-plumed lobelia plant attended by sunbirds, and for the highland rock hyrax, an endemic hyrax sub-species that is larger and thicker-furred than its lowland cousins.

Climbing Mt Kenya

What to Take

Consider the following to be a minimum checklist of necessary equipment. If you don't have your own equipment, items can be rented from some guiding associations. Prices vary, but expect to pay in the vicinity of KSh700/300/250/400 for a two-person tent/sleeping bag/pair of boots/stove per day.

➡ A good sleeping bag and a closed-cell foam mat or Thermarest if you're camping (nightly temperatures near the summit often drop to below –10°C).

➡ A good set of warm clothes (wool or synthetics – never cotton, as it traps moisture).

➡ Waterproof clothing (breathable fabric like Gore-Tex is best) as it can rain heavily any time of year.

➡ A decent pair of boots and sandals or light shoes (for the evening when your boots get wet).

→ Sunblock and sunglasses (at this altitude the sun can do some serious damage to your skin and eyes).

→ A tent, stove, basic cooking equipment, utensils, a 3L water container (per person) and water-purifying tablets (if you don't intend to stay in the huts along the way). Stove fuel in the form of petrol and kerosene (paraffin) is fairly easily found in towns.

→ If you have a mobile phone, take it along; reception on the mountain's higher reaches is actually very good.

→ Technical climbers and mountaineers should get a copy of the Mountain Club of Kenya (p68) *Guide to Mt Kenya & Kilimanjaro*. This substantial and comprehensive guide is available in bookshops or from MCK offices; MCK also has reasonably up-to-date mountain information posted on its website.

A few other things to remember:

→ If a porter is carrying your backpack, always keep essential clothing (warm- and wet-weather gear) in your day pack because you may become separated for hours at a time.

→ Don't sleep in clothes you've worn during the day because the sweat your clothes will have absorbed keeps them moist at night, reducing their heat-retention capabilities.

→ Fires are prohibited in the open except in an emergency; in any case, there's no wood once you get beyond 3300m.

Guides, Cooks & Porters

Don't underestimate the difficulty of the trek to Point Lenana. Unless you're a seasoned trekker with high-altitude experience and know how to read maps and use a compass, you'll be flirting with death by not taking a guide – people die on the mountain every year. A good guide will help set a sustainable pace, which should help you avoid headaches, nausea and other (sometimes more serious) effects of altitude sickness. And by spending at least three nights on the ascent, you'll enjoy yourself more too. Your guide should also be on the lookout for signs of hypothermia and dehydration in you (fluids and warm clothing go a long way towards preventing both) and be able to deal with the unpredictable weather. They will also hopefully dispense interesting information about Mt Kenya and its flora and fauna.

Having a porter for your gear is like travelling in a chauffeured Mercedes instead of a matatu. With both a porter and guide on your team, your appreciation of this mountain will be enhanced a hundredfold. If you hire a guide or porter who can also cook, you won't regret it.

The KWS issues vouchers to all registered guides and porters, who should also hold identity cards; they won't be allowed into the park without them.

Costs

Park fees must be factored into the overall cost of climbing Mt Kenya, as well as the costs of guides, food and tips.

Guides, Cooks & Porters

The cost of guides varies depending on the qualifications of the guide, whatever the last party paid and your own negotiating skills. You should expect to pay a minimum of US$30/25/20 per day for a guide/cook/porter.

Park Fees

Park fees for non-residents are adult/child US$52/26 per day. There is no discount on fees for staying longer. Note that KWS parks no longer accept cash, so you will have to pay at the gate with M-Pesa or a credit card. If you only have cash, you can get a bank deposit slip from any Kenya Commercial Bank or Standard Chartered Bank.

Tips

In addition to the actual cost of hiring guides, cooks and porters, tips are expected but these should only be paid for good service.

For a good guide who has completed the full trek with you, plan on a tip of about US$50 per group. Cook and porter tips should be around US$30 and US$20 respectively.

The Routes

There are at least seven different routes up Mt Kenya. Of those, we cover Naro Moru, the easiest and most popular, as well as Sirimon and Chogoria, which are excellent alternatives, and the exciting but demanding Summit Circuit, which circles Batian and Nelion, enabling you to mix and match ascending and descending routes. Other routes include the Timau Route and Burguret Route.

🏃 Naro Moru Route

Although the least scenic, this is the most straightforward and popular route and is still spectacular.

Starting in Naro Moru town, the first part of the route takes you along a gravel road through farmlands for some 13km (all the junctions are signposted) to the start of the forest. Another 5km brings you to the park entry gate (2400m), from where it's 8km to the road head and the Met Station Hut (3000m), where you stay for the night and acclimatise.

On the second day, set off through the forest (at about 3200m) and Teleki Valley to the moorland around so-called **Vertical Bog**; expect the going here to be, well, boggy. At a ridge the route divides into two. You can either take the higher path, which gives better views but is often wet, or the lower, which crosses the Naro Moru River and continues gently up to Mackinder's Camp (4200m). This part of the trek should take about 4½ hours. Here you can stay in the dormitories or camp.

On the third day you can either rest at Mackinder's Camp to acclimatise or aim for **Point Lenana** (4985m). This stretch takes three to six hours, so it is common to leave around 2am to reach the summit in time for sunrise. From the bunk-house, continue past the ranger station to a fork. Keep right and go across a swampy area, followed by a moraine, and then up a long scree slope – this is a long, hard slog. The KWS Austrian Hut (4790m) is three to four

---

ORGANISED TREKS

If you bargain hard, a package trek may end up costing only a little more than organising each logistical element of the trip separately. If you're keen to save money, think like a wildebeest and join a herd – the larger the group, the cheaper the per-person rate. Prices generally include guides, cooks and porters, park fees, meals and accommodation.

IntoAfrica (☑ Nairobi 0722511752, UK 0114-2555610; www.intoafrica.co.uk; 7-day treks from US$1695) Highly recommended by readers, IntoAfrica is an environmentally and culturally sensitive company offering both scheduled and exclusive seven-day trips ascending the Sirimon Route and descending Chogoria. All trips are calculated to ensure that local contractors earn a fair living wage from their work.

EWP (Executive Wilderness Programmes; ☑ UK 1550-721319; www.ewpnet.com/kenya; 3-/7-day trips from US$645/1445; ⊙ 9am-4.30pm) This UK company employs local guides and may be a good option if you want to book your travel before you arrive in Kenya. Prices get cheaper with more people, so try to get some friends to join you.

Mt Kenya Guides & Porters Safari Club (☑ 0723087042, 0726369611; www.mtkenya guides.com; per person per day from US$120) The most organised association of guides, cooks and porters in Naro Moru. A full-service tour, including a porter, food, transport and accommodation, will cost US$120 per person per day, though you can also just book a guide (US$20 per day) or a porter (US$15 per day).

KG Mountain Expeditions (☑ 0733606338, Nairobi 020-2033874; www.kenyaexpeditions. com) Run by a highly experienced mountaineer and a team of knowledgeable trekkers, KG offers all-inclusive scheduled treks.

Mountain Rock Safaris Resorts & Trekking Services (Bantu Mountain Lodge; ☑ 0722511752, Nairobi 020-242133; www.mountainrockkenya.com) Runs the Bantu Mountain Lodge (p175) near Naro Moru. Its popular four-day Naro Moru–Sirimon crossover trek costs US$650 per person.

Mountain View Tour Trekking Safaris (☑ 0722249439; mountainviewt@yahoo.com; guide per day from US$20) An association of local guides working together; the guides often approach independent travellers as they arrive in Naro Moru.

Naro Moru River Lodge (☑ 0708984002, 0708984005; www.naromoruriverlodge.com; 4-day trip per person US$719-1497) Runs a range of all-inclusive trips and operates **Met Station Hut** (p173) and **Mackinder's Camp** (p173) on the Naro Moru Route.

Mt Kenya Summit

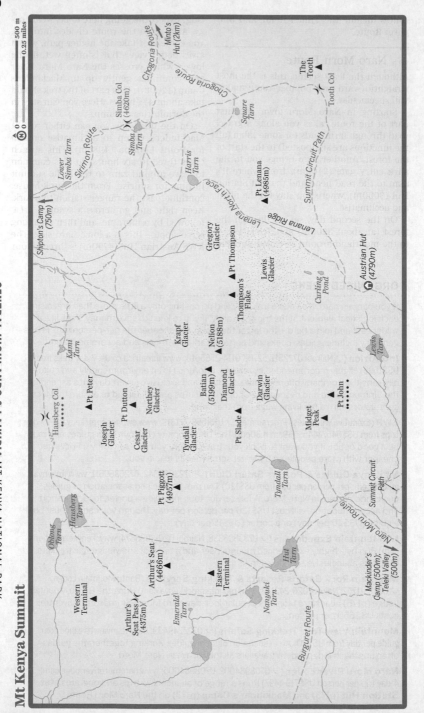

500 m
0.25 miles

Minto's Hut (2km)

Chogoria Route

The Tooth

Tooth Col

Square Tarn

Summit Circuit Path

Simba Col (4620m)

Lower Simba Tarn

Srimon Route

Simba Tarn

Harris Tarn

Pt Lenana (4985m)

Lenana Ridge

Shipton's Camp (750m)

Lenana North Face

Gregory Glacier

Pt Thompson

Lewis Glacier

Austrian Hut (4790m)

Curling Pond

Thompson's Flake

Krapf Glacier

Nelion (5188m)

Kami Tarn

Lewis Tarn

Hausberg Col

Pt Peter

Pt Dutton

Northey Glacier

Batian (5199m)

Diamond Glacier

Darwin Glacier

Pt John

Joseph Glacier

Cesar Glacier

Tyndall Glacier

Pt Slade

Midget Peak

Pt Piggott (4957m)

Hausberg Tarn

Oblong Tarn

Arthur's Seat (4666m)

Eastern Terminal

Tyndall Tarn

Summit Circuit Path

Naro Moru Route

Hut Tarn

Western Terminal

Arthur's Seat Pass (4375m)

Emerald Tarn

Namuki Tarn

Mackinder's Camp (500m); Teleki Valley (500m)

Burguret Route

hours from Mackinder's and about one hour below the summit of Lenana, so it's a good place to rest before the final push.

The section of the trek from Austrian Hut up to Point Lenana takes you up a narrow rocky path that traverses the south-west ridge parallel to the Lewis Glacier, which has shrunk more than 100m since the 1960s. Be careful, as the shrinkage has created serious danger of slippage along the path. A final climb or scramble brings you up onto the peak. In good weather it's fairly straightforward, but in bad weather you shouldn't attempt the summit unless you're experienced in mountain conditions or have a guide.

🏃 Sirimon Route

A popular alternative to Naro Moru, Sirimon has better scenery, greater flexibility and a gentler rate of ascent, but takes a day longer. It's well worth considering combining it with the Chogoria Route for a six- to seven-day traverse that really brings out the best of Mt Kenya.

The trek begins at the Sirimon Gate, 23km from Nanyuki, from where it's about a 9km walk through forest to Old Moses Hut (3300m), where you spend the first night.

On the second day you could head straight through the moorland for Shipton's Camp, but it is worth taking an extra acclimatisation day via Liki North Hut (3993m), a tiny place on the floor of a classic glacial valley. The actual hut is in poor shape and meant for porters, but it's a good campsite with a toilet and stream nearby.

On the third day, head up the western side of Liki North Valley and over the ridge into Mackinder's Valley, joining the direct route about 1½ hours in. After crossing the Liki River, follow the path for another 30 minutes until you reach the bunk-house at Shipton's Camp (4200m), which is set in a fantastic location right below Batian and Nelion.

From Shipton's you can push straight for Point Lenana (4985m), a tough 3½- to five-hour slog via Harris Tarn and the tricky north-face approach, or take the Summit Circuit in either direction around the peaks to reach Austrian Hut (4790m), about one hour below the summit. The left-hand (east) route past Simba Col (4620m) is shorter but steeper, while the right-hand (west) option

takes you on the Harris Tarn trail nearer the main peaks.

From Austrian Hut take the standard southwest traverse up to Point Lenana. If you're spending the night here, it's worth having a wander around to catch the views up to Batian and down the Lewis Glacier into the Teleki Valley.

🏃 Chogoria Route

This route crosses some of the most spectacular and varied scenery on Mt Kenya, and is often combined with the Sirimon Route (usually as the descent). The main reason this route is more popular as a descent is the 29km bottom stage. While not overly steep, climbing up that distance is much harder than descending it.

The only disadvantage with this route is the long distance between Chogoria and the park gate. These days most people drive, although it's a beautiful walk through farmland, rainforest and bamboo to the park gate. Most people spend the first night here, either camping at the gate or staying nearby in Meru Mt Kenya Lodge (3000m).

On the second day, head up through the forest to the trailhead (camping is possible here). From here it's another 7km over rolling foothills to the Hall Tarns area and **Minto's Hut** (4300m). Like Liki North, this place is only intended for porters, but makes for a decent campsite. Don't use the tarns here to wash anything, as careless trekkers have already polluted them.

From here follow the trail alongside the stunning **Gorges Valley** (another possible descent for the adventurous) and scramble up steep ridges to meet the Summit Circuit. It is possible to go straight for the north face or southwest ridge of Point Lenana, but stopping at Austrian Hut or detouring to Shipton's Camp gives you more time to enjoy the scenery.

Allow at least five days for the Chogoria Route, although a full week is better.

🏃 Summit Circuit

While everyone who summits Point Lenana gets a small taste of the spectacular Summit Circuit, few trekkers ever grab the beautiful beast by the horns and hike its entire length. The trail encircles the main peaks of Mt Kenya between the 4300m and 4800m contour lines and offers challenging terrain, fabulous views and a splendid opportunity to familiarise yourself with this complex mountain. It is also a fantastic way to acclimatise before bagging Point Lenana.

One of the many highlights along the route is a peek at Mt Kenya's southwest face, with the long, thin Diamond Couloir leading up to the **Gates of the Mists** between the summits of Batian and Nelion.

Depending on your level of fitness, this route can take between four and nine hours. Some fit souls can summit Point Lenana (from Austrian Hut or Shipton's Camp) and complete the Summit Circuit in the same day.

The trail can be deceptive at times, especially when fog rolls in, and some trekkers have become seriously lost between Tooth Col and Austrian Hut. It is imperative to take a guide.

◉ Sights

Shipton's Caves CAVE
Just before Shipton's Camp, along the Sirimon Route, you will find Shipton's Caves. You'll likely spend a night here to acclimatise, so ask your guide if they can take you to explore the caves, which are named after Eric Shipton, who was the first to ascend Nelion Peak in 1929. However, he's perhaps best known for giving a young sherpa, Tenzing Norgay, his first job as a porter on Mt Everest in 1935.

ⓘ COOKING AT ALTITUDE

Increased altitude creates unique cooking conditions. The major consideration is that the boiling point of water is considerably reduced. At 4500m, for example, water boils at 85°C; this is too low to sufficiently cook rice or lentils (pasta is better) and you won't be able to brew a good cup of tea (instant coffee is the answer). Cooking times and fuel usage are considerably increased as a result, so plan accordingly.

To avoid severe headaches caused by dehydration or altitude sickness, drink at least 3L of fluid per day and bring rehydration sachets. Water-purification tablets, available at most chemists, aren't a bad idea either (purifying water by boiling at this altitude would take close to 30 minutes).

Highland Castle LANDMARK
If you are trekking along the Burguret Route, you will likely camp just below the lava cliff of Highland Castle at 3700m. If time allows and you're adventurous enough, you can climb to the top of the castle-like formation to witness the incredible views of the Batian and Nelion peaks.

🛏 Sleeping

As well as the official sleeping options on each route, it is possible to camp anywhere on the mountain; the cost of camping is included in the four- to six-day park-fee packages payable at any gate. Most people camp near the huts or bunk-houses, as there are often toilets and water nearby.

Liki North Hut HUT
FREE If trekking the Sirimon Route, you will likely acclimatise here on the second night at 3993m. There is a river nearby, space to camp and a small hut that can provide shelter if needed.

Batian Guest House GUESTHOUSE $
(www.kws.go.ke/content/batian-guest-house; 8-bed banda US$180) Those needing a bit of luxury can sleep in lovely, KWS-run Batian Guest House, which sleeps eight people in several different bedrooms. You are required to book the entire house, however; it's not possible simply to book a room. It's around 1km from the Naro Moru Gate.

Austrian Hut HUT $
(www.kws.go.ke; dm KSh2000) The second-highest hut at 4790m, this makes a good base before the final ascent of Point Lenana. The dorm rooms are basic and you'll need a good sleeping bag to keep you warm at night, but what did you expect at this elevation?

Meru Mt Kenya Lodge CABIN $
(per person KSh2000) The only option besides camping on the Chogoria Route, this group of comfortable cabins is administered by **Meru South County Council** (☏0729390686; Chuka; per person from KSh2000). Ask your guide to reserve these in advance, as during peak season they can be booked out.

Old Moses Hut HUT $
(☏0718136539; www.mountainrockkenya.com; dm US$20) At 3300m and usually the first night's stop on the Sirimon Route. Campfires are allowed, but you'll have to supply

your own firewood. Book through Bantu Mountain Lodge (p175).

Met Station Hut
HUT $

(📞0708984002; www.naromoruriverlodge.com; dm US$26) One of three good bunk-houses along the Naro Moru Route, at 3000m. Beds can be hard to come by – book through Naro Moru River Lodge.

Shipton's Camp
HUT $

(📞0718136539; www.mountainrockkenya.com; dm US$20) Bunk-house at 4200m for the third night on the Sirimon Route. There is a tap and a pit latrine but no fires are allowed, so make sure you have a warm sleeping bag. Book through Bantu Mountain Lodge (p175).

Mackinder's Camp
HUT $

(📞0708984002; www.naromoruriverlodge.com; dm US$34) You're likely to spend your second night here, at 4200m on the Naro Moru Route, which has spectacular views of the different peaks. Book through Naro Moru River Lodge.

Sirimon Bandas
BANDAS $$

(www.kws.go.ke/content/sirimon-cottage; banda US$80) The excellent KWS-run Sirimon Bandas are located 9km from the Sirimon Gate and make for a comfortable place to acclimatise to the altitude before a climb. Each *banda* sleeps four, has a shower with hot water and a self-catering kitchen.

✗ Eating

You'll need to be totally self-sufficient if you're climbing Mt Kenya, as none of the lodges or camps on the route offer meals. However, most packages include cooks who both carry and prepare all meals for you on the way. Even if that is the case, take citrus fruits and/or citrus drinks as well as chocolate, sweets or dried fruit to keep your blood-sugar level up.

ℹ Getting There & Away

Short of hiring your own helicopter, the only way to reach the summit of Mt Kenya is on foot, and if you're starting your climb in the village of Naro Moru, you can set out directly from there. Naro Moru is a three-hour drive from Nairobi and is accessible in a 2WD car. If you are hiking the Sirimon or Chogoria routes, you may need a 4WD with high clearance to get to the gate, particularly if it has rained recently, though most trekking companies will pick you up from a nearby town for an extra fee.

AROUND MT KENYA

Naro Moru
📶 062 / POP 9000

Naro Moru may be little more than a string of shops and houses, with a couple of very basic hotels and a market, but it's the most popular starting point for treks up Mt Kenya.

🛏 Sleeping

Mt Kenya Guides & Porters Safari Club
BANDAS $

(📞0723087042; www.mtkenyaguides.com; per person KSh2300) Principally in the business of supplying guides and porters, this association has branched out with a couple of excellent-value cottages with open fires. Meals can be arranged on request and, obviously, organising a trek (p169) here is a breeze.

★ Nelion Hotel
HOTEL $$

(📞0714009219; www.the-nelion.co.ke; s/d from KSh10,000/16,000; 🅿🛜🏊) Offering 10 wooden log cabins complete with king-size beds, this is the top place to stay in the area. Just under 4km away from Naro Moru, the hotel is still quite tranquil. Families will love the pool and playground.

Creaky Cottage
COTTAGE $$

(📞0735965636; www.trout-tree.com/accommodation; cottage from KSh12,500) Located 200m from the Trout Tree Restaurant (p175), this self-contained cottage sleeps six. There is a kitchen, but meals can also be ordered from the restaurant. Ask about trout fishing – staff can cook your catch up at the restaurant.

Naro Moru River Lodge
LODGE $$

(📞0724082754; www.naromoruriverlodge.com; campsite/dm US$18/34, s/tw full board US$141/191, cottages from US$96; 🅿🛜🏊) A bit like a Swiss chalet, the River Lodge is a lovely collection of dark, cosy cottages and rooms embedded into a sloping hillside that overlooks the rushing Naro Moru River, 3km from town. All three classes of room are lovely, but the middle-of-the-road 'superior' option seems the best value of the lot.

Colobus Cottages
COTTAGE $$

(📞0722840195, 0753951720; www.colobuscottages.com; per person without breakfast KSh3500) These wooden cottages, some almost completely enveloped by the forest

Around Mt Kenya

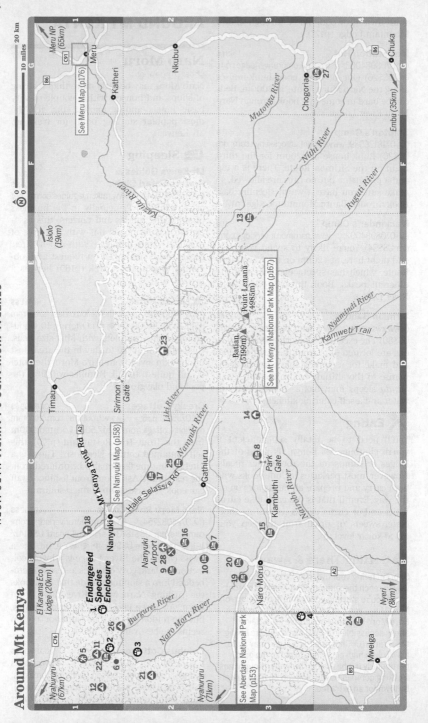

Around Mt Kenya

◎ **Top Sights**
1 Endangered Species Enclosure.............B1

◎ **Sights**
2 Chimpanzee Sanctuary..........................A1
Morani Information Centre.............(see 1)
Mt Kenya Wildlife
Conservancy Animal
Orphanage ....(see 17)
3 Ol Pejeta Conservancy A2
4 Solio Game Reserve................................A3

◎ **Activities, Courses & Tours**
5 Hippo Hide Walk......................................A1
Mountain Rock Safaris
Resorts & Trekking Services.......(see 7)
Mt Kenya Chogoria Guides &
Porters Association ....(see 27)
Mt Kenya Guides & Porters
Safari Club..................................(see 15)
Naro Moru River Lodge.................(see 19)
6 Rift Valley Adventures............................A1

◎ **Sleeping**
7 Bantu Mountain Lodge..........................B2
8 Batian Guest House................................C3
9 Colobus Cottages....................................B2

10 Creaky Cottage......................................B2
11 Ewaso Campsite.....................................A1
12 Kicheche Laikipia...................................A1
13 Meru Mt Kenya Lodge...........................E3
14 Met Station Hut...................................... C3
15 Mt Kenya Guides & Porters
Safari Club... B3
16 Mt Kenya Royal Cottages....................B2
17 Mt Kenya Safari Club...........................C2
18 Nanyuki River Camel Camp B1
19 Naro Moru River Lodge........................B3
20 Nelion Hotel..B3
21 Ngobit Campsite.....................................A2
Ol Lerai Campsite..........................(see 11)
22 Ol Pejeta House.......................................A1
23 Old Moses Hut..D2
24 Sandai Farm...A4
25 Sirimon Bandas......................................C2
26 Sweetwaters Serena Camp...................A1
27 Transit Motel...G4

◎ **Eating**
28 Barney's Bar & Restaurant...................B2
Morani's Restaurant........................(see 1)
Safari Diner..(see 1)
Trout Tree Restaurant................(see 10)
Tusks Restaurant ....(see 17)

overlooking the Burguret River, are simple but charmingly decorated inside. There's a fireplace in each, a barbecue area and a communal treetop bar. Note that the minimum booking is for two people. It's 2km off the main highway and best reached in a car with high clearance.

Mt Kenya Royal Cottages   COTTAGE $$
(☏0721470008; per person from KSh2500; P)
On a rise beside the highway, this relatively new place offers simple but well-priced cottages and a decent on-site restaurant. It's fine for a night – any longer and the proximity to the road will start to annoy. It's around 1km south of Nanyuki Airport (p159).

Mt Kenya Leisure Lodge   HOTEL $$
(☏0715724381; www.mtkenyaleisurelodge.com; s/d from US$80/144; P🕭🔲) Following renovations, this lodge now has a new wing, swimming pool and restaurant. The new wing still looks under construction and the rooms are spacious, though cold. The rooms in the old wing have more character, but could use some love. It is peaceful though and good for a post-hike relax before heading to the city.

Bantu Mountain Lodge   HOTEL $$
(☏0718136539, 0728057293; www.mountainrock kenya.com; camping US$10, s/d from US$65/100) This is a major base for Mt Kenya climbers and the operators of Old Moses Hut (p172) and Shipton's Camp (p173) on the mountain. Popular with overland trucks, there are three classes of rooms and like most hotels in this price bracket, the rooms are serviceable enough but need refurbishment. You can no longer pay in cash.

🍴 Eating

⭐ **Trout Tree Restaurant**   SEAFOOD $$$
(☏0726281704; www.trout-tree.com; Naro Moru-Nanyuki Hwy; mains KSh1100-1700; ⊙10am-4pm) Inhabiting a marvellous fig tree overlooking the Burguret River, alongside colobus monkeys and tree hyraxes, this is one of the most original places to eat in Kenya's Central Highlands. It doesn't do much else, but we never tire of the trout combinations – smoked trout and cucumber salad, trout chowder, trout curry, tandoori trout, whole grilled trout...char-grilled is best of all.

If you're lucky, you might be able to fish for your supper and have it cooked for you afterwards. Ask about Creaky Cottage (p173),

CENTRAL HIGHLANDS & LAIKIPIA NARO MORU

the fabulous riverside, self-contained house that sleeps six.

ⓘ Getting There & Away

There are plenty of buses and matatus heading to Nanyuki (KSh80, 30 minutes), Nyeri (KSh180, 45 minutes) and Nairobi (KSh600, three hours) from either the northbound or southbound bus parks.

Meru

♪ 064 / POP 240,900

Meru is the largest municipality in the Central Highlands and the epicentre of Kenyan production of *miraa*, a mild, leafy stimulant more widely known outside of Kenya as *khat*. The town itself is like a shot of the stuff: a briefly invigorating, slightly confusing head rush but you'll wonder what the point of it all was when the first effects wear off.

🛏 Sleeping

★ **Alba Hotel**   HOTEL **$$**
(☑0705556677, 072-8223344; www.albahotels. co.ke; Milimani Rd; s/d/tr KSh8500/10,200/12,700; P@🛰☒) With easily Meru's best rooms, this modern place has Western-style, Western-standard rooms with bright colours and modern furnishings. If you've only stayed here and in Nairobi, you might think this is the norm in Kenya – it's not.

Meru Slopes Hotel   HOTEL **$$**
(☑0738836295, 0711620219; www.meruslopes hotel.com; off Meru-Nairobi Hwy; s/d KSh5500/6500; P@🛰☒) A good choice in the town centre, Meru Slopes Hotel is behind the **Nakumatt Supermarket** (www.nakumatt.net; ⊙8.30am-8.30pm Mon-Sat, 10am-8pm Sun; P). It gets consistently good reviews from travellers – it's the sort of place that you won't remember years from now but won't hesitate to recommend to others.

Meru

🛏 **Sleeping**
1 Alba Hotel..A2
2 Meru Slopes Hotel................................A2

✪ **Eating**
3 Legends Restaurant C3
4 Nakumatt Supermarket A2
5 Royal Prince C3

ⓘ **Transport**
6 Bus & Matatu Stand............................C3
7 Matatu Stand B3

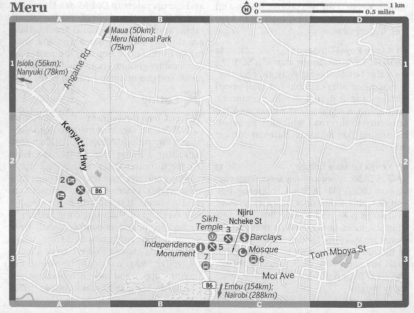

Meru

Maua (50km); Meru National Park (75km)

Isiolo (56km); Nanyuki (78km)

Angaine Rd

Kenyatta Hwy

B6

Sikh Temple

Njiru
Ncheke St

Barclays

Mosque

Independence Monument

Tom Mboya St

Moi Ave

B6 Embu (154km); Nairobi (288km)

Eating

Legends Restaurant KENYAN $
(Tom Mboya St; mains KSh100-250; ⊗8am-10pm)
Popular with locals, this restaurant is cheap
as chips, but has really good traditional Kenyan cuisine. Start with the samosas, then
have the beef stew with ugali and end with
a Kenyan tea.

Royal Prince KENYAN $
(Tom Mboya St; mains KSh250-450; ⊗noon-10pm)
There are two storeys of bustling eating
goodness at this cheap hotel. The downstairs restaurant specialises in all things
fried, while upstairs houses the '*choma*
zone', and also doubles as a bar during the
day and a club after dark.

ℹ Information

Barclays (Tom Mboya St; ⊗9am-4pm Mon-Fri,
to noon Sat) Branch with 24-hour ATM.

ℹ Getting There & Away

All transport leaves from the area between the
main mosque and the market at the eastern end
of the town centre.

You'll find regular **bus** departures throughout
the day from 6.45am onward to Embu (KSh400,
two hours), Thika (KSh400, 3½ hours) and
Nairobi (KSh500, five hours). There's also at
least one late-afternoon departure to Mombasa
(KSh1600, 12 hours).

Regular **matatus** also serve Nairobi (KSh750,
four hours), Thika (KSh650, 3½ hours), Embu
(KSh450, two hours), Nanyuki (KSh350, 1½
hours) and Isiolo (KSh300, 1½ hours).

Meru National Park

Welcome to one of Kenya's most underrated parks. Marred by serious poaching in
the 1980s and the subsequent murder of
George Adamson (of *Born Free* fame) in
1989, **Meru National Park** (☏061-2303094,
Nairobi 020-2310443; www.kws.org; adult/child
US$52/35; ⊗6am-7pm) fell off the tourist
map and has never quite managed to get
back on. This is a pity, because it has all the
essential ingredients for a classic safari destination, with some fine accommodation,
excellent prospects for seeing lions and
rhinos, and a landscape that incorporates
Hemingway-esque green hills, arid, Tsa-
vo-like savannah and fast-flowing streams
bordered by riverine forests, baobab trees
and doum palms. The advantage of being

ℹ **MERU NATIONAL PARK**

Why Go A pristine, seldom-visited
park with rhinos and lions where you'll
be guaranteed a 'congestion-free'
experience.

When to Go Because it falls within Mt
Kenya's eastern rain shadow, the park is
accessible year-round with a 4WD.

Practicalities There is no public
transport within the park but self-
drive safaris are possible as park
road junctions are numbered on the
ground and labelled on park maps.
Even with a park map, you may want to
hire a guide (under/over three hours
KSh1700/3000).

Budget Tips There is not a lot of accommodation in the area, so if you are
sticking to a budget it's best to camp
and bring in all the food and water you
will need for your stay.

one of Kenya's best-kept secrets is plain to
see – you're likely to have much of it all to
yourself.

⊙ Sights

Although this is a large park covering 870
sq km, most of the wildlife action is concentrated in the northern sector. The triangle
of largely open savannah between **Mururi Swamp**, **Leopard Rock Swamp** and
Mughwango Swamp is easily the park's
happiest hunting ground for lions and the
herbivores they stalk.

The park's most significant waterway,
Rojewero River, is a reliable place to view
hippos and crocodiles. To the south you may
want to check out **Elsa's Grave**, a stone memorial to the Adamson's star lioness. Access
to the adjacent Kora National Park is via the
bridge near **Adamson's Falls**.

ℹ **KORA NATIONAL PARK**

Entrance to Meru National Park also
entitles you to enter the adjacent Kora
National Park, which offers pristine
wilderness in an even wilder setting
than Meru. Visits into Kora must be
prearranged with Meru's warden at the
park headquarters.

Meru National Park

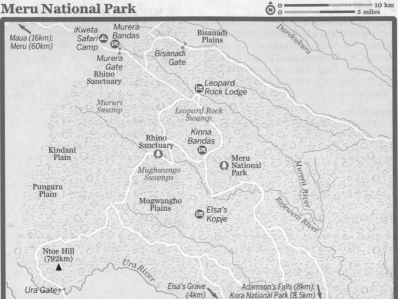

Meru National Park

0   10 km
0   5 miles

Maua (16km); Meru (60km)

iKweta Safari Camp

Murera Bandas

Murera Gate

Rhino Sanctuary

Bisanadi Plains

Bisanadi Gate

Darekukuru

Mururi Swamp

Leopard Rock Lodge

Leopard Rock Swamp

Rhino Sanctuary

Kinna Bandas

Meru National Park

Kindani Plain

Mughwango Swamps

Murera River

Punguru Plain

Mugwangho Plains

Elsa's Kopje

Rojewero River

Ntoe Hill (792km)

Ura River

Ura Gate

Elsa's Grave (4km)

Adamson's Falls (8km); Kora National Park (8.5km)

Rhino Sanctuary   NATIONAL PARK

(⊙6am-6pm) FREE A signposted hard right not long after entering Murera Gate takes you to Meru's 48-sq-km Rhino Sanctuary, one of the best places in Kenya to see wild rhinos. At last count, this fenced portion of the park was home to 25 black and 55 white rhinos, many of whom were reintroduced here from Lake Nakuru National Park after the disastrous poaching of the '80s.

☞ Tours

J Kirimi Safaris   SAFARI

(🖉0721683700; http://bestkenyasafari.com/meru-national-park-safari) John Kirimi of J Kirimi Safaris, a small safari operator, has a 4WD based in Maua (a small town 31km from the main gate). A full-day safari, including pick-up and drop-off at Meru town, costs around KSh18,000 per vehicle plus entrance costs.

🛏 Sleeping

★iKweta Safari Camp   TENTED CAMP **$$**

(🖉0705200050; www.ikwetasafaricamp.com; s/d full board US$86/143; P 🛜 🌊) This terrific place is just outside Meru National Park, 2.5km from Murera Gate on the road in

from Meru, so you can be inside the park in minutes. The semi-luxurious tents (with wi-fi) are outrageously good value and put to shame many tented camps that charge so much more for so much less.

The more-than-300 indigenous plants need a little time to mature, but when they do, this place will be even better. Most of the food served is grown in engaging host Susan's garden and is delicious. Even if you are not staying at the camp, you can make a booking to come for lunch or dinner. The name '*ikweta*' is Swahili for 'equator'.

Kinna Bandas   BANDAS **$$**

(🖉061-2303094; www.kws.go.ke; bandas US$80; 🌊) These three *bandas* each sleep two and are stocked with kerosene lanterns that add the right romanticism to a star-studded bush night. Located in the heart of the park, you can't get closer to the wildlife without the risk of being eaten by it. There's also a 10-bed guesthouse (US$250) and one four-bed cottage (US$160).

Murera Bandas   BANDAS **$$**

(🖉061-2303094; www.kws.go.ke; bandas US$80) The Murera camp, with plain wooden cottages and huts, isn't as charming as Kinna's, but it's a fine place to doss if everything is booked up. There's one two-bed *banda* with a TV, and six three-bed *bandas*.

★ Elsa's Kopje
BANDAS $$$

(☎0733333887, 0730127000; www.elsaskopje.com; s/d full board from US$843/1124; ☒) Plenty of hotels claim to blend into their environment, but Elsa's did so in such a seamless manner that the bar on chic ecosuites was permanently raised. Carved into Mugwangho Hill, these highly individualised 'three-walled' rooms open out onto views that *The Lion King* animators would have killed for.

Stone-hewn infinity pools plunge over the clifftops, while rock hyraxes play tag in your private garden. These features come with intense luxury pampering, wildlife drives, walking safaris and an utterly marvellous sense of being in a stunning, exclusive, remote corner of wildest Africa.

Leopard Rock Lodge
LODGE $$$

(☎0733920082, Nairobi 020-6000031; www.leopardmico.com; s/d full board US$570/980; ☒) This beautiful unfenced lodge lets the wildlife right in; keep an eye on your possessions, as the baboons and/or Sykes' monkeys will nick your stuff. Accommodation is in massive yet extremely comfortable *bandas,* the food is good and the location puts you right in the heart of the wildlife action.

ℹ Information

The KWS *Meru National Park Map* (KSh500), sometimes sold at the park gates, is helpful if you want to find your way around.

ℹ Getting There & Away

The park is roughly 1½ hours from Meru via the D484 Hwy. If you need a vehicle, J Kirimi Safaris (p178) offers full-day safari packages from KSh18,000 per vehicle.

Airkenya (p385) has twice-daily flights connecting Meru to Nairobi's Wilson Airport (adult/child one way US$268/186).

Chogoria

☏ 064 / POP 28,415

This town shares its name with the most difficult route up Mt Kenya. It's a friendly enough place but unless you're trekking, there's no real reason to stop here.

MERU'S LION STARS

When Joy Adamson wrote *Born Free* about her experience raising an orphaned lion cub called Elsa, few people predicted that the book would spend 13 weeks at the top of the *New York Times* bestseller list and go on to inspire a film that would become a worldwide hit.

Elsa, along with her two sisters, was orphaned when Joy's husband, George Adamson, was forced to kill their mother in self-defence while tracking a man-eater. But unlike her siblings, who were sent to European zoos, Elsa, the weakest of the litter, was kept by the Adamsons, who then spent two years educating her in the ways of lions before successfully releasing her into the wilds of what is today Meru National Park (p177).

The story of freed lions was not, unfortunately, always so simple, and one of Adamson's formerly captive lions, Boy, who starred in the movie, mauled Adamson's assistant to death; Adamson was forced to shoot the lion. Similar maulings occurred with other lions.

Even so, it was the success of Elsa's rehabilitation that inspired John Rendall and Ace Bourke to have their own lion, Christian (www.alioncalledchristian.com), shipped to George Adamson's camp in 1969 in the hope that he too could be returned to the wild. Christian was originally bought from Harrods department store and lived in a London basement below Rendall and Bourke's furniture shop. On learning that Christian had been successfully acclimatised, the men returned to Kenya and their reunion with Christian was filmed for a 1971 documentary.

More than 30 years later, edited footage of this reunion went viral on YouTube. It's a real tear-jerker, especially the part when Christian first recognises his old friends and comes bounding down a rocky slope and literally leaps into their arms, almost knocking the men off their feet in a 150kg demonstration of furry lion love.

☞ Tours

Mt Kenya Chogoria Guides & Porters Association   TREKKING

(☏ 0733676970; anthonytreks@yahoo.com; per person per day from US$120) A small association of guides, cooks and porters based at the Transit Motel, specialising in the Chogoria route up the mountain.

🛌 Sleeping

Transit Motel   MOTEL $

(☏ 0725609151; camping per person KSh300, s/d KSh1500/2000; P) If you haven't arranged your accommodation with one of the many touts offering Mt Kenya climbs, head to Transit Motel, 2km south of town. This is a large, friendly lodge with pleasant rooms (some with small balconies) and a decent restaurant (meals KSh550). Mt Kenya Chogoria Guides & Porters Association (p179) is also based here.

❶ Getting There & Away

Chogoria is 3km off the main B6 drag. In all likelihood an express matatu will drop you at either the Kiriani (southern) junction or the Kirurumwe (northern) junction, from where you will have to catch a *boda-boda* (motorcycle taxi) to town. Destinations include Meru (KSh220, one hour), Embu (KSh300, 1½ hours) and Nairobi (KSh500, four hours).

Embu

📞 068 / POP 67,864

This sleepy town is the unlikely capital of Eastern Province, but despite its local significance there's not a lot to do, and it's a long way from the mountain. The only reason to pass through is en route between Meru and Nairobi along the quieter back road. The town is at its best around October/November, when the local jacaranda trees are in full, purple bloom.

🛌 Sleeping

Izaak Walton Inn Hotel   HOTEL $

(☏ 0712781810; www.izaakwaltoninn.co.ke; Kenyatta Hwy; s/d KSh3500/4300; 🛜🏊) Set in a mature garden on the northern edge of town, this once-fine establishment is running down fast and is in urgent need of renovations or, at the very least, some maintenance and tender loving care. Rooms are promising but many seem not to have been fussed over in a while.

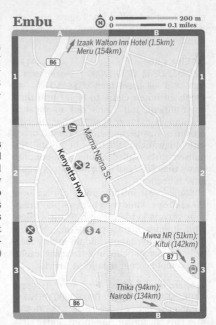

Embu — 0 / 200 m · 0 / 0.1 miles

Izaak Walton Inn Hotel (1.5km); Meru (154km)

Mwea NR (51km); Kitui (142km)

Thika (94km); Nairobi (134km)

Embu

🛏 **Sleeping**
1 Maina Highway Hotel A2

❌ **Eating**
2 Country View Downtown A2
3 Panesic Hotel A3

❶ **Information**
4 Barclays A3

❶ **Transport**
5 Bus & Matatu Stand B3

Maina Highway Hotel   HOTEL $

(☏ 068-2231789, 0722827700; www.mainahighwayhotel.com; off Meru–Nairobi Hwy; s/d KSh1500/2500; P🛜) Utterly unpromising from the outside, this simple place is the pick of the budget options. Rooms have mosquito nets and the central location is ideal, although noise can be a problem.

🍴 Eating

Country View Downtown   PUB FOOD $

(Kenyatta Hwy; mains KSh250-800; ⏱7.30am-late) Formerly Bomas pub, patrons are still afforded unadulterated views of downtown Embu, complete with acrid diesel fumes and views of the slightly depressing independence statue. Beers flow freely and good slabs of roast goat and ugali round out the experience. There is also a large patio away from the street.

Panesic Hotel INTERNATIONAL **$$**
(☎0707223715; mains KSh500-700; ⏰7am-9pm; 🅿📶) The food here is great value and only a few shillings more than the town's cheap eateries. Steaks come with a soup starter, mounds of veggies and starch (their phrasing) of your choice. The fruit cocktail is a vitamin-packed treat of layered avocado, mango and something-red juice. There's also a barbecue deck near the pool serving *nyama choma* and beer.

ℹ Information

Barclays (B7 Hwy; ⏰9am-4pm Mon-Fri, to noon Sat) ATM and foreign-exchange facilities.

ℹ Getting There & Away

Some buses call into the **Shell petrol station** (cnr Kenyatta Hwy & B7 Hwy; ⏰24hr) in the centre of town on their way to and from Nairobi and Mombasa. Buses to Nairobi arrive roughly every hour, though there is no set schedule; expect to pay between KSh200 and KSh400.

If you are in a rush, better to head south to the **bus and matatu stand** where numerous services depart for Chogoria (KSh300, 1½ hours), Meru (KSh450, two hours), Thika (KSh300, two hours), Nyeri (KSh320, two hours), Nanyuki (KSh400, 3½ hours), Nyahururu (KSh600, five hours), Nairobi (KSh400, three hours) and Nakuru (KSh750, six hours).

Ol Donyo Sabuk National Park

Tiny **Ol Donyo Sabuk National Park** (☎Nairobi 020-2062503; www.kws.go.ke; adult/child US$26/17; ⏰6am-7pm) covers little more than 20 sq km and is built around the summit and slopes of **Ol Donyo Sabuk** (2146m), known by the Kikuyu as Kilimambongo (Buffalo Mountain). The name fits, as buffaloes are one of the few animals that you may actually encounter here, aside from primates such as baboons, colobus monkeys and Sykes' monkeys in the montane forest that covers all but the hill's summit.

Because of the dangerous buffaloes, it is only possible to explore on foot if accompanied by a ranger (per half/full day KSh1720/3015). We found its signature 9km hike (three or four hours) to the summit on a dirt road to be disappointing and the views, while impressive, are slowly getting obscured by mobile-phone towers. More interesting is the weird Afro-alpine flora crowning the summit that you'd otherwise have to climb Mt Kenya to see.

'YOU WILL BUILD CASTLES'

'What does this stuff do?' we ask our driver.

'It gives you energy. When you chew this thing, you will build castles.'

That was our introduction to *miraa,* the small shoots and leaves that are chewed throughout the Mt Kenya area and Muslim parts of the country.

Some of the best *miraa* in the world is grown around Meru. Much of the demand is from Somalia and, since *miraa*'s potency is diminished 48 hours after picking, massively overladen pick-up trucks race at breakneck speed to Wilson Airport in Nairobi for the next flight to Mogadishu – get out of their way if you see them coming.

Chewing *miraa* pre-dates coffee drinking and is deeply rooted in the cultural traditions of some societies, especially in Muslim countries. It's usually chewed in company to encourage confidence, contentment and a flow of ideas. The active ingredient, cathinone, is closely related to amphetamine, and the euphoric effects can last for up to 24 hours, depending on how much is chewed.

Chewing too much can be habit-forming and has serious consequences, known as '*khat* syndrome'. Aggressive behaviour, nightmares and hallucinations are common mental side effects, while reduced appetite, malnourishment, constipation and brown teeth are common physical consequences.

Meru is a good place for curious travellers to give *miraa* a go. It's bitter and gives a brief high, followed by a long come-down. Note that *miraa* is illegal in neighbouring Tanzania (and, more recently, the UK, which decreed it a Class C drug in 2014), so best leave it out of the suitcase if you're heading that way.

WORTH A TRIP

THIKA

Thika is one of the most recognisable names to emerge from colonial Kenya, thanks to the eloquent memoir *The Flame Trees of Thika (Memories of an African Childhood)* by Elspeth Huxley. These days, in this sprawling modern city you'd be hard-pressed to find a tree, let alone a flame tree, but there is an opportunity to indulge in a little nostalgia before getting back on the highway and continuing on your way.

Sights

Karunguru Coffee Estate (☏0784420110, 0728765804; www.karungurucoffee.com; Kenyatta Rd; tour US$55; ⊗8am-6pm Mon-Fri, 10am-midnight Sat & Sun, tours 11am) This estate has been cultivating coffee since 1928, and its five-hour tours (which must be pre-booked) are outstanding, taking in an explanation of the estate's history, a tour of the various stages of coffee production, a buffet lunch in a stunning ballroom, coffee tasting and a visit to the estate's shop.

Chania Falls (Muranga Rd) The Chania Falls tumble over a rocky, tree-lined cliff, just in front of the restaurant of the Blue Post Hotel. The scene is delightfully appreciated from the porch of the restaurant with a stiff drink in one hand and a book in the other. There is a gated walkway on the hotel grounds that allows you to walk down to the falls' base (KSh400).

Thika Falls (Blue Post Hotel, Muranga Rd) Smaller than Chania Falls, Thika Falls are still impressive to watch. Located on the Blue Post Hotel grounds, you can watch the falls while your kids play on the large field next to the lookout. There are also barbecue facilities nearby, though you'll have to ask permission from the hotel reception to use them.

Sleeping

Blue Post Hotel (☏0721578245, 067-2222241; www.blueposthotel.co.ke; Muranga Rd; s/d/tr KSh6600/8800/11,400; P@�) With a history that outdates the town itself, the Blue Post still retains a faint whiff of the colonial. Undoubtedly it was the prime location, with grounds containing both the Chania and Thika Falls, that first attracted its original proprietors in 1908. Today the grounds (with a children's play area) attract Kenyan couples intent on tying the knot.

Getting There & Away

Thika's steady stream of matatus leave from the 'main stage' in the centre of town. Destinations include Nairobi (KSh150, one hour), Sagana (KSh200, one hour), Nyeri (KSh300, two hours) and Embu (KSh300, 1½ hours).

You can also catch one of the many matatus heading to Nairobi (KSh150, one hour) from a stop just outside the Blue Post Hotel.

🛏 Sleeping

Turacco Public Campsite CAMPGROUND $
(☏Nairobi 020-6000800; www.kws.co.ke; camping adult/child US$20/15) This pretty campsite is just after the main gate. Facilities include one long-drop toilet, a rusty tap and free firewood.

Sabuk House BANDAS $
(☏Nairobi 020-6000800; www.kws.go.ke; 10-bed house US$300) The most comfortable option in Ol Donyo Sabuk, this comfortable KWS *banda* is a little rundown but excellent value if you've enough people in your party to bring down per-person costs.

ⓘ Getting There & Away

From Thika, take the same matatu you would for **Fourteen Falls** (per person US$15, plus per camera US$5) but continue to the village of Ol Donyo Sabuk (KSh150, 50 minutes), from where it's a 2km walk along a straight dirt road to the gate.

Southeastern Kenya

Includes ➡

Namanga 185

Amboseli
National Park 185

Chyulu Hills
National Park 189

Tsavo West
National Park 190

Tsavo East
National Park 197

Voi 200

Taita Hills
Wildlife Sanctuary . . .201

Best Places to Eat

➡ Ol Donyo (p188)

➡ Campi ya Kanzi (p188)

➡ Finch Hatton's Safari Camp (p195)

➡ Severin Safari Camp (p195)

➡ Kilaguni Serena (p195)

Best Places to Stay

➡ Ol Donyo (p188)

➡ Campi ya Kanzi (p188)

➡ Finch Hatton's Safari Camp (p195)

➡ Tortilis Camp (p187)

➡ Lions Bluff Lodge (p203)

Why Go?

Southeastern Kenya is one of the great wildlife-watching destinations in Africa. Here you'll find a triumvirate of epic Kenyan parks – Amboseli, Tsavo West and Tsavo East – that are home to the Big Five and so much more. The landscapes, too, are something special, from Amboseli's backdrop of Africa's highest mountain, Mt Kilimanjaro, to the rugged beauty of Tsavo West's Ngulia Hills and the Chyulu Hills, Hemingway's Green Hills of Africa. Down here you'll also find smaller sanctuaries and so many exciting initiatives that combine conservation with community engagement. Many of these ensure that the chances to get to know the Maasai – the soulful human inhabitants of this land – on equal terms rank among the best in Kenya. And with good (if busy) roads and a newly minted rail link, it all adds up to Kenya at its wildest and yet most accessible.

When to Go
Voi

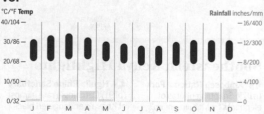

Jul–Oct This is prime time for watching wildlife in southern Kenyan parks; expect crowds.

Nov–Feb Good for watching birds and wildlife; November rains can be a minor inconvenience.

Mar–May Rains here can make roads impassable and wildlife disperses, but it changes yearly.

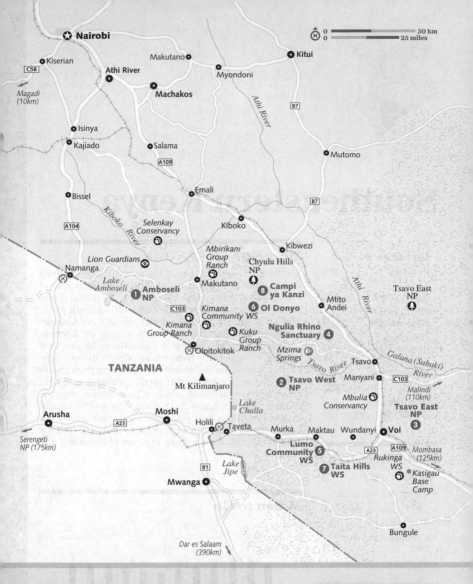

Southeastern Kenya Highlights

1 **Amboseli National Park** (p185) Snapping photos of elephants by Mt Kilimanjaro.

2 **Tsavo West National Park** (p190) Roaming the wilderness in search of leopards.

3 **Tsavo East National Park** (p197) Braving man-eating lions and red elephants in the back country.

4 **Ngulia Rhino Sanctuary** (p191) Catching a rare glimpse of Kenya's endangered black rhinos.

5 **Lumo Community Wildlife Sanctuary** (p202) The pick of the smaller sanctuaries.

6 **Ol Donyo** (p188) Contemplating Maasailand's

vast sweep from the heights of luxury.

7 **Taita Hills Wildlife Sanctuary** (p201) Learning about the region's fascinating WWI past.

8 **Campi ya Kanzi** (p188) Walking up into the Chyulu Hills in the company of a Maasai warrior.

SOUTH OF NAIROBI

Namanga

📍 045 / POP 12,000

In the shadow of low hills, Namanga sits adjacent to one of the busiest border crossings in East Africa. That said, it has a surprisingly relaxed atmosphere, and even the frontier itself has been streamlined to make the whole process more efficient.

🛏 Sleeping

Namanga River Hotel HOTEL **$**
(📞0724041375, 0725967676; www.facebook.com/namangariverhotel; off Namanga-Nairobi Rd; camping KSh750, s/d KSh5500/7000, deluxe KSh7500/9000; 🅿🛜🏊) For one last night in Kenya or to otherwise break up your travels, consider this shady campsite that offers some tidy cabins with TVs and mosquito nets. The deluxe rooms are only slightly larger than the standard ones, but come with mildly better bathrooms. There's also a decent bar-restaurant frequented by travellers drawn by the *nyama choma* (barbecued meats).

Namanga Maasai Hotel HOTEL **$**
(📞0750607069; off Namanga-Nairobi Rd; per person KSh1500) As basic as they come and really only for those on a real shoestring, the Namanga Maasai Hotel has unappealing digs in basic rooms arrayed around rather scruffy gardens.

❶ Getting There & Away

BUS & SHARED TAXI

Buses between Nairobi and Arusha pass through daily (KSh500 to KSh850, two hours). Matatus and Peugeots (shared taxis) also run here from the junction of River Rd and Ronald Ngala St in Nairobi (KSh550).

On the Tanzanian side of the border, nine-seater minivans run from the border to Arusha (two hours).

CAR & MOTORCYCLE

If you're driving, count on three hours to Nairobi or two hours to Arusha, once you've cleared immigration formalities.

If you're coming from Tanzania on your way to southeastern Kenya, there's a 4WD-only track that leads from Namanga to Amboseli National Park. It's a rough track, but infinitely preferable to travelling via Nairobi.

SOUTHEAST TO TSAVO

Amboseli National Park

Amboseli (📞0716493335, Nairobi 020-8029705; www.kws.go.ke; adult/child US$60/35; ⏱6am-6pm) belongs in the elite of Kenya's national parks, and it's easy to see why. Its signature attraction is the sight of hundreds of big-tusked elephants set against the backdrop of Africa's best views of Mt Kilimanjaro (5895m). Africa's highest peak broods over the southern boundary of the park, and while cloud cover can render the mountain's massive bulk invisible for much of the day, you'll be rewarded with stunning vistas when the weather clears, usually at dawn and/or dusk. Apart from guaranteed elephant sightings, you'll also see wildebeest and zebras, and you've a reasonable chance of spotting lions, cheetahs and hyenas. The park is also home to over 370 bird species, and it has an excellent array of lodges and an agreeably mild, dry climate.

---

❶ AMBOSELI NATIONAL PARK

Why Go To see big-tusked elephants, Africa's best Mt Kilimanjaro views, lions, cheetahs, hyenas, wildebeest and zebras, and rich birdlife.

When to Go Year-round. The dry season (July to October and January to February) is best for spotting wildlife, while November to March is the best time to see migratory birds. Much of the wildlife moves beyond the park during and immediately after the rains.

Practicalities The two most popular entrance gates are Iremito (accessible from Emali along the Nairobi–Mombasa highway) and Kimana (southeast). The two western approaches (Kitirua and Meshanani gates) are in poor condition. The park is accessible in 2WD, but 4WD is always the best option, particularly after rain.

Budget Tips Camp at a public campsite inside the park, or one of the private camps outside Kimana Gate. If you choose the latter, time your forays into the park carefully to make maximum use of the 24-hour entrance fee.

Amboseli National Park

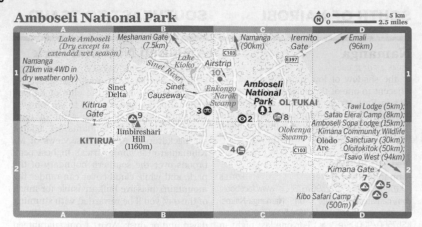

Amboseli National Park

◎ Top Sights
1 Amboseli National Park.......................C1

◎ Sights
2 Elephant Research Camp C1
3 Normatior (Observation Hill)..............B1

🛏 Sleeping
4 Amboseli Serena Lodge C2
5 Kibo Safari Camp D2
6 Kimana Camp D2
7 KWS Campsite D2
8 Ol Tukai Lodge.....................................C1
9 Tortilis Camp B1

ⓘ Transport
10 Airkenya C1

◎ Sights

The park's permanent swamps of **Enkongo Narok**, **Olokenya** and **Longinye** create a marshy belt across the middle of the park; this is where you'll encounter the most wildlife. Elephants love to wallow around in the muddy waters and you've a good chance of seeing hippos around the edge. For really close-up elephant encounters, **Sinet Causeway**, which crosses Enkongo Narok near (Normatior) Observation Hill, is often good; climb **Normatior** for fine views. The surrounding grasslands are home to grazing antelope, zebras and wildebeest, with spotted hyenas, cheetahs and lions sometimes lurking nearby; there's a reasonably reliable hyena den signposted northeast of the hill, which all the guides know about.

Birdlife is especially rich in these swamps when the migrants arrive in November.

If you're taking the road that runs east across the park to the Kimana Gate, watch for giraffes in the acacia woodlands; this is the best place inside the park for giraffe-spotting. We've also had excellent luck out here with cheetahs and lions.

At the time of writing, Ol Tukai Lodge (p187) was the only place offering **night drives** (per person US$80) and only to guests staying at the lodge.

Elephant Research Camp   NATURE CENTRE
(☏0714781699; www.elephanttrust.org; group of 10 or less US$800, group of more than 10 per person US$80; ⊙by prior appointment 3.30pm Mon-Fri) The elephants of Amboseli are among the most studied in the world, thanks largely to the work of Dr Cynthia Moss, whose books include *The Amboseli Elephants* and *Elephant Memories;* she was also behind the famous documentary DVD *Echo of the Elephants*. The research camp remains in operation in the heart of the park, under the guidance of the **Amboseli Trust for Elephants** (www.elephanttrust.org).

🛏 Sleeping

Kimana Camp   TENTED CAMP $
(☏0715059635; per person from US$31, camping US$10) A good deal within easy reach of Amboseli's main Kimana Gate, this dusty but great-value tented camp has 20 permanent tents and six cottages, all of which enjoy electricity and 24-hour hot water, although the bathrooms are extremely simple in both

cases. There's a restaurant, a kitchen that guests can use and views of Kilimanjaro.

KWS Campsite
CAMPGROUND $

(www.kws.go.ke; camping US$30) Just inside the park's southeastern boundary, the KWS campsite has toilets, an unreliable water supply (bring your own) and a small bar selling warm beer and soft drinks. It's fenced off from the wildlife, so you can walk around safely at night, though *don't* keep food in your tent, as baboons visit during the day looking for an uninvited feed.

★ Tawi Lodge
LODGE $$$

(Nairobi 020-2660080; www.tawilodge.com; s/d full board Jul-Sep US$530/820, rates vary rest of year; P❤️🏊) 🌿 Set on its own private 24-sq-km conservancy close to Kimana Gate and with its own airstrip, Tawi Lodge is our pick of the places southeast of the park. You've got the choice of going into Amboseli or exploring Tawi's own wildlife-rich area, while the cottages are refined, beautifully furnished and most come with fine Kili views. There's even an on-site spa, and night drives are possible.

★ Tortilis Camp
TENTED CAMP $$$

(0730127000, 045-622195; www.tortilis.com; s/d full board Jul-Oct US$678/904, family tent/private house US$2300/2800, rates vary rest of year; P🌐) 🌿 This wonderfully conceived site is one of the most exclusive ecolodges in Kenya, commanding a superb elevated spot with perfect Kilimanjaro vistas. The luxurious canvas tents have recently been given a facelift; the family rooms have the biggest wow factor we found in southern Kenya. The lavish meals, which are based on North Italian traditional recipes, feature herbs and vegetables from the huge on-site organic garden.

★ Ol Tukai Lodge
LODGE $$$

(0726249697, Nairobi 020-4445514; www.ol tukailodge.com; s/d/tr full board Jul-Oct US$410/520/730, Nov-Mar US$350/450/630, Apr-Jun US$170/315/435; P@🌐🏊) Lying at the heart of Amboseli, on the edge of a dense acacia forest, Ol Tukai is a splendidly refined lodge with soaring *makuti* (thatched roofs of palm leaves) and tranquil gardens defined by towering trees. Accommodation is in chalets, which are brought to life with vibrant zebra prints. The split-level bar has a sweeping Kili view and a pervading atmosphere of peace and luxury.

Kibo Safari Camp
TENTED CAMP $$$

(0721380539; www.kibosafaricamp.com; per person from US$160; P🌐🏊) Around 2km from Kimana Gate, Kibo Safari Camp gives you the experience of a tented camp without asking the prohibitive fees of the lodges inside the park proper; you can be inside the park soon after sunrise. The 72 tents and expansive grounds are beautifully kept and there are astonishing views of Kilimanjaro to be had, as well as a good restaurant serving high-quality buffet meals.

Satao Elerei Camp
TENTED CAMP $$$

(Nairobi 020-2434600; www.sataoelerai.com; s/d full board Jul-Oct US$545/820, rates vary rest of year; P🌐🏊) 🌿 The five lodge rooms are all well and good (and they are indeed very good), but we love this place for its nine supremely comfortable tents, each of which has its own private verandah and fabulous Kilimanjaro views when the weather's clear. It's signposted off the main track in from Oloitokitok, and is around 10km from Kimana Gate.

Amboseli Serena Lodge
LODGE $$$

(0735522361, Nairobi 020-2842000; www.serena hotels.com; s/d full board Jul-Oct US$282/392; @🌐🏊) A classically elegant property in Amboseli, the Serena is comprised of fiery-red adobe cottages, some of which (rooms 68 to 75) overlook the wildlife-rich Enkongo Narok swamp and are fringed by lush tropical gardens of blooming flowers and manicured shrubs. There are no Kilimanjaro views from the lodge. Service is excellent, as is the swimming pool and wi-fi connection.

ℹ️ Getting There & Away

AIR

Airkenya (www.airkenya.com; adult/child one way US$187/138) has daily flights between Nairobi's Wilson Airport (35 minutes) and Amboseli. You'll need to arrange with one of the lodges or a safari company for a vehicle to meet you at the airstrip, which is inside the park proper, near Ol Tukai Lodge. Most lodges within the park charge around US$40 for the transfer from the airstrip.

CAR & 4WD

There are four gates. Approaches to the park from the west (Kitirua and Meshanani gates) are in poor condition; the Iremito (northeast) and Kimana (southeast) gates are in better condition. The park is accessible in 2WD, but 4WD is always the best option, particularly after rain.

LODGES ALONG THE NAIROBI–MOMBASA ROAD

Hunter's Lodge (☑0721254174, 0727209509; www.madahotels.com; Nairobi-Mombasa Rd, Kiboko; s/d/tr US$60/80/100; P🖘❄) One of the longest-standing lodges in Kenya, having first opened in 1958, this property was overhauled in late 2014 and is now an excellent choice at Kiboko, 160km southeast of Nairobi (between Emali and Mtito Andei). It's set on 25 acres of leafy grounds. Rooms are large and comfortable with dark-wood furnishings and a suitably classic look.

Umani Springs (☑0733891996; www.sheldrickwildlifetrust.org; Kibwezi Forest; 5-bedroom lodge from US$600; P❄) A beautiful place to stay and wonderfully removed from the tourist scrum, this gracious, designer-renovated lodge is deep in the Kibwezi Forest, around 10km north of the Nairobi–Mombasa road. It's self-catering, so you'll need to bring in all your food, but there are staff (including a cook if required) and a real sense of having discovered your own private African retreat.

Around Amboseli

Greater Amboseli is a wonderful, complicated place. It's an integral part of the Maasai heartland and an intriguing wildlife-watching alternative to nearby Amboseli National Park. It's also ground zero for the future of wildlife on human-dominated landscapes and a place where some of the most exciting conservation work in Kenya is taking place. Throw in some terrific high-end places to stay and it all adds up to a fascinating mix.

The national park occupies less than 5% of the greater Amboseli ecosystem's 8000 sq km, and surrounding the park itself is a series of group Maasai ranches which are home, by one estimate, to around 30,000 Maasai, along with upwards of a million of their livestock. These ranches also occupy the ancient wildlife corridors that once connected Amboseli with northern Tanzania, the Athi Plains near Nairobi and even the Masai Mara.

⊙ Sights

Maasai Cattle Market   MARKET
(Kimana; ⊙ Tue) If you're in the Amboseli area on a Tuesday, consider stopping in the town of Kimana (along the paved road between Emali and Oloitokitok) for its weekly Maasai livestock market. It's an appealing slice of local life in an area where accessing same can be difficult and a rewarding complement to the national parks from which the Maasai are largely excluded.

🛏 Sleeping

**Muteleu Maasai
Traditional Village**   BUNGALOW $
(☑0720356430; www.mmaasaitraditionalvillage.com; Merrueshi; s/d incl breakfast US$30/50, full board US$70/120) Built in the style of a traditional Maasai village by local Maasai women, these ten Maasai huts make a refreshing alternative to the more upmarket lodges that are an Amboseli feature. The focus here is on cultural immersion in the local Maasai community rather than on watching wildlife, although it could equally be a base for visiting (or a waystation en route to) Amboseli.

★**Ol Donyo**   LODGE $$$
(☑Nairobi 020-600457; www.greatplainsconservation.com; s/d all-inclusive mid-Jun–Oct from US$1733/2310, rates vary rest of year; P🖘❄) ✎ Welcome to what could just be our favourite place to stay in Kenya. Built onto the foothills of Chyulu Hills at the remote eastern reaches of the 1113-sq-km Mbirikani Group Ranch, Ol Donyo is a temple to good taste grafted onto one of the loveliest corners of Africa.

★**Campi ya Kanzi**   TENTED CAMP $$$
(☑0720461300; www.maasai.com; s/d tented cottage US$950/1500, s/d tented suites US$1200/1900, conservation fee per adult/child from US$101/51; P🖘❄) ✎ Campi ya Kanzi is, quite simply, an outstanding place to stay. Set upon the slopes of the Chyulu Hills – these may have been Ernest Hemingway's 'Green Hills of Africa' and that sobriquet means so much more here than it does in Chyulu Hills National Park – accommodation here is in luxury tents scattered around an enormous ranch that is centred on a nostalgically decorated stone lodge.

Porini Amboseli Camp   TENTED CAMP $$$
(☑0722509200, Nairobi 020-7123129; www.porini.com; per person full board from US$394; P) ✎ Far removed from the tourist lodges in the park itself, this deliciously remote camp

inhabits the 748-sq-km Selenkay Conservancy (also known as Eselenkei Group Ranch) north of the national park. The tents are semi-luxurious without taking away from the remote feel. Although it's a good base for visiting the park, the conservancy is also worth exploring in its own right.

❶ Getting There & Away

The road between Emali (on the Nairobi–Mombasa road) and Oloitokitok (on the Kenya–Tanzania border) cuts through the heart of the area. It's the main access road for those who are driving, while matatus run up and down the road on a semi-regular basis.

Airkenya (p187) has flights from Nairobi's Wilson Airport into Amboseli airstrip (inside Amboseli National Park), while **Safarilink** (☑ Nairobi 020-6690000; www.flysafarilink.com; adult/child one way US$224/170) flies into an airstrip at Ol Donyo on Mbirikani Group Ranch.

Chyulu Hills National Park

One of Kenya's least-visited parks, **Chyulu Hills National Park** (☑0711574766, Nairobi 020-2626174; www.kws.go.ke/content/chyulu-hills-national-park; adult/child US$25/15; ◷6am-7pm) is a line of pretty green hills that rise above the arid plains between Amboseli and Tsavo West. The park is dominated by extinct volcanoes.

At the same time, this park is something of a disappointment – you're likely to see more herders with their cattle than wildlife, and poaching remains a problem here. The only reason to visit the park proper is **Leviathan**, one of the world's longest lava tubes, or some surprisingly dense cloud forest clinging (like the park border) to the ridgeline, and accessible by 4WD from the Nairobi–Mombasa road. Otherwise, admire the hills from afar (eg from

---

AMBOSELI CONSERVATION PROJECTS

Lion Guardians

In Maasai culture, young male warriors (the *moran*) have traditionally killed lions and other wild animals to prove their bravery and as an initiation rite into manhood. But one organisation has come up with an innovative way of honouring Maasai tradition while protecting lions in the process. The **Lion Guardians** (www.lionguardians.org), a cutting-edge and highly successful project, has taken many of these young, traditional warriors and turned them into Lion Guardians, whose task is to protect the Maasai and the lions from each other. Each Lion Guardian, most of whom are former lion killers, patrols a territory on the Maasai group ranches, keeping track of the lions, warning herders of lion locations and helping them to find lost livestock and even lost children. In areas where the Lion Guardians operate, lion killings (and livestock lost to lions) have fallen dramatically.

Maasailand Preservation Trust

Kuku in particular is the base for the Maasai Wilderness Conservation Trust (www.maasaiwilderness.org), which is run partly out of Campi ya Kanzi (p188) and has Hollywood star Edward Norton as the president of its US board of directors. The trust works closely with local communities in protecting these important wildlife habitats and corridors through programmes such as Simba Scouts (local Maasai rangers), environmental education, and Wildlife Pays (payments are made to local communities for the wildlife that lives on their land, instead of paying compensation for livestock losses after the fact).

Big Life Foundation

Mibirikani has been the centre for some excellent conservation work over the years. It began in 2004 (when lions were being killed in record numbers) with the Predator Compensation Fund (PCF), a scheme run by the Maasailand Preservation Trust. Designed to reduce human-wildlife conflict by paying monetary compensation to local Maasai herders for livestock killed by predators, the PCF is largely credited with turning the situation around.

In 2012, the Maasailand Preservation Trust was brought within the Big Life Foundation (www.biglife.org) which operates a paramilitary force of armed rangers who patrol the area to combat poaching. Run by veteran conservationist Richard Bonham and operating in part from Ol Donyo (p188), Big Life is widely touted as the reason why the poaching of elephants and rhinos – there's a small population of the latter on the western slopes of the Chyulu Hills – has largely passed Amboseli by.

neighbouring Tsavo West National Park) and consider visiting instead the hills' western slopes beyond the park borders – Ol Donyo (p188) and Campi ya Kanzi (p188) are two of the loveliest lodges in southeastern Kenya.

🏃 Activities

Savage Wilderness
CAVING

(📞0737835963; www.savagewilderness.org; per person per day US$250) Caving and trekking trips in the Chyulu Hills are possible with Savage Wilderness – they're based in Sagana a few hours to the north and while Chyulu Hills is not a part of their regular programme, but they do run four-day/three-night hiking and caving expeditions into the park upon request. Costs include park fees.

❶ Information

Chyulu Hills Park Headquarters Both the park entrance and the place to go for park information.

❶ Getting There & Away

The park headquarters, just outside Kibwezi about 41km northwest of Mtito Andei, is signposted off the Nairobi–Mombasa road.

You'll need your own vehicle to explore the park. Most tracks are accessible in a 2WD but a 4WD is preferable, especially after rains.

---

❶ TSAVO WEST NATIONAL PARK

Why Go For the dramatic scenery, wilderness and good mix of predators (lions, leopards, cheetahs and hyenas), prey (lesser kudus, gazelles, impalas) and other herbivores (elephants, rhinos, zebras, oryxes and giraffes).

When to Go Year-round. The dry season (May to October and January to March) is best for spotting wildlife. November to March is the best time to see migratory birds.

Practicalities Drive in from Mtito Andei or Tsavo Gate along the Nairobi–Mombasa road. There is a campsite close to the park entrance and lodges throughout the park.

Budget Tips Rent a matatu with other travellers in Mtito Andei; if staying in a lodge, June is much cheaper than July.

Tsavo West National Park
📄043

Welcome to the wilderness. **Tsavo West** (📞0720968527, Nairobi 0800597000, Nairobi 020-2384417; www.kws.go.ke/tsavo-west-national-park; adult/child US$52/35; ⏰6am-6pm) is one of Kenya's larger national parks (9065 sq km), covering a huge variety of landscapes from swamps, natural springs and rocky peaks to extinct volcanic cones, rolling plains and sharp outcrops dusted with greenery.

This is a park with a whiff of legend about it, first for its famous man-eating lions in the late 19th century and then for its devastating levels of poaching in the 1980s. Despite the latter, there's still plenty of wildlife here, although you'll have to work harder and be much more patient than in Amboseli or the Masai Mara; the foliage is generally denser and higher here. Put all of these things together, along with its dramatic scenery, fine lodges and sense of space, and this is one of Kenya's most rewarding parks.

◉ Sights

◉ Chyulu Gate & the West

The plains, rocky outcrops and light woodland between Kilaguni Serena Lodge and the Chyulu Gate are good for zebras and other herbivores, and sustain a healthy population of lions, leopards and spotted hyenas – the epic battle between rival hyena clans that we witnessed here on our last visit remains a favourite Tsavo memory.

★Mzima Springs
SPRING

Mzima Springs is an oasis of green in the west of the park that produces an incredible 250 million litres of fresh water a day. The springs, whose source rises in the Chyulu Hills, provides the bulk of Mombasa's fresh water. A walking trail leads along the shoreline. The drought in 2009 took a heavy toll on the springs' hippo population; the population is stable at around 20 individuals. There are also crocodiles and a wide variety of birdlife.

Poacher's Lookout
VIEWPOINT

A short distance northwest of Severin Safari Camp, this hilltop vantage point offers fine views out over the park, and especially fine views west to the plains of the Amboseli ecosystem and Mt Kilimanjaro.

★ Shetani Lava Flows LOOKOUT, VOLCANO

About 4km west of the Chyulu Gate of Tsavo West National Park, on the road to Amboseli, are the spectacular Shetani lava flows. 'Shetani' means 'devil' in Kiswahili: the flows were formed only a few hundred years ago and local peoples believed that it was the devil himself emerging from the earth. This vast expanse of folded black lava spreads for 50 sq km across the savannah near the Chyulu Hills, looking strangely as if Vesuvius dropped its comfort blanket here.

The last major eruption here is believed to have taken place around 200 years ago, but there are still few plants among the cinders. It's possible to follow the lava flows back from the Amboseli–Tsavo West road to the ruined cinder cone of Shetani. The views are spectacular, but you need to be wary of wildlife in this area, as there are predators about.

Nearby are the **Shetani Caves**, which are also a result of volcanic activity. You'll need a torch (flashlight) if you want to explore, but watch your footing on the razor-sharp rocks and keep an eye out for the local fauna – we've heard rumours that the caves are sometimes inhabited by hyenas, who don't take kindly to being disturbed. Some of the Tsavo West lodges charge US$50 per person for guided excursions out here.

Chaimu Crater & Roaring Rocks VIEWPOINT

Southeast of Kilaguni Serena Lodge, these two natural features offer stunning views of the Chyulu Hills and birds of prey circling high above the plains. The **Roaring Rocks** can be climbed in about 15 minutes; the name comes from the wind whistling up the escarpment and the persistent drone of cicadas. While there's little danger, the KWS does warn in its guidebook to the park that in **Chaimu Crater** 'be wary when exploring since the crater and lava may shelter snakes and large sleeping mammals'.

◉ Rhino Valley

This is a highly recommended area for wildlife watching, with plenty of antelope species keeping a careful eye out for the resident lions, leopards and cheetahs. You'll also see elephants, giraffes and, if you're lucky, black rhinos. Birdlife is also particularly diverse here. The signposted 'Rhino Valley Circuit' is a good place to start, and anywhere along the Mukui River's ponds and puddles is a place to watch and wait.

THE MOTHER OF ALL TRAFFIC JAMS

If you've ever driven along the Nairobi–Mombasa road, you'll be familiar with the endless procession of trucks and the times when you wonder whether you'll ever reach your destination at all. That's pretty standard for this road, but some days are, it seems, worse than others.

On 24 April 2016, for example, a truck overturned in heavy rains and traffic was unable to move for up to 12 hours. But it was six months earlier, in mid-November 2015, that things got *really* bad. Amid heavy rains, a section of the road near Taru, around halfway between Voi and Mombasa, was gridlocked for *three days*. The problem was compounded by trucks trying to go around the obstruction (or 'overlapping' in local parlance) and then becoming bogged in deep mud. Mombasa was effectively cut off from the Kenyan interior by land, impacting upon food supplies, business meetings and, of course, tourist itineraries.

Just one more reason to take the new Nairobi–Mombasa railway.

★ Ngulia Hills MOUNTAIN

Rising more than 600m above the valley floor and to a height of over 1800m above sea level, this jagged ridgeline ranks among the prettiest of all Tsavo landforms, providing as it does a backdrop to Rhino Valley. The hills can be climbed with permission from the **warden** (☑043-30049; tsavowestnp@kws.go.ke), while the peaks are also a recognised flyway (p196) for migrating birds heading south from late September through to November.

◉ Tsavo Gate & the East

Many visitors heading for Tsavo East National Park or Mombasa use this gate. Wildlife spotting in this eastern section of the park is challenging due to the quite dense foliage, but both leopards and lions are known to frequent the area.

★ Ngulia Rhino Sanctuary WILDLIFE RESERVE

(◷4-6pm) At the base of Ngulia Hills, this 90-sq-km area is surrounded by a 1m-high electric fence and provides a measure of security for around 80 of the park's highly endangered black rhinos. There are driving

Tsavo East & West National Parks

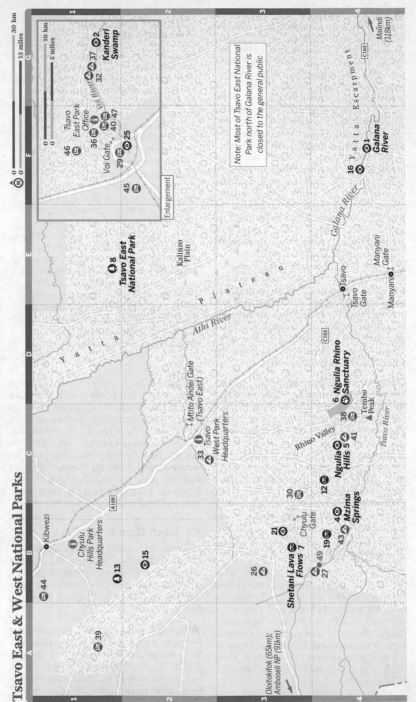

Note: Most of Tsavo East National Park north of the Galana River is closed to the general public

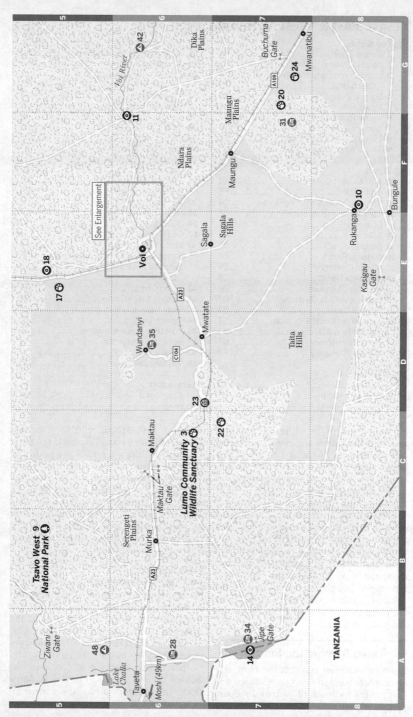

SOUTHEASTERN KENYA

Tsavo East & West National Parks

⊚ Top Sights
1 Galana River.................................. F4
2 Kanderi Swamp G1
3 Lumo Community Wildlife
  Sanctuary.................................C6
4 Mzima Springs..............................B4
5 Ngulia Hills...................................C4
6 Ngulia Rhino Sanctuary.........................D4
7 Shetani Lava Flows B3
8 Tsavo East National Park......................E1
9 Tsavo West National Park..................B5

⊚ Sights
10 African Shirt Company.......................... F8
11 Aruba Dam F6
12 Chaimu Crater & Roaring Rocks...........C4
13 Chyulu Hills National Park B1
   Crocodile Point................................(see 1)
14 Lake Jipe....................................... A7
15 Leviathan.......................................B2
16 Lugards Falls................................. F4
17 Mbulia Conservancy E5
18 Mudanda Rock.................................. E5
19 Poacher's Lookout B4
20 Rukinga Wildlife Sanctuary...................G7
21 Shetani Caves.................................B3
22 Taita Hills Wildlife Sanctuary................C7
23 Taita Hills WWI Museum D6
24 Tsavo Conservancy G7
25 Voi War Cemetery F2

ⓢ Sleeping
   Ashnil Aruba Lodge....................... (see 11)
26 Campi ya Kanzi.................................B3

   Cheetah Campsite...........................(see 3)
27 Finch Hatton's Safari Camp B4
28 Grogan's Castle Hotel A6
29 Impala Safari Lodge F1
   Kasigau Base Camp ....(see 10)
30 Kilaguni Serena Lodge C3
   Kitani Bandas...........................(see 43)
31 Kivuli Camp....................................... F7
32 KWS Campsite...............................G1
33 KWS Campsite...............................C2
34 Lake Jipe Safari Camp A7
35 Lavender Garden Hotel........................D6
   Leopards Lair ....(see 3)
36 Lion Hill Lodge.................................. F1
   Lions Bluff Lodge..........................(see 3)
37 Ndololo Safari Camp G1
38 Ngulia Safari Lodge C4
39 Ol Donyo...A1
40 Red Elephant Safari Lodge....................F1
41 Rhino Valley Lodge...........................C4
   Sarova Salt Lick Safari Lodge ......(see 22)
   Sarova Taita Hills Game
     Lodge.............................(see 23)
42 Satao Camp................................. G6
43 Severin Safari Camp B4
   Taita Research Station ....(see 35)
44 Umani Springs.................................B1
45 Voi Lutheran Guesthouse.....................F2
46 Voi Safari Lodge F1
47 Voi Wildlife Lodge...............................F1
48 Voyager Ziwani................................. A5

⊙ Transport
49 Safarilink B4

tracks and waterholes within the enclosed area, but the rhinos are mainly nocturnal and the chances of seeing one are slim – black rhinos, apart from being understandably shy and more active at night, are browsers, not grazers, and prefer to pass their time in thick undergrowth.

These archaic creatures are breeding successfully and around 15 have been released elsewhere in Tsavo West National Park. For all the security, one rhino was poached from inside the sanctuary in April 2014, with two more taken on 31 December 2016 amid reports of budget cuts and diminishing resources to fight poaching. Even so, there are plans to expand the boundaries of the sanctuary to the south.

⊙ Tsavo River & the South

Running west–east through the park, this lovely year-round river is green-shaded and surrounded for much of its path by doum palms. Along with Mzima Springs, the river provides aesthetic relief from the vast semi-arid habitats that dominate the park. The trees all along the river are known to shelter leopards.

South of the river, running down to the Ziwani and Maktau gates, the foliage is less dense, with cheetah sightings a possibility. This area has seen problems with poaching and the encroachment into the park by local herders – the further south you go, the less you're likely to see.

Lake Jipe   LAKE
This lake (pronounced ji-pay) lies at the extreme southwestern end of the park and is reached by a desperately dusty track from near Taveta. You can hire boats at the campsite to take you hippo and crocodile spotting on the lake (US$5). Huge herds of elephants come to the lake to drink, and it's particularly good for wildlife near the end of the dry season. Conversely, large flocks of migratory birds stop here from February to May.

🛏 Sleeping

Grogan's Castle Hotel
HOTEL $

(☑ 0717330228; www.facebook.com/Grogans Castle; Grogan's Hill, off Voi-Taveta Rd; s/d US$71/95) Feeling like a Mexican hacienda grafted onto the soils of Africa, this white-washed colonial relic has a lovely hilltop perch and is steeped in history – the building dates to late colonial times and takes its name from Ewart Grogan, the influential settler who built it. Although resurrected as a hotel in 2010, sadly the rooms aren't as well cared for as they could be.

KWS Campsite
CAMPGROUND $

(☑ 0720968527; www.kws.co.ke; Komboyo; camping US$20) This public campsite is at Komboyo, 8km from the Mtito Andei Gate. Facilities are basic, so be prepared to be self-sufficient, though there are at least toilets and cold-water showers.

★ Kitani Bandas
BANDAS $$

(☑ 0716833222, 041-2004154; www.severin safaricamp.com; bandas Jul-Mar US$125, Apr-Jun US$100; P🅿🛝) Run by the same people as Severin Safari Camp, Kitani is located 2km past its sister site, but is equally good value. These thatched concrete *bandas* (which have their own simple kitchens) have far more style than your average budget camp and you can use Severin's facilities (including the pool and free wi-fi). Great value, though do call ahead.

Lake Jipe Safari Camp
BUNGALOW $$

(☑ 0728284538, 0720911826; www.lakejipesafari camp.com; r full board from US$125; P🛜) With three safari tents and seven bandas, this simple place makes a decent base for Lake Jipe and the southern reaches of Tsavo West. It's lovely and quiet with Mt Kilimanjaro views just 500m back from the lakeshore. It's especially good for birdwatching (November to January), while reasonable concentrations of wildlife are drawn to the water around the end of the dry season.

★ Finch Hatton's Safari Camp
TENTED CAMP $$$

(☑ 0716021818, Nairobi 020-8030936; www. finchhattons.com; s/d full board Jul–mid-Oct US$1225/1960, family tent full board Jul–mid-Oct US$3240, rates vary rest of year; P🅿🛝) 🍃 This luxurious tented camp, arranged around a stream full of crocs and hippos, is now looking fancier than ever after a renovation. The 17 massive, glamorous tents have vast beds, huge verandahs and incredible outdoor bathrooms complete with copper bathtubs. There's a spa, gym and pool, courteous staff and a wonderfully stylish air to the place.

★ Severin Safari Camp
TENTED CAMP $$$

(☑ Nairobi 020-2684247; www.severinsafaricamp. com; s/d full board Jul-Mar US$252/388, Apr-Jun US$143/286, s/d ste full board Jul-Mar from US$379/506, Apr-Jun US$279/372; P🅿🛝) 🍃 This fantastic complex of thatched luxury tents just keeps getting better. There are lovely, spacious tents, a swimming pool and spa, and even a tented gym. The staff offer a personal touch (Manja and Juergen, a pastry chef, have been running this place since 2008), the food is outstanding and the tents are large and sumptuous despite costing considerably less than others elsewhere in the park.

Kilaguni Serena Lodge
LODGE $$$

(☑ 045-622376; www.serenahotels.com; s/d full board Jul-Oct US$243/342, rates vary rest of year; P@🛜🛝) As you'd expect from the upmarket Serena chain, this lodge is extremely comfortable with semi-luxurious, if slightly dated rooms. The centrepiece here is a splendid bar and restaurant with soaring thatched ceilings, volcanic stone and a panoramic bar overlooking a busy illuminated waterhole – the vista stretches all the way from Mt Kilimanjaro to the Chyulu Hills and has the wow factor upon arrival.

Voyager Ziwani
TENTED CAMP $$$

(☑ Nairobi 020-4446651; www.heritage-eastafrica. com; s/d full board US$165/220) Outside the southern boundary of the park but handy for exploring an area of the park that few travellers visit, Voyager Ziwani has lovely safari tents along a shady stretch of riverbank. If you're wanting to explore the more popular areas of the park further north it's quite a drive, but the setting is lovely and handy if you're going to/from Taita Hills or thereabouts.

Ngulia Safari Lodge
LODGE $$$

(☑ 043-30000; www.safari-hotels.com; s/d US$190/290; P🛝) Tsavo vantage points don't come any better than this – the views are simply magnificent and there's a waterhole right by the restaurant. It's all enough to make you forget that the building itself is a monstrosity and the rooms (especially the bathrooms) are tired and in need of an overhaul; the balcony views from all rooms are wonderful, especially rooms 6 and 7.

Rhino Valley Lodge TENTED CAMP $$$
(Ngulia Bandas; ☑ 043-30050; www.tsavo
lodgesandcamps.com; bandas full board s/d/tr
US$150/200/280; Ⓟ) Deep inside the park
on the slopes of the Ngulia Hills, this hill-
side camp is one of Tsavo's more reasonably
priced choices. The thatched stone cottages
and tents have lovely elevated perches with
sweeping views of Rhino Valley. The decor is
designer rustic with plenty of space and pri-
vate terraces. Self-catering is also an option
as many of the tents have small kitchens.

When things are quiet, it can feel a little
abandoned and maintenance is increasing-
ly an issue, but it's still a good deal. The
lodge is still signposted throughout the park
under its old name, Ngulia Bandas.

ⓘ Information

Tsavo West Park Headquarters The nearest
park entrance to Mtito Andei; there is limited
information here and a rather dusty interpreta-
tion centre.

MAPS
Tsavo West National Park map and guidebook is
available from Mtito Andei Gate.

ⓘ Getting There & Away

There are six gates into Tsavo West, but the main
access is just off the Nairobi–Mombasa road at
Mtito Andei and Tsavo gates. Payment can be
made at all gates.

THE NGULIA FLYWAY

Ngulia Safari Lodge (p195) may be past
its prime when it comes to its accom-
modation offering, but this means little
to the tens of thousands of European
and Asian Palearctic migrant bird spe-
cies that fly through here on their way
south from September to December.
The combination of a floodlit waterhole,
clifftop location and the fact that there
are no other settlements for miles
around attracts birds and birdwatchers
alike. Best of all, you can join in the
capture, tagging and release of species
which has been taking place here since
1969, usually in November or early
December. Highlights might include the
thrush nightingale, river warbler, march
warblers and a number of nightjar spe-
cies. Most Kenyan safari companies can
help make the arrangements, or you can
contact the lodge directly.

Safarilink (p189) has daily flights between
Nairobi's Wilson Airport and Tsavo West, with
airstrips near Finch Hatton's Camp and Kilaguni
Serena Lodge. You'll need to arrange with one of
the lodges or a safari company for a vehicle to
meet you at the airstrip.

Fuel is generally available at Kilaguni Serena
Lodge and Severin Safari Camp, but fill up before
entering the park.

The newly inaugurated Nairobi–Mombasa rail-
way stops at Mtito Andei – most lodges and tented
camps in the park offer transfers from the station.

Mbulia Conservancy

The 48-sq-km **Mbulia Conservancy** (con-
servation fee US$50) occupies part of an
important elephant corridor, and is also
an extension of the ecosystem inhabited
by Tsavo West National Park and its Ngulia
Rhino Sanctuary. Apart from the increas-
ing population of tusked giants and other
wildlife, the views from here out over the
plains towards the Taita and Ngulia Hills
are some of the most splendid in southeast-
ern Kenya.

Bordering the extreme southeastern cor-
ner of Tsavo West National Park, close to
the Nairobi–Mombasa highway, this con-
servancy inhabits what was, until recently,
a major hideout for poachers. While poach-
ing continues in adjacent areas, Mbulia
Conservancy uses a clever mix of carrot and
stick – careful community engagement and
an armed private ranger force – to ensure
the poachers don't return. It's clearly work-
ing, as wildlife has already begun to return.

🛏 Sleeping & Eating

There's only one place to stay inside the
conservancy – **Kipalo Hills** (☑ 0780240006;
www.h12africa.com; s/d all inclusive Jul, Aug & mid-
Dec–mid-Jan US$400/700, mid-Jan–Jun & Sep–
mid-Dec US$290/500, conservancy fee per person
year-round US$50; Ⓟ 🛜 🗗) 🅿 – which ensures
a sense of utter exclusivity.

All meals are included in the room rates
at Kipalo Hills.

ⓘ Getting There & Away

Many visitors fly into Tsavo West's Kilaguni
airstrip with Safarilink (p189), and combine their
transfer here (three hours) with a wildlife drive
through the national park.

If driving, ask for detailed directions – the
turn-off along the Nairobi–Mombasa road is
around 20km north of Voi.

Tsavo East National Park

📱 043

Kenya's largest national park, **Tsavo East** (📱 0722290009, 0775563672, Nairobi 020-600 0800; www.kws.go.ke/content/tsavo-east-national-park; adult/child US$52/35; ⊙ 6am-6pm), has an undeniable wild and primordial charm and is a terrific wildlife-watching destination. Although one of Kenya's largest rivers flows through the middle of the park, the landscape here is markedly flatter and drier and lacks the drama of Tsavo West. The flip side is that spotting wildlife is generally easier thanks to the thinly spread foliage.

Despite the size of the park, the area of most wildlife activity is actually quite compact – the northern section of the park is largely closed and can only be visited with advance permission due to the threat of banditry and ongoing campaigns against poachers. The demarcation point is the Galana River.

◉ Sights

Most people come to Tsavo East to see the famous red elephants of Tsavo – their colour comes from bathing in the red Tsavo mud (to keep the skin cool and prevent insect bites). The two Tsavo parks have the largest elephant populations of any Kenyan parks and include a third of the country's total, although herds are quite small. Lion and cheetah sightings are also common; unusually, the male lions are almost maneless.

Tsavo East is also notable as one of few places in southern Kenya where you can tick off some species usually seen only much further north. We've had luck here with the Somali ostrich (notable for its blue neck) and the gerenuk, an unusual breed of long-necked gazelle that 'browse' by standing on their hind legs and stretching their necks, as if yearning to be giraffes.

★ Galana River
RIVER

Running through the heart of the park and marking the northernmost point in the park that most visitors are allowed to visit, the Galana River, which combines the waters of the Tsavo and Athi Rivers, cuts a green gash across the dusty plains. Surprisingly few visitors make it even this far and sightings of crocs, hippos, lesser kudus, waterbucks, dik-diks and, to a lesser extent, lions and leopards are relatively common. Watch out also for the distinctive Somali ostrich.

There are several places along the flat-topped escarpments lining the river where you can get out of your vehicle (with due caution, of course). Most scenic are **Lugards Falls**, a wonderful landscape of water-sculpted channels and striated rocks, and **Crocodile Point**, where you may see abundant crocs and hippos. The trail that runs from the falls back to Voi follows a river and is good for wildlife-spotting, but the track is often impassable after rain.

The area north of the Galana River is dominated by the Yatta Escarpment, a vast prehistoric lava flow which is estimated by some to be the longest lava flow in the world at 300km. It's only accessible at present for those with a special permit.

★ Kanderi Swamp
RIVER

Around 10km from Voi Gate, the lovely area of green known as Kanderi Swamp is home to a resident pride of lions, and elephants also congregate near here; this is one of only two water sources in the park during the dry season. The landscape here has a lovely backdrop of distant hills. A number of vehicle tracks also follow the contours of the Voi River; keep an eye on the overhanging branches for leopards.

Aruba Dam
LAKE

Some 30km east of Voi Gate is the Aruba Dam, which spans the Voi River. It also attracts heavy concentrations of diverse wildlife; one of the park's regularly spotted lion prides ranges around here. Away to the east and southeast, all the way down to the

Buchuma Gate, the open grasslands provide the perfect habitat for cheetahs and sightings are more common here than almost anywhere else in southeastern Kenya.

Mudanda Rock MOUNTAIN

Towering over a natural dam near the Manyani Gate, this towering natural formation runs for over 1.5km. It attracts elephants in the dry season and is reminiscent of Australia's Uluru (Ayers Rock), albeit on a much smaller scale. Leopards and elephants are among the wildlife to watch out for here.

🛏 Sleeping

KWS Campsite CAMPGROUND $

(camping US$20) Decent site with toilets, showers and a communal kitchen. The location is good, as most safari vehicles don't loop down this way and there's some good wildlife-viewing down by the riverbank and in nearby Kanderi Swamp. You'll need to register at the gate and be entirely self-sufficient in food and water to stay here. Limited supplies are available in Voi.

Voi Wildlife Lodge LODGE $$

(☑0733201240, 0722201240; www.voiwildlife lodge.com; s/d full board from US$117/180; P⛱) Close to Voi Gate, this well-run place is actually a number of places in one. From the main property, there are fine views into the park from some of the recently renovated rooms as well as from the restaurant and viewing platform. At its Manyatta property, the tents have private plunge pools. It's a good deal in a good location just outside the park.

Red Elephant Safari Lodge LODGE $$

(☑0727112175; www.red-elephant-lodge.com; room/bungalow per person full board from US$80/120; P@⛱) One of the better budget places bordering Tsavo East, close to Voi, Red Elephant is popular with German travellers for its reasonable prices and attractive accommodation. The standard rooms have stone furnishings while the bush houses are lighter, come with mosquito nets and attractive yet simple Maasai prints. It's signposted off the main road into the park from Voi.

Lion Hill Lodge LODGE $$

(☑0735877431, Nairobi 020-8030828; www.lion hilllodge.com; s/d US$80/120) Just before the park entrance near Voi Gate, this quiet place sits atop an impossibly steep hill and the views that result from this location are extraordinary. The best views are from rooms 5 and 6, large rooms with balconies,

or, failing that, rooms 7 to 10 also boast fine panoramas. Tents are also available.

Voi Safari Lodge LODGE $$

(☑Mombasa 041-4718610; www.safari-hotels.com; s/d full board from US$66/121; 🛜⛱) Just 4km from Voi Gate, this is a long, low complex perched on the edge of an escarpment overlooking an incredible sweep of savannah. There's an attractive rock-cut swimming pool, as well as a natural waterhole that draws elephants, buffaloes and the occasional predator; a photographers' hide sits at the level of the waterhole. Rooms are attractive and many have superlative views.

Satao Camp TENTED CAMP $$$

(☑Nairobi 020-2434610; www.sataocamp.com; s/d full board Jul-Oct US$337/436, rates vary rest of year; P🛜) Located on the banks of the Voi River, this luxury camp was recently renovated and now looks better than ever. There are 20 canopied tents, all of which are perfectly spaced within sight of a waterhole that's known to draw lions, cheetahs and elephants on occasion. The elevated viewing tower and the sense of being far removed from the safari scrum are big selling points here.

A downside for families might be the lack of a swimming pool.

Ndololo Safari Camp TENTED CAMP $$$

(www.tsavolodgesandcamps.com; s/d/tr US$150/200/280) A well-priced tented camp in a good location close to Kanderi Swamp, Ndololo Safari Camp has a tight cluster of tents that are far more reasonably priced than most in southern Kenya.

Ashnil Aruba Lodge LODGE $$$

(☑Nairobi 020-4971008; www.ashnilhotels.com; s/d full board US$262/350; P@⛱) A stone's throw from the wildlife-rich Aruba Dam, this lodge has attractively decorated rooms decked out in safari prints, although it's the six luxury tents that are the real stars, with a far stronger sense of light and space than the rooms. In the heart of the park, it's an ideal starting point for most Tsavo East safaris.

ℹ Information

MAPS

The *Tsavo East National Park* map and guidebook is available from Voi Gate.

TOURIST INFORMATION

Tsavo East Park Office (☑0722290009) The park's eastern entrance; good for park information.

ℹ️ Getting There & Away

You'll need your own wheels to explore Tsavo East, and so even though it's perfectly easy to access the park on public transport from the town of Voi on the main road between Nairobi and Mombasa, it's not very useful unless you've got onward transport into the park booked. Fuel is available in Voi; fill up before entering the park.

A track through the park follows the Galana River from the Tsavo Gate to the Sala Gate; others fan out from Voi Gate. To access the park with your own vehicle use the following park gates:

➡ **to/from Nairobi or Tsavo West** Voi, Tsavo or Manyani gates.

➡ **to/from Mombasa** Sala or Buchuma gates.

Tsavo Conservancy

Although it's taking some time to take off, the area south of Voi and part of the Tsavo ecosystem is one to watch for the fusion of wildlife, conservation and community projects. Founded in 2013, the 1000-sq-km **Tsavo Conservancy** (☏0719159671; www.tsavoconservancy.com; adult/child US$30/20) represents seven ranches which have joined together to further the work of wildlife protection and programmes that help develop alternative income sources for local communities. The conservancy encompasses an important elephant corridor that's particularly busy at the end of the dry season, while night drives here also turn up some interesting sightings.

◎ Sights

African Shirt Company FACTORY
(www.theafricanshirtcompany.com; Kiteghe, Kasigau; ⊙hours vary) In 2009, Joan Hughes and Lindi Campbell Clause, two designers from Ireland and Kenya, set up this project which uses village workshops to employ and train the local community in tailoring; this is also production (and carbon-neutral) home base for the African Shirt Company. There are no set visiting hours but visits to the workshops can be arranged through Kasigau Base Camp (p200).

Rukinga Wildlife Sanctuary WILDLIFE RESERVE
(www.wildlifeworks.com; adult/child Tsavo Conservancy fee US$30/20) Begun in 1998, the 80,000-acre Rukinga Wildlife Sanctuary, at the heart of the Kasigau ecosystem, is reliable elephant country – Kasigau lies along a migration corridor between Tsavos East and

---

MAN-EATERS OF TSAVO

The famed 'man-eaters of Tsavo' were among the most dangerous lions to ever roam the planet. During the building of the Kenya–Uganda Railway in 1898, efforts soon came to a halt when railway workers started being dragged from their tents at night and devoured by two maneless male lions.

The surviving workers soon decided that the lions had to be ghosts or devils, which put the future of the railway in jeopardy. Engineer Lt Col John Henry Patterson created a series of ever more ingenious traps, but each time the lions evaded them, striking unerringly at weak points in the camp defences. Patterson was finally able to bag the first man-eater by hiding on a flimsy wooden scaffold baited with the corpse of a donkey. The second man-eater was dispatched a short time later, although it took six bullets to bring the massive beast down.

According to Patterson's calculations, the two lions killed and ate around 135 workers in less than one year. He detailed his experiences in the best-selling book *The Man-Eaters of Tsavo* (1907), which was later rather freely filmed as *Bwana Devil* (1952) and *The Ghost and the Darkness* (1996).

Patterson turned the two man-eaters into floor rugs. In 1924 he finally rid himself of the lions by selling their skins to the Chicago Field Museum for the sum of US$5000. The man-eaters of Tsavo were then stuffed and placed on permanent display, where they remain to this day.

Hypotheses vary as to why these lions became man-eaters. Tsavo lions have noticeably elevated levels of the male sex hormone testosterone. The pair themselves also had badly damaged teeth, which may have driven them to abandon their normal prey and become man-eaters. An outbreak of rinderpest (an infectious viral disease) might have decimated the lions' usual prey, forcing them to find alternative food sources. One final theory is that the man-eaters may have developed their taste for human flesh after growing accustomed to finding human bodies at the Tsavo River crossing, where slave caravans often crossed en route to Zanzibar.

TSAVO'S MANELESS LIONS

The lions of Tsavo have an image problem. For a start, they're known as man-eaters, thanks to the rather prolific man-eating exploits along the under-construction Kenya–Uganda Railway at the dawn of the 20th century. And then there's the issue of their manes: male Tsavo lions are known for their less-than-fulsome manes, with even fully grown and dominant males looking like subadult lions – their unkempt, scraggy manes are a far cry from those you'll see elsewhere, in the Masai Mara or Nakuru, for example.

The growth of a mane in a male lion signifies to the rest of the lion world that it has reached sexual maturity, associated as it is with testosterone. According to a study carried out by Dr Craig Packer, one of the world's foremost lion experts, the fuller and darker the mane, the more likely a male lion is to attract female lions looking for a mate. Male lions with longer, darker manes are also more likely to have offspring that survive for longer and are most likely to win male-on-male fights.

So why do Tsavo males, renowned as they are for their ferocity, have such inadequate manes? No-one knows. Some theories suggest that climate is to blame – heavy-maned lions suffer in the heat and lighter, thinner manes could be an evolutionary adaptation for lions living in hot climates. But male lions in similarly dry regions, such as the Kalahari Desert of southern Africa, have almost-universally impressive manes. West African lions, too, have similarly ragged manes to those of the Tsavo males, suggesting some possible link in the distant past. But no such link has yet been proven and whatever caused this genetic predisposition to less-than-hirsute facial profiles for now remains a mystery.

West, and the permanent population of just under 500 elephants swells to over 2000 around October and March. With more than 50 large mammal species (including Grevy's zebra and, sometimes, African wild dogs) and over 300 recorded bird species, there are some real surprises here.

🛌 Sleeping

Kivuli Camp BUNGALOW, CAMPGROUND $
(www.tsavoconservancy.com/visit-us/kivuli-camp; camping KSh500, s/d/f KSh4000/5000/6000; P @) Set in the heart of Rukinga Wildlife Sanctuary and with a lovely remote feeling surrounded by acacia woodland and Tsavo's distinctive red soils, Kivuli (formerly Camp Tsavo) has simple but nicely turned out circular thatched-roof bungalows which house double rooms, family rooms and dorms with bunk beds. There's also a fenced campsite.

Kasigau Base Camp CAMPGROUND, COTTAGES $
(☎0710755225, 0721365768; www.malewa.com; camping in own/hired tent KSh500/1000, cottages per person KSh2000; P) 🌿 This work in progress is an essential part of the Kasigau project, with good campsites, six attractive, locally built cottages and a range of activities that include hiking, abseiling and rock climbing in the surrounding hills. They can also arrange volunteering placements in local projects. Community visits can be arranged, as can meals (KSh750 per person).

🛈 Getting There & Away

For Kasigau Base Camp, Rukinga Wildlife Sanctuary and the African Shirt Company, if driving, head southeast of Voi along the Voi–Mombasa road. After around 30km, at the settlement of Maungu, turn right off the highway onto a red dirt road and continue for a further 30km to reach the village of Kiteghe, close to the foot of Mt Kasigau. Although occasional minibuses make the trip from Voi, you could end up waiting for a *very* long time.

For Kivuli Camp, the turn-off is signed as 'Rukinga', 5km southeast of Maungu. From the turn-off it's a further 11km along a dirt road.

Voi

☎043 / POP 45,485

Voi is a key service town at the intersection of the Nairobi–Mombasa road, the road to Moshi in Tanzania and the access road to the main Voi Gate of Tsavo East National Park. As such, much of its activity is designed around trying to catch the monetary crumbs that fall from the pockets of those changing transport, on safari or simply passing through. Think of it more as a place to get directions, fill up on petrol, change money and buy a newspaper or some snacks for the road, than as a place to linger.

👁 Sights

Voi War Cemetery CEMETERY
(Commonwealth War Graves; ☎0733633255, Nairobi 020-2604301; www.cwgc.org/find-a-cemetery/

cemetery/12214; ⊙6am-6pm Mon-Fri) FREE On the north side of the road just before the turn-off to Voi Gate on the eastern outskirts of town, this well-tended cemetery contains 137 graves, including 70 South African, 44 British, 12 'Rhodesian', nine East African and two Indian graves. If you find the gate locked, call one of the phone numbers to obtain the access code. Note, however, that the phones are only attended 8.30am to 12.30pm and from 1.30pm to 4.30pm Monday to Friday.

🛏 Sleeping

★ **Voi Lutheran Guesthouse** GUESTHOUSE $
(🖉 Nairobi 020-2668607; www.voiguesthouse.com; Bogesunds Farm, off Mombasa Rd; s/d incl breakfast KSh2300/3300, full board KSh3300/5300, per person incl breakfast/full board with shared bathroom KSh1500/2500) Easily the pick of the accommodation if you're not staying in the park, the Lutheran Guesthouse occupies a handsome house on a farm 1km west of the Nairobi–Mombasa road. Rooms have some colourful touches, with local basket decor and zebra-print shower curtains, and it's a much quieter choice than anywhere in town. The turn-off is 1km north of the Taveta turn-off along the main highway.

Impala Safari Lodge LODGE $$
(🖉 0750153694; www.impalasafarilodge.com; Edward Maganga Rd; s/d US$74/88; P❋🛜❄) In Voi but slightly removed from the main-road scrum, Impala Safari Lodge offers attractive safari tents in a secure compound. While the setting is more suburban than wilderness, the price is excellent and you're only a short drive from the national park.

ⓘ Getting There & Away

Frequent buses and matatus run to/from Mombasa (KSh250 to KSh600, three hours), and buses run to Nairobi (KSh600 to KSh1400, six hours). There are at least daily matatus to Wundanyi (KSh300, one hour) and Taveta (KSh550, two hours), on the Tanzanian border.

Voi also lies along the recently upgraded Nairobi–Mombasa railway line.

Taita Hills Wildlife Sanctuary

🖉 043
The Taita Hills, a fertile area of verdant hills and scrub forest, is a far cry from the semi-arid landscape of Tsavo. Within the hills is the **private wildlife sanctuary** (admission US$30), covering an area of 100 sq km – the landscape is dramatic and all the plains wildlife is here in abundance. Visiting involves a good mix of pretty landscapes, good birdwatching and decent mammal populations – nothing is guaranteed here but lions and elephants are frequently sighted.

👁 Sights

The sanctuary has three main focal points for wildlife watching. The **river valley** that runs east of the Sarova Taita Hills Game Lodge is good for birds of prey, while the open **grasslands** that rise gently south of the river and take up much of the park feed Grant's gazelles, impalas and hartebeests in numbers sufficient to sustain lions and cheetahs; elephants are also possible. At the southern reaches of the sanctuary, **Lion Rock** provides sanctuary for klipspringers and resting predators.

Taita Hills WWI Museum MUSEUM
(Sarova Taita Hills Game Lodge, Taita Hills Wildlife Sanctuary; ⊙24hr) FREE Occupying a corner of the lobby in the Sarova Taita Hills Game Lodge, this engaging little open-sided museum tells the story of WWI as it played out in East Africa. There are artefacts found on the nearby former battlefields (from bullets made in 1912 to glass shards from bottles of Indian hair oil), archival photos, informative and detailed panels on the course of the war and major personalities.

🛏 Sleeping

★ **Sarova Salt Lick Safari Lodge** LODGE $$$
(🖉 0728608765; www.sarovahotels.com; s/d full board US$132/192; P❋@❄) The centrepiece of the sanctuary, this original lodge calls to mind a traditional village of beehive huts on stilts, all connected by a web of walkways and overlooking a waterhole where elephants often come to drink. Rooms are a touch old-fashioned but the views outweigh such minor details and the hobbit-like structures really do make a great picture. Night drives are also possible.

Sarova Taita Hills Game Lodge LODGE $$$
(🖉 0728608765; www.sarovahotels.com; s/d/ste full board US$127/160/275; P❋@🛜❄) The older of the two Sarova properties within the sanctuary, this place has marginally better rooms and the service is more switched on (this is the main reception for both properties), but it's closer to the road and lacks

the waterhole-proximity and architectural personality of the Salt Lick. Don't miss its fine little museum (p201) in the lobby.

ℹ️ Getting There & Away

You'll need your own vehicle to get to the sanctuary, which is well signposted south of the dirt road from Voi to Taveta. While you could conceivably reach the sanctuary gate, around 1km off the main road by getting a Voi–Taveta matatu to drop you at the turn-off and arrange for a lodge vehicle to come down and pick you up, you'll still need wheels to explore the sanctuary itself – arranging these through the lodges can be expensive.

Lumo Community Wildlife Sanctuary

The innovative community-run **Lumo Community Wildlife Sanctuary** (☎0716119322, 0729265018; www.lumoconservancy.com; adult/child US$35/17) covers 657 sq km and was formed from three community-owned ranches in 1996, but only opened to the public in 2003. It's partly funded by the EU and involves local people at every stage of the project, from the park rangers to senior management. Big cats and elephants are regular highlights and the accommodation superb, making it a terrific all-round package.

You could easily spend three or four days taking in everything the sanctuary has to offer.

🏃 Activities

In addition to guided WWI Battlefield Tours to local wartime landmarks (watch for spent shell casings), there are wildlife drives – unlike in national parks, both day and night drives are possible – plus birdwatching and walking safaris. Traditional local dances and

---

TAITA HILLS & WWI

Though a remote wildlife sanctuary in southeastern Kenya might seem an unlikely location for a WWI museum, the wildlife-rich plains visible today conceal a lesser-known history: the area neighbouring Taita Hills Wildlife Sanctuary was one of the most important theatres of war in the early years of the East Africa Campaign.

While Germany fought Britain and the Allies in Europe, Britain and Germany conducted a low-level war to ensure neither gained ground in Africa. The German interest in Britain's Kenyan territories was focused on two primary targets.

The first was Mzima Springs (p190) in Tsavo West National Park, one of East Africa's most important permanent water supplies. The second target for the German incursions was a major railway bridge over the Tsavo River – if they could sever the supply and general transport artery that was the Mombasa–Uganda Railway, the German argument ran, the British would be in trouble.

On 15 August 1914, the first German soldiers crossed the border at Taveta and seized the town. These were the first shots of the East African Campaign on Kenyan soil, although the outnumbered British troops retreated almost immediately. The first major battle took place at Mile 27 along the Voi–Taveta road, around 1.5km from the museum. The first airfield in British East Africa was at Maktau and the Allies built their first fort of the war 5km from the Taita Hills Wildlife Sanctuary.

Although little remains of these incidents – the Voi War Cemetery (p200) is one of the few easily accessible landmarks to WWI – the museum (p201) gives an excellent overview. And while the sites of the actual battles can be impossible to find on your own, those with a particular interest in the campaign should contact **Willie Mwadilo** (☎0733931036; willie.mwadilo@sarovahotels.com; per group per day US$200), Lodge Manager at the Sarova Taita Hills Game Lodge (p201). With prior notice, he can show you around the museum for free, bringing to life many of its exhibits. With more advance warning, he can guide you around the region's sites.

One other landmark is found on the neighbouring Lumo Community Wildlife Sanctuary, scene of a battle that later formed part of the film *Shout at the Devil* starring Lee Marvin and Roger Moore. The sanctuary organises 'Battlefield Tours' which encompass the battlefield, as well as the ruins of a British wartime camp and a local WWI cemetery.

Another useful resource for those interested in pursuing this period of history further is The Great War in East Africa Association (www.gweaa.com), while Charles Miller's 1974 book *Battle for the Bundu: The First World War in East Africa* is one of few on the East African Campaign.

visits to local community projects can also be arranged.

Birdwatching

Birdwatching often takes a back seat to the mammals, but more than half of Kenya's 1070 species have been recorded in the area. Endemics to watch out for include the Taita thrush, Taita white-eye, Taita apalis, Abbott's starling and the southern banded snake eagle.

Wildlife Watching

The wildlife here is surprisingly varied – all the Big Five are here, and the night drives are especially good for nocturnal specialists such as lions, leopards, melanistic servals and aardwolves.

🛏 Sleeping

Cheetah Campsite CAMPGROUND $
(☑0733222420, 0717555498; www.lumo conservancy.com; Lumo Community Wildlife Sanctuary; camping from US$10, shelter US$20) Close to Lions Bluff Lodge, this shady, green-tinged campsite has levelled sites as well as running water, a communal kitchen, showers and toilets, and you can access the facilities at the lodge as required. Some sites have lovely views out over the plains. There's also a small shelter with space for four beds (with mosquito nets) – ideal for those not carrying their own camping gear.

★ Leopards Lair TENTED CAMP $$
(☑0733222420, 0717555498; www.lionsblufflodge. com/leopards-lair; Lumo Community Wildlife Sanctuary; s/d full board US$84/120) A fine addition to Lumo's portfolio of accommodation, this tented camp is outrageously good value by East African standards and the seven safari tents have a real sense of comfort-out-in-the-wilderness, blended with personal service and privately catered meals.

★ Lions Bluff Lodge LODGE $$
(☑0733222420, 0717555498; www.lionsblufflodge. com; s/d full board mid-Jul–mid-Sep & mid-Dec–mid-Jan US$84/120, per person rest of year US$80-95; 🅿🛜) 🌿 Built by the local community, these timber-and-canvas *bandas* with coconut-palm-thatched roofs get the balance right between being genuinely rustic yet supremely comfortable; most have exceptional views and there's a small waterhole. Food for the excellent meals is sourced almost exclusively from local farmers. It's an outstanding place to stay.

ℹ Getting There & Away

The sanctuary lies on the Voi–Taveta road and is well signposted. Wildlife drives and transfers can be arranged with advance notice (and for an additional cost) for those without their own vehicle for reaching and exploring the park.

Wundanyi

The provincial capital of Wundanyi is set high in the Taita Hills and is a refreshingly untouristy detour in the heart of the Taita homeland. Wildlife is scarce, but come here for a low-key, DIY cultural experience with some lovely landscapes thrown in.

Numerous trails criss-cross the cultivated terraced slopes around town, leading to dramatic gorges, waterfalls, cliffs and jagged outcrops. It's easy to find someone to act as a guide, but stout walking boots and a head for heights are essential. Other attractions in the hills include the butterflies of **Ngangao Forest**, a 6km matatu ride northwest to Werugha (KSh85); the huge granite **Wesu Rock** that overlooks Wundanyi; and the **Cave of Skulls** where the Taita people once put the skulls of their ancestors (and where the original African violets were discovered).

🛏 Sleeping

Taita Research Station GUESTHOUSE $
(☑0722287486, 0733849103; www.blogs.helsinki. fi/taita-research-station; dm KSh2500) Set up as a research station for Finnish scientists, this small and simple rest house offers basic facilities if they're not filled with visiting scientists.

Lavender Garden Hotel HOTEL $$
(☑0718922394, 0727750111; www.lavenderhotels kenya.com; r from US$70; 🅿🛜) Wundanyi's best place to stay has comfortable rooms with frilly decor, and front-facing rooms come with views of the corrugated rooftops of the town and the cloud-shrouded hills beyond. It's a good place to arrange excursions around the area.

ℹ Getting There & Away

Semi-frequent matatu services run between Wundanyi and Voi (KSh300, one hour). Leave Wundanyi no later than 8.30am if you want to connect with the morning buses to Nairobi from Voi.

Mombasa & the South Coast

Includes ➡

Mombasa 206

Shimba Hills
National Reserve 219

Tiwi Beach 220

Diani Beach 221

Funzi Island 228

Shimoni &
Wasini Island 229

Nyali 231

Bamburi 234

Shanzu Beach 236

Mtwapa 236

Best Places to Eat

➡ Tamarind Restaurant
(p234)

➡ Sails (p227)

➡ Nomad (p227)

➡ Monsoons (p237)

➡ Shehnai Restaurant (p214)

Best Places
to Stay

➡ Water Lovers (p225)

➡ The Maji (p226)

➡ AfroChic Diani Beach
(p225)

➡ Kenyaways Kite Village
(p225)

➡ Diani Backpackers (p224)

Why Go?

From the hypnotic port city of Mombasa south to the border with Tanzania, this stretch of Kenyan coast is anything but ordinary. Where else can you see snow-white beaches framed by *kayas* (sacred forests), soft-sailed dhows and elephant watering holes, all in one day, returning by night to your digs along one of the most beautiful beaches in Africa?

Governed by Swahili rhythms and the rise and fall of the tides, life here moves to its own beat. Thanks to the long interplay of Africa, India and Arabia, this coast feels wildly different from the rest of Kenya. Its people, the Swahili, have created a distinctive Indian Ocean society – built on trade with distant shores – that lends real romance to the coast's beaches and spice to its food, and to Mombasa, a city embraced by poets for many centuries.

When to Go
Mombasa

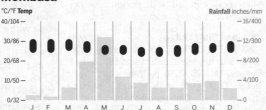

Jan–Mar Dolphins (and the occasional whale shark) fill the ocean and diving is at its best.

June–Sep The southeast trade winds are blowing, making the coast a kitesurfer's paradise.

Sep School-holiday crowds are gone, accommodation is cheaper and beaches are quieter.

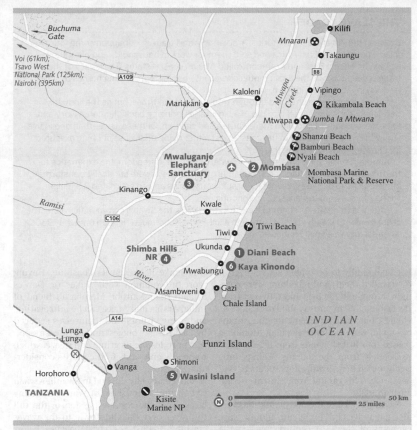

Mombasa & the South Coast Highlights

1 Diani Beach (p221)
Stepping barefoot onto the miles and miles of soft white sand, and later kitesurfing its waves.

2 Mombasa Old Town (p206) Exploring a centuries-old fort and shopping for spices and antiques in the labyrinthine streets of Mombasa's historical heart.

3 Mwaluganje Elephant Sanctuary (p220) Going elephant-spotting at this tremendous success of a local conservation project.

4 Shimba Hills National Reserve (p219) Tracking down tuskers and sable antelope and hiking to a splendid waterfall.

5 Wasini Island (p230) Diving into the emerald reef and soaking up the Swahili spirit on an island where time stands still.

6 Kaya Kinondo (p221) Finding god in the greenery at this sacred grove.

History

The coast's written history is essentially a tale of trade and conquest with outside forces. By the 1st century AD, Yemeni traders were in East Africa. Merchants traded spices, timber, gold, ivory, tortoise shell and rhinoceros horn, as well as slaves.

The mixture of Arabs, local Africans and Persian traders gave birth to the Swahili culture and language. But the Swahili were not the only inhabitants of the coast. Of particular note were the Mijikenda, or 'Nine Homesteads', a Bantu tribe who, 600 years ago, established themselves in *kayas* (sacred forests), which are dotted from the Tanzanian border to Malindi.

In the early 16th century the Portuguese took their turn at conquest. The Swahili did

THE SLAVE TRADE

Between the 7th and 19th centuries, Arab and Swahili traders kidnapped some four million people from East Africa and sold them for work in households and plantations across the Middle East and Arab-controlled African coastal states. The legacy of the trade is seen today in the chain motifs carved into doors (representing homes of slave traders) in Mombasa Old Town.

At first, slaves were obtained through trade with inland tribes, but as the 'industry' developed, caravans set off into the African interior, bringing back plundered ivory and tens of thousands of captured men, women and children. Of these, fewer than one in five survived the forced march to the coast, most either dying of disease or being executed for showing weakness along the way.

Although some slaves married their owners and gained freedom, the experience for the majority was much harsher. Thousands of African boys were surgically transformed into eunuchs to provide servants for Arabic households and an estimated 2.5 million young African women were sold as concubines.

After the trade was brought to a close in the 1870s, the Swahili communities along the coast went into steady decline, although illicit trading continued right up until the 1960s, when slavery was finally outlawed in Oman.

not take kindly to becoming slaves (even if they traded them) and rebellions were common throughout the 16th and 17th centuries. It's fashionable to portray the Portuguese as villains, but their replacements, the sultans of Oman, were no more popular. Mombasa passed into British hands from 1824 to 1826 to keep it from the sultans. Things only really quietened down after Sultan Seyyid Said moved his capital from Muscat to Zanzibar in 1832.

Said's huge coastal clove plantations created a massive need for labour, and the slave caravans of the 19th century marked the peak of the trade in human cargo. Through a mixture of political savvy and implied force, the British government pressured Said's son, Barghash, to ban the slave trade, marking the beginning of the end of Arab rule here.

As part of the treaty, the British East Africa Company took over administration of the Kenyan interior, and it took the opportunity to start construction of the East African Railway. A 16km-wide coastal strip was recognised as the sultan's territory and leased by the British from 1887. Upon independence in 1963, the last sultan of Zanzibar gifted this land to the new Kenyan government.

MOMBASA

♪ 041 / POP 915,101

Mombasa, a melting pot of languages and cultures from all sides of the Indian Ocean, waits like an exotic dessert for travellers who make it to Kenya's coastline. Having more in common with Dakar or Dar es Salaam than Nairobi, Mombasa's blend of India, Arabia and Africa can be intoxicating, and many visitors find themselves seduced by East Africa's biggest and most cosmopolitan port despite its grime and sleaze, which somehow only adds to the place's considerable charm.

Indeed, the city dubbed in Swahili *Kisiwa Cha Mvita* – the Island of War – has many faces, from the ecstatic passion of the call to prayer over the Old Town, to the waves crashing against the coral beaches below Fort Jesus and the sight of a Zanzibar-bound dhow slipping over the horizon. As the Swahili people themselves say in an old proverb: 'Mombasa is famous, but its waters are dangerously deep. Beware!'

History

Mombasa, which sits over the best deep-water harbour in East Africa, has always been an important town.

Travellers who come here are walking in the footsteps of Ibn Battuta, Marco Polo and Zhang He, which says something of this town's trade importance. Modern Mombasa traces its heritage back to the Thenashara Taifa (Twelve Nations), a Swahili clan that maintains an unbroken chain of traditions and customs stretching from the city's founding to this day. The date when those customs began – ie when Mombasa was born – is a little muddy, although it was already a thriving port by the 12th century.

Early in its life, Mombasa became a key link on Indian Ocean trade routes.

In 1498 Vasco da Gama became Mombasa's first Portuguese visitor. Two years later his countrymen returned and sacked the town, a habit they repeated in 1505 and 1528, when Nuno da Cunha captured Mombasa using what would become a time-honoured tactic: slick 'em up with diplomacy (offering to act as an ally in disputes with Malindi, Pemba and Zanzibar) then slap 'em down by force. Once again Mombasa was burnt to the ground.

In 1593 the Portuguese constructed the coral edifice of Fort Jesus as a way of saying, 'We're staying'. This act of architectural hubris led to frequent attacks by rebel forces and the ultimate expulsion of the Portuguese by Omani Arabs in 1698. But the Omanis were never that popular either, and the British, using a series of shifting alliances and brute force, turfed them out in 1870. All these power struggles, by the way, are the source of Mombasa's Island of War nickname.

Mombasa subsequently became the railhead for the Uganda railway and the most important city in British East Africa. In 1920, when Kenya became a fully fledged British colony, Mombasa was made capital of the separate British Coast Protectorate. Following Kenyan independence in 1963 the city fell into a torpor. It was the most important city in the region and the second largest in the country, but it was removed from the cut and thrust of Kenyan politics, whose focus had turned inland.

In the early 1990s violence briefly engulfed the city as supporters and opponents of the Islamic Party of Kenya clashed, but this has long since died down. During the 2007 elections, the coast, and Mombasa in particular, provided a rare peek into the policy platforms, rather than communal politics, of Raila Odinga and Mwai Kibaki. Neither politician could rely on a Kikuyu or Luo base here, and both campaigned on ideas, rather than appeals to tribalism. Odinga won the province by promising, in effect, a form of limited federation, which remains a hope of many Mombasan politicians who consider the coast culturally, economically and religiously distinct enough to warrant some form of self-governance.

Mombasa's outlawed separatist movement, known as the Mombasa Republican Council (MRC), listed grievances from land reform issues to economic marginalisation among reasons when it called for voters to boycott Kenya's 2013 presidential election. Nairobi imprisoned several of its key members over the years, and was jarred by its slogan, 'Pwani si Kenya' ('The coast is not Kenya'). Still, it continues to operate.

Mombasa's tensions were exacerbated in October 2013, when radical Muslim cleric Sheikh Ibrahim Rogo was killed by gunmen in the city. His supporters alleged that Kenyan security forces were involved in his murder. A second cleric, Sheikh Abubakar Shariff Ahmed, was killed in April 2014 under similar circumstances. Further jitters were felt in August 2017, preceding the hotly-contested general election, though violence in the city was kept to a minimum.

◉ Sights

★ Fort Jesus   MUSEUM
(www.museums.or.ke; Nkrumah Rd; adult/child KSh1200/600; ⊙8am-6pm) This 16th-century fort and Unesco World Heritage treasure is Mombasa's most visited site. The metre-thick walls, frescoed interiors, traces of European graffiti, Arabic inscriptions and Swahili embellishment aren't just evocative, they're a palimpsest of Mombasa's history and the coast writ in stone. You can climb on the battlements and explore its tree-shaded grounds.

The fort was built by the Portuguese in 1593 to serve as both symbol and headquarters of their permanent presence in this corner of the Indian Ocean. It's ironic, then, that the construction of the fort marked

---

MOMBASA'S OLD TOWN

If this cluster of beguiling streets seems familiar, it may be because you've seen the film *Inception* (2010); the chase scene featuring Leonardo DiCaprio was filmed here. The most characterful part of Mombasa is great for a wander, its houses characteristic of 19th-century Indian-style Zanzibari architecture, with ornately carved doors and window frames and fretwork balconies. Some parts of the Old Town can be a little sketchy, even during the day, such as the Leven Steps and Vasco da Gama's Well, so going around with a reliable local guide (such as Suleiman Sabdallah, p212) is not a bad idea.

Mombasa

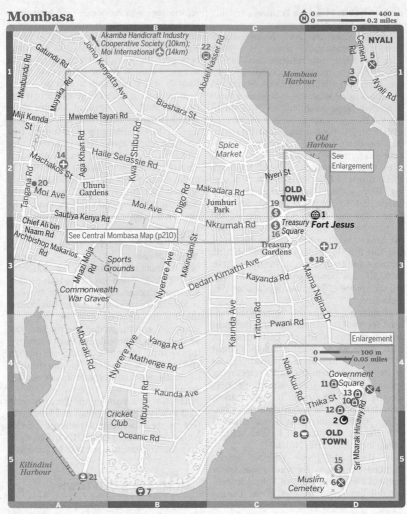

the beginning of the end of local Portuguese hegemony. Between Portuguese sailors, Omani soldiers and Swahili rebellions, the fort changed hands at least nine times between 1631 and the early 1870s, when it finally fell under British control and was used as a jail; it opened as a museum in 1960.

The fort was the final project completed by Giovanni Battista Cairati, whose buildings can be found throughout Portugal's eastern colonies, from Old Goa to Old Mombasa. The building is an opus of period military design – assuming the structure was

well manned, it would have been impossible to approach its walls without falling under the cone of interlocking fields of fire.

Within the fort compound, the **Mazrui Hall**, where flowery spirals fade across a wall topped with wooden lintels left by the Omani Arabs, is worthy of note. In another room, Portuguese sailors scratched graffiti that illustrates the multicultural naval identity of the Indian Ocean, leaving walls covered with four-pointed European frigates, three-pointed Arabic dhows and the coir-sewn 'camels of the ocean': the elegant Swahili *mtepe* (traditional sailing vessel).

Mombasa

◎ **Top Sights**
1 Fort Jesus...D2

◎ **Sights**
2 Mandhry Mosque...................................D5

◉ **Activities, Courses & Tours**
Tamarind Dhow..............................(see 3)

◉ **Sleeping**
3 Tamarind Village.....................................D1

◉ **Eating**
4 Forodhani Restaurant...........................D4
5 Ooh! Ice-Cream.......................................D1
Tamarind Restaurant....................(see 3)
6 The Fort..D5

◉ **Drinking & Nightlife**
7 Florida Club..B5
8 Jahazi Coffee House..............................C5

◎ **Shopping**
9 Imani Collective.......................................C5
10 Old Town Antiques and
Carvings..D4
11 Sanaa Gallery...D4
12 Sandal Shop..D4
13 Yusufi Antiques & Gallery.....................D4

◉ **Information**
14 AAR Mombasa Health Centre..............A2
15 Fort Jesus Forex Bureau.......................D5
16 Kenya Commercial Bank.......................C3
17 Mombasa Hospital..................................D3
18 Mombasa Immigration Office..............D3
19 Standard Chartered Bank.....................C2

◉ **Transport**
20 Glory Car Hire..A2
21 Likoni Car Ferry.......................................A5
22 Tawakal...C1

The **Omani house**, in the San Felipe bastion in the northwestern corner of the fort, was built in the late 18th century and has a small fishing dhow outside it. Inside there's a small exhibition of Omani jewellery, weaponry and other artefacts. The eastern wall includes an Omani audience hall and the Passage of the Arches, which leads under the pinkish-brown coral to a double-azure vista of sea floating under sky.

There's a **museum** in the centre of the fort that displays finds from 42 Portuguese warships that were sunk during the Omani Siege in 1697, from barnacled earthenware jars to Persian amulets and Chinese porcelain. Like the rest of the complex, they are poorly labelled and woefully displayed. Despite this, the fort is unmissable.

If you arrive early in the day, you may avoid group tours, but the same can't be said of the guides, official and unofficial, who will offer you tours the minute you approach the fort. Some of them can be quite useful and some can be duds. Unfortunately you'll have to use your judgement to suss out which is which. Official guides charge KSh1200 for a tour of Fort Jesus or the Old Town; unofficial guides charge whatever they can. If you don't want a tour, shake off your guide with a firm but polite 'no', or they'll launch into their spiel and expect a tip at the end. Alternatively, you can buy the Fort Jesus guide booklet from the ticket desk and go it alone.

Mandhry Mosque MOSQUE
(Sir Mbarak Hinawy Rd) Founded in 1570, Mandhry Mosque in the Old Town is the city's oldest, and an excellent example of Swahili architecture, which combines the elegant flourishes of Arabic style with the comforting, geometric patterns of African design – note, for example, the gently rounded minaret. Not open to visitors.

Spice Market MARKET
(Langoni Rd; ☉ sunrise to sunset) This market, which stretches along Nehru and Langoni Rds west of the Old Town, is an evocative, sensory overload – expect lots of jostling, yelling, wheeling, dealing and, of course, the exotic scent of stall upon stall of cardamom, pepper, turmeric and curry powders, with stalls along Langoni Rd selling delicious street food.

Jain Temple TEMPLE
(Langoni Rd; ☉ 10am-12.30pm) This Jain temple caters to believers of Gujarati origin, and the ornamental interior, with niches filled with brightly painted figurines of deities, is well worth a peek.

Lord Shiva Temple TEMPLE
(Mwinyi Ab Rd; ☉ 10am-12.30pm) Mombasa's large Hindu population doesn't lack for places of worship. The enormous Lord Shiva Temple is airy, open and set off by an interesting sculpture garden.

Central Mombasa

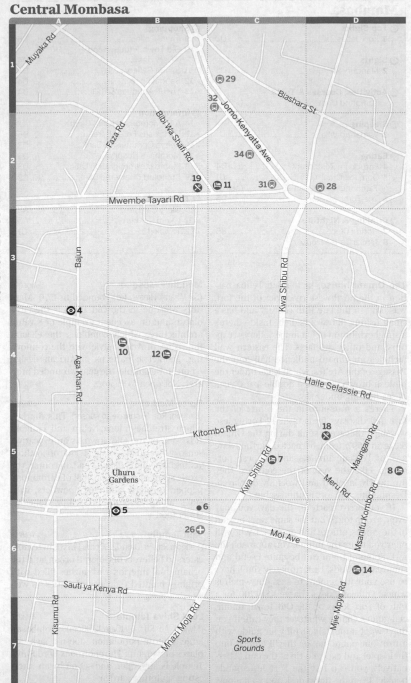

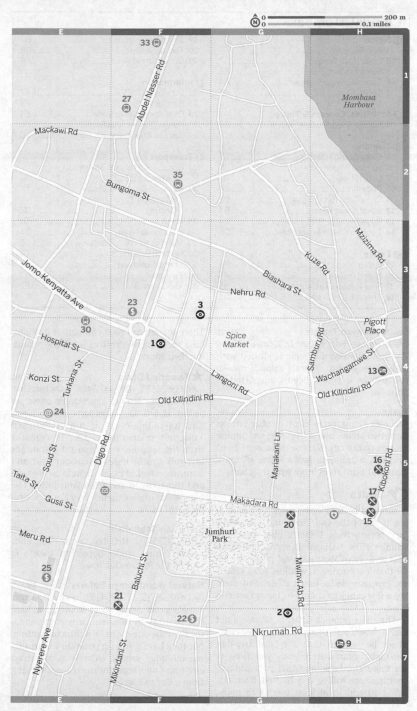

Central Mombasa

◎ **Sights**
1 Jain Temple...F4
2 Lord Shiva Temple.................................G7
3 Spice Market..F3
4 Swaminarayan Temple A4
5 Tusks..B6

⊕ **Activities, Courses & Tours**
6 Natural World Kenya Safaris.................B6

⊜ **Sleeping**
7 Glory Grand Hotel C5
8 Jundan Palace Hotel..............................D5
9 Lotus Hotel...H7
10 PrideInn B4
11 River Tana Rest House C2
12 Royal Court Hotel...................................B4
13 Royal Palace Hotel..................................H4
14 Sentrim Castle Royal Hotel...................D6

⊗ **Eating**
15 Barka..H6
16 Island Dishes..H5
17 New Recoda Restaurant H5
18 Shehnai Restaurant D5

19 Singh Restaurant....................................B2
20 Tarboush Cafe...G6
21 Urban Street Food..................................F6

ℹ **Information**
22 Barclays F7
23 Barclays F3
24 Blue Room Cyber Café...........................E4
25 Kenya Commercial Bank.......................E6
26 Sairose Pharmacy B6

ℹ **Transport**
27 Buses & Matatus to Malindi &
    Lamu.. F1
28 Buses to Arusha & Moshi
    (Mwembe Tayari Health
    Centre)... D2
29 Mash...C1
30 Matatus to Nyali......................................E4
31 Matatus to Voi & Wundanyi..................C2
32 Modern Coast...C1
33 Simba Coaches.. F1
34 Tahmeed...C2
35 TSS Express F2

Swaminarayan Temple   TEMPLE
(Haile Selassie Rd; ◷10am-12.30pm & 2-5pm)
The Swaminarayan Temple is stuffed with highlighter-bright murals that'll make you feel as if you've been transported to Mumbai.

Tusks   LANDMARK
(Mai Ave) Giant replicas of elephant tusks form two arches above Moi Ave, welcoming visitors to the city. Next to them are Uhuru Gardens, a tranquil, green space of fountains and giant trees hung with fruit bats.

☞ Tours

A number of tour companies offer standard tours of the Old Town and Fort Jesus (per person from US$60), plus safaris to Shimba Hills National Reserve and Tsavo East and Tsavo West national parks, famed for their easy access to wildlife. Most safaris are expensive lodge-based affairs, but there are a few camping safaris to Tsavo East and West.

The most popular safari is an overnight tour to Tsavo, and though most people enjoy these, be warned that a typical two-day, one-night safari barely gives you time to get there and back, and that your animal-spotting time will be very limited. It's much better to add in at least one extra night.

There are several tour companies in Mombasa that receive positive feedback regarding their tours.

★**Tamarind Dhow**   BOATING
(☑0733623583, 041-4471747; www.tamarind.co.ke; Cement Silo Rd; lunch/dinner cruise per person US$70/92; ◷ldeparts 1pm/6.30pm) This top-billing cruise is run by the posh Tamarind restaurant chain. It embarks from the jetty below Tamarind restaurant in Nyali and includes a harbour tour and fantastic meal. Prices include a cocktail and transport to and from your hotel. The two Jahazi dhows themselves are beautiful pieces of work.

Suleiman Sabdallah   WALKING
(☑0722478570) Reliable, knowledgeable, licensed tour guide happy to take you around the fort or Old Town.

Natural World Kenya Safaris   SAFARIS
(☑041-2226715, 0720894288; www.naturaltoursandsafaris.com; Jeneby House, Moi Ave) The hard sell prattled by the company 'representatives' on the street can be a little off-putting, but they have a solid reputation for arranging multiday safaris, as well as Mombasa city tours and trips to Tsavo East, ranging from a day to a week.

✿ Festivals & Events

★ **Mombasa Carnival**   FESTIVAL
(zainab@africaonline.co.ke; ⊙ Nov) Street festival, with a month of music, dance and other events.

Mombasa Triathlon   SPORTS
(☑ 0722714788; ⊙ Sep, Oct or Nov) Sporty types or keen spectators will enjoy this open competition, with a 1.5km swim, 40km bike ride and 10km run through the streets of Mombasa.

🛏 Sleeping

Mombasa has a number of decent hotels, though in general the more upmarket places tend to be far from the city centre. Dirt-cheap choices are in the busy area close to the bus stations on Abdel Nasser Rd and Jomo Kenyatta Ave. Lone female travellers might want to opt for something a little further up the price scale and away from the bus station area, which is rather sketchy.

Jundan Palace Hotel   HOTEL $
(☑ 0725376784, 0722200442; www.facebook.com/JundanHotel; Taita St; s/d/tr KSh2700/3400/4000; ✳ 🛜) The palace in the name may be entirely fanciful, but don't dismiss this city-centre cheapie immediately, as its rooms are far better than you'd expect from its market exterior and cramped lobby. Awaiting you upstairs are spotless tile-floored rooms with TVs and fridges. There's also the room number embroidered on each pillowcase in case you forget it.

Royal Palace Hotel   HOTEL $
(☑ 0722410168; www.facebook.com/royalpalacehotelmombasa; cnr Old Kilindini & Kibokoni Rds; s/d from KSh1500/2800) The style here is a bit Nigerian chic (over-the-top glitzy) and some of the rooms could do with a lick of paint, but there's a lovely rooftop terrace and the staff are welcoming. A perfectly fine budget option.

Glory Grand Hotel   BUSINESS HOTEL $
(☑ 041-2313564; Kwa Shibu Rd; s/d from KSh3500/4500) Neither glorious nor grand, this hotel is instead excellent value, with spruced-up rooms that hint at business-hotel style – minus the cost. Breakfast is simple, but it's a safe, convenient place to sleep and is located in a quiet(ish) area.

River Tana Rest House   GUESTHOUSE $
(☑ 0725806498; cnr Mwembe Tayari & Gatundu Rds; s/d KSh600/800) Probably the cheapest of Mombasa's safe guesthouses, this place isn't pretty on the outside, but the rooms are clean and your purse will thank you. Perfectly fine for a night or two and convenient for buses. Excellent Indian restaurant.

Lotus Hotel   HOTEL $$
(☑ 041-2313207; www.lotushotelmombasa.com; Cathedral Lane, off Nkrumah Rd; s/d US$50/75; ✳ 🛜) One of the best-value midrange options in Mombasa, the old-world Lotus is central and has clean, compact rooms with hot water and functioning air-conditioning. Staff are especially welcoming, and there are two bars downstairs to boot.

Royal Court Hotel   BUSINESS HOTEL $$
(☑ 0733412867; www.royalcourtmombasa.co.ke; Haile Selassie Rd; s/d KSh7700/10,500; ✳ 🛜 ♿) The swish lobby is the highlight of this stylish business hotel. Still, service and facilities are good, disabled access is a breeze and you get great views and food at the Roof Restaurant (on the roof), which also has a pool, and Malaika Brasserie. It wins points for charging everyone the same rates and for the spa and gym.

Prideinn   BUSINESS HOTEL $$
(☑ 0737999110; www.prideinn.co.ke; Haile Selassie Rd; s/d KSh5500/7000; ✳ 🛜) Right on Haile Selassie Rd, this hotel makes up in convenience what it lacks in soundproofing and charm. The rooms are business quality and well cared for and though superiors have kitchens, none of them are particularly fancy. A solid, mildly central option for a short Mombasa stay.

Sentrim Castle Royal Hotel   HISTORIC HOTEL $$
(☑ 041-2228790,0735339920;www.sentrim-hotels.net; Moi Ave; s/d/tr US$75/110/145; ✳ 🛜) With an impressive colonial exterior, Castle Royal harks back to glory days of yore. The service is friendly and helpful. The rooms have good bathrooms and flat-screen TVs, though the cheapest ones are overpriced and nothing special. There's a beautiful terrace looking out over the city. Due to road noise, be sure to get a room at the back.

🍴 Eating

Mombasa has a variety of cuisines on offer to match the breadth of its cultural influences. Explore the Old Town for cheap, authentic Swahili cuisine; if in doubt, follow the locals to find the best places. Most places are Muslim-run, so alcoholic drinks

STREET FOOD

Mombasa is good for street food: stalls sell samosas, bhajis, kebabs and the local take on pizza (meat and onions wrapped in soft dough and fried). A few dish out stew and ugali. For dessert, seek out *haluwa* (an Omani version of Turkish delight), fried taro root, sweet baobab seeds and sugared doughnuts.

are rarely on the menu and most places are closed until after sunset during Ramadan.

Island Dishes   KENYAN $

(☑ 0711122221; Kibokoni Rd; mains KSh150-350; ☺ 8am-11pm) Once your eyes have adjusted to the dazzling strip lights, feast them on the tasty menu at this very popular Swahili restaurant. *Mishikaki* (marinated, grilled meat kebabs), chicken tikka, fish with coconut, *mkate mayai* (Swahili pizza), fresh juices and all the usual favourites are on offer to eat in or take away, though the biryani is only available at lunchtime.

Barka   SWAHILI $

(☑ 0722991128; www.facebook.com/barka restaurantofficial; Makadara Rd; mains KSh400; ☺ 7am-10pm Mon-Sat) This canteen-style restaurant is constantly packed with ravenous locals – and you have to be ravenous to tackle one of the monster portions of mutton or chicken biryani. Cheap and cheerful. Takeaway available at extra cost.

★ Shehnai Restaurant   INDIAN $$

(☑ 0722871111; www.restaurantshehnai.com; Fatemi House, Mwindani Rd; mains KSh700-1500; ☺ noon-2pm & 7-10pm Tue-Sun; ☑) This reputable *mughlai* (North Indian) curry house is popular with the local Indian community and does delicious dishes such as *gosht palakwalla* (lamb with masala and spinach) and a superb chicken biryani. The staff are friendly and the entire place has an air of gentility absent elsewhere in Mombasa. There's no alcohol.

Forodhani Restaurant   INTERNATIONAL $$

(☑ 0724401551; Sri Mbarak Hinawy Rd; mains KSh350-1800; ☺ 8am-10pm; ☑☑) A very welcome addition to the Old Town dining scene, Forodhani has an appealing terrace overlooking the ocean. The menu is a crowd-pleasing, extensive list of Swahili and Indian dishes such as beef *mishikaki*

(marinated, grilled meat kebabs) and prawn curry, with lobster thermidor and chicken wings catering more to the international palate.

New Recoda Restaurant   SWAHILI $$

(☑ 0720436709; Kibokoni Rd; mains KSh400-700; ☺ 6am-11pm) The legendary, decades-old Moi Ave eatery has migrated to a new location, but the shish kebabs are as flavourful as ever. The coconut prawns and fruit juices also get high marks.

Urban Street Food   INTERNATIONAL $$

(☑ 0700907363; www.urbanstreetfood.co.ke; Nkrumah Rd; mains KSh500-750; ☺ 7am-11pm Mon-Sat; ☑) This textbook hip, yellow-walled place with an industrial vibe in central Mombasa does several things few other local establishments do, including great coffee, small plates of hummus, juicy burgers and gorgeous fresh juices. There's a distinct Middle Eastern slant to the otherwise international menu, with shawarma jostling with pizza and a selection of good breakfasts. Delivery is available.

Singh Restaurant   INDIAN $$

(☑ 0733702145; Mwembe Tayari Rd; mains KSh400-1200; ☺ noon-3pm & 7-10pm; ☑) A great Indian restaurant steeped in Mombasa history: the owner first opened the doors in 1962 to serve arriving and departing railway passengers. The decor is plain, but your tastebuds won't notice. Even things that don't sound great on paper, such as egg curry, are divine here. We rate the aubergine and okra dishes highly.

Tarboush Cafe   INTERNATIONAL $$

(Makadara Rd; mains KSh400-800; ☺ 8am-midnight) Most people come to this open-air, parkside restaurant for the chicken tikka and the beef *mishkaki* (marinated, grilled meat kebabs). Eat it with lovely soft naan bread, rice or chips. There's also a good range of Swahili staples and some curries.

The Fort   SEAFOOD $$$

(☑ 0722776399; www.thefort.co.ke; Nkrumah Rd; mains KSh1000-2000; ☺ noon-11pm Tue-Sun; ☑) Right opposite the entrance to Fort Jesus, Mombasa's main sight, this excellent restaurant is an obvious place for a meal after your visit. The speciality here is local seafood cooked in a variety of Swahili sauces, but there's lots of other choices, including seafood risotto and pizzas.

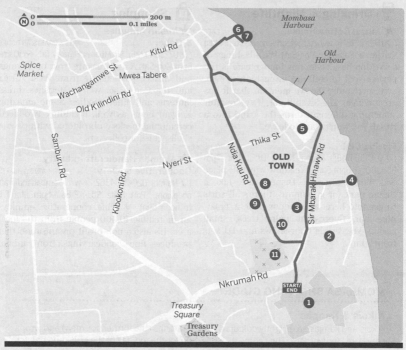

N 0 — 200 m
0 — 0.1 miles

Mombasa Harbour

Old Harbour

Spice Market

Kitui Rd

Wachangamwe St

Mwea Tabere

Old Kilindini Rd

Samburu Rd

Kibokoni Rd

Nyeri St

Ndia Kuu Rd

Thika St

OLD TOWN

Sir Mbarak Hinawy Rd

Nkrumah Rd

Treasury Square

Treasury Gardens

START/ END

🏃 City Walk
Mombasa Old Town

START FORT JESUS
END FORT JESUS
LENGTH ABOUT 1.5KM
DURATION ONE HOUR

Mombasa may not have the medieval charm of Lamu or Zanzibar, but the Old Town is a unique architectural blend of all who've influenced Swahili history and culture.

Start at **1 Fort Jesus** (p207). From here head past the colonial **2 Mombasa Club** onto Sir Mbarak Hinawy Rd, once the main access road to the port and still a lively thoroughfare.

On the left, **3 Africa Hotel** was one of only three hotels in the city at the turn of the 20th century. If you take a quick jaunt to your right you'll hit the water and see the restored facades of **4 old houses**.

Turn the corner at the end of the street and you'll enter **5 Government Sq**, the largest open space in the Old Town. The buildings lining the square used to hold some of the city's key administrative offices.

Heading out of the square you'll need to hang a right towards Mombasa Harbour. Here you'll find the **6 Leven Steps**, which lead down past a great view of the ships docking in the harbour to **7 Vasco da Gama's Well**, a reservoir that supposedly never dries.

Returning to Ndia Kuu Rd, the final stages of your route can be as direct or as tangential as you wish – diverting into side streets is highly recommended. The winding alleyways linking Old Town towards Digo Rd are lively with market traders. Heading this way will eventually land you in the city spice market.

If you do stick to Ndia Kuu Rd, you'll see a lot of nicely restored traditional buildings, including the **8 Balcony House**, so named for obvious reasons; **9 Edward St Rose**, the former chemist, which retains its original engraved-glass panel; and **10 Ali's Curio Market**, one of the better-preserved balcony houses. Pass the Muslim **11 cemetery** and you're back at Fort Jesus.

Drinking & Nightlife

⭐ Jahazi Coffee House   CAFE

(📞0738277975; www.jahazicoffeehouse.com; Ndia Kuu Rd; ⏰8am-7pm Mon-Sat) With lashings of sexy Mombasa style, this lounge cafe is the perfect spot to chill out in cushion-strewn, arty surrounds. Did we mention that it has great coffee? The Swahili pot, if you're after something different, turns the grind into a ritual. You won't want to leave.

Florida Club   CLUB

(📞0701568746; Mama Ngina Dr; after 7pm KSh300; ⏰6pm-6am) We know why this place was named after the Disney state. Like a theme park for grown-ups, there's all sorts to get into here: an outdoor pool, a 'crazy' blue bar, fluorescent palm trees, small casino, Vegas-style floor shows and DJ sets from 7pm.

🛍 Shopping

⭐ Yusufi Antiques & Gallery   ARTS & CRAFTS, ANTIQUES

(📞0723849226; Sir Mbarak Hinawy Rd; ⏰10am-6pm Mon-Sat) A real treasure trove of carvings and masks, particularly from West Africa and the Congo, as well as fetishes, brass lanterns and other goodies. Some amazing Kenyan items as well, including two-faced ceremonial masks embroidered with cowrie shells. One for collectors.

⭐ Akamba Handicraft Industry Cooperative Society   ARTS & CRAFTS

(📞Nairobi 020-2654362; www.akambahandicraft coop.com; Port Reitz Rd; ⏰8am-5pm Mon-Fri, to noon Sun) 🌿 This cooperative employs an incredible 10,000 people from the local area. It's also a non-profit organisation that produces fine woodcarvings, from animal

---

MOMBASA SHOPPING GUIDE

Kikois & Kangas

Kikois and kangas are brightly coloured woven sarongs (the former, for men) and wraps (the latter, for women). They come as a pair, one for the top half of the body and one for the bottom, and are marked with Swahili proverbs. Head to Biashara St, west of the Digo Rd intersection (just north of the spice market). You may need to bargain, but what you get is generally what you pay for – bank on about KSh600 for a pair of cheap kangas or a *kikoi*. *Kofia* (the handmade caps worn by Muslim men) are also crafted here; a really excellent one can cost up to KSh2500.

Tailored Outfits

Mombasa has an incredible number of skilled tailors and you can have a safari suit or shirt custom-made in a day or two for no more than US$30. There are numerous tailors on Nehru Rd, behind the spice market. You can either buy some stylish printed fabric beforehand or have your tailor assist.

Wood Carvings & Masks

Sri Mbaraki Hinawy Rd in the Old Town is the place to search for true collectors' items, with a rich selection of antiques, masks and carvings, particularly from west and central Africa.

Gifts & Souvenirs

For fair-trade gifts, the purchase of which empowers the residents of one enterprising Kenyan village, check out the Imani Collective (p217) in the Old Town. Run by a non-profit organisation, the Akamba Handicraft Industry Cooperative Society near the airport is a terrific place for all sorts of Kenyan crafts, from animal carvings and masks to polished calabash bowls and toys.

Spices

Saffron, cinnamon, cloves, cardamom, curry powder from India...no visit to Mombasa is complete without a stop at the famous spice market (p209). Prices aren't fixed, so start bargaining only once you're sure you want to buy something. You'll also likely be offered other kinds of 'spices', such as miraa (twigs and shoots that are chewed as a stimulant) and pan.

shapes and polished calabash bowls to stick-thin Maasai figures, replica Maasai shields, salad spoons and elaborate masks. Kwa Hola/Magongo matatus (minibuses) run right past the gates from the Kobil petrol station on Jomo Kenyatta Ave. Very fair prices.

Sandal Shop SHOES
(off Sir Mbarak Hinawy Rd; ⊙7am-6pm Mon-Sat) You're likely to see these attractive leather sandals with beading embroidery all over Kenya. Watch them being made at this cobblers shop and buy them for the fairest prices around (from KSh500).

Imani Collective GIFTS & SOUVENIRS
(www.imanicollective.com; Ndia Kuu Rd; ⊙8.30am-5pm Mon-Sat) ✎ Fair trade woven items, bags, embroidered cushions, soft toys and other appealing gifts, created by a collective of over 50 men and women from Mtepeni village in the Kilifi district along the coast.

Old Town Antiques and Carvings ARTS & CRAFTS
(✎0725792955; Sir Mbarak Hinawy Rd; ⊙10am-6pm Mon-Sat) Good selection of collectors' items – Central and West African masks and carvings – as well as numerous Kenyan small carvings of animals.

Sanaa Gallery ARTS & CRAFTS
(Government Sq; ⊙8am-6pm Mon-Sat) A good place to check out traditional furniture-making, or if you're looking for an attractive yet bulky souvenir to ship home.

ⓘ Information

DANGERS & ANNOYANCES
Sensible precautions should be taken, such as avoiding poorly lit streets after dark and not displaying your valuables. When in doubt, hailing a tuk-tuk is an easy (and cheap) answer. Women may expect a bit more attention if walking alone through the Old Town. Two pickpocketing and bag-snatching hotspots are the junction of Jomo Kenyatta Ave and Mwembe Tayari Rd – the departure point for many buses and matatus – and the Likoni ferry, which tends to get jam-packed.

EMERGENCY
Central Police Station (✎999; Makadara Rd)

INTERNET ACCESS
Blue Room Cyber Café (✎041-224021; www.facebook.com/brcafe; Haile Selassie Rd; per min KSh2; ⊙9am-10pm)

MEDICAL SERVICES
The following are the best medical services in Mombasa.
AAR Mombasa Health Centre (✎0731191067; www.aar-healthcare.com; Pereira Bldg, Machakos St, off Moi Ave; ⊙24hr) Around-the-clock medical clinic.
Mombasa Hospital (✎0733333655, 041-2312191; www.mombasahospital.com; off Mama Ngina Dr) Best private hospital in the region.
Sairose Pharmacy (✎0733320201; Moi Ave; ⊙7am-10pm Mon-Sat, 9am-10pm Sun) Open late.

MONEY
Outside business hours you can change money at most major hotels, although rates are usually poor. ATMs can be found everywhere and nearly all accept international credit and debit cards.
Kenya Commercial Bank (Nkrumah Rd) With ATM. Another on **Moi Ave** (Moi Ave).
Barclays (Digo Rd) Has an ATM, as does another branch on **Nkrumah Rd** (Nkrumah Rd).
Fort Jesus Forex Bureau (✎041-316717; Ndia Kuu Rd; ⊙9am-5pm Mon-Fri) Currency exchange.
Standard Chartered Bank (Treasury Sq, Nkrumah Rd) With ATM.

POST
Post Office (✎041-227705; Digo Rd; ⊙9am-5pm Mon-Fri, to 1pm Sat)

TOURIST INFORMATION
There is currently no tourist information office in Mombasa. Hotels, travel agencies and your fellow travellers are your best bet for up-to-date travel information about the city and its surroundings.

ⓘ Getting There & Away

AIR
From Moi International Airport (p382), around 9km northwest of central Mombasa, there are up to a dozen flights to Nairobi (from US$55) daily with Fly540 (www.fly540.com) and Kenya Airways (www.kenya-airways.com). There is also a daily flight to Lamu (US$90) with Skyward Express (www.skywardexpress.co.ke) and one to Zanzibar (US$140) with Fly540. From a separate terminal, Mombasa Air Safari (www.mombasaairsafari.com) connects Mombasa with airstrips in the Masai Mara.

BUS & MATATU
Most bus offices are on either Jomo Kenyatta Ave or Abdel Nasser Rd. Services to Malindi and Lamu leave from Abdel Nasser Rd, while buses to Nairobi and destinations in Tanzania leave

from the junction of Jomo Kenyatta Ave and Mwembe Tayari Rd.

For buses and matatus to the beaches and towns south of Mombasa, you first need to get off the island on the **Likoni ferry**. Frequent matatus run from Nyerere Ave to the transport stand by the ferry terminal. Walk off the ferry and pick up transport on the other side.

If all goes according to plan, a cable car across the Likoni Channel will become operational in 2019.

To Nairobi

There are dozens of daily departures in both directions (mostly in the early morning and late evening). Daytime services take at least eight hours, and overnight trips take 10 to 12 hours, and are not terribly recommended.

The trip isn't particularly comfortable, although it's not bad for an African bus ride, but note that the Nairobi–Mombasa road is accident prone. Speedometers with an 80km/h limit fitted on buses and matatus have eased the problem somewhat, but some drivers continue to flout rules. Theft is also an issue on this route: as much as it disappoints us to say so, don't accept food and drink from fellow travellers; we've heard too many stories of *wazungu* (white people – both tourists and Kenyans) being drugged and mugged on this route. Most trips, however, are crime and accident free.

Fares vary from KSh700 to KSh2200, with Modern Coast (p384) the swishest (and most expensive) of the lot. Mash (p384) is also a good bet. Most companies have at least four departures daily. Several companies go to Kisumu and Lake Victoria, but all go via Nairobi first.

Matatus to Voi and Wundanyi (Mwembe Tayari Rd), towards Nairobi, depart from the junction of Mwembe Tayari Rd and Jomo Kenyatta Ave.

North to Malindi and Lamu

There are numerous daily buses and matatus heading up the coast to Malindi, leaving from in front of the Noor Mosque on Abdel Nasser Rd. Buses take up to three hours (around KSh700) and matatus take about two hours (KSh500 rising to KSh700 during holidays and very busy periods).

Tahmeed (p384), **Tawakal** (☑ 0722550111; Abdel Nasser Rd), **Simba** (☑ 0707471410; Abdel Nasser Rd) and **TSS Express** (p384) have buses to Lamu (KSh800 to KSh1200), most leaving at around 7am (report 30 minutes early) from their offices on Abdel Nasser Rd and Jomo Kenyatta Ave. Tawakal is considered to be the most comfortable and reliable. Buses take around seven hours to reach the Lamu ferry at Mokoke and travel via Malindi. At research time, buses had to join an armed

convoy between Garsen and Witu, as that stretch of road north of Malindi is known for intermittent banditry.

Matatus to Nyali (Jomo Kenyatta Ave) depart from Jomo Kenyatta Ave.

South to Diani Beach and Lunga Lunga

Regular buses and matatus leave from the far side of the Likoni ferry terminal and travel along the southern coast.

To Tanzania

Mash, **Modern Coast**, **Tahmeed** and **TSS Express** (p384) have daily departures to Dar es Salaam (KSh1400 to KSh2200, 10 to 12 hours) via Tanga from their offices on Jomo Kenyatta Ave, near the junction with Mwembe Tayari Rd. Dubious-looking **buses to Arusha and Moshi** (Jomo Kenyatta Ave) leave from in front of the Mwembe Tayari Health Centre in the morning or evening.

TRAIN

From the **Mombasa Terminus** (Mombasa-Nairobi Rd; ⊘ ticket sales 7am-4pm), the new high-speed *Madaraka Express* connects Mombasa and Nairobi (economy/1st class KSh700/3000, 4½ hours). Departures from Mombasa are at 9am daily; at research time, tickets could only be purchased at the train station with cash.

ⓘ Getting Around

TO/FROM THE AIRPORT & TRAIN STATION

Moi International Airport (p382) There is no public transport from the airport. Taxi fare to central Mombasa is KSh2000. A tuk-tuk to the airport costs KSh1000, plus parking fee of KSh60.

Mombasa Terminus The *Madaraka Express* train from Nairobi arrives at the newly built Mombasa Terminus, 18km from the city, and is met by taxis and matatus. A taxi into Mombasa costs around KSh2500, while matatus drop passengers off by the former train station in the centre for KSh150. Tuk-tuks are not allowed in the train station car park, but if you walk out to the main road (around 300m), you'll find them waiting at the junction.

BOAT

The **Likoni ferry** (www.kenyaferry.co.ke) connects Mombasa island with the southern mainland, so if you want to head to Diani Beach or any points south of there, you have to take the ferry unless you want to travel hours out of your way.

There's a crossing roughly every 15 minutes between 5am and 12.30am, and hourly outside these times. It's free for pedestrians and cyclists, KSh150 per car, KSh190 per 4WD and

KSh270 for a pick-up or big safari jeep. To get to the jetty from the centre of town, take a Likoni matatu from Digo Rd. Do also note that there can be long waits at rush hour on this route, so plan your trip accordingly.

CAR & MOTORCYCLE
Glory Car Hire (📱0722388729; www.glory kenya.com; Moi Ave) is a reliable local choice for rentals. Cars with drivers can also be arranged for as little as KSH3500 per day.

MATATU, TAXI & TUK-TUK
Matatus charge between KSh30 and KSh50 for short trips. There are also plenty of three-wheeled tuk-tuks about, which run from about KSh50 to KSh200 for a bit of open-air transit. These two are the main forms of transport in Mombasa.

Taxis are expensive and hard to find. Ask your hotel to call one for you. Assume it'll cost KSh2500 from the train station to the city centre.

SOUTH OF MOMBASA

Shimba Hills National Reserve

Cool and grassy, this 320-sq-km **national reserve** (📱0704467855; www.kws.org; adult/child US$22/13; ⏱6am-6pm) makes an easy day trip from Diani Beach. Its lush hills are home to sable antelope, elephants, warthogs, baboons, buffaloes and Masai giraffes, as well as 300 species of butterfly. The sable antelope have made a stunning recovery here after their numbers dropped to less than 120 in 1970.

In 2005 the elephant population reached an amazing 600 – far too many for this tiny space. Instead of culling the herds, KWS organised an unprecedented US$3.2 million translocation operation to reduce the pressure on the habitat, capturing no fewer than 400 elephants and moving them to Tsavo East National Park, a wildlife reserve between Mombasa and Nairobi.

There are more than 150km of tracks that criss-cross the reserve.

◉ Sights

Sheldrick Falls — WATERFALL
These pretty 21m-high falls are laced with lianas and greenery, and have a natural plunge pool. Free, two-hour, 2km walks,

---

---

organised by the KWS, depart from the Sheldrick Falls ranger post at 10am and 2pm daily.

Elephant Hill — VIEWPOINT
With the best viewpoint in the reserve, this hill is the place to see elephants. It affords lovely views out over the valley towards the ocean. Armed rangers will escort you once you reach the entry point to the hill.

Marere Dam — VIEWPOINT
A watering hole that attracts animals, including elephants. Also a great birdwatching spot.

🛏 Sleeping

Shimba Hills Lodge — LODGE $$$
(📱0711367345; www.shimbalodge.net; Kinango Rd; r from US$160) Entered by a separate park gate from the main entrance, this dark timber lodge features an attractive interior, strewn with numerous Congolese and West African carvings. The rooms are snug, bright and come with welcome splashes of

DON'T MISS

MWALUGANJE ELEPHANT SANCTUARY

Opened in October 1995 to create a corridor along an elephant migration route between Shimba Hills and Mwaluganje Forest Reserve, and comprising 240 sq km of ruggedly beautiful country along the valley of the Cha Shimba River, this **sanctuary** (☑0721765476; www.elephantmwaluganje.co.ke; adult/child US$15/2, vehicles KSh150-300; ⊙6am-6pm) is home to one of the densest concentrations of pachyderms on the continent (150 or so, to be precise). Sightings of these magnificent beasts are guaranteed, and the reserve's relative remoteness means that you're unlikely to have to share them with many other visitors. All this makes Mwaluganje more suitable for those who've done a few safaris elsewhere and are after a wilder, more pristine experience. The drier country means the wildlife in Mwaluganje differs slightly from that of wetter and greener Shimba Hills, especially so when it comes to the birds.

This sanctuary is a good example of community-based conservation, with local people acting as stakeholders in the project.

The rather fine **Mwaluganje Elephant Camp** (☑0721765476; camping KSh1000, s/d US$170/245) has very plush safari tents overlooking a waterhole. If you can't afford the fancy-pants tents, then camp in your own tent at the campsite, located near the main gate. The setting is sublime (though rocks make things tricky for tent pegs). It's as genuine an African wilderness experience as you can ask for.

Getting There & Away

The main entrance to the sanctuary is about 13km northeast of Shimba Hills National Reserve, on the road to Kinango. A shorter route runs from Kwale to the Golini Gate, passing the Mwaluganje ticket office. It's only 5km but the track is 4WD only. The roads inside the park are pretty rough and a 4WD is the only way to get around. Some Mombasa- and Diani-based operators offer organised tours.

colourful art. The highlight is the wildlife seen from the boardwalk, which looks out over a forest clearing with a small lake.

ⓘ Getting There & Away

Shimba Hills is 40km south of Mombasa. The majority of the roads inside the park are accessible by city car during the drier months, with only a couple of tracks designated 4WD only. During the rainy season you'll need a 4WD to enter the reserve.

Every safari company in Mombasa and Diani Beach offers trips to Shimba Hills (half-day tours per person from US$75). If you're travelling with others, renting a car in Mombasa may be the cheapest way to go.

Tiwi Beach

☑040

The sleepy, shaded and secluded antithesis to nearby Diani Beach, Tiwi makes a lovely, quiet, cottage-style escape by the ocean. The wide, white beach is studded with skinny palms and there is very little in the way of beach boys. Tiwi also has a beautiful coral reef, part of which teems with starfish of all

shapes and colours. A stable, pool-like area between the shore and the coral is great for swimming and snorkelling.

🛏 Sleeping

With a few exceptions, Tiwi doesn't provide the all-in-one package experience of the high-end resorts to the south. The name of the game here is small, self-catered cottages, which can be a real joy for couples and groups. All of these places are located off the unnamed dirt track that runs parallel to the main highway and the beach.

Twiga Lodge　　　　　　　　　HOTEL $
(☑0721577614; twigakenya@gmail.com; camping KSh500, older s/d KSh2000/3500, new s/d KSh3500/5300) This secluded overlanders' favourite is great fun when there's a crowd staying, with *makuti* (thatched-roof) lodgings peeking at the ocean from between the venerable baobab trees. The older rooms are extremely basic and in dire need of TLC – opt for one of the newer, tiled rooms with sea views. The on-site restaurant serves mainly seafood (mains KSh400 to KSh600).

Sand Island Beach Cottages   COTTAGE $$
(☑ 0722395005; www.sandislandbeach.com; cottages US$120-200; 🐾) Named after the spit of sand exposed by low tide, Sand Island consists of 10 spacious, airy, self-catering cottages overlooking the sand. Each has its own style – Pweza cottage, for example, features furniture made from salvaged Swahili doors – and all have colourful quilts and shady terraces. It's signposted from the main Tiwi Beach road and lies 3.5km along a dirt track.

Coral Cove Cottages   COTTAGE $$
(☑ 0722732797; www.coralcove.tiwibeach.com; cottages KSh5500-8600) A good self-catering option, offering simple, colourful cottages within sight of the ocean. Expect a warm welcome – from the menagerie of dogs, cats, ducks and rescued parrots, as well as from host Kerstin – and cottages furnished with everything you might need for a weekend hideaway. The turn-off is next to the one for Twiga.

ℹ Getting There & Away

To get to Tiwi, turn left off the main highway (A14) about 18km south of Mombasa (or right if you're coming from Diani) and follow the track until it terminates at a north–south T-junction.

Buses and matatus on the road between the Likoni ferry crossing and Ukunda can drop you at the start of either track down to Tiwi (KSh100). The **Tiwi bus stop** or the southern turn-off, known locally as Tiwi 'spot', is much easier to find. Although it's only 3.5km to the beach, both access roads are notorious for muggings, so take a *boda-boda* (around KSh200), a taxi (KSh500) or hang around for a lift. If you're heading back to the highway, any of the accommodation places can call ahead for a taxi.

Diani Beach

☑ 040 / POP 62,529
With a flawless, long stretch of white-sand beach hugged by lush forest and kissed by surfable waves, it's no wonder Diani Beach is so popular. This resort town scores points with a diverse crowd: party people, families, honeymooners, backpackers and water-sports enthusiasts.

But if that sounds like your typical resort town, think again. Diani has some of the best accommodation in Kenya, from budget party hostels to funky kitesurfing lodges and intimate honeymoon spots. Most places are spread along the beach road, hidden behind a line of forest.

When lazing in a hammock gets tiring, visit the coral mosques with their archways that overlook the open ocean, venture into the sacred forests where guides hug trees that speak in their ancestors' voices, or take in the monkey sanctuary – all are good ways to experience more of the coast than the considerable charms of sun and sand.

◉ Sights

★ Colobus
Conservation Centre   WILDLIFE RESERVE
(☑ 0711479453; www.colobusconservation.org; Diani Beach Rd; tours adult/child KSh750/250; ⊙ 8am-4.30pm Mon-Sat) Notice the monkeys clambering on rope ladders over the road? The 'colobridges' are the work of the Colobus Conservation Centre, which aims to protect the Angolan black-and-white colobus monkey, a once-common species now restricted to some 5000 monkeys in a few isolated pockets of forest south of Mombasa. It runs excellent tours of its headquarters, where you'll likely get to see a few orphaned or injured colobus, Sykes' and vervet monkeys undergoing the process of rehabilitation to the wild.

With advance notice the centre can organise forest walks (per person KSh1000) in search of wilder primates and other creatures. There's also a wildly popular volunteer programme, costing from €750 for three weeks.

★ Kaya Kinondo   FOREST
(☑ 0722446916; www.kaya-kinondo-kenya.com; Diani Beach Rd; KSh1000; ⊙ 8am-5pm) This forest, sacred to the Digo people, is the only one of the area's sacred forests that's open to visitors. Visiting this small grove is a nature walk, historical journey and cultural experience. As you make your way across tangled roots and chunks of ancient coral, the guide points out various plants used in traditional medicine, and there's the chance to transmit your fears and worries to an ancient tree by hugging it. Expect to tip your guide.

Before entering the Kaya Kinondo you have to remove head wear, promise not to kiss anyone inside the grove, wrap a black *kaniki* (sarong) around your waist and go with a guide, who will explain the significance of some of the 187 plant species inside. They include the 'pimple tree', a

MOMBASA & THE SOUTH COAST DIANI BEACH

LOCAL KNOWLEDGE

BEST BEACHES

Beaches, beaches everywhere, but which is the best? We think you'll never want to stop building sandcastles on the following beaches:

Tiwi Beach Sunny, sandy and empty.

Diani Beach Despite the tourist resorts and the crowds, Diani Beach is a stunning, miles-long expanse of sugary-white sand.

Takaungu The very definition of a perfect beach.

known cure for acne; a palm believed to be 1050 years old; snatches of coral; and the rather self-explanatory 'Viagra tree'. Enormous liana swings (go on, try it) and strangling fig trees abound.

Many *kaya* (sacred forests) have been identified in this area, all of which were originally home to Mijikenda villages. The Mijikenda (Nine Homesteads) are actually nine subtribes – Chonyi, Digo, Duruma, Giriama, Jibana, Kambe, Kauma, Rabai and Ribe – united, to a degree, by culture, history and language. Yet each of the tribes remains distinct and speaks its own dialect of the Mijikenda language. Still, there's a binding factor between the Nine Homesteads, and between the modern Mijikenda and their ancestors: their shared veneration of the *kaya*.

This historical connection becomes concrete when you enter the woods and realise – and there's no other word that fits here – they simply feel old.

Many trees are about 600 years old, which corresponds to the arrival of the first Mijikenda from Singwaya, their semi-legendary homeland in southern Somalia. Cutting vegetation within the *kaya* is strictly prohibited – visitors may not even take a stray twig or leaf from the forest.

The preserved forests do not just facilitate dialogue with the ancestors, they also provide a direct link to ecosystems that have been clear-felled out of existence elsewhere. Kaya Kinondo contains five possible endemic species, and 140 tree species classified as 'rare', within its 30 hectares – the space of a suburban residential block.

The main purpose of the *kaya* was to house the villages of the Mijikenda, which were located in a large central clearing.

Entering the centre of a *kaya* required ritual knowledge to proceed through concentric circles of sacredness surrounding the node of the village. Sacred talismans and spells were supposed to cause hallucinations that disoriented enemies who attacked the forest.

The *kaya* were largely abandoned in the 1940s and conservative strains of Islam and Christianity have denigrated their value to the Mijikenda, but thanks to their Unesco World Heritage status, they will hopefully be preserved for future visitors. The *kaya* have lasted 600 years; with luck, the wind will speak through their branches for much longer.

Kongo Mosque
MOSQUE

(Diani Beach Rd; donation KSh100; ⊙ dawn-dusk) At the far northern end of the beach road (follow the faded sign behind the Jacaranda Resort) is the 16th-century Kongo Mosque – Diani's last surviving relic of the ancient Swahili civilisations that once controlled the coast, and one of a tiny handful of coral mosques still in use in Kenya. The baobab-studded beach is a wonderful picnic spot and the mosque is worth a peek in spite of an unsympathetic contemporary extension.

🏃 Activities

Diani Beach is a superb destination for active travellers, with numerous water sports on offer, from diving and snorkelling to kitesurfing and windsurfing. If you want to take it easy, there are relaxing day-long dhow cruises, and if you want an extra jolt of adrenaline, skydiving is also an option.

★ H$_2$O Extreme
KITESURFING

(📞 0721495876; www.h2o-extreme.com; Diani Beach Rd, Kenyaways Kite Village) The best-regarded kitesurfing outfit in Diani offers half-day beginner courses for €100, as well as windsurfing and stand up paddle boarding (SUP) lessons (per hour €25). You can also rent SUPs (per hour €10), kitesurfing equipment (per hour €40), single and two-person sea kayaks (per hour €25), and body boards (per hour €10).

★ Pilli Pipa
WATER SPORTS

(📞 0722205120, 0724442555; www.pillipipa.com; Diani Beach Rd, Colliers Centre; from KSh7500) The reputable dive school Pilli Pipa offers excellent dhow safaris, dolphin-spotting trips, whale watching, night dives and snorkelling trips to Kisite Marine National Park (p230).

Tiwi & Diani Beaches

Tiwi & Diani Beaches

⊙ Sights
1	Kongo Mosque	B2

✦ Activities, Courses & Tours
2	Coral Spirit	B3
	Diani Bikes	(see 18)
	Diani Marine	(see 7)
	Diving the Crab	(see 19)
3	Fredlink Tours	B4
4	Pilli Pipa	B3
5	Skydive Diani	B4

⊟ Sleeping
6	AfroChic Diani Beach	B3
	Coral Cove Cottages	(see 13)
7	Diani Marine Village	B4
	Flamboyant	(see 15)
8	Leopard Beach Resort & Spa	B3
9	Sand Island Beach Cottages	B1
10	Stilts Eco-Lodge	B4
11	Swahili Beach Hotel	B3
12	The Maji	B3
13	Twiga Lodge	B2
14	Water Lovers	B4

✕ Eating
15	Ali Barbour's Cave Restaurant	B4
16	Aniello's	B3
17	Coast Dishes	B3
18	Kokkos Cafe Bistro	B4
19	Nomad	B5
20	Rongai	A3
	Shanshin-Ka	(see 18)
21	Swahili Pot/African Pot	A3

⊙ Drinking & Nightlife
	Forty Thieves Beach Bar	(see 15)
22	Shakatak	B5

ⓘ Information
23	Barclays	B3
24	Forex Bureau	B4
25	Kenya Commercial Bank	B4

ⓘ Transport
26	Glory Car Hire	B4
27	Tiwi Bus Stop	A1

Skydive Diani
ADVENTURE SPORTS

(☏ 0701300400; www.skydivediani.com; Diani Beach Rd, nr Forty Thieves Beach Bar) Set up by a British Army parachutist and a professional skydiver (among others), this highly professional outfit – the only one of its kind in East Africa – lets you live the most intense 50 seconds of your life by letting you fall 3500m over Kenya's coastal reefs. Go for a tandem jump (US$350), or the Accelerated Freefall course (US$2600).

Diving the Crab
DIVING

(☏ 0723108108; www.divingthecrab.com; Diani Beach Rd, Sands at Nomad) Highly established, professional diving outfit located by Nomad restaurant. PADI open-water courses cost €480, with dives for kids from €35 and two-tank dives costing €106.

Diani Marine
DIVING

(☏ 0707629061; www.dianimarine.com; Diani Beach Rd, Diani Marine Village) This highly regarded, German-run centre provides its own accommodation. PADI open-water diving courses cost €495, with single dives from €90.

DHOW TRIPS

The salty breeze and the high seas: it's a sailor's life for you and me. There's no more romantic way to explore the Kenyan coast than sailing by dhow (a traditional sailing boat that's been used here for centuries) past slivers of sand, offshore coral islands and reefs bubbling with colourful fish. Several companies offer dhow trips in the Kisite Marine National Park (p230), with pick-ups from Diani and departures from Shimoni. Pilli Pipa (p222) is probably the best known, but there are several other operators in Diani. Dhow trips (per person US$115 to US$135) usually include a couple of snorkelling or diving stops and a big lunch spread.

Coastal Microlights   GLIDING
(📞0727177700; kenyawild@gmail.com; Diani Beach Rd, Kenyaways Kite Village) The pilot picks you up from your lodgings and takes off in his microlight off Diani Beach outside Kenyaways Kite Village at low tide, spending 20 to 30 minutes flying low over the jungle and the reef.

East African Whale Shark Trust   BOATING
(📞0720293156; www.giantsharks.org; Diani Beach Rd, Blue Marlin) This is an excellent conservation body monitoring populations of the world's largest fish – the harmless, plankton-feeding whale shark. In February and March (the busiest time for whale sharks) it occasionally offers whale shark encounters to paying guests.

Trip costs vary, depending on how much sponsorship money has been raised, but averages US$150 per person, with a minimum of six people needed for a trip.

🧭 Tours

★ Diani Bikes   CYCLING
(📞0713959668; www.dianibikes.com; Diani Beach Rd; tours per person €25-35) This cycling outfit gets rave reviews from travellers for their engaging tours that include visiting the Kaya Kinondo and a typical rural Kenyan village, and nature trails good for spotting colobus monkeys. The Beach Ride is the longest (five hours) and includes a canoe trip through mangroves.

Coral Spirit   BOATING
(📞0716440223; www.coralspirit.com; Diani Beach Rd, Centrepoint; dhow trips US$115) Of the three companies that run popular dhow/snorkelling trips in the Kisite Marine National Park (p230), Coral Spirit is the only one that docks at Wasini Island for lunch.

🎪 Festivals & Events

Diani Rules   SPORTS
(www.dianirules.com; 🕐 Jun) This entertaining charity sports tournament, in aid of the Kwale District Eye Centre, is held at Diani Sea Lodge around the first weekend of June. It's more an expat event than a tourist attraction, but if you're staying locally there's every chance you'll be invited to watch or asked to join a team.

🛏 Sleeping

★ Diani Backpackers   HOSTEL $
(📞0700713666; www.dianibackpackers.com; off Diani Beach Rd; camping KSh600, dm KSh1300-1500, r KSh2600-4000; 🅿🛜🏊) Stylish and secure, Diani Backpackers has airy dorms, our favourite being Baobab, with an actual baobab growing through its middle, and comfortable private rooms (one with own bath). Come to party at the 24-hour bar and pool, or chill out in the lush garden.

Bidi Badu   HOTEL $
(📞0721131415; http://bidibadubeachresort.com; Diani Beach Rd; s/d from €30/45; ❄🛜🏊) At the southern end of Diani Beach, backpackers strike gold with the most unlikely of combinations: glorious beach access and low prices. It's essentially a hostel on the beach, with three categories of rooms, a superb beachfront restaurant (try the coconut prawns), a pool and volleyball nets. Cheapest rooms share facilities.

Stilts Eco-Lodge   LODGE $
(📞0706889539; www.kenyabackpacker.com; Diani Beach Rd; camping KSh1200, s/d safari tent KSh4500/5200, s/d cottage KSh3600/4400; 🅿🛜) 🌿 This rustic haven gives backpackers and eco-conscious travellers four lodging options: tents on wooden platforms amid riotous greenery, luxurious, fan-cooled safari tents with own bathrooms, thatched treehouses with terraces and somewhat dark, monkey-proof cottages. A breezy, *makuti* bar rises from the coastal forest, with sofas, wi-fi, food and drinks, plus visits from the resident bush babies.

★**Kenyaways Kite Village** BOUTIQUE HOTEL **$$**
(☎0726126204, 0739760733; www.thekenyaway.com; Diani Beach Rd; s/d from US$55/80; 🛜🍽) ⚑ This small, stylish kitesurfing lodge is one of our favourite places to stay in Diani. The gorgeously rustic rooms are simple but lovely, with painted timber bed frames, whitewashed walls and a sea breeze. Downstairs there's a good beachside bar and restaurant that attracts surfers and a chilled-out crowd. Friendly staff and a superb stretch of beach seal the deal.

Kinondo Poa RESORT **$$**
(☎0792717054; www.kinondopoaresort.com; Diani Beach Rd; s/d US$105/158; ❄🛜🍽) Just around the corner from the sacred Kaya Kinondo grove, at the southern end of Diani Beach, this intimate resort clusters around an attractive pool. The 10 mangrove-beamed, *makuti* rooms are a study in tranquillity; the on-site restaurant can serve meals on the guests' private patios if they want a little privacy.

Diani Marine Village BOUTIQUE HOTEL **$$**
(☎0707629060, Nairobi 020-2650426; www.dianimarine.com/village; Diani Beach Rd; s/d €55/90; ❄🛜🍽) The huge rooms at this dive resort are more than just a little appealing. With stone floors, a modern Swahili style and a beautiful pool and gardens, this place represents superb value for money. The complimentary breakfast is fit for a king.

Flamboyant RESORT **$$**
(☎0733411110; www.flamboyant.co; Diani Beach Rd; s/d from KSh7000/11,000; ❄🛜🍽) This intimate boutique hotel has breathtaking beach views, 10 rooms, each with a slightly different colour scheme, from peach to cerulean, and excellent bathrooms. The star of the show is a fantastic pool complex.

★**Water Lovers** HOTEL **$$$**
(☎0735790535; www.waterlovers.it; Diani Beach Rd; r €250-569; 🅿🛜🍽) ⚑ Beautiful, peaceful and intimate, Water Lovers has eight rooms and one villa, all designed with aesthetics, sustainability and love in mind. The furniture is a mix of Swahili wood and Italian pottery, and the wonderful staff will cater for every need. As you might expect from Italian owners, there's a great private restaurant serving organic fare and homemade pasta.

★**AfroChic Diani Beach** BOUTIQUE HOTEL **$$$**
(☎0730127000; www.afrochicdiani.com; Diani Beach Rd; r per person US$380-637; ❄🛜🍽) With just 10 individually decorated rooms and an elegant lobby and common area filled with West African carvings, this intimate hotel is all about attention to detail.

JOIN THE DOTS: ON THE COASTAL BACKPACKER TRAIL

There's so much to see along Kenya's stunning coastline. If you're travelling on a budget and after cheap, safe and fun digs, there's no better option than to follow the backpacker trail.

Starting in **Diani Beach**, bunk down at Diani Backpackers (p224), inside a lovely house with a lush garden. You'll meet the owners behind the 24-hour bar. Alternatively, get your very own slice of white-sand paradise by bedding down at the budget Bidi Badu (p224) resort at the southern end of Diani Beach, complete with an excellent seafood restaurant. Next stop is the beachside Mombasa suburb of Nyali, where your best budget pick is the lively Tulia House Backpackers (p233), a good base for exploring Mombasa Island.

From there, board a bus to **Kilifi**, home of Distant Relatives (p240) ecolodge, where there's always a good crowd, some beautiful gardens in which to chill out, and plenty of tours that showcase the best of local culture and nature. At the time of research, **Malindi** and **Watamu** still lacked good backpackers' hostels, but north of Malindi, on a deserted stretch of a superb kitesurfing beach, you can camp at the Barefoot Beach Camp (p251) or else stay at a rustic budget banda (thatched-roof hut) at Che Shale (p251), Kenyan capital of kitesurfing. There are also some great budget digs on the banks of Mida Creek, from the rustic Mida Ecocamp (p248) to the friendly luxury hotel turned hostel, Merry Crab Cove (p248), with free boat drop-offs and pick-ups from Watamu. On Lamu island, Jambo House (p257) and Baitul Noor House (p257) mark the end of the line.

We love the hand-carved bed frames and Maasai-beading chairs. The food makes the best of seasonal produce and is served 'anywhere, anytime', be it in your room or by the pool.

★ **The Maji** HOTEL $$$
(☑ 0773178873/4; http://themaji-com; Diani Beach Rd; r US$120-576; P 🛜 🏊) Among the loveliest of Diani's beachfront boutique hotels, the Maji – which means 'water' in Swahili – is simply gorgeous. The water feature in the beautiful Swahili lobby is surrounded by West African carvings, with welcome touches of contemporary art throughout. Each of the 15 rooms has its own vibe, but all have enormous beds, high ceilings and lovely bathrooms. Bliss.

Swahili Beach Hotel RESORT $$$
(☑ 0707730753; www.swahilibeach.com; Diani Beach Rd; s/d from KSh15,000/25,000; ❄ 🛜 🏊) Just south of Palm Ave, this elegant resort is all Moorish chic, with latticed screens, soaring ceilings, Moroccan-style mihrab headboards and reflecting pools that resemble those at the Taj Mahal. Five excellent restaurants, three pools (including one for scuba diving and one infinity pool), vast rooms with sunken tubs, beach bar, and spa are among the perks.

Leopard Beach Resort & Spa RESORT $$$
(☑ 0724255280, Nairobi 020-2049270; www.leopardbeachresort.com; Diani Beach Rd; r per person half board from US$220; P ❄ 🛜 🏊) As beach resorts go, Leopard is rated among the best in Africa. Rooms are spacious, with king-sized beds and West African art, while splurge-worthy sea-view villas come with Jacuzzis. Trees, lianas and a riot of flowers give the vast property a jungle feel, swimming pools abound and the restaurants (yes, there are four) serve excellent fusion fare.

Four Twenty South COTTAGE $$$
(☑ 0722901806; www.fourtwentysouth.com; Diani Beach Rd, Galu; beach houses US$275-1200; P ❄ 🛜) Named after the latitude of this gorgeous, remote beach, Four Twenty South has six rustic-chic cottages. Each comes with a personal chef (who may have cordon bleu credentials), stylish beach furniture, fresh flowers and creative decor. The welcome is warm and there's attention to detail. Great for groups. Turn left after KFI supermarket and follow the signs.

✖ Eating

Swahili Pot/African Pot KENYAN $
(Palm Ave, Coral Beach Cottages; mains KSh250-400; ☉ 7am-10pm) This place and its culinary siblings (there are two other branches, one about halfway down the beach access road and another at Ukunda junction) do excellent traditional African and Swahili dishes. The title comes from the gimmick of selecting a meat and having it cooked in a variety of sauces and marinades, all of which are highly rated.

Coast Dishes KENYAN $
(☑ 0722410745; Palm Ave, Ukunda; mains KSh450; ☉ 6am-11pm) Want to give the overpriced tourist restaurants a miss? Want to eat where the locals eat? Coast Dishes ticks both of these boxes and, if you're sensible, you'll opt for a steaming great bowl of biryani, the house special.

Rongai KENYAN $
(Ukunda–Ramisi Rd; mains KSh300; ☉ noon-10pm) This rowdy joint is a popular place for *nyama choma* (barbecued meat) – if you've been missing your roast meat and boiled maize, Rongai's here for you.

★ **Shanshin-Ka** JAPANESE $$
(☑ 0720747803; Diani Beach Rd; mains KSh400-950; ☉ 10am-10pm Tue-Sat, 12.30-10pm Sun) A spartan aesthetic and a full menu of authentic Japanese dishes are Shanshin-Ka's two distinguishing features. The portions of teriyaki, udon, tempura and yakitori dishes are generous, the sushi rolls are excellent (we're particular fans of Dynamite), the fruit juices are terrific and there's even a free palate cleanser in the form of fresh fruit at the end.

Kokkos Cafe Bistro INTERNATIONAL $$
(☑ 0721565567; www.facebook.com/KokkosCafe Bistro; Diani Beach Rd; mains KSh680-1150; ☉ 7.30am-10.30pm Mon-Sat, 8.30am-4pm Sun) This roadside crowd-pleaser is your one-stop shop for anything from good coffee and banoffee pie to daily specials such as baked oysters and BBQ pork ribs. Saturday is ribs night, while Tuesday features burger and beer specials.

Lymington's KENYAN $$
(☑ 0714632801; www.thekenyaway.com; Diani Beach Rd; mains KSh800-1300; ☉ 8am-10.30pm; 🛜) Lymington's sits right on the beach, within Kenyaways Kite Village. Lounge on the sofas beneath the magnificent baobab tree or take a breezy table overlooking the

gorgeous white sand. The menu is a short and sweet mix of the likes of smoked sailfish, spaghetti carbonara and garlic prawns, while the bar serves excellent cocktails and ice-cold Tuskers.

Aniello's ITALIAN $$
(☑0717590523; Diani Beach Rd, Colliers Centre; mains KSh450-900; ☺10am-11pm; ℗) This thoroughly authentic Italian restaurant is a mainstay among holidaymakers in Diani, and is a great place to enjoy an evening out among the local Italian community. Also good to pick up a pizza to take away.

★Nomad SEAFOOD $$$
(☑0735373888; www.thesandsatnomad.com; Diani Beach Rd, Sands at Nomad; mains KSh690-3590; ☺7.30am-10.30pm; ☏) One of the best restaurants in Diani, Nomad benefits from stellar sea views from its terrace and a talented chef who cooks up such culinary magic as seared yellowfin tuna with smoked aubergine and ginger and coconut crab. The sushi is among Kenya's best as well.

★Sails SEAFOOD $$$
(☑0716863884; www.almanararesort.com/sails; Diani Beach Rd, Almanara Luxury Villas Resort; mains KSh1200-2700; ☺noon-2pm & 6.30-10.30pm Wed-Mon; ℗☏☑) By far the most stylish place to eat in Diani, Sails is gorgeous: a canopy of billowing white canvas separates the restaurant from the stars, while waiters serve up fine dishes, particularly seafood, including Zanzibar-style snapper, steamed ginger crab and smoked Malindi sailfish. Reservations highly recommended in the evening.

Ali Barbour's Cave Restaurant SEAFOOD $$$
(☑0714456131; www.alibarbours.co; Diani Beach Rd; mains KSh1100-4950; ☺from 7pm; ☏) For a theme restaurant set in a coral cave, this is actually quite good and not cheesy at all. The focus is seafood and steak, cooked up poshly and perfect for a special dinner. It's served under the stars, jagged rocks and fairy lights.

Drinking & Nightlife

★Forty Thieves Beach Bar BAR
(☑0712294873; www.facebook.com/40beach bar; Diani Beach Rd; ☺8am-midnight Sun-Thu, 8am-dawn Fri & Sat; ☏) A legendary beachside boozer with sand floors and waves crashing onto the shore just metres from the long wooden bar, Forty Thieves is a Diani Beach institution and you'll find it busy with daytime drinkers and football watchers at any time. Come the evenings, it's always full. The Sunday roast is a big hit.

Shakatak CLUB
(☑0708498177; Diani Beach Rd; ☺7pm-4am) The only nightclub in Diani not attached to a hotel is Shakatak. It's quite hilariously seedy, but can be fun once you know what to expect. Like most big Kenyan clubs, food is served at all hours.

ⓘ Information

DANGERS & ANNOYANCES
Take taxis at night and try not to be on the beach by yourself after dark. Beachfront hotels have security guards and if you have to walk a short distance along the beach in the evening, some will oblige you by lighting your way or even walking with you. Souvenir sellers are an everyday nuisance, sex tourism is pretty evident and beach touts can be a bit of a hassle – you'll hear a lot of, 'Hey, one love, one love' Rasta-speak spouted by guys trying to sell you drugs or scam you into supporting fake charities for 'local schools'.

MONEY
Barclays (Diani Beach Rd, Barclays Centre) With ATM.
Forex Bureau (Diani Beach Rd; ☺9am-5pm Mon-Fri) Currency exchange.
Kenya Commercial Bank (Diani Beach Rd) With ATM.

POST
Diani Beach Post Office (Diani Beach Rd; ☺9am-5pm Mon-Fri, to 1pm Sat)

ⓘ Getting There & Away

The town of Ukunda, which is basically a traffic junction on the main Mombasa–Tanzania road, is the turn-off point for Diani Beach. From here a sealed road runs about 2.5km to a T-junction with the beach road, where you'll find everything Diani has to offer.

Do note that if you're travelling from Mombasa, you'll need to use the Likoni car ferry (p218) to reach Diani Beach. The five-minute crossing runs regularly, but the entire thing will slow down your journey and there can be delays at rush hour. From Diani to Mombasa, via the Likoni ferry, bank on one to two hours' driving time, depending on traffic.

AIR
From **Ukunda Airstrip** (☑0711305051) there are at least three flights per day to Nairobi (from US$48) with **Fly540** (www.fly540.com), **FlySAX** (www.fly-sax.com) and **Airkenya** (www.airkenya. com). Many hotels along Diani Beach offer free

pick-up from the airstrip; otherwise you're looking at a minimum taxi fare of KSh700.

BUS & MATATU

Numerous matatus run south from the Likoni ferry in Mombasa directly to Ukunda (KSh200, 30 minutes), the junction for Diani, and onwards to Msambweni and Lunga Lunga. From Ukunda, matatus run to the beach (KSh70) all day; check before boarding to see if it's a 'Reef' (heading north along the strip, then south) or 'Neptune' (south beach only) service.

CAR & MOTORCYLE

Motorcycles can be hired from **Fredlink Tours** (p36). A full motorcycle licence, passport and credit card or cash deposit are required for rental. The company also arranges motorcycle safaris.

You can rent cars from **Glory Car Hire** (☑ 0721315335; www.glorykenya.com; Diani Beach Rd, Diani Shopping Centre).

TAXI

Taxis, boda-bodas and tuk-tuks hang around Ukunda junction and all the main shopping centres, and most hotels and restaurants will also have a couple waiting at night. Boda-bodas are the cheapest of the lot, with short hops costing from KSh100; tuk-tuks are a little pricier. Much depends on your negotiating skills.

Gazi & Chale Island

☑ 040

About 20km south of Diani, off the main road, is soporific Gazi, a friendly Digo village on the edge of a mangrove-filled bay. Its historical claim to fame rests on the shoulders of Mazrui leader Sheikh Mbaruk bin Rashid, who led the unsuccessful Mazrui Rebellion against the British in 1895. Today, the main attraction is an excellent mangrove boardwalk.

🏃 Activities

Mangrove Boardwalk   BIRDWATCHING
(KSh200; ⊙ 8am-4pm) Run by a local women's group, this boardwalk is a sun-blanched, pleasantly rickety affair that winds back into a wine-dark lagoon webbed over by red, orange, green and grey mangrove trees as, nearby, the husks of old dhows bake into driftwood on the sand. Best birdwatching opportunities are early in the morning or later in the afternoon.

Previously, the mangroves were cut for timber, which led to extreme beach erosion; today, both the shore and the mangroves are being restored and a glut of entrepreneurial activities has grown around the boardwalk, including oyster farming and bee keeping. The fee for the walk goes into improving the boardwalk, buying school textbooks and paying teachers at local schools.

🛌 Sleeping

Homestay accommodation is available in Gazi in the house just behind the telephone mast (ask around – everyone knows it) for around KSh1500 per person, while Chale Island boasts a single luxury resort.

The Sands at Chale Island   RESORT $$$
(☑ 0725546879;   www.thesandsatchaleisland. com; r/banda/ste from US$188/314/628; ❄ ❀) The only private island resort on the tip of a sacred sliver of land originally caused controversy for wiping out a chunk of native forest (they've since replanted and much of the island is now a nature reserve). Bright, spacious rooms with Swahili-style beds and local art, and gorgeous sea views from pretty much everywhere, plus a spa and seafood restaurant.

❶ Getting There & Away

Matatus dashing between the Likoni ferry crossing and the border with Tanzania can drop you off at the Gazi turn-off, from where you can catch a boda-boda. A private boat from the Chale Island resort picks up guests at the end of the beach road running south from Diani; airport pick-ups also available.

Funzi Island

Funzi is a small mangrove island about 35km south of Diani that tends to be visited as part of birdwatching and croc-spotting day tours organised through agencies and hotels to the north.

If you arrive independently, you can generally count on the permanent presence of an accompanying guide from the moment you land, which is actually no bad thing, as he'll show you around the island and can arrange a homestay.

🏃 Activities

You can negotiate individual dolphin- and crocodile-spotting trips up the Ramisi River from the mainland village of Bodo.

Various water sports are possible to organise for guests of Funzi Keys Lodge.

Sleeping

Homestays in the village can be sorted for around KSh1000 to KSh1500 per person, per night, or there is the luxurious beachside Funzi Keys Lodge. Camping wild is also an option if you're self-sufficient.

Funzi Keys Lodge RESORT $$$
(☑0733900446, 0700617855; www.thefunzikeys.com; per person full board US$220-330; ✳✳) Rustic yet chic, this mangrove-creek resort has plenty of get-away-from-it-all appeal. The cottages are spacious and some have sunken bathtubs that look out over the ocean. Expect a warm welcome, good food and few distractions that don't involve the natural surroundings. Two nights minimum. Water sports arranged at extra cost. The resort was undergoing renovation at research time.

❶ Getting There & Away

To get to Bodo, the mainland jumping off point for Funzi, take a matatu from Ukunda towards Lunga Lunga and ask for the Bodo turn-off (KSh150). The village lies another 1.5km along a sandy track – you can take a *boda-boda* for around KSh150, or get someone to show you the way.

Arranging your own boat access to the island is easy if you're in a group: boatmen in Bodo ask around KSh3500 per person with a minimum of three people required (or one person with a really big wallet!).

Shimoni & Wasini Island

Shimoni

☑040

The fishing village of Shimoni, the site of alleged slave caves, has a tranquil Swahili vibe. As it is the departure point for boats to Wasini Island, Shimoni is mostly visited as part of a package tour that includes the island and a dhow trip to Kisite Marine National Park (p230). This does mean the chilled nature of the village is disrupted when convoys of tour buses rock up in the mornings during high season. Independent travellers tend to get pounced on by boat captains as soon as they make an appearance.

◉ Sights

Slave Caves HISTORIC SITE
(KSh400; ⊙8.30-10.30am & 1.30-6pm) These caves are where slaves were supposedly kept before being loaded onto boats and shipped to Zanzibar. A custodian takes you around the dank caverns to illustrate this little-discussed part of East African history. Actual evidence that slaves were kept here consists solely of iron rings in the rocks, but as piles of empty votive rosewater bottles indicate, the site definitely has significance for locals.

☆ Activities

Shimoni is the jumping-off point for dhow and boat tours of the Kisite Marine National Park (p230). If you've signed up for an organised dhow trip in Diani, all the fees and paperwork are taken care of. If coming independently, it's up to you to pay the marine park fee at the **office** (☑0723929766; www.kws.go.ke; ⊙8am-6pm) here and negotiate with one of the local boat captains. They tend to have life jackets and snorkelling gear on board; inspect it before setting off, though.

Shimoni Reef FISHING
(☑0733939359, 0727486961; www.shimonireeflodge.com; half-day/full-day fishing trips US$700/900) The Pemba Channel is world famous for deep-sea fishing, and Shimoni Reef can arrange a variety of offshore fishing trips for up to four people per charter boat.

Sleeping

Camp Eden Bandas COTTAGE $
(☑0723929766; www.kws.org; banda KSh5000, camping KSh2000) These seven basic but cosy *bandas* (thatched-roof huts) are owned and managed by the KWS. There's a kitchen (with some cooking equipment) and shared bathroom facilities. The compound is located about 200m south of Shimoni, and there's usually a ranger around to assist. You can also camp in the grounds.

Shimoni Gardens BANDAS $
(☑0722630638; per person KSh2500) This cluster of 15 tiny *bandas* sits amid tranquil, leafy grounds 2.5km south of Shimoni pier. While there's no room to swing a cat in any of them, you will find either twin beds or a snug double in each one, along with a bathroom that would suit Thumbelina. A *banda* is set aside as a guest kitchen.

Shimoni Reef Lodge
LODGE $$

(📞 0722270826, 0725643733; www.shimonireef
lodge.com; s/d/ste US$100/130/155; 🌊) This
waterfront base for deep-sea fishing and
diving with a saltwater pool and an average
(though beautifully situated) restaurant is
a tranquil spot. The whitewashed rooms,
although spacious and bright, aren't particu-
larly luxurious – they're best enjoyed after a
day on the ocean wave.

Betty's Camp
LODGE $$

(📞 0722434709; s/d US$70/90) This small,
pretty fishing camp usually attracts serious
(yet budget-minded) deep-sea-fishing types,
so expect lots of chat about such things.
The rooms and the fan-cooled safari tents
are simple, but nicely furnished, and there's
always a friendly welcome and some good
seafood on the grill.

ℹ️ Getting There & Away

There are matatus every hour or so between the
Likoni ferry crossing and Shimoni (KSh350, 1½
hours) until about 6pm. Matatus heading to the
Tanzanian border from Ukunda (for Diani Beach)
can drop you at the Shimoni turn-off, where you
can catch a *boda-boda* for around KSh150.

Wasini Island
🕐 040

The final pearl in the tropical beach neck-
lace that stretches south of Mombasa is the
idyllic island of Wasini, located about 76km
south of the Likoni ferry crossing. With its
faded white alleyways, Swahili fishing vibe
and fat, mottled trees, this tiny island (it's
only 5km long) feels like a distant relative of
Lamu and Zanzibar. It's ripe with the ingredients required for a perfect backpacker
beachside hideaway: it has that sit-under-
a-mango-tree-and-do-nothing-all-day vibe,
a coastline licked with pockets of white
sand and Kisite Marine National Park, the
most gorgeous snorkelling reef on the coast.
In fact, the only things it doesn't have are
regular electricity, banana-pancake traveller
cafes, backpacker hostels, and cars, and it's
all the better for it.

👁 Sights

It's worth poking about the ancient Swahili
ruins and the coral gardens, a bizarre landscape of exposed coral reefs with a boardwalk (KSh200) for viewing, on the edge of
Wasini village.

★ Kisite Marine National Park
NATIONAL PARK

(www.kws.org; adult/child US$25/13) Off the south
coast of Wasini, this gorgeous marine park,
which also incorporates the Mpunguti Marine
National Reserve and the two tiny Penguti
islands, is one of the best in Kenya. The park
covers 28 sq km of pristine coral reefs and
offers colourful diving and snorkelling, with
frequent dolphin and turtle sightings. The
marine park is accessible by dhow tour from
Diani Beach or private boat hired in Wasini
(per person from KSh2500 to KSh3000).

The best time to dive and snorkel is
between October and March. Diving and
snorkelling in June, July and August can
mean poorer visibility and rougher seas,
though the weather is changeable. During
the monsoon season you can snorkel over
the coral gardens – enquire about prices
opposite the pier in Wasini.

Mkwiro
VILLAGE

Mkwiro is a small village on the unvisited
eastern end of Wasini Island. The gorgeous
hour-long walk from Wasini village, through
woodlands, past tiny hamlets and along
the edge of mangrove forests, is more than
reason enough to visit. There are some wonderful, calm swimming spots around the village. Local children are sure to take you by
the hand and show you the best swimming
places.

The Mkwiro Youth Group can help you
dig a little deeper into village life by organising village tours and cooking classes. It's
all a little vague and prices are highly flexible, but the man you need to speak to about
organising these is Shafii Vuyaa.

🏃 Activities

★ Charlie Claw's
WATER SPORTS

(📞 0722205155/6; www.wasini.com) This highly
regarded outfit offers diving and snorkelling
trips to Kisite, as well as to Mako Koko reef
a few kilometres west. Dhow sunset cruises
are also on offer. Some of the day excursions
include lunch at its eponymous restaurant
on Wasini Island, where they cook up a seafood feast of grilled crab and seared Swahili
beef steaks.

Diving & Snorkelling

Besides Wasini-based operators, Pilli Pipa
(p222) and Coral Spirit (p224) in Diani
Beach also operate snorkelling and diving
tours to Kisite Marine National Park.

Paradise Divers
DIVING

(☎ 0718778372; www.paradisediver.net) On the eastern side of Wasini, this outfit offers diving and snorkelling trips to the marine park, starting at €45 per day, as well as discover scuba dives (€60) and full PADI certification courses (from €250). It also has a small lodge at which you can stay.

Fishing

While the idea of wrestling a huge marlin on the open sea has macho allure, catches of billfish in the Indian Ocean are getting smaller all the time. The biggest threat to game fish is overfishing by commercial tuna companies, which routinely hook other pelagic fish as so-called 'bycatch'. Pollution and falling stocks of prey are also having a serious knock-on effect. Some large species are believed to have declined by as much as 80% since the 1970s. Sharks are particularly vulnerable.

You can do your bit to help sustain shark and billfish populations by tagging your catch and releasing it back into the ocean. Most deep-sea-fishing companies provide anglers with a souvenir photo and official recognition of their catch, then release the fish to fight another day, carrying tags that will allow scientists to discover more about these magnificent predators.

🛏 Sleeping

Blue Monkey Cottages
COTTAGE $

(☎ 0715756952; http://wasini.net/blue-monkey-beach-cottages; s/d/tr KSh2500/3300/3900) 🏐 Made entirely of local materials – salvaged coral, stone, shells, driftwood, palm-thatched roofs – these rustic cottages on the outskirts of Wasini village are drowning in bougainvillea. The private beach, delicious Swahili food (vegan and seafood meals KSh380 to KSh720) and a feeling of disconnectedness, helped by the relative seclusion and reliance on solar power, are the things that lure travellers here.

Mpunguti Lodge
HOTEL $

(☎ 0710562494, 0700010026; wasinimpunguti original@yahoo.com; r from KSh3000) The 10 rooms here, which overlook the delicious turquoise ocean, are uncomplicated, with mosquito nets, flush toilets and small verandahs. Running water is collected in barrels. The food is excellent (ask for the seagrass starter) and it's a common lunch stop for boat trips. It's on the edge of Wasini village.

★ Paradise Lodge
LODGE $$

(☎ 0718778372; www.paradisediver.net; per person safari tent €60, r €75-85) This friendly little dive lodge on the eastern side of Wasini has a range of simple but colourful rooms (the most expensive with en suite), plus two furnished safari tents. Diving trips can also be arranged. You can sleep here independently, or as part of a diving tour.

ℹ Getting There & Away

Although most people come to Wasini on organised tours, you can cross the channel by motorboat (per person from KSh2000) or by simple wooden vessel with the islanders (KSh350) from the mainland village of Shimoni – head to its pier to assess your options.

Lunga Lunga

There isn't much at Lunga Lunga apart from the Tanzanian border crossing, which is open 24 hours. It's 6.5km from the Kenyan border post to the Tanzanian border post at Horohoro.

ℹ Information

If exchanging Kenyan shillings for Tanzanian ones, be aware that the exchange rate is better on the Tanzanian side of the border.

ℹ Getting There & Away

Boda-bodas run between the two border posts throughout the day (KSh150, if you're lucky). From Horohoro, there are numerous matatus (around KSh1700) and buses (KSh2400, three hours) to Tanga. Matatus from Lunga Lunga to the Likoni ferry crossing cost KSh350. It's possible to get from Lunga Lunga to Dar es Salaam on the same day, provided you get to the Kenyan border early in the morning. From Tanga, it takes around five hours to get to Dar by public transport.

NORTH OF MOMBASA

Nyali

☎ 041

Mombasa's most popular northern beach suburb, Nyali is a good alternative to staying on Mombasa Island. What it lacks in Mombasa's hustle and bustle it makes up for in amenities – there's a nice selection of places

North of Mombasa

0 ─────── 2 km
0 ─────── 1 mile

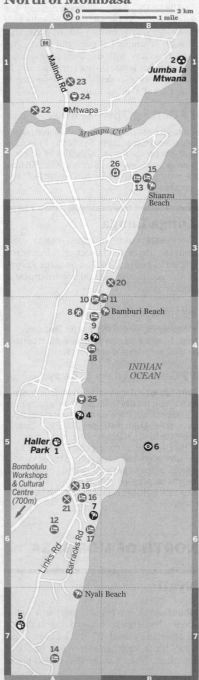

North of Mombasa

◎ **Top Sights**
1	Haller Park	A5
2	Jumba la Mtwana	B1

◎ **Sights**
3	Bamburi Beach	A4
4	Kenyatta Beach	A5
5	Mamba Village Crocodile Farm	A7
6	Mombasa Marine National Park & Reserve	B5
7	Nyali Beach	A6

◎ **Activities, Courses & Tours**
8	Bamburi Forest Trails	A4

◎ **Sleeping**
9	Bamburi Beach Hotel	A4
10	Kahama Hotel	A4
11	Kenya Bay	B4
12	L'Torec	A6
13	Mombasa Safari Inn	B2
14	Nyali Beach Hotel	A7
15	Serena Beach Hotel & Spa Kenya	B2
16	Tulia House Backpackers	A6
17	Voyager	A6
18	Whitesands Sarova Hotel	A4

◎ **Eating**
19	10 Street	A5
	Cafesserie	(see 19)
	Il Covo	(see 11)
20	Imani Dhow Restaurant	B3
21	Java House Nyali	A6
	La Veranda	(see 19)
	Monsoons	(see 2)
22	Moorings Restaurant	A2
23	Mumtaz	A1
	Yul's	(see 9)

◎ **Drinking & Nightlife**
24	Casuarina	A1
	Kahama Sports Bar	(see 10)
25	Pirates	A5

◎ **Shopping**
26	Shanzu Transitional Workshop	B2

to sleep and eat, and the sand is but a hop, skip and jump away.

◎ Sights

Nyali Beach BEACH
(off Mombasa–Malindi Rd) This attractive strip of white sand practically disappears at high tide – particularly its northern end. At the southern end of the beach, look out for Shiva Cave with its phallic stalagmites; visiting it will supposedly enhance your fertility.

Mamba Village Crocodile Farm ZOO

(📞 0729403670; Links Rd; adult/child KSh800/400; ⊗8.30am-7pm) This is the largest reptile farm in Kenya, with guided tours taking you past several pools where you can see the crocs in various stages of development: from babies to the 100-year-old Big Daddy, who's 5m long. There's a small serpentarian as well. Be aware that some of the smaller crocodiles here become handbags and fried reptile bites at the on-site restaurant, so this place is not for everyone. Crocodile feeding time is at 5pm.

🛏 Sleeping

⭐ Tulia House Backpackers HOSTEL $

(📞 0722668163, 0711955999; www.tuliahouse.com; off Links Rd; camping KSh650, hammock/dm/s/d KSh1150/1450/3700/4400; 🅿️🛜🏊) Backpackers seem to love Tulia. It's clean, well-run and knows how to party. Accommodation is in well-kept dorms, hammocks and good private rooms, while the emerald-green pool is the setting for BBQs, swimwear contests and games of beer pong. Expect a warm welcome, tonnes of local info and just as much fun.

L'Torec B&B $

(📞 0727300025; www.facebook.com/Ltorec; off Links Rd; r KSh4000; ❄️🛜🏊) A 10-minute walk (or KSh50 tuk-tuk ride) from the heart of Nyali, this secure B&B has a few spacious rooms clustered around the pool. Tranquillity reigns. If taking public transport, ask for the Nyali Healthcare turn-off.

Nyali Beach Hotel RESORT $$

(📞 0727228344, 0733700533; www.nyali-international.com; Beach Rd; s/d from KSh7295/10,845; ❄️@🏊) At the southern end of the beach, the oldest resort in Nyali has been given a contemporary facelift. It's a vast property with smart, tiled rooms with welcome splashes of colour, and three-bedroom villas for groups. Plus points are the horseshoe-shaped bar, two beautiful pools, the equally beautiful gardens and the even more beautiful beach it fronts.

⭐ Tamarind Village APARTMENT $$$

(📞 0722205160, 0733623583; www.tamarind.co.ke; Cement Silo Rd; s/d/tr KSh17,000/27,000/34,000; 🅿️❄️🛜🏊) These beautiful self-catering apartments are brought to you by the owners of the excellent Tamarind restaurant (right next door) and Nairobi's Carnivore (p77). Whitewashed, spacious and stylish,

there are few lovelier places to sleep in the Mombasa area. And you won't beat the view from those balconies, which stretches all the way to Mombasa's Old Town.

Voyager RESORT $$$

(📞 Nairobi 020-444 6651; www.heritage-eastafrica.com/welcome-heritage-hotels; s/d from US$138/184; ❄️🛜🏊) From the soaring, *makuti* reception to the three pools, cliff-top bar, and ship-shape, colour-coded rooms, this is Nyali's top beach resort. In keeping with the hotel's nautical theme, guests are referred to as passengers and, every day, Voyager 'sets sail' to a new destination (look for the country's flag in reception), honoured by key dishes at the excellent restaurant.

🍴 Eating

10 Street FAST FOOD $

(📞 0706101010; www.facebook.com/10street mombasa; Mahesh Doshi Rd; mains KSh390-790; ⊗24hr; 🛜) Catering both to midnight and regular munchers, this round-the-clock fast-food joint has baffling decor (vintage red telephone box, menacing wide-angle shot of pigeons), friendly service and very good burgers. Choose from the list of 10 mains and pair them with one of 10 sides and 10 drinks. Poached eggs and hash browns fortify the early risers.

Java House Nyali CAFE $

(📞 0718543579; www.nairobijavahouse.com; Links Rd, Nyali Centre; mains KSh360-920; ⊗7am-10pm Mon-Fri, 8am-11pm Sat, 8am-10pm Sun; ❄️🛜) We know, we know. It's a chain, but it's Kenyan and it's a good one. Java House's coffee always goes down a treat, and we're big fans of its BLT sandwiches and milkshakes. The Nyali branch has enough in the way of hot drinks, pastries, burgers and salads to cure the worst bout of homesickness.

Ooh! Ice-Cream ICE CREAM $

(Nyali Rd; per scoop KSh140; ⊗noon-10pm) Even if this friendly, air-conditioned place didn't serve fantastic ice creams, we'd still consider including it just because of the name!

⭐ Cafesserie CAFE $$

(📞 Nairobi 020-202 3769; http://citymall.co.ke/cafesserie; Mombasa–Malindi Rd, Nyali City Mall; mains KSh790-1480; ⊗7am-midnight; 🅿️❄️🛜🍴) Inside Nyali City mall, Cafesserie has the best selection of cakes on the coast. But it doesn't end there: the breezy, chilled-out place has a crowd-pleaser menu of brunch items, bagel sandwiches and heartier mains, such as masala fish. Add some fresh fruit juices, lattes and Tuskers, and we can't think why you wouldn't want to eat there. A lot.

★ **Tamarind Restaurant** FUSION $$$
(☑0722205160; www.tamarind.co.ke; Cement Silos Rd; mains from KSh1300; ⊗noon-3pm & 7-10pm; 🅿 🛜 ⚡) Without doubt the finest restaurant around Mombasa, Tamarind looks out over the harbour. Laced with high white arches, this refined restaurant has a superb menu that looks to Asia for inspiration and includes things such as tamarind seafood salad, black pepper crab and twice-cooked pork belly. We highly rate the mangrove oysters, the desserts and the boozy coffees.

La Veranda ITALIAN $$$
(☑0733774436; 2nd Ave, Maheshi Doshi Rd; mains KSh900-1600; ⊗10am-3pm & 6-10.30pm Tue-Fri, 10am-10.30pm Sat & Sun; ⚡) This reliable Italian restaurant is behind Nakumatt Nyali shopping centre, with a big pizza oven, al fresco dining on the verandah and reasonable prices.

🛍 **Shopping**

★ **Bombolulu Workshops & Cultural Centre** ARTS & CRAFTS
(☑0723560933; www.apdkbombolulu.org; Nyali Rd; adult/child KSh750/350, workshops & showroom free; ⊗8am-5pm Mon-Sat, 10am-3pm Sun) This non-profit organisation produces crafts of a high standard and gives vocational training to physically disabled people. Visit the workshops and showroom to buy jewellery, leatherwork, sisal bags, carvings and textiles. The turn-off for the centre is about 3km north of Nyali Bridge. Bombolulu matatus run here from Msanifu Kombo Rd, and Bamburi services also pass the centre.

ℹ **Getting There & Away**

From Mombasa, Nyali Beach is reached via Nyali Rd, which branches off the main road north just after Nyali Bridge. There are regular matatus to and from Mombasa (KSh50).

Bamburi

☑041
Bamburi merges with neighbouring Nyali to create one long Mombasa holiday strip. Either place works fine as a base for exploring Mombasa Old Town. Kenyatta Beach, near the south end of Bamburi, thumps to the beat of holidaying Kenyans. Alternatively, Bamburi makes a good day trip from Mombasa; many resorts offer day passes to nonguests.

⊙ **Sights**

★ **Haller Park** WILDLIFE RESERVE
(☑0722410064; Mombasa–Malindi Rd; adult/child KSh1400/700; ⊗8am-5pm) This lovely wildlife sanctuary, part of the Baobab Adventure complex, includes a fish farm and reptile park. Guided walks around the park last about 1½ hours, or else you can wander the trails that meander through casuarine groves by yourself. There are some friendly giraffes to feed, some enormous tortoises making their way around the grounds, and you can also spot the resident hippos and impalas and attend the hippo- and croc-feeding sessions.

In a nice example of environmentalism and entrepreneurship finding common ground, Baobab Adventure is the child of seemingly unlikely parents: Bamburi Cement and a group of conservationists. Bamburi Cement has funded the rehabilitation of its own former cement works. The various parts of the Baobab Adventure, including forest trails, are well signposted from the highway north of Mombasa and have well-marked bus stops.

Kenyatta Beach BEACH
(off Mombasa–Malindi Rd) Busy with vacationing Kenyan families and snack sellers peddling their wares, Kenyatta Beach is the place to come if you're looking for a totally local scene. There are various family-friendly attractions, including a go-kart track and a complete absence of the beach boys who haunt other beaches.

Bamburi Beach BEACH
(off Mombasa–Malindi Rd) Lined with a couple dozen hotels, Bamburi Beach is a 6km stretch of palm-shaded white sand. Outside low tide, the waters are good for swimming, and there's some decent snorkelling towards the northern end of the beach.

Mombasa Marine National Park & Reserve MARINE RESERVE
(☑Nairobi 020-2317371; www.kws.org; adult/child US$17/13) The offshore Mombasa Marine National Park and Reserve has impressive marine life, although it cops some

pollution from industry in the area. You can hire glass-bottomed boats for a couple of hours for around KSh2500 (excluding park fees), but you'll need to be seriously silver-tongued to whittle the price down that low.

🏃 Activities

Bamburi Forest Trails WALKING, CYCLING
(Mombasa–Malindi Rd; adult/child KSh600/300; ⊙8am-6pm) This network of walking and cycling trails passes through reforested cement workings, with a butterfly pavilion and terrace (it's also known as the Butterfly Pavilion) from which to catch the sunset. It's located within the Baobab Adventure site. Bicycle rental costs KSh300 per hour.

🛏 Sleeping

Kenya Bay RESORT $$
(☑0725991500, 041-5487600; www.kenyabay.com; off Mombasa–Malindi Rd; s/d from KSh5600/9400; P❄🛜🛏) Between the Kahama Hotel and the excellent Il Covo restaurant, Kenya Bay is one of the oldest resorts on the block, but it's in decent shape. The spacious rooms are generic looking, but fan out nicely around the gardens and pool, with patios and balconies for ocean views. There's a small spa, a beach bar and a decent seafood restaurant.

Kahama Hotel RESORT $$
(☑0725961791, 041-5485395; www.kahama hotel.co.ke; off Mombasa–Malindi Rd; s/d from KSh6750/6950; ❄🛜🛏) Sometimes business hotels seem too impersonal, holiday resorts too package-deal and boutique hotels too expensive. Thankfully, there's intimate Kahama, which marries all three and does a mighty fine job of it. This Bamburi branch has the most spacious rooms of the lot, with stylish Swahili touches, large pool and an on-site bar/restaurant with live music. It gets our vote.

★Whitesands Sarova Hotel RESORT $$$
(☑0709111000, Nairobi 020-2767000; www.sarova hotels.com; off Mombasa–Malindi Rd; s/d half board from US$161/196; ❄🛜🛏) Whitesands is beautiful: a seafront Swahili castle of airy corridors, marble accents and wooden detailing uplifted by every flash, modern amenity you can imagine, from interconnecting, waterfall-fed pools and fine-dining restaurant specialising in seafood to a great spa and full range of PADI diving courses. It's considered one of the best high-end resorts on the coast, with good reason.

Bamburi Beach Hotel RESORT $$$
(☑041-5485611; www.bamburibeachkenya.com; off Mombasa–Malindi Rd; s/d half board €203/298; ❄🛜🛏) This tidy little complex has direct access to the beach and a choice of appealing, bamboo-finished hotel rooms (nab a sea-facing one) and self-catering rooms (with outdoor kitchens). There's a nice beachfront bar with a big, shaggy *makuti*. There's a terrific pool as well.

🍴 Eating

Yul's PIZZA $$
(☑0715012311; Mombasa–Malindi Rd; mains from KSh850; ⊙noon-11pm) This beachfront pizzeria makes *the* best ice cream in town. (We've never heard anyone disagree.) The pizzas are pretty good too, as are the burgers, only rivalled by the views out to sea. Good for an atmospheric dinner or a long lunch.

★Imani Dhow Restaurant SEAFOOD $$$
(☑0722284682; off Mombasa–Malindi Rd, Severin Sea Lodge; mains KSh1100-3800) This traditional Zanzibari dhow on the grounds of Severin Sea Lodge is Bamburi's most atmospheric restaurant, complete with creaky wooden floors and ceiling and evening mood lighting. Go for flambee crab, Swahili-style prawns or push the boat out with their signature lobster dish. The alcohol-infused coffees are good, too.

Il Covo ITALIAN $$$
(☑0722709800; www.ilcovomombasa.com; off Mombasa–Malindi Rd; mains KSh650-2250; P🛜) You'll find salt-licked walls, white tablecloths and – if you eat in the intimate little cove at the end – breakers crashing beneath your feet at this charming Italian/Japanese spot. The tuna carpaccio starter and the fresh Kilifi oysters are tasty stuff. We rate the fish more highly than the pasta. After dark, the attached nightclub gets going.

🍸 Drinking & Nightlife

Kahama Sports Bar SPORTS BAR
(off Mombasa–Malindi Rd, Kahama Hotel; ⊙noon-late; 🛜) This sleek sports bar, part of the same complex as the Kahama Hotel, has more big screens than you can count, plus disco-ball lighting, burgers and beers on tap. It attracts a mixed local and foreign crowd. The couches inside the gazebo are quieter than the main bar.

Pirates — CLUB
(off Mombasa–Malindi Rd, Kenyatta Beach; Fri & Sat KSh200; ⊙ Wed-Sat) A huge complex of water slides and bars transforms into the strip's rowdiest nightclub in high season, blazing into the small hours. During the day it's a typical beach-bar area, complete with attendant beach-boy hassle.

ⓘ Getting There & Away
Matatus run from Mombasa to Bamburi for KSh100. If you're driving yourself, be aware that the roads near Kenyatta Beach can be *insane* on weekends with a combination of matatus and drunk holidaymakers.

Shanzu Beach
📞 041

The coastline here is beautiful, but it's dominated by all-inclusive resorts. Outside of these areas, Shanzu is not much more than a highway fuel stop and string of seedy bars. It's located just north of Bamburi.

🛏 Sleeping

Mombasa Safari Inn — HOTEL $
(📞 0733430996, 0733925736; www.mombasa-safari-inn.com; Shanzu Tourist Rd; s/d/tr KSh1350/1900/2400; 📶) This small, cheerful and authentically Kenyan place has a few basic but adequate rooms set behind a busy bar that may as well be sponsored by Tusker, so many advertising posters does it have.

★ Serena Beach Hotel & Spa Kenya — RESORT $$$
(📞 0732125000, 0727424201; www.serenahotels.com; Serena Rd; r from US$179; ※@🛜🏊) ♻ This lovely, polished resort is extensive and is styled on a traditional Swahili village – the pathways around the tree-filled complex even have street names. The split-level rooms are equally impressive, the hotel's eco-rating is Gold and there's a plethora of extras that makes you not want to leave: excellent seafood restaurant, swim-up bar, Turtle Watch programme, PADI dive school...

🛍 Shopping

Shanzu Transitional Workshop — ARTS & CRAFTS
(📞 0733994007; shanzuworkshop@yahoo.com; off Shanzu Tourist Rd; ⊙ 9am-12.30pm & 2-6pm Mon-Sat) Run by the Mombasa Girl Guides Association, this centre provides training for handicapped young women and sells their crafts for them. Pick up some decent leatherwork, clothing and jewellery here.

ⓘ Getting There & Away
Public transport plying the route between Mombasa and Malindi or Mtwapa passes the turn-off to Shanzu (KSh100), where a crowd of *boda-bodas* (motorcycle taxis) tout for rides to the hotels (KSh50). Hourly matatus from Mtwapa stop at the resorts (KSh150) before heading to Mombasa.

Mtwapa
📞 041 / POP 48,625

Locals call Mtwapa the Las Vegas of Kenya, because the town sleeps by day and parties by night. Many expats settle down around here, and although Mtwapa's bars are far more seedy than they are shiny, it's a friendly enough place. There's little reason to spend the night here, but Mtwapa is the gateway to some of the coast's most impressive ruins, and there are a couple of excellent restaurants here. The businesses with red mood lighting and names such as 'Escort Lodge' and 'Best Lady Bar' attract a particular type of clientele.

⦿ Sights

★ Jumba la Mtwana — RUINS
(www.museums.or.ke; adult/child KSh500/250; ⊙ 8am-6pm) These Swahili ruins, just north of Mtwapa Creek, have as much archaeological grandeur as the more famous Gede ruins. Jumba la Mtwana means 'Big House of Slaves' and locals believe the town was an important slave port in the 14th or 15th century. There's a small museum on Swahili culture, an excellent restaurant by the sea, and the custodian gives excellent tours for a small gratuity. The ruins are down a 3km access road, 2km north of Mtwapa Creek bridge.

The remains of buildings, with their exposed foundations for mangrove beam poles, ablution tanks, the heft of the resident baobabs and the twisting arms of 600-year-old trees – leftover from what may have been a nearby *kaya* (sacred grove) – are quite magical. In the dying evening light, your imagination will be able to run riot with thoughts of lost treasures, ghosts, pirates and abandoned cities.

Slaves may or may not have been traded here, but turtle shell, rhino horn and ambergris (sperm-whale intestinal secretions, used for perfume) all were. In return, Jumba received goods such as Chinese dishes, the fragments of which can be seen in the floors of some buildings today. While here, keep your eyes peeled for the upper-wall holes that mark where mangrove support beams were affixed, the many cisterns that point to the Swahilis' keenness on hygiene, the **House of Many Doors**, which is believed to have been a guesthouse, and dried-out, 40m-deep wells. You'd be remiss to miss the **Mosque by the Sea**, which overlooks a crystal-sharp vista of the Indian Ocean.

Notice the Arabic inscription on the stela adjacent to the nearby graveyard: 'Every Soul Shall Taste Death'. Underneath is a small hole representing the opening all humans must pass through on the way to paradise.

Eating

Mumtaz
KENYAN $
(Mombasa–Malindi Rd; meals KSh350; ⊙11am-late) The best-value *nyama choma* joint in town also offers big plates of chicken, other kinds of meat, and chapati, served with a soda. A popular local hangout.

Moorings Restaurant
SEAFOOD $$
(☑0736547923, Nairobi 020-213828; www.themoorings.co.ke; mains KSh700-1400; ⊙10am-10pm Tue-Sun) This legendary restaurant is on a floating pontoon on the north bank of Mtwapa Creek. It's a fine place for a beer and serves great seafood and international dishes with a view. The turn-off is just after the Mtwapa bridge on the Mombasa–Malindi road – follow the signs down to the water's edge.

★ Monsoons
ITALIAN $$$
(☑041-2012666; Jumba la Mtwana; mains KSh950-2700; ⊙11.30am-5.30pm Mon-Sat, 11am-6pm Sun) As you stumble over the tangled tree roots of the Jumba la Mtwana ruins, delicious smells propel you towards the beach. A thatched hut perched above the blue of the Indian Ocean is not where you'd expect to find the region's best Italian restaurant, but there it is! Grilled seafood is the speciality here, paired with Italian wines.

Drinking & Nightlife

Casuarina
BAR
(☑0713918920; Mombasa–Malindi Rd; ⊙24hr) The first bar to get going in Mtwapa, Casuarina always makes for a fun night out, with some good dancing and decent grilled food to chase the booze down. Everyone from ladies of negotiable affection to expats and fishing tourists seems to agree.

❶ Getting There & Away

Regular matatus run from Mtwapa to Mombasa (KSh200) and Kilifi (KSh150).

Lamu &
the North Coast

Includes ➡

South of Lamu 240
Kilifi 240
Watamu 242
Arabuko Sokoke
Forest Reserve 247
Mida Creek 247
Gede Ruins 250
Malindi 250
Lamu Archipelago 255
Lamu Island 255
Manda Island 266
Paté Island 266
Kiwayu Island 268

Why Go?

Prepare to fall under the spell of this hypnotic part of Kenya's Indian Ocean coastline, where the exotic permeates everything, blending spice, soul and sand. The attractions of this slice of paradise have historically not been lost on anyone lucky enough to visit, whether it be Portuguese explorers, Cushitic Somalis, Bantu-speaking Mijikenda, cattle-herding Orma, Italian holidaymakers or, of course, the Swahili. Many of these people stayed on and have left their own mark on the coast, from the ancient ruins at Gede to the holiday resorts built by Italians in more recent times.

Watamu and Malindi remain popular beach destinations for Europeans; Mida Creek is a haven for birdwatchers and vagabonds in search of shooting stars; and Lamu archipelago beckons with its mazelike Swahili villages, bohemian artist/yoga vibe and the promise of waterborne adventure as you sail between the islands on a traditional dhow.

Best Places to Eat

➡ Peponi (p264)

➡ Crab Shack (p248)

➡ Baby Marrow (p253)

➡ Nautilus (p241)

➡ Pilipan Restaurant (p246)

Best Places to Stay

➡ Watamu Treehouse (p245)

➡ Kizingo (p265)

➡ Che Shale (p251)

➡ Mike's Camp (p269)

➡ Merry Crab Cove (p248)

When to Go
Lamu

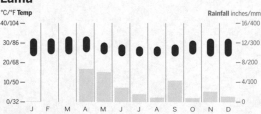

Jul–Sep Lamu is aglow in the wake of Eid; satisfy your sweet tooth with a visit to the island's night markets.

Oct–Mar The light *matilai* wind blows softly, clearing the water for fantastic snorkelling and diving.

Feb & Mar Artists and yoga practitioners convene on Lamu Island.

Garissa (75km); Thika (380km)

Garissa (75km); Thika (380km)

SOMALIA

0 ——— 50 km
0 ——— 25 miles

N

Arawale NR

Hola

Dodori River

Ijara

Boni NR

Tana River National Primate Reserve

Duldul River

Bodhei

Dodori NR

B8

Kiunga Marine NR

Bargoni

Paté Island

Kiwayu Island

Lamu Archipelago **1**

Tana

Hindi

Paté

Manda Island

Garsen

Lamu

Matondoni

Takwa

Witu C112

Kipungani

Shela

Lamu Island

Kipini

Mpeketoni

Lamu Archipelago

River

Ungwana

Mwana

Shaka

Ungwana Bay

B8

INDIAN OCEAN

Gandi

Marafa Depression **7**

Galana

Marafa

Gongoni

River

Manyani (75km)

C103

Mambrui

Rare

River

Gede

Malindi **6**

Malindi Marine NP

Arabuko Sokoke FR

Watamu **2**

Bamba

Mida Creek

Watamu Marine NP

Malindi Marine NR

Kilifi **3**

B8

Vuma Cliffs **8**

Lamu & the North Coast Highlights

1 **Lamu Archipelago** (p255) Hopping by dhow between stunning islands and delving into centuries-old Swahili culture.

2 **Watamu** (p242) Coming face-to-face with serpents and reef fish while diving.

3 **Kilifi** (p240) Embracing this Swahili village and high-fiving Mother Nature on the bank of Kilifi Creek.

4 **Mida Creek** (p247) Exploring the mangroves before watching shooting stars outside your thatched hut.

5 **Gede Ruins** (p250) Discovering the ruins of an ancient Swahili city for the first time.

6 **Malindi** (p250) Tucking into Italian food on the coast.

7 **Marafa Depression** (p254) Travelling across a jagged Mars-like landscape in the middle of the countryside.

8 **Vuma Cliffs** (p240) Watching the raging sea pummel the cliffs at this wild end-of-the-world spot.

SOUTH OF LAMU

Kilifi

📱 041 / POP 44,257

A passionate group of Kenyans and expats have transformed Kilifi from a sweet but soporific backwater into a stunning place renowned for its eco-projects and clean, green, joyful living.

Gorgeous beach houses stand atop the creek, yachts dance in the bay and warm waves wash fantasy beaches buttered with lashings of soft white sand. You'll find orange groves and hermit crabs, fresh oysters and pizza ovens, permaculture projects and sailing schools, beach barbecues and night swimming. And you might even spot a whale shark migration from the windy brink of Vuma Cliffs.

The town is also home to a renowned medical research centre, so with a steady stream of doctors, sailors, backpackers, aid workers, artists and yogis passing through, you'll never be short of crew with whom to share those oysters.

👁 Sights

★ Vuma Cliffs   NATURAL FEATURE

(Takaungu) Just outside the village of Takaungu, you fly on the back of a motorbike down dirt roads, past spiky fields of sisal and giant baobabs towering above maize crops. Abruptly, the land ends in jagged black coral cliffs, pounded relentlessly by the rolling waves of the Indian Ocean. It's a desolate and lonely place that seems like a secret portal into Scotland rather than the Kenyan coast. Motorbikes to the cliffs are organised by Distant Relatives (KSh1500 for one or two people).

Bofa Beach   BEACH

(Bofa Rd) Bofa Beach is a wide slash of white sand, with swaying palms and rolling Indian Ocean surf. It's the stuff of which fantasies are made. A path to the left of Kilifi Bay Beach Resort (p241) takes you there.

Mnarani   RUINS

(adult/child KSh500/250; ⊘7am-6pm) The partly excavated, atmospheric ruins of the Swahili city of Mnarani are high on a bluff just west of the old ferry landing stage on the southern bank of Kilifi Creek. The best-preserved ruin is the Great Mosque, with its finely carved inscription around the mihrab (prayer niche showing the direction of Mecca). Under the minaret lies the skeleton of the supposed founder of the town.

Kilifi Creek   CREEK

This might be the only place where we wouldn't mind being up the creek without a paddle. It's just gorgeous, from the cliffs jutting up out of the water, to the hermit crabs scooting along the shoreline. Boat hire can easily be arranged, and there are lots of lovely spots for wild, romantic camping.

🏃 Activities

★ Buccaneer Diving   DIVING

(📞0714757763; www.buccaneerdiving.com; 2-tank dive US$130; ⊘Oct-Apr) The lovely Tim runs this excellent diving centre over at Mnarani Club (p241), covering everything from the basics to instructor-level dives and cave and wreck exploration. PADI open water from US$595.

Three Degrees South   BOATING

(📞0714783915, 0714757763; www.3degreessouth. co.ke; 3-day course KSh24,500) This British Royal Yachting Association–affiliated sailing school is one of the best places to learn on the East African coast. Expect expert tuition for beginners and advanced sailors, serious attention to safety and a vast expanse of (beautiful) empty space. Windsurfing courses on Kilifi Creek also offered.

🛏 Sleeping

★ Distant Relatives   HOSTEL, LODGE $

(📞0702232323; www.kilifibackpackers.com; camping KSh800, dm/s/d/bandas KSh1500/3500/4500/6000, tents KSh3000; 🅿🛜❄) 🍃 Both an ecolodge and a backpackers, this place gets it so right. The fantastic owners, staff and guests have created a living, breathing space that's a haven for everyone. Expect good vibes, good people and good conscience. We love the pizza oven and the amazing bamboo showers. Follow the signs for around 2km from opposite Tusky's Supermarket on the main road.

Bofa Bay Beach Resort   RESORT $

(📞0703110995; off Bofa Rd; tents KSh2500, s/d from KSh3500/4500; 🅿❄🛜❄) A slightly dishevelled yellow building a three-minute walk from the blindingly beautiful beach of the same name, Bofa Bay has some posh safari tents with fancy showers and showy rugs. The rooms are spotless, though your back won't thank you for the cheap mattresses. There's a lovely garden restaurant and thimble-sized dipping pool.

★ Takashack
COTTAGE $$

(bruceryrie@yahoo.com; Takaungu beach; whole house KSh7500; P) On gorgeous Takaungu beach and off the electricity grid, this eclectic, relaxed three-bedroom house makes a great escape. Catch the sunrise from the top floor, taste the fish curry and ginger prawns cooked by Nickson the caretaker, jump in the ocean and, after dark, watch the house light up from the glow of amber hurricane lanterns. Email bookings only.

Mnarani Club
RESORT $$

(Nairobi 020-8070501/2; www.mnarani.co.za; off Mombasa-Malindi Rd; s/d from US$117/196; P❄️📶🏊) This big resort sits on the edge of Kilifi Creek, close to Mnarani ruins. There's a gorgeous curved infinity pool, a decent restaurant, a spa and lots of extras, such as diving and sailing schools, on-site. The creek-view rooms are the nicest.

Kilifi Bay Beach Resort
RESORT $$$

(0722202564; www.madahotels.com; Bofa Rd; s/d from €176/221; ❄️📶🏊) This polished, *makuti* (thatched-roofed) place sits right on the beach and has a series of bright, comfortable, Swahili-themed rooms with high beds and sea- or garden-view patios. Three bars and a lovely pool in a jungled garden are some of the perks. It's about 5km north of Kilifi, on the coast road.

✖️ Eating

Kilifi Members Club
KENYAN $

(0733560725; mains KSh300-600; 8am-11pm) Atop a cliff on the edge of the bay, this restaurant/bar has the best location in Kilifi. Unfortunately, not all of the staff seem so thrilled to be here. But never mind that;

chow down on some good chicken barbecue or stop by for sundowners.

Wild Living Cafe
CAFE $$

(0791183312; Malindi-Mombasa Rd; mains from KSh600; 8am-7pm; 📶) The picnic tables under the trees and the welcoming interior of this *makuti* cafe entice travellers to break their journey here and indulge in some barbecued meats, paninis, cakes, tasty coffee and smoothies. Buy your Zanzibar spices here also.

Distant Relatives Restaurant
INTERNATIONAL $$

(0702232323; www.kilifibackpackers.com; mains KSh600-1200; noon-10pm) Even if you're not staying here, join your distant relatives for dinner at this great, laid-back eatery atop Kilifi Creek. We rate the bacon-and-avo sandwiches, the beetroot-and-hummus veggie bowls and the steaks. Friday is pizza night (there's a pizza oven) and Tuesday is burger night. The breakfast smoothies are the best we tried on the coast.

Boatyard
SEAFOOD $$

(0721590502; www.facebook.com/KilifiBoatyard; mains from KSh700; 7am-7pm) Jetties and boats, fresh crab and fries, salty air... there's nothing better than a long, lazy meal at the Boatyard, especially when it involves fresh oysters (oyster night is Saturday), fish and chips or full English breakfasts for homesick Brits. This is a great place to meet enthusiastic deep-sea fishermen and yachting old sea salts.

★ Nautilus
SEAFOOD $$$

(0713762748; Old Ferry Rd; mains KSh1000-2500; noon-3pm & 6-11pm Tue-Sun) We're still dining out on our last memory of dinner at Nautilus. This Swiss-owned restaurant offers fine, romantic dining with gorgeous

---

ECO-TISTICAL: THE BEST GREEN PROJECTS ON THE COAST

Distant Relatives, a backpackers and ecolodge in Kilifi, is an ecosystem in its own right, with a beautiful garden that serves as the basis for permaculture projects. Beds are made from neem trees, mattresses are stuffed with cotton from kapok trees and coat hangers are made from empty wine bottles. Permaculture design courses, taught by big East African names, are held here frequently, covering everything from grafting to composting toilets. The ecolodge does a great deal to support the local community, offering traditional Swahili meals with local families, supporting local seamstresses and more.

Wild Living (p242) conservation centre is a beautiful 53-hectare conservancy on the outskirts of Kilifi. It serves as a training centre for farmers interested in eco-charcoal production and aloe farming. The shop and cafe can arrange tours of the site.

views over the water and a warm welcome. The wine is good, the oysters are even better and the prawns in spicy coconut milk top the lot.

Drinking & Nightlife

Felix Unique Collections JUICE BAR
(Kibaoni St; ⊙8am-5pm Mon-Sat) Felix Unique Collection might not be what we would name our juice bar if we had one – especially if we wanted to make it into an acronym – but the blender geniuses here turn out fantastic avocado, passion-fruit, tamarind and mango juice, which is probably why they have a juice bar and we don't.

De Coffee Pub BAR
(☑0726363437; Biashara St; ⊙8am-late; 🛜) You can disco dance on caffeine (and alcoholic things) at this popular nightspot. *Nyama choma* (barbecued meat) is on the grill, wi-fi is on the house and drinks are on (well, actually behind) the bar. There's a slightly posh VIP area.

Shopping

★ Kilifi

Design Collective FASHION & ACCESSORIES
(☑0700246463; Malindi-Mombasa Rd; ⊙9am-6pm Tue-Sun) Right next to the Wild Living Cafe (p241) on the southern outskirts of Kilifi, this excellent shop showcases the wares of four local, ecofriendly Fair Trade designers and cooperatives: leather bags, purses, clutches and belts by Zinj; colourful shirts and dresses by Duka; lampshades and containers made of baobab seed pods by Seedling; and 4Shore T-shirts with Kenyan themes.

★ Zinj FASHION & ACCESSORIES
(☑0728282288; www.zinjdesign.com; Takaungu; ⊙8am-4.30pm Mon-Fri, to noon Sat) This home-run design store of international reputation is located near the southern edge of Kilifi Creek. You'll find stylish leather bags adorned with Maasai-style beading (from KSh9000), clutches and purses (from KSh2500), belts (from KSh3500) and sandals.

Wild Living FASHION & ACCESSORIES
(☑0791183312; Mombasa-Malindi Rd; ⊙8am-6pm) Stock up on baobab oil, moringa powder, charcoal briquettes for the barbecue and – why not? – hats made from soft Ugandan bark at this innovative eco-shop that's been incorporated into the namesake cafe

on the edge of Kilifi. Tours of its excellent conservation centre can also be arranged.

❶ Getting There & Away

All buses and matatus (minibuses) travelling between Mombasa and Malindi stop at Kilifi.

Watamu

☑042 / POP 10,030
Laid-back little Watamu looks out over the Indian Ocean and enjoys a blinding white-sand beach and a soft breeze coming off the water. It's a gorgeous slice of coastline and one that includes its own marine national park. As well as its natural endowments, great dining scene and laid-back village vibe, Watamu makes an excellent base from which to explore the nearby Gede ruins, Arabuko Sokoke Forest Reserve and the mangrove-fringed waterways of Mida Creek.

◉ Sights

★ Bio-Ken Snake Farm & Laboratory SERPENTARIUM
(Map p244; ☑emergency snakebite 0718290324; www.bio-ken.com; Jacaranda Rd; adult/child KSh1000/500; ⊙10am-noon & 2-5pm) This humble-looking place is one of the world's most renowned snake research centres. Bio-Ken specialises in antivenin research and acts as an emergency service for snakebite victims throughout the region. Passionate guides lead excellent 45-minute tours (included in the price), during which they introduce you to such deadly beauties as the black spitting cobra, black mamba, horned viper, puff adder, and the innocuous-looking but deadly twig snake for whose venom there's no cure.

★ Watamu Turtle Watch WILDLIFE RESERVE
(Map p244; ☑0713759627; www.watamuturtles. com; Turtle Bay Rd; suggested donation KSh300; ⊙2-4pm Mon, 9.30am-noon & 2-4pm Tue-Fri, 9.30am-noon Sat) 🌿 This excellent organisation protects the approximately 50 hawksbill and green turtles that lay their eggs on Watamu Beach. The centre provides much-needed education in the local community about the fragility of sea turtles, and actively patrols for people selling turtle shell. At the trust's rehabilitation centre you can normally see turtles being treated for injury or illness and learn about these magnificent creatures. It's a very worthwhile visit.

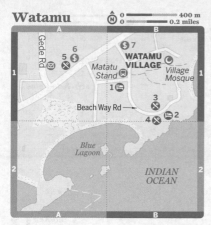

Watamu

Watamu

🛌 **Sleeping**
1 Barracuda Inn B1
2 Seawhispers Inn B1

🍴 **Eating**
3 Ascot Residence...............................B1
4 Bahati Gelateria Italiana.....................B1
5 Bistro Watamu..................................A1

ℹ️ **Information**
6 Barclays..A1
7 Kenya Commercial Bank....................B1

Watamu Marine National Park
NATIONAL PARK

(Map p244; www.kws.go.ke/content/watamu-marine-national-park-reserve; adult/child US$20/15; ⏰8am-6pm) The southern part of Malindi Marine National Park, this reserve includes some magnificent coral reefs, abundant fish life and sea turtles. To get here to snorkel and dive, you'll need a boat, which is easy enough to hire at the KWS office (p246), where you pay the park fees, at the end of the coast road. Boat operators ask anywhere from KSh2500 to KSh5000 for two people for two hours; it's all negotiable. Alternatively, arrange trips with recommended watersports operators.

🏃 Activities

Tribe Kitesurfing KITESURFING
(Map p244; ✆0718553355; www.tribe-watersports.com; Turtle Bay Rd; ⏰9am-5pm) This excellent outfit is your go-to place for kitesurfing courses (three-day beginner course US$330) and equipment in Watamu. It also offers stand up paddle boarding 'surfaris', and rents boards (US$22 per hour).

Alleycat Big Game Fishing FISHING
(Map p244; ✆0722734788; www.alleycatfishing.com; Turtle Bay Rd, Ocean Sports Resort) Runs dedicated, tailored deep-sea fishing safaris for around US$700 per day.

Mwamba Field Study Centre WILDLIFE
(Map p244; ✆Nairobi 020-2335865; www.arocha.or.ke; Plot 28, Watamu Beach) This Christian conservation society, based out of the namesake guesthouse, is involved in various worthwhile projects, from ringing endangered bird species and protecting vulnerable coastal ecosystems to sponsoring the education of local children. Guests at their guesthouse are welcome to participate in various conservation-related activities.

Diving

Watamu is one of the top diving destinations along the Kenyan coast, with 16 main sites to choose from and a good mix of reef and wreck diving. Diving is best between October and March, when the visibility is optimal and seas are calmest. Aqua Ventures runs highly professional diving trips to the likes of Moray Reef, famous for its giant eel, and Drummers' Reef, with its sea turtles, rays and shoals of Napoleon wrasse. Diving fees do not include the daily marine park fee of US$20.

⭐ Aqua Ventures ADVENTURE SPORTS
(Map p244; ✆0733906577, 0703628102; www.diveinkenya.com; Turtle Bay Rd, Ocean Sports Resort; dives from €45) Veteran diving outfit operated by British ex-military. It's the only British Sub-Aqua Club (BSAC) Premier Centre in Kenya and a full range of dives and courses is on offer, from five-day PADI open water (US$590) to night dives and wreck dives.

Snorkelling

Ocean Sports (Map p244; ✆0734195227; www.oceansports.net; Turtle Bay Rd, Ocean Sports) organises two-hour snorkelling outings in glass-bottomed boats to the coral gardens of the Watamu Marine National Park for around US$40 per person, with equipment provided, and another snorkelling stop in Mida Creek at high tide. Watamu Treehouse (p245) arranges more innovative snorkelling outings, with stand up paddle boarding to one or two of the best snorkelling sites.

Around Watamu

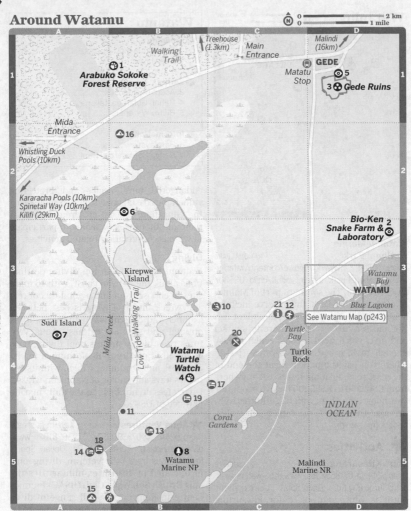

N 0 —————— 2 km
   0 —————— 1 mile

Arabuko Sokoke Forest Reserve 1

Treehouse (1.3km)
Walking Trail
Main Entrance
Malindi (16km)
GEDE
Matatu Stop
5
3 **Gede Ruins**

Mida Entrance

Whistling Duck Pools (10km)

16

Kararacha Pools (10km);
Spinetail Way (10km);
Kilifi (29km)

6

Bio-Ken Snake Farm & Laboratory 2

Kirepwe Island

Watamu Bay
WATAMU
Blue Lagoon

10   21 12

See Watamu Map (p243)

Sudi Island 7

Mida Creek

Low Tide Walking Trail

20

Turtle Bay
Turtle Rock

Watamu Turtle Watch 4

17

19

INDIAN OCEAN

11

13

Coral Gardens

18
14

8
Watamu Marine NP

Malindi Marine NR

15   9

Kayaking & Stand Up Paddle Boarding

If you're after straight-up gear rental, Tribe (p243) has SUPs for hire, while Ocean Sports (p243) rents sea kayaks. However, if you're looking for a guided kayaking or SUP trip into the Mida Creek mangroves or in the Watamu Marine National Park, Watamu Treehouse (p245) organises highly recommended trips for guests and nonguests alike.

Yoga

Nonguests are welcome to attend yoga sessions at the Watamu Treehouse (p245).

🛏 Sleeping

Mwamba Field Study Centre

GUESTHOUSE $

(Map p244; ☐ Nairobi 020-2335865; www.arocha. or.ke; Plot 28, Watamu Beach; per person KSh2500, full board KSh3500; ☎) ✆ This lovely guesthouse, set amid a pleasant garden and thick woods, is just a short wander from the beach. Run by a Christian conservation society, it's a fantastic deal with simple, clean and charming rooms with bright colour schemes and the noise of waves crashing onto the beach as you drift off to sleep.

LAMU & THE NORTH COAST WATAMU

Around Watamu

◎ **Top Sights**
1 Arabuko Sokoke Forest Reserve B1
2 Bio-Ken Snake Farm & Laboratory.......D3
3 Gede Ruins...D1
4 Watamu Turtle Watch...........................B4

◎ **Sights**
5 Kipepeo Butterfly Farm.........................D1
6 Kirepwe Island..B2
7 Sudi Island..A4
8 Watamu Marine National Park.............B5

◎ **Activities, Courses & Tours**
Alleycat Big Game Fishing............(see 12)
Aqua Ventures...............................(see 12)
9 Mida Creek Boardwalk..........................A5
10 Mida Creek Community
Ecotourism...C3
11 Mida Dhow..B4
Mwamba Field Study Centre........(see 17)
12 Ocean Sports...C3

Treehouse Paddleboarding..........(see 19)
Tribe Kitesurfing.............................(see 4)

◎ **Sleeping**
Hemingway's...................................(see 12)
13 Kobe Suite Resort.................................. B5
14 Merry Crab Cove.....................................A5
15 Mida Creek Camping Site.....................A5
16 Mida Ecocamp...B2
17 Mwamba Field Study Centre................C4
Ocean Sports ....(see 12)
18 Rock and Sea...A5
19 Watamu Treehouse...............................B4

◎ **Eating**
Crab Shack......................................(see 10)
Ocean Sports Restaurant.............(see 12)
20 Pilipan Restaurant.................................C4

◎ **Information**
21 Kenya Marine Park Office.....................C3

LAMU & THE NORTH COAST WATAMU

Seawhispers Inn
GUESTHOUSE **$**
(Map p243; ☑ 0719448609; Watamu Beach Rd; r/
apt KSh3000/6500) If you want to be as central as possible and as cheaply as possible without slumming it, friendly Seawhispers has a clutch of spotless, fan-cooled rooms opening out into a narrow passageway drowning in bougainvillea. No frills and no wi-fi.

★ Kobe Suite Resort
BOUTIQUE HOTEL **$$**
(Map p244; ☑ 0722658951; www.kobesuite resort.com; Turtle Bay Rd; s/d US$110/130; ❄️🛜🏊) With five rooms facing Kenya's best beach and a further 18 set back around a second saltwater pool, this boutique hotel works a sleek, dreamy vibe. Expect Swahili archways, bougainvillea window frames, brushed concrete surfaces and a minimalist feel. The garden hides intimate coves and a fire pit, there's a beautiful rooftop terrace and the restaurant serves fine Italian food.

Barracuda Inn
HOTEL **$$**
(Map p243; ☑ 0701578688, 0701028754; www. barracuda-inn.com; off Beach Way Rd; r/tr KSh7200/10,400; ❄️🛜🏊) With beach access and *makuti* buildings clustered around a large pool, this is a great midrange option if you want to be in the thick of the action and desire some creature comforts without splurging on a resort. Rooms on the ground floor tend to be the largest.

Ocean Sports
RESORT **$$**
(Map p244; ☑ 0734195227; www.oceansports.net; Turtle Bay Rd; s/d from KSh7100/12,800, ste from KSh19,360; @🛜🏊) With oodles of water sports based on its premises, Ocean Sports is true to its name. There's a pool and diving trips, as well as a tennis court and ultimate frisbee. It has pretty, glassed-in rooms in a garden setting, ranging from split-level suites with king-sized beds dominating the rooms, to more humble standard rooms with rain-head showers.

★ Watamu Treehouse
BOUTIQUE HOTEL **$$$**
(Map p244; ☑ 0712810055; www.treehouse.co.ke; Turtle Bay Rd; s/d US$100/200; 🛜) A wonder of recycled stained-glass windows, curvy walls of brushed concrete, nooks with sofas for sunset-watching and gnarled railings made of coconut wood, this twin-towered tree-house retreat rises from a sea of greenery. The seven plush, whitewashed rooms with rain-head showers are open to the elements, and this is a tranquil space for relaxation, yoga, paddle boarding and tasty, healthy meals.

Hemingway's
BOUTIQUE HOTEL **$$$**
(Map p244; ☑ 020-2295000; www.hemingways-watamu.com; s/d US$170/390; 🅿️❄️🛜🏊) Hemingway spent his gin-fuelled holidays around here, and his namesake hotel has everything you'd expect from a coastal resort. Closed for reconstruction when we

ON THE TRAIL OF THE ELEPHANT SHREW

'The most interesting thing about the golden-rumped elephant shrew,' says our guide, pausing for effect as we push back lianas inside the Arabuko Sokoke Forest Reserve, 'is its forgetfulness.' We're surprised. We thought perhaps it would be its shiny golden bum, its elephantine trunk, or the fact that the male lives in mixed-sex couples but frequents other females on the side.

But no. 'Here in the forest, the shrew's forgetfulness has saved its life. It's the reason it continues to thrive here,' he says. 'People say that if they catch and kill an elephant shrew, they will lose their memory, too. So nobody touches them.'

We walk past tall tamarind trees (an accidental import from India), medicinal plants and brilliant blue-and-orange African tiger moths. We spot flying handkerchief butterflies and tiny duikers, prehistoric zamia plants and parasitic trees that have squeezed all life from their reluctant hosts. We see gigantic termite mounds and deadly orange fungus. But still no golden-rumped elephant shrews.

And then, a red-capped robin flutters into view. 'Aha,' whispers our guide, explaining that this small bird has a symbiotic relationship with the shrew, feeding on the insects that escape its nozzle and, in turn, alerting the rodent to predators. 'A shrew must be nearby...' And then we see it, scooting across the forest floor, its glorious golden rump reflecting the afternoon sun.

visited, it was due to reopen in December 2017. Expect all the same luxuries as before – deluxe doubles come with large tubs and plush ocean-facing beds – plus a new state-of-the-art spa and gym.

✖ Eating

★ Bahati Gelateria Italiana   GELATO $

(Map p243; ☏ 0724079856; Watamu Beach Rd; gelato scoop KSh120; ☺ 7am-6pm Wed-Sun) In a village where gelato joints sit cheek by jowl, the oldest one is still the best, with Anna and Andrea enticing customers with scoops of rich chocolate pistachio and other flavours. Great pastries and coffee, too.

Bistro Watamu   CAFE $

(Map p243; ☏ 0727988524; off Turtle Bay Rd; cakes from KSh250; ☺ 8am-5pm) Opening onto a little garden area, this pretty coffee shop has freshly baked cakes, gooey brownies, pastries and quiches, plus decent coffee.

★ Pilipan Restaurant   FUSION $$$

(Map p244; ☏ 0736724099; Turtle Bay Rd; mains KSh800-2000; ☺ noon-2.30pm & 6-10pm Tue-Sun; P ☎) Set on a breezy Swahili-style outdoor terrace looking down on mangrove-strewn Prawn Lake, Pilipan turns up Watamu's chic factor, particularly after sunset, when the place is lit with twinkling fairy lights and candles. The mostly-Indian-but-not-quite menu includes sambal squid, Camembert samosas, tuna carpaccio and malabar prawn curry. There's a stylish bar area for aperitifs and sundowners.

★ Ocean Sports Restaurant   INTERNATIONAL $$$

(Map p244; ☏ 0734195227; Turtle Bay Rd, Ocean Sports Resort; mains from KSh800; ☺ 6am-10pm; P ☎) This popular place is spread along a breeze-blown terrace and has some plusher seating inside. Expect sandwiches, burgers, great salads and finer dining such as seared tuna and other seafood creations. It's atmospheric at night, when the ocean rock formations glow under the moon. That's also when the music gets louder and the party starts.

Ascot Residence   ITALIAN $$$

(Map p243; ☏ 0721267761; Beach Way Rd, Ascot Hotel; mains KSh800-1650; ☺ 11.30am-2pm & 6-10pm Tue-Sun) A favourite for romantic dinners, Ascot consistently gets good feedback and is famous for its wood-fired pizzas. It occasionally closes during the low season.

ℹ Information

MONEY

Barclays (Map p243; Jacaranda Rd, Watamu Supermarket)
Kenya Commercial Bank (Map p243; Beach Way Rd) Has an ATM.

POST

Post Office (Map p243; Gede Rd; ☺ 9am-5pm Mon-Fri)

TOURIST INFORMATION

Kenya Marine Park Office (Map p244; www.kws.go.ke; Turtle Bay Rd; ☺8am-5pm) Marine park entry fees (US$20/day) payable here.

ⓘ Getting There & Away

Watamu is about a two-hour drive north of Mombasa and about a 40-minute drive south of Malindi. Matatus run regularly between the three destinations. Heading north, they depart from the **matatu stand** (Map p243) in Watamu village; southbound vans leave from the **matatu stop** (Map p244) near the Gede ruins. Matatus to Malindi charge KSh150; to Mombasa they charge KSh500 to KSh700.

Arabuko Sokoke Forest Reserve

This 420-sq-km tract of natural forest – the largest indigenous coastal forest remaining in East Africa – is most famous as the home of the golden-rumped elephant shrew. Yes, you read that right – it's a guinea-pig-sized rodent with a long furry trunk and a (mostly) monogamous streak, and the **Arabuko Sokoke Forest Reserve** (Map p244; ☏0729295382; www.kenyaforestservice.org; Mombasa-Malindi Rd; adult/child US$20/10; ☺6am-6pm) is its only natural habitat.

Besides this marvellous creature, the forest is home to about 240 bird species, including the Amani sunbird, the Clarke's weaver and the Sokoke scops owl – Africa's smallest owl. More than 33 species of snakes slither through the undergrowth and shy water-bucks hide behind mahogany trees. The forest's other denizens include the elephant shrews' largest relative, the elephant, as well as the shy Aders' duiker (miniature antelope), Sykes' monkeys and yellow baboons.

An overnight stay (or very early arrival) greatly increases your chances of spotting wildlife.

🛏 Sleeping

Treehouse   TREEHOUSE $
(camping US$15) Pitch your tent on this platform high up in a tree, overlooking an elephant watering hole. No facilities but great wildlife encounters!

Kararacha Camping   CAMPGROUND $
(camping US$15) Basic campsite near the Kararacha entrance to the reserve, with cold showers and pit toilets.

ⓘ Information

The visitor centre near the main entrance was being rebuilt when we visited, but there was a trail map on a noticeboard and a warden on duty who could help organise guided walks (KSh1500 for two hours).

ⓘ Getting There & Away

The forest is just off the main Malindi–Mombasa road. The main entrance is about 1.5km west of the turn-off to Gede and Watamu, while the Mida entrance is about 3km further south, and the Kararacha entrance is another 11km or so south of Mida. Buses and matatus between Mombasa and Malindi can drop you at either entrance. From Watamu, matatus to Malindi can drop you at the main junction.

Mida Creek

Hugged by silver-tinged mudflats flowing with tiny ghost and fiddler crabs and long tides, 32-sq-km-Mida Creek is a place where the creeping marriage of land and water is epitomised by a mangrove forest and the salty, fresh scent of wind over an estuary. Eight types of mangroves thrive here, along with dozens of species of birds, including the rare crab plover. Giriama people live next to the creek, maintaining a boardwalk for birdwatchers and offering accommodation to those keen on experiencing a local way of life. Mida Creek is at its best at dawn, sunset, and in the clear evenings when the stars rain down on you. Explore it by stand up paddle board, canoe or boat.

◎ Sights

Sudi Island   ISLAND
(Map p244) This uninhabited island on the far side of Mida Creek makes an interesting excursion. It is very green (at least during the rainy season) and there are all sorts of curious creatures around. Local fishermen can canoe you across from the Mida Creek boardwalk, or the Mida Eco-Camp (p248) can organise a trip.

Kirepwe Island   ISLAND
(Map p244) Mida Ecocamp (p248) organises day trips (KSh3500) to this quiet island just across the estuary. The ruins are atmospheric and you can visit a Giriama village and stop for a fisherman's lunch.

🏃 Activities

★ Treehouse Paddleboarding
WATER SPORTS

(Map p244; ☑ 0712810055; www.treehouse.co.ke) Watamu Treehouse (p245) arranges tours of Mida Creek by stand up paddle board. Paddle out at dawn through the narrow, overgrown side channels and go for a dip among the mangroves, or do a two-hour jaunt to the famed local Crab Shack and pair sunset viewing with crab samosas.

Mida Creek Community Ecotourism
CANOEING

(Map p244; per person from KSh1000) The Giriama community that manages the excellent Crab Shack offers canoe rides around Mida Creek, from sunset paddles and trips to Kirepwe Island to specially arranged birdwatching jaunts.

Mida Creek Boardwalk
WALKING

(Map p244; adult/child KSh300/200, guides KSh500; ⏰ 6am-6pm) Excellent Giriama guides will take you through the water-laced landscape of the creek and through the mangroves on a seriously rickety walkway that needs an upgrade. At its culmination, a bird hide looks out over the surrounding wetlands. This is a community project, so your visit helps the local Giriama people. Canoe trips (from KSh700) can be arranged from here.

👉 Tours

Mida Dhow
BOATING

(Map p244; ☑ 0713462999; www.facebook.com/MidaDhow; per person from €70) Moored on the north side of the creek, this traditional dhow takes you on an atmospheric sunset whirl around Mida Creek, complete with dinner and drinks.

🛏 Sleeping

Mida Ecocamp
CAMPGROUND $

(Map p244; ☑ 0729213042; www.midaecocamp.com; camping KSh500, huts per person KSh900-1400) 🌿 This relaxed ecocamp has *the* most perfect position, between the forest, the creek and the stars. Accommodation is in atmospheric traditional huts – choose from Zanzibar (duplex with a breezy upper terrace), Giriama (haystack with amiable face and raised platform beds) and Swahili (square, with a thatched roof). The eco-credentials stretch to solar panels, renewable materials and a serious Giriama community focus.

Mida Creek Camping Site
CAMPGROUND $

(Map p244; ☑ 0703881043, 0727894173; camping KSh500, banda KSh1000) Staying at this basic campsite in this friendly Giriama village, right near the Mida Creek boardwalk, is a great way to interact with locals and to see the amazing light show of stars above the creek at night. Meals of fish and coconut rice (KSh800) are available.

★ Merry Crab Cove
HOSTEL $$

(Map p244; ☑ 0792295131; www.mcc-guesthouse-backpackers.net; Uyombo; dm KSh1800, d KSh6500-8500; 🛜🌀) We challenge you to find a lovelier backpackers' spot on Kenya's north coast! A converted luxury resort, the Merry Crab retains the rain-head showers and sumptuous room design, with a saltwater pool, own beach and sunset-watching terrace. The delightful owners make guests feel like family, and boat transfers to Watamu are organised. By road, follow signs for Rock and Sea.

Rock and Sea
DESIGN HOTEL $$$

(Map p244; ☑ 0722658951; ste €400; 🛜🌀) This ambitious ecolodge consists of just four rooms – three in plexi 'eco-bubbles' and a brushed concrete one next to a 2000-year-old baobab, crowned with a sunset-watching platform. Its hillock location gives it the best views of Mida Creek and the restaurant is great for sundowners. Speedboat transfers from Watamu are available, or follow the signs from Matasangoni turn-off for 4.5km.

🍴 Eating

★ Crab Shack
SEAFOOD $$

(Map p244; ☑ 0725315562; mains KSh800-1200; ⏰ 10am-8pm) Crab samosas, grilled calamari and steamed fish await at the end of a mangrove boardwalk, overlooking Mida Creek. This lovely Giriama-run spot is a favourite for sunset-watching, too. It's a 3km walk or *boda-boda* (motorcycle taxi) ride along the road directly opposite Turtle Bay Hotel. Follow the signs for Mida Creek Community Ecotourism Enterprizes at the crossroads.

ℹ Getting There & Away

Any bus travelling between Mombasa and Malindi can drop you on the main road near the turn-offs for Mida Creek boardwalk, and the Mida Ecocamp, from where it's a pleasant, leafy, 20-minute walk to the water.

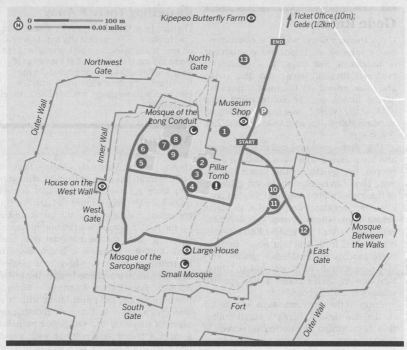

Walking Tour
Gede Ruins

START GEDE RUINS ENTRANCE
FINISH GEDE RUINS MUSEUM
LENGTH 1.5KM; ONE TO 1½ HOURS

Gede is Kenya's most visitor-friendly archaeological site. Most of the excavated buildings are concentrated near the entrance, but there are dozens of other ruins scattered through the forest.

On your right as you enter the compound is the **1** **Dated Tomb**, so called because of the inscription on the wall, featuring the Muslim date corresponding to 1399. Near it, inside the wall, is the **2** **Tomb of the Fluted Pillar**, which is characteristic of such pillar designs found along the East African coast.

Past the tomb, next to the **3** **House of the Long Court**, the **4** **Great Mosque** is one of Gede's most significant buildings. The entrance was on the side of a long rectangular prayer hall, with the mihrab (prayer niche that faces Mecca) obscured behind rows of stone pillars.

Behind the mosque are the ruins of an extensive **5** **palace**. One of the most interesting

things found within the ruins was an earthenware jar containing a *fingo* (charm), thought to attract djinns (guardian spirits) who would drive trespassers insane. The palace also has a fine **6** **pillar tomb**; its hexagonal shape is unique to East Africa.

Just off to the right from the palace is a **7** **tree** with steps leading high up into its canopy for a bird's-eye view of the site.

Along the path past the tomb are around 11 old **8** **Swahili houses**. They're each named after particular features of their design, or objects found in them by archaeologists, such as the House of Scissors and the House of the Iron Lamp. The **9** **House of the Cistern** is particularly interesting, with ancient illustrations incised into the plaster walls.

The other excavations include the **10** **House of the Dhow**, the **11** **House of the Double Court** and the nearby **12** **Mosque of the Three Aisles**, which has the largest well at Gede.

On the way out you'll find an excellent little **13** **museum**.

Gede Ruins

If you thought Kenya was all about nature, you're missing an important component of its charm: lost cities. The remains of medieval Swahili towns dot the coast, and many would say the most impressive of the bunch are the **Gede ruins** (Map p244; ☑ 0723359652; www.museums.or.ke; off Mombasa-Malindi Rd; adult/child KSh500/250; ☻ 8am-6pm).

This series of coral palaces, mosques and townhouses, which once housed 3000 people, lies quietly in the jungle's green grip. Here, archaeologists found evidence of the cosmopolitan nature of Swahili society: silver necklaces decorated with Maria Teresa coins (from Europe) and Arabic calligraphy (from the Middle East), vermicelli makers from Asia that would become pasta moulds in the Mediterranean, Persian sabres, Arab coffee pots, Indian lamps, Egyptian or Syrian cobalt glass, Spanish scissors and Ming porcelain.

Entry to the dusty **museum** is included in the site ticket. There's a small collection of excavated Chinese coins, porcelain bowls, weapons, terracotta pots and other items found here.

History

Gede, which reached its peak in the 15th century, was inexplicably abandoned in the 17th or 18th century. Some theories point to disease and famine, others blame guerrilla attacks by Somalian Galla people and cannibalistic Zimba from near Malawi, or punitive expeditions from Mombasa. Or Gede ran out of water – at some stage the water table here dropped rapidly and the 40m-deep wells dried up.

◉ Sights

Kipepeo Butterfly Farm　　　　FARM
(Map p244; ☑ 0719671161; www.kipepeo.org; off Mombasa-Malindi Rd; adult/child incl guided tour KSh100/50; ☻ 8am-5pm) 🖉 Visit this butterfly centre on a Friday morning, and you might spot exotic pupae being packed for export to the UK and USA. The farm pays locals to collect live pupae from Arabuko Sokoke Forest Reserve and the money is then ploughed back into conservation of the forests. The price includes a (brief) guided tour and, of course, dozens of dazzling butterflies flitting around.

ℹ Getting There & Away

The ruins lie off the main highway, on the access road to Watamu. The easiest way to get here is on any matatu plying the main highway between Mombasa and Malindi. Get off at the village of Gede and follow the well-signposted dirt road from there – it's about a 10-minute walk. Tuk-tuks from Watamu charge around KSh200 to get you here.

Malindi

☑ 042 / POP 84,154

Having hosted Vasco da Gama's fleet in 1498, Malindi has been welcoming strangers ever since. It's a bustling town that doesn't quite have the architecture of Lamu or the easy-going charm of Watamu, but it makes up for it with several worthwhile historical sights, its own marine national park and some fantastic stretches of beach. Beloved by Italians – many of whom have settled here (particularly Sicilians back in the 1970s, allegedly fleeing from Interpol) – Malindi has been feeling the pinch lately, with economic depression in Europe impacting on much of its visitor market. Still, it remains a melting pot of local cultures with a rich and fascinating history. Wander through the alleys of the atmospheric old town, dine on terrific Italian food beside the Indian Ocean or take a plunge into the crystal-clear waters of the national park, and you'll discover for yourself that Malindi is quite the charmer.

◉ Sights

Vasco da Gama Pillar　　　　LANDMARK
(off Mama Ngina Rd; adult/child KSh500/250; ☻ 8am-6pm) More impressive for what it represents (the genesis of the Age of Exploration) than the edifice itself. Erected by the Portuguese explorer Vasco da Gama as a navigational aid in 1498, the coral column is topped by a cross made of Lisbon stone, which almost certainly dates from the explorer's time. There are good views from here down the coast and out over the ocean.

Malindi Marine National Park　　　　NATIONAL PARK
(www.kws.go.ke; adult/child US$20/15; ☻ 6am-6pm) The oldest marine park in Kenya covers 213 sq km of powder-blue fish, organ-pipe coral, green sea turtles and beds of Thalassia seagrass. If you're extremely lucky, you may spot mako and whale sharks. Unfortunately, these reefs have suffered (and continue to suffer) extensive damage, evidenced

by the piles of seashells on sale in Malindi. Monsoon-generated waves can reduce visibility from June to September.

The cost of a boat trip depends on your bargaining skills, but expect a two-hour outing to cost around KSh2500, with glass-bottom boats from around KSh3500 for two hours.

House of Columns
HISTORIC BUILDING

(Mama Ngina Rd; adult/child KSh500/250; ⊙8am-6pm) This building is a good example of traditional Swahili architecture and contains a peculiar exhibit on marine ecology – on the first and only coelacanth ever to turn up in Malindi waters.

🏃 Activities

Malindi is one of the top destinations in the world for **kitesurfing**, with the best seasons being July to September and January to April. The best place to learn is at Che Shale, the kitesurfing camp/beach retreat north of Malindi, partially responsible for introducing the sport to the area. A three-day course for beginners costs €340.

Blue Fin
DIVING

(☑0722261242; www.bluefindiving.com; Mama Ngina Rd) With the marine park just offshore from Malindi, scuba diving is a popular activity, although the visibility is greatly reduced by silt between March and June. Blue Fin is reputable and operates out of several resorts in town. Open water courses from €360.

👉 Tours

Aqua Ventures
DIVING

(☑0703628102; www.diveinkenya.com; Mama Ngina Rd) Based at the **Driftwood Beach Club** (☑0721724489; www.driftwoodclub.com; s/d from KSh7300/14,500; ❀ 🛜 🌊), Aqua Ventures is one of the best diving outfits in town. Dives start at US$50, but buying a package reduces the cost considerably.

🛏 Sleeping

Dagama's Inn
INN $

(☑0701864446, 0722357591; Mama Ngina Rd; s/d excl breakfast KSh1200/1400) This friendly little place is a real seaside travellers' inn – that's to say that seamen prop up the bar with mermaid stories, and drunken sailors make eyes at the barmaid. The rooms are spacious but simple. If you can get hot water out of those rusty water-storage tanks, you're a better person than us.

Lutheran Guest House
GUESTHOUSE $

(☑0723766278; lutheranmalindi@gmail.com; r KSh1400, bungalows KSh2700) If you need quiet, this religious centre (which accepts guests of all stripes) is a nice option. Like most church-run places in Kenya, everything here is a little cleaner, staff are earnestly friendly and alcohol is strictly prohibited.

★Che Shale
BANDAS $$

(☑0722230931; www.cheshale.com; s €45-180, d €90-180; 🛜) Three kinds of people make their way to this camp on Mambrui Beach, 25km north of Malindi: kitesurfers, foodies and tranquillity seekers. Choose between three types of *bandas* (thatched-roof huts), all crafted from local materials: basic (shared loo outside), beachfront (king-sized bed, relaxation space on the porch) and luxury (even snazzier). The excellent restaurant's mangrove crab dishes are unique on the coast.

★Barefoot Beach Camp
TENTED CAMP $$

(☑0722421351; www.barefootbeachcampkenya.com; camping KSh1000, r with half board KSh6500) Venture 25km from Malindi, and you can have Mambrui North Beach almost to yourselves at this intimate and relaxed camp, run by fantastic hosts. Glamp in one of five luxury safari tents with sumptuous beds and bathrooms, or camp out. Gourmet seafood dishes are served here; book 24 hours in advance if not staying at the camp.

★Villa Fortuna Malindi
GUESTHOUSE $$

(☑0735923507; Crocodile Rd; r KSh5650-8400; ❀ 🛜 🌊) Drowning in a riot of bougainvillea, this *makuti* guesthouse overlooks a kidney-shaped pool in a secure, gated property. The warm welcome from the owners and their tiny dogs and cats is second to none. It's down an unlit dirt road from Marine Park Rd, so take a *boda-boda* (KSh100) in the evenings.

Scorpio Villas
RESORT $$

(☑0700437680; Mnarani Rd; s/d/tr from KSh7800/9700/15,900; 🅿 🛜 🌊) Right by the ocean, with four pools and within walking distance of some good restaurants, Italian-owned Scorpio Villas offers excellent value for money. The 48 rooms follow the hotel theme – gorgeous dark wood, four-poster beds, white linen sofas and Swahili carvings – while the bathrooms have huge monsoon showers.

Malindi

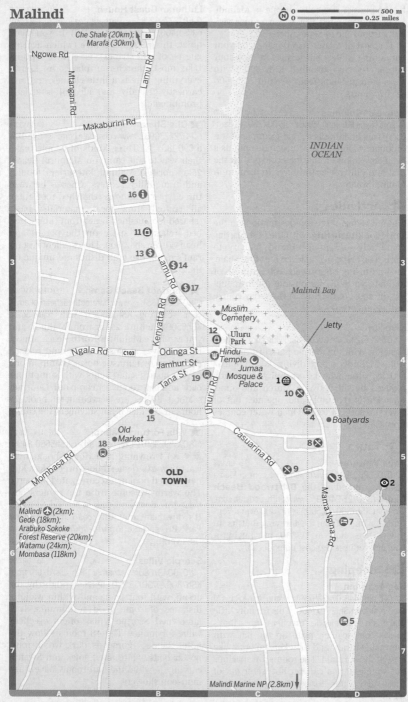

Che Shale (20km);
Marafa (30km)

B8

Ngowe Rd

Mtangani Rd

Lamu Rd

Makaburini Rd

INDIAN
OCEAN

6

16

11

13

Lamu Rd

14

Kenyatta Rd

17

Malindi Bay

Muslim
Cemetery

Jetty

12

Uluru
Park

Ngala Rd

C103

Odinga St

Hindu
Temple

Jamhuri St

Jumaa
Mosque &
Palace

Tana St

19

1

10

Uhuru Rd

4

Boatyards

15

8

Old
Market

9

18

3

2

Mombasa Rd

OLD
TOWN

Casuarina Rd

Mama Ngina Rd

7

Malindi ✈ (2km);
Gede (18km);
Arabuko Sokoke
Forest Reserve (20km);
Watamu (24km);
Mombasa (118km)

5

Malindi Marine NP (2.8km)

0   500 m
0   0.25 miles

Malindi

⊙ Sights
1 House of Columns.................................C4
2 Vasco da Gama Pillar.........................D5

⊕ Activities, Courses & Tours
Aqua Ventures................................(see 5)
3 Blue Fin..D5

⊜ Sleeping
4 Dagama's Inn.....................................D5
5 Driftwood Beach Club......................D7
6 Lutheran Guest House......................B2
7 Scorpio Villas....................................D6

⊗ Eating
8 Baby Marrow.....................................D5
9 Dreamland...C5
10 Osteria...C4

⊜ Shopping
11 Mizizi Ya Afrika.................................B3
12 Our Shop..C4
Rosanis..(see 12)

ⓘ Information
13 Barclays...B3
14 Dollar Forex Bureau..........................B3
15 Malindi Immigration Office...............B5
16 Malindi Tourist Office........................B2
17 Standard Chartered Bank.................B3

ⓘ Transport
18 New Malindi Bus Station...................A5
19 Simba Coaches..................................B4
Tahmeed.......................................(see 19)
Tawakal...(see 19)

✖ Eating

Dreamland
KENYAN $

(Casuarina Rd; mains around KSh400; ⊘ noon-10pm Mon-Sat) The outer walls look a bit like the children's ward of a hospital, but there's nothing sterile about this circular roadside lunch spot. Expect friendly service, local banter and a blaring TV. The fresh juice is good.

★ Rosada
ITALIAN $$$

(☑ 0700501813; off Casuarina Rd; mains from KSh800; ⊘ 8am-10pm Nov-Feb, until 5pm Mar-Oct; ☏) Right on the sand, Rosada is a chilled beach bar with great cocktails and some wonderful views out over the marine park. Monday night is a popular beach party, which sees dancing on the beach once the sun has gone down. The food gets rave reviews, particularly the pizzas.

★ Baby Marrow
ITALIAN, SEAFOOD $$$

(☑ 0700766704; Mama Ngina Rd; mains KSh800-2200; ⊘ noon-3pm & 7-11pm, evenings only in low season; ☏) This standout restaurant is not only one of the best on the coast, but in the entire country. Think leafy, intimate setting, *makuti* roof, and bold contemporary art, while the charming staff bring you house specialities such as smoked sailfish, pizza bianca, vodka sorbet or Sicilian ice cream. The jungle bar is a good spot for a digestif.

Osteria
ITALIAN $$$

(☑ 0725525665; www.osteriadelchianti.com/malindi; Mama Ngina Rd; mains KSh800-2600; ⊘ noon-3pm & 6.30pm-midnight; ☏) Pictures of vintage celebrities deck the wall at this, one of the best Italian places in Malindi. There's a formal dining room, which is great for an evening meal, and a breezy (read: mosquito-y in the evenings) terrace where you can eat such classics as spaghetti vongole and risotto al prosecco. Gelato rounds things off. Another branch on Casuarina Beach.

🛍 Shopping

★ Our Shop
ARTS & CRAFTS

(☑ 0721723779; Lamu Rd; ⊘ 9am-1pm & 3-6.30pm Mon-Sat) ✏ We really wish it were our shop, stocked as it is with cowrie-studded Congolese and West African carvings and masks to tempt collectors. Some great affordable and unusual fashion accessories, too, in the shape of clutches and handbags made out of recycled cement bags and rice sacks by Kenyan seamstresses.

Rosanis
JEWELLERY

(Uhuru Rd; ⊘ 8.30am-6pm Mon-Sat) The main thing here is an extensive collection of antique silver jewellery from Lamu. Dig around, and you can also pick up some antique compasses and sextants, some malachite items and carvings.

Mizizi Ya Afrika
GIFTS & SOUVENIRS

(Lamu Rd; ⊘ 9am-6pm Mon-Sat) This boutique take on a souvenir shop sells some beautiful carved calabashes, bowls, carvings from West Africa and Zanzibar, masks and jewellery. Smaller branch next to Uhuru Park.

DON'T MISS

MARAFA DEPRESSION

One of the more intriguing sights inland from the north Kenyan coast is **Marafa Depression** (KSh800, guide KSh500; ⊗7am-7pm), known as Hell's Kitchen or Nyari ('the place broken by itself'). About 30km northeast of Malindi, it's an eroded sandstone gorge where jungle, red rock and cliffs heave themselves into a single stunning Mars-like landscape. You can take an organised tour, take a taxi (KSh9000), drive, or catch a morning matatu from Mombasa Rd in Malindi to Marafa village (KSh200, 2½ hours) and walk for 20 minutes.

The depression is currently managed as a local tourism concern by Marafa village, with the steep admission costs going into village programmes. A guide will walk you around the lip of the gorge and into its heart of sandstone spikes and melted-candle-like formations, and tell the story of Hell's Kitchen. Which goes like so: a rich family was so careless with their wealth that they bathed themselves in the valuable milk of their cows. God became angry with this excess and sank the family homestead into the earth. The white and red walls of the depression mark the milk and blood of the family painted over the gorge walls. The more mundane explanation? The depression is a chunk of sandstone that's geologically distinct from the surrounding rock and more susceptible to wind and rain erosion.

There are two very basic places to stay if needed (KSh1000), plus a restaurant right next to the gorge.

If you come by private transport, it's worth making a day trip of it and enjoying the beautiful African countryside, with its fields of maize studded with chunky baobab trees, mud houses with *makuti* roofs and cattle herders tending their beasts.

❶ Information

DANGERS & ANNOYANCES

Being on the beach alone at night is asking for trouble, as is walking along any quiet beach back road at night. Avoid the far northern end of the beach, or any deserted patches of sand, as muggings are common. There are lots of guys selling drugs, so remember: everything is illegal. Drug sales often turn into stings, with the collusive druggie getting a cut of whatever fee police demand from you (if they don't throw you in jail).

MONEY

Barclays (Lamu Rd) With ATM.

Dollar Forex Bureau (Lamu Rd; ⊗9am-6pm Mon-Sat) Rates may be slightly better here than at the banks.

Standard Chartered Bank (Lamu Rd, Stanchart Arcade) With ATM.

POST

Post Office (Kenyatta Rd; ⊗9am-5pm Mon-Fri, to 1pm Sat)

TOURIST INFORMATION

Malindi Tourist Office (☑042-2120747; Lamu Rd, Malindi Complex; ⊗8am-12.30pm & 2-4.30pm Mon-Fri) Not a great deal of information on the area, but it's the place to register your complaints if you've had a bad experience with a local tour operator.

❶ Getting There & Away

AIR

Malindi Airport (☑042-2131201; https://kaa.go.ke/airports/our-airports/malindi-airport; off Mombasa-Malindi Rd) has up to four daily flights to Nairobi (from US$47 one way, one hour) with AirKenya (www.airkenya.com), Fly540 (www.fly540.com) and Fly-SAX (www.fly-sax.com), and a daily flight to Lamu (from US$59 one way, 25 minutes) with Fly540.

BUS & MATATU

Bus-company offices are found opposite the old market in the centre of Malindi. The main bus companies are **Tahmeed** (☑0711756970; Jamhuri St), **Tawakal** (☑0705090122; Jamhuri St) and **Simba Coaches** (☑0774471112; Tana St), and they all run services to Lamu, Mombasa and Nairobi (via Mombasa).

Lamu

There are usually at least six buses a day to Lamu (around KSh1000, but this can rise in periods of high demand, five to six hours). They depart from Mombasa around 7am and 9am and swing by their Malindi offices around 9am and 11am. Tawakal is the biggest and most reliable operator.

Mombasa

There are numerous daily buses and matatus to Mombasa (bus/matatu KSh450/500, two hours), departing from the **New Malindi Bus**

Station (off Mombasa-Malindi Rd). During periods of high demand, fares can rise to KSh700.

Nairobi

All the main bus companies have daily departures to Nairobi, via Mombasa, at around 7am and/or 7pm (KSh900 to KSh3200, 12 to 14 hours).

Watamu

Matatus to Watamu (KSh150, one hour) leave from the not-very-new New Malindi Bus Station on the edge of town.

ⓘ Getting Around

You can rent bicycles from most hotels for around KSh700 per day. Tuk-tuks are ubiquitous – a short hop through town should cost around KSh150 to KSh200. *Boda-bodas* are even cheaper – KSh50 to KSh100 for a short hop. A taxi to the airport is around KSh1000 and a tuk-tuk is KSh200. However, these are official prices and you'll need the gift of the gab to actually bargain down to this.

LAMU ARCHIPELAGO

The Arabs called them the 'Seven Isles of Eryaya', while sailors called them a welcome port of call when en route to, or from, India. Hundreds of expats who've fallen irrevocably in love with these islands call them home, as do the Swahili, who trace the deepest roots of their culture to here.

Few would dispute the Lamu archipelago forms the most evocative destination on the Kenyan coast. It's the best of several travelling worlds: medieval stone towns of narrow streets, charming architecture, tropical-island paradise, delicious local cuisine and star-heavy nights that are pregnant with the smell of spice and possibility. Choose your calling: bustling Lamu Town, a pungent, lively Unesco site; Shela Beach, an idyllic spot that attracts the majority of Lamu's visitors; Manda Island and its resorts; little-visited Paté Island with its traditional villages and beguiling ruins; or remote Kiwayu Island, an adventure destination often reached by dhow.

Lamu Island

With its centuries-old Swahili settlements, a couple of gorgeous beaches, and culture and architecture distinctive from what you encounter elsewhere along the Kenyan coast, Lamu is beguiling. Whether you're looking to lose yourself in the fragrant labyrinth of tiny streets in Lamu Town and spend hours admiring carved Omani and Swahili doorways, or whether you're

Lamu Archipelago

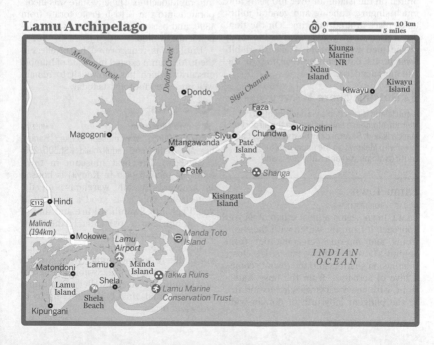

looking for a peaceful beachfront stay replete with yoga, art and fusion food in Shela village, Lamu has something to satisfy most travellers.

🎊 Festivals & Events

Lamu Painters' Festival ART
(www.lamupaintersfestival.org; ⊘Feb) Draws contemporary artists and work from across Africa and Europe.

Lamu Yoga Festival SPORTS
(www.lamuyoga.org; ⊘Mar) Can't make it to India? Practise yoga in the Indian Ocean instead. First held in 2014, this festival spills across Shela, Manda and Lamu, and includes workshops, classes and meditation. It culminates in one big beach party featuring drummers and acrobats. Typically in March.

Lamu Cultural Festival CULTURAL
(⊘Nov) Exact dates for this colourful carnival vary each year, but it often falls in November. Expect donkey and dhow races, Swahili poets and island dancing.

Maulid Festival RELIGIOUS
(www.lamu.org/maulid-celebration.html; ⊘Dec/Jan) Marking the birth of the Prophet Mohammed, this festival has been celebrated on the island for over 100 years and much singing, dancing and general jollity takes place around this time. On the final day a procession heads down to the tomb of the man who started it all, Ali Habib Swaleh. Its date shifts according to the Islamic calendar.

❶ Getting There & Away

Lamu Island is reachable via daily flights from Nairobi, Mombasa and Malindi via the airport on Manda Island. Several daily boats connect Lamu Town with Mokowe on the mainland (for buses south to Mombasa) and with Paté Island.

Lamu Town
📞042 / POP 13,243

Lamu Town seems almost ethereal as you approach it from the water, with the shopfronts and mosques creeping out from behind a forest of dhow masts. Up close, the illusion shatters and the town becomes a hive of activity – from the busy waterfront, with heavy carts wheeled to and fro, to the pungent labyrinth of donkey-wide

alleyways, along which women whisper by in full-length *bui-bui* (black cover-all worn by some Islamic women outside the home) and stray cats hunt for scraps. Your nostrils are assaulted with blue smoke from meat grilling over open fires, donkey dung and the organic scent of the cured wooden shutters on houses built of stone and coral. Many visitors call this town – the oldest living town in East Africa, a Unesco World Heritage Site and arguably the most complete Swahili town in existence – one of the highlights of their trip to Kenya.

History

In pre-Arab times the islands were home to the Bajun, but their traditions vanished almost entirely with the arrival of the Arabs.

In the 19th century, the soldiers of Lamu caught the warriors of Paté on open mud at low tide and slaughtered them. This victory, plus the cash cows of ivory and slavery, made Lamu a splendidly wealthy place, and most of the fine Swahili houses that survive today were built during this period.

It all came to an end in 1873, when the British forced Sultan Barghash of Zanzibar to close down the slave markets. With the abolition of slavery, the economy went into rapid decline. The city-state was incorporated into the British Protectorate from 1890, and became part of Kenya with independence in 1963.

Until it was 'rediscovered' by travellers in the 1970s, Lamu existed in a state of humble obscurity, which has allowed it to remain well preserved for tourists today.

◉ Sights

★ Lamu Museum MUSEUM
(📞0721660645; www.museums.or.ke; Harambee Ave, Waterfront; adult/child KSh500/250; ⊘8am-6pm) The best museum in town (and the second best in Kenya) is housed in a grand Swahili warehouse on the waterfront. This is as good a gateway as you'll get into Swahili culture and that of the archipelago in particular. Exhibitions focus on boat-building, domestic life and weddings, the intricate door carvings that you're likely to encounter (from Swahili and Omani to Kijumwa, Swabu and Bajun) and traditional silver jewellery. Don't miss the ceremonial *siwa* (side-blow) horns of ivory and brass.

LAMU'S LAYOUT

Lamu Town realises Swahili urban-planning conventions like few other places in the world. Within the seemingly random conglomeration of streets is a patchwork of neighbourhoods and districts divided by family hierarchy, social standing and profession.

There are 28 *mitaa* (districts) in Lamu, with names that range from the functional, such as Madukani (Place of Shopping), to the esoteric, such as Makadara (Eternal Destiny), to the funny, such as Kivundoni (Smelly Place). In addition, the town is divided into two halves: the north, Zena (Beauteous), and the south, Suudi (Fortunate).

This division stems from the traditional contempt of the Zijoho (Arab-Swahili elite) for trade. The Zena half of town is, to this day, where the grandest houses are to be found, while the main markets, noisy activity and – to be frank – poorer residents are generally on the Suudi side of the tracks. Note that the construction/restoration of grand houses by foreigners has disrupted this dynamic, but it's still present – you'll notice most of these new villas are on the Zena side of town.

Donkey Sanctuary WILDLIFE RESERVE
(Harambee Ave; ⊙9am-1pm Mon-Fri) FREE A man without a donkey *is* a donkey, claims one Swahili proverb. Or, as the staff of this sanctuary might tell you, a man who doesn't look after his donkey *is* a donkey. With around 3000 donkeys active on Lamu, *Equus asinus* is the main form of transport here. Visitors are free to visit the sanctuary and learn about its work – donations appreciated.

Lamu Market MARKET
(next to Lamu Fort) Atmospheric and somewhat chaotic, this quintessential Lamu market is best visited early in the morning. Bargain for fresh tuna and sailfish, wade through alleys teeming with stray cats and goats, and experience Lamu at its craziest. If you're sick of seafood, this is the place to find your fruit and veg.

Lamu Fort FORTRESS
(www.museums.or.ke; Main Sq; adult/child KSh500/200; ⊙8am-6pm) This squat castle was built by the Sultan of Paté between 1810 and 1823. From 1910 right up to 1984 it was used as a prison. It now houses the island's library, which holds one of the best collections of Swahili poetry and Lamu reference work in Kenya, while the upstairs walkway is a gallery space for temporary exhibitions (stunning photos of the Tana River delta, when we visited). Entry is free with a ticket for Lamu Museum.

Swahili House MUSEUM
(www.museums.or.ke; adult/child KSh500/250; ⊙8am-6pm) This preserved 16th-century Swahili house, tucked away to the side of Yumbe Guest House, in a tranquil courtyard with a well, is beautiful. The entry fee for viewing the two sleeping galleries and upstairs kitchen is very hard to justify, though, especially as half the hotels in Lamu are as well preserved.

🛏 Sleeping

⭐ **Jambo House** B&B $
(☑0713411714; www.jambohouse.com; s/d from KSh1400/1800; ❇🛜) Hands down the best place in town for budget travellers, this friendly guesthouse is owned by German world traveller Arnold, a treasure trove of all things Lamu. He tells guests what they can do in Lamu and how to do it, and dishes out maps of the town. Five snug rooms and a hearty breakfast seal the deal.

Baitul Noor House HOSTEL $
(☑0725220271, 0723760296; www.facebook.com/lamubackpackers; dm/s/d KSh1300/1800/2900; ❀🛜) 🗲 From the Arabic for 'house of light', this 16th-century townhouse is a stylish backpackers joint that guests rate highly for the warm hospitality. The dorms are lovely and ecofriendly, featuring extra-long beds, homemade soaps and solar reading lamps. Don't miss the roof terrace and the downstairs restaurant, which does lobster suppers for lemonade pockets. Helpful staff can arrange excursions.

Stone House Hotel BOUTIQUE HOTEL $
(☑0722528377, 0736699417; www.stonehousehotellamu.com; r KSh2000-4500; 🛜) This Swahili mansion is set into a tourist-free backstreet and is notable for its fine, white-washed walls and fantastic rooftop, which includes a good restaurant (no alcohol) with

Lamu Town

0 — 100 m
0 — 0.05 miles

Mokowe
(Mainland)
(5km)

*INDIAN
OCEAN*

11

Harambee Ave

10

18

14

2

12

6

*Matondoni
(6km)*

19

**Lamu
Museum**
1

*Manda Island
(Airport)
(1km)*

Main
Jetty

Catholic
Church

*Bohora
Mosque*

15

*Dhow
Moorings*

21

Kenyatta Rd

7

Kipungani
(10km)

8

13

Tawakal

22

District
Commissioner's
Office

New
Jetty

4

9

5

*Shiaithna-
Asheri Mosque*

Tahmeed

3

Simba

17

20

Shela (Inland Track)
(3.5km)

*Tamarind
Cafe (300m);
Shela (3km)*

16

Lamu Town

⊙ Top Sights
1 Lamu Museum.....................................C3

⊙ Sights
2 Donkey Sanctuary...............................C2
3 German Post Office Museum...............C6
4 Lamu Fort..C5
5 Lamu Market.......................................C5
6 Swahili House.....................................B2

⊜ Sleeping
7 Amu House..C4
8 Baitul Noor House...............................C5
9 Jambo House.......................................B5
10 Jannat House.......................................A1
11 Lamu House..B1
12 Stone House Hotel..............................B2
13 Subira House.......................................C5

⊗ Eating
14 Bustani Café..A2
15 Hapa Hapa...C3
    Moonrise.....................................(see 11)
16 Olympic Restaurant D7
17 Whispers Cafe....................................D6

⊛ Shopping
    Baraka Gallery..............................(see 17)
18 Old Town Art & Crafts........................B1
19 Slim Silversmith.................................B3

ⓘ Information
20 Ibnusina Clinic....................................D7
21 Kenya Commercial Bank.....................C4
22 Lamu Immigration Office.....................C5

excellent views over the town and waterfront. The rooms are spacious and nicely decorated, and it's easily one of the better-value options in town.

Amu House B&B $
(☑ 0792558449, 0717308131; www.amuhouse kenya.com; s/d/tr KSh2500/3500/2500; ❄) A winner during the hottest months, this beautifully restored 16th-century Swahili house is one of the coolest places on the island. Friendly manager/musician Kesh houses his guests in seven rooms, decked out in traditional style, and there's a breezy rooftop chill-out terrace with hammocks for relaxation. No wi-fi just yet.

Subira House GUESTHOUSE $$
(☑ 0726916686, 0707293832; www.subirahouse. com; s/d from KSh6000/9000; ❄☎) 🍃 This Swedish-owned property features graceful arches and twin gardens with wells. The Sultan of Zanzibar knew a thing or two about style when he built the house 200 years ago. As well as seven stylish bedrooms (the ones at the top are smaller but brighter and breezier), there are relaxing common spaces and serious eco-credentials. We rate the restaurant highly.

Jannat House HOTEL $$
(☑ 0708569892, 0714969831; www.jannathouse lamu.com; s/d US$39/59; ☎☎) This old merchant's house gives the impression of genteel decay, with creeping plants taking over the inner courtyard. The main draws here are the pool and the bar, both rare luxuries on the Lamu guesthouse scene. Rooms on

the upper floors are much better than those lower down. Various multiday dhow trips on offer.

★ Lamu House BOUTIQUE HOTEL $$$
(☑ 0792469577; www.lamuhouse.com; Harambee Ave; r US$150-200; ☎☎) In a town where every building wants to top the preservation stakes, Lamu House stands out. It consists of two fused Swahili villas. Each of its handful of rooms is individually decorated and comes with a breezy private terrace, while the common spaces are a riot of woodcarvings and art. The excellent Moonrise restaurant serves fine Swahili cuisine.

✕ Eating

Hapa Hapa INTERNATIONAL $
(☑ 0712526215; Harambee Ave; mains from KSh450; ⊗ 8am-11pm) For a decent but cheap feed right on the seafront, Hapa Hapa is a safe bet. It offers good seafood curries and substandard international fare, but the kitchen is clean and there's usually a good crowd around.

Bustani Café CAFE $
(☑ 0722859594; meals KSh350-600; ⊗ hours vary) This pretty garden cafe has tables set about a lily-bedecked pond. The small menu includes lots of healthy salads, smoothies and various snack foods. It also contains a decent bookshop.

★ Whispers Cafe CAFE $$
(Kenyatta Rd; mains KSh400-950; ⊗ 9am-2pm & 4-6.30pm Mon-Sat; ☎) You know how sometimes you just need that escape into the

🏃 Town Walk
Lamu

START LAMU MAIN JETTY
FINISH LAMU MAIN JETTY
LENGTH APPROXIMATELY 4KM; ONE TO 1½ HOURS

The best, indeed only, way to see Lamu Town is on foot. Few experiences compare with exploring the far backstreets, where you can wander amid wafts of cardamom and carbolic and watch the town's agile cats scaling the coral walls. There are so many wonderful Swahili houses that it's pointless for us to recommend specific examples – keep your eyes open wherever you go, and don't forget to look up.

Starting at the ❶ **main jetty**, head north past the ❷ **Lamu Museum** (p256) and along the waterfront until you reach the ❸ **door-carving workshops**.

From here head onto Kenyatta Rd, passing an original Swahili ❹ **well**, and into the alleys towards the ❺ **Swahili House museum** (p257). Once you've had your fill of domestic insights, take any route back towards the main street.

After you've hit the main square and the ❻ **fort** (p257), take a right to see the crumbled remains of the 14th-century ❼ **Pwani Mosque**, one of Lamu's oldest buildings – an Arabic inscription is still visible on the wall. From here you can head round and browse the covered ❽ **market** (p257) then negotiate your way towards the bright, Saudi-funded ❾ **Riyadha Mosque**, the centre of Lamu's religious scene.

Now you can take as long or as short a route as you like back to the waterfront. Stroll along the promenade, diverting for the ❿ **German Post Office Museum** – the door is another amazing example of Swahili carving. If you're feeling the pace, take a rest and shoot the breeze on the ⓫ **baraza ya wazee** ('old men's bench') outside the stucco minarets of the ⓬ **Shiaithna-Asheri Mosque**.

Carrying on up Harambee Ave will bring you back to the main jetty.

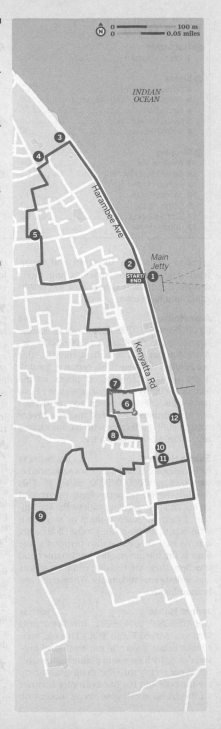

world of magazines and fresh pastries? Welcome to Whispers. For a real cappuccino, light meals, mega juices and smoothies, or the best desserts in town, this cafe with a garden, set in the same building as the Baraka Gallery, is just the ticket.

Olympic Restaurant
AFRICAN $$

(☏ 0728667692; Harambee Ave; mains KSh500-1000) The family that runs the Olympic makes you feel as if you've come home every time you enter, and their food, particularly the curries and biriyani, is excellent. There are few better ways to spend a Lamu night than with a cold mug of passion-fruit juice and the noir-ish view of the docks here, at the ramshackle end of town.

Tamarind Cafe
SEAFOOD $$

(☏ 0710500760; mains KSh600-1400; ☉noon-9pm) Built around a sturdy tamarind tree, this wonky tree house–restaurant overlooks the dhows on the waterfront. Lobster, prawns, squid and catch of the day are all present on the menu and simply prepared, and there's a friendly cat that'll climb all over you.

★ Moonrise
FUSION $$$

(☏ 0708073164; Harambee Ave, Lamu House; mains KSh900-1550; ☉7am-10pm; ☎) Particularly strong when it comes to seafood dishes and slightly set back from the waterfront, this is the best restaurant in town. Feast on the likes of fish tacos with mango salsa, ginger crab with coconut rice and such crowd pleasers as chicken and chips.

🛍 Shopping

★ Baraka Gallery
ART

(☏ 042-4633399; Kenyatta Rd; ☉9am-1pm & 3.30-6pm) This upmarket gallery is *the* place to come if you're a serious Africana collector. There are pieces from all over the continent and beyond, from affordable Kenyan belts with Maasai bead embroidery to ceremonial Yoruba masks, central African carvings, heavy Yemeni silver jewellery and gorgeous handwoven shell embroidery.

Slim Silversmith
JEWELLERY

(Kenyatta Rd; ☉9am-12.30pm & 2.30-6pm Mon-Sat) The most charismatic of the local silversmiths is a chap called Slim, whose silversmith shop sells beautiful rings created from ancient cuttings of coloured tiles.

Old Town Art & Crafts
ARTS & CRAFTS

(☏ 0715577614; Kenyatta Rd; ☉9am-6pm) This is a good place to shop for prints and paintings, handbags made from recycled materials, woven sisal bags and small Kenyan masks. The ebony woodcarvings of animals are best avoided as it's an endangered wood, often harvested illegally.

ℹ Information

DANGERS & ANNOYANCES

The biggest hassle is the constant stream of volunteers to be your guide. The beach boys will come at you the minute you step off the boat, offering drugs, tours and hotel bookings (for which they receive a commission), but a firm 'No, thanks' is usually sufficient. It can be worth having a guide to explore Lamu Town properly, but make sure it's a licensed guide. Recommendations from fellow travellers may be valuable.

The town's sanitation system is overtaxed by overpopulation. This can make for some hairy, stinky times of overflow (especially given all the donkey crap lying around) – watch your step here after it rains.

LGBT+ TRAVELLERS

Lamu has long been popular for its relaxed, tolerant atmosphere, but it does have Muslim views of what's acceptable behaviour. Whatever your sexuality, it's best to keep public displays of affection to a minimum and respect local attitudes to modesty.

MEDICAL SERVICES

Ibnusina Clinic (☏ 0721447985; Kenyatta Rd; ☉24hr) The best emergency and nonemergency medical care on the island.

MONEY

Local shopkeepers may be able to help with changing money.

Kenya Commercial Bank (Harambee Ave) The main bank on Lamu, with an ATM (Visa only). Several other ATMs along the waterfront.

POST

Post Office (Kenyatta Rd; ☉9am-5pm Mon-Fri, to 1pm Sat) Postal services and phonecards.

TOURIST INFORMATION

Rumour has it that a tourist office will open in the not too distant future somewhere along the waterfront. In the meantime, http://lamutourism.org is an excellent source of local info.

WOMEN TRAVELLERS

Female travellers should note that most Lamurians hold strong religious and cultural values and

DHOW TRIPS

More than the bustle of markets or the call to prayer, the pitch of 'We take dhow trip, see mangroves, eat fish and coconut rice' is the unyielding chorus of Lamu's voices when you first arrive. That said, taking a dhow trip (and seeing the mangroves and eating fish and coconut rice) is generally fun, though this depends to a large degree on your captain. Guesthouses such as Jambo House (p257) work with several reliable captains and it's good to get recommendations from other travellers. There's a real joy to kicking it on the boards under the sunny sky, with the mangroves drifting by in island time while snacking on spiced fish.

Trips include dhow racing excursions (learning how to tack and race these amazingly agile vessels is quite something), sunset sails, adventures to Kipungani and Manda Island, deep-reef fishing and even three-day trips south along the coast to Kilifi (from US$120 per person).

Prices vary, depending on where you want to go, who you go with and how long you go for. With bargaining you could pay around KSh2500 per person in a group of four or five people, on a half-day basis. Don't hand over any money until the day of departure, except perhaps a small advance for food. On long trips, it's best to organise your own drinks. A hat and sunscreen are essential.

may be deeply offended by revealing clothing. There have been some isolated incidents of rape, which locals say were sparked by tourists refusing to cover up. That may outrage some Western ears, but the fact remains that you risk getting into trouble if you walk around in small shorts and low-cut tops. There are kilometres of deserted beaches on which you can walk around butt naked if you choose, but we urge you to respect cultural norms in built-up areas.

Getting There & Away

AIR

Lamu Airport is on Manda Island, and boats across the channel to Lamu cost KSh100. You'll be met by 'guides' at the airport who will offer to carry your bags to the hotel of your choice for a small consideration (about KSh200). Many double as touts, so be cautious about accepting the first price you're quoted when you get to your hotel.

There are several daily flights to Nairobi (from US$108, two hours) with Fly540 (www.fly540. com), Airkenya (www.airkenya.com), Skyward Express (www.skywardexpress.co.ke) and Safarilink (www.flysafarilink.com). Safarilink and Airkenya fly to Nairobi Wilson. A single Skyward Express flight serves Mombasa (US$80, 45 minutes, daily) while Fly540 and Fly-SAX (www. fly-sax.com) fly daily to Malindi (US$45, 30 minutes).

BUS

There are booking offices for the main bus companies either on Kenyatta Rd or along the waterfront. Buses leave from the jetty on the mainland and dock at Lamu's main jetty. The going rate for a trip to Mombasa (eight to nine hours) is KSh1100 to KSh1300. Most buses leave between 7am and 8am (11am and 1pm departures with Tawakal); the first connecting *mtabotis* (motorboat taxis) leave Lamu Town between 6am and 6.30am. Book bus tickets in advance and be on time; buses leave on the dot and will resell the seats of late-coming passengers further up the line. The most reliable companies are **Simba** (☑ 0707471110, 0707471111; off Kenyatta Rd), **Tahmeed** (☑ 0724581015, 0724581004; Kenyatta Rd) and **Tawakal** (☑ 0705090122; Kenyatta Rd); Tawakal is the fastest.

At the time of writing, armed guards were on every Lamu-bound bus from Mombasa and all vehicles were required to travel in convoy between Witu and Garsen.

Coming from Mombasa to Lamu, buses will drop you at the mainland jetty at Mokowe. From there you can either catch a *mtaboti* (KSh100, 30 minutes) or a speedboat (KSh150, 10 minutes). Don't listen to touts who try to tell you that you need to charter your own *mtaboti*.

Getting Around

Boats to the airstrip on Manda Island (KSh100) leave from the **main jetty** (Harambee Ave) about an hour before the flights leave. In theory, you have to be at the airport an hour before your flight.

Plenty of motorised dhows run to Shela throughout the day until around sunset from the **new jetty** (Harambee Ave); these cost about KSh100 per person if you share a boat with others or KSh500 if you don't. After dark, boat captains charge KSh1500 between Lamu Town and Shela.

There are also daily boats between Lamu and Paté Island (KSh200 to KSh250, two hours).

Shela

📍 042

The destination of choice of the majority of tourists who come to Lamu Island, Shela is like a smaller version of Lamu Town put through a high-end wringer, with the presence of artists, designers and yoga retreats adding a bohemian touch. It's a cleaner, more compact warren of dirt and sand streets, with a lot more expats, numerous lodgings and the best dining in the Lamu archipelago. Another plus is the long, lovely stretch of beach and a link to a specific slice of coast culture – the locals speak a distinct dialect, of which they're quite proud.

◉ Sights & Activities

There's reasonable windsurfing in the channel between Shela and Manda Island, while the water-sports centre at Peponi Hotel (p264) runs all kinds of activities of the damp sort, including diving, snorkelling, windsurfing and kayaking.

★ Shela Beach   BEACH

Most people are here for the beach – a 12km-long, wide sweep of pristine white sand where you're guaranteed an isolated spot (at least if you're prepared to walk some way) to catch some rays. Swimming is possible, but there are places with strong rip currents – particularly around The Fort hotel (p264) – so get some local advice before venturing into the water.

🛏 Sleeping

Shella White House   B&B $
(☑ 0722698059; s/d KSh2900/4200; ❄️ 🛜 🏊) Terrific value, and just metres away from the beach, this centrally located B&B comprises a clutch of snug rooms with four-poster beds and a breezy rooftop terrace. There's pool access as well, and a delicious breakfast thrown in.

Dudu Villas & Lamu Backpackers   HOSTEL $
(☑ 0729906827, 0717081488; www.facebook.com/duduvillasbackpackers; camping KSh500, dm/s/d KSh1200/1500/2600; ❄️ 🛜) This place is as budget as it gets in Shela, with room for

several tents inside the large, sandy garden, and several anonymous-looking, fan-cooled dorms with mosquito nets and porches.

★ Jua House   B&B $$
(☑ 0796517937; www.juahouse.com; s/d KSh5700/7300, ste KSh10,300; ❄️ 🛜) This five-storey house rises above the sleepy, donkey-filled alleyways of Shela. Apart from the warm welcome and plenty of advice from owner Thomas and his staff, there's a fantastic rooftop terrace with all-encompassing views, chill-out spaces and seven tastefully decorated, spotless rooms. The rooftop suite with private terrace is a worthy splurge.

Fatuma's Tower   BOUTIQUE HOTEL $$
(☑ 0722277138; www.fatumastower.com; s/d from €50/95; ❄️ 🛜 🏊) 🐾 This restored 200-year-old tower, once owned by a Swahili noblewoman, is a peaceful yoga retreat at the back of the village. The 10 rooms are individually decorated and decked out with antiques, with solar-powered showers. There's a small plunge pool and the healthy meals, big on seafood and fresh fruit, get rave reviews from guests.

Banana House & Wellness Centre   BOUTIQUE HOTEL $$
(☑ 0721275538, 0722618574; www.bananahouse-lamu.com; s/d US$89/129, penthouse US$185-239; ❄️ 🛜 🏊) 🐾 Arranged around a tranquil, flower-filled courtyard with a small pool, this is Lamu's premier yoga retreat and is a generally tranquil place to while away a few days. The 16 rooms are bright and airy; we love the recycled glass art, cosy nooks for relaxing in and the open-air massage terrace, and the Kenyan-Dutch owners arrange quality tours of Lamu.

Bahari Guest House   GUESTHOUSE $$
(☑ 0722901643; info@shellabahari.co.ke; s/d KSh6000/8000; ❄️ 🛜) Right on the seafront as you round the corner to Peponi, a clutch of whitewashed, self-contained rooms with heavy four-poster beds catches the sea breeze. Snap up a room facing the ocean if you can. During the low season prices are negotiable.

Stopover Guest House   GUESTHOUSE $$
(☑ 0731398895; s/d from KSh5200/6200, ste KSh10,400; ❄️ 🛜) If walking to Shela from Lamu Town, one of the first places you come to on the waterfront is this beautiful

guesthouse of pure-white unfussy lines. Rooms are spacious, airy, bright and crisp, and a salt wind through your carved window shutters is the best alarm clock imaginable. It's above the popular restaurant of the same name.

★**Kijani Hotel** BOUTIQUE HOTEL **$$$**
(☑0733545264, 0725545264; www.kijani-lamu. com; s/d €139/199; ✹🛜🛏) With 10 spacious, palatially decorated rooms scattered across three traditional Swahili houses and overlooking the beach, this tranquil spot sits in the shade of centuries-old baobab trees. Luxuriant tropical gardens, two pools and one of the best restaurants in Lamu – serving clever fusion food and doubling as an art gallery – make this an excellent upmarket choice.

★**Peponi Hotel** BOUTIQUE HOTEL **$$$**
(☑0703790411, 0722203082; www.peponi-lamu. com; s/d from US$220/280; ☺closed May & Jun; ✹🛜🛏) 🏊 Wonderfully situated right on the waterfront, this is the beating heart of Shela. Owner Carol knows everything there is to know about Lamu (and provides her guests with handy maps); the 28 characterful, Swahili-style rooms (some with private terraces) all face the sea; the staff arrange all manner of water sports; and the restaurant is the best in Lamu. Winner.

On top of all that, the hotel is responsible for the sea turtle protection project on Manda Island; stop by and talk to Famau about it.

The Fort BOUTIQUE HOTEL **$$$**
(www.thefortshela.com; d from US$215; ✹🛜) Built to resemble an Omani-style fort and fully staffed, this former private home overlooks a deserted stretch of Shela Beach. Its glorious isolation, its somewhat rustic rooms and the intermittent electricity are of considerable appeal to those who come to switch off. Bring a torch for the 10-minute evening walk into the village. Online bookings only.

✖ Eating

Luq Tabassam Cafe KENYAN **$**
(samosas KSh200; ☺9am-6pm) This craftshop-cum-cafe serves the tastiest samosas in Lamu – spicy, flavourful triangles with vegetable, prawn or meat filling. Wash them down with a tamarind juice.

Rangaleni Café KENYAN **$**
(meals KSh250-400; ☺noon-9pm Mon-Sat) The best of the Shela cheapies. Hidden away in the alleys behind the shorefront mosque, this tiny greeny-turquoise cafe does the usual stews and ugali (a staple made from maize or cassava flour, or both).

Sea Suq KENYAN **$$**
(mains KSh400-900; ☺11.30am-9pm) Casual little cafe that serves good samosas and other snacks, and more substantial mains such as Swahili pizzas and seafood, chicken or mutton biriyani.

Stopover Restaurant SEAFOOD **$$**
(☑0731398895; mains KSh700-1700; ☺noon-10pm) There are waterfront restaurants all over the place, but the Stopover's friendly staff and excellent grub (of the spicy Swahili-seafood sort) make it a cut above the competition, particularly the seafood curries. Great fruit juices, too.

★**Peponi** FUSION **$$$**
(☑0722203082; mains KSh1000-2950; ☺noon-2.30pm & 7-11pm; 🛜) We're still waxing lyrical about our last meal at this amazing restaurant. Choose between global offerings, such as tuna ceviche, Philly cheese steak sandwich and BBQ fish, or get your fill of mostly Italian dishes, such as gnocchi with wild mushrooms. The chocolate cake with pistachio ice cream is worth every penny.

★**Kijani Restaurant** FUSION **$$$**
(☑0733545264; mains KSh1150-1500; ☺12.30-2.30pm & 7-10pm) On the premises of Kijani Hotel, this excellent new restaurant has a daily changing menu that combines fresh local ingredients with global influences. Go on, treat yourself to Tahitian-style fish, miso-grilled aubergine or tamarind crab. Eat surrounded by local art or on the breezy, semiprivate terrace overlooking the sea.

🍷 Drinking & Nightlife

Peponi's Bar BAR
(☑0722203082; ☺noon-late) Naturally, the bar at a Swiss-owned Kenyan hotel with an Italian name has to resemble an English pub. Pretty much everyone on Shela finds their way to the sunset-watching terrace to happily drift into insolvency over a pricey but expertly mixed sundowner or three.

🔒 Shopping

In contrast to Lamu Town, famed for its heavier traditional crafts such as woodwork, Shela has a high concentration of shops that focus more on high-quality clothing, jewellery, unusual gifts and accessories.

Rift   FASHION & ACCESSORIES
(📞0700337534; www.rift-africa.com; ⊘9am-5.30pm Mon-Sat) Beautiful handmade leather bags, wallets and belts.

Baraka Gallery   ARTS & CRAFTS
(⊘10.30am-1.30pm & 3-6pm) Some beautiful, high-end masks from Central and West Africa of interest to serious collectors, plus more affordable items such as beautiful cutlery, jewellery and handbags embroidered with cowrie shells.

4Shore   FASHION & ACCESSORIES
(www.4shore.org; ⊘9am-2pm & 3-6pm) Kenyan-made clothing, from T-shirts by 4Shore to colourful shirts by Duka, plus clever gifts made of baobab seed pods by Seedling.

Leah's Designs   ARTS & CRAFTS
(📞0726049202; ⊘10am-6pm Mon-Sat) Handmade *kikois* (woven cloths) made by Leah herself (from KSh600), plus a selection of handbags and beaded sandals.

Aman   FASHION & ACCESSORIES
(📞0733455821; ⊘9am-1pm & 2.30-6pm) High-end fashion and accessories by Kenyan designers. You can also get your garments tailored to order.

ℹ️ Information

DANGERS & ANNOYANCES

It's not advisable to walk between Shela and Lamu Town after dark, as muggings occasionally occur. Don't take valuables with you if venturing on a long walk along Shela Beach. There are dangerous rip tides around the Fort hotel, a short walk along the beach from Shela proper.

If you find yourself wandering Shela's warren of streets, local children will helpfully enquire if you're lost and then solicit financial contributions for giving you directions. Ignore them.

TOURIST INFORMATION

A comprehensive source of info on all things Lamu is http://lamutourism.org.

ℹ️ Getting There & Away

You can take a motorised dhow here from the new jetty in Lamu (KSh100 per person if you share the boat, KSh500 if it's just you). Alternatively, you can walk it in about 40 minutes along the waterfront road and shoreline. Evening boats between Shela and Lamu charge KSh1500. Boats directly to the airport cost KSh1000.

Matondoni & Kipungani

🎵 042

The best place to see dhows being built is the village of **Matondoni**, in the island's northwest. It's a peaceful little fishing village that receives few visitors, so the welcome is always warm.

Kipungani, 'the place of fresh air', is a small village at Lamu Island's southwest tip where locals make straw mats, baskets, hats and *kifumbu* (woven strainer), used to squeeze milk from mashed coconut. Tea and snacks can be arranged and there's the beautiful, empty Kizingo Beach nearby.

This part of the island also offers some of Kenya's best kitesurfing, though you'll have to bring your own gear. There's no backdrop quite like it.

🛏️ Sleeping

⭐ Kizingo   BANDAS $$$
(📞0722901544, 0712575261; www.kizingo.com; s/d full board US$180/240; 🅿️@🛜🎬) 🏴 The owners describe this beautiful spot as 'no news, no shoes', which says it all really. It's at the end of the 12km stretch of beach that begins in Shela (a little beyond Kipungani). The bar serves up refreshing cocktails, the food is healthy and hip, and hostess Mary-Jo always has great stories to tell.

Kipungani Explorer   BANDAS $$$
(📞0722903152; www.heritage-eastafrica.com; s/d full board from US$277/410; ⊘Jul-Mar; 🛜🎬) 🏴 This resort is quite luxurious, in a rustic, end-of-the-world, *banda*-on-the-beach kind of way. The 13 *bandas* are made solely of local materials, and nonmotorised water sports and kiddie-friendly activities are included in the price. The resort deserves a shout-out for employing local villagers as staff, funding school projects, experimenting with solar and wind power, and sourcing food from village fishermen.

ℹ️ Getting There & Away

It's possible to walk to Kipungani from Shela (four hours), but it's a long, exposed and hot walk. Kipungani is an hour's walk from Matondoni, but the path can be hard to find. A boat from Shela costs around KSh2000.

Manda Island

Manda is a quiet lattice of dune and mangroves a short hop and jump across from Shela. The island has just started to feel the claws of development, and the appealing long beach facing Lamu is backed by a couple of places to stay and several huge private villas. Beyond the beach, traditional life continues unabated in a local fishing village, and a small Orma settlement looks after a Shela-based green turtle conservation project that visitors can take part in. And if you take a dhow or speedboat to the Takwa ruins, particularly atmospheric around sunset, you can visualise a once-great city that once dominated this peaceful backwater.

👁 Sights

★ Takwa Ruins
RUINS

(adult/child KSh500/250; ⊘ 6.30am-6pm) What sets these ruins, the remains of a city that existed between the 15th and 17th centuries, apart from other archaeological sites on the coast? Quiet. When you're here and the light shatters in the trees, which have grown over some 100 ruined Mecca-aligned houses, you feel as if the ruins are speaking to you in the breeze. The ruins are only reachable during high tide; boat trips from Shela cost around KSh5000 for up to four people.

🏃 Activities

Lamu Marine Conservation Trust
WILDLIFE WATCHING

(http://tusk.org/lamu-marine-conservation-project; turtle hatching trip per person KSh1500) 🕭 Started in 1992 by the owners of Peponi Hotel (p264) in Shela, this excellent project works with local fishing communities to conserve endangered sea turtle species of the Lamu archipelago. Turtles are monitored, tagged and released into the sea, and visitors may witness the life-affirming turtle hatchings and release on Manda Island in July and August.

Manda Toto Island
SNORKELLING

Just off the northeast coast of Manda is Manda Toto Island, which offers some of the best snorkelling possibilities in the archipelago. The only way to get here is by dhow – a full day (there and back) from Lamu typically costs around KSh5500 for up to four people.

🛏 Sleeping

Diamond Beach Village
BANDAS $$

(⤸0720915001; www.diamondbeachvillage.com; s/d KSh5000/10,000; 🕭) This is one of those Robinson Crusoe–style hideouts; but don't worry, that doesn't mean it's basic. The breezy, en-suite, coconut-thatch and mangrove wood *bandas* (thatched-roof huts) are adorned with driftwood and shell art. If you want a different view of the world, opt for the eccentric tree house perched in the branches of an old baobab tree.

★ Majlis
RESORT $$$

(⤸0773777066, 0708073126; www.themajlis resorts.com; per person full board from US$210; P🅿❄@🛜🏊) From the acacia-tree-shaded pool overlooked by a hookah bar to the daring driftwood-and-metal sculptures that dot the property, this luxury resort dazzles with its style and amenities. All rooms are spacious, with Swahili-style beds, splashes of contemporary art, rain-shower bathrooms and relaxation terraces. A spa and all manner of water sports are on offer. Glassed-in rooms are the only downside.

Manda Bay
RESORT $$$

(⤸0712579999, 0713785152; www.mandabay. com; r from KSh15,000) This luxury resort on the northern end of the island benefits from the wonderfully tranquil location, the hospitality of gregarious Debbie and Fuzz, and wonderfully comfortable, spacious rooms, decorated in Swahili style. The food (including vegetarian options) is highly rated by guests and numerous water sports keep the active busy. Also arranges boat trips to Takwa ruins.

ℹ Getting There & Away

The trip across to Manda from Shela takes five minutes and costs KSh300. From Lamu Town it's more likely to be around KSh600.

Paté Island

Paté is a tranquil island of green brush, silver tidal flats and coconut trees, bisected by red dirt tracks. You can walk over the island in about seven hours (excluding lots of stopping time for chats and cups of tea with locals).

As isolated from the modern world as Paté is, this was once the dominant island of the archipelago. 'None who go to Paté returns; what returns is wailing', goes one archipelago song. Whether this refers to military battles or the slave trade that was conducted through here is unknown, but the warning certainly doesn't apply now – most people return from Paté with a peaceful smile.

You're likely to experience great hospitality here – residents are either not used to tourists and consider them a happy novelty, or work in the tourism industry in Lamu and appreciate you making the effort to come all the way out here.

◉ Sights

To get the most out of a trip to Paté Island, it's well worth having a little local help. Mansur Ile (p268) is a top guide to the island's historical sites; Lamu Museum may also be able to arrange guides. It's best to arrange this in advance.

Nabahani Ruins

RUINS

(◷24hr) Located just outside Paté Town, these ruins are slowly vanishing under a riot of tropical vegetation and banana plantations. There is nothing to stop you from wandering among the tombs, ancient mosques and other crumbling buildings, with local farmers growing edible crops and

tobacco in the plots between the ruins. It's worth getting a guide in advance to point out the **Mosque with the Two Mihrabs** and the remains of a **Portuguese house**.

At night, no local will venture into the ruins because they fear the djinn (guardian spirits) rumoured to inhabit them. Lamu Museum (p256) may be able to organise a guide.

Shanga
ARCHAEOLOGICAL SITE

(◷24hr) **FREE** Shanga, south of the village of Siyu, is the world's most complete example of a medieval Swahili town. Arguably the oldest archaeological site on the Kenyan coast, it includes the ruins or foundations of some 130 houses and 300 tombs. Be on the lookout for a 21-sided pillar tomb topped by a 15th-century celadon bowl, five town gates, 'Lamu' arches constructed of sandstone bedrock, coral ragstone and sand gathered from the nearby dunes, and tablets marked with Arabic inscriptions.

Siyu
VILLAGE

It's hard to believe today that Siyu was once the major city of the Lamu archipelago, with 30,000 inhabitants and several major universities. The only remnant of this glory is an enormous intact **fort**, which, given its emergence from the abandoned mangrove

LAMU & THE NORTH COAST PATÉ ISLAND

SWAHILI ARCHITECTURE

The Swahili culture has produced one of the most distinctive forms of architecture in Africa, if not the world. Once considered a stepchild of Arabic building styles, Swahili architecture, while owing some of its aesthetic to the Middle East, is more accurately a reflection of African design, partly influenced by the Arab (and Persian, Indian and even Mediterranean) worlds.

One of the most important concepts of Swahili space is marking the line between the public and private, while also occasionally blurring those borders. So, for example, you'll see Lamu stoops (semicovered doorway areas or porches) that exist in the public arena of the street but also serve as a pathway into the private realm of the home. The use of stoops as a place for conversation further blends these inner and outer worlds. Inside the home the emphasis is on creating an airy, natural interior that contrasts with the exterior's constricting network of narrow streets. The use of open space also facilitates breezes that serve as natural air-conditioning.

You will find large courtyards, day beds placed on balconies and porches that all provide a sense of horizon within a town where the streets can only accommodate a single donkey. Other elements include dakas (verandahs), which again sit in the transitional zone between the street and home and also provide open areas; vidaka (wall niches) that either contain a small decorative curio or serve a decorative purpose in their own right; and mambrui (pillars), which are used extensively in Swahili mosques.

Also note how the 'front' of a house tends to face north. This may be because of the Muslim concept of qiblah, the direction towards Mecca in which Muslims are supposed to pray (a Swahili term for north is upande ya kibla). Or it may be for sunlight protection.

and coconut forest, is quite dramatic. Today Siyu is a small village with a whole lot of donkeys. Locals will happily put you up with a meal for about KSh500 to KSh600.

Paté
VILLAGE

Paté vllage, on the west side of the island, is a maze of streets carved out of orange and brown coral ragstone. The modern village itself is almost identical in design and construction to the nearby ruins and, in fact, the two merge almost seamlessly into one another. A footpath leads down from Kitokwe (upper town) to Mitaaguu (lower town), where the dhows and boats to Lamu dock.

Faza
VILLAGE

Connected to the mainland by a causeway, the biggest settlement on the island has a chequered history. Faza was almost totally destroyed by the Paté town citizens in the 13th century, then again by the Portuguese in 1586 or 1587 (accounts differ, but it is known that the Portuguese chopped off the local sheik's head and preserved it in salt). With the demise of slavery, Faza faded away, but its status as an administrative centre is breathing some life back into the place.

⟨⟩ Tours

Mansur Ile
TOUR

(☑ 0717165311) A top guide to the island's historical sites, Mansur Ile worked on many of the original excavations, knows the island intimately and speaks superb English. Contact him in advance.

🛏 Sleeping

Chundwa Ecolodge Homestay
HOMESTAY

(Chundwa) This friendly homestay between Faza and Kizingitini is run by a helpful family that can organise trips around Paté Island.

Umra Homestay
HOMESTAY

(☑ 0715555581; Chundwa) This place gives travellers a good taste of village life.

Pwani Guest Gouse
GUESTHOUSE $

(☑ 0722523885, 0704767925; Faza; r KSh500) The Ritz it ain't, but it is the only place to stay in Faza. It's right on the waterfront and the clutch of simple rooms (with mosquito nets) catch the breeze. And, amazingly, some of the rooms are en suite (though they wouldn't pass a white-glove inspection). Talk to the young owner about getting meals organised.

ⓘ Information

The only two mobile phone networks that work on Paté are Safaricom and Orange.

ⓘ Getting There & Away

There is usually at least one public boat daily from Lamu to Mtangawanda (KSh200, two hours). Some boats continue to Faza (KSh250, another two hours) and Kizingitini (an additional KSh150, another hour), also stopping at the mouth of the channel to Siyu (KSh100), where small boats transfer passengers to shore. Boats leave from the main jetty in Lamu Town. Times depend on the tides, but it can be tricky finding out when they go, as everyone you ask will tell you something different! It's normally around one or two hours before high tide. At research time, boats were leaving around 4am both from Lamu and Paté.

Coming back from Paté, there is usually one daily boat from Mtangawanda and another that originates in Faza and calls at Mtangawanda, where the crew play 'How Many People Can You Fit In One Boat'. The journey can be cramped and life jackets absent.

A bunch of matatus meet the boats and run to Paté Town (KSh100), Siyu (KSh150), Faza (KSh200) and other villages.

ⓘ Getting Around

There are few vehicles on the island and the matatus are very infrequent. Your best bet is to take a matatu from the boat dock to the village where you'll be staying and organise transport around the island from there. You can usually get someone to take you around on the back of a motorbike for around KSh1000 to KSh1500 for a few hours. Walking is also an option if you have plenty of time.

Kiwayu Island
☑ 042

Cut by a dazzling white sandbar and stippled with rocks that are home to huge oysters, Kiwayu is a wonder. At the far northeast end of the archipelago, Kiwayu has a population of a couple of hundred people and is part of the Kiunga Marine National Reserve. Gloriously remote, it's a long, narrow ridge of sand and baobab trees surrounded by reefs, with a long beach stretching down the eastern side of the island. Standing at the tallest point and surveying your surroundings at sunset will probably be one of the defining experiences of your time on the coast.

Three things draw travellers here: the glorious isolation, the striking scenery – from the rugged hilltop views to the baobab- and coconut-tree-studded beaches – and friendly, low-key local culture. For those who like to take it slow, the three-day dhow trip from Lamu, with dugong, sea turtle and dolphin sightings, is another highlight.

👁 Sights & Activities

Kiunga Marine
National Reserve   MARINE RESERVE
(www.kws.go.ke; entry adult/child US$17/13) This stunning, little-visited marine reserve covers 270 sq km and includes beautiful coral reefs. The reefs are ideal for snorkelling and whale sharks can be spotted in season. You need to charter a boat to get out here.

🛏 Sleeping

Abubakar Khatib Ali   HOMESTAY $
(☑0703776307; Kiwayu Village; per person KSh1000) Friendly Abu puts up travellers at his humble home and can arrange home-cooked meals.

Kaka Mutua Isaguu   HOMESTAY $$
(☑0702719274; Kiwayu Village; per person KSh3000) On the edge of Kiwayu village, this local couple have a basic twin room and a couple of spartan thatched huts for rent at rather optimistic prices. Meals included.

★ Mike's Camp   BANDAS $$$
(☑0724262816; www.mikescampkiwayu.com; Kiwayu; r per person from US$200; @ 🕿) 🍴
From its blustery hilltop location, seven spacious, glorious *bandas* made from all-natural materials with ecofriendly bucket showers look down at the ocean. There's a breezy common area with books on Kenya's wildlife, and owner Mike organises numerous activities, from waterskiing and kiting to ocean kayaking and deep-sea fishing. Speedboat pickups from Lamu arranged.

Champali Camp   BANDAS $$$
(☑0723487145; www.champali.co.ke; Kiwayu; whole camp KSh28,000) Overlooking a mangrove creek towards the southern end of the island, this camp is ideal for groups or families on a dhow sailing trip. You pay for the whole camp, which can host up to 10 people in three comfortable *bandas*, each with coconut-palm thatching.

ℹ Getting There & Away

If you'd like to travel (slowly, slowly) by dhow, you can arrange this on Lamu. Three-night trips cost between KSh50,000 and KSh70,000, including food, fuel, snorkelling gear and two nights on Kiwayu. A return journey by speedboat from Lamu will set you back around KSh25,000 and around KSh6500 from Paté Island. There are no public boats between Lamu and Kiwayu; you can take a public boat to Paté, from where unscheduled boats run between the two islands every other day or so, depending on the locals' needs.

Northern Kenya

Includes ➡

Isiolo 271

Samburu, Buffalo
Springs & Shaba
National Reserves . . .275

Marsabit 279

Marsabit
National Park 281

Moyale 282

Maralal 284

South Horr 287

Lake Turkana 288

Loyangalani 288

Lodwar 292

Best Places to Eat

➡ Saku Guest House (p281)

➡ Sasaab Lodge (p279)

➡ Cradle Tented Camp (p293)

Best Places to Stay

➡ Desert Rose (p287)

➡ Cradle Tented Camp (p293)

➡ Sasaab Lodge (p279)

➡ Elephant Watch Camp (p277)

Why Go?

Calling all explorers! We dare you to challenge yourself against some of the most exciting wilderness in Africa. Step forward only if you're able to withstand appalling roads, searing heat, clouds of dust torn by relentless winds, primitive food and accommodation, vast distances and more than a hint of danger.

The rewards include memories of vast, shattered lava deserts, camel herders walking their animals to lost oases, fog-shrouded mountains full of mysterious creatures, pre-historic islands crawling with massive reptiles, and jokes shared with traditionally dressed warriors. Additional perks include camel trekking through piles of peachy dunes, elephant encounters in scrubby acacia woodlands and the chance to walk barefoot along the fabled shores of a sea of jade.

When to Go
Loyangalani

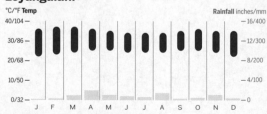

Jun Head to Loyangalani for the Lake Turkana Festival.

Aug Saddle up a camel and race through the Maralal International Camel Derby.

Nov–Dec It's marginally cooler in the northern deserts.

ISIOLO TO MOYALE

For most people this route means one of two things: the wildlife riches of the Samburu ecosystem, or the road to the cultural riches of Ethiopia. But in between and beyond, this area has much more to offer. You can drink tea and track wildlife with the Samburu people, climb mist-shrouded volcanoes in the desert, blaze trails in untrammelled mountains and get so far off the beaten track you'll start to wonder whether you're still on the same planet. All told, this massive wilderness offers something to anyone whose heart sings with adventure.

Isiolo

☑ 064 / POP 143,294

Isiolo is where anticipation and excitement first start to send your heart aflutter. This vital pit stop on the long road north to Ethiopia from central Kenya is a true frontier town, a place on the edge, torn between the cool, verdant highlands just to the south and the scorching badlands – home of nomads and bandits – to the north. On a more practical note, it's also the last place with decent facilities until Maralal or Marsabit.

Among the first things you'll undoubtedly notice is the large Somali population (descendants of WWI veterans who settled here) and the striking faces of Boran, Samburu and Turkana people walking the streets. It's this mix of people, cultures and religions that's the most interesting thing about Isiolo. Nowhere is this mixture better illustrated than in the hectic market.

🛏 Sleeping

Rangeland Hotel COTTAGE $
(☑0710114030; A2 Hwy; camping per person KSh1000, s/d bungalow KSh4000/5000; P🛜) About 4km south of town, this is a nice option for those with their own set of wheels. The sunny campground has bickering weaver birds and busy rock hyraxes in abundance, as well as neat-and-tidy stone bungalows with hot showers. Many people come to laze around in the gardens at the weekend, but during the week it's quiet.

Moti Peal Hotel HOTEL $
(☑064-5352400; www.moti.co.ke; s/d KSh2500/3500; 🛜) This smart place markets itself as the 'Pearl of Isiolo'. This actually says more about the state of Isiolo than the quality of

the hotel, but even so it's very clean, well run and has friendly management.

Josera Guest House HOTEL $
(☑0728059274; r KSh1500-2000) Excellent-value sky-blue rooms that range from tiny cubes to those large enough to swing a backpack. All have hot showers and there's a decent in-house restaurant.

Bomen Hotel HOTEL $
(☑0721698849; Great North Rd; s/tw KSh2500/3500; P🛜) The NGOs' favourite home, the Bomen Hotel has the town's most toe-curlingly frilly pink bed sheets! It also has TVs, shared terraces with views and unfailingly polite staff.

🍴 Eating

101 Supermarket SUPERMARKET $
(⊙8am-6pm) Northbound self-caterers should head here for provisions, as there's very little available elsewhere. The supermarket doesn't have lots of fresh food though, so best to head to the daily market near the mosque for that.

Bomen Hotel KENYAN $$
(☑0721698849; meals KSh400-650; ⊙6am-10.30pm; 🛜) A rare place serving more than the local usuals, with fried tilapia (Nile perch), pepper steak, goulash and curries up for grabs. Has an attached bar with comfy couches and cheap beer.

ⓘ Information

Banks are scarce in the north, so plan ahead.
Barclays (Hospital Rd; ⊙9am-4pm Mon-Fri, to noon Sat) With an ATM.
Kenya Commercial Bank (Hospital Rd; ⊙8.30am-3pm Mon-Fri, to noon Sat) With an ATM and foreign exchange.

ⓘ Getting There & Away

AIR
At the time of research, the **Isiolo International Airport** (HKIS; ☑0728165349) had just opened but was not yet operational. Passenger flights were slated to be available from Nairobi in late 2017. The airport is also supposed to offer international flights to Somalia and South Sudan.

BUS & MATATU
Most of the bus companies serve Nairobi (KSh600, 4½ hours), with buses generally leaving between 5.30am and 6.30am from outside their respective offices on the main road through town. They also stop at the matatu and bus stand just south of the market.

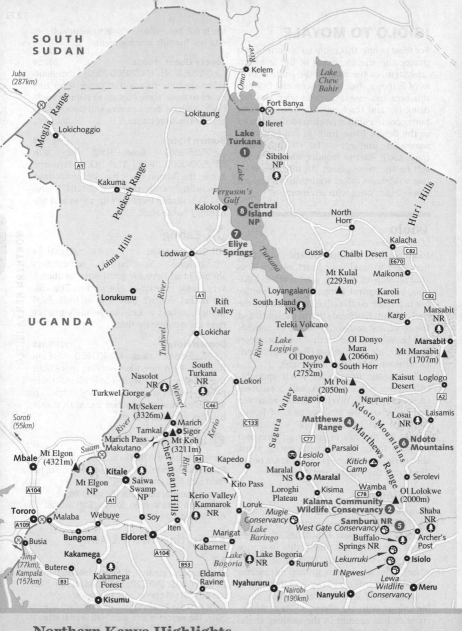

Northern Kenya Highlights

1 Lake Turkana (p288)
Blasting over the plains of darkness to this 'Sea of Jade'.

2 Kalama Community Wildlife Conservancy (p278)
Enjoying a private slab of wild Africa.

3 Marsabit National Park (p281) Searching for forest elephants in an ocean of sand.

4 Matthews Range (p279)
Exploring the remote and little-visited forests.

5 Samburu National Reserve (p275) Realising that zebras *do* change their

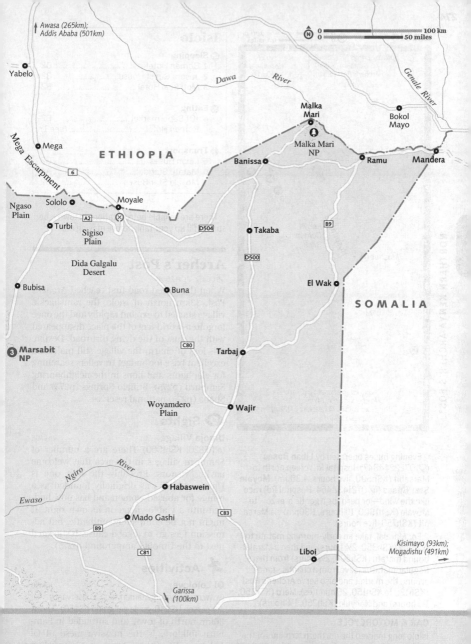

Awasa (265km);
Addis Ababa (501km)

Dawa River

Genale River

Yabelo

Malka Mari

Bokol Mayo

Mega

E T H I O P I A

Malka Mari NP

Mega Escarpment

Banissa

Ramu

Mandera

6

Ngaso Plain

Sololo

Moyale

Turbi

A2

Sigiso Plain

D504

Takaba

B9

Dida Galgalu Desert

Bubisa

Buna

D500

El Wak

S O M A L I A

③ Marsabit NP

C80

Tarbaj

Woyamdero Plain

Wajir

Ngiro River

Habaswein

C83

Ewaso

Mado Gashi

B9

C81

Liboi

Kisimayo (93km);
Mogadishu (491km)

Garissa (100km)

stripes, and ostriches change
their legs.

⑥ Ndoto Mountains (p279)
Leading your camel to water
during a camel safari.

⑦ Eliye Springs (p293)
Relaxing under palm trees on
remote sandy shores.

**⑧ Central Island National
Park** (p294) Having an

adventure surrounded by
14,000 Nile crocodiles.

Isiolo

N
0 — 200 m
0 — 0.1 miles

Buffalo Springs NR (28km);
Samburu (28km);
Archer's Post (33km)
A2

District
Hospital
(350m)

Barclays $
5
7

4 2
X
1
3

Hospital Rd

Kenya
Commercial
Bank

Mosque

A2

6

Isiolo International ✈ (2km);
Rangeland Hotel (4km);
Lewa Wildlife Conservancy (12km);
Il Ngwesi (32km)

Isiolo

Sleeping
1 Bomen Hotel..B2
2 Josera Guest House............................B2
3 Moti Peal Hotel B2

Eating
4 101 Supermarket..................................B2
Bomen Hotel.................................(see 1)

Transport
5 Liban Buses...B2
6 Matatu Stand.......................................A4
7 Moyale Star Buses..............................B2

There are reliable petrol stations in town – be sure to fill up your tank before moving on.

Evening buses operated by **Liban Buses** (📞 0722244847; Hospital Rd) creep north to Marsabit (KSh500, five hours, 4.30pm). **Moyale Star Buses** (📞 0721438454; Hospital Rd) race like the wind – or perhaps a gentle breeze – to Moyale (KSh1500, 10 hours, 1.30pm) via Marsabit (KSh750, five hours).

For Maralal, take an early-morning matatu to Wamba (KSh350, 2½ hours) and then a Maralal-bound matatu (KSh500, 2½ hours) from there. Regular matatus leave from a chaotic stand around the market and also serve Archer's Post (KSh130 to KSh150, 25 minutes), Meru (KSh150, 1½ hours) and Nanyuki (KSh250, 1¾ hours).

CAR & MOTORCYCLE
Isiolo long marked the northern terminus of the sealed road system, but now a new Chinese-built road extends all the way to Moyale. If you are just travelling to Marsabit or Moyale, a 4WD is not necessary, but is required if you are planning to veer off the highway towards Lake Turkana or one of the parks.

Archer's Post

📞 064 / POP 2500

When the sealed road first reached Archer's Post, 33km north of Isiolo, the ramshackle village started to expand rapidly and the once forgotten-world feel of the place disappeared with the dust of the dying dirt road. Despite this loss of charm the village still makes an excellent base for budget travellers searching for elephants and lions in the neighbouring Samburu (p275), Buffalo Springs (p275) and Shaba (p275) national reserves.

⊙ Sights

Umoja Village   VILLAGE

(off E820; KSh1000) There are a number of Samburu villages in the area that welcome paying visitors. Probably the best one is Umoja, which was originally founded as a refuge for abused women and has now budded into a viable village in its own right. It might not be completely authentic, but admission fees go to a good cause. It's located next to the Umoja Campground (p275).

🏃 Activities

Ol Lolokwe   HIKING

(www.nrt-kenya.org/namunyak; conservancy fee per person US$40, guide per group US$50) About 30km north of town, and shrouded in Samburu folklore, is the massive mesa of Ol Lolokwe. It's a very tough but rewarding day hike (five hours just to climb it) and, at sunset, light radiating off its rusty bluffs is seen for miles around. The mountain is renowned for its raptors and has Kenya's biggest population of Rüppell's vultures.

🛏 Sleeping

Umoja Campground   CAMPGROUND $
(☎ 0721659717; camping US$10, s/d banda
KSh2000/3000) 🏊 Sitting on the Ewaso Ngiro River's banks between town and Archer's
Post Gate, this option has clean and comfortable *bandas* but bring your own mosquito
net. The campground is OK (it's seen better
days), there is a chilled cafe (meals available
on request) and occasional big-nosed, big-
eared visitors come in from the reserves.

ℹ Getting There & Away

There are matatus (KSh300, 1½ hours) and buses (KSh200, 1¾ hours) to Wamba that leave when
full (most departures are in the morning). Matatus go to Isiolo (KSh130, 25 minutes) throughout
the day. Transport to Marsabit is often full when
it passes through Archer's – to be safe, return to
Isiolo and catch the bus from there.

There are reliable petrol stations here; make
sure you have a full tank if you plan to spend a
few days in the reserves.

Samburu, Buffalo Springs & Shaba National Reserves

Blistered with termite skyscrapers, cleaved by
the muddy Ewaso Ngiro River and heaving
with heavyweight animals, this triumvirate of
national reserves has a beauty that is unsur-
passed, as well as a population of creatures
that occur in no other major Kenyan park.
These species include the blue-legged Somali
ostrich, endangered Grevy's zebra, beisa oryx,
reticulated giraffe and gerenuk – gazelles that
dearly wish to be giraffes. Despite covering
just 300 sq km, the reserves' variety of landscapes and vegetation is amazing.

◉ Sights

Shaba National Reserve is the most physically beautiful of the reserves, but it often
has less visible wildlife. The open savannahs, scrub desert and verdant river foliage
in Samburu and Buffalo Springs virtually
guarantee close encounters with elephants
and all the other wildlife. The best wildlife
viewing is almost always along the banks of
the Ewaso Ngiro in Samburu.

Samburu National Reserve   NATIONAL PARK
(adult/child US$70/40, vehicle KSh1000; ⊘ 6am-
6pm) The most popular park in northern
Kenya, Samburu's dominant feature is the
Ewaso Ngiro River, which slices through the

otherwise bone-dry country. The river acts
as a magnet for thirsty animals, and large
numbers of elephants, Grevy's zebras, giraffes and lions gather along the riverbanks.

**Buffalo Springs
National Reserve**   NATIONAL PARK
(adult/child US$70/40, vehicle KSh1000; ⊘ 6am-
6pm) The twin sister of Samburu National
Reserve, which sits on the opposite, northern side of the river, Buffalo Springs has a
wide variety of animals, including lots of
elephants, but surprisingly few safari-goers,
which helps make it a joy to explore.

Shaba National Reserve   NATIONAL PARK
(adult/child US$70/40, vehicle KSh1000; ⊘ 6am-
6pm) Shaba, with its great rocky kopjes
(isolated hills), natural springs and doum
palms, is more beautiful than Samburu and
Buffalo Springs. It is also much less visited,
so you'll almost have it to yourself.

🛏 Sleeping

Each reserve is blessed with at least two luxury lodges and several campsites. The five
public campsites (camping US$10) close to
Gare Mara Gate in Buffalo Springs National

ℹ **SAMBURU, BUFFALO
SPRINGS & SHABA
NATIONAL RESERVES**

Why Go To see some of Kenya's most
unique creatures in a compelling and
beautiful desert landscape. Samburu is
also one of the best places in the country to see elephants. Crowds of visitors
are non-existent.

When to Go There's little rain in these
parts so it's possible to visit year-round,
but between November and March
animals congregate near the Ewaso
Ngiro River.

Practicalities Isiolo is the main gateway
town. Conveniently, for the moment at
least, Buffalo Springs, Shaba and Samburu entries are interchangeable, so
you only pay once, even if you're visiting
all three in one day. You must buy your
ticket at the gate to the park in which
you're staying.

Budget Tips You can camp in any of
the reserves (but you mostly need to be
self-sufficient). However, you'll still need
a vehicle to get around. These can be
hired by the half-day in Archer's Post.

NORTHERN KENYA

Samburu & Buffalo Springs National Reserves

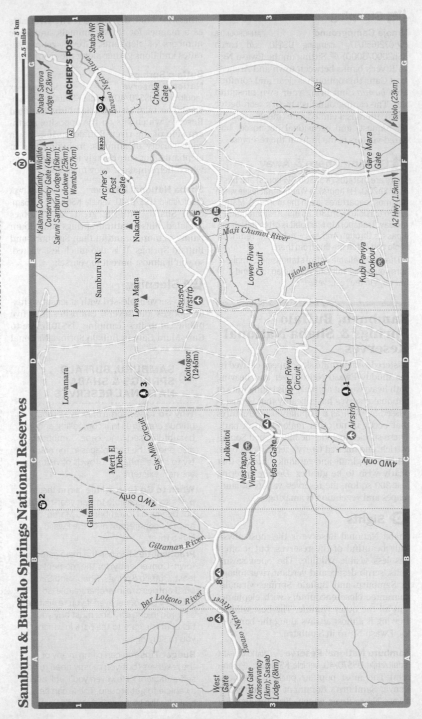

Shaba Sarova Lodge (2.8km)
Shaba NR (3km)
Ewaso Ngiro River
Choka Gate
A2
Gare Mara Gate
Isiolo (23km)
A2 Hwy (1.5km)
Kubi Panya Lookout
Isiolo River
Lower River Circuit
Maji Chumvi River
Nakadeli
Archer's Post Gate
B320
Kalama Community Wildlife Conservancy Gate (4km); Saruni Samburu Lodge (16km); Ol Lolokwe (25km); Wamba (57km)
Samburu NR
Lowa Mara
Disused Airstrip
Lowamara
Koitogor (1245m)
Upper River Circuit
Merti El Debe
Six-Mile Circuit
Giltaman
4WD only
Giltaman River
Nashapa Viewpoint
Loikoitoi
Uaso Gate
Bar Lolgoto River
Ewaso Ngiro River
West Gate
West Gate Conservancy (1km); Sassab Lodge (8km)
Airstrip
4WD only

5 km
2.5 miles

Samburu & Buffalo Springs National Reserves

◎ **Sights**
1 Buffalo Springs National
  Reserve...D4
2 Kalama Community Wildlife
  Conservancy...................................C1
3 Samburu National Reserve....................D2
4 Umoja Village..G1

🛏 **Sleeping**
5 Elephant Bedroom..................................E2
6 Elephant Watch Camp A2
7 Riverside Camp................................... C3
8 Samburu Intrepids Club B2
  Samburu Public Campsite ....(see 7)
9 Samburu Simba Lodge........................E2
  Umoja Campground.......................(see 4)

Reserve (p275) are overgrown, hard to find and have absolutely no facilities or water. For toilets, showers and less solitude, camp in Samburu (p275).

🛏 Samburu National Reserve

Samburu Public Campsite   CAMPGROUND $
(Samburu NR; camping US$35) The main public campsite is close to the park headquarters. It lacks even the most basic facilities and there are lots of baboons with light fingers. Arrange your stay at the park gates.

Riverside Camp   TENTED CAMP $
(Edwards Camp; ☎ 0721252737, 0721108032; per person KSh1500, per person full board KSh3000) On the northern bank of the Ewaso Ngiro River, the scrappy (and hot) dark canvas safari tents here might not climb as luxuriously high as some of the big-boy lodges but, let's face it, this is much more authentic Africa. Meals can be prepared on request. It's very close to the park headquarters.

★ Elephant Watch Camp   TENTED CAMP $$$
(☎ 0713037886, 0731596437; www.elephant watchportfolio.com; s/d all-inclusive US$809/1618; ⊙ closed Apr–10 May & Nov–10 Dec) 🏅 Undoubtedly the most unique and memorable place to stay in Samburu. Massive thatched roofs cling to crooked acacia branches and tower over cosy, palatial, eight-sided tents and large, grass-mat-clad terraces. Natural materials dominate the exteriors, bright textiles the interiors, and the bathrooms are stunning. The owners are renowned elephant experts and a visit to their elephant research centre is included.

Elephant Bedroom   TENTED CAMP $$$
(☎ Nairobi 020-4450035; www.atua-enkop.com; s/d all-inclusive US$395/580; ☀) Twelve absolutely superb riverfront tents that are so luxurious even budding princesses will feel a little overwhelmed by the surroundings. Exactly how luxurious are we talking? Well,

when was the last time you saw a tent that came with a private plunge pool?

Samburu Intrepids Club   TENTED CAMP $$$
(☎ Nairobi 020-4446651; www.heritage-east africa.com; s/d full board US$305/395; 🐾☀) Situated along a gorgeous stretch of river, the tents here are placed very close and cosy to each other, which rather reduces privacy, but despite this it's one of the cheaper and better-value luxury options in the reserve. Intrepids stands out for the child-friendly activities on offer, including spear throwing and making of bows and arrows.

🛏 Buffalo Springs National Reserve

Samburu Simba Lodge   LODGE $$$
(☎ 0729407162, Nairobi 020-2012243; www.simba lodges.com; s/d full board US$550/630; @☀) It doesn't exactly blend harmoniously into the countryside, but this large lodge, with accommodation in big rooms scattered over several blocks, is ideal for those who prefer something other than canvas between them and the wildlife. It's one of the few options in Buffalo Springs.

🛏 Shaba National Reserve

Joy's Camp   TENTED CAMP $$$
(☎ 0730127000; www.joyscamp.com; s/d all-inclusive from US$671/894; 🐾☀) 🏅 Once the home of Joy Adamson, of *Born Free* fame, this is now an outrageously luxurious camp in Shaba's remotest corner. The accommodation is in 'tents', but these tents aren't like others – they come with underfloor lighting, lots of stained glass and giant, walk-in rain showers.

Other pluses are an absolute lack of other safari vehicles in the surrounds, superb food (sorry, overnight guests only) and an infinity pool where you can wallow while overlooking a swamp filled with buffaloes.

Shaba Sarova Lodge
LODGE $$$

(✓0728603590; www.sarovahotels.com; s/d full board from US$270/315; @🔊🌐) This place nestles on the Ewaso Ngiro River and its pathways intertwine with frog-filled streams and ponds. There's a large pool and natural springs flow through the gorgeous open-air bar. The rooms are very comfortable with lots of Africana-style art. The lodge leaves bait along the river to attract crocodiles, so sightings are guaranteed.

❶ Getting There & Away

Airkenya (p385) and Safarilink (p385) have frequent flights from Nairobi's Wilson Airport to **Samburu**. You can also fly into **Kalama**, which is roughly 40km north of the parks.

The vehicle-less can try to wangle a 4WD and driver in Archer's Post or Isiolo for about US$100 per half-day.

The bridge between Samburu and **Buffalo Springs** has repeatedly collapsed for years due to flooding and mismanagement. Currently, the bridge cannot be crossed so if you want to visit both Samburu and Buffalo Springs, you'll need to make a long detour back to Archer's Post and the main A2 road, which can take up to three hours. Petrol is available in Archer's Post.

Samburu Area Conservancies

Kalama Community Wildlife Conservancy

Eight kilometres north of Archer's Post, and abutting the northern boundary of Samburu National Reserve (p275), is the 384-sq-km **Kalama Community Wildlife Conservancy** (✓0721463930; www.nrt-kenya.org/kalama; conservation fee incl in accommodation price), which opened in 2004. Although the conservancy is home to Grevy's zebras, elephants and reticulated giraffes, among others, and acts as a vital wildlife corridor for animals migrating between the Samburu and Marsabit areas, its drier habitat means animals are considerably less visible than in Samburu. On a more positive note, you will pretty much have the place to yourself. It can also be used as a base for safaris in nearby reserves and, best of all, walking is allowed, unlike in Samburu.

Only guests of the lodge or those booked for camping are allowed to enter the conservancy. The conservation fee is included in the cost of the camping.

🛏 Sleeping

Nasha Campsite
CAMPGROUND $

(✓0701295357; www.nrt-kenya.org; camping KSh2000) Sheltered by a natural rock amphitheatre and with shade provided by acacia trees, this campground is more secluded than Lgoita and is a great base for the many treks around the conservancy. We recommend hiring at least two guides (KSh1000 per day) – one to guide you on the hikes and one to watch your campsite.

Lgoita Campsite
CAMPGROUND $

(✓0701295357; www.nrt-kenya.org; camping KSh2000) Set at the base of a vertical rock formation, this is a great location for access to the many hikes available in the camp. Hire a guide for KSh1000 per day.

★ Saruni Samburu Lodge
LODGE $$$

(✓0735950903; www.sarunisamburu.com; s/d all-inclusive US$780/1560, conservation fee per person per night US$116; 🔊🌐) 𝒫 So perfectly designed is Saruni Samburu Lodge, the only accommodation other than camping within the conservancy, that its 'tents' virtually melt into the rocky bluff on which it's located. And when we say tents we do, of course, mean tents with stone bathtubs, designerchic furnishings and views that are quite simply out of this world.

Throw in an infinity pool, superb Italian–Kenyan fusion cooking and attentive staff, and you get a place that gives any hotel in the world a run for its money. Prices include safaris, most drinks, airstrip transfers and almost anything else you can imagine.

❶ Getting There & Away

The conservancy is about a five-hour drive from Nairobi on good roads, and only 43km north of Isiolo. A 4WD with high clearance is recommended once inside the conservancy.

West Gate Community Conservancy

West of Samburu National Reserve is this amazing conservancy – its thorny acacia scrub is home to several thousand Samburu people and a healthy, and growing, population of large mammals, including up to 500 Grevy's zebras. As in Samburu, the Ewaso Ngiro River flows through the conservancy and is the focus of interest for the area's wildlife. However, most of the animals here are much more jumpy and elusive than those in the reserve proper. Regardless, this

NDOTO MOUNTAINS

Climbing from the Korante Plain's sands are the magnificent rusty bluffs and ridges of the Ndoto Mountains. Kept a virtual secret from the travelling world by their remote location, the Ndotos abound with hiking, climbing and bouldering potential. **Mt Poi** (2050m), which resembles the world's largest bread loaf from some angles, is a technical climber's dream – its sheer 800m north face begs to be bagged. If you're fit and have a whole day to spare, it's a great hike to the summit and the views are extraordinary.

The tiny village of **Ngurunit** is the best base for your adventures and is interesting in its own right, with captivating, traditionally dressed Samburu people living in simple, yet elegantly woven, grass huts.

conservancy is a brilliant example of how conservation and the needs of local people can facilitate each other.

Note that the conservancy is only accessible if you are staying at Sasaab Lodge; the conservancy's fees are included in the lodge's nightly rates.

🛏 Sleeping

⭐**Sasaab Lodge** LODGE $$$
(☑ Nairobi 020-5020888; www.thesafaricollection. com; s/d all-inclusive US$1445/2850; 🖥🍴) 🏊 Hands down the most extravagant, yet serene, place to stay in northern Kenya. Its half-dozen Moorish-style 'tents' (each the size of a small house) have high-thatched roofs, private plunge pools, stunning river views from the beds...and the showers...and the toilets...

The food is some of the best in any of the top lodges, and there's a breathtaking infinity pool that seems to merge seamlessly into river and savannah views.

❶ Getting There & Away

The conservancy is roughly a three-hour drive from Nanyuki. You can enter through the southern gate by passing through the Samburu National Reserve (p275). If you are coming from the north, you can reach the gate via the C79 highway, which splits the conservancy and the Namunyak Wildlife Conservancy to the north. You will need a 4WD, especially during and after the rainy season.

Matthews Range

West of the remarkable flat-topped Ol Lolokwe (p274) mountain, and north of Wamba, is the Matthews Range. The name might sound tame but, rest assured, this is real African wilderness, full of 1000 adventures. These forests and dramatic slopes support a wealth of wildlife, including elephants, lions, buffaloes and Kenya's most important wild dog population. With few roads and almost no facilities, the mountains reward only those willing to go the extra kilometre on foot.

In 1995 the local Samburu communities collectively formed a Trust to look after the **Namunyak Wildlife Conservancy**, now one of Kenya's most successful community conservation programmes.

🛏 Sleeping

⭐**Kitich Camp** TENTED CAMP $$$
(☑ 0730127000; www.kitichcamp.com; s/d all-inclusive US$562/936; ⊘ closed Apr–mid-Jun & Nov–mid-Dec; 🅿🛜) One of the remotest camps in Kenya, Kitich falls squarely into the luxury-tented-camp category, but staying here is unquestionably a wild-Africa experience. Elephants pass through the camp almost daily and exploration of the thick forests is done on foot with expert Samburu trackers. This is a unique safari experience and one of the most exciting places to stay in Kenya.

❶ Getting There & Away

Matatus run from Isiolo (KSh350) and Maralal (KSh400) to Wamba, but you'll need your own transport from there to head into the range. The drive from Wamba takes approximately two hours, though in the rainy season this may be much longer if the roads become impassable, in which case you'll need to take an alternative route. Four-wheel drive is essential. **Kitich Camp** can arrange a transfer from Kalama airstrip (KSh20,000 per vehicle).

Marsabit

☑ 069 / POP 5000

The small town of Marsabit sits on the side of a 6300-sq-km shield volcano, the surface of which is peppered with 180 cinder cones and 22 volcanic craters, many of which house lakes – or at least they do when the rains have been kind. While the town is less attractive than its surrounds, which also comprise the enormous 1500-sq-km **Marsabit National Reserve** and the smaller Marsabit National Park (p281), it's an interesting and lively place, thanks to colourful nomads passing through and a lively market.

◉ Sights

Shurr Community Conservancy
WILDLIFE RESERVE

(www.nrt-kenya.org/shurr) Established in 2013, and immediately to the east of Marsabit, this conservancy has a lot of potential and there's more wildlife around here than many people realise, though there are currently no visitor facilities.

⎚ Sleeping

Chicho
GUESTHOUSE $

(☑0706153827; www.chichohotel.com; off Post Office Rd; s/d KSh2500/3500; P☎) Located very close to the post office (p281), but up a quiet side road, this family-run place has colourful rooms with some character, small bathrooms with hot water and bed sheets that will shock you with their absence of dubious stains! All up it's the best bet in the town centre. You must book your meals in advance.

THE KING OF MARSABIT

The main entrance to Marsabit National Park (p281) is called the Ahmed Gate, named after one of the most famous elephants in Kenya. Ahmed the elephant was known as the King of Marsabit due to his enormous tusks. His tusks were so large that he was the first, and only, elephant to be declared a national treasure and was granted presidential protection by President Jomo Kenyatta in 1970 to prevent him from being poached. Personal bodyguards were assigned to Ahmed, who would stay as close as possible to prevent any attacks against the regal pachyderm.

Ahmed was a loner and quite elusive, for an elephant, and so the stories about him became legend after several years. It is said that when he died in 1974, he was not found lying on his side, but was half leaning against a tree, resting on his tusks. Ahmed can still be seen today, as an exhibit at the Kenya National Museum in Nairobi.

Nomads Trail Hotel
HOTEL $

(☑0726560846; A2 Hwy; s/d old rooms KSh1800/2700, new rooms KSh2500/3700; P☎) The rooms here are prim and proper and all have attached bathrooms that come with – wait for it – real hot water from a real shower! Upstairs are some newer rooms that, for Marsabit, are surprisingly posh. There is also a restaurant serving decent fare.

JeyJey Centre
HOTEL $

(☑0728808801/2; A2 Hwy; camping KSh300, s/d/tw with shared bathroom KSh800/1200/1800, d KSh1350; P) This mud-brick castle bedecked in flowers is something of a travellers' centre and is always bursting with road-hardened souls. Basic rooms with mosquito nets surround a courtyard, and bathrooms (even shared ones) sport on-demand hot water. There's also an unattractive campground.

Saku Guest House
HOTEL $$

(☑0799189160; www.sakuguesthousemarsabit.com; s/d KSh2200/5000; P☎) Built in 2017, this is the poshest place to stay in Marsabit. The rooms are large and each comes with a clean bed and TV. If you are looking for a splurge, try the VIP rooms (KSh7000), which have a widescreen TV, lounge and four-poster bed.

Jirime Hotel & Resort
HOTEL $$

(☑0727383639, 0724942941; www.jirimehotel.com; A2 Hwy; camping KSh500, s/d KSh3000/5000; P☎) ⌗ Located 2.5km north of town on the road to Moyale, this place has little in the way of character but has big, tiled en-suite rooms, lots of peace and quiet, a decent in-house restaurant and pretty good wi-fi. Camping is also possible.

✗ Eating

JeyJey Centre
KENYAN $

(A2 Hwy; meals KSh300-500; ☺11am-7pm) Inside the popular hotel of the same name, JeyJey serves local favourites as well as the odd curry. Take a good book to read while your food is prepared, particularly if you order anything out of the ordinary.

Five Steers Hotel
KENYAN $

(A2 Hwy; meals KSh250-450; ☺8am-8pm) With a wooden fenced-off terrace, this place is the height of Marsabit style. There is no menu, so just ask what the special is for the day. The owner is a good source of information on onward transport.

Marsabit

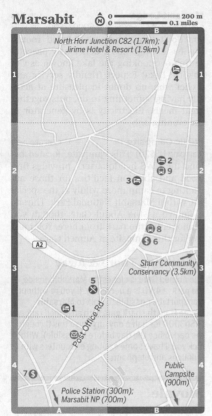

North Horr Junction C82 (1.7km);
Jirime Hotel & Resort (1.9km)

Shurr Community
Conservancy (3.5km)

Public
Campsite
(900m)

Police Station (300m);
Marsabit NP (700m)

Marsabit

Sleeping
1 Chicho... A3
2 JeyJey Centre B2
3 Nomads Trail Hotel B2
4 Saku Guest House................................. B1

Eating
5 Five Steers Hotel A3
   JeyJey Centre ....(see 2)
   Saku Guest House........................(see 4)

Information
6 Co-operative Bank B3
7 Kenya Commercial Bank.................... A4

Transport
8 Liban Buses.. B3
9 Moyale Liner Buses............................. B2

Getting There & Away

Although improved security means convoys and armed guards are no longer being used to Moyale or Isiolo, it's still wise to get the latest security and Ethiopian border information from locals and the **police station** (24hr) before leaving town. As a rule, if buses and trucks travel in a convoy, or take armed soldiers on board, you should too!

There is little public transport to Lake Turkana, but enquire at the larger hotels to catch a lift with a local heading towards North Horr.

BUS

With the completion of the paved road from Moyale to Isiolo, the number of bus companies serving the route has exploded. Most are situated on the main road near the JeyJey Centre (p280). **Moyale Liner Buses** (0705614600; www. moyaleliner.co.ke) connect Marsabit to Moyale daily (KSh800, six hours, 5.30pm). Heading south, both Moyale Liner and **Liban Buses** (0715099446; A2 Hwy) run to Isiolo (KSh700, six hours) and Nairobi (KSh1700, eight hours).

CAR & MOTORCYCLE

The road north and south of Marsabit is now completely paved and accessible with a normal car. However, if you are looking to venture to **Marsabit National Park** or towards Lake Turkana, a 4WD is a necessity. There are several petrol stations on the main road.

Marsabit National Park

Within the larger national reserve, this small **park** (www.kws.go.ke; adult/child US$30/20; 6am-7pm), nestled on Mt Marsabit's upper slopes, is coated in thick

★**Saku Guest House** KENYAN $$
(0799189160; www.sakuguesthousemarsabit. com; mains KSh300-700; 6am-10pm; P) The restaurant on the 2nd floor of the Saku Guest House (p280) is spotlessly clean and bright. The menu (yes, there is an actual menu!) is varied and has the most choice of any restaurant in the area. We recommend the King Saku Marsabit, a spicy chicken dish large enough to share.

Information

MONEY

Co-operative Bank (A2 Hwy; 8.30am-4pm Mon-Fri, to noon Sat) Has an ATM that works with foreign Visa cards.

Kenya Commercial Bank (off Post Office Rd; 8.30am-4pm Mon-Fri, to noon Sat) With ATM.

POST

Post Office (Post Office Rd; 7.45am-6pm Mon-Fri, 9am-4pm Sat)

Marsabit National Park

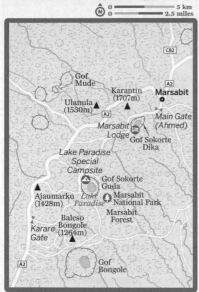

forests and contains a wide variety of wildlife, including leopards, elephants (some with huge tusks) and buffaloes. The park forms a key point on an elephant migration route that extends as far as the slopes of Mt Kenya. The dense forest makes spotting wildlife very difficult, but fortunately help is at hand in the form of a couple of natural clearings with semi-permanent lakes, where animal sightings are almost guaranteed.

This is a very climate-affected park. In the increasingly common years when the rains fail, the park very quickly turns brown, parched and apparently lifeless. In more generous years the vegetation positively glows green, the lakes fill with water and animals seem to reappear from nowhere.

🛌 Sleeping

Lake Paradise Special
Campsite   CAMPGROUND $
(www.kws.go.ke; camping US$35) This picturesque site, with nothing but a dried-up lake bed and firewood, is the only place to camp in the park. Due to roaming buffaloes and elephants, a ranger must be present when you camp here.

Marsabit Lodge   LODGE $$
(☑ 0726625477; s/tw KSh6000/7500; P) If you don't mind the rather faded rooms, this basic lodge has a deliciously peaceful setting overlooking the lake known as Gof Sokorte Dika. Expect friendly service and a chef who, no doubt in pleasure at actually having something to do, puts together great meals. Electricity is by generator in the evening only.

Public Campsite   CAMPGROUND $
(camping US$20) This campsite, located behind the KWS headquarters, provides firewood and ablution facilities for those not wanting to camp more wildly at the special site within Marsabit National Park. The site is known as the Abdul Gate, though you cannot enter the park from here. You must pay for this campsite at Ahmed Gate.

❶ Getting There & Away

The Ahmed Gate is closest to Marsabit. Inside the park, a 4WD is a necessity. If you're without transport it's possible to walk to **Marsabit Lodge** from the park gate with an armed ranger (KSh3000 for half a day; organise this through the park office the day before if possible). With luck you'll have some exciting encounters with buffaloes and elephants.

Moyale

☑ 069 / POP 34,314

Let's be honest. Nobody comes to Moyale to see Moyale; people come because it's the gateway to one of the world's most fascinating countries – Ethiopia. In stark contrast to the solitary journey here, Moyale's small, sandy streets burst with activity. The town's Ethiopian half is more developed, complete with sealed roads, and there's a palpable difference in its atmosphere.

While the drive to Moyale from Marsabit is no longer hard, it is still immensely rewarding. Leaving the misty highlands of Marsabit, you drop onto the bleak-by-name, bleak-by-nature **Dida Galgalu Desert** (Plains of Darkness) and trundle for endless hours through a magnificent monotony of black, sunburnt lava rock. The only sign of life, aside from the odd nomad and his camels, is the hamlet of **Bubisa**, a fly-blown place marked on few maps, where broken-looking people sit chewing *miraa* (leaves and shoots that are chewed as a stimulant). Then it's onwards over an empty landscape until you reach the tiny village of **Turbi**, sheltered by two small, forested peaks. These can be climbed in half a day, but take a guide as there's a lot of wildlife and wild people in these parts. If you were to get stuck here for the night, there are a couple of very meagre places to stay. For security's sake, however, it's best to push on to Moyale. After Turbi, scrubby thorn bushes replace lava desert and, in the distance, the mountain vastness of Ethiopia springs up and tantalises.

🛏 Sleeping

Al-Yusra Hotel   HOTEL $
(📞 0727165801; s/d KSh2500/3000; 🛜) Big news, folks! Kenyan Moyale finally has a decent place to stay! OK, let's not go overboard. It's hardly fantastic, but it does have running water that's sometimes even hot and no strange creatures sharing your bed.

Moyale 🧭 ⓝ | 0 ———— 200 m / 0 ———— 0.1 miles

You can't miss it. It's by far the town's tallest building, which also houses a clinic.

Sessi Guesthouse   HOTEL $
(r per person with shared bathroom KSh750; 🅿) This place, a short way out of the centre, is clean (well, clean for Moyale) and fairly quiet. It does double as a timber yard, with several stray dogs lurking outside, but for this price, what did you expect?

🍴 Eating

If you are travelling to Ethiopia, it's best to wait until you're there to eat. Moyale's restaurants are lacking.

Prison Canteen   KENYAN $
(meals KSh150-350; ⊘10am-late) Set up just outside the prison for the staff, this canteen offers ample room to eat *nyama choma* (barbecued meat) and drink slightly warm beer surrounded by locals.

ℹ Information

MONEY
Kenya Commercial Bank (A2 Hwy; ⊘8.30am-4pm Mon-Fri, to 1pm Sat) Has an ATM and MoneyGram services.

The Commercial Bank of Ethiopia, 2km inside Ethiopia from the border, changes travellers cheques as well as US dollars and euros. While it doesn't exchange Kenyan shillings, many hawkers will swap them for Ethiopian birr on the way to Ethiopia.

POST
Post Office (www.posta.co.ke; ⊘7.45am-6pm Mon-Fri, 9am-4pm Sat)

ℹ Getting There & Away

Onward transport from both sides of the frontier leaves before the border opens, so cross straight to the other side if you arrive early enough. Otherwise you'll get stuck here for an extra day.

Moyale Raha Buses (📞 0712620784) and other companies leave town daily for Marsabit (KSh800, two to three hours). With the recent improvements in the road between Moyale and Marsabit, it's now possible to get from Moyale to Isiolo, or even Nairobi, in one very long day. Drivers should note that petrol on the Ethiopian side of Moyale is half the cost of that in Kenya.

On the Ethiopian side, a bus leaves for Addis Ababa each morning at around 5am, though it takes two days, so you might want to break the journey at any number of fascinating places in southern Ethiopia.

VISAS & BORDER CROSSINGS

Entry & Exit Formalities

It used to be possible to cross to the Ethiopian side of Moyale without a visa for a few hours to see what you were missing (which isn't really very much at all), but this is no longer permitted. The border is open from 6am to 6pm daily. If you are entering with a vehicle, you'll have to visit Ethiopian Customs. The process is all a bit confusing, but the officers will want to see that you have car insurance that covers the amount of the car or, failing that, will ask you to pay a security deposit. They were unsure how you would get this deposit back if you are not returning to the border, but were confident that, somehow, it would work itself out...

Visas

If entering Ethiopia, be aware that visas aren't available at the border, nor at the Ethiopian embassy in Nairobi for non-residents of Kenya. Also be aware that you cannot use an e-visa to enter Ethiopia via borders – e-visas are only for airport arrivals. The Kenyan Border Post was being moved to a new building at the time of research, but you should still expect a bit of a wait before you're allowed to leave (or enter) the country. The Ethiopian Immigration Post is tucked off the road as you enter Ethiopia – ask locals for directions and don't even think about entering without a valid visa.

If you're coming from the other way, three-month Kenyan tourist visas (US$50) are available at the border for most Western nationalities.

MARALAL TO TURKANA'S EASTERN SHORE

Journeying to a beautiful Jade Sea shouldn't be something that's easy to do, and this route, the ultimate Kenyan adventure, is certainly not easy. Your backside will take a battering, but you'll be rewarded 1000 times over with memories of vibrant tribes, camel caravans running into a red sunset, mesmerising volcanic landscapes and, of course, the north's greatest jewel – Lake Turkana.

Maralal

📞 065 / POP 24,612

Maralal is the kind of place where you should spend some time. After all, the town's most famous former resident was one of the greatest explorers of the 20th century, Wilfred Thesiger, and if he decided that Maralal was the perfect place for retirement, then it must be doing something right. Yet, few people choose to take the time to enjoy it, most stopping only for a night en route to Lake Turkana. The lucky ones tend to be those using the erratic public transport, as they end up delayed here for enough time to appreciate the town.

Sights

Maralal National Sanctuary WILDLIFE RESERVE

FREE This sanctuary, home to zebras, impalas and other wildlife, once completely surrounded the town. Today it only covers a small patch of land around what's left of the Maralal Safari Lodge. The lodge closed down several years ago, but you can still drive into the sanctuary and animals still roam inside. It's not much, but if you *really* want to see impalas and won't be able to go to a proper reserve, then it is worth a quick visit.

🏃 Activities

Loroghi Hills Circuit TREKKING

The Loroghi Hills Circuit, which takes in one of Kenya's most astounding vistas, Lesiolo (p286), is a rewarding five-day (78km) trek. Somewhat shorter walks are possible by just strolling aimlessly around the high country and down the paths linking the *shambas* (small plots) that surround the town.

A local guide is a necessity for the circuit; you should be able to find one by enquiring at your accommodation.

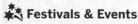 Festivals & Events

Inaugurated in 1990, the annual **Maralal International Camel Derby** is one of the biggest events in Kenya, attracting riders and spectators from around the world in mid- to late August. The derby is now run by Nairobi-based Adventure 360 Africa (www.adventure360africa.com). The parties surrounding the event are justifiably well known, and worth the trip for many visitors.

However, if you'd rather just get involved in some fast-moving camel action, the derby's first race has your name written all over it – it's for amateur camel riders! It's a butt-jarring 11km journey. Don't even start feeling sorry for your backside – the professional riders cover 42km.

🛏 Sleeping

Sunbird Guest House GUESTHOUSE $
(☎0720654567; s/d KSh1000/2000; 🅿🛜) The single rooms are starting to look a little old and damp but, by and large, this very friendly place has quiet, clean and comfortable rooms with nice linen, mosquito nets and hot water in the bathrooms. The courtyard has a sunny, garden vibe and there's a pleasant restaurant serving healthy fried stuff.

Cheers Guest House GUESTHOUSE $
(☎0722655877; s/d KSh1000/1500; 🅿🛜) A long-time favourite, this well-run place has small single rooms and smart doubles with friendly staff, mosquito nets and safe parking in the courtyard. The in-house restaurant (mains KSh280 to KSh560), which

serves all your fried Kenyan favourites, is one of the town's better places to eat.

★Samburu Guest House HOTEL $$
(☎0725363471; www.samburuguesthouse.com; s/d KSh2500/5000; 🅿🛜) With a new wing, this hotel has been modernised, with large beds, mosquito nets and TVs in each room. Request a room in the new wing for extra comfort. There is also a restaurant attached that serves good Kenyan fare.

🍴 Eating

Coast Dishes KENYAN $
(mains KSh80-300) While the atmosphere is far from coastal, this place, run by a couple from the sultry coast, offers daily dishes such as pilau – it's made with goat rather than fish or chicken, but it will still whet your appetite.

Pop Inn Hotel KENYAN $
(meals KSh150-250; ⊘7am-8pm) This zebra-striped building has decent Kenyan staples and is popular with locals.

ℹ Information

MEDICAL SERVICES
Maralal Medical Clinic (Sanctuary Rd; ⊘8am-6pm) Small clinic with dishevelled facilities on Maralal's main road.

Maralal

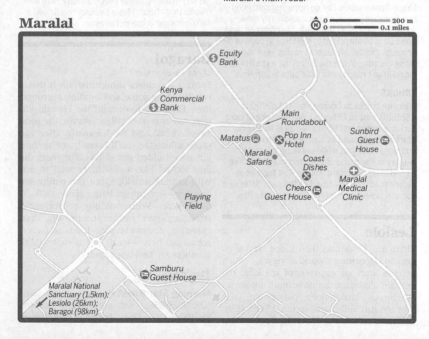

MONEY

Equity Bank (☉ 8am-4.30pm Mon-Fri, to noon Sat) A more reliable ATM than that at KCB.

Kenya Commercial Bank (☉ 8.30am-4pm Mon-Fri, to noon Sat) Behind the market, with an ATM, but staff can be a bit stroppy when presented with foreign Visa cards.

❶ Getting There & Away

BUS & MATATU

Matatus serve Nyahururu (KSh500, three to four hours), Rumuruti (KSh300 to KSh400, 2½ hours) and Wamba (KSh500, 3½ hours). For Nairobi you need to change in Nyahururu. Reaching Isiolo involves staying overnight in Wamba to catch the early-morning southbound matatu.

There are buses too, which look like they're crossed with a tank, heading to Baragoi (KSh500) at around 11am every morning. As there is still no regular transport north from there, it's more pleasant to wait in Maralal for something heading further north. **Maralal Safaris** (☏ 0721808017; ☉ 9am-5pm) is able to book onward bus travel and sometimes has connections to trucks heading north.

Most **local transport** (C77 Hwy) leaves from the main roundabout.

CAR & MOTORCYCLE

The 130km drive from Nyahururu to Maralal along the C77 is bumpy but straightforward, despite the tarmac running out just before the Mugie Conservancy (we do hope you said goodbye, because you won't see it again any time soon). Punctures on this route are common, and don't be at all surprised to see large groups of elephants, giraffes and zebras racing your vehicle along the edge of the road. Fuel up, as petrol and diesel aren't readily available until South Horr.

TRUCKS

Waits for trucks to Loyangalani (KSh1000 to KSh1500, nine to 12 hours), on the shore of Lake Turkana, might last from a few days to a week. Start asking around as soon as you arrive in town and remember that while breaking the truck journey in Baragoi or South Horr may seem like a good idea, you might have to wait for a week before another truck trundles through. After rain you can expect prices for all transport to rise.

Lesiolo

There are views and then there are views. Lesiolo (meaning 'world's view'), which perches atop an escarpment marking the Loroghi Plateau's dramatic end, offers an outrageous 120km-deep panoramic view over the Rift Valley and serrated Taita Hills. Lesiolo is part of the **Malasso Ecotourism**

Project and a viewing fee (KSh500) is now charged – pricey, but worth every penny. There is also a truly rewarding hike here, the Lesiolo Loop.

🏃 Activities

The **Lesiolo Loop** is a spectacular and gruelling 12km trek (four to five hours) that takes you down the escarpment to the valley floor and then slowly brings you back up again. A guide is essential for this trek – arrange one through locals in Lesiolo (expect to pay KSh1000 per day).

🛏 Sleeping & Eating

It's possible to camp (US$10 per adult) at Lesiolo and the viewing fee is waived if you do so. There's water (collected rain that will need treatment), crude toilets and a whole lot of cow patties to go with the astounding view.

There are no restaurants or shops here, so make sure you come prepared with water and food.

❶ Getting There & Away

Head north from Maralal towards Baragoi for 17km and the Malasso Ecotourism Project sign marks the turn-off for Lesiolo. Several more signs and helpful locals will point you the rest of the way. Patience and erratic transport can get you to the village of Poror, an easy 9km walk (two to three hours) from Lesiolo. You'll need a 4WD if driving in the wet season.

Baragoi

 065 / POP 20,000

Baragoi is a dusty, diminutive town that is enveloped by some spellbinding surroundings. The long descent off the Loroghi Plateau towards the village serves up some sweet vistas, and for kilometre after gorgeous kilometre you'll literally see nothing but tree-studded grasslands. For years this area looked like it should be wall to wall with grazing antelope, but the reality was that very few things larger than a dik-dik lived here. With wildlife conservancies stretching ever further northward, that's changing, and we've seen herds of Grevy's zebras out here – locals tell us that wildlife numbers are building rapidly.

🛏 Sleeping

Morning Star Guest House   HOTEL $
(☏ 0790734856; s/d with shared bathroom KSh400/800) The bougainvillea-dressed

NORTHERN KENYA LESIOLO

Morning Star Guest House provides for a night's kip – though it doesn't supply the peg you'll need to place over your nose before entering the communal toilets.

ℹ️ Getting There & Away

The dirt track from Maralal to Baragoi is very rocky in places, but still one of the better stretches of road in this area. Even so, if there has been any rain it becomes treacherous. The drive takes a minimum of three hours.

There are now daily buses to Maralal (KSh500, three hours); these leave from **Star Station Filling** (⊘ 6am-8pm), which sells expensive petrol, but it is the only station between South Horr and Maralal.

South Horr

☑ 069 / POP 9753

South Horr, surrounded by flowering trees, is the next village north of Baragoi and sits in an acacia-paved valley beneath the towering peaks of **Ol Donyo Nyiro** (2752m) and **Ol Donyo Mara** (2066m). Despite the delightful craggy scenery, your eyes will rarely look up from the enchanting Samburu herders who gather in the wavering trees' shadows.

This is fantastic walking country – easy hikes are possible on the valley's forested lower slopes, while more motivated souls can try to bag Ol Donyo Nyiro's peak. In either case, ask your hotel to arrange a guide (around KSh1000 per day) because these woodlands are haunted by all manner of

---

WINDS OF CHANGE

Northern Kenya has wind. Lots of it. And it's integral to Africa's biggest wind farm, the new **Lake Turkana Wind Power** project. The Dutch consortium behind the farm built 365 giant wind turbines on the southeast corner of Lake Turkana, which can generate 300MW, or a quarter of Kenya's current installed power. Despite several hold-ups, the project was completed two months ahead of schedule in 2017. However, while the turbines are ready to go, the Kenyan government has yet to complete the transmission line that connects the wind farm to its end users, so the facility is still inactive. The transmission line was expected to be completed in early 2018.

---

large, toothy creatures who'd love a passing hiker for lunch.

🛏️ Sleeping

Samburu Sports Centre Guesthouse
BANDAS $

(☑ 0720334561; www.safarisportscamp.com; off the C77; per person tent KSh500, hut with shared bathroom KSh1000, banda KSh1500; 🛜) One of the only places to stay in South Horr, this sports centre usually functions as a sports camp for local children. There is a full-size basketball court and a restaurant (you must give advance notice). The *bandas* look quaint from the outside with a porch and chairs, but the huts are actually the cleanest rooms available.

Desert Rose
LODGE $$$

(☑ 0721840150, 0729403131; www.desertrose kenya.com; s/d all-inclusive US$735/1250; 🏊) Your first thought on seeing this incredible lodge is likely to be 'How?' How did anyone find this location, about as far as you can get from Nairobi and yet still in Kenya? How did anyone conjure up the idea of building a lodge here? And how on earth did they manage to do it?

We don't know the answers, but we're certainly glad someone did because this lodge, which seems to have grown out of the mountainside, is probably the most architecturally impressive lodge in Kenya and certainly the remotest. Heavy hardwood and the local rock have been chipped and carved into furnishings, and many of the rooms are totally open plan with nothing but a mosquito net protecting you from the elements. A stay here isn't about classic safaris but, rather, it's about easy relaxation, great food and, most importantly, getting to know the beautiful Samburu people and going on wild fly-in adventures to the terrifyingly forbidding Sugata Valley or up to Lake Turkana.

Most guests fly in by private charter or helicopter, but the adventurous can drive in up an almost-vertical section of the mountain. All visitors must give advance notice.

ℹ️ Getting There & Away

The road between Baragoi and South Horr is in reasonable shape (for northern Kenya). There are buses every other day to Maralal (KSh1000, four to five hours). Stock up on fuel before heading north – there is pricey petrol at the **Samburu Sports Centre**, which is one of the only pumps between Marsabit and Maralal.

North to Lake Turkana

Travelling north from South Horr, the scrub desert suddenly scatters and you're greeted by vast volcanic armies of shimmering bowling-ball-sized boulders, cinder cones and reddish-purple hues. If this arresting and barren Martian landscape doesn't take your breath away, the first sight of the sparkling Jade Sea a few kilometres north certainly will.

As you descend to the lake, South Island stands proudly before you, while Teleki Volcano's geometrically perfect cone lurks on Turkana's southern shore. Since you've probably pulled over for the moment, looking for your swimming kit, we thought we'd warn you that Turkana has the world's largest crocodile population.

LAKE TURKANA'S EASTERN SHORE

Loyangalani

🎵 069 / POP 16,965

Standing in utter contrast to the dour desert shades surrounding it, tiny Loyangalani assaults all your senses in one crazy explosion of clashing colours, feather headdresses and blood-red robes. Overlooking Lake Turkana and surrounded by small ridges of pillow lava (evidence that this area used to be underwater), the sandy streets of this one-camel town are a meeting point of the great northern tribes: Turkana and Samburu, Gabbra and El Molo. It's one of the most exotic corners of Kenya and a fitting reward after the hard journey here.

👁 Sights

South Island National Park   NATIONAL PARK

(adult/child US$22/13) Designated a World Heritage Site by Unesco in 1997, this 39-sq-km purplish volcanic island is completely barren (minus some rock art) and uninhabited, apart from large populations of crocodiles, venomous snakes and feral goats. Spending the night at a **special campsite** (US$35), which is close to the main dock, makes for an even eerier trip. Visit the **KWS headquarters** (📞 0727332834; www.kws. go.ke) to pay the entry fee and book a boat (boats can also be hired from Palm Shade Camp and Malabo Resort).

In calm weather a speedboat can reach the island in 30 minutes and circumnavigate it in another hour. If winds crop up, trip times can easily double. As speedboats are somewhat limited in number, you will probably end up in something much more sedate: reckon on a six-hour return trip, for which you will pay about KSh20,000 at a minimum.

Mt Kulal   MOUNTAIN

Mt Kulal (2293m) dominates Lake Turkana's eastern horizon and its forested volcanic flanks offer some serious hiking possibilities. This fertile lost world in the middle of the desert is home to some unique creatures, including the Mt Kulal chameleon, a beautiful lizard first recorded in only 2003.

No matter what the local guides tell you, trekking to the summit from Loyangalani in a day isn't feasible. Plan on several days for a return trip. Guides (KSh1000 per day) and donkeys (KSh500 per day) to carry your gear can be hired in Loyangalani, or you can part with considerable sums of cash (KSh30,000 to KSh40,000) for a lift up Mt Kulal to the villages of Arapal or Gatab. From there you can head for the summit and spend a long day (eight to 10 hours) hiking back down to the base of the mountain.

If you pass by Arapal, be sure to whistle a tune at the **singing wells** where the Samburu gather water (and sing while doing so – hence the name).

LAKE TURKANA FACTS

➡ Lake Turkana, the world's largest permanent desert lake, has a shoreline that's longer than Kenya's entire Indian Ocean coast.

➡ The lake's water level was over 100m higher some 10,000 years ago and used to feed the mighty Nile. Environmentalists have claimed that the Gibe 3 Dam in Ethiopia has caused the lake's water level to drop 1.5m and some shores have receded by almost 2km.

➡ The first Europeans to reach the lake were Austrian explorers Teleki and von Höhnel in 1888. They proudly named it Lake Rudolf, after the Austrian Crown Prince at the time. It wasn't until the 1970s that the Kiswahili name Turkana was adopted.

Loyangalani Desert Museum   MUSEUM

(adult/child KSh500/250) Standing on a bluff above the lake several kilometres north of town, this museum covers the history and cultures of northern Kenya. The rooms contain lots of photo-heavy displays, but it's seriously overpriced. Opening hours are basically whenever an interested person comes along. There is also accommodation available, which has the best views in Loyangalani.

⭐ Festivals & Events

Held in mid-June, the **Lake Turkana Festival** (http://laketurkanaculturalfestival. com) is a jamboree of all that's colourful in the tribes of northern Kenya. Originally organised by the German embassy, it is now run by Kenya's tourism board, KWS and National Museums of Kenya. If you want to see people in their tribal best, there's no better time to be in Loyangalani.

🛏 Sleeping

⭐ Malabo Resort   BANDAS $

(☑0722381548, 0724705800; www.malaboresort. co.ke; camping KSh750, hut from KSh2000, banda KSh2500; P) For our money, this is the best place to stay in Loyangalani, just a few hundred metres north of the village and with slight lake views. There's a range of decent *bandas* with arty wooden beds and attached bathrooms, or there are thatched huts based on a traditional Turkana design. The bar-restaurant area is a good place to hang out.

Palm Shade Camp   BANDAS $

(☑0726714768; camping KSh600, s/tw hut with shared bathroom KSh1000/2000, s/d KSh2400/4800; P) Drop your tent on the grass beneath acacias and doum palms, lie back in one of the clean, tiled, newly constructed rooms, or crash in the tidy domed huts with their unique meshed cut-out walls that let in light and heavenly evening breezes. The manager is an endless source of information on travel in the area.

Loyangalani Desert Museum   BANDAS $

(banda KSh1500; P🏊) The Desert Museum has a dozen *bandas* on the bluff overlooking the lake. The views are the best you will find in Loyangalani, though the *bandas* are slightly unkempt. There's no kitchen, so you'll have to travel to town to find food.

Request one of the 'old' *bandas*, which, for some reason, are cleaner and seem in better shape than the 'new' *bandas*.

EL MOLO VILLAGES

The El Molo tribe, which is one of Africa's smallest, lives on the lake shore just north of Loyangalani in the villages of **Layeni** and **Komote**. Although outwardly similar to the Turkana, the El Molo are linguistically linked to the Somali and Rendille people. Unfortunately, the last speaker of their traditional language died before the turn of the millennium. Visiting their villages (KSh1000 per person, negotiable) is something of a circus and you shouldn't expect to see many people traditionally dressed.

🍴 Eating

Cold Drink Hotel   KENYAN $

(meals KSh100-300; ☉7am-8pm) Not just cold drinks but also, according to locals, the finest eating experience in all of Turkana country, which sadly might actually be true. It's a bit of an institution as it was the town's first hotel, so it's well known by travellers and is good for more authentic Loyangalani food (compared to what's offered at the newer hotels).

ℹ Getting There & Away

Trucks loaded with fish (and soon-to-be-smelly passengers) leave Loyangalani for Maralal (around KSh1000, nine to 12 hours) once or twice a week at best. Trucks heading in any other direction are even rarer and locals talk of waits of between a week and a month for transport to North Horr (around KSh1000). There are buses roughly every other day to Marsabit (KSh1000), but if you are in a hurry, you can try to catch a ride with a truck. When trucks do travel to Marsabit, they tend to take the slightly easier southern route via Kargi and charge a flexible KSh1000. It's better to travel from Loyangalani to North Horr, rather than the other way around, because with buses every other day from North Horr to Marsabit you won't get stuck for more than a night – going from North Horr to Loyangalani could mean waiting in North Horr for a week or more. This would be bad.

If you're travelling in your own vehicle, you have two options to reach Marsabit: continue northeast from Loyangalani across the dark stones of the Chalbi Desert towards North Horr, or head 67km south towards South Horr and take the eastern turn-off via Kargi. The 270km Chalbi route (10 to 12 hours) is hard in the dry season and impossible after rain. It's also wise to ask for directions every chance you get, otherwise it's easy to take the wrong track and not realise until hours later. This would also be bad. The 241km southern route (six to seven hours) via the Karoli Desert and Kargi is composed of compacted sands and is marginally less difficult in the rainy season.

The Catholic mission occasionally sells petrol out of the barrel, but prices are exorbitant.

North Horr

📞 069 / POP 5000

On the map, North Horr stands out like a beacon from all that surrounding desert, but once you finally drag your weary and battered self onto its sand-washed streets, the reality of this drab town is a little disappointing. Don't miss the **water source** on the edge of town, where hundreds of camels, goats and weathered nomadic faces come each day. Taking photos is not appreciated.

🛏️ Sleeping

North Horr Mazingira Women Group Lodge BANDAS $

(banda from KSh300; 🅿️) Despite the name, there are no women at this lodge, either working or staying. The *bandas* are passable, with comfortable beds, clean linen and mosquito nets. It's also one of the only places in town that serves beer, so expect groups of men congregating after dark. They're incredibly friendly, so grab a bottle of Tusker and pull up a chair...

Gallasa Diqa Womens Group Lodge HUT $

(hut KSh300) The half-dozen basic huts of the Gallasa Diqa Womens Group Lodge are located slightly outside of town at the western end. Luxury they're not; authentic they are. These huts are likely to be quieter than the ones at the Mazingira Women Group Lodge.

ℹ️ Getting There & Away

As well as occasional trucks and 4WDs, **Chalbi Buses** (📞 0705095511) now operates buses (that look like tanks) every second day between North Horr and Marsabit (KSh800) via Kalacha (KSh400). Only very rarely does anything venture to Loyangalani. There is no set price for the Loyangalani leg, but expect to pay around KSh1000.

Don't be at all surprised if you get stuck here for anything between a couple of days and a couple of weeks. Even in the dry season the 'roads' are often impassable and after rain it's completely out of the question. Whichever way you're heading, it's a road to adventure – blasting over the plains of darkness, destined for a sea of jade, is nothing short of magical.

TURKANA: PAVED WITH 'BLACK GOLD'

Northern Kenya, long ignored by the ruling elite in Nairobi, became much more in favour after 2012 when British company Tullow Oil discovered 'black gold' in the South Lokichar Basin. Further oil discoveries were made in 2017, which is likely to result in more companies heading up north looking for reserves. While not all Kenyans in the area are happy about the exploration, the development has resulted in improved infrastructure for the region. The area around Lokichar now has access to electricity, clean water and, eventually, a paved road up to Lodwar.

The Eldoret–Kitale–Lokichar–Amosing road project was launched in 2016 and will stretch almost 300km right to the border with South Sudan. The road will transport the oil from Turkana to Mombasa and is expected to be completed by 2018, though at the time of research the roads outside of Lodwar were still untouched.

Kalacha

📞 065 / POP 7937

Huddled around a permanent oasis in the middle of the Chalbi Desert, the acacia- and doum-palm-pocked village of Kalacha is home to the fascinating Gabbra people. There's little to see and do, but the sense of isolation is magnificent and the sight of camels, released from their night corrals and kicking up the dust on the way to the grazing grounds, will remain with you forever. Don't miss the cartoon-like biblical murals in the church, a prelude for those travellers heading north to Ethiopia. Some rock paintings and carvings can be found in a canyon near the **Afgaba** waterhole, not far from Kalacha – take a guide.

🛏️ Sleeping

Chalbi Safari Resort Kalacha HUT $

(campsites KSh400, tw huts per person KSh1000; 🅿️) Managed by the friendly Abdul, this is an excellent choice with several immaculate *bandas* and a sun-battered camping area.

ℹ Getting There & Away

Coming from Marsabit, the road winds down off the mountains and sinks into a mass of black lava rocks. Slowly the land becomes ever more barren until finally you hit the blank expanse of the Chalbi Desert, which is featureless, sandy and blisteringly hot. It's a spectacular ride through a clutter-free world, where the only signs of life are occasional camels heading to the wells in the bustling village of Maikona. Don't drive this route without a heavy-duty 4WD and an experienced local guide. The C82 road splits roughly 85km north of Marsabit – it's a quicker route to turn left onto the E670 rather than continue straight on the C82.

Buses stop at Kalacha every other day on their way between North Horr (KSh700) and Marsabit (KSh500).

MARICH TO TURKANA'S WESTERN SHORE

Despite boasting some of northern Kenya's greatest attributes, such as copious kilometres of Jade Sea shoreline, striking volcanic landscapes, ample wildlife and vivid Turkana tribes, this remote corner of the country has seen relatively few visitors. However, this may change if the highway north of Lokichar is completed, but at the time of research that was not looking likely to happen any time soon.

Marich to Lodwar

The spectacular descent from Marich Pass, north of Kitale, through the lush, cultivated Cherangani Hills leads to arid surroundings, with sisal plants, cactus trees and acacias lining both the road and the chocolate-brown Morun River. Just north, the minuscule village of Marich marks your entrance into northern Kenya. Welcome to adventure!

🏃 Activities

There is an abundance of trekking potential in the area, and the Marich Pass Field Studies Centre offers English-speaking Pokot and Turkana guides for half-day (US$9) or full-day (US$14) excursions.

Wei-wei Valley TREKKING
A 13km (one way) and vertically challenged (only 300m elevation gain) trek is possible up the Wei-wei Valley from Sigor to Tamkal.

Cherangani Hills TREKKING
The Cherangani Hills, covered in thick forest, are actually the fourth-highest mountain range in Kenya. There is a plethora of hiking options and several of them are quite gentle slopes through open farmland and sheltered valleys. Many people consider these intensely farmed and deeply forested hills to be one of the most beautiful corners of the country.

Mt Koh TREKKING
Reaching the dome of Mt Koh (3211m), which soars some 1500m above the adjacent plains, is a hard but rewarding two-day slog. The hike leaves from the Marich Pass Field Studies Centre.

Mt Sekerr TREKKING
Although the northern plains may beckon, it's worth heading into the hills for some eye-popping and leg-loving hiking action. Mt Sekerr (3326m), also known as Mt Mtelo, is a few kilometres northwest of Marich and can be climbed comfortably in a three-day round trip via the agricultural plots of the Pokot tribe, passing through forest and open moors.

🛏 Sleeping

Marich Pass Field Studies Centre CAMPGROUND, BANDAS $
(www.gg.rhul.ac.uk/MarichPass; camping US$7, dm US$8, s/tw US$26/35, with shared bathroom US$16/21) Just north of Marich village, this is essentially a residential facility for visiting student groups, but it also makes a great base for independent travellers. The centre occupies a beautiful site alongside the misty Morun River and is surrounded by dense bush and woodland. Facilities include a

---

THE GIBE 3 DAM CONTROVERSY

Over the border in Ethiopia, the massive Gibe 3 hydroelectric dam opened in December 2016. The controversial dam aims to produce 15,000MW of electricity by 2021, which will make Ethiopia one of the largest producers and consumers of renewable energy on the continent. However, Kenyan environmentalists complain the project will affect the Omo River that runs into Lake Turkana, resulting in dropping water levels, livelihood losses and increased local conflicts.

DON'T MISS

SIBILOI NATIONAL PARK

A Unesco World Heritage Site, and probably Kenya's most remote national park, **Sibiloi** (www.kws.go.ke; adult/child US$22/13) is located up the eastern shore of Lake Turkana and covers 1570 sq km. It was here that Dr Richard Leakey discovered the skull of a *Homo habilis* believed to be 2.5 million years old, and where others have unearthed evidence of *Homo erectus*.

The National Museums of Kenya (NMK; www.museums.or.ke) maintains a small museum and Koobi Fora (www.kfrp.com) has a research base. Best to contact all of the following before venturing in this direction: staff of the Loyangalani Desert Museum (p289; you'll have to go in person), the KWS and NMK.

Wild Frontiers (satellite phone 088216-43334103; www.wildfrontierskenya.com) is one of the best-regarded camel safari operators. Its safaris help support the Milgis Trust (www.milgistrustkenya.com), which works with local communities to preserve the pastoral way of life and the wildlife of northern Kenya.

Getting There & Away

In the dry season it's a tricky seven-hour drive north from Loyangalani to Sibiloi. You will need a guide from either KWS or the Loyangalani Desert Museum (p289). Hiring a jeep in Loyangalani will work out at around KSh40,000 per day. It's also possible to hire a boat (KSh30,000 to KSh40,000 return, with an overnight stop) from Ferguson's Gulf on the western side of the lake.

---

secure campground as well as a tatty dorm and simple, comfortable *bandas*.

The centre can organise guides for walks around the hills (half/full day US$9/14).

ℹ Getting There & Away

The stretch of the scenic A1 Hwy from Kitale to the Marich Pass via Makutano is often described as 'Kenya's most spectacular tarmac road'.

Buses plying the A1 between Kitale and Lodwar can drop you anywhere along the route, whether at Marich or the **field studies centre**. You may be asked to pay the full fare to Lodwar (KSh1500), but a smile and some patient negotiating should reduce the cost.

The road north of the Marich Pass is still a bit of a mess, however, so a 4WD is recommended for trips up-country. Hopefully that won't be necessary forever, as the recent discovery of oil around Lokichar means this section of road is slated to be improved.

Lodwar

054 / POP 48,316

Besides Lokichoggio near the South Sudan border, Lodwar is the only town of any size in the northwest. Barren volcanic hills skirted by traditional Turkana dwellings sit north of town and make for impressive sunrise vistas. Lodwar has outgrown its days as just an isolated administrative outpost of the Northern Frontier District and has now become the major service centre for the region. If you're visiting Lake Turkana, you'll find it convenient to stay here for at least one night.

🛏 Sleeping

Nawoitorong Guest House   HOTEL $

(0704911947; camping KSh300, s/tw with shared bathroom KSh800/1500, cottages KSh1400-2000; P) Built entirely out of local materials and run by a local women's group, Nawoitorong is a solid budget option and the only one for campers. Thatched roofs alleviate the need for fans and all rooms have mosquito tents, which staff will set up for you. It also houses a handicraft shop, perfect for souvenirs.

Lodwar Lodge   HOTEL $

(0796263253; r KSh1000-1500; P) Slightly tatty concrete cottages that are fairly clean and secure. Though worn, it's much less so than other town-centre options. Tends to get quite noisy at night as the bar is close to the accommodation. However, the bar has a pool table, so you can always challenge some locals to a game if you can't sleep.

Ceamo Prestige Lodge   HOTEL $$

(0721555565, 0718999703; www.ceamolodge. com; s/d KSh6500/8500; P🌢🗏) A short way out of town, this new place is also Lodwar's flashest place to stay, with large, cool, quiet, tiled rooms in a bungalow setting. It might be Lodwar's finest but it's still very overpriced. The attached restaurant/pub is probably your best bet for some *nyama choma* (KSh10,000) and a cold beer.

★ **Cradle Tented Camp**   TENTED CAMP **$$$**
(📞0722870214; www.thetentedcradlecamp.comp; tent US$150; P❄🛜🏊) When not escaping the Turkana heat in the large swimming pool, you can relax on your balcony in front of your large tent, which comes complete with TV, minibar and luxurious bathroom.

✕ Eating

Nawoitorong Guest House   KENYAN **$**
(meals KSh250-450; ⊙7am-8pm) Burgers and toasted sandwiches join local curries and various meaty fried dishes on the menu, all served in an open-air *boma* on the large grounds. It offers the most pleasant dining experience in the region, but give staff time – lots of it – to prepare dinner!

Salama Hotel   KENYAN **$**
(meals KSh80-150; ⊙6am-9pm) The most popular place in the town centre. The culinary highlight of the Salama has to be its giant bowl of pilau. There's always a crowd of people here waiting for buses to depart.

ℹ Information

MEDICAL SERVICES
Lodwar District Hospital (📞0775996389; ⊙24hr)

MONEY
Kenya Commercial Bank (⊙8.30am-4pm Mon-Fri, to noon Sat) Has an ATM and changes cash and travellers cheques.

POLICE STATIONS
Lodwar Police Station (⊙24hr) The station commander speaks excellent English in case you run into trouble.

POST
Post Office (⊙7.45am-6pm Mon-Fri, 9am-4pm Sat) If there was any out-of-the-way place in the country to send a postcard, this is it. Unfortunately, Lodwar does not actually sell postcards so a letter will have to do.

ℹ Getting There & Away

Fly540 (p385) runs frequent flights from Nairobi to **Lodwar Airport**, via Eldoret, for around US$150 (two hours).

There are regular buses plying the long route south departing from the **bus station** (📞0727096551). For more local travel, several operators offer services to Kitale (KSh2000, 8½ hours), with departures from close to Salama

Hotel. The use of matatus is unknown here – most operators use bike taxis instead.

To get to Eliye Springs or Ferguson's Gulf, you can ask your hotel to sort out a private car for you (KSh70,000 per day). Your other option is on the back of a bike taxi, which is the cheapest option (KSh30,000) but not the most comfortable. Never accept the first price offered to you – these are negotiable and you are likely to get it cheaper if you have time to shop around.

There are several reliable petrol stations in Lodwar. Note that petrol becomes much more scarce if you venture outside of town, so make sure you stock up.

Eliye Springs
📞 054 / POP 5000

Spring water percolates out of crumbling bluffs, and oodles of palms bring a taste of the tropics to the remote sandy shores of Lake Turkana. Down on the slippery shore, children play in the lake's warm waters, while Central Island (p294) lurks magically on the distant horizon. Eliye Springs is the best place to get a taste of the lake's western shore.

🛏 Sleeping

Eliye Springs Resort   RESORT **$$**
(📞0703891810; www.eliyespringsresort.com; camping KSh600, hut per person with shared bathroom KSh1800, r/luxury boma per person KSh4200/10,800; P) For many years all that stood on the shores of Eliye Springs was the shell of an abandoned lodge, but it's been brought back to life by a German with a passion for Turkana. The resort has a mixture of self-contained rooms and traditional Turkana huts made of sticks. Camping is also available, as are meals.

The resort offers a variety of activities, such as big-game fishing, boat trips to Central Island (p294) or Sibiloi National Park (p292), and aerial flights over Turkana country.

ℹ Getting There & Away

The turn-off for Eliye Springs is signposted a short way along the Lodwar–Kalokol road. The gravel is easy to follow until it suddenly peters out and you're faced with a fork in the road – stay left. The rest of the way is a mix of gravel, deep sand and even deeper sand, which can turn into a muddy nightmare in the wet season. Over the really bad sections, locals have constructed a 'road' out of palm fronds, which means that on a good day, normal cars can even make it here (though expect to do a bit of pushing and

CENTRAL ISLAND NATIONAL PARK

Bursting from the depths of Lake Turkana, and home to thousands of living dinosaurs, is the Jurassic world of **Central Island** (www.kws.go.ke; adult/child US$22/13) volcano, last seen belching molten sulphur and steam just over three decades ago. It's one of the most otherworldly places in Kenya. Quiet today, its stormy volcanic history is told by the numerous craters scarring its weathered facade. Several craters have coalesced to form three sizeable lakes, one of which is home to thousands of fish that occur nowhere else.

Both a national park and Unesco World Heritage Site, Central Island is an intriguing place to visit. Budding Crocodile Dundee types will love the 14,000 or so Nile crocodiles, some of which are massive, that flock here at certain times of year (May is the most crocodile-friendly month, but there are some crocs here year-round). The most northerly crater lake, which is saline, attracts blushing pink flocks of flamingos.

Central Island Campsite (☑ 0800597000; www.kws.go.ke; camping US$20) is the only accommodation option on the island. Located close to the dock, it is the ideal setting-off point for treks around the island. Unlike at **South Island National Park** (p288), there are trees to which you can tie your tent.

Getting There & Away

Hiring a boat from Ferguson's Gulf or Eliye Springs is the only option to get here. It's easiest to head to the KWS camp (www.kws.go.ke) in Ferguson's Gulf and ask them to sort out a boat for you (KSh15,000); alternatively, try the **Eliye Springs Resort** (p293; boats KSh18,000).

KWS can also put you in touch with locals who have boats to try to haggle the price down to around KSh10,000. Don't ever think about being cheap and taking a sailboat – the 10km trip and the sudden squalls that terrorise the lake's waters aren't to be taken lightly.

shoving). There is also a route to Eliye Springs that goes by the **Lodwar District Hospital**, but only take this route if you are with a local and in a 4WD. Petrol is only available in Lodwar, so make sure you have a good supply before heading to Eliye Springs or Ferguson's Gulf.

There is also an airstrip close to the water. Contact Eliye Springs Resort (p293) for more information on chartering a plane from **Lodwar Airport** (p293; US$160 per person).

If you don't have your own vehicle, you can usually arrange a private car and driver in Lodwar for about KSh7000, including waiting time, or hop on the back of a *boda-boda* (bike taxi) for KSh1500. If you're staying overnight, you'll have to arrange transport back to Lodwar for roughly the same amount.

Ferguson's Gulf

☑ 054 / POP 2100

If you're planning on visiting Central Island National Park or Sibiloi National Park (p292), Ferguson's Gulf is the best (and cheapest) place to arrange a boat. While more accessible than Eliye Springs, it has none of its southern neighbour's charm. Fishing boats in various states of disrepair litter its grubby western beach and a definite feeling of bleakness pervades.

🛏 Sleeping & Eating

There are a few budget options in town, one being the makeshift campsite on the KWS grounds (www.kws.go.ke; KSh1000 per person). If you are looking for luxury, you are in the wrong place.

You are guaranteed to find fish on the menu at the few small restaurants in town, but there is not much else. If you are going to Central Island, it would be best to stock up on essentials in Lodwar.

ℹ Getting There & Away

Few people in Lodwar have heard of Ferguson's Gulf, so you need to ask around for transport to nearby Kalokol, which is 75km north along a road littered with potholes. Ferguson's Gulf is only a few kilometres from there. Enquire at your accommodation in Lodwar about renting a private car and driver (KSh70,000) or you can hop on a *boda-boda* for KSh30,000.

There is also a small airstrip in Kalokol that can be accessed by charter flights; Eliye Springs Resort (p293) can organise these from Lodwar.

The KWS (www.kws.go.ke) can organise boats to **Central Island** (KSh15,000), **Sibiloi** (p292; KSh30,000) and **South Island** (p288; KSh80,000).

Understand
Kenya

KENYA TODAY................................296

Despite ethnic tensions, a robust political climate and an election fraught with peril, Kenya is marching forward with confidence. Find out why.

HISTORY......................................298

Join us on a journey that begins with prehistoric humans, detours via colonial struggles and traces the complicated independence years.

TRIBES OF KENYA...........................310

We take you behind the stereotypes and into the traditions of Kenya's major ethnic groups.

DAILY LIFE...................................315

What holds Kenya together? What's it like to be a Kenyan woman? Find out what makes Kenyans tick.

THE ARTS....................................317

Kenyans love their music and are justly proud of their literary and cinematic output. We give you the low-down.

KENYAN CUISINE............................321

From lavishly laid safari tables to Kenyan kitchen staples, we tell you everything you need to know about Kenya's food.

ENVIRONMENT...............................351

We cover the signature Kenyan landforms and the country's most pressing environmental issues in great detail.

NATIONAL PARKS & RESERVES............S362

National parks are the centrepiece for many of Kenya's attractions and we help you to explore them all.

Kenya Today

Life in Kenya is as complicated as ever, but there's a lot to suggest that the country is moving in the right direction. High (and consistent) economic growth levels and a muscular democratic scene that seems to have survived yet another fiercely disputed election, along with improving security and a dynamic cultural scene, are all signs that Kenya is an increasingly good place to live. However, age-old problems such as drought, a growing population and conflict over shrinking resources remain.

Best in Print

Out of Africa (Karen Blixen, aka Isak Dinesen; 1937) The definitive account of colonial Kenya.

The Tree Where Man was Born (Peter Matthiessen; 1972) Still the best book written about East Africa, its wildlife and its people.

The Flame Trees of Thika (Elspeth Huxley; 1959) A marvellously told colonial memoir.

Petals of Blood (Ngũgĩ wa Thiong'o; 1977) Four Kenyans struggle to come to terms with their newly independent country.

One Day I Will Write about This Place: A Memoir (Binyavanga Wainaina; 2011) A modern Kenyan childhood as told by one of its most exciting writers.

Best on Film

The Great Rift (2010) BBC documentary about the Rift Valley.

Echo of the Elephants (1993) Elephants of Amboseli National Park.

Enough is Enough (2004) Critically acclaimed portrayal of the Mau Mau uprising.

Born Free (1966) Lions of legend return to the wild.

Out of Africa (1985) Caused a generation to dream of Africa.

The Constant Gardener (2005) Gripping Hollywood story set in Kenya.

Climbing Out of Poverty?

Kenya's economy is booming, and neither natural disasters, postelection violence or war with Somalia can shake the country's confidence that Kenya is on the up. There's just one problem: only a small percentage of Kenyans see the benefits of the growing prosperity. And many don't trust their politicians – hardly surprising when Kenya's leaders are among the richest people in the country while unemployment sits at around 40%, a staggering 50% of Kenyans live below the poverty line and the prices of basic foodstuffs are soaring. By one estimate, Kenya would require an annual growth rate of 11% for the prosperity gains to even begin to trickle down to poorer sectors of society. Although Kenya has shown some gains in recent years, the Human Development Index (which measures the wellbeing of a country, taking into account life expectancy, education and standard of living) ranked Kenya at a fairly dismal 146 out of 188 countries in 2016, while the country's income gap between rich and poor remains within the 10 worst in the world.

The Challenges of Democracy

Ever since the widespread political and ethnic violence that followed the disputed 2007 elections, when more than 1000 people were killed, Kenya and its friends hold their collective breath whenever the country goes to the polls. Thankfully, Kenya's hotly contested 2017 elections ended peacefully. And then, in an event unprecedented in African politics, Kenya's highest court ruled in favour of an opposition challenge, the elections were annulled and new elections were scheduled. It was a landmark moment in Kenya's road to democracy. Sadly, however, the rerun was boycotted by the opposition, one of the country's electoral commissioners fled to the US, and barely one-third of Kenyans cast their ballots (compared with 80% in the first round). Although Uhuru Kenyatta was declared the winner, the future appears more uncertain than ever. Just when Kenyans thought they had survived another election...

The Coming Environmental Crisis?

Drought has always stalked East Africa, with some parts of Kenya just one failed rainy season from a major crisis. For all the growth in Kenya's urban middle class, much of the population continues to live at subsistence levels, wholly dependent upon the rains that sustain their crops or provide grazing for their livestock. Often these people live alongside wildlife-rich national parks or private ranches and conservancies that are closed to them despite having what could be prime grazing or agricultural lands within their borders. Failed rains in 2016 and again the following year, especially in the country's north and west, prompted the large-scale movement of armed herders and gangs onto the Laikipia Plateau where many of the ranches are owned by white Kenyans. One prominent conservationist was killed, another was critically injured, and a number of lodges were burned to the ground. Things have quietened down since then, but there are fears that these may be the first shots in a coming war in a country with a rapidly growing population, increasingly unpredictable rains and fiercely contested yet scarce resources.

War & Peace

In October 2011, for the first time in its independent history, Kenya went to war. The spark for such a drastic move was a series of cross-border raids allegedly carried out by al-Shabaab, an al-Qaeda-affiliated Somali group. Kenya initially paid a high price for its involvement in Somalia. Major terrorist attacks in 2013, 2014 and 2015, coupled with a consistently high death toll among Kenyan soldiers serving in Somalia, left many Kenyans wondering whether Kenya's Somali mission was actually inflaming tensions. A couple of years later, the government has yet to publicly articulate its exit strategy, but a crackdown and greater military presence *within* Kenya has eased many of those concerns – with each month that passes without a terrorist incident on Kenyan soil, the more the country grows in confidence. One thorny (and related) issue does remain unresolved: Kenya's government has promised to close the notorious Dadaab Refugee camp, the largest in the world with over 300,000 Somalis living there. When it does happen, expect rising tensions along the Somali border, where safety and stability are already precarious.

AREA: **580,367 SQ KM**

POPULATION: **47.7 MILLION**

AVERAGE AGE: **19.5 YEARS**

GDP PER CAPITA: **US$3400**

LIFE EXPECTANCY: **64 YEARS**

UNEMPLOYMENT: **40%**

URBAN POPULATION AS % OF TOTAL: **25.6%**

if Kenya were 100 people

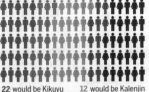

22 would be Kikuyu
14 would be Luhya
13 would be Luo
12 would be Kalenjin
11 would be Akamba
28 would be other

belief systems
(% of population)

83 Christian
11 Muslim
2 Traditional Religions
4 Other

population per sq km

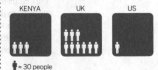

KENYA   UK   US

👤 ≈ 30 people

History

Africa's Great Rift Valley is where human beings first walked upright upon the earth. Ever since, Kenya's story has unfolded as a fascinating tale of ancient connections across the seas, the ravages of slavery and a colonial occupation that continues to mark the country to this day. Now independent with a chance to chart its own course, Kenya has become an East African powerhouse whose stunning diversity has proved to be both curse and blessing in equal measure.

Prehistoric Sites

Cradle of
Humankind exhibit
(National Museum,
Nairobi)

Sibiloi National
Park (Northern
Kenya)

Olorgasailie
Prehistoric Site
(Southern Rift
Valley)

Hyrax Hill
Prehistoric Site
(Southern Rift
Valley)

Kariandusi
(Southern Rift
Valley)

The First Kenyans

The Tugen Hills

In 1959 British paleoanthropologist Mary Leakey discovered the earliest recorded hominid fossil at Olduvai Gorge in Tanzania, causing a scientific sensation. Following this, palaeontologists digging in the Tugen Hills, west of Lake Baringo, unearthed one of the most diverse and densely packed accumulations of fossil bone in Africa. Bedded down in lava flows and representing a unique archaeological record in Africa, the fossil beds incorporate that most elusive period of human history between 14 and four million years ago when the largely primate *Kenyapithecus* evolved into our earliest bipedal ancestor *Australopithecus afarensis*.

In the sandy clay, seven of the 18 hominoid specimens known from that period were found. The jaw fragment at five million years old represents the closest ancestor of *A afarensis*, a family band that left their footprints on the Laetoli mud pan (Tanzania) 3.7 million years ago, while a fragment of skull, dating from 2.4 million years ago, represents the earliest-known specimen of our own genus, *Homo*.

Lake Turkana

In 1969 Richard Leakey – son of veteran archaeologists Louis and Mary – shifted his attentions to Lake Turkana in Kenya's north, where he turned up dozens of fossil sites, including a completely new hominid specimen – *Homo habilis* (able man).

TIMELINE

3,700,000 BC

A group of early hominids walk across the Laetoli pan, moving away from the volcano. Their footsteps take them to the grasslands of the Serengeti plains.

1,760,000 BC

In 2011 archaeologists announce the discovery at Lake Turkana of a four-sided hand axe dubbed by scientists the 'Swiss army knife' of the Stone Age.

1,600,000 BC

In 1984 Kamoya Kimeu discovers the Turkana Boy, a nearly complete skeleton of an 11- or 12-year-old hominid boy who died 1.6 million years ago near Lake Turkana.

Prior to the Leakey discovery it was thought that there were only two species of proto-humans: the 'robust' hominids and the 'gracile' hominids, which eventually gave rise to modern humans. However, the Turkana finds demonstrated that the different species lived at the same time and even shared resources – advancing the Leakey theory that evolution was more complex than a simple linear progression.

In 1984 Kamoya Kimeu (a member of the Leakey expedition) uncovered the spectacular remains of a young boy's skeleton dating back 1.6 million years. Standing at a height of 1.6m tall, the boy was appreciably bigger than his *H habilis* contemporary. His longer limbs and striding gait were also more characteristic of modern human physiology, and his larger brain suggested greater cognitive ability. *H erectus* was the biggest and brainiest hominid to date and was the longest surviving and most widely dispersed of all the ancestral toolmakers, disappearing from the fossil records a mere 70,000 years ago.

From these remarkable evolutionary leaps it was but a small step to our closest ancestors, *H sapiens,* who made an appearance around 130,000 years ago.

Kenya's Ancestors
Ten thousand years ago, Africa was unrecognisable: the Sahara was a green and pleasant land, and much of Kenya was uninhabitable because its tropical forests and swamps were inhabited by the deadly tsetse fly, which is fatal to cattle and people. Over the five millennia that followed, a changing climate saw the tsetse belt drop south, Kenya's grasslands began to spread and migrating peoples from the north began to populate what we now know as Kenya. Soon, the peoples of the continent began to converge on East Africa.

The first arrivals were a Cushitic-speaking population, who moved south with their domestic stock from Ethiopia. At the same time a population of Nilote speakers from the Sudan moved into the western highlands of the Rift Valley (the Maasai, Luo, Samburu and Turkana tribes are their modern-day descendants). These pastoralists shared the region with the indigenous Khoikhoi (ancestors of the modern-day San), who had occupied the land for thousands of years.

Africa's fourth linguistic family, the Bantu speakers, arrived from the Niger Delta around 1000 BC. Soon they became East Africa's largest ethnolinguistic family, which they remain today. Kenya's largest tribe, the Kikuyu, along with the Gusii, Akamba and Meru tribes, are all descended from them.

For more on Kenya's fossil finds look up www.leakeyfoundation.org. Members can even sign up for trips with the Leakeys themselves.

100,000 BC	2000–1000 BC	400 BC	AD 200–300
Homo sapiens strike out to colonise the world, moving into the eastern Mediterranean. By 40,000 years ago they reach Asia and Australia and 10,000 years later are settled across Europe.	Immigrant groups colonise sub-Saharan Africa. First Cushites from Ethiopia move into central Kenya, followed by Nilote speakers from Sudan. Finally, they're joined by Bantu speakers from Nigeria and Cameroon.	Azania (as the East African coast was then called) is known to the peoples of the Mediterranean and becomes an important trading post for the Greeks.	With the introduction of the camel, trans-Saharan journeys become practicable and profitable. The news of large gold deposits undoubtedly spurs Arab ambitions and interests in the continent.

Arabs, Swahili & Portuguese

The Land of Zanj

It was in the 8th century that Arab dhows began docking regularly in East African ports as part of their annual trade migration. In their wake, Arabs set up trading posts along the seaboard, intermarrying with Africans and creating a cosmopolitan culture that, in time, became known as Swahili. Before long there were Arab-Swahili city states all along the coast from Somalia to Mozambique; the remains of many of these settlements can still be seen, most notably at Gede.

By the 10th century the 'Land of Zanj' (the present-day coastal region of Kenya and Tanzania) was exporting leopard skins, tortoiseshell, rhino horns, ivory and, most importantly, slaves and gold to Arabia and India. Ports included Shanga, Gede, Lamu and Mombasa as well as Zanzibar (Tanzania). Kilwa, 300km south of Zanzibar, marked the southernmost limit of travel for Arab dhows. For over 700 years, up to 1450, the Islamic world was virtually the only external influence on sub-Saharan Africa.

The word *swahili* originates from the Arabic word *sawahil*, which means 'of the coast'. It refers both to the Swahili language (most accurately called Kiswahili), as well as the Islamic people of the coast.

Portuguese East Africa

Arab-Swahili domination on the coast received its first serious challenge with the arrival of the Portuguese in the 15th century, spurred by the tales of gold and riches that traders brought back from their travels. In 1497, for example, while on his pioneering voyage along the coastline of South and East Africa, Vasco da Gama found Arab dhows

EAST AFRICAN SLAVES

Slaves left Africa via the Sahara, the Red Sea, the Atlantic and the East African coast. The total estimated number of slaves exported from tropical Africa between 1500 and the late 1800s is put at 18 million; two million of them came from East Africa. By its height in the 18th century, the slave trade had touched every region on the continent.

In East Africa, around 50,000 slaves passed through the markets every year – nearly 44% of the total population of the coast. Overall, close to 600,000 slaves were sold through the Zanzibar market between 1830 and 1873, when a treaty with Britain paved the way for the end of the trade. It's true that slavery was already an established fact of African life before the advent of the slave trade. But enslavement for sale, the importation of foreign goods and the sheer scale of Europe's involvement were radical departures from everything that had gone before. The social, psychological and economic impact changed the fate of the continent forever.

AD 800	10th century	1415	1492–1505
Muslims from Arabia and Persia begin to dock in East African ports. Soon they establish Arab-Swahili states and trading depots along the coast from Somalia to Mozambique.	The 'Land of Zanj' along East Africa's coast becomes known for its exotic export goods, including leopard skins, tortoiseshell, rhino horns, ivory, slaves and gold, predominantly to Arabia and India.	Chinese fleets visit East Africa in the early 15th century. In 1415 a giraffe is transported to Beijing and presented by Malindi envoys to the emperor himself.	Dom Francisco de Almeida's armada begins the Portuguese conquest of Kenya. Mombasa falls in 1505, followed by towns like Barawa (Somalia), Kilwa, Moçambique and Sofala, up and down the coast.

at the Zambezi delta loaded with gold dust. During the same period Europe was desperately short of labour as it struggled to recover from the effects of the Black Death (1347–51). The plantations of southern Europe were initially worked by captive Muslims and Slavic peoples (hence the word 'slaves'), but with access to Africa a whole new labour market opened up.

The Portuguese consolidated their position on the East African coast through blatant force and terror, justifying their actions as battles in a Christian war against Islam. They sailed their heavily armed vessels into the harbours of important Swahili towns, demanding submission to the rule of Portugal and payment of large annual tributes. Towns that refused were attacked, their possessions seized and resisters killed. Zanzibar was the first Swahili town to be taken in this manner (in 1503). Malindi formed an alliance with the Portuguese, which hastened the fall of Mombasa in 1505.

British East Africa
Securing Control

In 1884 European powers met in Germany for the Berlin conference. Here behind closed doors they decided the fate of the African continent. No African leaders, let alone ordinary Africans, were invited to attend, nor were they consulted.

The colonial settlement of Kenya dates from 1885, when Germany established a protectorate over the sultan of Zanzibar's coastal possessions. In 1888 Sir William Mackinnon received a royal charter and concessionary rights to develop trade in the region under the aegis of the British East Africa Company (BEAC). Seeking to consolidate its East African territories, Germany traded its coastal holdings in return for sole rights over Tanganyika (Tanzania) in 1890. Still, it was only when the BEAC ran into financial difficulties in 1895 that the British government finally stepped in to establish formal control through the East African Protectorate.

British Kenya

Initially, British influence was confined to the coastal area, and any presence in the interior was restricted to isolated settlers and explorers. Maasai resistance began to crack following a brutal civil war between the Ilmaasai and Iloikop groups and the simultaneous arrival of rinderpest (a cattle disease), cholera, smallpox and famine. The British were able to negotiate a treaty with the Maasai, allowing

---

Swahili Ruins

Gede (North Coast)

Jumba la Mtwana (south of Mombasa)

Mnarani (south of Mombasa)

Takwa (North Coast)

Shanga (North Coast)

Wasini Island (south of Mombasa)

HISTORY BRITISH EAST AFRICA

In order to force the indigenous population into the labour market, the British introduced a hut tax in 1901. This could only be paid in cash, so Africans had to seek paid work.

1593	1729	1807–73	1883–84
The Portuguese construct the coral Fort Jesus in Mombasa. Accounts from the garrison at Mombasa record the first evidence of maize production in Africa.	The Portuguese grip on East Africa ends in 1698, when Mombasa falls to Baluchi Arabs from Oman after a 33-month siege. In 1729 the Portuguese leave the Kenyan coast for good.	Legislation abolishing the slave trade is enacted in Britain in 1807. Another 65 years pass before Sultan Barghash of Zanzibar bans the slave trade on the East African coast.	British Explorer Joseph Thomson crosses Maasailand en route to Lake Victoria then returns to the coast, an important forerunner to Britain's colonial push inland.

THE LORD OF HAPPY VALLEY

During the colonial heyday, Happy Valley (the highland area outside Nairobi) played host to an eccentric cast of British elites with a reputation for fondness for drinking, drug abuse and wife swapping. However, few can rival Hugh Cholmondeley (1870–1931), third baron of Delamere.

Lord Delamere first set foot on the African continent in 1891 to hunt lions in then British Somaliland; he is widely credited with coining the term 'white hunter'. By the early 1900s, Lord Delamere owned more than 120,000 hectares of land and was one of Kenya's most influential colonists. For more than 20 years, he doggedly farmed his vast country estates by mere trial and error, experimenting with various crop strains from around the British Empire.

At the Norfolk Hotel, which still bears a bar-restaurant named in his honour, Lord Delamere once rode his horse through the dining room, wooing dinner guests with his ability to leap over banquet tables.

In his later years, Lord Delamere established himself as a firebrand politician determined to protect British holdings in Africa. Often described as the 'Cecil Rhodes of Kenya', he once wrote of his support for the 'extension of European civilisation', stating that the British were 'superior to heterogeneous African races only now emerging from centuries of relative barbarism'.

In 2005 charges were dropped against Lord Delamere's great-grandson, Baron Thomas Cholmondeley, who had been accused of shooting a Maasai game warden. One year later, a poacher was shot on Cholmondeley's property and in 2009 Cholmondeley was sentenced to eight months' imprisonment for manslaughter. The police spokesman on the case was reported as saying, 'The Delameres used to be untouchable. But that's all changed now.' Cholmondeley died of complications after surgery in 2016, aged 48.

the British to drive the Mombasa–Uganda railway line through the heart of Maasai grazing lands.

The completion of the railway enabled the British administration to relocate from Mombasa to more temperate Nairobi. Although the Maasai suffered the worst annexations of land, being restricted to designated reserves, the Kikuyu from Mt Kenya and the Aberdares (areas of white settlement) came to nurse a particular grievance about their alienation from the land.

By 1912 settlers had established themselves in the highlands and set up mixed agricultural farms, turning a profit for the colony for the first time. These first outposts, Naivasha and the Ngong Hills, are still heavily white-settled areas today.

1884–93	1884–85	1888	1890
A decade known by the Maasai as *enkidaaroto* ('the disaster') as drought, a rinderpest epidemic and civil war severely weaken the Maasai resistance to Britain's colonial advance.	The Berlin Conference convenes and Africa is divided into colonial territories. Today the continent is divided into 54 states, more than four times the number in South America.	Sir William Mackinnon establishes the British East Africa Company (BEAC) in Mombasa. Its focus is the exportation of goods and agriculture and the construction of the East African Railway.	Waiyaki Wa Henya, a Kikuyu chief who signed a treaty with Frederick Lugard of the BEAC under pressure, burns down Lugard's Fort. Waiyaki is abducted two years later and murdered.

The colonial process was interrupted by WWI, when two-thirds of the 3000 white settlers in Kenya formed impromptu cavalry units and marched against Germans in neighbouring Tanganyika. Colonisation resumed after the war, under a scheme by which white veterans of the European campaign were offered subsidised land in the highlands around Nairobi. The net effect was a huge upsurge in the white Kenyan population, from 9000 in 1920 to 80,000 in the 1950s.

The Road to Independence
Nationalist Stirrings

Although largely peaceful and a period of economic growth, the interwar years were to see the fomenting of early nationalist aspirations. Grievances over land appropriation and displacement were only exacerbated in 1920, when, after considerable lobbying from white settlers, Kenya was transformed into a Crown Colony. A Legislative Council was established but Africans were barred from political participation (right up until 1944). In reaction to their exclusion, the Kikuyu tribe, Kenya's most populous group and the one under the greatest pressure from European settlers, founded the Young Kikuyu Association, led by Harry Thuku. This was to become the Kenya African Union (KAU), a nationalist organisation demanding access to white-owned land.

One passionate advocate for the movement was a young man called Johnstone Kamau, later known as Jomo Kenyatta. When this early activism fell on deaf ears he joined the more outspoken Kikuyu Central Association; the association was promptly banned.

In 1929, with money supplied by Indian communists, Kenyatta sailed for London to plead the Kikuyu case with the British colonial secretary, who declined to meet with him. While in London, Kenyatta met with a group called the League Against Imperialism, which took him to Moscow and Berlin, back to Nairobi and then back to London, where he stayed for the next 15 years. During this time, he studied revolutionary tactics in Moscow and built up the Pan-African Federation with Hastings Banda (who later became the president of Malawi) and Kwame Nkrumah (later president of Ghana).

The War Years

Although African nationalists made impressive headway, it was the advent of WWII that was to ultimately bring about the rapid demise of colonialism in Africa. In 1941, in a desperate bid for survival, British Premier Winston Churchill crossed the Atlantic to plead for

Red Strangers: The White Tribe of Kenya (CS Nicholls; 2005) offers a sympathetic perspective on colonialism, examining Kenya's white settler population before and after independence. For a light-hearted look at the era, try *The Ghosts of Happy Valley: Searching for the Lost World of Africa's Infamous Aristocrats* (Juliet Barnes; 2013).

Africans and Africa played a key role in WWII. The East African Carrier Corps consisted of over 400,000 men, and the development of the atom bomb was entirely dependent on uranium from the Congo.

1895	1899	1901	1914
After experiencing serious financial difficulties, BEAC hands over to the British government, which becomes responsible for Kenya through the East African Protectorate.	Nairobi is founded in an area of rivers, plains and swamps traditionally known by the Maasai as *uaso nairobi* (cold water). Residents have to carry guns to defend against wild animals.	The East African Railway links the coast with Uganda. The construction of the line sees a huge influx of Indians, who provide the bulk of skilled labour.	The first shots of WWI in East Africa are fired near Taveta. Although the war on East African soil would later expand, Kenya's Taita Hills was an important battleground in the early years.

Weep Not, Child (1964), by Kenya's most famous novelist, Ngũgĩ wa Thiong'o, tells of British occupation and the effects of the Mau Mau on the lives of black Kenyans. His 2010 memoir *Dreams in a Time of War* is a patiently told chronicle of his childhood in colonial Kenya.

American aid. The resulting Atlantic Charter (1942), which Churchill negotiated with President Roosevelt, enshrined the end of colonialism in the third clause, which stated self-determination for all colonies as one of the postwar objectives.

In October 1945 the sixth Pan-African Congress was convened in Manchester, England. For the first time this was predominantly a congress of Africa's young leaders. Kwame Nkrumah and Jomo Kenyatta were there, along with trade unionists, lawyers, teachers and writers from all over Africa. By the time Kenyatta returned to Kenya in 1946, he was the leader of a bona fide Kenyan liberation movement.

Mau Mau

Although Kenyatta appeared willing to act as the British government's accredited Kenyan representative within a developing constitutional framework, militant factions among the KAU had a more radical agenda. When in 1951 Ghana became the first African country to achieve independence, it raised the stakes even higher.

Starting with small-scale terror operations, bands of guerrillas began to intimidate white settlers, threatening their farms and anyone deemed to be a collaborator. Their aim: to drive white settlers from the land and reclaim it. Kenyatta's role in the Mau Mau rebellion, as it came to be known, was equivocal. At a public meeting in 1952, he denounced the movement, but he was arrested along with other Kikuyu politicians and sentenced to seven years' hard labour for 'masterminding' the plot.

Four years of intense military operations ensued. The various Mau Mau units came together under the umbrella of the Kenya Land Freedom Army, led by Dedan Kimathi, and outright guerrilla warfare followed, with the British declaring a state of emergency in 1952.

The first major Kenyan film to tackle the thorny subject of the Mau Mau uprising, Kibaara Kaugi's *Enough is Enough* (2005), is a fictionalised biopic of Wamuyu wa Gakuru, a Kikuyu woman who became a famed guerrilla fighter.

By 1956 the Mau Mau had been quelled and Dedan Kimathi was publicly hanged on the orders of the British policeman Colonel Henderson (who was later deported from Kenya for crimes against humanity). But Kenyatta was to continue the struggle following his release in 1959. Soon even white Kenyans began to feel the winds of change, and in 1960 the British government officially announced its plan to transfer power to a democratically elected African government. Independence was scheduled for December 1963, accompanied by grants and loans of US$100 million to enable the Kenyan assembly to buy out European farmers in the highlands and restore the land to local tribes.

1918–39	1920	1929	1931
The interwar period facilitates economic activity. Famine relief and campaigns against epidemic diseases are established in the colonies, stimulating a 37.5% increase in Africa's population.	Kenya is declared a Crown Colony. Africans are barred from the Legislative Council. The next year the first nationalist organisation, the Kenya African Union (KAU), is established and presses for land rights.	Jomo Kenyatta sails for London, beginning 15 years of travels in his bid to drum up support for Kenyan independence. During this period, he helps build up the Pan-African Federation.	Lord Delamere dies at the age of 61. He had helped to lay the foundations for Kenya's agricultural economy, but personified the deeply resented policies of the British colonial government.

It had been a long time coming, but Kenya finally became independent on 12 December 1963.

Independent Kenya

Harambee

The political handover began in earnest in 1962 with Kenyatta's election to a newly constituted parliament. To ensure a smooth transition of power, Kenyatta's party, the Kenya African National Union (KANU), which advocated a unitary, centralised government, joined forces with the Kenya African Democratic Union (KADU), which favoured *majimbo,* a federal set-up. *Harambee,* meaning 'pulling together', was seen as more important than political factionalism, and KADU voluntarily dissolved in 1964, leaving Kenyatta and KANU in full control.

It is difficult to overstate the optimism that accompanied those early days of postcolonial independence. Kenyatta took pains to allay the fears of white settlers, declaring 'I have suffered imprisonment and detention; but that is gone, and I am not going to remember it. Let us join hands and work for the benefit of Kenya'. But the nascent economy was vulnerable and the political landscape was barely developed. As a result the consolidation of power by the new ruling elite nurtured an authoritarian regime.

One-Party State

Although considered an African success story, the Kenyatta regime failed to undertake the essential task of deconstructing the colonial state in favour of a system with greater relevance to the aspirations of the average Kenyan. The *majimbo* (federalist) system – advocated by KADU and agreed upon in the run-up to independence – was such a system, but it died with the party in 1964.

Power was not only being centralised in Nairobi, but increasingly also in the hands of the president. The consolidation of presidential power was buttressed by a series of constitutional amendments, culminating in the Constitutional Amendment Act No 16 of 1969, which empowered the president to control the civil service. The effects were disastrous. Subsequent years saw widespread discrimination in favour of Kenyatta's own tribe, the Kikuyu. The Trade Union Disputes Act made industrial action illegal and when KADU tried to reassemble as the Kenya People's Union (KPU) it was banned. Corruption soon became a problem at all levels of the power structure and the political arena contracted. Barely a decade after independence, much of the optimism had evaporated.

In 2013 the British government agreed to pay £19.9 million in costs and compensation to more than 5000 elderly Kenyans who suffered torture and abuse during the Mau Mau uprising in the 1950s.

Historical Reads

Through Masai Land (Joseph Thomson; 1887)

Out of Africa (Karen Blixen; 1937)

The Flame Trees of Thika (Elspeth Huxley; 1959)

Nine Faces of Kenya (Elspeth Huxley; 1990)

1930s	1942	1946	1946–48
Thousands of European settlers occupy the Central Highlands, farming tea and coffee. The land claims of the area's million-plus members of the Kikuyu tribe are not recognised in European terms.	The Atlantic Charter, signed by Winston Churchill and President Roosevelt, guarantees self-determination for the colonies as a postwar objective. The charter also gives America access to African markets.	Jomo Kenyatta completes his anthropology degree and returns to Kenya as head of the KAU. The British government views him as its accredited representative in the independence handover.	To separate the region's wildlife from Nairobi's burgeoning human population, Nairobi National Park becomes British East Africa's first national park. Amboseli National Reserve is gazetted two years later.

The Moi Years

Kenyatta was succeeded in 1978 by his vice-president, Daniel arap Moi. A Kalenjin, Moi was regarded by establishment power brokers as a suitable front man for their interests, as his tribe was relatively small and beholden to the Kikuyu.

On assumption of power, Moi sought to consolidate his regime by marginalising those who had campaigned to stop him from succeeding Kenyatta. Lacking a capital base of his own upon which he could build and maintain a patron-client network, and faced with shrinking economic opportunities, Moi resorted to the politics of exclusion. He reconfigured the financial, legal, political and administrative institutions. For instance, a constitutional amendment in 1982 made Kenya a de jure one-party state, while another in 1986 removed the security of tenure for the attorney-general, comptroller, auditor general and High Court judges, making all these positions personally beholden to the president. These developments had the effect of transforming Kenya from an 'imperial state' under Kenyatta to a 'personal state' under Moi.

Winds of Change

By the late 1980s, most Kenyans had had enough. Following the widely contested 1988 elections, Charles Rubia and Kenneth Matiba joined forces to call for the freedom to form alternative political parties and stated their plan to hold a political rally in Nairobi on 7 July without a licence. Though the duo was detained prior to their intended meeting, people turned out anyway, only to be met with brutal police retaliation. Twenty people were killed and police arrested a slew of politicians, human-rights activists and journalists.

The rally, known thereafter as Saba Saba ('Seven Seven' in Kiswahili), was a pivotal event in the push for a multiparty Kenya. The following year, the Forum for the Restoration of Democracy (FORD) was formed, led by Jaramogi Oginga Odinga, a powerful Luo politician and former vice-president under Jomo Kenyatta. FORD was initially banned and Odinga arrested, but the resulting outcry led to his release and, finally, a change in the constitution that allowed opposition parties to register for the first time.

Faced with a foreign debt of nearly US$9 billion and blanket suspension of foreign aid, Moi was pressured into holding multiparty elections in early 1992, but independent observers reported a litany of electoral inconsistencies. Just as worrying, about 2000 people were killed during ethnic clashes in the Rift Valley, widely believed to have been triggered by government agitation.

Kenya: Between Hope & Despair, 1963–2011 (2011), by Daniel Branch, covers the 2007 election and its aftermath in searing detail. The encyclopaedic *Kenya: A History Since Independence* (2011), by Charles Hornsby, is another meticulously researched study of Kenya's history postindependence.

1952–56	1963	1966	1978
The British declare a state of emergency during the Mau Mau rebellion. By 1956 nearly 2000 Kikuyu loyalists and 11,500 Mau Mau have been killed. Thirty-two white settlers die.	Kenya gains independence; Jomo Kenyatta becomes president. In the same year the Organisation of African Unity is established, aimed at providing Africa with an independent voice in world affairs.	The Kenya People's Union is formed by Jaramogi Oginga Odinga. Following unrest at a presidential visit to Nyanza Province the party is banned; Kenya becomes a de facto one-party state.	Kenyatta is succeeded by his vice-president, Daniel arap Moi, who goes on to become one of the most enduring 'Big Men' of Africa, ruling for the next 25 years.

In 1992 Moi secured only 37% of the votes cast against a combined opposition tally of 63%, but he held on to power. The same results were replicated in the 1997 elections, when Moi once again secured victory with 40% of the votes cast against 60% of the opposition. After the 1997 elections, KANU was forced to bow to mounting pressure and initiate some changes: some Draconian colonial laws were repealed, as was the requirement for licences to hold political rallies.

On 7 August 1998, Islamic extremists bombed the US embassies in Nairobi and Dar es Salaam in Tanzania, killing more than 200 people and bringing al-Qaeda and Osama bin Laden to international attention for the first time. The effect on the Kenyan economy was devastating. It would take four years to rebuild the shattered tourism industry.

The Kibaki Years & Beyond

Democratic Kenya

Having been beaten twice in the 1992 and 1997 elections due to disunity, 12 opposition groups united to form the National Alliance Rainbow Coalition (NARC). With Moi's presidency due to end in 2002, many feared that he would alter the constitution again to retain his position. This time, though, he announced his intention to retire.

Moi put his weight firmly behind Uhuru Kenyatta, the son of Jomo Kenyatta, as his successor, but the support garnered by NARC ensured a resounding victory for the party, with 62% of the vote. Mwai Kibaki was inaugurated as Kenya's third president on 30 December 2002.

When Kibaki assumed office in January 2003, donors were highly supportive of the new government and its pledges to end corruption. In 2003–04, donors contributed billions of dollars to the fight against corruption, including support for the office of a newly appointed anticorruption 'czar'.

Corruption Continues

Despite initial positive signs it became clear by mid-2004 that large-scale corruption was still a considerable problem in Kenya. Western diplomats alleged that corruption had cost the treasury US$1 billion since Kibaki took office. In February 2005 the British high commissioner, Sir Edward Clay, denounced the 'massive looting' of state resources by senior government politicians, including sitting cabinet ministers. Within days, Kibaki's anticorruption 'czar', John Githongo, resigned and went into exile amid rumours of death threats related

Michela Wrong's *It's Our Turn to Eat: The Story of a Kenyan Whistleblower* (2009) is a searing insight into Kenya's battle against corruption. Taking centre stage is John Githongo, the anticorruption 'czar' who fled into exile after unearthing corruption at the highest level.

1982	1993	1998	2002
The Universities Academic Staff Union (UASU), one of the few credible opposition groups remaining, is banned. This leads to a short-lived coup by the air force.	In August 1993 inflation reaches a record 100% and the government's budget deficit is over 10% of GDP. Donors suspend aid to Kenya and insist on wide-ranging economic reforms.	Terrorist attacks shake US embassies in Nairobi and Dar es Salaam, killing more than 200 people. The effect on the Kenyan economy is devastating.	Mwai Kibaki wins the 2002 election as leader of the National Alliance Rainbow Coalition (NARC). For the first time in Kenya the ballot box elects a president by popular vote.

to his investigation of high-level politicians. He has since returned to the country at the head of an anticorruption NGO. With Githongo's release of a damning, detailed dossier in February 2006, Kibaki was forced to remove three ministers from their cabinet positions.

At the root of the difficulties in fighting corruption were the conditions that brought Kibaki to power. The slow march to democratisation in Kenya has been attributed to the personalised nature of politics, where focus is placed on individuals with ethnic support bases rather than institutions. To maximise his electoral chances, Kibaki's coalition also included a number of KANU officials who were deeply implicated in the worst abuses of the Moi regime. Indebted to such people for power, Kibaki was only ever able to effect a half-hearted reshuffle of his cabinet. He also allowed his ministers a wide margin of manoeuvre to guarantee their continued support.

But the Kibaki government did at least succeed in making primary and secondary education more accessible for ordinary Kenyans, while state control over the economy was loosened.

Things Fall Apart

On 27 December 2007, Kenya held presidential, parliamentary and local elections. While the parliamentary and local-government elections were largely considered credible, the presidential elections were marred by serious irregularities, reported by both Kenyan and international election monitors, and by independent nongovernmental observers. Nonetheless, the Electoral Commission declared Mwai Kibaki the winner, triggering a wave of violence across the country.

The Rift Valley, Western Highlands, Nyanza Province and Mombasa – areas afflicted by years of political machination, previous election violence and large-scale displacement – exploded in ugly ethnic confrontations. The violence left more than 1000 people dead and over 600,000 people homeless.

Fearing for the stability of the most stable linchpin of East Africa, former UN secretary-general Kofi Annan and a panel of 'Eminent African Persons' flew to Kenya to mediate talks. A power-sharing agreement was signed on 28 February 2008 between President Kibaki and Raila Odinga, the leader of the ODM opposition. The coalition provided for the establishment of a prime ministerial position (to be filled by Odinga), as well as a division of cabinet posts according to the parties' representation in parliament.

The Kenyatta–Odinga rivalry is nothing new. In the 1960s, Odinga's father, Jaramogi Oginga Odinga, was the loyal deputy to Kenya's first postindependence president, Uhuru's father, Jomo Kenyatta. The two fell out in 1969 and Odinga served prison time before becoming a leading opposition figure until his death in 1994.

2007	2010	2012	4 March 2013
Kenyans go to the polls again. The outcome is contested amid bloody clashes. International mediation finally brings about a power-sharing agreement in April 2008.	The radically overhauled constitution is approved by 67% of Kenya's voters. It provides for judicial independence, devolves powers to the regions and incorporates a bill of rights.	Oil is discovered in the Lake Turkana area, generating great excitement across the country at the prospect of Kenya becoming a major oil-producing nation.	Uhuru Kenyatta, son of independent Kenya's first president, wins presidential elections with 50.07% of the vote, thereby crossing the 50% threshold required to avoid a run-off poll.

309

Rebuilding Confidence

Despite some difficult moments, the fragile coalition government stood the test of time. Arguably its most important success was the progressive 2010 constitution, which was passed in a referendum by 67% of Kenya's voters. Among the key elements of this new constitution are the devolution of powers to Kenya's regions, the introduction of a bill of rights and the separation of judicial, executive and legislative powers.

In 2013 Uhuru Kenyatta won hotly contested presidential elections, claiming 50.07% of the vote and thereby avoiding the need for a run-off election against Raila Odinga. Despite widespread reports of irregularities in the conduct of the elections, the Supreme Court upheld the result and postelection violence was minimal. Kenya breathed a huge sigh of relief.

In 2017, largely peaceful presidential elections resulted in another victory for incumbent Kenyatta. However, when the opposition challenged the outcome in court, the Supreme Court annulled the results and ordered fresh elections due to irregularities. The opposition boycotted the election and although President Kenyatta won, voter turnout was low and there was considerable uncertainty about the political road ahead.

HISTORY THE KIBAKI YEARS & BEYOND

21 September 2013	2014	April 2015	2016–17
Four armed supporters of Somalia's militant al-Shabaab group attack Westgate Shopping Mall in an upmarket area of Nairobi. The siege lasts for days and ends with 67 people dead, including the attackers.	The International Criminal Court (ICC) drops charges against President Uhuru Kenyatta due to a lack of evidence. The charges relate to the postelection violence in 2007.	Al-Shabaab militants from Somalia kill 148 people in a terrorist attack on Garissa University College in northwestern Kenya.	A devastating drought grips much of Kenya, especially in the north, and the government declares a national disaster.

Tribes of Kenya

The tribe remains an important aspect of a Kenyan's identity: upon meeting a fellow Kenyan, the first question on anyone's mind is, 'What tribe do you come from?' Although we have divided Kenya's tribes into geographical areas, this is a guide only, as you'll find Kenyans from most tribal groupings well beyond their traditional lands. In the same way, distinctions between many tribal groups are slowly being eroded as people move to major cities for work, and intermarry.

Rift Valley & Central Kenya

Kikuyu (also Gikikuyu)

The Kikuyu make up 22% of the population and are Kenya's largest and most influential tribe. This tribe contributed the country's first president, Jomo Kenyatta, and its current one, his son, Uhuru Kenyatta. Famously warlike, the Kikuyu overran the lands of the Athi and Gumba tribes, becoming hugely populous in the process. Now their heartland surrounds Mt Kenya, although they also represent the largest proportion of people living in Kenya's major cities. With territory bordering that of the Maasai, the tribes share many cultural similarities due to intermarriage. The administration of the *mwaki* (clans) was originally taken care of by a council of elders, with a good deal of importance being placed on the role of the witch doctor, the medicine man and the blacksmith. Initiation rites consist of ritual circumcision for boys and genital mutilation for girls (although the latter is slowly becoming less common). Each group of youths of the same age belongs to a *riikaan* (age-set) and passes through the various stages of life, and their associated rituals, together. Subgroups of the Kikuyu include the Embu, Ndia and Mbeere.

The Kikuyu are renowned for their entrepreneurial skills and for popping up everywhere in Kenya (the Kikuyu name Kamau is as common as Smith is in Britain).

Kalenjin

The Kalenjin (12% of the population) comprise the Nandi, Kipsigis, Eleyo, Marakwet, Pokot and Tugen (former president Daniel arap Moi's people), and occupy the western edge of the central Rift Valley area. They first migrated to the area west of Lake Turkana from southern Sudan around 2000 years ago, but gradually filtered south as the climate became harsher. The Kipsigis have a love of cattle rustling, which continues to cause strife between them and neighbouring tribes. However, the tribe is most famous for producing Kenya's Olympic runners (75% of all the top runners in Kenya are Kalenjin). As with most tribes, the Kalenjin are organised into age-sets. Administration of the law is carried out at the *kok* (an informal court led by the clan's elders).

Meru

Originally from the coast, the Meru now occupy the northeastern slopes of Mt Kenya and represent 6% of Kenya's population. Up until 1974 the Meru were led by a chief (the *mogwe*), but upon his death the last incumbent converted to Christianity. Strangely, many of their tribal stories mirror the traditional tales of the Old Testament. The practice of ancestor worship, however, is still widespread. They have long been governed by an elected council of elders *(njuuri)*, making them the only tribe practising a structured form of democratic governance prior to colonialism. The Meru now live on some of the most fertile farmland in Kenya and grow numerous cash crops. Subgroups of the Meru include the Chuka, Igembe, Igoji, Tharaka, Muthambi, Tigania and Imenti.

Samburu

Closely related to the Maasai, and speaking the same language, the Samburu occupy an arid area directly north of Mt Kenya and make up around 0.5% of the population. It seems that when the Maasai migrated to the area from Sudan, some headed east and became the Samburu. Like the Maasai, they have retained their traditional way of life as nomadic pastoralists, depending for their survival on their livestock. They live in small villages of five to eight families, divided into age-sets, and they continue to practise traditional rites like male and female circumcision and polygamy. After marriage, women traditionally leave their clan, and their social status is much lower than that of men. Samburu women wear similar colourful bead necklaces to the Maasai. Like the Maasai and Rendille, Samburu warriors paste their hair with red ochre to create a visor to shield their eyes from the sun.

Western Kenya

Luhya

Made up of 18 different groups (the largest being the Bukusu), the Bantu-speaking Luhya are the second-largest group in Kenya, representing 14% of the population. They occupy a relatively small, high-density area of the country in the Western Highlands centred on Kakamega. In the past, the Luhya were skilled metal workers, forging knives and tools that were traded with other groups, but today most Luhya are agriculturists, farming groundnuts, sesame and maize. Smallholders also grow cash crops, such as cotton and sugar cane. Many Luhya are superstitious and still have a strong belief in witchcraft. Traditional costumes and rituals are becoming less common with each passing year.

Luo

The tribe of former US President Barack Obama's father, the Luo live on the shores of Lake Victoria and are Kenya's third-largest tribal group with 13% of the population. Though originally a cattle-herding people like the Maasai, their herds suffered terribly from the rinderpest outbreak in the 1890s so they switched to fishing and subsistence agriculture. During the struggle for independence, many of the country's leading politicians and trade unionists were Luo. Socially, the Luo are unusual among Kenya's tribes in that they don't practise circumcision for either sex. The family unit is part of a larger grouping of *dhoot* (families), several of which in turn make up an *ogandi* (group of geographically related people), each led by a *ruoth* (chief). The Luo have two major recreational passions, soccer and music, and there are many distinctive Luo instruments made from gourds and gut or wire strings.

Gusii (Kisii)

The Gusii (6% of the population) occupy the Western Highlands, east of Lake Victoria, forming a small Bantu-speaking island in a mainly Nilotic-speaking area. Primarily cattle-herders and crop-cultivators, they farm Kenya's cash crops – tea, coffee and pyrethrum – as well as market vegetables. They are also well known for their basketry and distinctive, rounded soapstone carvings. Like many other tribal groups, Gusii society is clan based, with everyone organised into age-sets.

The Meru are active in the cultivation of *miraa*, the stems of which contain a stimulant similar to amphetamines, which are exported to Somalia and Yemen.

TRIBES OF KENYA WESTERN KENYA

Medicine men *(abanyamorigo),* in particular, hold a highly respected and privileged position, performing the role of doctor and social worker. One of their more peculiar practices is trepanning: the removal of sections of the skull or spine to aid maladies such as backache or concussion.

Southern Kenya

Akamba (also Kamba)

The region east of Nairobi towards Tsavo National Park is the traditional homeland of the Bantu-speaking Akamba who make up 11% of the population. Great traders in ivory, beer, honey, iron weapons and ornaments, they traditionally plied their trade between Lake Victoria and the coast, and north to Lake Turkana. In particular, they traded with the Maasai and Kikuyu for food stocks. Highly regarded by the British for their fighting ability, they were drafted in large numbers into the British army. After WWI the British tried to limit their cattle stocks and settled more Europeans in their tribal territories. In response, the Akamba marched en masse to Nairobi to squat peacefully at Kariokor Market in protest, forcing the administration to relent. Nowadays, they are more famous for their elegant *makonde*-style (ebony) carving. Akamba society is clan based with all adolescents going through initiation rites at about the age of 12.

Maasai

Despite representing only a small proportion of the total population (2%), the Maasai are, for many, the definitive symbol of Kenya. With a reputation as fierce warriors, the tribe has largely managed to stay outside the mainstream of development in Kenya and still maintains large cattle herds along the Tanzanian border. The British gazetted the Masai Mara National Reserve in the early 1960s, displacing the Maasai, and they slowly continued to annexe more and more Maasai land. Resettlement programmes have met with limited success as the Maasai traditionally scorn agriculture and land ownership. The Maasai still have a distinctive style and traditional age-grade social structure, and circumcision is still widely practised for both men and women. Women typically wear large plate-like bead necklaces, while the men typically wear a red-checked *shuka* (blanket) and carry a distinctive ball-ended club. Blood and meat are the mainstays of the Maasai diet, supplemented by a drink called *mursik,* made from milk fermented with charcoal, which has been shown to lower cholesterol.

Taita

The Taita people, making up 0.1% of the population, came originally from what is now Tanzania, and first settled in the region around Voi and Taveta in Kenya's far southeast around 10 centuries ago. The Taita language belongs to the Bantu group of languages and is similar to Swahili, although such is their interaction with other tribes that their language has imported many words from neighbouring tribes, including the Kikuyu. Taita social life was traditionally dispersed and strongly territorial, with each clan inhabiting a discrete area of the Taita Hills, south of what is now Tsavo West National Park. It was only after colonialism that a collective sense of Taita identity developed in earnest, a process accelerated by the intrusion of the railway through Taita lands; Mwangeka, a Taita hero, was lauded for his resistance to colonial rule. Taita religion was largely animist in nature, with sacred meeting places and elaborate burial rituals the defining features, although few Taita now live according to traditional ways.

The Rosen Publishing Group (www. rosenpublishing. com) publishes the *Heritage Library of African Peoples,* aimed at late-primary and early-secondary school students. Although the entire East Africa set is available, individual titles (such as *Luo, Kikuyu, Maasai* and *Samburu*) are also easy to track down.

The Worlds of a Maasai Warrior: An Autobiography (1988), by Tepilit Ole Saitoti, presents an intriguing perspective on the juxtaposition of traditional and modern in East Africa.

Northern Kenya

Borana

The Borana are one of the cattle-herding Oromo peoples, indigenous to Ethiopia, who migrated south into northern Kenya and make up less than 0.1% of the population. They are now concentrated around Marsabit and Isiolo. The Borana observe strict role segregation between men and women – men being responsible for care of the herds while women are in charge of children and day-to-day life. Borana groups may pack up camp and move up to four times a year, depending on weather conditions and available grazing land. As a nomadic group their reliance on oral history is strong, with many traditions passed on through song.

Turkana

Originally from Karamojong in northeastern Uganda, the Turkana live in the virtual desert country of Kenya's northwest and make up 1.5% of Kenya's population. Like the Samburu and the Maasai (with whom they are linguistically linked), the Turkana are primarily cattle herders, although fishing on the waters of Lake Turkana and small-scale farming is on the increase. Traditional costume and practices are still commonplace, although the Turkana are one of the few tribes to have voluntarily given up the practice of circumcision. Men typically cover part of their hair with mud, which is then painted blue and decorated with ostrich and other feathers, and, despite the intense heat, their main garment is a woollen blanket. A woman's attire is dictated by her marital and maternal status; the marriage ritual itself is quite unusual and involves kidnapping the bride. Tattooing is also common. Men were traditionally tattooed on the shoulders for killing an enemy – the right shoulder for killing a man, the left for a woman. Witch doctors and prophets are held in high regard, and scars on someone's lower stomach are usually a sign of a witch doctor's attempt to cast out an undesirable spirit using incisions.

A surprising number of Turkana men still wear markings on their shoulders to indicate they have killed another man.

THE MAASAI & THEIR CATTLE

The Maasai tell the following story. One of the Maasai gods, Naiteru-Kop, was wandering the earth at the beginning of time and there he found a Dorobo man – 'Dorobo' is a derogatory Maasai word used to describe hunter-gatherer groups – who lived with a snake, a cow and an elephant. The man killed the snake and the elephant, but the elephant's calf escaped and came upon Le-eyo, a Maasai man to whom he told the story of the Dorobo.

The elephant calf took Le-eyo to the Dorobo man's compound, where Le-eyo heard Naiteru-Kop, the Maasai god, calling out to the Dorobo man and telling him to come out the next morning. Having heard this, it was Le-eyo who emerged first the following morning and asked Naiteru-Kop what to do next. Following the god's instructions, Le-eyo built a large enclosure, with a little hut of branches and grasses on one side. He then slaughtered a thin calf, but did not eat it, instead laying out the calf's hide, and piling the meat high on top. He then built a large fire, and threw the meat upon it.

A great storm swept over the land. With the storm clouds overhead, a leather cord dropped from the sky into Le-eyo's compound, and down the cord came cattle until Le-eyo's compound was full of these animals. One of the cattle stuck its hoof through the hut's wall, and Le-eyo called out, frightened. Upon Le-eyo's cry, the cattle stopped falling from the sky. Naiteru-Kop called out to Le-eyo: 'These are all the cattle you will receive, because your cry stopped them coming. But they are yours to look after, and you will live with them.'

Since that day, the Dorobo have been hunters and the Maasai have herded their cattle, convinced that all the cattle in the world belong to them.

El-Molo

This tiny tribal group (less than 0.1% of the population) has strong links with the Rendille, their close neighbours. The El-Molo rely on Lake Turkana for their existence, living on a diet mainly of fish and occasionally crocodiles, turtles and other wildlife. Hippos are hunted from doum-palm rafts, and great social status is given to a warrior who kills a hippo. Intermarriage with other tribes and abandonment of the nomadic lifestyle have helped to raise their numbers to about 4000, now living on the mainland near Loyangalani.

Gabbra

This small pastoral tribe (less than 0.1% of the population) lives in the far north of Kenya, from the eastern shore of Lake Turkana up into Ethiopia. Many Gabbra converted to Islam during the time of slavery. Traditional beliefs include the appointment of an *abba-olla* (father of the village), who oversees the moral and physical wellbeing of the tribe. Fathers and sons form strong relationships, and marriage provides a lasting bond between clans. Polygamy is still practised by the Gabbra, although it is becoming less common. Gabbra men usually wear turbans and white cotton robes, while women wear kangas, thin pieces of brightly coloured cotton. The Gabbra are famous for their bravery, hunting lions, rhino and elephants.

Rendille

For a detailed and respected analysis of the role of ethnicity in Kenyan politics, read the reports on Kenya's 2017 elections by the International Crisis Group (ICG; www.crisisgroup. org/africa/horn-africa/kenya).

The Rendille are pastoralists who live in small nomadic communities in the rocky Kaisut Desert in Kenya's northeast and make up less than 0.1% of the population. They have strong economic and kinship links with the Samburu and rely heavily on camels for many of their daily needs, including food, milk, clothing, trade and transport. Camels are bled by opening a vein in the neck with a blunt arrow or knife. The blood is then drunk on its own or mixed with milk. Rendille society is strongly bound by family ties centred on monogamous couples. Mothers have high status and the eldest son inherits the family wealth. It is dishonourable for a Rendille to refuse to grant a loan, so even the poorest Rendille often has claims to at least a few camels and goats. Rendille warriors often sport a distinctive visor-like hairstyle, dyed with red ochre, while women may wear several kilos of beads.

Coastal Kenya

Swahili

Although the people of the coast do not have a common heritage, they do have a linguistic link: Kiswahili (commonly referred to as Swahili), a Bantu-based language that evolved as a means of communication between Africans and the Arabs, Persians and Portuguese who colonised the East African coast; the word *swahili* is a derivative of the Arabic word for coast – *sawahil*. The cultural origins of the Swahili, who make up 0.6% of the population, come from intermarriage between the Arabs and Persians with African slaves from the 7th century onwards. In fact, many anthropologists consider the Swahili a cultural tribe brought together by trade routes rather than a tribe of distinct biological lineage. A largely urban tribe, they occupy coastal cities like Mombasa, Malindi, Lamu and Stone Town (Zanzibar); and given the historical Arab influence, the Swahili largely practise Islam.

Daily Life

It can be hard work being Kenyan. While most are proud to be Kenyan, national identity is only one way among many in which Kenyans understand their world. Unlike in neighbouring Tanzania, where being Tanzanian is placed above all else, in Kenya family ties, tribal affiliations, the pull of religion and gender roles are all prominent issues and each plays a significant role in the daily lives of ordinary people. The result is a fascinating, if complicated, mosaic.

Traditional Cultures, Modern Country

Traditional cultures are what hold Kenya together. Respect for one's elders, firmly held religious beliefs, traditional gender roles and the tradition of *ujamaa* (familyhood) create a well-defined social structure with stiff moral mores at its core.

Extended family provides a further layer of support, which is increasingly important as parents migrate to cities for lucrative work, leaving their children to be cared for by grandparents, aunts and uncles. This fluid system has also enabled many to deal with the devastation wrought by the HIV/AIDS epidemic – Kenya has the 12th-highest HIV prevalence rate among adults (5.4%) in the world.

Historically the majority of Kenyans were either farmers or cattle herders with family clans based in small interconnected villages. Even today, as traditional rural life gives way to a frenetic urban pace, this strong sense of community remains.

Grafted onto these traditional foundations of culture, family and community, education is also critical to understanding modern Kenya. Kenya sends more students to the US to study than any other African country, and adult literacy stood at an impressive 78% in 2015. The generation of educated Kenyans who came of age in the 1980s is now making itself heard: Kenyans abroad have started to invest seriously in the country, Nairobi's business landscape is changing rapidly and a new middle class is demanding new apartment blocks and cars.

One Country, Many Tribes

Kenya is home to more than 40 tribal groups. Although most have coexisted quite peacefully since independence, the ethnocentric bias of government and civil-service appointments has led to escalating unrest and

Fast Facts

Urban population: 25.6%

Life expectancy: 64 years

Female/male literacy: 74.9/78%

Annual deaths from HIV/AIDS: 36,000

People living with HIV/AIDS: 1.6 million

THE INDIAN INFLUENCE

Kenya's first permanent settlers from the Indian subcontinent were indentured workers, brought here from Gujarat and the Punjab by the British to build the Uganda Railway. After the railway was finished, the British allowed many workers to stay and start up businesses, and hundreds of *dukas* (small shops) were set up across the country.

After WWII the Indian community came to control large sectors of the East African economy, and still does to some degree. However, few gave their active support to the black nationalist movements in the run-up to independence, despite being urged to do so by India's prime minister, and many were hesitant to accept local citizenship after independence. This earned the widespread distrust of the African community. Thankfully, however, Kenya escaped the anti-Asian pogroms that plagued Uganda.

In the 2016 United Nations Development Program (UNDP) Human Development Index, which is based on a number of economic and quality-of-life indicators, Kenya ranked 146th out of 188 countries.

disaffection. During the hotly contested elections of 1992, 1997 and 2007, clashes between two major tribes, the Kikuyu and Luo, bolstered by allegiances with other smaller tribes like the Kalenjin, resulted in deaths and mass displacement.

One positive step came with the adoption of the 2010 constitution, which recognises the rights of ethnic minorities and even calls for the cabinet to 'reflect the regional and ethnic diversity of the people of Kenya'.

Some analysts point out that election violence and ethnic tensions have more to do with economic inequality than with tribalism – they insist that there are only two tribes in Kenya: the rich and the poor.

Christian Interior, Muslim Coast

As a result of intense missionary activity, the majority of Kenyans outside the coastal and eastern provinces are Christians (including some home-grown African Christian groups that do not owe any allegiance to the major Western groups). Hard-core evangelism has made some significant inroads and many groups from the US have a strong following.

In the country's east, the majority of Kenyans are Sunni Muslims. They make up about 11% of the population.

Women in Kenya

During Kenya's struggle for independence, many women fought alongside the men, but their sacrifice was largely forgotten when independence came. At the Lancaster House conference in the early 1960s, where Kenya's independence constitution was negotiated, just one out of around 70 Kenyan delegates was a woman and the resulting constitution made no mention of women's rights.

In Ngũgĩ wa Thiong'o's *Petals of Blood* (1977), Wanja the barmaid sums up the situation for women in newly independent Kenya: '...with us girls the future seemed vague... as if we knew that no matter what efforts we put into our studies, our road led to the kitchen or the bedroom'.

Under the 2010 constitution things improved, at least on paper: women are described as a disadvantaged group, and the bill guarantees equal treatment for men and women, protects against discrimination on the basis of gender, calls on the state to undertake affirmative-action policies and sets aside 47 special seats for women in parliament – as a result, 19% of MPs in 2014 were women, compared with 1% in 1990.

Even so, major discrepancies remain in the ways in which women and men have access to essential services and resources, such as land and credit, while traditional gender roles still largely prevail.

Kenyan women are increasingly able to access educational opportunities and, particularly in the cities, are slowly coming to play a more prominent role in public life. In rural areas traditional gender roles are observed, although women are accorded status and respect as mothers, wives, healers and teachers.

FEMALE GENITAL MUTILATION

Female genital mutilation (FGM), often termed 'female circumcision', is still widespread across Africa, including throughout Kenya. In some parts of tribal Kenya more than 90% of women and girls are subjected to FGM.

The term FGM covers a wide range of procedures, from a small, mainly symbolic cut to the total removal of the clitoris and external genitalia (known as infibulation). The effects of FGM can be fatal. Other side effects, including chronic infections, the spread of HIV, infertility, severe bleeding and lifelong pain during sex, are not uncommon.

FGM is now banned in Kenya for girls aged under 17, but the ritual still has widespread support in some communities; attempts to stamp out FGM are widely perceived as part of a Western conspiracy to undermine African cultural identity. Many local women's groups, such as the community project Ntanira na Mugambo (Circumcision Through Words), are working towards preserving the rite-of-passage aspect of FGM without any surgery.

The Arts

Kenya is arguably the leading cultural powerhouse of East Africa, with Nairobi in particular one of the most dynamic spaces for the arts. Often these arts provide not only a powerful medium for expressing African culture but also a means for expressing the dreams and frustrations of the poor and disenfranchised, and that's where Kenyan artists and performers really find their voice. Kenyan musicians and writers are particularly worth watching out for.

Music

With its diversity of indigenous languages and cultures, Kenya has a rich and exciting music scene. Influences, most notably from the nearby Democratic Republic of Congo and Tanzania, have helped to diversify the sounds. More recently reggae and hip-hop have permeated the pop scene.

The live music scene in Nairobi is excellent and a variety of clubs cater for traditional and contemporary musical tastes. A good reference is the *Daily Nation*, which publishes weekly Top 10 African, international and gospel charts and countrywide gig listings on Saturday. Beyond Nairobi, take what you can get.

Outside Influences

The Congolese styles of rumba and soukous, known collectively as *lingala*, were first introduced into Kenya by artists such as Samba Mapangala (who is still playing) in the 1960s and have come to dominate most of East Africa. This upbeat party music is characterised by clean guitar licks and a driving *cavacha* drum rhythm.

Music from Tanzania was influential in the early 1970s, when the band Simba Wanyika helped create Swahili rumba, which was taken up by bands like the Maroon Commandos and Les Wanyika.

Popular bands today are heavily influenced by benga, soukous and also Western music, with lyrics generally in Kiswahili. These include bands such as Them Mushrooms (now reinvented as Uyoya) and Safari Sound. For upbeat dance tunes, Ogopa DJs, Nameless, Redsan and Deux Vultures are popular acts.

Home-Grown Styles

Kenyan bands were also active during the 1960s, producing some of the most popular songs in Africa, including Fadhili William's famous *Malaika* (Angel), and *Jambo Bwana,* Kenya's unofficial anthem, written and recorded by the hugely influential Them Mushrooms.

Benga is the contemporary dance music of Kenya. It refers to the dominant style of Luo pop music, which originated in western Kenya and spread throughout the country in the 1960s, being taken up by Akamba and Kikuyu musicians. The music is characterised by clear electric guitar riffs and a bounding bass rhythm. Some well-known exponents of benga include DO Misiani (a Luo) and his group Shirati Jazz, which has been around since the 1960s and is still churning out the hits. You should also look out for Globestyle, Victoria Kings and Ambira Boys.

Music Resources

African Music Encyclopedia (www. africanmusic.org)

AfricMusic (www. africmusic.com)

Sterns Music (www.sternsmusic. com)

African Hip Hop (www.african-hiphop.com)

Contemporary Kikuyu music often borrows from benga. Stars include Sam Chege, Francis Rugwiti and Daniel 'Councillor' Kamau, who was popular in the 1970s and is still going strong.

Taarab, the music of the East African coast, originally only played at Swahili weddings and other special occasions, has been given a new lease of life by coastal pop singer Malika.

Rap, Hip-Hop & Other Styles

American-influenced gangster rap and hip-hop are also on the rise, including such acts as Necessary Noize, Poxi Presha and Hardstone. The slums of Nairobi have proved to be particularly fertile for local rap music. In 2004 Dutch producer Nynke Nauta gathered rappers from the Eastlands slums of Nairobi and formed a collective, Nairobi Yetu. The resultant album, *Kilio Cha Haki* (A Cry for Justice), featuring raps in Sheng (a mix of KiSwahili, English and ethnic languages), has been internationally recognised as a poignant fusion of ghetto angst and the joy of making music.

Kenya pioneered the African version of the reggaeton style (a blend of reggae, hip-hop and traditional music), which is now popular in the US and UK. Dancehall is also huge here.

Other names to keep an eye or ear out for include Prezzo (Kenya's king of bling), Nonini (a controversial women-and-booze rapper), Nazizi (female MC from Necessary Noize) and Mercy Myra (Kenya's biggest female R&B artist).

Literature

There are plenty of novels, plays and biographies by contemporary Kenyan authors, but they can be hard to find outside the country. The backlist of the Heinemann African Writers Series offers an accessible collection of such works.

A KENYAN PLAYLIST

➡ *Nairobi Beat: Kenyan Pop Music Today* (1989) Regional sounds including Luo, Kikuyu, Akamba, Luhya, Swahili and Congolese.

➡ *Journey* (Jabali Afrika; 1996) Stirring acoustic sounds complete with drums, congas, shakers and bells.

➡ *Amigo* (Les Wanyika; 1998) Swahili rumba from one of Kenya's most influential bands.

➡ *Nuting but de Stone* (1999) Phenomenally popular compilation combining African lyrics with American urban sounds and Caribbean ragga.

➡ *Kenyan: The First Chapter* (2000) Kenya's home-grown blend of African lyrics with R&B, house, reggae and dancehall genres.

➡ *Necessary Noize* (Necessary Noize 2; 2000) Hip-hop, reggae and R&B that produced numerous hits.

➡ *Nairobbery* (K-South; 2002) The landmark hip-hop album that launched the careers of this popular band.

➡ *Yahweh* (Esther Wahome; 2003) The hit 'Kuna Dawa' from this album improbably crossed over from gospel song to nightclub hit.

➡ *Kilio Cha Haki – A Cry for Justice* (2004) Groundbreaking rap in Sheng (a mix of Kiswahili, English and ethnic languages).

➡ *Mama Africa* (Suzanna Owiyo; 2009) Afropop from the Tracy Chapman of Kenya.

➡ *82* (Just a Band; 2009) Experimental Afro-fusion that Kenya fell in love with.

➡ *Magic in the Air* (Mayonde; 2015) Debut pop album from a talent to watch.

➡ *Tusk at Hand* (Parking Lot Grass; 2015) Hard-rock protest songs sung in Swahili.

Ngũgĩ wa Thiong'o

Ngũgĩ wa Thiong'o (1938–) is uncompromisingly radical, and his harrowing criticism of the neocolonialist politics of the Kenyan establishment landed him in jail for a year (described in his *Detained: A Writer's Prison Diary;* 1982), lost him his job at Nairobi University and forced him into exile. In 2004 he returned to Kenya but he and his wife were injured in a home invasion in Nairobi and he returned to the US where he now lives.

His works include *Petals of Blood* (1977), *Matigari* (1987), *The River Between* (1965), *A Grain of Wheat* (1967), *Devil on the Cross* (1980) and *Wizard of the Crow* (2006), which was shortlisted for the 2007 Commonwealth Writers' Prize. As a statement about the importance of reviving African languages as cultural media, Ngũgĩ wa Thiong'o wrote *Wizard of the Crow* in Gikuyu and then translated it himself into English. His latest works are memoirs: *Dreams in a Time of War* (2010), *In the House of the Interpreter* (2012) and *Birth of a Dream Weaver: A Memoir of a Writer's Awakening* (2016). All his works, whether fiction or nonfiction, offer insightful portraits of Kenyan life.

Meja Mwangi

Meja Mwangi (1948–) writes both for adults and children with a focus on social issues and urban dislocation. He has a mischievous sense of humour that threads its way right through his books. Notable titles include *The Return of Shaka* (1989), *Weapon of Hunger* (1989), *The Cockroach Dance* (1979), *The Last Plague* (2000) and *The Big Chiefs* (2007). His *Mzungu Boy* (2006), winner of the Children's Africana Book Award in 2006, depicts the friendship of white and black Kenyan boys at the time of the Mau Mau uprising.

Binyavanga Wainana

One of Kenya's rising stars on the literary front is Binyavanga Wainaina (1971–), who won the Caine Prize for African Writing in July 2002. The award-winning piece was the short story 'Discovering Home', about a young Kenyan working in Cape Town who returns to his parents' village in Kenya for a year. His *One Day I Will Write about This Place: A Memoir* (2011) is a fascinating portrait of a middle-class Kenyan upbringing.

In the aftermath of the 2008 postelection crisis, Wainaina helped form the Concerned Kenyan Writers (CKW) group. CKW aims to inspire and unite Kenyans and show them that there is a pay-off in peace and nationhood; it also seeks to counter the 'Dark Continent' reporting by the international media in the wake of the violence. In 2014 *Time* named him one of the 100 Most Influential People in the World.

Contemporary Women Writers

The first female Kenyan writer of note in the modern era was Grace Ogot (1930–2015), the first woman to have her work published by the East African Publishing House. Her work includes *Land Without Thunder* (1968), *The Strange Bride* (1989), *The Graduate* (1980) and *The Island of Tears* (1980). Born in Nyanza Province, she set many of her stories against the scenic background of Lake Victoria, offering an insight into Luo culture in precolonial Kenya.

Another interesting writer is Margaret Atieno Ogola (1958–2011), the author of the celebrated novel *The River and the Source* (1994) and its sequel, *I Swear by Apollo* (2002), which follow the lives of four generations of Kenyan women in a rapidly evolving country.

Other books of note are Marjorie Magoye's *The Present Moment* (1987), which follows the life of a group of elderly women in a Christian refuge, and *The Man from Pretoria* (1975) by Kenyan conservationist and journalist Hilary Ngweno. Moraa Gitaa's *Crucible for Silver and Furnace for*

Facing the Lion (2003) is Joseph Lekuton's simple but beautifully crafted memoir of how he grew up as a poor Maasai boy, who, through a series of incredible twists and turns, ends up in the US studying for an MBA.

To follow the work of contemporary writers, look out for *Kwani?* (www.kwani. org), Kenya's first literary journal, established by Binyavanga Wainaina in 2003. Nairobi-based, it facilitates the production and distribution of Kenyan literature and hosts an annual literary festival that attracts a growing number of pan-African names.

Gold (2008) follows the relationship between an HIV-positive African woman and an Italian tourist; her *Shifting Sands* (2012) is also worth tracking down.

Cinema

Kenya's underfunded film industry has struggled to establish itself, but the Zanzibar International Film Festival (ZIFF) in neighbouring Tanzania, one of the region's premier cultural events, has helped to bring East African filmmakers to the fore. One such auteur is Kibaara Kaugi, whose *Enough is Enough* (2004), a brave exploration of the Mau Mau uprising, garnered critical praise.

In 2005 the government established the Kenya Film Commission (KFC; www.kenyafilmcommission.com), which aims to support and promote the Kenyan film industry. One notable success since its inception is *Kibera Kid* (2006), a short film set in the Kibera slum, written and directed by Nathan Collett. It tells the story of 12-year-old Otieno, an orphan living with a gang of thieves, who must make a choice between gang life and redemption. Featuring a cast of children, all of whom live in Kibera, the film played at film festivals worldwide.

Filmed in Kenya

Born Free (1966)

Out of Africa (1985)

I Dreamed of Africa (2000)

Lara Croft Tomb Raider: The Cradle of Life (2003)

The Constant Gardener (2005)

Painting

Kenya has a diverse artistic heritage, and there's a wealth of artistic talent in the country, practising both traditional painting and all manner of sculpture, printing, mixed media and graffiti. Nairobi has a number of excellent galleries; for an overview of the local scene, visit the Go-Down Arts Centre (p60) in Nairobi.

Textiles & Jewellery

Women throughout East Africa wear brightly coloured lengths of printed cotton cloth, typically with Swahili sayings printed along the edge, known as kanga. Many of the sayings are social commentary or messages, often indirectly worded, or containing puns and double meanings. Others are local forms of advertising, such as the logos of political parties.

In coastal areas, you'll also see the *kikoi*, which is made of a more thickly textured cotton, usually featuring striped or plaid patterns, and traditionally worn by men. Also common are batik-print cottons depicting everyday scenes, animal motifs or geometrical patterns.

Jewellery, especially beaded jewellery, is particularly beautiful among the Maasai and the Turkana. It is used in ceremonies as well as in everyday life, and often indicates the wearer's wealth and marital status.

Nairobi Art Galleries

Circle Art Gallery

Go-Down Arts Centre

Tazama Art Gallery

Kuona Trust Centre for the Visual Arts

Woodcarvings & Sculpture

Woodcarving was only introduced into Kenya in the early 20th century. Mutisya Munge, an Akamba man, is considered the father of Kenyan woodcarving, having brought the tradition from Tanzania's Makonde people to Kenya following WWI. Kenya's woodcarving industry has grown exponentially in the century since, although recent shortages of increasingly endangered hardwoods have presented major challenges to the industry. While woodcarvings from Kenya may lack the sophistication and cultural resonance of those from Central and West Africa, the carvings' subjects range from representations of the spirit and animal worlds to stylised human figures.

Carvings rendered in soapstone from the village of Tabaka, close to Kisii in the Western Highlands, are among the most attractive of Kenyan handicrafts. These sculptures take on numerous forms, but the abstract figures of embracing couples are the genre's undoubted highpoint.

Kenyan Cuisine

The Kenyan culinary tradition has generally emphasised feeding the masses as efficiently as possible, with little room for flair or innovation. Most meals are centred on ugali, a thick, doughlike mass made from maize and/or cassava flour. While traditional fare may be bland but filling, there are some treats to be found. Many memorable eating experiences in Kenya are likely to revolve around dining al fresco in a safari camp, surrounded by the sights and sounds of the African bush.

Staples & Specialities

Counting Carbs

Kenyan cuisine has few culinary masterpieces and is mainly survival food, offering the maximum opportunity to fill up at minimum cost. Most meals in Kenya consist largely of heavy starches.

In addition to ugali, Kenyans rely on potatoes, rice, chapati and *matoke*. The rice-based dishes, biryani and pilau, are clearly derived from Persia – they should be delicately spiced with saffron and star anise, and liberally sprinkled with carrot and raisins. The chapati is identical to its Indian predecessor, while *matoke* is mashed green plantains that, when well prepared, can taste like buttery, lightly whipped mashed potato. Also look out for *irio* (or *kienyeji*), made from mashed greens, potato and boiled corn or beans; *mukimo*, a kind of hash made from sweet potatoes, corn, beans and plantains; and *githeri*, a mix of beans and corn.

Flesh & Bone

Kenyans are enthusiastic carnivores and their unofficial national dish, *nyama choma* (barbecued meat), is a red-blooded, hands-on affair. Most places have their own on-site butchery, and *nyama choma* is usually purchased by weight, often as a single hunk of meat. Half a kilogram is usually enough for one person (taking into account bone and gristle). It'll be brought out to you chopped into small bite-sized bits, often with a salad or vegetable mash and greens.

THE ART OF EATING UGALI

A meal wouldn't be a meal in Kenya without ugali. Ugali is made from boiled grains cooked into a thick porridge until it sets hard, then served up in flat (and rather dense) slabs. It's incredibly stodgy and tends to sit in the stomach like a brick, but most Kenyans swear by it – it will fill you up after a long day's safari, but it won't set your taste buds a-tingle.

In general, good ugali should be neither too dry nor too sticky, which makes it easy to enjoy as a finger food. Take some with the right hand from the communal pot (your left hand is used for wiping – and we don't mean your mouth!), roll it into a small ball with the fingers, making an indentation with your thumb, and dip it into the accompanying sauce. Eating with your hand is a bit of an art, but after a few tries it starts to feel natural. Don't soak the ugali too long (to avoid it breaking up in the sauce), and keep your hand lower than your elbow (except when actually eating) so the sauce doesn't drip down your forearm.

Goat is the most common meat, and *can* be surprisingly tender, but you'll see chicken, beef and some game animals (ostrich and crocodile) in upmarket places. Don't expect *nyama choma* to melt in the mouth – its chewiness is probably indicative of the long and eventful life of the animal you're consuming and you'll need a good half-hour at the end of the meal to work over your gums with a toothpick. We find that copious quantities of Tusker beer also tend to help it go down.

In addition to *nyama choma,* Kenyans are fond of meat-based stews, which help make their carb-rich diet more palatable. Again, goat, chicken and beef, as well as mutton, are the most common cuts on the menu, though they tend to be pretty tough, despite being cooked for hours on end.

For a refreshingly African take on Kenyan cooking, with an emphasis on home cooking rather than restaurants, check out Talking to Nelly (www.talkingtonelly.com), a food blog from a Mombasa-based foodie.

Fruit & Vegetables

Ugali (and most Kenyan dishes for that matter) is usually served with *sukuma wiki* (braised or stewed spinach). *Sukuma wiki* in Kiswahili means literally 'stretch the week', the implication being that it's so cheap it allows the householder to stretch the budget until the next weekly pay cheque. Despite its widespread availability, a dish of well-cooked *sukuma wiki* with tomatoes, stock and capsicum makes a refreshing change from the abundance of meat in other recipes.

Depending on the place and the season, you can buy mangoes, pawpaws, pineapples, passion fruit, guavas, oranges, custard apples, bananas (of many varieties), tree tomatoes and coconuts. Chewing on a piece of sugar cane is also a great way to end a meal.

Kenyan Classics

Breakfast in Kenya is generally a simple affair consisting of chai accompanied by a *mandazi* (semisweet doughnut). *Mandazi* are best in the morning when they're freshly made – they become ever more rubbery and less appetising as the day goes on. Another traditional breakfast dish is *uji* (a thin, sweet porridge made from bean, millet or other flour); it's similar to ugali and best served warm, with lashings of milk and brown sugar.

On the coast, Swahili dishes reflect the history of contact with Arabs and other Indian Ocean traders, and incorporate the produce of the region; the results can be excellent. Grilled fish or octopus will be a highlight of any menu, while coconut and spices such as cloves and cinnamon feature prominently.

The large South Asian presence in East Africa means that Indian food commonly appears on menus throughout Kenya. Most restaurants serve curries and Indian-inspired dishes, such as masala chips (ie chips with a curry sauce), while authentic Indian restaurants in Nairobi and along the coast and elsewhere serve traditional dishes from the subcontinent.

WE DARE YOU

If you're lucky (!) and game (more to the point), you may be able to try various cattle-derived products beloved of the pastoral tribes of Kenya. Samburu, Pokot and Maasai warriors have a taste for cattle blood. The blood is taken straight from the jugular, which does no permanent damage to the cattle, but it's certainly an acquired taste. *Mursik* is made from milk fermented with ash, and is served in smoked gourds. It tastes and smells pungent, but it contains compounds that reduce cholesterol, enabling the Maasai to live quite healthily on a diet of red meat, milk and blood. You may be able to sample it at villages or homestays in the Masai Mara National Reserve or near Amboseli National Park.

Drinks

Tea & Coffee

Despite the fact that Kenya grows some excellent tea and coffee, getting a decent cup of either can be difficult. Quite simply, the best stuff is exported.

Chai is the national obsession, and although it's drunk in large quantities, it bears little resemblance to what you might be used to. As in India, the tea, milk and masses of sugar are boiled together and stewed for ages and the result is milky and very sweet – it may be too sickly for some, but the brew might just grow on you. Spiced masala chai with cardamom and cinnamon is very pleasant and rejuvenating. For tea without milk ask for chai *kavu*.

As for coffee, it's often sweet, milky and made with a bare minimum of instant coffee. However, in Nairobi and larger towns, there is a steadily increasing number of coffee houses serving very good Kenyan coffee, and you can usually get a passable filter coffee at better hotels. With all the Italian tourists who visit the coast, you can at least get a decent cappuccino or espresso pretty much anywhere between Diani Beach and Lamu.

Water & Juices

With all the fresh fruit that's available in Kenya, the juices on offer are, not surprisingly, breathtakingly good. All are made using modern blenders, so there's no point asking for a fruit juice during a power cut. Although you can get juices made from almost any fruit, the nation's favourite is passion fruit. It's known locally just as 'passion'. However, be wary of fruit juices watered down with unpurified water (tap water is best avoided) – double-check they're using bottled or purified water. Bottled water is widely available, even in remote areas for the most part.

Beer

Kenya has a thriving local brewing industry, and formidable quantities of beer are consumed day and night. You'll usually be given a choice of 'warm' or 'cold' beer. 'Why warm?', you might well ask. Curiously, most Kenyans appear to prefer it that way, despite the fact that room temperature in Kenya is a lot hotter than room temperature in the USA or Europe.

The local beers are Tusker, Pilsner and White Cap, all manufactured by Kenya Breweries and sold in 500mL bottles. Tusker comes in three varieties: Tusker Export, Tusker Malt Lager and just plain Tusker. Tusker Export is a stronger version of ordinary Tusker lager, while Tusker Malt has a fuller taste. Locally produced foreign labels include Castle (a South African beer) and Guinness, though the Kenyan version is nothing like the genuine Irish article.

Nairobi in particular is witnessing a rise in craft or boutique breweries that increasingly offer an alternative to the long-standing mass-produced beers. Some of the better new kids on the block include Brew (p80), Sierra Premium (p80) and Sirville Brewery (p80); the latter clearly has an eye on the tourist market with beers like Mara Pils, Tsavo Lager, Amboseli Ale and Aberdare Bitter Ale.

Wine

Kenya has a fledgling wine industry, and the Lake Naivasha Colombard wines are generally quite good. This is something that cannot be said about the most commonly encountered Kenyan wine – pawpaw wine. Quite how anyone came up with the idea of trying to reproduce

For the low-down on various Kenyan recipes, including the ubiquitous ugali and *sukuma wiki*, check out the excellent All Kenyan Recipes (www.allkenyanrecipes.com). You can also buy the companion *Explore the Kenyan Kitchen* (Mary W Plancherel, 2017) through the website.

The most long-lasting impact that Portuguese explorers had on Kenya was in the culinary field. Portuguese travellers introduced maize, cassava, potatoes and chillies from South America – all of which are now staples of the Kenyan diet.

DOS & DON'TS

For Kenyans, a shared meal and eating out of a communal dish are expressions of solidarity between hosts and guests: here are a few tips to help you get into the spirit of things.

→ If you're invited to eat and aren't hungry, it's OK to say that you've just eaten, but try to share a few bites of the meal in recognition of the bond with your hosts.

→ If eating in someone's home or *manyatta* (Maasai village), leave a small amount on your plate to show your hosts that you've been satisfied.

→ Don't take the last bit of food from the communal bowl – your hosts may worry that they haven't provided enough.

→ Never, *ever* handle food with the left hand!

→ If others are eating with their hand, do the same, even if cutlery is provided.

→ Defer to your hosts for customs that you aren't sure about.

a drink made from grapes using pawpaw remains a mystery, but the result tastes foul and smells even worse.

You can get South African, European and even Australian wine by the glass in upmarket restaurants in major cities and tourist areas.

Cocktails

A popular Kenyan cocktail is *dawa,* which translates from the Kiswahili as 'medicine'. Clearly based on the Brazilian *caipirinha,* it's made with vodka, lime and honey. We suggest you enjoy a tipple at sunset in a bar overlooking the coast, or out on the savannah plains – both experiences can certainly have a therapeutic effect on mind and body.

Home Brew

Although it is strictly illegal for the public to brew or distil liquor, it remains a way of life for many Kenyans. *Pombe* is the local beer, usually a fermented brew made with bananas or millet and sugar. It shouldn't do you any harm. The same cannot be said for the distilled drinks known locally as *chang'a,* which are laced with genuine poisons. In 2005, 48 people died near Machakos after drinking a bad batch of *chang'a.* A further 84 were hospitalised and treated with vodka to reduce the effect of methyl alcohol poisoning – such events are not uncommon. Perhaps the most dangerous *chang'a* comes from Kisii, and is fermented with marijuana twigs, cactus mash, battery alkaline and formalin. Don't touch it.

Where to Eat & Drink

'Hotels' & Restaurants

The most basic local eateries are usually known as 'hotels' or *hotelis,* and they often open only during the daytime. You may find yourself having dinner at 5pm if you rely on eating at these places. However, even in smaller towns it's usually possible to find a restaurant that offers a more varied menu at a higher price. Often these places are affiliated with the town's midrange and top-end hotels, and are usually open in the evening.

You'll find that many of the big nightclubs also serve food until late into the night.

Menus, where they exist in the cheaper places, are usually just a chalked list on a board. In more upmarket restaurants, they're usually written only in English.

Cooking the East African Way (Constance Nabwire and Bertha Vining Montgomery, 2001) combines easy-to-follow recipes from across the region with interesting text on culinary traditions in Kenya and elsewhere.

Quick Eats

Eating fast food has taken off in a big way and virtually every town has a place serving greasy-but-cheap chips, burgers, sausages, pizzas and fried chicken. Lashings of tomato and chilli sauce are present to help lubricate things. A number of South African fast-food chains have taken hold in Nairobi, such as the ubiquitous Steers.

On the streets in Kenya, you may encounter roasted corn cobs and deep-fried yams, which are eaten hot with a squeeze of lemon juice and a sprinkling of chilli powder. *Sambusas,* deep-fried pastry triangles stuffed with spiced mincemeat, are good for snacking on the run, and are obvious descendants of the Indian samosa.

Something you don't come across often, but which is an excellent snack, is *mkate mayai* (literally 'bread eggs'), a wheat dough pancake, filled with minced meat and egg and fried on a hotplate.

On the coast street food is more common and you'll find cassava chips, chapatis and *mishikaki* (marinated grilled meat kebabs, usually beef).

Pilau flavoured with spices and stock is the signature dish at traditional Swahili weddings. The expression 'going to eat pilau' means to go to a wedding.

Vegetarians & Vegans

Vegetarian visitors are likely to struggle, as meat features in most meals and many vegetable dishes are cooked in meat stock. But, with a bit of scouting around, you should be able to find something. You may find yourself eating a lot of *sukuma wiki* (braised or stewed spinach served with tomatoes, stock and capsicum), while other traditional dishes such as *githeri* (a bean-and-corn mix) are hearty, if not particularly inspiring, options. Beans and avocado will also figure prominently in any vegetarian's culinary encounters in Kenya. Many Indian restaurants will provide a vegetarian *thali* (an all-you-can-eat meal, usually with lentils) that should fill you up. Buying fresh fruit and vegetables in local markets can help relieve the tedium of trying to order around the meat on restaurant menus.

Note that most tour operators are willing to cater to special dietary requests, such as vegetarian, vegan, kosher or halal, with advance notice.

Menu Decoder

bia	beer
biryani	rice dish, sometimes in a casserole form often served with chicken or meat
chai	tea
chai ya asubuhi	breakfast
chakula cha jioni	dinner
chakula cha mchana	lunch
chakula kutoka bahari	seafood
chapati	Indian-style bread
chenye viungo	spicy
chipsi mayai	puffy omelette with chips mixed in
chumvi	salt
githeri	a mix of beans and corn
irio	mashed greens, potato and boiled corn or beans (also called *kienyeji*)
jusi	juice
kaa	crab
kahawa	coffee
karanga	peanut

kiazi	potato
kienyeji	mashed greens, potato and boiled corn or beans (also called *irio*)
kiti moto	fried or roasted pork bits, sold by the kilogram, served with salad and fried plantain
kuku	chicken
kumbwe	snack
maji	water
maji ya machungwa	orange juice
maji ya madini	mineral water
mandazi	a semisweet doughnut served warm, with lashings of milk and brown sugar
masala chai	tea with cardamom and cinnamon
matoke	mashed green plantains
maziwa	milk
mboga	vegetable
mchuzi	sauce, sometimes with bits of beef and vegetables
mgahawa	restaurant
mishikaki	marinated grilled meat kebabs, usually beef
mkate mayai	literally 'bread eggs'; a wheat dough pancake, filled with minced meat and egg and fried on a hotplate
mkate wa kumimina	sesame-seed bread, found along the coast
mtindi	cultured milk, usually sold in small bags and delicious on a hot day
mukimo	sweet potatoes, corn, beans and plantains
mwanakondoo	lamb
nyama	meat
nyama choma	seasoned barbecued meat
nyama mbuzi	mutton
nyama nguruwe	pork
nyama ng'ombe	beef
nyama ya ndama	veal
pilau	rice dish, often served with chicken, meat or seafood, sometimes cooked in broth (a coastal speciality)
pilipili	pepper
posho	Ugandan version of ugali
samaki	fish
sambusas	deep-fried pastry triangles stuffed with spiced mincemeat; similar to Indian samosas
sukari	sugar
sukuma wiki	braised or stewed spinach
tambi	pasta
ugali	thick, doughlike mass made from maize and/or cassava flour
uji	thin, sweet porridge made from bean, millet or other flour
vitambua	small rice cakes resembling tiny, thick pancakes
wali	cooked rice
wali na kuku/samaki/ nyama/maharagwe	cooked white rice with chicken/fish/meat/beans

Above Elephant herd, Amboseli National Park (p185)

Wildlife & Habitat

East Africa is synonymous with safaris, and Kenya is where it all began. From US President Theodore Roosevelt in 1909 to Joy Adamson's *Born Free* to Karen Blixen's sweeping tale *Out of Africa*, Kenya forms the centrepiece of our popular image of Africa. And for good reason – it is one of the best places in the world to see wildlife. You will never forget the shimmering carpets of zebras and wildebeest, or the spine-tingling roars of lions at night.

– David Lukas

TRAVEL STOCK / SHUTTERSTOCK ©

1. Leopard **2.** Lions **3.** Cheetah cubs

3

Big Cats

The three big cats – leopard, lion and cheetah – provide the high point for so many memorable safaris. The presence of these apex predators, even the mere suggestion that they may be nearby, is enough to draw the savannah taut with attention. It's the lion's gravitas, roaring at night, stalking at sunset. It's the elusive leopard that remains hidden while in plain view. And it's the cheetah in a fluid blur of hunting perfection.

Leopard

Weight 30–60kg (female), 40–90kg (male); length 170–300cm More common than you realise, the leopard relies on expert camouflage to stay hidden. During the day you might only spot one reclining in a tree after it twitches its tail, but at night there is no mistaking their bone-chilling groans.

Best seen: Masai Mara NR, Olare-Orok Conservancy, Tsavo West NP.

Lion

Weight 120–150kg (female), 150–225kg (male); length 210–275cm (female), 240–350cm (male) Those lions sprawled lazily in the shade are actually Africa's most feared predators. Equipped with teeth that tear effortlessly through bone and tendon, they can take down an animal as large as a bull giraffe. Each group of adults (a pride) is based around generations of females that do the majority of the hunting; swaggering males typically fight among themselves and eat what the females catch.

Best seen: Masai Mara NR, Naboisho, Mara North and Olare-Orok Conservancies, Laikipia, Amboseli NP.

Cheetah

Weight 40–60kg; length 200–220cm The cheetah is a world-class sprinter. Although it reaches speeds of 112km/h, the cheetah runs out of steam after 300m and must cool down for 30 minutes before hunting again. This speed comes at another cost – the cheetah is so well adapted for running that it lacks the strength and teeth to defend its food or cubs from attack by other large predators.

Best seen: Masai Mara NR, Naboisho and Mara North Conservancies, Amboseli NP, Tsavo East NP.

Small Cats

While big cats get the lion's share of attention from tourists, Kenya's small cats are equally interesting though much harder to spot. You won't find these cats chasing down gazelles or wildebeest; instead look for them slinking around in search of rodents or making incredible leaps to snatch birds out of the air.

Caracal

Weight 8–19kg; length 80–120cm The caracal is a gorgeous tawny cat with long, pointy ears. This African version of the northern lynx has jacked-up hind legs like a feline dragster. These beanpole kickers enable this slender cat to make vertical leaps of 3m and swat birds in flight.

Best seen: Widespread in Kenya's parks, although difficult to spot.

Wildcat

Weight 3–6.5kg; length 65–100cm If you see what looks like a tabby wandering the plains of Kenya you're probably seeing a wildcat, the direct ancestor of our domesticated housecat. Occurring wherever there are abundant mice and rats, the wildcat is readily found on the outskirts of villages, where it can be best identified by its unmarked rufous ears and longish legs.

Best seen: Widespread but difficult to spot.

Serval

Weight 6–18kg; length 90–130cm Twice as large as a housecat but with long legs and large ears, the beautifully spotted serval is adapted for walking in tall grass and making prodigious leaps to catch rodents and birds. More diurnal than most cats, it may be seen tossing food in the air and playing with it.

Best seen: Masai Mara NR, Aberdare NP (black servals).

1. Caracal 2. Wildcats 3. Serval

SEKAR B / SHUTTERSTOCK ©

Savannah Primates

East Africa is the evolutionary cradle of primate diversity, giving rise to more than 30 species of monkeys, apes and prosimians (the 'primitive' ancestors of modern primates), all of which have dextrous hands and feet. Several species have evolved to living on the ground where they are vulnerable to lions and hyenas.

Vervet Monkey

Weight 4–8kg; length 90–140cm Each troop of vervets is composed of females who defend a home range passed down from generation to generation, while males fight each other for bragging rights and access to females. Check out the extraordinary blue and scarlet colours of their sexual organs when aroused.

Best seen: Saiwa Swamp NP, but widespread throughout the country.

Olive Baboon

Weight 11–30kg (female), 22–50kg (male); length 95–180cm Although the formidable olive baboon has 5cm-long fangs and can kill a leopard, its best defence may consist of running up trees and showering intruders with liquid excrement. Intelligent and opportunistic, troops of these greenish baboons are common in western Kenya, while much paler yellow baboons range over the eastern half of the country.

Best seen: Lake Nakuru NP, but widespread throughout the country.

Patas Monkey

Weight 7–25kg; length 110–160cm A unique subspecies of this widespread West African monkey lives on the Serengeti Plains. Russet-backed and slender bodied with lanky legs, this remarkable monkey is the fastest primate in the world – able to sprint 55km/h as it races towards the nearest trees. Still, quite a few adults are eaten by carnivores so Patas monkeys have a very high reproductive rate.

Best seen: Segera Ranch.

1. Vervet monkeys 2. Olive baboons 3. Patas monkey

1. Black-and-white colobuses 2. De Brazza's monkey
3. Lesser galago

Forest Primates

Forest primates are a diverse group that live entirely in trees. These agile, long-limbed primates generally stay in the upper canopy where they search for leaves and arboreal fruits. It might take the expert eyes of a professional guide to help you find some of these species.

Black-and-White Colobus

Weight 10–23kg; length 115–165cm Also known as the guereza, the black-and-white colobus is one of Kenya's most popular primates due to the flowing white frills of hair arrayed across its black body. Like all colobus, this agile primate has a hook-shaped hand, so it can swing through the trees with the greatest of ease. When two troops run into each other, expect to see a real show.

Best seen: Kakamega Forest, Mt Elgon NP.

De Brazza's Monkey

Weight 4–8kg; length 90–135cm Riverside forests of west-central Kenya are home to this rare and colourful monkey. Despite glaring red eyebrows and big bushy white beards, de Brazza's monkeys are surprisingly inconspicuous due to their grizzled upperparts and habit of sitting motionless for up to eight hours. In the early morning and late afternoon they ascend to higher branches to eat fruit and sunbathe.

Best seen: Kakamega Forest, Mt Elgon NP, Saiwa Swamp NP.

Lesser Galago

Weight 100–300g; length 40cm A squirrel-sized nocturnal creature with a doglike face and huge eyes, the lesser galago belongs to a group of prosimians that have changed little in 60 million years. Best known for its frequent bawling cries (hence the common name 'bushbaby'), the galago would be rarely seen except that it readily visits feeding stations at many popular safari lodges. Living in a world of darkness, galagos communicate with each other through scent and sound.

Best seen: Widespread throughout Kenya.

Cud-Chewing Mammals

Africa is arguably most famous for its astounding variety of ungulates – hoofed mammals that include everything from buffaloes to giraffes. In this large family cud-chewing antelope are particularly numerous, with 40 different species in East Africa alone.

MICHELE B / SHUTTERSTOCK ©

Gerenuk

Weight 30–50kg; length 160–200cm
Adapted for life in semi-arid brush, the gerenuk stands on its hind legs to reach 2m-high branches with its giraffelike neck.
　Best seen: Samburu NR, Amboseli NP.

Thomson's Gazelle

Weight 15–35kg; length 95–150cm This long-legged antelope is built for speed. In southern Kenya an estimated 400,000 migrate in great herds, along with zebras and wildebeest.
　Best seen: Masai Mara NR, Mara North and Naboisho Conservancies, Amboseli NP, Tsavo East NP.

Wildebeest

Weight 140–290kg; length 230–340cm Few animals evoke the spirit of the African plain as much as the wildebeest. Over a million gather on the Masai Mara alone, where they form vast, constantly moving herds.
　Best seen: Masai Mara NR.

Waterbuck

Weight 160–300kg; length 210–275cm If you're going to see any antelope on safari, it's likely to be the big, shaggy and, some say, smelly waterbuck. However, their numbers fluctuate dramatically between wet and dry years.
　Best seen: Widespread throughout Kenya.

African Buffalo (Cape Buffalo)

Weight 250–850kg; length 220–420cm
Imagine a cow on steroids then add a par-ticularly fearsome set of curling horns and you get the massive African buffalo. Thank goodness they're usually docile.
　Best seen: Lake Nakuru NP, Masai Mara NR, but widespread throughout southern and central Kenya.

2

1. Gerenuk 2. Thomson's gazelle 3. Wildebeest 4. Waterbuck

4

1. Elephants 2. Plains zebras 3. Reticulated giraffes
4. Grevy's zebras

Hoofed Mammals

The continent has a surprising diversity of hoofed animals. Those that don't chew cuds occur over a much broader range of habitats than the cud-chewing antelope. They have been at home in Africa for millions of years. Without human intervention, Africa would be ruled by elephants, zebras, hippos and warthogs.

Grevy's Zebra

Weight 350–450kg; length 290–375cm This large and distinctive zebra is restricted to the semi-arid plains of northern Kenya, where it mingles with the plains zebra. Look for the thinner black stripes that do not extend down onto its white belly.

Best seen: Lewa and Ol Pejeta Conservancies, Segera Ranch, Meru NP, Samburu NR.

Plains Zebra

Weight 175–320kg; length 260–300cm My oh my, those plains zebras sure have some wicked stripes. Although each animal is as distinctly marked as a fingerprint, scientists still aren't sure what function these patterns serve. Do they help zebras recognise each other?

Best seen: Widespread throughout southern and central Kenya.

Giraffe

Weight 450–1200kg (female), 1800–2000kg (male); height 3.5–5.2m The giraffe does such a good job of reaching up to grab high branches, but stretching down to get a simple drink of water is difficult. Though they stroll along casually, a healthy giraffe can outrun most predators.

Best seen: Masai Mara (Masai giraffes), Lake Nakuru NP (Rothschild's giraffes), Samburu NR (reticulated giraffes).

African Elephant

Weight 2200–3500kg (female), 4000–6300kg (male); height 2.4–3.4m (female), 3–4m (male) No one stands around when a bull elephant rumbles out of the brush. Though the elephant is commonly referred to as 'the king of beasts', elephant society is ruled by a lineage of elder females.

Best seen: Amboseli NP, Tsavo East NP, Masai Mara NR, Samburu NR.

More Hoofed Mammals

This sampling of miscellaneous hoofed animals highlights the astonishing diversity in this major group of African wildlife. Every visitor wants to see elephants and giraffes, but don't pass up a chance to watch hyraxes or warthogs.

Warthog

Weight 45–75kg (female), 60–150kg (male); length 140–200cm Despite their fearsome appearance and sinister tusks, only the big males are safe from lions, cheetahs and hyenas. When attacked, warthogs run for burrows and reverse backside in, while slashing wildly with their tusks.

Best seen: Widespread throughout Kenya.

Black Rhinoceros

Weight 700–1400kg; length 350–450cm Pity the black rhinoceros for having a horn worth more than gold. Once widespread and abundant south of the Sahara, the rhino has been poached to the brink of extinction. Unfortunately, females may only give birth every five years.

Best seen: Ol Pejeta Conservancy, Lake Nakuru NP, Nairobi NP, Meru NP.

Hippopotamus

Weight 510–3200kg; length 320–400cm The hippopotamus is one strange creature. Designed like a floating beanbag with tiny legs, the 3000kg hippo spends its time in or very near water chowing down on aquatic plants. Placid? No way! Hippos have tremendous ferocity and strength when provoked.

Best seen: Masai Mara NR, Tsavo West NP.

Rock Hyrax

Weight 1.8–5.5kg; length 40–60cm It doesn't seem like it, but those funny tail-less squirrels lounging around on rocks are an ancient cousin to the elephant. You won't see some of the features that rock hyraxes share with their larger kin, but look for tusks when one yawns.

Best seen: Easily spotted in many of Kenya's parks.

1. Warthog 2. Black rhino 3. Hippos 4. Rock hyraxes

1. Golden jackal 2. Wild dogs 3. Spotted hyena
4. Banded mongoose

Carnivores

It is a sign of Africa's ecological richness that the continent supports a remarkable variety of predators. Expect the unexpected and you'll return home with a lifetime of memories!

Golden Jackal

Weight 6–15kg; length 85–130cm Despite its trim, diminutive form, the jackal fearlessly stakes a claim at the dining table of the African plain while holding hungry vultures and much stronger hyenas at bay.

Best seen: Masai Mara NR.

African Wild Dog

Weight 20–35kg; length 100–150cm Organised in complex hierarchies with strict rules of conduct, these social canids are incredibly efficient hunters. They run in packs of 20 to 60 to chase down antelope and other animals.

Best seen: Borana Conservancy, Il Ngwesi Group Ranch.

Spotted Hyena

Weight 40–90kg; length 125–215cm Living in groups that are ruled by females (who grow penis-like sexual organs), hyenas are savage fighters that use their bone-crushing jaws to disembowel terrified prey on the run or battle with lions.

Best seen: Widespread and easily seen throughout Kenya's parks.

Banded Mongoose

Weight 1.5–2kg; length 45–75cm Bounding across the savannah on their morning foraging excursions, a family of mongooses is a delightful sight. Not particularly speedy, they find delicious snacks, such as toads, scorpions and slugs.

Best seen: Easily spotted in many parks.

Common Genet

Weight 1–2kg; length 80–100cm Though nocturnal, these slender, agile hunters are readily observed slinking along roadsides or scrambling among the rafters of safari lodges. They look like a cross between a cat and a raccoon, but are easily recognised by their cream-coloured bodies and leopard-like spotting.

Best seen: Easily spotted in many parks.

Birds of Prey

ANUP SHAH / GETTY IMAGES ©

Kenya has nearly 100 species of hawks, eagles, vultures and owls. With a range from the songbird-sized pygmy kestrel to the massive lammergeier, this is one of the best places in the world to see an incredible variety of birds of prey.

Lappet-Faced Vulture

Length 115cm It's not a pretty sight when gore-encrusted vultures take over a rotting carcass that no other scavenger wants, but it's the way nature works. The monstrous lappet-faced vulture, a giant among vultures, gets its fill before other vultures move in.

Best seen: Masai Mara NR.

Secretary Bird

Length 100cm With the body of an eagle and the legs of a crane, the secretary bird stands 1.3m tall and walks up to 20km a day in search of vipers, cobras and other snakes.

Best seen: Masai Mara NR, Amboseli NP.

African Fish Eagle

Length 75cm With a wingspan over 2m, this replica of the American bald eagle is most familiar for its loud ringing vocalisations, which have become known as 'the voice of Africa'.

Best seen: Amboseli NP, Lake Nakuru NP.

Bateleur

Length 60cm French for 'tightrope-walker', this eagle's name refers to its distinctive low-flying aerial acrobatics. At close hand, look for its bold colour pattern and scarlet face.

Best seen: Widespread throughout southern and central Kenya.

Augur Buzzard

Length 55cm Perhaps Kenya's most common raptor, the augur buzzard occupies a wide range of wild and cultivated habitats. One of their hunting strategies is to float motionless in the air by riding the wind then swoop down quickly to catch unwary critters.

Best seen: Widespread throughout southern and central Kenya.

1. Lappet-faced vulture 2. African fish eagle 3. Secretary bird
4. Bateleur

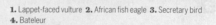

1. Saddle-billed stork 2. Lesser flamingos
3. Ostrich 4. Lilac-breasted roller

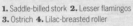

2

DR AJAY KUMAR SINGH / SHUTTERSTOCK ©

Other Birds

Birdwatchers from all over the world travel to Kenya in search of the country's 1100 species of bird – an astounding number by any measure – including every shape and colour imaginable.

Saddle-Billed Stork

Height 150cm; wingspan 270cm The saddle-billed stork is one of the more remarkably coloured of Kenya's birds. As if the 270cm wingspan wasn't impressive enough, check out its brilliant-red-coloured kneecaps and bill.

Best seen: Tsavo West NP.

Lesser Flamingo

Length 1m Coloured deep rose-pink and gathering by the hundreds of thousands on shimmering salt lakes, lesser flamingos create some of the most dramatic wildlife spectacles found in Africa, especially when they all fly at once or perform synchronised courtship displays.

Best seen: Lake Magadi, Lake Bogoria NR, Lake Nakuru NP (depending on the year).

Ostrich

Height 200–270cm Standing tall and weighing upwards of 130kg, these ancient flightless birds escape predators by running at 70km/h or lying flat on the ground to resemble a pile of dirt.

Best seen: Widespread throughout southern Kenya; Laikipia and Samburu NR (Somali ostrich).

Lilac-Breasted Roller

Length 35–38cm Nearly everyone on safari gets to know the lilac-breasted roller. It gets its name from its tendency to 'roll' from side to side in flight to show off its iridescent blues, purples and greens.

Best seen: Commonly seen throughout Kenya.

Vulturine Guineafowl

Length 70cm Take an electric-blue chicken, drape black-and-white speckled feathers over its body and place an elegant ruff around its neck, and you have a pretty flamboyant bird. Look for guineafowl walking around in groups in semi-arid areas.

Best seen: Tsavo West NP.

4

Habitats

Nearly all of Kenya's wildlife occupies a specific type of habitat. You will hear rangers and fellow travellers refer to these habitats repeatedly as they describe where to search for animals. If this is your first time in Kenya, some of these habitats and their seasonal rhythms take some getting used to, but your wildlife-viewing experience will be greatly enhanced if you learn how to recognise these habitats and the animals you might expect to find in each one.

High Mountains

Kenya is remarkable for having extensive high-mountain habitats, including unexpected snowy crags and glaciers that are located right on the equator, a habitat that is very rare anywhere else in East Africa. The massive extinct volcanoes of Mt Elgon and Mt Kenya are islands of montane forests, bogs, giant heathers and moorlands that are perched high above the surrounding lowlands. The few animals that survive here are uniquely adapted to these bizarre landscapes.

Semi-arid Desert

Much of eastern and northern Kenya sees so little rainfall that shrubs and hardy grasses, rather than trees, are the dominant vegetation. This is not the classic landscape that many visitors come to see and it doesn't seem like a great place for wildlife, but the patient observer will be richly rewarded. While it's true that the lack of water restricts larger animals such as zebras, gazelles and antelope to areas around waterholes, this habitat explodes with plant and animal life whenever it rains. During the dry season many plants shed their leaves to conserve water and grazing animals move on in search of food and water.

Savannah

Savannah is *the* classic East African landscape – broad, rolling grasslands dotted with lone acacia trees. The openness and vastness of this landscape make it a perfect home for large herds of grazing zebras and wildebeest, in addition to fast-sprinting predators like cheetahs, and

it's the best habitat for seeing large numbers of animals. Savannah develops in areas where there are long wet seasons alternating with long dry seasons, creating ideal conditions for the growth of dense, nutritious grasses. Shaped by fire and grazing animals, savannah is a dynamic habitat in constant flux with adjacent woodlands.

Rivers & Lakes

Since vast areas of Kenya are extremely dry, at least on a seasonal basis, any source of water is a mecca for wildlife. Everything from slow-moving rivers to shallow lakes and muddy wallows attract steady streams of birds and mammals; one of the best ways to watch wildlife is to sit quietly near watering holes. Some of the highly saline and alkaline lakes of the Rift Valley, such as Lake Nakuru and Lake Bogoria, attract fantastic numbers of birds, including African fish eagles, shorebirds and ducks, as well as flocks of over a million flamingos.

1. Lake Nakuru National Park (p102)
2. Ewaso Ngiro River, Samburu National Reserve (p275)

Lion in Masai Mara National Reserve (p112)

Environment

Kenya's natural environment is at once inspiring and troubled. The country is home to some of East Africa's most beautiful landscapes, from its signature savannah to palm-fringed coast with sky-high mountains, parched deserts and dense forests in between. But Kenya faces a slew of environmental issues that challenge the very sustainability of its future, with impacts upon everything from food security to the viability of protected areas. Like so many things Kenyan, it's a complicated, fascinating story.

The Land

Kenya, as the cliché goes, is Africa in microcosm, and in the case of its landscapes, the cliché happens to be true. Within Kenya's borders you'll find astonishing variety, from deserts to tropical coast and snowcapped mountains, from sweeping savannah grasslands to dense forests. And running through the heart of it all is the Great Rift Valley.

Kenya: A Natural History (2012), by Stephen Spawls and Glenn Matthews, covers everything from wildlife to geology and just about everything in between. It's a terrific resource, if a little eclectic in parts.

Great Rift Valley

The Great Rift Valley is one of Africa's defining landforms and this great gouge in the planet cuts a swathe through the heart of Kenya. It was formed some eight million years ago, when Mother Earth tried to rip Africa in two. Africa bent, Africa buckled, but Africa never gave in.

The Rift Valley is part of the Afro-Arabian rift system that stretches 5500km from the salty shores of the Dead Sea to the palm trees of Mozambique, passing through the Red Sea, Ethiopia, Kenya, Tanzania and Malawi en route. A western branch forms a string of lakes (Albert, Edward, Kivu and Tanganyika) in the centre of the continent, joining the main system at the tip of Lake Malawi. The East African section of the rift 'failed' and now only the Red Sea rift continues, slowly separating Africa from the Middle East. The Rift's path through Kenya can be traced through Lake Turkana, the Cherangani Hills and Lakes Baringo, Bogoria, Nakuru, Elmenteita, Naivasha and Magadi.

The Rift created Africa's highest mountains – including Mt Kenya, Mt Elgon, Mt Kilimanjaro (across the border in Tanzania) and the Virunga Range (in the Democratic Republic of the Congo; DRC, formerly Zaïre) – most of which began as volcanoes. Most of the volcanoes that line the valley are now extinct, but no fewer than 30 remain active and, according to local legend, Mt Longonot erupted as recently as the 1860s. This continuing activity supports a considerable number of hot springs and provides ideal conditions for geothermal power plants (in Hell's Gate National Park and the Menengai Crater, for example), which are increasingly important for Kenya's energy supply, if controversial from an environmental perspective.

The Savannah

The African savannah is a quintessentially African landform, so much so that it covers an estimated two-thirds of the African land mass. In Kenya, the most famous sweeps of savannah are found in the country's west (particularly in the Masai Mara National Reserve) and south.

The East African savannah was formed during the Rift's great upheavals, when volcanic lava and ash rained down upon the lands surrounding the Rift's volcanoes, covering the landscape in fertile but shallow soils. Grasses, that most successful of plant forms, flourished as they needed little depth for their roots to grow. The perfectly adapted acacia aside, however, no other plants were able to colonise the savannah: their roots were starved of space and nourishment.

The result is sweeping plains that are home to some of the richest concentrations of wildlife on earth. The term itself refers to a grasslands ecosystem sustained by an annual cycle of wet and dry seasons. While trees may be (and usually are) present in savannah ecosystems, such trees do not, under the strict definition of the term, form a closed canopy.

The Coast

Along the coast of East Africa, warm currents in the Indian Ocean provide perfect conditions for coral growth, resulting in beautiful underwater coral reefs.

Mangroves

Wasini Island

Funzi Island

Gazi Island

Mida Creek

Coral reefs are the most biologically diverse marine ecosystems on earth, rivalled only by tropical rainforests on land. Corals grow over geologic time – ie over millennia rather than the decades that mammals live – and have been in existence for about 200 million years. The delicately balanced marine environment of the coral reef relies on the interaction of hard and soft corals, sponges, fish, turtles, dolphins and other marine life forms.

Coral reefs also rely on mangroves, the salt-tolerant trees with submerged roots that form a nursery and breeding ground for birds and most of the marine life that migrates to the reef. Mangroves trap and produce nutrients for food and habitat, stabilise the shoreline and filter pollutants from the land base. Both coral reefs and the mangrove colonies that support them are under threat from factors such as oil exploration and extraction, coastal degradation, deforestation and global warming.

Forests

Kenya's forests border the great rainforest systems of central Africa, and western Kenya once formed part of the mighty Guineo-Congolian forest ecosystem. Few vestiges remain and just 6.2% of Kenyan territory is now covered by forest. The process of clearing these forests began with Kenya's colonial rulers, who saw in the land's fertility great potential for the vast tea plantations that now provide critical export

CONCRETE & SAND

Driving around Kenya, especially along the southern and eastern outskirts of Nairobi, it can feel as if every second factory is a cement factory. This highly competitive industry is a major player in Kenya's rapidly developing economy, but the industry's demand for sand – especially with so many major infrastructure projects underway, such as the expansion of the national railway – is causing concerns among conservationists. In particular, the dredging from sand has already begun to impact upon the beaches of Tiwi and the sea turtles that nest in the area, while a number of rivers have been seriously degraded as well. The Kilome Ikolya River in Makueni County in southeastern Kenya has been particularly affected with massive erosion, dying trees, disappearing water and violence – in 2011 a police officer who tried to confront illegal sand harvesters was killed.

RIFT LAKES RISING

Whether alkaline or freshwater, Kenya's lakes have experienced an as-yet-unexplained rise in water levels. For some lakes, these rises have been by metres, engulfing shorelines and beyond, forcing some businesses to close, maps to be redrawn and reducing the salinity of the lakes in some cases; the latter problem has caused the flamingos to go elsewhere. Hardest hit have been Baringo, Bogoria, Elmenteita and Nakuru, with Lake Naivasha also experiencing rising water levels.

The most likely explanation is that tectonic plates well below the surface have shifted, causing changes in water flows, although nobody knows for how long these new watery boundaries will remain as they are.

revenue to Kenya. The clearing of the land has continued apace ever since as Kenya's population soars and the need for land for agriculture has increased. The Kakamega Forest has been protected just in time and shows what most of western Kenya must have once looked like. Other important forest areas include those covering 2000 sq km of the slopes of Mt Kenya, the Arabuko Sokoke Forest Reserve (the largest surviving tract of coastal forest in East Africa), Mt Elgon National Park and Aberdare National Park.

Six sites in Kenya are included on the Unesco World Heritage list: Mt Kenya, the Lake Turkana national parks, Lamu's Old Town, Fort Jesus in Mombasa, the Mijikenda *kayas* (sacred forests) and the lake system in the Great Rift Valley.

Deserts

Much of northern Kenya is extremely arid, with rainfall of less than 100mm a year. A number of contiguous deserts occupy the territory between Lake Turkana's eastern shore and the Ethiopian and Somali borders. The largest and best known of these is the Chalbi Desert, centred on North Horr and Kalacha, and formed by an ancient lake bed. Other deserts of northern Kenya include the Kaisut Desert (between Marsabit and South Horr) and the Dida Galgalu Desert (close to the Ethiopian border, near Moyale).

Parts of southern Kenya are also considered arid or semi-arid, thanks largely to the looming hulk of Mt Kilimanjaro, which diverts rain elsewhere. One of these is the Nyiri Desert, which lies roughly between Lake Magadi and Amboseli National Park.

Lakes & Wetlands

Lake Victoria, which is shared between Uganda, Tanzania and Kenya, is Africa's largest freshwater lake (and the second largest by area in the world after the USA's Lake Superior). Its surface covers an area of over 68,000 sq km, with only 20% of the lake lying within Kenyan territory. Water levels fluctuate widely, depending largely on the rains, with depths never more than 80m and more often lower than 10m.

Most of Kenya's section of Lake Victoria is taken over by the Winam Gulf, a 100km-long, 50km-wide arm of the lake with a shoreline of almost 550km and an average depth of 6m. A fast-growing population around the gulf's shoreline has caused massive environmental problems, such as siltation, sedimentation and toxic pollution (primarily pesticides and untreated sewage), although the major issue has been the invasion of water hyacinth since the late 1980s. The millions of dollars ploughed into solving the problem largely rid the gulf of hyacinth by 2005, but the gulf remains highly susceptible to the plant's clutches.

Aside from Lake Victoria in the west, Kenya has numerous small volcanic lakes, as well as a sea of jade, otherwise known by the more

WHICH FIELD GUIDE

Having trouble telling a dik-dik from a klipspringer? A serval from a caracal? Field guides, apart from being damned interesting to read, can be invaluable tools for identifying animals while on safari. Our favourites:

➡ *A Field Guide to the Carnivores of the World* (Luke Hunter; 2011) Wonderfully illustrated and filled with fascinating detail.

➡ *The Kingdon Field Guide to African Mammals* (Jonathan Kingdon; 2nd ed, 2015) The latest edition of the classic field guide covering over 1150 species. There's also the travel-friendly *Kingdon Pocket Guide to African Mammals* (2016).

➡ *The Behavior Guide to African Mammals* (Richard Despard Estes; 1991) Classic study of the behaviour of mammal species. Estes' follow-up *The Safari Companion: A Guide to Watching African Mammals* (1993) is an excellent, slightly more accessible alternative.

➡ *Birds of Kenya and Northern Tanzania* (Dale A Zimmerman, David J Pearson and Donald A Turner; 2005) The birding field guide of choice for East Africa.

➡ *Jonathan Scott's Safari Guide to East African Animals* and *Jonathan Scott's Safari Guide to East African Birds,* both published first in 1998 but updated since, are wonderful safari companions with fine photos by Angela Scott.

In the UK, an excellent source for wildlife and nature titles is Subbuteo Natural History Books Ltd (www.wildlifebooks.com), while in Australia, check out Andrew Isles Natural History Books (www.andrewisles.com); both accept international mail orders.

boring name of Lake Turkana, which straddles the Ethiopian border in the north. The main alkaline lakes in the Rift Valley include Bogoria, Nakuru, Elmenteita, Magadi and Oloiden. These shallow soda lakes, formed by the valley's lack of decent drainage, experience high evaporation rates, which further concentrates the alkalinity. The strangely soapy and smelly waters are, however, the perfect environment for the growth of microscopic blue-green algae, which in turn feed lesser flamingos, tiny crustaceans (food for greater flamingos) and insect larvae (food for soda-resistant fish).

Not all of the Rift Valley's lakes are alkaline; freshwater lakes include Baringo and Naivasha.

In 2011 the global significance of Kenya's Rift Valley lake system (primarily Lakes Nakuru, Elmenteita and Bogoria) was recognised when it was inscribed on Unesco's list of World Heritage Sites. Five of the Rift Valley's lakes – Baringo, Bogoria, Elmenteita, Naivasha and Nakuru – have also been listed on the Ramsar List of Wetlands of International Importance, and represent important habitats for wintering waterbirds from the north.

Rivers

One of Kenya's most important rivers is the Athi/Galana River system. The Athi River passes east of Nairobi, joins the Tsavo River (which passes through the Tsavo West National Park), and the two then feed into the Galana River, which cuts Tsavo East National Park in two. The Athi/Galana River then empties into the Indian Ocean close to Malindi. The Tana River is the country's other major river, rising northeast of Nairobi and emptying into the Indian Ocean between Malindi and Lamu.

Environmental Issues

Kenya faces a daunting slew of environmental issues, among them deforestation, desertification, threats to endangered species and the impacts of tourism. In response, Kenya's private conservation community has taken matters into its own hands with, in many cases, exceptional results.

Deforestation

More than half of Africa's forests have been destroyed over the last century, and forest destruction continues on a large scale in parts of Kenya – today, less than 3% of the country's original forest cover remains. Land grabbing, charcoal burning, agricultural encroachment, the spiralling use of firewood and illegal logging have all taken their toll over the years. However, millions of Kenyans (and the majority of hotels, lodges and restaurants) still rely on wood and charcoal for cooking fuel, so travellers to the country will almost certainly contribute to this deforestation, whether they like it or not.

Native hardwood, such as ebony and mahogany, is often used to make the popular carved wooden statue souvenirs sold in Kenya. Although this industry supports thousands of local families who may otherwise be without an income, it also consumes an estimated 80,000 trees annually. The World Wide Fund for Nature (WWF) and Unesco campaigned to promote the use of common, faster-growing trees, and many handicraft cooperatives now use wood taken from forests managed by the Forest Stewardship Council. If you buy a carving, ask if the wood is sourced from managed forests.

Desertification

Northern and eastern Kenya are home to some of the most marginal lands in East Africa. Pastoralists have eked out a similarly marginal existence here for centuries, but recurring droughts have seriously degraded the land, making it increasingly susceptible to creeping desertification and erosion. As a consequence, the UN estimates that the livelihoods of around 3.5 million herders may be under medium- to long-term threat.

And desertification, at least in its early stages, may even begin to encroach upon the most unlikely places. The fertile lands of Kenya's Central Highlands rank among Africa's most agriculturally productive, but therein lies their peril: here, around three-quarters of Kenya's population crowds into just 12% of the land, with the result that soils are being rapidly depleted through overexploitation – one of the early warning signs of desertification.

Endangered Species

Many of Kenya's major predators and herbivores have become endangered over the past few decades, because of poisoning, the ongoing destruction of their natural habitat and merciless poaching for ivory, skins, horn and bushmeat.

Elephants

Elephants are numerous in many areas of Kenya, but this hasn't always been so and their survival is one of world conservation's most enduring success stories.

In the 1970s and 1980s, the numbers of African elephants on the continent plummeted from an estimated 1.3 million to around 500,000 due to widespread poaching. In Kenya, elephant numbers fell from

Game Changer: Animal Rights & the Fate of Africa's Wildlife (2012), by Glen Martin, is a provocative look at wildlife conservation, covering Kenya, Tanzania and Namibia.

In 2016, 27 years after then-President Daniel arap Moi dramatically burned 12 tonnes of ivory in Nairobi National Park and with poaching again on the rise, President Jomo Kenyatta burned 100 tonnes of ivory at the same site. The bonfire amounted to tusks from 6000 elephants or 5% of global ivory stocks.

45,000 in 1976 to just 5400 in 1988. The slaughter ended only in 1989 when the trade in ivory was banned under the Convention on International Trade in Endangered Species (CITES). When the ban was established, world raw-ivory prices plummeted by 90% and the market for poaching and smuggling was radically reduced. The same year, Kenyan President Daniel arap Moi dramatically burned 12 tonnes of ivory in Nairobi National Park as a symbol of Kenya's resolve in the battle against poachers.

Yet poaching still hasn't been stamped out entirely and attacks continue to happen. The Great Elephant Census of 2016 (www.greatelephantcensus.com) estimated that there were around 26,000 elephants in Kenya today, and the country is one of the few places in Africa where elephant numbers are growing, although admittedly very slowly.

Based in Kenya and run by the respected Dr Iain Douglas-Hamilton, Save the Elephants (www.savetheelephants.org) is one of the pre-eminent NGOs working with elephants in Africa, while one of the longest-running studies of elephants on the planet, Amboseli Trust for Elephants (www.elephanttrust.org) is overseen by Dr Cynthia Moss and is based inside Amboseli National Park.

Rhinoceroses

These inoffensive vegetarians are armed with impressive horns that have made them the target of both hunters and poachers – rhino numbers plummeted to the brink of extinction during the 20th century and the illegal trade in rhino horns is still driven by their use in traditional medicines in Asian countries.

There are two species of rhino – black and white – both of which are predominantly found in savannah regions. The black rhino is probably Kenya's most endangered large mammal. It is also often described as Kenya's indigenous rhino – historically, the white rhino was not found

POACHING'S RETURN

A recent upsurge in the poaching of both elephants (for their tusks) and rhinos (for their horns) has conservationists worried we may soon be facing a return to the dark days of the 1980s.

Talk to many in the conservation community and they'll tell you that it was in 2009 that the crisis again began to take hold. It was in the following year that Lewa Wildlife Conservancy lost its first rhinos to poaching in almost three decades and Africa has lost more than 30,000 elephants a year since 2010. In 2014, for the first time in decades, a critical threshold was crossed when more elephants were being killed on the continent than were being born.

While numbers of poached animals in Kenya remain relatively low, all of the major rhino sanctuaries – Nairobi National Park, Lake Nakuru National Park, Lewa Wildlife Conservancy, Solio Game Reserve, Ol Pejeta Conservancy, Ngulia Rhino Sanctuary in Tsavo West National Park – have lost rhinos to poachers in recent years. Most worrying of all is that each of these have extremely high security and sophisticated anti-poaching programmes.

For elephants, poaching hotspots include the northern half of Tsavo East National Park (which is off-limits for travellers), the community lands just outside the southern boundary of Tsavo West National Park, and the lands surrounding Samburu National Reserve.

The KWS, while denying that poaching has reached crisis levels in Kenya, remains on the frontline in the war against poaching, but other organisations are also active, such as the Big Life Foundation (www.biglife.org).

in Kenya. Pursued by heavily armed gangs, the black rhino's numbers fell from an estimated 20,000 in the 1970s to barely 300 a decade later. Numbers are slowly recovering (rhinos are notoriously slow breeders), with an estimated 600 to 700 black rhinos surviving in the wild in Kenya, which represents around one-sixth of Africa's total (or close to 90% of the world population for the eastern subspecies of black rhino). Despite some poaching incidents, Kenya's black rhino population almost doubled in the decade to 2016.

Although numbers are quite small in Kenya, the survival of the white rhino is an environmental conservation success story, having been brought back from the brink of extinction in South Africa through captive breeding. The KWS estimates that Kenya is home to 350 to 375 white rhinos in the wild. At Ol Pejeta Conservancy in Laikipia you can see the last three remaining northern white rhinos (a subspecies of the white rhino) left in the world.

Rhino Ark (www.rhinoark.org) is one organisation that raises funds to create rhino sanctuaries, or to build fences around national parks, as it has done in Aberdare National Park. Donations are always appreciated.

Lions

Lions may be the easiest of Kenya's big cats to spot – leopards are notoriously secretive and largely keep to the undergrowth, while cheetahs live in similarly low-density populations and can also prove elusive. But don't let appearances fool you: the lion may be the most imperilled of Africa's three big cats.

Fewer than 30,000 lions are thought to remain in Africa (there is a tiny, highly inbred population of Asian lions in the Gir Forest in Gujarat state in India), although most conservationists agree that the number is most likely considerably below that figure. In Kenya, fewer than 2000 are thought to survive, although this, too, is feared to be an overestimate. Although there are small, scattered prides around the country, in Lake Nakuru National Park and northern Kenya, the only viable lion populations in the long term are those in Laikipia (estimated at around 270 lions), Maasailand and the two Tsavo parks (around 700 lions in the entire Tsavo ecosystem).

And numbers are falling alarmingly, possibly by as many as 100 lions per year, thanks primarily to human encroachment, habitat loss and the resulting human–wildlife conflict. The poisoning of lions (as well as scavengers and other predators), either in retaliation for lions killing livestock or encroaching onto farming lands, has also reached dangerous levels, to the extent that some lion conservationists predict that the lion could become extinct in Kenya within 20 years.

Important work is being done in the world of lion conservation, including by Ewaso Lions (www.ewasolions.org), Lion Guardians (www.lionguardians.org) and the Maasai Wilderness Conservation Trust (www.maasaiwilderness.org).

Grevy's Zebras

Kenya (along with neighbouring Ethiopia) is home to the last surviving wild populations of Grevy's zebra. Grevy's zebras are distinguished from other zebra species by having narrow stripes everywhere but with bellies free from stripes. In the 1970s, approximately 15,000 Grevy's zebras were thought to survive in the wild. Just 2500 are estimated to remain and less than 1% of the Grevy zebra's historical range lies within protected areas.

White rhinos aren't white at all – the name comes from the Dutch word *wijd*, which means wide and refers to the white rhino's wide lip (the black rhino has a pointed lip).

ENVIRONMENT ENVIRONMENTAL ISSUES

Where to See Grevy's Zebras

Lewa Wildlife Conservancy

Ol Pejeta Conservancy

Segera Ranch

Meru National Park

Samburu National Reserve

WILDLIFE WATCHING – THE BASICS

➡ Most animals are naturally wary of people, so to minimise their distress (or aggression) keep as quiet as possible, avoid sudden movements and wear subdued colours when in the field.

➡ Avoid direct eye contact, particularly with primates, as this is seen as a challenge and may provoke aggressive behaviour.

➡ Good binoculars are an invaluable aid to observing wildlife at a distance and are essential for birdwatching.

➡ When on foot, stay downwind of animals wherever possible – they'll smell you long before they see or hear you.

➡ Never get out of your vehicle unless it's safe to do so.

➡ Always obey park regulations, including traffic speed limits; thousands of animals are needlessly killed on African roads every year.

➡ Follow your guide's instructions at all times – it may mean the difference between life and death on a walking safari.

➡ Never get between a mother and her young.

➡ Exercise care when boating or swimming, and be particularly aware of the dangers posed by crocodiles and hippos.

➡ Never feed wild animals – it encourages scavenging, may adversely affect their health, and can cause animals to become aggressive towards each other and humans.

Giraffes

One of the most worrying developments in recent years has been the downgrading of the giraffe by the International Union for the Conservation of Nature (www.iucnredlist.org) from Least Concern in 2010 to Vulnerable in 2016. The world's tallest land mammal remains widespread across eastern and southern Africa, but a precipitous 40% decline (from an estimated 151,702 to 163,452 individuals in 1985 to 97,562 in 2015) has brought the species' fate into sharp focus.

The main threats to the giraffe are illegal hunting, habitat loss, increasing human–wildlife conflict, civil conflict and encroaching human settlements.

Rothschild Giraffes

The most endangered of the nine giraffe subspecies, the Rothschild's giraffe has recently been hauled back from the brink of extinction. At the forefront of the fight to save Rothschild's giraffe (which, unlike other subspecies, has distinctive white 'stockings' with no orange-and-black markings below the knee) has been the Giraffe Centre (p61) in Nairobi – visiting here is a fascinating experience, and helps further the attempts to save the giraffes and facilitate their return to the wild.

Cheetahs

The fastest land animal on earth (it can reach speeds of 75km/h in the first two seconds of its pursuit and at full speed may reach 115km/h), the cheetah in full flight is one of the most thrilling sights in the African wild. Cheetahs inhabit mostly open country, from the savannah to the desert, and they're most easily spotted in the major national parks of Kenya, Tanzania, Namibia, Botswana, South Africa and Zambia. A small number of cheetahs are also believed to survive in the Sahara of Algeria and Niger.

At the end of 2016, a scientific study confirmed what many conservationists in the field had long feared – the cheetah is in trouble. The latest estimates suggest that just 7100 cheetahs remain in the wild, all of which live in Africa save for an isolated population of around 50 in the deserts and mountains of central Iran.

Of the estimated 6600 adult cheetahs that remain, the IUCN argued that there were just under 2000 cheetahs left in East Africa; between one-half and two-thirds are in southern Africa. More specifically, the IUCN estimated a population of 710 for the Serengeti–Mara–Amboseli–Tsavo regions, plus a further 450 spread across Samburu and the Laikipia Plateau.

The major causes of the cheetah's decline are shrinking habitats and human encroachment, which results in increasing conflict between cheetahs and farmers; more than three-quarters of Africa's wild cheetahs live outside protected areas. Other problems include the smuggling of cheetah cubs out of the continent for sale as pets – baby cheetahs sell for as much as US$10,000 on the black market – with more than 1200 trafficked off the continent over the past decade, 85% of whom died in transit.

Organisations such as the Mara Cheetah Project (www.mara cheetahs.org) and the Namibia-based Cheetah Conservation Fund (www.cheetah.org) are at the forefront of efforts to mitigate this conflict and are worth contacting to find out more.

Panthera (www.panthera.org) is another conservation organisation working on prgrams to support cheetahs and other wild cats.

Private Versus Public Conservation

Kenya Wildlife Service (KWS)

Conservation in Kenya has, for over two decades, been in the hands of the government-run KWS (www.kws.org) and few would dispute that it has done a pretty impressive job. In the dark years of the 1970s and '80s when poaching was rampant, a staggering number of Kenya's rhinos and elephants were slaughtered and many KWS officers were in league with poachers. It all changed after the famous palaeontologist Dr Richard Leakey cleaned up the organisation in the 1980s and '90s. A core part of his policy was arming KWS rangers with modern weapons and high-speed vehicles, and allowing them to shoot poachers on sight. Even so, with poaching again on the rise, KWS rangers continue to lose their lives every year in battles with poachers.

GOOD WILDLIFE READS

➤ The Tree Where Man Was Born (Peter Matthiessen; 1972) Classic, lyrical account of wildlife and traditional peoples in East Africa.

➤ A Primate's Memoir: Love, Death and Baboons in East Africa (Robert M Sapolsky; 2002) Wonderfully told memoir of working among the baboons of East Africa.

➤ Ivory, Apes & Peacocks: Animals, adventure and discovery in the wild places of Africa (Alan Root; 2012) Picaresque tale of the life of the late Alan Root, one of the pioneers in wildlife documentary film-making.

➤ The Big Cat Man: An Autobiography (Jonathon Scott; 2016) Jonathon Scott has been the companion to a generation of safari goers and armchair travellers. His autobiography is typically warm-hearted.

➤ Don't Run, Whatever You Do: My Adventures as a Safari Guide (Peter Allison; 2007) Light-hearted romp through adventures and misadventures of a safari guide. Set in Botswana but could easily be Kenya.

The East African Wildlife Society (www.eawildlife. org), based in Nairobi, is the most prominent conservation body in the region and a good source of information. It also publishes *SWARA* magazine, a stalwart of the conservation scene and much of which is available online for members.

Despite their excellent work in fighting poaching and maintaining Kenya's protected areas, the KWS is limited in what it can achieve. For a start, in times of shrinking government revenues, funding remains a major issue in how well the KWS can fulfil its mandate.

Just as importantly, much of Kenya's wildlife lives beyond national park and other publicly protected boundaries. In such an environment, the KWS has shown itself to be at times intransigent in handling incidents of human–wildlife conflict in the communities that surround national park areas. As a result, there is a widespread perception among some communities that the KWS is more interested in looking after wildlife than it is in protecting local people. In response, the KWS has in recent years been working hard to improve its community relations, particularly in and around Amboseli National Park.

Private Conservancies

For all the success of KWS, there seems to be little doubt that the future of conservation in Kenya lies in private hands.

Much of it began up on the Laikipia Plateau and surrounding areas, on large cattle ranches which had, in many cases, been owned by the same family of white settlers since colonial times. One of the first to turn its attention to conservation was Lewa Downs, now the Lewa Wildlife Conservancy (p162), which in 1983 set aside part of its land as a rhino sanctuary. Lewa remains a standard bearer for the conservancy model and there are now more than 40 such conservancies scattered across Laikipia and northern regions, with more around the Masai Mara.

While wildlife conservation is a primary focus of nearly all conservancies – these places often have the resources to work more intensively on specific conservation issues than national parks and reserves can – community engagement and development are considered equally important. Most often this consists of funding local schools, health centres and other development projects. By giving local communities a stake in the protection of wildlife, so the argument goes, they are more likely to protect the wildlife in their midst.

Another important element of the conservancy model includes making tourism pay its way. In almost all of the conservancies, access to conservancy land is restricted to those staying at the exclusive and often extremely expensive lodges and tented camps. Most also charge a conservancy fee (usually around US$100 per day), which goes directly to local community projects and wildlife programmes. All of this means a far more intimate safari experience as well as a much-reduced impact upon the land when compared with mass tourism.

Yet another advantage of visiting a private conservancy is that the range of activities on offer far exceeds what is possible in national parks. At the most basic level, this means off-road driving (to get you *really* close to the wildlife), night drives and walking safaris. Horseback safaris and visits to local communities are among the other possibilities, although you'll usually pay extra for these.

One exception to the overall rule, and it's a significant one, is Ol Pejeta Conservancy (p160). Although similar in terms of wildlife protection programmes and community engagement, it has opened its doors to the public and receives tens of thousands of visitors every year. The experience of visiting Ol Pejeta is akin to visiting a national park but with a whole lot of really cool activities thrown in.

The private conservancies of the Laikipia Plateau in particular have produced some startling results – without a single national park or reserve in the area, Laikipia has become a major safari destination,

BANNING PLASTIC BAGS

At the end of August 2017, Kenya introduced one of the world's strictest laws against the use of plastic carrier bags. The law, which survived a High Court challenge and warnings of 80,000 job losses in the plastic-bag-production industry, allows for those who break the law to be sentenced to four years in prison or face a US$38,000 fine. In practice, in the first months of the law's implementation, police were instructed to warn those who violate the laws and confiscate the offending bags.

No-one who has travelled in Kenya could doubt the need for such a law, with plastic bags filling the countryside and vacant plots of land, especially in Kenyan cities. In addition to being an eyesore, plastic bags have the potential to impact upon public health: for example, grazing cattle feed on the bags, with up to 20 polythene bags pulled from the stomach of just one cow in one Nairobi abattoir The government estimates that before the ban Kenyans used 24 million plastic bags every month. And travellers are certainly not exempt – if you're arriving by air with duty-free plastic shopping bags, the bags will be taken from you before you leave the airport.

Later in 2017, the government announced a further ban, this time on taking plastic water bottles into Nairobi National Park and the nearby Karura Forest. It seems likely that the ban will be extended to cover all national parks in the not-too-distant future.

and is proving to be a particularly important area for viable populations of endangered black rhinos, Grevy's zebras, African wild dogs and lions. In fact, the black rhino may well have disappeared forever from Kenya were it not for the Laikipia conservancies.

Community Conservancies

Similar in focus to private ranches, community conservancies are an extension of the private conservancy model. Rather than being owned by wealthy owners or families, community conservancies are communally owned by entire communities and administered by community representatives. These communities treat wildlife as a natural resource and take serious action to protect the animals' wellbeing, whether by combating poaching with increased security or by modifying their herding activities to minimise human–animal conflict and environmental damage.

With financial and logistical support from many sources, including Lewa Wildlife Conservancy (LWC), Laikipia Wildlife Forum (LWF) and the Northern Ranchlands Trust (NRT), these communities have in many cases built ecolodges whose income now provides much-needed funds for their education, health and humanitarian projects.

Northern Kenya appears to provide particularly fertile ground for the community conservancy model – fine examples include the Maasai of Il Ngwesi, Laikipia Maasai of Lekurruki and the Samburu within the Matthews Range – but there are also some excellent examples on the Maasai Group Ranches around Amboseli National Park and in the Masai Mara region.

Renewable Energy

The use of renewable energy has been slow to catch on in Kenya. Many top-end lodges attempt to pursue sound environmental practices – the use of solar energy is increasingly widespread – but these remain very much in the minority. And many of these top-end lodges suggest that you travel to them by air, which surely cancels out any gains of having solar-powered hot water in your shower. Expect fossil fuels to continue to drive Kenya's economy.

National Parks & Reserves

Kenya's national parks and reserves rate among the best in Africa. Around 10% of the country's land area is protected by law – that means, at least in theory, no human habitation, no grazing and no hunting within park boundaries. The parks range from the 15.5-sq-km Saiwa Swamp National Park to the massive, almost 21,000-sq-km Tsavo East and West national parks. Together they embrace a wide range of habitats and ecosystems and contain an extraordinary repository of Africa's wildlife.

History

The idea of setting aside protected areas began during colonial times, and in many cases this meant authorities forcibly evicting the local peoples from their traditional lands. Local anger was fuelled by the fact that many parks were set aside as hunting reserves for white hunters with anything but conservation on their minds. In 1946 Nairobi National Park became the first park in British East Africa. Now, there are 22 national parks, plus numerous marine parks and national reserves – the KWS administers 33 protected areas in total.

Many of the parks came under siege in the 1970s and 1980s when poaching became endemic. In response, President Moi grabbed international headlines when, in 1989, he set fire to a stockpile of 12 tonnes of ivory in Nairobi National Park and appointed Richard Leakey to the head of the Wildlife Conservation and Management Department

NATIONAL PARKS VERSUS RESERVES

If you go onto the website of the Kenya Wildlife Service (KWS; www.kws.org) looking for information on the Masai Mara National Reserve or Samburu National Reserve, you'll be disappointed. That's because Kenya's parks and reserves are divided into those that are administered by the national government (this includes all national parks and some national reserves, such as Kakamega Forest National Reserve) and those administered by local communities (such as the Masai Mara and Lake Bogoria national reserves).

The difference is significant from a local perspective, less so in terms of your experience on safari. It all comes down to revenues. The entry fees for parks administered by the KWS go directly into the coffers of the national government, with a proportion, in theory at least, returned to the local communities. In the case of the locally administered reserves, revenues go to the local county council, which forwards some revenue on to the national government and, again in theory, uses the money for the benefit of local communities.

The whole issue came to national and international attention in 2005 when President Kibaki announced plans to de-gazette Amboseli National Park and turn it into a reserve administered by the Maasai-dominated Kajiado County Council. His motives remained unclear, although cynics suggested it may have been a ploy to win over the Maasai vote in advance of a crucial national referendum on constitutional reform. Conservationists cried foul and the move was declared illegal by Kenya's High Court in 2011.

MAJOR NATIONAL PARKS & RESERVES

PARK/RESERVE	HABITATS	WILDLIFE	ACTIVITIES	BEST TIME TO VISIT
Aberdare National Park	dramatic highlands, waterfalls, rainforest	elephants, black rhinos, bongo antelope, black leopards, black servals	trekking, fishing, gliding	year-round
Amboseli National Park	dry plains, scrub forest	elephants, buffaloes, lions, antelope, birds	wildlife drives	Jun–Feb
Arabuko Sokoke Forest Reserve	coastal forest	Sokoke scops owls, Clarke's weavers, birds, elephant shrews, elephants	bird tours, walking, cycling	year-round
Hell's Gate National Park	dramatic rocky outcrops, gorges	elands, giraffes, lions, birds of prey	cycling, walking	year-round
Kakamega Forest Reserve	virgin tropical rainforest	de Brazza's monkeys, red-tailed monkeys, flying squirrels, 330 bird species	walking, birdwatching	year-round
Lake Bogoria National Reserve	scenic soda lake	greater kudus, leopards	birdwatching, walking, hot springs	year-round
Lake Nakuru National Park	hilly grassland, alkaline lakeland	flamingos, black & white rhinos, over 400 bird species, lions, leopards	wildlife drives	year-round
Masai Mara National Reserve	savannah, grassland	Big Five, antelope, cheetahs, hyenas, wildebeest migration	wildlife drives, ballooning	Jul–Oct
Meru National Park	rainforest, swamplands, grasslands	rhinos, elephants, lions, cheetahs, lesser kudus	wildlife drives, fishing	year-round
Mt Elgon National Park	extinct volcano, rainforest	elephants, black-and-white-colobus monkeys, de Brazza's monkeys, over 240 bird species	walking, trekking, fishing	Dec–Feb
Mt Kenya National Park	rainforest, moorland, glacial mountain	elephants, buffaloes, mountain flora	trekking, climbing	Jan & Feb, Aug & Sep
Nairobi National Park	open plains with urban backdrop	black rhinos, lions, leopards, over 400 bird species, cheetahs, giraffes	wildlife drives	year-round
Saiwa Swamp National Park	swamplands, riverine forest	sitatunga antelope, otters, black-and-white colobus monkeys, over 370 bird species	walking, birdwatching	year-round
Samburu, Buffalo Springs & Shaba National Reserves	semi-arid open savannah	elephants, leopards, gerenuks, crocodiles, Grevy's zebras	wildlife drives	year-round
Shimba Hills National Reserve	densely forested hills	elephants, sable antelope, leopards	walking, forest tours	year-round
Tsavo West & East National Parks	sweeping plains, ancient volcanic cones	Big Five, cheetahs, giraffes, hippos, crocodiles, around 500 bird species	rock climbing, wildlife drives	year-round

(WMCD), which became the KWS a year later. Leakey is largely credited with saving Kenya's wildlife, but his methods were hugely controversial: he declared war on poachers by forming elite and well-armed anti-poaching units with orders to shoot on sight.

Things are much quieter these days in the national parks, although poaching remains a problem.

Visiting National Parks & Reserves

Going on safari is an integral part of the Kenyan experience, and the wildlife and scenery can be extraordinary. Even in more popular parks such as Masai Mara National Reserve and Amboseli National Park, which can become massively overcrowded in high season (July to October and January to February, although KWS maintains high-season prices into March), this natural splendour is likely to be your most enduring memory.

Park & Reserve Entry

All KWS entry fees must now be paid by credit card or via the M-Pesa phone app. The rationale behind the move to prohibit the use of cash to pay park entry fees was to eliminate corruption by KWS staff.

Entry Fees

The KWS has a number of categories for parks and reserves. Rates for Kenyan citizens and residents are available from the KWS website.

Further costs in the land-based parks and reserves include KSh300 for vehicles with fewer than six seats and KSh1030 for larger vehicles.

It's important to remember that the entry fees for parks and reserves only entitle you to stay for a 24-hour period, and you pay an additional fee of the same amount for each day you are inside the park, even if you don't leave the park during that period. Not all parks allow you to leave the park and re-enter under the same ticket, so always check the situation and be sure of your plans before you pay for a multiday ticket.

Marine Parks

Kisite Marine National Park (Wasini Island)

Kiunga Marine National Reserve (Kiwayu Island)

Malindi Marine National Park (near Malindia)

Mombasa Marine National Park & Reserve (Bamburi Beach)

Watamu Marine National Park (Watamu)

NATIONAL PARKS & RESERVES FEES

KWS CATEGORY	PARK/RESERVE	NONRESIDENT ADULT/CHILD (US$)	CAMPING NON-RESIDENT ADULT/ CHILD (US$)
N/A	Masai Mara	80/45	20/15
Premium	Amboseli, Lake Nakuru	60/35	30/25
Wilderness	Meru, Tsavo East, Tsavo West	52/35	20/15
Aberdare National Park	Aberdare	52/26	20/15
Urban Safari	Nairobi National Park	43/22	20/15
Mountain Climbing (Day Trip)	Mt Kenya	52/26	20/15
Mountain Climbing (4-Day Package)	Mt Kenya	208/104	20/15
Scenic & Special Interest A	Hell's Gate, Mt Elgon, Ol Donyo Sabuk, Mt Longonot	26/17	20/15
Scenic & Special Interest B	Chyulu, Marsabit, Arabuko Sokoke, Kakamega, Shimba Hills, all other KWS parks	22/13	20/15
Marine Parks	Kisite, Malindi, Watamu, Mombasa, Kiunga	17/13	n/a

CATTLE-FREE NATIONAL PARKS?

Nothing seems to disappoint visitors to Kenya's national parks more than the sight of herders shepherding their livestock to water sources within park boundaries. In the words of former KWS head Dr Richard Leakey: 'People don't pay a lot of money to see cattle'. The issue is, however, a complicated one.

On the one hand, what you are seeing is far from a natural African environment. For thousands of years people, and their herds of cattle, lived happily (and sustainably) alongside the wildlife, and their actions helped to shape the landscapes of East Africa. But with the advent of conservation and national parks, many of Kenya's tribal peoples, particularly pastoralists such as the Maasai and Samburu, found themselves and their cattle excluded from their ancestral lands or waterholes of last resort, often with little or no compensation or alternative incomes provided (although, of course, some do now make a living through tourism and conservation).

Having been pushed onto marginal lands and with limited access to alternative water sources in times of drought, many have been forced to forgo their traditional livelihoods and have taken to leading sedentary lifestyles. Those that continue as herders have little choice but to overgraze their lands. Such policies of exclusion tend to reinforce the perception among local peoples that wildlife belongs to the government and brings few benefits to local communities. This position is passionately argued in the excellent (if slightly dated) book *No Man's Land: An Investigative Journey Through Kenya & Tanzania* (2003) by George Monbiot.

At the same time, tourism is a major (and much-needed) source of revenue for Kenya and most visitors to Kenya want to experience a natural wilderness – on the surface at least, the national parks and reserves appear to provide this Eden-esque slice of Africa. It also remains questionable whether allowing herders and their livestock to graze within park boundaries would alleviate the pressures on overexploited land and traditional cultures, or would instead simply lead to the degradation of Kenya's last remaining areas of relatively pristine wilderness.

Things get even more complicated when talking about private and community conservancies. Many Laikipia and Mara conservancies – Ol Pejeta Conservancy and Segera Ranch are two prominent examples – consider livestock to be an important part of habitat management, arguing that well-maintained livestock herds can help reduce tick infestations for wildlife. Carefully controlled grazing can also, they argue, actually assist in the regeneration of grassland ecosystems.

Private Conservancies

The widespread conversion of private cattle ranches or community lands into wildlife or community conservancies adds a whole new dimension to your safari experience in Kenya.

In the case of private conservancies, many are open only to those who pay to stay at one of the (usually exclusive) lodges or tented camps within the conservancy's boundaries. Such restrictions sometimes, but don't always, apply to the community conservancies. Most also charge a conservation fee – often around US$100 per person per day – whose proceeds go directly to wildlife conservation or community development projects.

One exception is Ol Pejeta Conservancy (p160), which is open to the public (adult/child US$85/42) – it's the closest conservancy experience to visiting a national park, but with fun activities thrown in.

In all cases, these conservancies are free to set their own rules, and these are invariably far less restrictive than those imposed by the KWS. The two most obvious examples are that both walking safaris (usually accompanied by an armed guide or ranger) and night game drives are permitted on the conservancies. Other activities – including, in some cases, horse riding – are also possible.

For an evocative and beautifully written picture of Kenya's physical, environmental and cultural make-up, track down Peter Matthiessen's classic, *The Tree Where Man was Born* (1972), an account of the author's epic journey through East Africa in the 1960s.

MAJOR CONSERVANCIES

CONSERVANCY OR RESERVE	HABITATS	WILDLIFE	ACTIVITIES	BEST TIME TO VISIT
Borana Conservancy	hills, light woodland, savannah	rhinos, African wild dogs, lions	walking, birdwatching	Jun–Feb
Il Ngwesi Group Ranch	light woodland, hills	rhinos	walking, cultural visits	Jun–Feb
Kalama Community Wildlife Conservancy	semi-arid savannah, woodland	Grevy's zebras, reticulated giraffes, elephants	walking, night drives	Jun–Feb
Kuku Group Ranch	light woodland, mountain foothills	big cats, plains wildlife	walking, night drives	Jun–Feb
Lekurruki Community Ranch	indigenous forest, open savannah	elephants, big cats	walking, birdwatching	Jun–Feb
Lewa Wildlife Conservancy	savannah, riverine woodland	black & white rhinos, lions, leopards, cheetahs, elephants, Grevy's zebras, Somali ostriches	walking, community visits, horse riding, quad biking, flying	Jun–Feb
Maji Moto Group Ranch	savannah	plains wildlife	Maasai cultural encounters	Jun–Feb
Mara North Conservancy	savannah	big cats, plains wildlife	walking, night drives, cultural encounters	Jun–Feb
Mbirikani Group Ranch	savannah, Chyulu Hills	elephants, big cats, giraffes	walking, running, horse riding	Jun–Feb
Naboisho Conservancy	savannah, acacia woodlands	big cats, elephants, plains wildlife	walking, cultural encounters	Jun–Feb
Ol Pejeta Conservancy	savannah, light woodland	Big Five, black rhinos	walking, night drives, lion-tracking, birdwatching	Jun–Feb
Olare-Orok Conservancy	savannah, acacia woodlands	big cats, plains wildlife	walking, cultural encounters, night drives	Jun–Feb
Olderikesi Conservancy	savannah, acacia woodlands	big cats	walking, night drives	Jun–Feb
Segera Ranch	savannah, river valleys	big cats, Grevy's zebras, elephants, Patas monkeys, elephants	walking, flying, night drives	Jun–Feb
Selenkay Conservancy	semi-arid savannah	lions, elephants, giraffes	walking, night drives, Maasai cultural encounters	Jun–Feb
Siana, Isaaten and Leleshwa-Olarro	forests, swamps, grasslands	big cats, elephants	walking, cultural encounters	Jun–Feb
West Gate Community Conservancy	semi-arid acacia woodland, riverine woodland	Grevy's zebras, big cats, African wild dogs	walking, night drives, Samburu cultural encounters	Jun–Feb

Survival Guide

DIRECTORY A–Z ... 368

Accommodation........ 368
Bargaining............. 370
Customs Regulations ... 370
Dangers & Annoyances.. 370
Discount Cards........ 373
Electricity 373
Embassies &
Consulates 373
Etiquette 373
Food 374
Holidays.............. 374
Insurance............. 374
Internet Access........ 375
Language Courses 375
Legal Matters 376
Maps................. 376
Media 376
Money............... 376
Opening Hours 377
Photography 377
Post................. 378
Smoking.............. 378
Taxes & Refunds....... 378
Telephone 378
Time 378
Toilets............... 378
Tourist
Information 378
Travellers with
Disabilities............ 378

Visas................. 379
Volunteering 380
Women Travellers....... 381
Work 381

TRANSPORT 382

GETTING THERE
& AWAY 382
Entering the Country.... 382
Air 382
Land 383
Sea & Lake 384
GETTING AROUND 385
Air 385
Bicycle 385
Boat 386
Bus 386
Car & Motorcycle....... 386
Hitchhiking 390
Local Transport........ 390

HEALTH 392

Health Insurance 392
Medical Checklist....... 392
Availability &
Cost of Health Care..... 393
Infectious Diseases 393
Traveller's Diarrhoea 396
Environmental Hazards .. 396

LANGUAGE 397

Directory A–Z

Accommodation

Kenya has numerous accommodation options to suit all budgets. Budget travellers have plenty of choice in towns, far less in national parks.

Hotels The main accommodation in towns, from budget places up to five-star business hotels (larger cities only).

Safari lodges & tented camps From midrange to high levels of luxury in national parks, conservancies and other remote areas.

Camping Often the only budget accommodation in national parks and reserves.

Bandas Traditional-style huts and cottages, usually self-catering and sometimes found in national parks.

Beach resorts Large complexes along the coast with plenty of facilities but often little personality.

Seasons

➜ High-season prices usually run from July (sometimes June) to October, from January until February, and include Easter and Christmas, although there may be slight variations in some regions. Sometimes high season is also referred to as peak season. Low season usually covers the rest of the year, although many lodges and top-end hotels also have intermediate shoulder seasons.

➜ On the coast, peak times tend to be July, August and December to March, and a range of lower rates can apply for the rest of the year.

➜ During the low season many companies offer excellent deals on accommodation on the coast and in the main wildlife parks, often working with airlines to create packages aimed at the local and expat market.

Prices

All-inclusive & full board It's worth remembering that many places, particularly places in national parks or other remote areas, offer full-board-only rates – prices may, therefore, seem higher than you'd expect, but less so once you factor in three meals a day. Some also offer what are called all-inclusive or 'package rates' that include full board accommodation but also things such as game drives, transfers and other extras.

Dual pricing Kenya also operates on a dual pricing system, particularly in midrange and top-end places – nonresidents pay significantly more (often double or triple the price) than Kenyan (or other East African) residents. When things are quiet, you may be able to get the residents' rate if you ask, but don't count on it.

Currencies Hotels and other places to stay in Kenya quote their prices in a variety of currencies, usually US dollars or Kenyan shillings (KSh). In almost all cases you can pay in dollars, shillings, euros and (sometimes) other foreign currencies.

Accommodation Types

BANDAS

Bandas are Kenyan-style huts and cottages, usually with some kind of kitchen and bathroom, which offer

---

USEFUL ACCOMMODATION RESOURCES

Ecotourism Kenya (www.ecotourismkenya.org) Certification of many hotels based on their environmental and sustainability practices.

Uniglobe Let's Go Travel (www.uniglobeletsgotravel.com) Information on almost all the major hotels and lodges in Kenya, giving price ranges and descriptions.

Expert Africa (www.expertafrica.com) Detailed firsthand reviews of (mostly safari) accommodation by Expert Africa staff as well as traveller feedback.

excellent value. Although there are numerous private examples, there are also Kenya Wildlife Service (KWS) *bandas* at some national parks – some are wooden huts, some are thatched stone huts and some are small brick bungalows with solar-powered lights.

Facilities range from basic dorms and squat toilets to kitchens and hot water provided by wood-burning stoves. In such places, you'll need to bring all your own food, drinking water, bedding and firewood.

Although originally aimed at budget travellers, an increasing variety of places are calling *bandas* huts, which are decidedly midrange in price and quality.

BEACH RESORTS

Much of the coast, from Diani Beach to Malindi, is taken up by huge luxury beach resorts. Most offer a fairly similar experience, with swimming pools, water sports, bars, restaurants, mobs of souvenir vendors on the beach and 'tribal' dance shows in the evening. They aren't all bad, especially if you want good children's facilities, and a handful of them have been very sensitively designed. Note that many of these places will close in early summer, generally from May to mid-June or July.

CAMPING

There are many opportunities for camping in Kenya, and although gear can be hired in Nairobi and around Mt Kenya, it's worth considering bringing a tent with you.

Public campsites There are KWS campsites in just about every national park or reserve. These are usually very basic, with a toilet block with a couple of pit toilets, a water tap, perhaps public showers and very little else. They cost US$30/25 per adult/child in Amboseli and

Lake Nakuru national parks, begin at US$20 per person in Masai Mara National Reserve and US$20/15 in all other parks.

Special campsites As well as these permanent campsites, KWS also runs so-called 'special' campsites in most national parks. These sites move every year and have even fewer facilities than the standard camps, but cost more because of their wilder locations and set-up costs. They cost US$50/25 per adult/child in Amboseli and Lake Nakuru, US$35/20 elsewhere; a reservation fee of KSh7500 per week is payable on top of the relevant camping fee.

Private campsites Private sites are rare, but they offer more facilities and may hire out tents if you don't have your own. It's sometimes possible to camp in the grounds of some hotels in rural towns, and Nairobi has some good private campsites. Camping in the bush is possible but unless you're doing it with an organised trip or a guide, security is a major concern – don't even think about it on the coast.

HOSTELS

The only youth hostel affiliated with Hostelling International (HI) is in Nairobi. It has good basic facilities and is a pleasant enough place to stay, but there are plenty of other cheaper choices that are just as good. Other

places that call themselves 'youth hostels' are not members of HI, and standards are variable.

HOTELS & GUESTHOUSES

Real bottom-end hotels (often known as 'board and lodgings' to distinguish them from *hotelis*, which are often only restaurants) are widely used as brothels, and tend to be very rundown. Security at these places is virtually non-existent, though the better ones are set around courtyards, and are clean if not exactly comfortable.

Proper hotels and guesthouses come in many different shapes and sizes. As well as the top-end Western companies, there are a number of small Kenyan chains offering reliable standards across a handful of properties in particular towns or regions, and also plenty of private, family-run establishments.

Self-catering options are common on the coast, where they're often the only midpriced alternative to the top-end resorts, but not so much in other parts of the country. A few fancier places offer modern kitchens, but more often than not the so-called kitchenettes will be a side room with a small fridge and portable gas stove.

Terms you will come across in Kenya include 'self-contained', which just means a room with its own private bathroom, and 'all-inclusive', which generally means all meals, certain drinks and possibly some activities should be included. 'Full board' accommodation includes three meals a day, while 'half board' generally means breakfast and dinner are included.

RENTAL HOUSES

Renting a private house is a popular option on the coast, particularly for groups on longer stays, and many expats let out their holiday homes when they're not using them.

Properties range from restored Swahili houses on the northern islands to luxurious colonial mansions inland, and while they're seldom cheap, the experience will often be something pretty special.

Papers and noticeboards in Nairobi and along the coast are good places to find out about rentals, as is old-fashioned word of mouth. You could also try www. airbnb.com.au/s/Kenya.

SAFARI LODGES

Hidden away inside or on the edges of national parks and wildlife conservancies are some fantastic safari lodges. These are usually visited as part of organised safaris, and you'll pay much more if you just turn up and ask for a room.

Some of the older places trade heavily on their more glorious past, but the best places feature five-star rooms, soaring *makuti*-roofed bars (with a thatched roof of palm leaves) and restaurants overlooking waterholes full of wildlife. Staying in at least one good safari lodge while you're in Kenya is recommended.

Rates tend to fall significantly in the low season.

TENTED CAMPS

As well as lodges, many parks and conservancies contain some fantastic luxury tented camps. These places tend to occupy wonderfully remote settings, usually by rivers or other natural locations, and feature large, comfortable, semi-permanent safari tents with beds, furniture, bathrooms (usually with hot running water) and often some kind of external roof thatch to keep the rain out;

you sleep surrounded by the sounds of the African bush.

Most of the camps are very upmarket and the tents are pretty much hotel rooms under canvas. The really exclusive properties occupy locations so isolated that guests fly in and out on charter planes.

Bargaining

As a general rule, bargaining is expected in markets and street stalls, especially those that sell handicrafts aimed at tourists. It is sometimes possible to negotiate a discount for taxis (especially if chartered for a set period) and accommodation (depending on the season), but this varies from one place to the next. Most other prices are usually fixed.

Customs Regulations

There are strict laws about taking wildlife products out of Kenya. The export of products made from elephant, rhino and sea turtle are prohibited. The collection of coral is also not allowed. Ostrich eggs will be confiscated unless you can prove you bought them from a certified ostrich farm. Always check to see what permits are required, especially for the export of any plants, insects and shells.

Allowable quantities you can bring into Kenya are:

Alcohol 1L

Cigarettes 200

Cigars 50

Perfume 250mL

Pipe tobacco 250g

Dangers & Annoyances

While Kenya can be quite a safe destination, there are still plenty of pitfalls for the

---

PRACTICALITIES

Newspapers & magazines The *Daily Nation* (www. nation.co.ke), the *Standard* (www.standardmedia.co.ke), the *Star* (www.the-star.co.ke), the *East African* (www. theeastafrican.co.ke) and the *New African* (newafrican-magazine.com).

TV KBC and NTV, formerly KTN, are the main national TV stations. CNN, Sky and BBC networks are also widely available on satellite or cable (DSTV).

Radio KBC Radio broadcasts across the country on various FM frequencies. BBC World Service is easily accessible.

Smoking Banned in restaurants, bars and enclosed public areas, with expensive fines for breaches.

Weights & measures The metric system is used.

unwary or inexperienced traveller, from everyday irritations to more serious threats.

➡ Always take a taxi from door to door after dark in cities, especially Nairobi.

➡ Avoid deserted beach areas at night.

➡ Keep all of your valuables locked safely away, especially when out and about in Nairobi, or when spending a day at the beach.

➡ Never travel major inter-city roads at night due to the heightened risk of road accidents.

➡ Keep a close eye on travel advisories issued by foreign governments.

Is It Safe?

As of late 2017, most Western governments were advising against all but essential travel within 60km of the Kenya–Somali border as well as the entire coast from Malindi to the Somali border (except Lamu and Manda islands). The rest of the country was largely considered to be safe for travellers, but check the most recent reports to be sure.

Such advisories can be important when it comes to travel insurance – check with your insurance company about your specific itinerary before finalising tickets, hotels etc.

It is also worth checking the prevailing situation in Laikipia, after violence affected a handful of ranches and lodges in 2017.

Hotel Security

Although hotels give you room keys, it is recommended that you carry a padlock for your backpack or suitcase as an extra deterrent. Furthermore, don't invite trouble by leaving valuables, cash or important documents lying around your room or in an unlocked bag.

> ## STREET KIDS
>
> Nairobi in particular has huge problems with street children, many of whom are AIDS orphans, who trail foreigners around asking for food or change. It's up to you whether you give, but it's debatable how much your donations will help as the older boys operate like a minimafia, extorting money from the younger kids. If you want to help out, money might be better donated to a charity, such as the Consortium for Street Children (www.streetchildren.org), which works to improve conditions for these children.

Upmarket hotels will have safes (either in the room or at reception) where you can keep your money and passport (and sometimes even your laptop), so it's advised that you take advantage of them. It's usually best not to carry any valuables on the street, but when your budget accommodation is a bit rough around the edges you'll find yourself faced with a difficult choice and may want to consider hiding your valuables on your person and carrying them with you at all times. Of course, use discretion, as muggings do happen in large towns and cities. Sadly, theft is perhaps the number-one complaint of travellers in Kenya, so it can't hurt to take a few extra precautions.

Banditry

Northeast The ongoing conflict in Somalia has had an effect on the stability and safety of northern and northeastern Kenya – the latter is considered extremely dangerous and has been for years thanks to bandits and poachers. AK-47s have been flowing into the country for many years, and the newspapers are filled with stories of hold-ups, shoot-outs, cattle rustling and general lawlessness. Visitors to Lamu should fly if possible.

Northwest In the northwest, the main problem is armed tribal wars and cattle rustling across the South Sudanese

border. There are Kenyan *shiftas* (bandits) too, of course, but cross-border problems seem to account for most of the trouble in the north of the country.

Risk Despite all the headlines, tourists are rarely targeted, as most of the violence and robberies take place far from the main tourist routes. Security has also improved considerably in previously high-risk areas, such as the Isiolo–Marsabit and Marsabit–Moyale routes. However, you should check the situation locally before taking these roads, and should avoid Garissa County altogether.

South Sudan & Ethiopia borders The areas along the South Sudanese and Ethiopian borders are sometimes considered risky – check the situation carefully if you're planning to travel overland between either country and Kenya.

Crime

Even the staunchest Kenyan patriot will readily admit that one of the country's biggest problems is crime. It ranges from petty snatch theft and mugging to violent armed robbery, carjacking and, of course, white-collar crime and corruption. As a visitor you needn't feel paranoid, but you should always keep your wits about you, particularly at night.

Although crime is a fact of life in Kenya, it needn't spoil your trip. Above all, don't make the mistake of distrusting everyone you meet – the honest souls you encounter will far outnumber any crooks who cross your path.

Precautions Perhaps the best advice for when you're walking around cities and towns is not to carry anything valuable with you – that includes jewellery, watches, cameras, bumbags, daypacks and money. Most hotels provide a safe or secure place for valuables, although you should also be cautious of the security at some budget places.

Mugging While pickpocketing and bag snatching are the most common crimes, armed muggings do occur in Nairobi and on the coast. Always take taxis after dark.

Snatch & run Snatching crimes happen more in crowds. If you suddenly feel there are too many people around you, or think you are being followed, dive straight into a shop and ask for help.

Luggage This is an obvious signal to criminals that you've just arrived. When arriving anywhere by bus, it's sensible to take a 'ship-to-shore' approach, getting a taxi directly from the bus station to your hotel. You'll have plenty of time to explore once you've safely stowed your belongings. Also, don't read a guidebook or look at maps on the street – it attracts unwanted attention.

Reporting crime In the event of a crime, you should report it to the police, but this can be a real procedure. You'll need to get a police report if you intend to make an insurance claim. In the event of a snatch theft, think twice before yelling 'Thief!' It's not unknown for people to administer summary justice on the spot, often with fatal results for the criminal. In Nairobi, the **tourist helpline** (☏020-604767; ⏱24hr) is a free service for tourists in trouble. It is a good nationwide network and works closely with the police and local authorities.

Money

With street crime a way of life in Nairobi, you should be doubly careful with your money. Don't overlook the obvious and leave money lying around your hotel room in plain view. However well you get on with the staff, there will be some who are unlikely to resist a free month's wages if they've got a family to feed.

Hotel safes The safest policy is to leave most of it in the hotel (or room) safe and just carry enough cash for that day. If you don't actually need your credit card or cash with you, they'll almost always be safer locked away in your hotel safe.

Money belts If you do need to carry larger sums around, a money belt worn under your clothes is the safest option to guard against snatch thefts. However, be aware that muggers will usually be expecting this.

Other tricks More ingenious tricks include tucking money into a length of elasticised bandage on your arm or leg, or creating a hidden pocket inside your trousers with a small stash for emergencies.

Scams

Expensive stories At some point in Kenya you'll almost certainly come across people who play on the emotions and gullibility of foreigners. Nairobi is a particular hotspot, with 'friendly' approaches a daily, if not hourly, occurrence. People with tales about being refugees or having sick relatives can sound very convincing, but they all end up asking for cash. It's OK to talk to these people if they're not actively hassling you, but you should probably ignore any requests for money.

Over-friendly strangers Be sceptical of strangers who claim to recognise you in the street, especially if they're vague about exactly where they know you from – it's unlikely that any ordinary person is going to be *this* excited by seeing you twice. Anyone who makes a big show of inviting you into the hospitality of their home also probably has ulterior motives. The usual trick is to bestow some kind of gift upon the delighted traveller, who is then emotionally blackmailed into reciprocating.

Car scams Tourists with cars also face potential rip-offs. Don't trust people who gesticulate wildly to indicate that your front wheels are wobbling; if you stop, you'll probably be relieved of your valuables. Another trick is to splash oil on your wheels, then tell you the wheel bearings, differential or something else has failed, and direct you to a nearby garage where their friends will 'fix' the problem – for a substantial fee, of course.

GOVERNMENT TRAVEL ADVICE

The following government websites offer travel advisories and information for travellers:

Australian Department of Foreign Affairs & Trade (www.smartraveller.gov.au)

Canadian Department of Foreign Affairs & International Trade (www.voyage.gc.ca)

France Diplomatie (www.diplomatie.gouv.fr)

Italian Ministero degli Affari Esteri (www.viaggiaresicuri.mae.aci.it)

New Zealand Ministry of Foreign Affairs & Trade (www.safetravel.govt.nz)

UK Foreign & Commonwealth Office (www.gov.uk/foreign-travel-advice)

US Department of State (www.travel.state.gov)

Terrorism

Terrorism is, unfortunately, something you have to consider when visiting Kenya, although the vast majority of the country is safe to visit. Remember that reports of an attack in, for example, Mombasa is likely to have very little impact upon the safety of visiting the Masai Mara or even Tsavo East National Park.

The country has come under major terrorist attack on at least three occasions: in August 1998 the US embassy in Nairobi was bombed; in November 2002 the Paradise Hotel, north of Mombasa, was car-bombed at the same time as a rocket attack on an Israeli jet; and in September 2013 terrorists attacked the upscale Westgate Shopping Mall in Nairobi. Since then, security has been tightened considerably.

Road Accidents

Kenya has an extremely high rate of road accidents and perhaps the most widespread threat to your safety comes from travelling on the region's roads. Road conditions vary, but driving standards are often poor and high speeds are common. Tips for minimising the risk of becoming a road statistic:

➡ Avoid night travel.

➡ A full-sized bus is usually safer than a minibus.

➡ If travelling in a shared taxi or minibus, avoid taking the seat next to the driver.

Discount Cards

Residence permits Very favourable admission fees and accommodation rates around the country.

Seniors No concessions.

Student cards Concession rates at museums and some other attractions; the ISIC card should be widely recognised.

Electricity

Type G
230V/50Hz

Embassies & Consulates

Australian High Commission (Map p56; ☎020-4277100; www.kenya.embassy.gov.au; ICIPE House, Riverside Dr, Nairobi; ⏰9-11am Mon-Thu)

Canadian High Commission (☎020-3663000; www.canadainternational.gc.ca/kenya/Index.aspx?lang=eng; Limuru Rd, Gigiri, Nairobi; ⏰7.30am-4pm Mon-Thu, to 1pm Fri)

Ethiopian Embassy (Map p56; ☎0722207025, 020-2732050; State House Ave, Nairobi; ⏰9am-noon Mon-Fri)

French Embassy (☎07605555; www.ambafrance-ke.org; Peponi Gardens, Nairobi; ⏰8.30am-1pm & 2-5.30pm Mon-Thu, 8.30am-1pm Fri)

German Embassy (☎020-4262100; www.nairobi.diplo.de; 113 Riverside Dr, Nairobi; ⏰8am-12.30pm Mon-Fri)

Netherlands Embassy (Map p56; ☎020-4288000; www.netherlandsworldwide.nl/countries/kenya; Riverside Lane, Nairobi; ⏰9-10.45am Mon, 8.30-10.45am Tue-Thu)

South Sudan Embassy (Map p62; ☎0729790144; 2nd fl, Senteu Plaza, Galana Rd, Nairobi; ⏰9am-5pm Mon-Thu, to noon Fri)

Tanzanian Embassy (Map p66; ☎020-2311948; www.tanzaniahc.or.ke; Reinsurance Plaza, Aga Khan Walk, Nairobi; ⏰8.30am-2pm Mon-Fri)

Uganda High Commission (Consular Section) (Map p66; ☎020-4445420, 020-311814; www.nairobi.mofa.go.ug; 1st fl, Uganda House, Kenyatta Ave, Nairobi; ⏰9am-noon Mon-Fri) The consular section is in the city centre. There's also the High Commission office further out.

UK High Commission (Map p56; ☎020-2844000; www.gov.uk/world/organisations/british-high-commission-nairobi; Upper Hill Rd, Nairobi; ⏰7am-4pm Mon-Thu, to 1pm Fri)

US Embassy (☎020-3636000; https://ke.usembassy.gov; United Nations Ave, Nairobi; ⏰8am-4.30pm Mon-Fri)

Etiquette

➡ **Greetings** Greetings are important. Never launch into a conversation, even when just asking for directions, without first greeting the person with whom you're speaking. Learning a few words in Swahili helps.

➡ **Eating** If eating in someone's home, leave a small amount on your plate to show your hosts that you've been satisfied. Never, ever handle food with the left hand! If others are eating with their hand, do the same, even if cutlery is provided.

➡ **Interactions with children** Don't hand out sweets or pens to children on the streets, since it encourages begging.

➡ **Be patient** If you're in a frustrating situation, be patient, friendly and considerate. Never lose your temper as a confrontational attitude won't go down well.

➡ **Taking photos** Always ask before taking photos of people. Never photograph someone if they don't want you to. If you agree to send someone a photo, make sure you do so.

Food

See Kenyan Cuisine (p321) for details.

Holidays
Public Holidays

New Year's Day 1 January

Good Friday and Easter Monday March/April

Labour Day 1 May

Madaraka Day 1 June

Moi Day 10 October

Kenyatta Day 20 October

Independence Day 12 December

Christmas Day 25 December

Boxing Day 26 December

Islamic Holidays
Islamic festivals and holidays are particularly significant on the coast. Many eateries there close until after sundown during the Muslim fasting month of Ramadan. Islamic holidays vary in date according to the lunar calendar.

School Holidays
➡ Kenyan schools run on a three-term system much like the British education establishments on which they were originally modelled, although summer vacations tend to be shorter.

➡ Holidays usually fall in April (one month), August (one month) and December (five weeks).

➡ As few Kenyan families can afford to stay in tourist hotels, these holidays mostly have little impact on visitors, but more people will travel during these periods and popular public areas like the coastal beaches will be that bit more crowded.

Insurance

Two words: get some! A travel-insurance policy to cover theft, loss and medical problems is a

very sensible precaution. Worldwide travel insurance is available at www.lonelyplanet.com/travel-insurance. You can buy, extend and claim online anytime – even if you're already on the road.

➡ Some policies specifically exclude 'dangerous activities', which can even include motorcycling, scuba diving and trekking. If such activities are on your agenda, you'll need a fully comprehensive policy, which may be more expensive. Using a locally acquired motorcycle licence may not be valid under your policy.

➡ You may prefer a policy that pays doctors or hospitals directly rather than you having to pay on the spot and claim later. If you have to claim later, make sure you keep all documentation.

➡ Some policies ask you to call back (reverse charges) to a centre in your home country where an immediate assessment of your problem is made. Be aware that reverse-charge calls are only possible to certain countries from Kenya.

➡ Check that the policy covers ambulances or an emergency flight home.

Local Agencies
If you're travelling through Africa for some time or heading to more remote corners of the country, consider signing up with a local service. Check with your insurance company that

ISLAMIC HOLIDAYS

HOLIDAY	2018	2019	2020
Ramadan begins	16 May	6 May	24 Apr
Eid al-Fitr (end of Ramadan)	15 Jun	4 Jun	24 May
Eid al-Adha (Feast of Sacrifice)	21 Aug	11 Aug	31 Jul
New Year begins	11 Sep (1440)	31 Aug (1441)	20 Aug (1442)
Maulid (Prophet Mohammed's birthday)	20 Nov	9 Nov	29 Oct

you can contact the local service direct in the event of a serious emergency without having to confirm it with your company at home first.

AAR Health Services (☎0734225225; www.aar-healthcare.com/ke; 2nd fl, Williamson House, Fourth Ngong Ave, Nairobi) Comprehensive medical network that covers Kenya, Tanzania and Uganda and offers a road and local service as well as emergency air evacuation to any suitable medical facility in East Africa. In addition to Nairobi, there's also a Mombasa office (☎0731191067).

Flying Doctors Service (☎0206993000; www.amref.org) Part of the African Medical and Research Foundation (AMREF), with a 24-hour air-ambulance service out of Nairobi's Wilson Airport.

Internet Access

Wi-fi You'll find wi-fi in all but the very cheapest or most remote hotels, though speeds vary enormously. Many wildlife lodges have wi-fi access, but it tends to be highly unreliable. Budget and midrange lodges rarely have internet access at all.

Mobile networks Safaricom, Telkom and Airtel are your best bets for internet access on your phone. Data is cheap and speeds are generally decent, especially compared to other countries in East Africa.

Language Courses

Taking a Swahili-language course (or any course) entitles you to a 'Pupil's Pass', which is an immigration permit allowing continuous stays of up to 12 months.

You may have to battle with bureaucracy and the process may take months, but it can be worth it, especially as you will then have resident status in Kenya during your stay.

ACK Language & Orientation School (Map p56; ☎0718233085, 020-2721893; www.acklanguageschool.org; Bishops Rd, Upper Hill, Nairobi) The Anglican Church runs full-time Swahili courses of varying levels lasting 14 weeks and taking up to five hours a day. Private tuition is available on a flexible part-time schedule.

Language Center Ltd (Map p62; ☎020-3870610, 0721495774; www.language-cntr.com; Ndemi Close, Nairobi) A good Swahili centre offering a variety of study options ranging from private hourly lessons to daily group courses.

LGBT+ TRAVELLERS

Negativity towards homosexuality is widespread in Kenya and recent events ensure that it's a brave gay or lesbian Kenyan who comes out of the closet. Frequent denunciations by those in power have created a toxic atmosphere of homophobia, which sometimes spills over into violence and, more often, into government harassment. In July 2014, for example, 40 people were arrested for 'suspected homosexuality' in a Nairobi nightclub.

Underlying all of this is a penal code that states that homosexual (and attempted homosexual) behaviour is punishable by up to 14 years in prison. Attitudes may be slowly shifting, however – in 2015 Kenya's High Court ruled in favour of the National Gay and Lesbian Coalition of Kenya being able to register as an NGO, something that had previously been rejected multiple times due to homosexuality's illegality in Kenya. This has at least given gay people in Kenya a voice and is the first step on the long path towards legalisation. No law currently prohibits discrimination on the basis of sexual orientation.

The main challenge to the acceptance of gay and lesbian lifestyles in Kenya is religion. Nearly all churches and mosques maintain a vociferously anti-gay position, and this is amplified by the presence of homophobic American churches that actively campaign in Kenya against gay rights. In early 2014 star author Binyavanga Wainaina revealed publicly that he was gay to protest against a resurgence in anti-gay laws and public debate across Africa. A few others have followed suit, but visibility for gay people remains extremely low.

While there are very few prosecutions under the law, it is certainly better to be discreet as a gay foreigner in Kenya. Some local con artists do a good line in blackmail, picking up foreigners then threatening to expose them to the police.

Useful Resources

David Tours (www.davidtravel.com) Can arrange anything from balloon safaris to luxurious coastal hideaways, all with a gay focus.

Gay and Lesbian Coalition of Kenya (GALCK; www.galck.org) Local advocacy group that keeps a low profile but that it exists at all in the public domain represents a scrap of progress.

Global Gayz (www.globalgayz.com/africa/kenya) Links to Kenyan gay issues.

Legal Matters

All drugs except *miraa* (a leafy shoot chewed as a stimulant) are illegal in Kenya. Marijuana (commonly called *bhang*) is widely available but illegal; possession carries a penalty of up to 10 years in prison. Dealers are common on the beaches north and south of Mombasa and frequently set up travellers for sting operations for real or phoney cops to extort money.

African prisons are unbelievably harsh places – don't take the risk. Note that *miraa* is illegal in Tanzania, so if you do develop a taste for the stuff in Kenya, you should leave it behind when heading south.

Maps

Country Maps

➔ The *Tourist Map of Kenya* gives good detail, as does the *Kenya Route Map;* both cost around KSh250.

➔ Marco Polo's 1:1,000,000 *Shell Euro Karte Kenya,* Geocenter's *Kenya* (1:1,000,000) and IGN's *Carte Touristique: Kenya* (1:1,000,000) are useful overview maps that are widely available in Europe. The scale and clarity are very good, but the locations of some minor features are inaccurate.

➔ For those planning a longer trip in southern and East Africa, Michelin's 1:4,000,000 *Map 955 (Africa Central and South)* is very useful.

National Park Maps

Most maps to Kenya's national parks might look a bit flimsy on detail (you won't get much in the way of topographical detail), but they include the numbered junctions in the national parks.

Tourist maps Macmillan publishes a series of maps to the wildlife parks and these are not bad value at around KSh250 each (three are available in Europe: *Amboseli, Masai Mara* and *Tsavo East & West*). Tourist Maps also publishes a national park series for roughly the same price. The maps by the KWS are similar.

Survey of Kenya The most detailed and thorough maps are published by the Survey of Kenya, but the majority are out of date and many are also out of print. The better bookshops in Nairobi usually have copies of the most important maps, including *Amboseli National Park* (SK 87), *Masai Mara Game Reserve* (SK 86), *Meru National Park* (SK 65), *Tsavo East National Park* (SK 82) and *Tsavo West National Park* (SK 78).

Kenya Institute of Surveying & Mapping (☎020-8561484; off Thika Rd, Nairobi) It may be worth a visit to this office, but this can take all day and there's no guarantee it will have any more stock than the bookshops.

Media

Newspapers & magazines The Daily Nation (www.nation.co.ke), the Standard (www.standardmedia.co.ke), the Star (www.the-star.co.ke), the East African (www.theeastafrican.co.ke) and the New African (newafricanmagazine.com).

TV KBC and NTV, formerly KTN, are the main national TV stations. CNN, Sky and BBC networks are also widely available on satellite or cable (DSTV).

Radio KBC Radio broadcasts across the country on various FM frequencies. BBC World Service is easily accessible.

Money

All banks change US dollars, euros and UK pounds into Kenyan shillings. ATMs can be found in medium-sized towns, so bring cash and a debit or credit card.

ATMs

Virtually all banks in Kenya now have ATMs, most of which accept international credit and debit cards. Barclays Bank has easily the most reliable machines for international withdrawals, with ATMs in most larger Kenyan towns. Standard Chartered and Kenya Commercial Bank are also good options. Whichever bank you use, the international data link still goes down occasionally, so don't rely on being able to withdraw money whenever you need it, and always keep a reasonable amount of cash on hand.

Black Market

With deregulation, the black market has almost vanished, and the handful of money changers who still wander the streets offering 'good rates' are usually involved in scams. The exception is at land border crossings, where money changers are often the only option (or will try to convince you that they are). Most offer reasonable

---

US DOLLAR TRICKS

➔ When getting US currency to take to Kenya, make sure you get US$100 bills manufactured in 2006 or later. Most banks and just about all businesses simply won't accept those that were printed earlier.

➔ If changing money at a foreign exchange bureau or other moneychanger, watch out for differing small-bill (US$10) and large-bill (US$100) rates; the larger bills usually get the better exchange rates.

rates, although you should be careful not to get short-changed or scammed during any transaction.

Cash

The unit of currency is the Kenyan shilling (KSh), which is made up of 100 cents. Notes in circulation are KSh1000, 500, 200, 100, 50 and 20, and there are also coins of KSh40, 20, 10, five and one. Locally the shilling is commonly known as a 'bob', after the old English term for a one-shilling coin. The shilling has been relatively stable over the last few years, maintaining fairly constant rates against the US dollar, euro and UK pound.

Changing Money

While most major currencies can be exchanged in Nairobi and Mombasa, once away from these two centres you'll run into problems with currencies other than US dollars, UK pounds and euros.

Credit Cards

Credit cards are becoming increasingly popular. Visa and Mastercard are now widely accepted in midrange and top-end hotels, top-end restaurants and some shops.

Exchange Rates

Australia	A$1	KSh84
Canada	C$1	KSh86
Europe	€1	KSh125
Japan	¥100	KSh94
New Zealand	NZ$1	KSh76
UK	UK£1	KSh142
US	US$1	KSh105

For current exchange rates, see www.xe.com.

Moneychangers

The best places to change money are foreign exchange or 'forex' bureaus, which can be found everywhere

and usually don't charge commission. The rates for the main bureaus in Nairobi are published in the *Daily Nation* newspaper.

International Transfers

M-Pesa Kenyans swear by M-Pesa, a quick and easy way of transferring money via mobile networks.

Western Union (⌧Australia 1800-173833, New Zealand 0800-005253, UK 0808-2349168, USA 1800-3256000; www.westernunion.com) Western Union Postbank, a branch of the Kenyan Post Office, is the regional agent for Western Union, the global money-transfer company. Using its service is an easy way (if the phones are working) of receiving money in Kenya. Senders should contact Western Union to find the location of their nearest agency. Handily, the sender pays all the charges and there's a Postbank in most towns, often in the post office or close by.

Tipping

➡ **Hotel porters** Tips expected in upmarket hotels (from KSh200).

➡ **Restaurants** Service charge of 10% often added to the bill plus 16% VAT and 2% catering levy.

➡ **Taxi drivers** As fares are negotiated in advance, no need to tip unless they provide you with exceptional service.

➡ **Tour guides, safari drivers & cooks** Gratuity is expected at the end of your tour/trip. Count on around US$10 to US$15 per day per group.

Travellers Cheques

Travellers cheques are next to useless in Kenya – very few banks or foreign exchange bureaus accept them and those that do, do so reluctantly and charge high commissions.

Opening Hours

Opening hours can vary throughout the year, particularly in tourist areas, less so in larger cities. We've provided high-season opening hours; hours will generally decrease in the shoulder and low seasons.

Banks 9am–3pm or 4pm Monday to Friday, 9am–noon Saturday

Post offices 8.30am–5pm Monday to Friday, 9am–noon Saturday

Restaurants 11.30am–2pm or 3pm and 5pm or 6pm–9pm; some remain open between lunch and dinner

Shops 9am–5pm Monday to Friday, 9am–noon Saturday; some stay open later and open on Sundays

Supermarkets 8.30am–8.30pm Monday to Saturday, 10am–8pm Saturday

Photography

➡ Photographing people remains a sensitive issue in Kenya – it is advisable to ask permission first. Some ethnic groups, including the Maasai, may request money for you to take their photo.

➡ You should never get your camera out at border crossings or near government or army buildings – even bridges can sometimes be classed as sensitive areas.

Taking Pictures

Light As the natural light in Kenya can be extremely strong, morning and evening are the best times to take photos.

Filters A plain UV filter can also be a good idea to take the harshness out of daylight pictures.

Lenses and tripods SLR cameras and zoom lenses are best for serious wildlife photography. When using long lenses you'll find that a tripod can be close to essential.

Vibrations If in a safari minibus or other vehicle, ask your driver to switch off the engine to avoid vibrations affecting your photo.

Post

Service The Kenyan postal system is run by Posta (www.posta.co.ke). Letters sent from Kenya rarely go astray but can take up to two weeks to reach Australia or the USA.

Parcels If sent by surface mail, parcels take three to six months to reach Europe, while airmail parcels take around a week.

Courier Most things arrive eventually, although there is still a problem with theft within the system. Curios, clothes and textiles will be OK, but if your parcel contains anything of obvious value, send it by courier. Posta has its own courier service, EMS, which is considerably cheaper than the big international courier companies. The best place to send parcels from is the main post office in Nairobi.

Smoking

Banned in restaurants, bars and enclosed public areas, with expensive fines for breaches.

Taxes & Refunds

Quoted prices and tariffs usually include all local taxes, but always ask if you're unsure.

There is no system of sales-tax refunds for tourists who purchase items in Kenya.

Telephone

Landlines continue to be used by most businesses in Kenya, but otherwise the mobile phone is king. Prices are low, data is fast and coverage is excellent in most towns and cities.

Mobile Phones

Buy a SIM card from one of the Kenyan mobile-phone companies: Safaricom (www.safaricom.co.ke), Airtel (www.africa.airtel.com/kenya) or Telkom (www.telkom.co.ke). SIM cards cost about KSh100 and you can then buy top-up scratch cards and use them either for data or calling credit.

Phone Codes

➡ Kenya's regions have area codes that must be dialled, followed by the local number.

➡ The international dialling code for Kenya is 254.

➡ When dialling Kenya from abroad, drop the first zero in the area code.

Time

Kenya is three hours ahead of Greenwich Mean Time (GMT) year-round.

Toilets

➡ Toilets vary from pits (quite literally) to full-flush, luxury conveniences that can spring up in the most unlikely places.

➡ Nearly all hotels sport flushable sit-down toilets, but seats in cheaper places may be a rare commodity – either they're a prized souvenir for trophy hunters or there's a vast stockpile of lost lids somewhere...

➡ Public toilets in towns are almost equally rare, but there are a few slightly less-than-emetic pay conveniences in Nairobi if you've only got a penny to spend.

➡ In upmarket bush camps you may be confronted with real toilets or a long drop covered with some sort of seating arrangement.

➡ Things are less pleasant when camping in the wildlife parks. Squatting on crumbling concrete is common.

➡ When trekking it's good practice to take soiled toilet paper out of the park with you (consider carrying sealable bags for this purpose).

Tourist Information

Considering the extent to which the country relies on tourism, it's incredible to think that there is still no tourist office in Nairobi. There are a tiny handful of information offices elsewhere in the country, ranging from helpful private concerns to underfunded government offices; most can at least provide basic maps of the town and brochures on local businesses and attractions, but precious little else.

Tourist Offices Abroad

The Ministry of Tourism (www.tourism.go.ke) maintains a number of overseas offices, including in the UK and some European countries, but they're pretty useless and most only provide information by telephone, post or email.

Travellers with Disabilities

Travelling in Kenya is not easy for people with a physical disability, but it's not impossible. Very few tourist companies and facilities are geared for travellers with disabilities, and those that are tend to be restricted to the expensive hotels and lodges. However, Kenyans are generally very accommodating and willing to offer whatever assistance they can. Visually or hearing-impaired travellers, though, will find it very hard to get by without an able-bodied companion.

In Nairobi, only the ex-London taxi cabs are spacious enough to accommodate a wheelchair, but some safari companies are accustomed to taking people with a disability out on safari.

Kenyan Services

Beach resorts Many of the top-end beach resorts on the coast have facilities for the disabled, whether it's a few token ramps or fully equipped rooms with handrails and bath tubs.

On safari Other places may have varying degrees of disabled access, but in Amboseli National Park, **Ol Tukai Lodge** (Map p186; ☑0726249697, Nairobi 020-4445514; www.oltukai lodge.com; s/d/tr full board Jul-Oct US$410/520/730, Nov-Mar US$350/450/630, Apr-Jun US$170/315/435; ☑@🖇🏊) has two accessible cottages, while in Lake Nakuru National Park, **Lake Nakuru Lodge** (Map p103; ☑0720404480, Nairobi 020-2687056; www.lakenakurulodge.com; s/d/tr full board Jul-Mar from US$300/400/500, Apr-Jun from US$200/300/380; ☑@🖇🏊) has a handful of accessible rooms.

Useful Resources

Download Lonely Planet's free Accessible Travel guide from http://lptravel.to/AccessibleTravel.

Association for the Physically Disabled of Kenya (APDK; ☑020-2324372; APDK House, Lagos Rd, Nairobi) Kenyan group that may be able to help visitors with a disability.

Society for Accessible Travel and Hospitality (☑212-447 7284; www.sath.org; USA) A good resource that gives advice on how to travel with a wheelchair, kidney disease, sight impairment or deafness. The website has a section called 'African Safaris' (type 'Kenya' into the search box).

Visas

Visas, needed by most foreign nationals, are straightforward. An e-visa scheme (www.evisa.go.ke) is the simplest way to apply, pay and receive a visa almost instantly.

Visa on arrival Tourist visas can still be obtained on arrival at all three international airports and at the country's land borders with Uganda and Tanzania. This applies to Europeans, Australians, New Zealanders, Americans and Canadians, although citizens from a few smaller Commonwealth countries are exempt. Visas cost US$50/€40/£30 and are valid for three months from the date of entry. Tourist visas can be extended for a further three-month period. Check before travelling whether the visa-on-arrival scheme has been replaced by the e-visa, which must be applied for in advance.

E-visa The Kenyan government's online visa portal (www.evisa.go.ke) issues single-entry tourist visas (US$51) valid for up to 90 days from the date of entry, as well as transit visas (US$21). Simply register, apply and pay online, and once it's approved (within two business days) you'll be sent a PDF visa document to print out, which you then present on entry to Kenya.

Single-entry visas Under the East African partnership system, visiting Tanzania or Uganda and returning to Kenya does not invalidate a single-entry Kenyan visa, so there's no need to get a multiple-entry visa unless you plan to go further afield. Always check the latest entry requirements with embassies before travel.

Prearranged visas It's also possible to get visas from Kenyan diplomatic missions overseas, but the only reasons to do so are if you come from a country not eligible for an on-arrival visa, you want to get a multiple-entry visa, or you need longer than three months in the country. If this is

---

EAST AFRICA TOURIST VISA

The East Africa Tourist Visa scheme issues tourists with a 90-day, multiple-entry visa that covers travel to Kenya, Uganda and Rwanda for a single fee of US$100. These visas are available upon arrival at Jomo Kenyatta International Airport in Nairobi, and at most land crossings.

Applications can also be made prior to travelling to the region, either at an embassy or consulate for one of the three countries in your home country or online. Although requirements vary from embassy to embassy, most applications require a single passport photo and a letter to the embassy outlining your travel plans. With the visa duly in your passport, your first port of call must be the country through which you applied for the visa, whereafter there are no restrictions on travelling in and out of the three countries. No visa extensions are possible.

Apart from convenience, the East African Tourist Visa could save you money, with individual visas for most (but not all) nationalities costing US$50 for Kenya, US$50 for Uganda and US$30 for Rwanda.

For more information and links to online application forms, see www.visiteastafrica.org.

VISAS FOR NEIGHBOURING COUNTRIES

COUNTRY	VISA AVAILABLE?	VISA FEE (US$)	PASSPORT PHOTOS	ISSUE TIME	NOTES
Ethiopia	Yes	50	1	same day	Must show that it was not possible to obtain your Ethiopian visa in your home country.
Somalia	No	-	-	-	-
South Sudan	Yes (3-month, single entry)	100	2	48hr	Collect form 8.30am-10pm; must have letter of invitation; must pay visa fee at bank.
Tanzania	Yes (3-month, single entry)	50 (US nationals 100)	1	same day	-
Uganda	Yes (3-month, single entry)	50	1	same day	-

the case for you, apply well in advance, especially if you're doing it by mail.

Visa Extensions

Visas can be renewed at immigration offices during normal office hours, and extensions are usually issued on a same-day basis. Staff at the immigration offices are generally friendly and helpful, but the process takes a while.

Requirements You'll need two passport photos for a three-month extension, and prices tend to vary widely depending on the office and the whims of the immigration officials. You also need to fill out a form registering as an alien if you're going to be staying more than 90 days.

Immigration offices Offices only open Monday to Friday; note that the smaller offices may sometimes refer travellers back to Nairobi or Mombasa for visa extensions.

Kisumu Immigration Office (Map p128; Nyanza Bldg, cnr Jomo Kenyatta Hwy & Awuor Otiende Rd, Kisumu; ⊙9am-3pm Mon-Fri)

Lamu Immigration Office (Map p258; ☑042-6330321; off Kenyatta Rd; ⊙9am-5pm Mon-Fri) Travellers are sometimes referred to Mombasa.

Malindi Immigration Office (Map p252; ☑042-2120149; Casuarina Rd)

Mombasa Immigration Office (☑041-311745; Uhuru ni Kari Bldg, Mama Ngina Dr; ⊙9am-5pm Mon-Fri)

Nairobi Immigration Office (Map p66; ☑020-222022; Nyayo House, cnr Kenyatta Ave & Uhuru Hwy; ⊙8am-4pm Mon-Fri) Visa extensions can be obtained at this office, around the side of Nairobi's once-feared main administrative building.

Visas for Onward Travel

Since Nairobi is a common gateway city to East Africa and the city centre is easy to get around, many travellers spend some time here picking up visas for other countries that they intend to visit. But be warned: although officially issuing visas again, the Ethiopian embassy in Nairobi was not issuing tourist visas for a number of years and the situation could change again. Call the embassy to check.

Most embassies will want you to pay visa fees in US dollars, and most open for visa applications from 9am to noon, with visa pick-ups around 3pm or 4pm. Again, contact the embassy in

question to check the times as these change regularly in Nairobi.

Volunteering

There are a large number of volunteers in Kenya, and volunteering can be a great way to reduce the ecological footprint of your trip. As a general rule, volunteering works best for both the traveller and the organisation in question if you treat it as a genuine commitment rather than simply a fun extension of your trip. It's also preferable if you have a particular skill to bring to the experience, especially one that cannot be satisfied by local people.

Keep in mind that there is no such thing as a perfect volunteer placement. Generally speaking, you'll get as much out of a programme as you're willing to put into it; the vast majority of volunteers in Kenya walk away all the better for the experience.

Note that for any volunteering work involving children, you'll require a criminal background check from your home country and/or previous countries of residence.

Kenyan Organisations

A Rocha Kenya (☎042-2332023, Nairobi 020-2335865; www.arocha.or.ke) Programmes (including Mida Ecocamp) near the Arabuko Sokoke Forest and Mida Creek. Also operates the Mwamba Field Study Centre at Watamu Beach.

Watamu Turtle Watch (Map p244;☎0713759627; www.watamuturtles.com; Turtle Bay Rd; suggested donation KSh300; ⊗2-4pm Mon, 9.30am-noon & 2-4pm Tue-Fri, 9.30am-noon Sat) 🌊 Helps protect the marine turtles that come to Watamu to lay eggs on the beach.

International Organisations

The following international organisations are good places to start gathering information on volunteering, although they won't necessarily always have projects on the go in Kenya.

Australian Volunteers International (www.australianvolunteers.com)

Coordinating Committee for International Voluntary Service (www.ccivs.org)

Earthwatch (www.earthwatch.org)

Idealist (www.idealist.org)

International Volunteer Programs Association (www.volunteerinternational.org)

Peace Corps (www.peacecorps.gov)

Step Together Volunteering (www.step-together.org.uk)

UN Volunteers (www.unv.org)

Voluntary Service Overseas (www.vso.org.uk)

Volunteer Abroad (www.goabroad.com/volunteer-abroad)

Volunteer Service Abroad (www.vsa.org.nz)

Worldwide Experience (www.worldwideexperience.com)

Women Travellers

In their day-to-day lives, Kenyans are generally respectful towards women, although solo women in bars will attract a lot of interest from would-be suitors.

Trouble spots In most areas of Kenya, and certainly on safari, women are unlikely to experience any difficulties. The only place you are likely to have problems is at the beach resorts on the coast, where women may be approached by male prostitutes as well as local aspiring Romeos. It's always best to cover your legs and shoulders when away from the beach so as not to offend local sensibilities.

Safety Women should avoid walking around at night. The ugly fact is that while men are likely just to be robbed without violence, rape is a real risk for women. Lone night walks along the beach or through quiet city streets are a bad idea and criminals usually work in gangs, so take a taxi, even if you're in a group.

Discrimination Regrettably, black women in the company of white men are often assumed to be prostitutes, and can face all kinds of discrimination from hotels and security guards as well as approaches from Kenyan hustlers offering to help rip off the white 'customer'. Again, the worst of this can be avoided by taking taxis between hotels and restaurants etc.

Work

Availability It's difficult, although by no means impossible, for foreigners to find jobs in Kenya. The most likely areas in which employment might be found are in the safari business, teaching, advertising and journalism. Except for teaching, it's unlikely you'll see jobs advertised, and the only way you'll find out about them is to spend a lot of time with resident expats. As in most countries, the rule is that if a local can be found to do the job, there's no need to hire a foreigner.

Disaster work The most fruitful area in which to look for work, assuming that you have the relevant skills, is the 'disaster industry'. Nairobi is awash with UN and other aid agencies servicing the famines in Somalia and South Sudan and the refugee camps along the Kenyan border with those countries. Keep in mind that the work is tough and often dangerous, and pay is usually very low.

Paperwork Work permits and resident visas are not easy to arrange. A prospective employer may be able to sort out the necessary paperwork for you, but otherwise you'll find yourself spending a lot of time and money at the **Nairobi immigration office** (Map p66; ☎020-222022; Nyayo House, cnr Kenyatta Ave & Uhuru Hwy; ⊗8am-4pm Mon-Fri).

Transport

GETTING THERE & AWAY

Nairobi is a major African hub with numerous African and international airlines connecting Kenya to the world. By African standards, flights between Kenya and the rest of Africa or further afield are common and relatively cheap, and flying is by far the most convenient way to get to Kenya.

Kenya is also a popular and relatively easy waystation for those travelling overland between southern Africa and Egypt. Finding your way here can be tricky – with several war zones in the vicinity – and such journeys should only be considered after serious planning and preparation. But they're certainly possible, and it's rarely Kenya that causes problems.

Flights, cars and tours can be booked online at lonely planet.com/bookings.

Entering the Country

Entering Kenya is generally pleasingly straightforward, particularly at the international airports, which are no different from most Western terminals.

Visas, needed by most foreign nationals, are straightforward. An e-visa scheme (www.evisa.go.ke) has now been rolled out and is the simplest way to apply, pay and receive a visa almost instantly. It is expected to replace the visa-on-arrival

scheme soon. Contact your nearest Kenyan diplomatic office to get the most up-to-date information.

Passport

There are no restrictions on which nationalities can enter Kenya, but you will need a passport with a validity of more than six months.

Air

Airports

Kenya has three international airports; check out the website www.kaa.go.ke for further information.

Jomo Kenyatta International Airport (NBO; Map p62; ✆020-6822111, 0722205061; www.kaa.go.ke) Most international Nairobi flights to and from use this airport, 15km southeast of the city. There are two international terminals and a smaller domestic terminal; you can easily walk between them.

Moi International Airport (MBA; ✆041-3433211) In Mombasa, 9km west of the city centre, Kenya's second-busiest international airport. Apart from flights to Zanzibar, mainly used by charter airlines and domestic flights.

Wilson Airport (WIL; Map p62; ✆0724255343, 0724256837; www.kaa.go.ke) Located 6km south of Nairobi's city centre on Langata Rd. Has some flights between Nairobi and Kilimanjaro International Airport or Mwanza in Tanzania, as well as scheduled and charter domestic flights.

Airlines

The main national airline carrier is **Kenya Airways** (✆Nairobi 020-3274747; www.kenya-airways.com). It has a generally good safety record.

Other international airlines flying to Nairobi include the following:

Air Mauritius (✆Nairobi 020-822805; www.airmauritius.com)

British Airways (Map 66; ✆Nairobi 020-3277400; www.britishairways.com; Mama Ngina St)

Daallo Airlines (✆Nairobi 020-317318; www.daallo.com)

Egypt Air (Map p66; ✆Nairobi 020-2226821; www.egyptair.com.eg; City Hall Way)

Emirates (Map p66; ✆Nairobi 020-7602519; www.emirates.com; Uhuru Hwy)

Ethiopian Airlines (Map p66; ✆Nairobi 020-2296000; www.ethiopianairlines.com; Standard St)

KLM (Map p66; ✆Nairobi 020-2958210; www.klm.com; Loita St)

Precision Air (✆Nairobi 020-3274282; www.precisionairtz.com)

Qatar Airways (Map p66; ✆Nairobi 020-2800000; www.qatarairways.com; Loita St)

Rwandair (✆Nairobi 020-343870; www.rwandair.com)

South African Airways (✆Nairobi 020-2247342; www.flysaa.com)

Swiss International Airlines (✆Nairobi 020-2666967; www.swiss.com; Limuru Rd)

Thomson Airways (www.thomson.co.uk)

Tickets

Seasons It's important to note that flight availability and prices are highly seasonal. Conveniently for Europeans, the cheapest fares usually coincide with the European summer holidays, from June to September.

Charter flights It's also worth checking out cheap charter flights to Mombasa from Europe, although these will probably be part of a package deal to a hotel resort on the coast. Prices are often absurdly cheap and there's no obligation to stay at the resort you're booked into.

Onward tickets If you enter Nairobi with no onward or return ticket you may incur the wrath of immigration, and be forced to buy one on the spot – an uncommon but expensive exercise.

Departure Tax

Departure tax is included in the price of a ticket.

Land

Ethiopia

Security With ongoing problems in South Sudan and Somalia, Ethiopia offers the only viable overland route into Kenya from the north. The security situation around the main entry point at Moyale is changeable – the border is usually open, but security problems often force its closure. Most foreign governments warn against travel to areas of Kenya bordering Ethiopia and, sometimes, along the highway between Isiolo and Moyale. Even so, cattle- and goat-rustling are rife, triggering frequent cross-border tribal wars, so check the security situation carefully before attempting this crossing.

Visas Theoretically Ethiopian visas can be issued at the Ethiopian embassy in Nairobi, but expect a number of hurdles, including having to provide a letter of introduction from your own embassy in Nairobi, which is likely to be hard to get. Persistence generally pays off, however, so if you have plenty of time, it should be possible to get an Ethiopian visa eventually.

CAR & MOTORCYCLE

Those coming to Kenya with their own vehicle could also enter at Fort Banya, on the northeastern tip of Lake Turkana, but it's a risky route with few fuel stops. There's no border post; you must already possess a Kenyan visa and get it stamped on arrival in Nairobi. Immigration are quite used to this, but not having an Ethiopian exit stamp can be a problem if you want to re-enter Ethiopia.

PUBLIC TRANSPORT

There were no cross-border bus services at the time of writing. If you don't have your own transport from Moyale, there's a daily bus between Moyale and Marsabit (KSh800), while lifts can be arranged with the trucks (KSh500).

From immigration on the Ethiopian side of town it's a 2km walk to the Ethiopian and Kenyan customs posts. A yellow-fever vaccination is required to cross either border at Moyale. Unless you fancy being vaccinated at the border, get your jabs in advance and keep the certificate with your passport. A cholera vaccination may also be required.

Somalia

There's no way you can pass overland between Kenya and war-ravaged Somalia at present, as the Kenyan government has closed the border to try to stop the flow of poachers, bandits and weapons into Kenya. Kidnappings, armed conflict and banditry are rife in the area close to the border. If you ignore the warnings and somehow survive, don't expect your travel insurance to help if you need assistance.

South Sudan

Kenya's border with South Sudan is one of East Africa's more remote border crossings – check with the South Sudanese **embassy** (Map p62; ☏0729790144; 2nd fl, Senteu Plaza, Galana Rd; ◷9am-5pm Mon-Thu, to noon Fri) in Nairobi to see whether it's open to foreign travellers. Most visitors travelling between the two countries fly from Nairobi to Juba, although with continued unrest and the growing threat of famine and war, very few are currently making the journey.

Tanzania

The main land borders between Kenya and Tanzania are at Namanga, Loitokitok, Taveta, Isebania and Lunga Lunga, and can be reached by public transport. There are no train services between the two countries.

There are also no border crossings open between the Serengeti and the Masai Mara – the closest crossings are at Sirari to the west and (much further away) Namanga to the east. Reports suggest that Kenya would like to open the crossing, but Tanzania remains resolutely opposed. With that being the case, it is highly unlikely that any of the direct Serengeti–Mara border crossings will open in the foreseeable future.

Although all of the routes may be done in stages using a combination of buses and local matatus (minibuses), there are six main routes to/from Tanzania:

➡ Mombasa–Tanga/Dar es Salaam

➡ Mombasa–Arusha/Moshi

➡ Nairobi–Arusha/Moshi (via Namanga)

➡ Nairobi–Moshi (via Loitokitok)

➡ Nairobi–Dar es Salaam

➡ Nairobi–Mwanza

NAMANGA

The busiest of the Kenya–Tanzania crossings, Namanga (open 24 hours) is for those travelling between Nairobi and Arusha (Tanzania). A recent upgrading of the infrastructure here means that all essential business – yellow-fever checks, immigration, vehicle paperwork and an exchange counter – can be transacted within one building at each of the crossings and with touts largely kept beyond the fence – a vast improvement on what went before.

Numerous bus companies offer cross-border services from Nairobi to Arusha, but the most convenient and comfortable option between Moshi or Arusha and Nairobi are the shuttle buses that depart daily. Numerous companies make the trip, among them **Riverside Shuttle** (Map p66; ☑0722328595; www. riverside-shuttle.com).

LOITOKITOK

The border crossing at Loitokitok (open 6am to 8pm) is generally hassle-free but there's no cross-border transport of any kind – you'll need your own wheels.

TAVETA

The Taveta crossing (open 6am to 8pm) connects Voi (and/or Mombasa) with Moshi (Tanzania).

Tahmeed (☑0729356561) has a daily bus from Moshi to Mombasa via Voi. Otherwise, you'll need to do the journey in stages. Matatus run from Voi to Taveta, then you'll then need to take a *boda-boda* (motorcycle taxi) for the 3km to the Tanzanian border post. From there, *dalla-dallas* go frequently between the border town of Holili and Moshi.

ISEBANIA

The Isebania–Sirari crossing is in Kenya's far southwest, and is convenient for travelling between western Kenya (including the Masai Mara or Lake Victoria) and the Serengeti or western Tanzania.

At the time of writing, there was no currency-exchange office on the Kenyan side of the border but, despite what the Kenyan touts will tell you, there is an exchange counter in the next room to the immigration desks on the Tanzanian side.

There are currently no direct buses over the border. Buses run from numerous points in western Kenya (including Kisii and Homa Bay) to Isebania. It is easy to walk between the two border posts.

LUNGA LUNGA

Lunga Lunga (open 6am to 8pm) is the closest border

crossing to the coast, and connects Mombasa with Tanga and/or Dar es Salaam.

Mash (www.masheastafrica. com), **Modern Coast** (www. modern.co.ke), **Tahmeed** (☑0729356561; and **TSS Express** (☑0704137202) have daily departures from Mombasa to Dar es Salaam via Tanga. There's nowhere official to change money at the border. Touts here charge extortionate rates, and it's difficult to get rid of Kenyan shillings once in Tanga, so plan accordingly.

Uganda

The main border posts between Kenya and Uganda are at Busia and Malaba; the latter is an alternative if you're travelling via Kisumu. There's plenty of cross-border transport, including long-haul bus services between Nairobi and Kampala. Trekkers in either the Ugandan or Kenyan national parks on Mt Elgon also have the option of walking over the border.

BUSIA

The main border crossing is at Busia on the direct route between Kampala and Nairobi via Kisumu. From Kisumu, there are three daily **Easy Coach** (Map p128; www. easycoach.co.ke; Jomo Kenyatta Hwy) departures for Kampala (KSh1500). Otherwise, take a matatu to Busia, then a minibus from Busia to Jinja (USh10,000, two hours). The border crossing is straightforward, although please be wary of moneychangers here: check every aspect of your transaction very carefully.

Many travellers avoid local transport altogether and opt for the direct buses running between Kampala and Nairobi, which range from luxurious to basic. You can also pick up these buses (or get dropped off on your way into Uganda) in Jinja. The full journey takes about 12 to 13 hours. From the Kenyan side, we recommend **Easy Coach** (Map p66; ☑0726354301, 0738200301; www.easycoach. co.ke; Haile Selassie Ave) and **Modern Coast**

Express (Oxygen; Map p66; ☑0737940000, 0705700888; www.modern.co.ke; cnr Cross Lane & Accra Rd). If travelling from Nairobi or Nakuru, prices include a meal at the halfway point. Various other companies have cheaper, basic services, which depart from the Accra Rd area in Nairobi.

MALABA

The second-busiest Kenya–Uganda border crossing is through Malaba, a bit north of Busia and just east of Tororo (Uganda). It will be most convenient for those travelling between Uganda and Eldoret. **Kampala Coach** has twice daily Eldoret–Kampala services. **Mash Bus** (☑0730889000; www. masheastafrica.com) is another possibility.

There are also regular matatus to Malaba from Cross Rd in Nairobi. The Ugandan and Kenyan border posts at Malaba are about 1km apart, so you can walk or take a *boda-boda*. Once you get across the border, there are frequent matatus until the late afternoon to Kampala, Jinja and Tororo.

SUAM

The Suam border crossing, beyond which lies the Kenyan city of Kitale, may be convenient if you're visiting Mt Elgon and not walking across, but this is a pretty rough route with infrequent public transport.

Sea & Lake

At the time of writing there were no international ferries operating on the coast or Lake Victoria, although there's been talk for years of a cross-lake ferry service between Kenya, Tanzania and Uganda.

Tanzania

It's theoretically possible to travel by dhow between Mombasa and the Tanzanian islands of Pemba and Zanzibar, but first of all you'll have to find a captain who's making the journey and then you'll have to bargain hard to

OVERLAND TOURS

Most people come to Kenya on safari but it's also possible to reach the country as part of an overland truck tour originating in Europe or other parts of Africa – many also start in Nairobi bound for other places in Africa. Most companies are based in the UK or South Africa.

Because most people prefer to travel north to south, overland truck companies sometimes drive empty trucks back from South Africa's Cape Town, Victoria Falls and Harare, and will sometimes transport travellers back up to Arusha (Tanzania) or Nairobi (Kenya) for negotiable knock-down prices. Ask around in backpacker hang-outs in the departure towns for tips on when these trucks may be leaving.

Acacia Expeditions (www.acacia-africa.com) Covers East and southern Africa with some small-group options.

Africa Travel Co (www.africatravelco.com) Focuses on East and southern Africa.

Dragoman (www.dragoman.co.uk) There are few places in Africa it doesn't go, with good links to trips across the continent.

Oasis Overland (www.oasisoverland.co.uk) A range of East and southern African overland trips, as well as some more conventional tours.

pay a reasonable amount for the trip. The best place to ask about sailings is at Shimoni. There's a tiny immigration post there, but there's no guarantee they'll stamp your passport so you might have to go back to Mombasa for an exit stamp.

GETTING AROUND

Air

Airlines in Kenya

Including the national carrier, Kenya Airways, a handful of domestic operators of varying sizes run scheduled flights within Kenya. Destinations served are predominantly around the coast and the popular national parks, where the highest density of tourist activity takes place. Most operate small planes and many of the 'airports', especially those in the parks, are dirt airstrips with very few if any facilities.

With all airlines, be sure to book well in advance (this is essential during the tourist high season). You should also remember to reconfirm your return flights 72 hours before departure, especially those that connect with an international flight. Otherwise, you may find that your seat has been reallocated. All of the following airlines fly to Nairobi.

Airkenya (☎Nairobi 020-3916000; www.airkenya.com; Wilson Airport, Nairobi) Amboseli, Diani Beach, Lamu, Lewa, Malindi, Masai Mara, Meru, Mombasa, Nakuru, Nanyuki and Samburu.

Fly540 (☎0710540540; www.fly540.com; Wilson Airport) Eldoret, Kisumu, Lamu, Lodwar, Malindi, Masai Mara and Mombasa.

Jambo Jet (☎Nairobi 020-3274545; www.jambojet.com) Subsidiary of Kenya Airways that flies to Diani Beach, Eldoret, Kisumu, Lamu, Malindi and Mombasa.

Kenya Airways (☎Nairobi 020-3274747; www.kenya-airways.com) Kisumu, Malindi and Mombasa.

Mombasa Air Safari (☎0734400400; www.mombasaairsafari.com) Amboseli, Diani Beach, Kisumu, Lamu, Malindi, Masai Mara, Meru, Mombasa, Samburu and Tsavo West.

Safarilink (☎Nairobi 020-6690000; www.flysafarilink.com) Amboseli, Diani Beach, Kiwayu, Lamu, Lewa Downs, Loisaba, Masai Mara, Naivasha, Nanyuki, Samburu, Shaba and Tsavo West.

CHARTER AIRLINES

Chartering a small plane saves you time and is the only realistic way to get to some parts of Kenya. However, it's an expensive affair and may only be worth considering if you can get a group together. There are dozens of charter companies operating out of Nairobi's **Wilson Airport** (p382).

Blue Bird Aviation (☎0732189000; www.bluebirdaviation.com)

Boskovic Air Charters (☎020-6006364; www.boskovicaircharters.com)

Bicycle

Loads of Kenyans get around by bicycle, and while it can be tough for those who are not used to the roads or climate, plenty of hardy visiting cyclists tour the country every year.

Safety Whatever you do, if you intend to cycle here, do as the locals do and get off the road whenever you hear a car coming. And no matter how experienced you are, it would be tantamount to suicide to attempt the road from Nairobi to Mombasa, or from Nairobi to Nakuru, on a bicycle.

Rural touring Cycling is easier in rural areas, and you'll usually receive a warm welcome in any villages you pass through. Many local people operate boda-bodas, so repair shops are quite common along the roadside. Be wary of cycling on dirt roads as punctures from thorn trees are a major problem.

Mountain biking The hills of Kenya are not particularly steep but can be long and hard. You can expect to cover around 80km per day in the hills of the Western Highlands, somewhat more where the country is flatter. Hell's Gate National Park, near Naivasha, is particularly popular for mountain biking, but you can also explore on two wheels around Mt Kenya, the Masai Mara and Ol Pejeta Conservancy.

Hire It's possible to hire road and mountain bikes in an increasing number of places, usually for KSh600 to KSh1000 per day. Few places require a deposit, unless their machines are particularly new or sophisticated.

Boat

The only ferry transport on Lake Victoria at the time of writing is across the Winam Gulf between Mbita Point (near Homa Bay) and Luanda Kotieno, where matatus go to Kisumu. You might also find motorised canoes to Mfangano Island from Mbita Point.

Dhow

Sailing on a traditional Swahili dhow along the East African coast is one of Kenya's most memorable experiences. And, unlike on Lake Victoria, a good number of traditional routes are very much still in use. Dhows are commonly used to get around the islands in the Lamu archipelago and the mangrove islands south of Mombasa.

Facilities For the most part, these trips operate more like dhow safaris than public transport. Although some trips are luxurious, the trips out of Lamu are more basic. When night comes you simply bed down wherever there is space. Seafood is freshly caught and cooked on board on charcoal burners, or else barbecued on the beach on surrounding islands.

Propulsion Most of the smaller boats rely on the wind to get around, so it's quite common to end up becalmed until the wind picks up again. The more commercial boats, however, have been fitted with outboard motors so that progress can be made even when there's no wind. Larger dhows are all motorised

and some of them don't even have sails.

Bus

Services Kenya has an extensive network of long- and short-haul bus routes, with particularly good coverage of the areas around Nairobi, the coast and the western regions. Services thin out the further from the capital you get, particularly in the north, and there are still plenty of places where you'll be reliant on matatus.

Operators Buses are operated by a variety of private companies that offer varying levels of comfort, convenience and roadworthiness. They're considerably cheaper than taking the train or flying and, as a rule, services are frequent, fast and can be quite comfortable.

Facilities In general, if you travel during daylight hours, buses are a fairly safe way to get around – you'll certainly be safer in a bus than in a matatu. The best coaches are saved for long-haul and international routes, and offer DVD movies, drinks, toilets and reclining airline-style seats; some of the newer ones even have wi-fi. On shorter local routes, however, you may find yourself on something resembling a battered school bus.

Seating tips Whatever kind of conveyance you find yourself in, don't sit at the back (you'll be thrown around like a rag doll on Kenyan roads) or right at the front (you'll be the first to die in a head-on collision, plus you'll be able to see the oncoming traffic, which is usually best left to the driver or those with nerves of steel).

Safety There are a few security considerations to think about when taking a bus in Kenya. Some routes, most notably the roads from Malindi to Lamu and Isiolo to Marsabit, have been prone to attacks by *shiftas* (bandits) in the past; check things out locally before you travel. Another possible risk is drugged food and drink: it is best to politely refuse any offers of drinks or snacks from strangers.

The main national bus operators in Kenya:

Busways (☏020-2227650) Western Kenya and the coast.

Coastline Safaris (Coast Bus; ☏0722206446; www.coastbus. com) Western and southern Kenya, Mombasa.

Dreamline Executive (☏0731777799) Nairobi, Mombasa and Malindi.

Easy Coach (Map p66; ☏0726354301, 0738200301; www.easycoach.co.ke; Haile Selassie Ave) Rift Valley and western Kenya.

Modern Coast Express (Oxygen; Map p66;☏0737940000, 0705700888; www.modern. co.ke; cnr Cross Lane & Accra Rd) Nairobi, Mombasa, Malindi and western Kenya.

Costs

Kenyan buses are pretty economical, with fares starting at around KSh150 for an hour-long journey between towns, while fares between Nairobi and Mombasa begin at KSh600 for the standard journey and can go as high as KSh2000 for premium services.

Reservations

Most bus companies have offices or ticket agents at important stops along their routes, where you can book a seat. For short trips between towns, reservations aren't generally necessary, but for popular longer routes, particularly Nairobi–Kisumu and Nairobi–Mombasa, buying your ticket at least a day in advance is highly recommended.

Car & Motorcycle

Many travellers bring their own vehicles into Kenya as part of overland trips and, expense notwithstanding, it's a great way to see the country at your own pace. Otherwise, there are numerous car-hire companies that can rent you anything from a small hatchback to a 4WD, although hire rates are very high.

MAJOR BUS ROUTES

FROM	TO	PRICE (US$)	DURATION (HR)	COMPANY
Mombasa	Tanga	10	4	Modern Coast Express
Mombasa	Dar es Salaam	15-20	5-8	Modern Coast Express
Nairobi	Moshi	40-45	7½	Riverside Shuttle
Nairobi	Arusha	35	5½	Riverside Shuttle
Nairobi	Kampala	30	10-12	Modern Coast Express
Nakuru	Kampala	25	11-12	Easy Coach

If you're a seasoned driver in African conditions, hiring a sturdy vehicle can also open up relatively inaccessible corners of the country. However, do be aware that Kenyan drivers are some of the most dangerous in the world, and be prepared to have to pull off the main Nairobi–Mombasa highway in order to avoid collisions with oncoming overtaking trucks in your lane. This is definitely not a place for inexperienced or nervous drivers.

If you don't fancy driving yourself, hiring a vehicle with a driver rarely costs a lot more, but then of course you have to pay for the driver's food and accommodation and that quickly adds up.

A useful organisation is the **Automobile Association of Kenya** (Map p62; www.aakenya.co.ke).

Bringing Your Own Vehicle

Paperwork Drivers of cars and riders of motorbikes will need the vehicle's registration papers, liability insurance and driving licence; although not necessary, an International Driving Permit (IDP) is also a good idea. You may also need a *Carnet de passage en douane,* which is effectively a passport for the vehicle and acts as a temporary waiver of import duty. The *carnet* may also need to specify any expensive spare parts that you're planning to carry with you, such as a gearbox. This is necessary when travelling in many countries in Africa, and is designed to prevent car-import rackets. Contact your local automobile association for details

about all documentation well in advance of your departure.

Shipping If you're planning to ship your vehicle to Kenya, be aware that port charges in the country are very high. For example, a Land Rover shipped from the Middle East to Mombasa is likely to cost more than US$1000 just to get off the ship and out of the port – this is almost as much as the cost of the shipping itself! Putting a vehicle onto a ship in the Mombasa port can cost another US$750 on top of this. There are numerous shipping agents in Nairobi and Mombasa willing to arrange everything for you, but check all the costs in advance.

Driving Licence

An IDP is not necessary in Kenya as most foreign licences are accepted, but it can be useful. If you have a British photo-card licence, be sure to bring the counterfoil, as the date you passed your driving test (something car-hire companies may want to know) isn't printed on the card itself.

Fuel & Spare Parts

Fuel prices Generally lower outside the capital, but can creep up to frighteningly high prices in remote areas and inside national parks, where petrol stations are scarce and you may end up buying dodgy supplies out of barrels from roadside vendors.

Availability Petrol, spare parts and repair shops are readily available at all border towns, though if you're coming from Ethiopia you should plan your supplies carefully, as stops are few and far between on the rough northern roads.

Parts Even if it's an older-model vehicle, local spare-parts suppliers in Kenya are very unlikely to have every little part you might need, so carry as many such parts as you can. Belt breakages are probably the most common disaster you can expect, so bring several spares.

Fire equipment Note that you can be fined by the police for not having a fire triangle and an extinguisher, although the latter is more often asked for in neighbouring Tanzania.

Car Hire

Hiring a vehicle to tour Kenya (or at least the national parks) is an expensive way of seeing the country, but it does give you freedom of movement and is sometimes the only way of getting to more remote parts of the country. However, unless you're sharing with a sufficient number of people, it's likely to cost more than you'd pay for an organised camping safari with all meals.

Four-wheel drive Unless you're just planning on travelling on the main routes between towns, you'll need a 4WD vehicle. Few of the car-hire companies will let you drive 2WD vehicles on dirt roads, including those in the national parks, and if you ignore this proscription and have an accident you'll be personally liable for any damage to the vehicle.

Driver requirements A minimum age of between 23 and 25 years usually applies for hirers. Some companies require you to have been driving for at least two years. An IDP is not required, but you will need to show your passport.

Vehicle condition It's generally true to say that the more you pay for a vehicle, the better its condition will be. The larger companies are usually in a better financial position to keep their fleet in good order. Always be sure to check the brakes, the tyres (including the spare), the windscreen wipers and the lights before you set off.

Breakdowns The other factor to consider is what the company will do for you (if anything) if you have a serious breakdown. The major hire companies *may* deliver a replacement vehicle and make arrangements for recovery of the other vehicle at their expense, but with most companies you'll have to get the vehicle fixed and back on the road yourself, and then try to claim a refund.

Crossing borders If you plan to take the car across international borders, check whether the company allows this – many don't, and those that do charge for the privilege.

COSTS

Starting rates for hire almost always sound very reasonable, but once you factor in mileage and the various types of insurance, you'll be lucky to pay less than US$50 per day for a saloon car, US$80 per day for a small 4WD or US$150 per day for a proper 4WD.

Kilometre limit Hiring a vehicle with unlimited kilometres is the best way to go.

Insurance costs Rates are usually quoted without insurance, with the option of paying a daily rate (usually around KSh1500 to KSh3000) for insurance against collision damage and theft. It would be financial suicide to hire a car in Kenya without both kinds of insurance. Otherwise you'll be responsible for the full value of the vehicle if it's damaged or stolen.

Excess Even if you have collision and theft insurance, you'll still be liable for an excess of anywhere between KSh5000 to KSh150,000 (depending on the company) if something happens to the vehicle; always check this before signing. You can usually reduce the excess to zero by paying another KSh1500 to KSh2500 per day for an excess loss waiver. Note that tyres, damaged windscreens and loss of the tool kit are always the hirer's responsibility.

Tax As a last sting in the tail (unless you've been quoted an all-inclusive rate), you'll be charged 16% value added tax (VAT) on top of the total cost of hiring the vehicle.

Petrol And a final warning: always return the vehicle with a full tank of petrol; if you don't, the company will charge you twice the going rate to fill up.

DRIVER RATES

While hiring a 'chauffeur' may sound like a luxury, it can actually be a very good idea in Kenya for both financial and safety reasons.

Costs Most companies will provide a driver for anywhere

ROAD DISTANCES (KM)

	Busia	Embu	Isiolo	Kakamega	Kericho	Kisumu	Kitale	Lodwar	Malindi	Meru	Mombasa	Nairobi	Nakuru	Namanga	Nanyuki
Embu	610														
Isiolo	569	184													
Kakamega	95	525	481												
Kericho	218	395	351	130											
Kisumu	138	475	431	50	80										
Kitale	154	511	467	109	230	158									
Lodwar	440	691	735	395	522	443	285								
Malindi	1087	657	877	999	869	949	985	1141							
Meru	565	154	56	477	347	427	463	729	864						
Mombasa	969	618	759	881	751	831	867	1120	118	746					
Nairobi	482	131	272	394	264	368	380	599	605	259	521				
Nakuru	325	288	244	237	107	211	223	442	762	240	644	157			
Namanga	661	314	524	596	469	548	563	779	430	468	409	180	337		
Nanyuki	487	131	84	399	269	349	385	651	795	78	677	190	175	380	
Nyeri	508	88	140	420	290	370	406	601	752	136	634	150	151	330	58
Voi	811	460	601	723	593	673	709	960	281	588	160	329	486	249	519	476

between US$5 and US$40 per day – the big advantage of this is that the car is covered by the company's insurance, so you don't have to pay any of the various waivers and won't be liable for any excess in the case of an accident (though tyres, windows etc remain your responsibility).

Advantages In addition, having someone in the car who speaks Swahili, knows the roads and is used to Kenyan driving conditions can be absolutely priceless, especially in remote areas. Most drivers will also look after the car at night so you don't have to worry about it, and they'll often go massively out of their way to help you fulfil your travel plans.

Disadvantages On the other hand, it will leave one less seat free in the car, reducing the number of people you can have sharing the cost in the first place.

HIRE AGENCIES

We recommend the following local and international hire companies. Be aware that some places offering car hire in Kenya online are scammers. Never wire money to anyone, and double-check the reputation of a company before entering into a contract.

Adventure Upgrade Safaris (Map p66; ✆020-228725, 0722529228; www.adventureupgradesafaris.co.ke; Tom Mboya St, Nairobi) An excellent local company with a good range of vehicles and drivers.

Avis (Map p62; ✆0703046500, 020-2966500; www.avis.co.ke; Xylon Complex, Mombasa Rd, Nairobi) Has outlets in Nairobi, at Jomo Kenyatta Airport, Mombasa and Mombasa airport.

Budget (Map p66; ✆020-652144; www.budget.co.ke; College House, University Way, Nairobi) Offers car hire at both the airport and downtown Nairobi. Also has an office at Mombasa airport.

Central Rent-a-Car (Map p66; ✆020-2222888; www.carhirekenya.com; Ground fl, 680 Hotel Building, Muindi Mbingu St, Nairobi) Long-standing car-hire agency with

4WDs, SUVs and normal cars at competitive rates.

Market Car Hire (Map p56; ✆020-225797, 0722515053; www.marketcarhire.com; 6th fl, Tower 2, The Mirage, Chiromo Rd, Nairobi) Local car-hire firm with a solid reputation that has been operating for 40 years.

Roadtrip Kenya (Map p62; ✆0791959998; www.roadtripkenya.com; Jungle Junction, Kongoni Rd, Langata) New arrivals in Nairobi, this long-standing Dutch-run agency has been working in Uganda and Tanzania for years and offers excellent value, local knowledge and support.

Insurance

Driving in Kenya without insurance would be an idiotic thing to do. If coming in your own vehicle, it's best to arrange cover before you leave. Liability insurance is not always available in advance for Kenya; you may be required to purchase some at certain borders if you enter overland, otherwise you will effectively be travelling uninsured.

Most car-hire agencies in Kenya offer some kind of insurance.

Parking

In small towns and villages parking is usually free, but there's a pay-parking system in Nairobi, Mombasa, Nakuru, Nyeri, Nanyuki and other main towns. Attendants issue one-day parking permits for around KSh100, valid anywhere in town. If you don't get a permit, you're liable to be

wheel-clamped, and getting your vehicle back will cost you a few thousand shillings. With that said, it's always worth staying in a hotel with secure parking if possible.

Road Conditions

Road conditions vary widely in Kenya, from flat, smooth highways to dirt tracks and steep, rocky pathways. Many roads are severely eroded at the edges, reducing the carriageway to a single lane, which is usually occupied by whichever vehicle is bigger in any given situation.

Trouble spots The roads in the north and east of the country are particularly poor, although the situation is improving. The main Mombasa–Nairobi–Malaba road (A104) is badly worn in places due to the constant flow of traffic, but has improved in recent years. The never-ending stream of trucks along this main route through the country will slow travel times considerably.

National parks Roads in national parks are all made of *murram* (dirt) and many have eroded into bone-shaking corrugations through overuse by safari vehicles. Keep your speed down, slowly increasing until you find a suitable speed (when the rattling stops), and be careful when driving after rain. Although some dirt roads can be negotiated in a 2WD vehicle, you're much safer in a 4WD.

Road Hazards

The slightest breakdown can leave you stranded for hours in the bush, so always carry drinking water, emergency

---

BRIBES

Although things have improved, police will still stop you and will most likely ask you for a small 'donation' or, as Kenyans say, the police will let you know that they are 'hungry'. To prevent being taken advantage of, always ask for an official receipt – this goes a long way in stopping corruption. Also, always ask for their police number and check it against their ID card as there are plenty of con artists running about. If you're ever asked to go to court, consider saying yes as you just might call their bluff and save yourself a bit of cash.

food and, if possible, spare fuel.

Vehicles The biggest hazard on Kenyan roads is simply the other vehicles on them, and driving defensively is essential. Ironically, the most dangerous roads in Kenya are probably the well-maintained ones, which allow drivers to go fast enough to do really serious damage in a crash.

Potholes On poor roads, potholes are a dual problem: driving into them can damage your vehicle or cause you to lose control, and sudden avoidance manoeuvres from other vehicles are a constant threat.

People & livestock On all roads, be very careful of pedestrians and cyclists. Animals are another major hazard in rural areas, be it monkeys, herds of goats and cattle, or lone chickens with a death wish.

Acacia thorns These are a common problem if you're driving in remote areas, as they'll pierce even the toughest tyres.

Bandits Certain routes have a reputation for banditry, particularly the Garsen–Garissa–Thika road, which is still essentially off limits to travellers. The road from Isiolo to Marsabit and Moyale has improved considerably security-wise in the last few years, while some coast roads between Lamu and Malindi remain subject to occasional insecurity. Seek local advice before driving any of these routes.

Road Rules

➡ You'll need your wits about you if you're going to tackle driving in Kenya. Driving practices here are some of the worst in the world and all are carried out at breakneck speed. Indicators, lights, horns and hand signals can mean anything from 'I'm about to overtake' to 'Hello *mzungu* (white person)!' or 'Let's play chicken with that elephant', and should never be taken at face value.

➡ Driving is on the left-hand side of the road, but Kenyans habitually drive on the wrong side of the road whenever they see a pothole, an animal or simply a break

in the traffic – flashing your lights at the vehicle hurtling towards you should be enough to persuade the driver to get back into their own lane.

➡ Never drive at night unless you absolutely have to, as few cars have adequate headlights and the roads are full of pedestrians and cyclists. Drunk driving is also very common.

➡ Note that foreign-registered vehicles with a seating capacity of more than six people are not allowed into Kenyan national parks and reserves; jeeps should be fine, but VW Kombis and other campervans may have problems.

Hitchhiking

Hitchhiking is never entirely safe in any country, and we don't recommend it. Travellers who hitch should understand they are taking a small but potentially serious risk. It's safer to travel in pairs and let someone know where you are planning to go. Also beware of drunken drivers. Although it's risky, many locals have no choice but to hitch, so people will know what you're doing if you try to flag down cars.

Signalling The traditional thumb signal will probably be understood, but locals use a palm-downwards wave to get cars to stop.

Contributions Many Kenyan drivers expect a contribution towards petrol or some kind of gift from foreign passengers, so make it clear from the outset if you are expecting a free ride.

National parks If you're hoping to hitch into the national parks, dream on! You'll get further asking around for travel companions in Nairobi or any of the gateway towns.

Local hitchers On the other side of the wheel, foreign drivers will be approached regularly by Kenyan hitchers demanding free rides – giving a lift to a carload of

Maasai is certainly a memorable cultural experience.

Local Transport

Boat

There are few public ferry services in Kenya. One in regular use is the Likoni ferry between the mainland and Mombasa island, which runs throughout the day and night and is free for foot passengers (vehicles pay a small toll).

On Lake Victoria, there's a ferry from Mbita to Luanda Kotieno (handy for onward travel to Kisumu). Boats also travel between Mbita and Mfangano Island, but it's a fairly unreliable service, safety is a concern and they only leave when *very* full.

Boda-Boda

Boda-bodas are common in areas where standard taxis are hard to find, and also operate in smaller towns and cities such as Nakuru or Kisumu. There's a particular proliferation on the coast, where the bicycle boys also double as touts, guides and drug dealers in tourist areas. A short ride should cost around KSh100 or so.

Bus

Nairobi is the only city with an effective municipal bus service, although few travellers use it and most locals take private matatus. Routes cover the suburbs and outlying areas during daylight hours. Metro Shuttle and private City Hopper services also run to areas such as Kenyatta Airport and Karen. Safety is rarely a serious concern.

Matatu

Local matatus are the main means of getting around for local people, and any reasonably sized city or town will have plenty of services covering every major road and suburb.

Fares These start at around KSh40 and may reach KSh100 for longer routes in Nairobi.

Vehicles The vehicles themselves can be anything from dilapidated Peugeot 504 pick-ups with a cab on the back to big 20-seater minibuses. The most common are white Nissan minibuses (many local people prefer the name 'Nissans' to matatus).

Shared Taxi

Shared Peugeot taxis are a good alternative to matatus. The vehicles are usually Peugeot 505 station wagons that take seven to nine passengers and leave when full.

Peugeots take less time to reach their destinations than matatus as they fill quicker and go from point to point without stopping, and so are slightly more expensive. Many companies have offices around the Accra, Cross and River Rds area in Nairobi, and serve destinations mostly in the north and west of the country.

Taxi

Even the smallest Kenyan towns generally have at least one banged-up old taxi for easy access to outlying areas or even more remote villages, and you'll find cabs on virtually every corner in the larger cities, especially in Nairobi and Mombasa, where taking a taxi at night is virtually mandatory.

Fares These are invariably negotiable and start around KSh350 to KSh600 for short journeys. Since few taxis in Kenya actually have functioning meters (or drivers who adhere to them), it's advisable that you agree on the fare prior to setting out. This will inevitably save you the time and trouble of arguing with your cabbie over the fare.

Bookings Most people pick up cabs from taxi ranks on the street, but some companies will take phone bookings and most hotels can order you a ride.

Tuk-Tuk

They're an incongruous sight outside southeast Asia, but several Kenyan towns and cities have these distinctive motorised minitaxis. The highest concentration is in Malindi, but they're also in Nairobi, Mombasa, Nakuru, Machakos and Diani Beach; Watamu has a handful of less sophisticated motorised rickshaws. Fares are negotiable, but should be at least KSh100 less than the equivalent taxi rate for a short journey (and you wouldn't want to take them on a long one!).

Matatu

Matatu, usually in the form of minivans, are the workhorses of Kenya's transport system. Apart from in the remote northern areas, where you'll rely on occasional buses or paid lifts on trucks, you can almost always find a matatu going to the next town or further afield, so long as it's not too late in the day. Simply ask around among the drivers at the local matatu stand or 'stage'. Matatus leave when full and the fares are fixed. It's unlikely you will be charged more than other passengers.

Safety Despite a periodic government drive to regulate the matatu industry, matatus remain notorious for dangerous driving, overcrowding and general shady business. A passenger backlash has seen a small but growing trend in more responsible matatu companies offering less crowding, safer driving and generally better security on intercity services. Mololine Prestige Shuttle is one of these plying the route from Nairobi to Kisumu or Nakuru.

Accidents As with buses, roads are usually busy enough for a slight shunt to be the most likely accident, though of course congestion never stops drivers jockeying for position like it's the Kenya Derby. Wherever you go, remember that most matatu crashes are head-on collisions – under no circumstances should you sit in the 'death seat' next to the matatu driver. Play it safe and sit in the middle seats away from the window.

Train

The Uganda Railway was once the main trade artery in East Africa and, after massive investment, will be again. Inaugurated in 2017, the new high-speed Nairobi–Mombasa rail service has cut travelling time from 18 hours (the old train service) to just 4½ hours. It's faster, cheaper and safer than taking the bus. The service stops in Mtito Andei and Voi.

The line – operated by Kenya Railways – will eventually extend to Naivasha as well (with a branch line to Kisumu), and then on to Kampala in Uganda, if all goes to plan.

CLASSES & COSTS

There are two classes on Kenyan trains – as all services are seat only, the difference between the two is all to do with comfort.

Services are likely to increase over the coming years, but for now there's one 9am departure daily in each direction. From Nairobi, services stop at Mtito Andei (one way 2nd/1st class KSh360/1490, 2¼ hours) and Voi (KSh510/2130, 3½ hours) en route to Mombasa (KSh900/3000, 4½ hours).

RESERVATIONS

There are booking offices at the train stations in Nairobi (Syokimau Railway Station) and Mombasa, and at present it's recommended that you show up in person; online and phone booking services have been promised, but were not yet operational at the time of writing.

Health

Africa certainly has an impressive selection of tropical and other diseases, but you're much more likely to get a bout of diarrhoea, a cold or an infected mosquito bite than anything exotic. If you stay up-to-date with your vaccinations and take some basic preventive measures, you'd be pretty unlucky to succumb to most of the other health hazards on offer. When it comes to injuries (as opposed to illness), the most likely reason for needing medical help in Kenya is as a result of road accidents.

BEFORE YOU GO

It's tempting to leave all the preparations to the last minute – don't! Many vaccines don't take effect until two weeks after you've been immunised, so visit a doctor four to eight weeks before departure. Ask your doctor for an International Certificate of Vaccination (known in some countries as the yellow booklet), which will list all the vaccinations you've received. This is mandatory for the African countries that require proof of yellow fever vaccination upon entry, which includes Kenya and its neighbours, but it's a good idea to carry it anyway wherever you travel.

Health Insurance

Fee payment Find out in advance whether your insurance plan will make payments directly to providers or will reimburse you later for overseas health expenditures (many doctors expect payment in cash).

Emergency transport It's vital to ensure that your travel insurance will cover the emergency transport required to get you to a hospital in a major city, to better medical facilities elsewhere in Africa, or all the way home, by air and with a medical attendant if necessary. Not all insurance covers this, so check the contract carefully.

Medical assistance If you need medical help, your insurance company might be able to locate the nearest hospital or clinic, or you can ask at your hotel. In an emergency, contact your embassy or consulate.

Air evacuation Membership of the African Medical & Research Foundation (AMREF; www.amref. org) provides an air-evacuation service in medical emergencies in Kenya, as well as air-ambulance transfers between medical facilities. Money paid by members for this service goes into providing grassroots medical assistance for local people.

Medical Checklist

It's a very good idea to carry a medical and first-aid kit with you, to help yourself in the case of minor illness or injury. If you're travelling through an area where malaria is a problem, particularly an area where falciparum malaria predominates, consider taking a self-diagnostic kit that can identify malaria in the blood from a finger prick.

Following is a list of other items you should consider bringing:

➡ Acetaminophen (paracetamol) or aspirin

➡ Acetazolamide (Diamox) for altitude sickness (prescription only)

➡ Adhesive or paper tape

➡ Antibacterial ointment (eg Bactroban) for cuts and abrasions (prescription only)

➡ Antibiotics (prescription only), eg ciprofloxacin (Ciproxin) or norfloxacin (Utinor)

RECOMMENDED VACCINATIONS

The World Health Organization (www.who.int/en) recommends that all travellers be covered for diphtheria, tetanus, measles, mumps, rubella and polio, as well as for hepatitis B, regardless of their destination.

According to the Centers for Disease Control & Prevention (www.cdc.gov), the following vaccinations are recommended for Kenya: hepatitis A, hepatitis B, meningococcal meningitis, rabies and typhoid, and boosters for tetanus, diphtheria, polio and measles. It is also necessary to be vaccinated against yellow fever.

- → Antidiarrhoeal drugs (eg loperamide)
- → Antihistamines (for hay fever and allergic reactions)
- → Anti-inflammatory drugs (eg ibuprofen)
- → Antimalaria pills
- → Bandages, gauze
- → DEET insect repellent
- → Iodine tablets (for water purification)
- → Oral rehydration salts
- → Permethrin-containing insect spray for clothing, tents and bed nets
- → Pocket knife
- → Scissors, safety pins, tweezers
- → Steroid cream or hydrocortisone cream (for allergic rashes)
- → Sunscreen
- → Syringes, sterile needles and fluids if travelling to remote areas
- → Thermometer

IN KENYA

Availability & Cost of Health Care

Standards of care Health care in Kenya is varied: it can be excellent in Nairobi, which generally has well-trained doctors and nurses, but is often patchy off the beaten track, even in Mombasa. Medicine and even sterile dressings and intravenous fluids might need to be purchased from a local pharmacy. The standard of dental care is equally variable, and there is an increased risk of hepatitis B and HIV transmission from poorly sterilised equipment.

Hospitals By and large, public hospitals in Kenya offer the cheapest service, but will have the least up-to-date equipment and medications; mission hospitals (where donations are the usual form of payment) often have more reasonable facilities; and private hospitals and clinics are more expensive but tend to have more advanced drugs and equipment and better-trained medical staff.

Drugs Most drugs can be purchased over the counter without a prescription. Many drugs for sale in Kenya might be ineffective; they might be counterfeit or might not have been stored in the right conditions. The most common examples of counterfeit drugs are malaria tablets and expensive antibiotics, such as ciprofloxacin. Most drugs are available in Nairobi, but remote villages will be lucky to have a couple of paracetamol tablets. It is strongly recommended that you bring all medication from home.

Contraception The availability and efficacy of contraception cannot be relied upon – bring all you'll need.

Blood transfusion There is a high risk of contracting HIV from infected blood if you receive a blood transfusion in Kenya. The Blood Care Foundation (www.bloodcare.org.uk) is a useful source of safe, screened blood, which can be transported to any part of the world within 24 hours.

Infectious Diseases

It's a formidable list but, as we say, a few precautions go a long way...

Bilharzia (Schistosomiasis)

This disease is spread by flukes (minute worms) that are carried by a species of freshwater snail. The parasites penetrate human skin as people paddle or swim and then migrate to the bladder or bowel. Paddling or swimming in suspect freshwater lakes or slow-running rivers should be avoided. There may be no symptoms. However, there may be a transient fever and rash, and advanced cases may have blood in the stool or in the urine. A blood test can detect antibodies if you might have been exposed, and treatment is then possible in specialist travel or infectious-disease clinics. If not treated, the infection can cause kidney failure or permanent bowel damage.

Cholera

Cholera is usually only a problem during natural or other disasters – eg floods, earthquakes or war – although small outbreaks can also occur at other times. Travellers are rarely affected, although there was an outbreak in a Nairobi conference hotel when we were in town. The disease is caused by a bacterium and spread via contaminated drinking water. The main symptom is profuse watery diarrhoea, which causes debilitation if fluids are not replaced quickly. Most cases of cholera can be avoided by drinking only clean water and by avoiding potentially contaminated food. Treatment is by fluid replacement (orally or via a drip), but sometimes antibiotics are needed. Self-treatment is not advised.

Dengue Fever (Break-Bone Fever)

Dengue fever, spread through the bite of mosquitoes, causes a feverish illness with headache and muscle pains similar to those experienced with a bad, prolonged attack of influenza. There might be a rash. Mosquito bites should be avoided whenever possible. This disease is present in Kenya. Self-treatment consists of paracetamol and rest.

Diphtheria

Found in all of Africa, diphtheria is spread through close respiratory contact. It usually causes a high temperature and a severe sore throat. A membrane can form across the throat, requiring a tracheotomy to prevent suffocation. Vaccination is recommended for those likely to be in close contact with the locals in infected areas. This is more important for long stays than for short-term trips. The vaccine is given as an injection alone or with tetanus, and lasts 10 years.

Hepatitis A

Hepatitis A is spread through contaminated food (particularly shellfish) and water. It causes jaundice and, although it is rarely fatal, it can cause prolonged lethargy. If you're recovering from hepatitis A, you shouldn't drink alcohol for up to six months afterwards, but once you've recovered, there won't be any long-term problems. The first symptoms include dark urine and a yellow colour to the whites of the eyes. Sometimes a fever and abdominal pain might be present. Hepatitis A vaccine (Avaxim, Vaqta, Havrix) is given as an injection: a single dose will give protection for up to a year, and a booster after a year gives 10-year protection. Hepatitis A and typhoid vaccines can also be given as a single-dose vaccine, with hepatyrix or viatim.

Hepatitis B

Hepatitis B is spread through infected blood, contaminated needles and sexual intercourse. It can also be spread from an infected mother to the baby during childbirth. Hepatitis B affects the liver, which causes jaundice and occasionally liver failure. Most people recover completely, but some people might be chronic carriers of the virus, which could lead eventually to cirrhosis or liver cancer. Those visiting high-risk areas for long periods or those with increased social or occupational risk should be immunised. A course will give protection for at least five years. It can be given over four weeks or six months.

HIV

Human immunodeficiency virus (HIV), the virus that causes acquired immune deficiency syndrome (AIDS), is an enormous problem in Kenya, where the infection rate is around 6.1% of the adult population. The virus is spread through infected blood and blood products, by sexual intercourse with an infected partner, and from an infected mother to her baby during childbirth or breastfeeding. It can be spread through 'blood to blood' contacts, such as with contaminated instruments during medical, dental, acupuncture and other body-piercing procedures, and through sharing intravenous

needles. If you think you might have been exposed to HIV, a blood test is necessary; a three-month gap after exposure and before testing is required to allow antibodies to appear in the blood.

Malaria

Malaria is a major health scourge in Kenya. Infection rates vary with the season (higher in the rainy season) and climate, so check out the situation before departure. The incidence of malarial transmission at altitudes higher than 2000m is rare.

Malaria is caused by a parasite in the bloodstream spread via the bite of the female anopheles mosquito. There are several types, falciparum malaria being the most dangerous and the predominant form in Kenya. Unlike most other diseases regularly encountered by travellers, there is no vaccination against malaria (yet). However, several different drugs are used to prevent malaria and new ones are in the pipeline. Up-to-date advice from a travel-health clinic is essential, as some medication is more suitable for some travellers than others. The pattern of drug-resistant malaria is changing rapidly, so what was advised several years ago might no longer be the case.

SYMPTOMS

Malaria can affect people in several ways. Anyone who develops a fever while in a malarial area should assume malarial infection until a blood test proves negative, even if you've been taking antimalarial medication. Treatment in hospital is essential, and if patients enter the late stage of the disease the death rate may still be as high as 10%, even in the best intensive-care facilities.

➡ The early stages include headaches, fevers, generalised aches and pains, and malaise, often mistaken for flu. Other symptoms can include abdominal pain, diarrhoea and a cough.

➡ If not treated, the next stage can develop within 24 hours, particularly if falciparum malaria is the parasite: jaundice, reduced consciousness and coma (known as cerebral malaria).

SIDE EFFECTS & RISKS

Many travellers are under the impression that malaria is a mild illness, that treatment is always easy and successful, and that taking antimalarial drugs causes more illness through side effects than actually getting malaria. Unfortunately, this is not true. Side effects of the medication depend on the drug being taken. These side effects are not universal, and can be minimised by taking medication correctly, such as with food.

➡ Doxycycline can cause heartburn, sunburn and indigestion.

➡ Mefloquine (Larium) can cause anxiety attacks, insomnia and nightmares, and (rarely) severe psychiatric disorders.

➡ Chloroquine can cause nausea and hair loss.

➡ Proguanil can cause mouth ulcers.
If you decide that you really do not wish to take antimalarial drugs, you must understand the risks, and be obsessive about avoiding mosquito bites. Use nets and insect repellent, and report any fever or flu-like symptoms to a doctor as soon as possible.

Some people advocate homeopathic preparations against malaria, such as Demal200, but as yet there is no conclusive evidence that this is effective, and many homeopaths do not recommend their use.

Some people should not take a particular antimalarial drug; eg people with epilepsy should avoid mefloquine, and doxycycline should not be taken by pregnant women or children younger than 12 years. Malaria in pregnancy frequently results in miscarriage or premature labour and the risks to both mother and foetus during pregnancy are

THE ANTIMALARIAL A TO D

A – Awareness of the risk. No medication is totally effective, but protection of up to 95% is achievable with most drugs, as long as other measures have been taken.

B – Bites: avoid at all costs. Sleep in a screened room, use a mosquito spray or coils; sleep under a permethrin-impregnated net at night. Cover up at night with long trousers and long sleeves, preferably with permethrin-treated clothing. Apply appropriate repellent to all areas of exposed skin in the evenings.

C – Chemical prevention (ie antimalarial drugs) is usually needed in malaria-infected areas. Expert advice is needed as the resistance patterns of the parasite can change, and new drugs are in development. Not all antimalarial drugs are suitable for everyone. Most antimalarial drugs need to be started at least a week in advance and continued for four weeks after the last possible exposure to malaria.

D – Diagnosis. If you have a fever or flu-like illness within a year of travel to a malaria-infected area, malaria is a possibility, and immediate medical attention is necessary.

considerable. Travel in Kenya when pregnant should be carefully considered.

STAND-BY TREATMENT
If you're going to be in remote areas or far from major towns, consider carrying with you a stand-by treatment. Emergency stand-by treatments should be seen as emergency treatment aimed at saving the patient's life and not as a routine way of self-medicating. It should be used only if you will be far from medical facilities and have been advised about the symptoms of malaria and how to use the medication. Medical advice should be sought as soon as possible to confirm whether the treatment has been successful.

The type of stand-by treatment used will depend on local conditions, such as drug resistance, and on what antimalarial drugs were being used before stand-by treatment. This is worthwhile because you want to avoid contracting a particularly serious form, such as cerebral malaria, which can be fatal within 24 hours. Self-diagnostic kits, which can identify malaria in the blood from a finger prick, are also available in the West.

Meningococcal Meningitis

Meningococcal infection is spread through close respiratory contact and is more likely to be contracted in crowded situations, such as dormitories, buses and clubs. Infection is uncommon in travellers. Vaccination is recommended for long stays and is especially important towards the end of the dry season. Symptoms include a fever, severe headache, neck stiffness and a red rash. Immediate medical treatment is necessary.

The ACWY vaccine is recommended for all travellers in sub-Saharan Africa. This vaccine is different from the meningococcal meningitis C vaccine given to children and adolescents in some countries; it is safe to be given both types of vaccine.

Rabies

Rabies is spread by the bites or licks of an infected animal on broken skin. It is always fatal once the clinical symptoms start (which might be up to several months after an infected bite), so post-bite vaccination should be taken as soon as possible. Post-bite vaccination (whether or not you've been vaccinated before the bite) prevents the virus from spreading to the central nervous system.

Animal handlers should be vaccinated, as should those travelling to remote areas where a reliable source of post-bite vaccine is not available within 24 hours. To prevent the disease, three injections are needed over a month. If you have not been vaccinated and receive a bite, you will need a course of five injections starting 24 hours or as soon as possible after the injury. If you have been vaccinated, you will need fewer post-bite injections, and have more time to seek medical help.

Rift Valley Fever

This fever is spread occasionally via mosquito bites and is rarely fatal. The symptoms are a fever and flu-like illness.

Typhoid

This illness is spread through handling food or drinking water that has been contaminated by infected human faeces. The first symptom of infection is usually a fever or a pink rash on the abdomen. Sometimes septicaemia (blood poisoning) can also occur. A typhoid vaccine (typhim Vi, typherix) will give protection for three years. In some countries, the oral vaccine Vivotif is also available. Antibiotics are usually given as treatment, and death is rare unless septicaemia occurs.

Yellow Fever

You should carry a certificate as evidence of vaccination against yellow fever if you've recently been in an infected country, to avoid immigration problems. For a full list of countries where yellow fever exists, visit the website of the World Health Organization (www.who.int) or the Centers for Disease Control & Prevention (www.cdc.gov/travel/blusheet.htm). A traveller without a legally required up-to-date certificate could possibly be vaccinated and detained in isolation at the port of arrival for up to 10 days, or even repatriated.

Yellow fever is spread by infected mosquitoes. Symptoms range from a flu-like illness to severe hepatitis (liver inflammation), jaundice and death. Vaccination must be given at a designated clinic and is valid for 10 years. It's a live vaccine and must not be given to immunocompromised people or pregnant women. For visitors to Kenya, vaccination is not mandatory (unless you're arriving from a country where yellow fever is present, such as Tanzania and Uganda) but is strongly recommended.

Traveller's Diarrhoea

Although it's not inevitable that you will get diarrhoea while travelling in Kenya, it's certainly possible. Diarrhoea is the most common travel-related illness, and sometimes simply dietary changes, such as increased spices or oils, are the cause.

Prevention To help prevent diarrhoea, avoid tap water. You should also only eat fresh fruits or vegetables if cooked or peeled, and be wary of dairy products that might contain unpasteurised milk. Although freshly cooked food can often be safe, plates or serving utensils might be dirty, so be highly selective when eating food from street vendors (ensure that cooked food is piping hot right through).

Treatment If you develop diarrhoea, drink plenty of fluids, preferably an oral rehydration solution containing water (lots), and some salt and sugar. A few loose stools don't require treatment but if you start having more than four or five stools a day, you should start taking an antibiotic (usually a quinoline drug, such as ciprofloxacin or norfloxacin) and an antidiarrhoeal agent (eg loperamide) if you are not within easy reach of a toilet. If diarrhoea is bloody, persists for more than 72 hours or is accompanied by fever, shaking chills or abdominal pain, seek medical attention.

Amoebic Dysentery

Contracted by eating contaminated food and water, amoebic dysentery causes blood and mucus in the faeces. It can be relatively mild and tends to come on gradually, but seek medical advice if you think you have the illness as it won't clear up without treatment (which is with specific antibiotics).

Giardiasis

Giardiasis, like amoebic dysentery, is caused by contaminated food or water. The illness usually appears a week or more after exposure to the parasite. It might cause only a short-lived bout of typical traveller's diarrhoea, but may cause persistent diarrhoea. Ideally, seek medical advice if you suspect you have giardiasis, but if you are in a remote area you could start a course of antibiotics.

Environmental Hazards

Heat Exhaustion

This condition occurs following heavy sweating and excessive fluid loss with inadequate replacement of fluids and salt, and is particularly common in hot climates when taking unaccustomed exercise before full acclimatisation.

Symptoms include headache, dizziness and tiredness. Dehydration is already happening by the time you feel thirsty – aim to drink sufficient water to produce pale, diluted urine.

Self-treatment: fluid replacement with water and/or fruit juice, and cooling by cold water and fans. The treatment of the salt-loss component consists of consuming salty fluids such as soup, and adding a little more salt to foods than usual.

Heatstroke

Heat exhaustion is a precursor to the much more serious condition of heatstroke. In this case there is damage to the sweating mechanism, with an excessive rise in body temperature; irrational and hyperactive behaviour; and eventually loss of consciousness and death. Rapid cooling by spraying the body with water and fanning the body is ideal. Emergency fluid and electrolyte replacement is usually also required by intravenous drip.

Insect Bites & Stings

Mosquitoes might not always carry malaria or dengue fever, but they (and other insects) can cause irritation and infected bites. Use DEET-based repellents, also effective against sand flies.

Scorpions are frequently found in arid or dry climates. They can cause a painful bite that is sometimes life-threatening. If you are bitten by a scorpion, seek immediate medical assistance.

Snake Bites

Basically, avoid getting bitten! Don't walk barefoot, and don't stick your hand into holes or cracks. If bitten, do not panic. Immobilise the bitten limb with a splint (such as a stick) and apply a bandage over the site, with firm pressure – similar to bandaging a sprain. Do not apply a tourniquet, or cut or suck the bite. Get medical help as soon as possible so antivenene can be given if needed. It will also help if you are able to provide doctors with a detailed description of the snake so that they can identify the species and treat you correctly.

TAP WATER

Never drink tap water unless it has been boiled, filtered or chemically disinfected (such as with iodine tablets). Never drink from streams, rivers and lakes. It's also best to avoid drinking from pumps and wells – some do bring pure water to the surface, but the presence of animals can still contaminate supplies.

Language

Swahili is the national language of Kenya (as well as Tanzania). It's also the key language of communication in the wider East African region. This makes it one of the most widely spoken African languages. Although the number of speakers of Swahili throughout East Africa is estimated to be more than 50 million, it's the mother tongue of only about 5 million people, and is predominantly used as a second language or a lingua franca by speakers of other African languages. Swahili belongs to the Bantu group of languages from the Niger-Congo family and can be traced back to the first millenium AD. It's hardly surprising that in an area as vast as East Africa many different dialects of Swahili can be found, but you shouldn't have problems being understood in Kenya (or in the wider region) if you stick to the standard coastal form, as used in this book.

Most sounds in Swahili have equivalents in English. In our coloured pronunciation guides, ay should be read as in 'say', oh as the 'o' in 'role', dh as the 'th' in 'this', and th as in 'thing'. Note also that the sound ng can be found at the start of words in Swahili, and that Swahili speakers make only a slight distinction between r and l – instead of the hard 'r', try pronouncing a light 'd'. In Swahili, words are almost always stressed on the second-last syllable. In our pronunciation guides, the stressed syllables are in italics.

BASICS

Jambo is a pidgin Swahili word, used to greet tourists who are presumed not to understand the language. If people assume you can speak a little Swahili, they might use the following greetings:

Hello. (general)	*Habari?*	ha·*ba*·ree
Hello. (respectful)	*Shikamoo.*	shee·ka·*moh*
Goodbye.	*Tutaonana.*	too·ta·oh·*na*·na
Good ...	*Habari za ...?*	ha·*ba*·ree za ...
morning	*asubuhi*	a·soo·*boo*·hee

afternoon	*mchana*	m·*cha*·na
evening	*jioni*	jee·oh·nee

Yes.	*Ndiyo.*	n·*dee*·yoh
No.	*Hapana.*	ha·*pa*·na
Please.	*Tafadhali.*	ta·fa·*dha*·lee
Thank you (very much).	*Asante (sana).*	a·*san*·tay (*sa*·na)
You're welcome.	*Karibu.*	ka·*ree*·boo
Excuse me.	*Samahani.*	sa·ma·*ha*·nee
Sorry.	*Pole.*	*poh*·lay

How are you?
Habari?   ha·*ba*·ree

I'm fine.
Nzuri./Salama./Safi.   n·*zoo*·ree/sa·*la*·ma/*sa*·fee

If things are just OK, add *tu* too (only) after any of the above replies. If things are really good, add *sana sa*·na (very) or *kabisa* ka·*bee*·sa (totally) instead of *tu*.

What's your name?
Jina lako nani?   jee·na la·*ko* koh *na*·nee

My name is ...
Jina langu ni ...   jee·na lan·goo nee ...

Do you speak English?
Unasema Kiingereza?   oo·na·*say*·ma kee·een·gay·*ray*·za

I don't understand.
Sielewi.   see·ay·*lay*·wee

WANT MORE?

For in-depth language information and handy phrases, check out Lonely Planet's *Swahili Phrasebook*. You'll find it at **shop.lonelyplanet.com**, or you can buy Lonely Planet's iPhone phrasebooks at the Apple App Store.

ACCOMMODATION

Where's a ...?	... iko wapi?	... ee·koh wa·pee
campsite	Uwanja wa kambi	oo·wan·ja wa kam·bee
guesthouse	Gesti	gay·stee
hotel	Hoteli	hoh·tay·lee
youth hostel	Hosteli ya vijana	hoh·stay·lee ya vee·ja·na

Do you have a ... room?	Kuna chumba kwa ...?	koo·na choom·ba kwa ...
double (one bed)	watu wawili, kitanda kimoja	wa·too wa·wee·lee kee·tan·da kee·moh·ja
single	mtu mmoja	m·too m·moh·ja
twin (two beds)	watu wawili, vitanda viwili	wa·too wa·wee·lee vee·tan·da vee·wee·lee

How much is it per ...?	Ni bei gani kwa ...?	nee bay ga·ne kwa ...
day	siku	see·koo
person	mtu	m·too
air-con	a/c	ay·see
bathroom	bafuni	ba·foo·nee
key	ufunguo	oo·foon·goo·oh
toilet	choo	choh
window	dirisha	dee·ree·sha

DIRECTIONS

Where's the ...?
... iko wapi?　　　　... ee·koh wa·pee

What's the address?
Anwani ni nini?　　　an·wa·nee nee nee·nee

How do I get there?
Nifikaje?　　　　　nee·fee·ka·jay

How far is it?
Ni umbali gani?　　　nee oom·ba·lee ga·nee

Can you show me (on the map)?
Unaweza　　　　　oo·na·way·za
kunionyesha　　　koo·nee·oh·nyay·sha
(katika ramani)?　　(ka·tee·ka ra·ma·nee)

It's ...	Iko ...	ee·koh ...
behind ...	nyuma ya ...	nyoo·ma ya ...
in front of ...	mbele ya ...	m·bay·lay ya ...
near ...	karibu na ...	ka·ree·boo na ...
next to ...	jirani ya ...	jee·ra·nee ya ...
on the corner	pembeni	paym·bay·nee
opposite ...	ng'ambo ya ...	ng·am·boh ya ...
straight ahead	moja kwa moja	moh·ja kwa moh·ja

KEY PATTERNS

To get by in Swahili, mix and match these simple patterns with words of your choice:

When's (the next bus)?
(Basi ijayo)　　　　(ba·see ee·ja·yoh)
itaondoka lini?　　　ee·ta·ohn·doh·ka lee·nee

Where's (the station)?
(Stesheni) iko　　　(stay·shay·nee) ee·koh
wapi?　　　　　wa·pee

How much is (a room)?
(Chumba) ni　　　(choom·ba) nee
bei gani?　　　　bay ga·nee

I'm looking for (a hotel).
Natafuta (hoteli).　　na·ta·foo·ta (hoh·tay·lee)

Do you have (a map)?
Una (ramani)?　　　oo·na (ra·ma·nee)

Please bring (the bill).
Lete (bili).　　　　lay·tay (bee·lee)

I'd like (the menu).
Nataka (menyu).　　na·ta·ka (may·nyoo)

I have (a reservation).
Nina (buking).　　　nee·na (boo·keeng)

Turn ...	Geuza ...	gay·oo·za ...
at the corner	kwenye kona	kway·nyay koh·na
at the traffic lights	kwenye taa za barabarani	kway·nyay ta za ba·ra·ba·ra·nee
left	kushoto	koo·shoh·toh
right	kulia	koo·lee·a

EATING & DRINKING

I'd like to reserve a table for ...	Nataka kuhifadhi meza kwa ...	na·ta·ka koo·hee·fa·dhee may·za kwa ...
(two) people	watu (wawili)	wa·too (wa·wee·lee)
(eight) o'clock	saa (mbili)	sa (m·bee·lee)

I'd like the menu.
Naomba menyu.　　na·ohm·ba may·nyoo

What would you recommend?
Chakula gani ni　　cha·koo·la ga·nee nee
kizuri?　　　　　kee·zoo·ree

Do you have vegetarian food?
Mna chakula　　　m·na cha·koo·la
bila nyama?　　　bee·la nya·ma

I'll have that.
Nataka hicho.　　　na·ta·ka hee·choh

Cheers!
Heri!　　　　　　　　hay·ree

That was delicious!
Chakula kitamu sana!　cha·koo·la kee·ta·moo sa·na

Please bring the bill.
Lete bili.　　　　　　lay·tay bee·lee

I don't eat ...	*Sili ...*	see·lee ...
butter	*siagi*	see·a·gee
eggs	*mayai*	ma·ya·ee
red meat	*nyama*	nya·ma

mutton	*nyama mbuzi*	nya·ma m·boo·zee
oyster	*chaza*	cha·za
pork	*nyama nguruwe*	nya·ma n·goo·roo·way
seafood	*chakula kutoka bahari*	cha·koo·la koo·toh·ka ba·ha·ree
squid	*ngisi*	n·gee·see
tuna	*jodari*	joh·da·ree
veal	*nyama ya ndama*	nya·ma ya n·da·ma

Key Words

bottle	*chupa*	choo·pa
bowl	*bakuli*	ba·koo·lee
breakfast	*chai ya asubuhi*	cha·ee ya a·soo·boo·hee
cold	*baridi*	ba·ree·dee
dinner	*chakula cha jioni*	cha·koo·la cha jee·oh·nee
dish	*chakula*	cha·koo·la
fork	*uma*	oo·ma
glass	*glesi*	glay·see
halal	*halali*	ha·la·lee
hot	*joto*	joh·toh
knife	*kisu*	kee·soo
kosher	*halali*	ha·la·lee
lunch	*chakula cha mchana*	cha·koo·la cha m·cha·na
market	*soko*	soh·koh
plate	*sahani*	sa·ha·nee
restaurant	*mgahawa*	m·ga·ha·wa
snack	*kumbwe*	koom·bway
spicy	*chenye viungo*	chay·nyay vee·oon·goh
spoon	*kijiko*	kee·jee·koh
with	*na*	na
without	*bila*	bee·la

Meat & Fish

beef	*nyama ng'ombe*	nya·ma ng·ohm·bay
chicken	*kuku*	koo·koo
crab	*kaa*	ka
fish	*samaki*	sa·ma·kee
hering	*heringi*	hay·reen·gee
lamb	*mwanakondoo*	mwa·na·kohn·doh
meat	*nyama*	nya·ma

Fruit & Vegetables

apple	*tofaa*	toh·fa
banana	*ndizi*	n·dee·zee
cabbage	*kabichi*	ka·bee·chee
carrot	*karoti*	ka·roh·tee
eggplant	*biringani*	bee·reen·ga·nee
fruit	*tunda*	toon·da
grapefruit	*balungi*	ba·loon·gee
grapes	*zabibu*	za·bee·boo
guava	*pera*	pay·ra
lemon	*limau*	lee·ma·oo
lentils	*dengu*	dayn·goo
mango	*embe*	aym·bay
onion	*kitunguu*	kee·toon·goo
orange	*chungwa*	choon·gwa
peanut	*karanga*	ka·ran·ga
pineapple	*nanasi*	na·na·see
potato	*kiazi*	kee·a·zee
spinach	*mchicha*	m·chee·cha
tomato	*nyanya*	nya·nya
vegetable	*mboga*	m·boh·ga

SIGNS

Mahali Pa Kuingia	Entrance
Mahali Pa Kutoka	Exit
Imefunguliwa	Open
Imefungwa	Closed
Maelezo	Information
Ni Marufuku	Prohibited
Choo/Msalani	Toilets
Wanaume	Men
Wanawake	Women

Other

bread	mkate	m·ka·tay
butter	siagi	see·a·gee
cheese	jibini	jee·bee·nee
egg	yai	ya·ee
honey	asali	a·sa·lee
jam	jamu	ja·moo
pasta	tambi	tam·bee
pepper	pilipili	pee·lee·pee·lee
rice (cooked)	wali	wa·lee
salt	chumvi	choom·vee
sugar	sukari	soo·ka·ree

Drinks

beer	bia	bee·a
coffee	kahawa	ka·ha·wa
juice	jusi	joo·see
milk	maziwa	ma·zee·wa
mineral water	maji ya madini	ma·jee ya ma·dee·nee
orange juice	maji ya machungwa	ma·jee ya ma·choon·gwa
red wine	mvinyo mwekundu	m·vee·nyoh mway·koon·doo
soft drink	soda	soh·da
sparkling wine	mvinyo yenye mapovu	m·vee·nyoh yay·nyay ma·poh·voo
tea	chai	cha·ee
water	maji	ma·jee
white wine	mvinyo mweupe	m·vee·nyoh mway·oo·pay

EMERGENCIES

| Help! | Saidia! | sa·ee·dee·a |
| Go away! | Toka! | toh·ka |

I'm lost.
Nimejipotea. — nee·may·jee·poh·tay·a

QUESTION WORDS

How?	Namna?	nam·na
What?	Nini?	nee·nee
When?	Wakati?	wa·ka·tee
Where?	Wapi?	wa·pee
Which?	Gani?	ga·nee
Who?	Nani?	na·nee
Why?	Kwa nini?	kwa nee·nee

Call the police.
Waite polisi. — wa·ee·tay poh·lee·see

Call a doctor.
Mwite daktari. — m·wee·tay dak·ta·ree

I'm sick.
Mimi ni mgonjwa. — mee·mee nee m·gohn·jwa

It hurts here.
Inauma hapa. — ee·na·oo·ma ha·pa

I'm allergic to (antibiotics).
Nina mzio wa (viuavijasumu). — nee·na m·zee·oh wa (vee·oo·a·vee·ja·soo·moo)

Where's the toilet?
Choo kiko wapi? — choh kee·koh wa·pee

SHOPPING & SERVICES

I'd like to buy ...
Nataka kununua ... — na·ta·ka koo·noo·noo·a ...

I'm just looking.
Naangalia tu. — na·an·ga·lee·a too

Can I look at it?
Naomba nione. — na·ohm·ba nee·oh·nay

I don't like it.
Sipendi. — see·payn·dee

How much is it?
Ni bei gani? — ni bay ga·nee

That's too expensive.
Ni ghali mno. — nee ga·lee m·noh

Please lower the price.
Punguza bei. — poon·goo·za bay

There's a mistake in the bill.
Kuna kosa kwenye bili. — koo·na koh·sa kwayn·yay bee·lee

ATM	mashine ya kutolea pesa	ma·shee·nay ya koo·toh·lay·a pay·sa
post office	posta	poh·sta
public phone	simu ya mtaani	see·moo ya m·ta·nee
tourist office	ofisi ya watalii	o·fee·see ya wa·ta·lee

TIME & DATES

Keep in mind that the Swahili time system starts six hours later than the international one – it begins at sunrise which occurs at about 6am year-round. Therefore, saa mbili sa m·bee·lee (lit: clocks two) means '2 o'clock Swahili time' and '8 o'clock international time'.

What time is it?
Ni saa ngapi? — nee sa n·ga·pee

It's (10) o'clock.
Ni saa (nne). — nee sa (n·nay)

Half past (10).
Ni saa (nne) na nusu. — nee sa (n·nay) na noo·soo

morning	*asubuhi*	a·soo·*boo*·hee
afternoon	*mchana*	m·*cha*·na
evening	*jioni*	jee·*oh*·nee
yesterday	*jana*	*ja*·na
today	*leo*	*lay*·oh
tomorrow	*kesho*	*kay*·shoh
Monday	*Jumatatu*	joo·ma·*ta*·too
Tuesday	*Jumanne*	joo·ma·*n*·nay
Wednesday	*Jumatano*	joo·ma·*ta*·noh
Thursday	*Alhamisi*	al·ha·*mee*·see
Friday	*Ijumaa*	ee·joo·*ma*
Saturday	*Jumamosi*	joo·ma·*moh*·see
Sunday	*Jumapili*	joo·ma·*pee*·lee

TRANSPORT

Public Transport

Which ...	*... ipi*	... ee·pee
goes to	*huenda*	hoo·*ayn*·da
(Mbeya)?	*(Mbeya)?*	(m·*bay*·a)
bus	*Basi*	*ba*·see
ferry	*Kivuko*	kee·*voo*·koh
minibus	*Matatu*	ma·*ta*·too
train	*Treni*	*tray*·nee
When's the	*Basi ...*	*ba*·see ...
... bus?	*itaondoka*	ee·ta·ohn·*doh*·ka
	lini?	*lee*·nee
first	*ya kwanza*	ya *kwan*·za
last	*ya mwisho*	ya *mwee*·shoh
next	*ijayo*	ee·*ja*·yoh
A ... ticket	*Tiketi moja*	tee·*kay*·tee *moh*·ja
to (Iringa).	*ya ... kwenda*	ya ... *kwayn*·da
	(Iringa).	(ee·*reen*·ga)
1st-class	*daraja la*	da·*ra*·ja la
	kwanza	*kwan*·za
2nd-class	*daraja la*	da·*ra*·ja la
	pili	*pee*·lee
one-way	*kwenda tu*	*kwayn*·da too
return	*kwenda na*	*kwayn*·da na
	kurudi	koo·*roo*·dee

What time does it get to (Kisuma)?
Itafika (Kisumu) ee·ta·*fee*·ka (kee·*soo*·moo)
saa ngapi? sa n·*ga*·pee

Does it stop at (Tanga)?
Linasimama (Tanga)? lee·na·see·*ma*·ma (*tan*·ga)

I'd like to get off at (Bagamoyo).
Nataka kushusha na·*ta*·ka koo·*shoo*·sha
(Bagamoyo). (ba·ga·*moh*·yoh)

NUMBERS

1	*moja*	*moh*·ja
2	*mbili*	m·*bee*·lee
3	*tatu*	*ta*·too
4	*nne*	*n*·nay
5	*tano*	*ta*·noh
6	*sita*	*see*·ta
7	*saba*	*sa*·ba
8	*nane*	*na*·nay
9	*tisa*	*tee*·sa
10	*kumi*	*koo*·mee
20	*ishirini*	ee·shee·*ree*·nee
30	*thelathini*	thay·la·*thee*·nee
40	*arobaini*	a·roh·ba·ee·nee
50	*hamsini*	ham·*see*·nee
60	*sitini*	see·*tee*·nee
70	*sabini*	sa·*bee*·nee
80	*themanini*	thay·ma·*nee*·nee
90	*tisini*	tee·*see*·nee
100	*mia moja*	*mee*·a *moh*·ja
1000	*elfu*	*ayl*·foo

Driving & Cycling

I'd like to	*Nataka*	na·*ta*·ka
hire a ...	*kukodi ...*	koo·*koh*·dee ...
4WD	*forbaifor*	fohr·ba·ee·fohr
bicycle	*baisikeli*	ba·ee·see·*kay*·lee
car	*gari*	*ga*·ree
motorbike	*pikipiki*	pee·kee·*pee*·kee
diesel	*dizeli*	dee·*zay*·lee
regular	*kawaida*	ka·wa·ee·da
unleaded	*isiyo na*	ee·*see*·yoh na
	risasi	ree·*sa*·see

Is this the road to (Embu)?
Hii ni barabara hee nee ba·ra·ba·ra
kwenda (Embu)? *kwayn*·da (aym·boo)

Where's a petrol station?
Kituo cha mafuta kee·*too*·oh cha ma·*foo*·ta
kiko wapi? *kee*·ko wa·pee

(How long) Can I park here?
Naweza kuegesha na·*way*·za koo·ay·*gay*·sha
hapa (kwa muda gani)? *ha*·pa (kwa *moo*·da ga·ni)

I need a mechanic.
Nahitaji fundi. na·hee·*ta*·jee foon·dee

I have a flat tyre.
Nina pancha. nee·na *pan*·cha

I've run out of petrol.
Mafuta yamekwisha. ma·*foo*·ta ya·*may*·*kwee*·sha

GLOSSARY

The following are some common words you are likely to come across when in Kenya.

abanyamorigo – medicine man

askari – security guard, watchman

bakshishi – tip (gratuity)

banda – thatched-roof hut with wooden or earthen walls or simple wood-and-stone accommodation

bao – traditional African board game

barabara – an avenue, highway, motorway or road

beach boys – self-appointed guides, touts, hustlers and dealers on the coast

bhang – marijuana

boda-boda – motorcycle or bike taxi

boma – village

bui-bui – black cover-all garment worn by Islamic women outside the home

cardphone – phone that takes a phonecard

chai – tea, but also a bribe

chang'a – dangerous homemade alcoholic brew containing methyl alcohol

choo – toilet; pronounced *cho*

dhow – traditional Arab sailing vessel

duka – small shop or kiosk selling household basics

fundi – repair man or woman who fixes clothing or cars, or is in the building trades; also an expert

gof – volcanic crater

hakuna matata – no problem; watch out – this often means there is a problem!

harambee – the concept of community self-help; voluntary fundraising; a cornerstone of Kenyatta's ideology

hatari – danger

hoteli – basic local eatery; sometimes also called simply 'hotel'

ito – wooden 'eyes' painted on a dhow to allow it to see obstacles in the water

jinga! – crazy!; also used as an adjective

jua kali – literally 'fierce sun'; usually an outdoor vehicle-repair shop or market

kachumbari – tomato-and-onion salsa

kali – fierce or ferocious; eg *hatari mbwa kali* – 'danger fierce dog'

kanga – printed cotton wraparound incorporating a Swahili proverb; worn by many women both inside and outside the home

KANU – Kenya African National Union

kifungua chupa – bottle opener

kikoi – striped cotton sarong traditionally worn by men

kiondo – woven basket

kitu kidogo – 'a little something'; a bribe

kofia – cap worn by Muslim men

KWS – Kenya Wildlife Service

lugga – dry river bed, mainly in northern Kenya

makonde – woodcarving style, originally from southern Tanzania

makuti – thatch made with palm leaves used for roofing buildings, mainly on the coast

malaya – prostitute

mandazi – a semisweet doughnut served warm, with lashings of milk and brown sugar

manyatta – Maasai or Samburu livestock camp often surrounded by a circle of thorn bushes

masala chai – tea with cardamom and cinnamon

mataha – mashed beans, potatoes, maize and green vegetables

matatu – public minibuses used throughout the country

matoke – mashed plantains (green bananas)

mboga – vegetables

miraa – bundles of leafy shoots that are chewed as a stimulant and appetite suppressant

mkate mayai – fried, wheat pancake filled with mincemeat and raw egg; literally 'bread eggs'

moran – Maasai or Samburu warrior (plural *morani*)

murram – dirt or part-gravel road

mursik – milk drink fermented with cow's urine and ashes

mwizi – a thief

mzee – an old man or respected elder

mzungu – white person (plural *wazungu*)

NARC – National Alliance Rainbow Coalition

Ng'oroko – Turkana bandits

Nissan – see *matatu*

nyama choma – barbecued meat, often goat

Nyayo – a cornerstone of Moi's political ideology, meaning 'footsteps'; to follow in the footsteps of Jomo Kenyatta

panga – machete, carried by most people in the countryside and often by thieves in the cities

parking boys – unemployed youths or young men who will assist in parking a vehicle and guard it while the owner is absent

pesa – money

Peugeot – shared taxi

pombe – Kenyan beer, usually made with millet and sugar

rafiki – friend; as in 'my friend, you want safari?'

rondavel – circular hut, usually a thatched building with a conical roof safari – 'journey' in Kiswahili

sambusa – deep-fried pastry triangles stuffed with spiced mincemeat; similar to Indian samosa

shamba – small farm or plot of land

shifta – bandit

shilingi – money

shuka – Maasai blanket

sigana – traditional African performance form containing narration, song, music, dance, chant, ritual, mask, movement, banter and poetry

sis – white Kenyan slang for 'yuck'

siwa – ornately carved ivory wind instrument, unique to the coastal region and often used for fanfare at weddings

sukuma wiki – braised or stewed spinach

Tusker – Kenyan beer

ugali – staple made from maize or cassava flour, or both

uhuru – freedom or independence

uji – thin, sweet porridge made from bean, millet or other flour

vitambua – small rice cakes resembling tiny, thick pancakes

wa benzi – someone driving a Mercedes-Benz car bought with, it's implied, the proceeds of corruption

wali – cooked rice

wali na kuku/samaki/nyama/ maharagwe – cooked white rice with chicken/fish/meat/beans

wananchi – workers or 'the people' (singular mwananchi)

wazungu – white people (singular mzungu)

LANGUAGE GLOSSARY

Behind the Scenes

SEND US YOUR FEEDBACK

We love to hear from travellers – your comments keep us on our toes and help make our books better. Our well-travelled team reads every word on what you loved or loathed about this book. Although we cannot reply individually to your submissions, we always guarantee that your feedback goes straight to the appropriate authors, in time for the next edition. Each person who sends us information is thanked in the next edition – the most useful submissions are rewarded with a selection of digital PDF chapters.

Visit **lonelyplanet.com/contact** to submit your updates and suggestions or to ask for help. Our award-winning website also features inspirational travel stories, news and discussions.

Note: We may edit, reproduce and incorporate your comments in Lonely Planet products such as guidebooks, websites and digital products, so let us know if you don't want your comments reproduced or your name acknowledged. For a copy of our privacy policy visit lonelyplanet.com/privacy.

OUR READERS

Many thanks to the travellers who used the last edition and wrote to us with helpful hints, useful advice and interesting anecdotes:

Benedek Csorba, Charlie Beard, Claire Pictor, David Pavlita, Elena Corona, Erinna Foley-Fisher, Hannah Hayden, Ivana Motylova & Martin Ondrusek, Keith McGhie, Mark Rowlatt, Matt Todd, Nora Nord, Patrícia Nabiço, Sam Pictor.

WRITER THANKS

Anthony Ham

Heartfelt thanks to Matt Phillips, my Africa friend and editor of long standing for continuing to entrust me with a corner of the earth I adore. Warmest thanks also to Peter Ndirangu Wamae, another companion of the African road over many years. Carole and Donald Boag were wonderful hosts in the Serengeti, and thanks to Mary Fitzpatrick for her enduring wisdom. To my family, Marina, Carlota and Valentina: thank you for sharing my love of Africa and for giving me so many special memories there.

Shawn Duthie

Thank you to my wife, Lucy, for looking after Kai while I had fun in Kenya. Many thanks also to the staff at Lonely Planet, particularly Matt Phillips, Neill Coen and Paul Clammer for all of the advice and support. In Kenya, my utmost thanks to everyone who helped with information and advice, especially Rob Andrew, Sophie Grant and my drinking buddies in North Horr.

Anna Kaminski

I'd like to thank Matt for entrusting me with the Kenyan coast, Stuart for the advice, and everyone who helped me along the way. In particular: Carol in Shela, Rachel on Manda, Arnold and Kesh in Lamu town, Paul in Watamu, Suleiman in Mombasa, my driver Fauz, my wonderful hosts in Malindi and Diani, my Kaya Kinondo guide, and the boat captains who got me to Paté and Kiwayu islands safely.

ACKNOWLEDGEMENTS

Climate map data adapted from Peel MC, Finlayson BL & McMahon TA (2007) 'Updated World Map of the Köppen-Geiger Climate Classification', *Hydrology and Earth System Sciences*, 11, 1633–44.

Cover photograph: A herd of zebras, Masai Mara, Kenya, Mohammed Alnaser/500px ©

THIS BOOK

This 10th edition of Lonely Planet's *Kenya* guidebook was researched and written by Anthony Ham, Shawn Duthie and Anna Kaminski. The Wildlife & Habitat chapter was written by David Lukas. The previous edition was written by Stuart Butler, Anthony Ham and Kate Thomas. The 8th edition was written by Stuart Butler, Anthony Ham and Dean Starnes, with contributing author David Lukas (Wildlife & Habitat).

This guidebook was produced by the following:

Destination Editor
Matt Phillips

Product Editors Hannah Cartmel, Elizabeth Jones, Sandie Kestell

Senior Cartographer
Diana Von Holdt

Book Designer Wibowo Rusli

Cartographer
Mick Garrett

Assisting Editors Janet Austin, Sarah Bailey, Judith Bamber, Michelle Bennett, Melanie Dankel, Rosie Nicholson, Kristin Odijk, Maja Vatrić

Cover Researcher
Naomi Parker

Thanks to Will Allen, Kate Chapman, Grace Dobell, Kate Kiely, Alison Lyall, Anne Mason, Lauren O'Connell, Lyahna Spencer, Tony Wheeler

Index

A

Aberdare National Park
152-4, **153**
Aberdares 17, 51, 150-4, **17**
accommodation 47,
49, 368-70, **23**, *see
also individual locations*
language 398
activities 24-5, 40-4, 47,
44, *see also individual
activities*
Adamson, George 17, 177
Adamson, Joy 92, 179
African Heritage House 65
African Shirt Company 199
African wild dogs 343
air travel 382-3, 385
airports 19
Akamba people 312
altitude, cooking at 172
Amboseli Elephants, The
186
Amboseli National Park 9,
185-7, **186**, **9**
amoebic dysentery 396
animals, *see individual
species*
antelopes 133
Rhino Valley 191
Saiwa Swamp National
Park 147
Shimba Hills National
Reserve 219-20
Arabuko Sokoke Forest
Reserve 247
archaeological sites
Gede Ruins 249
Hyrax Hill Prehistoric
Site 100
Kariandusi 99
Mnarani 240
Nabahani Ruins 267
Olorgesailie Prehistoric
Site 89

Map Pages **000**
Photo Pages **000**

Rock Paintings 133
Shanga 267
Takwa Ruins 266
Thimlich Ohinga
Archaeological Site 131
Archer's Post 274-5
area codes 19
art galleries, *see* museums
& galleries
arts 317-20, *see also
individual arts*
Aruba Dam 197-8

B

Baboon Cliffs 102
baboons 333, **332**, *see
also* primates
Arabuko Sokoke Forest
Reserve 247
Baboon Cliffs 102
Mt Elgon National Park
144
Mt Susua 92
Ol Donyo Sabuk National
Park 181
Samburu National
Reserve 277
Shimba Hills National
Reserve 219
Shompole Coservancy 90
Thomson's Falls 155
backpacking
Diani Beach 225
Baden-Powell, Lord 150
Baden-Powell's Grave 150
Bajun 256
ballooning 41, **44**
Masai Mara National
Reserve 116
Bamburi Beach 234-6
banditry 371
Baragoi 286-7
bargaining 370
Barghash, Sultan 256
bathrooms 378
bats 144, 146
Battuta, Ibn 206

beaches 22, 29, 46, 52
Bamburi Beach 234-6
Bofa Beach 240
Kenyatta Beach 234
Nyali Beach 231-4
Shanzu Beach 236
Shela Beach 263
Tiwi Beach 220-1
Watamu 17, **17**
beer 323, 324
bicycle travel, *see* cycling
Big Cat Diary 116
big cats
Mugie Sanctuary 157
Big Five 16, 27
Lumo Community Wildlife
Sanctuary 203
Ol Pejeta Conservancy
160
Saiwa Swamp National
Park 147
bilharzia (schistosomiasis)
393
birds **13**, **17**
bateleurs 344, **345**
buzzards 344
eagles 344, **345**
flamingos 347, **347**
lilac-breasted rollers
347, **347**
ostriches 347, **346**
secretary birds 344, **344**
storks 347, **346**
vultures 344, **344**
vulturine guineafowls 347
birdwatching 20, 25, 51, 52
Arabuko Sokoke Forest
Reserve 247
Chale Island 228
Gazi 228
Lake Baringo 108
Lake Bogoria 107
Lumo Community Wildlife
Sanctuary 203
Ol Pejeta Conservancy
161-2

Ruma National Park 131
safaris 35
Shrompole
Conservancy 90
black market 376-7
Blixen, Karen 64-5, 78, 86
boat travel 384, 386
boat trips 127, 248, *see also*
dhow trips
bongo
Mt Kenya Wildlife
Conservancy Animal
Orphanage 157
books 296, 304, 312, 318-20
environment 351, 365
field guides 354
history 303, 305
politics 306, 309
Rift Valley 100
wildlife 355, 359
women 316
Borana Conservancy 165
Borana people 313
border crossings 383-4
Lunga Lunga 231
Moyale 284
Born Free 17, 92, 177, 179
British colonisation 207
British East Africa 301-3
budget 19, 369, 374
budget safaris 37
Buffalo Circuit 99
Buffalo Springs National
Reserve 275-8, **276**
buffaloes 336
Masai Mara National
Reserve 113
Mt Elgon National Park
144
Segera Ranch 160
Solio Game Reserve 154
Bukusu Circumcision
Festival 140
bus travel 386, 387
bushbucks
Masai Mara National
Reserve 113

Mt Elgon National Park
144
business hours 19
butterflies 52
Kipepeo Butterfly Farm
250

C
Cairati, Giovanni Battista
208
camel derby 284-5
camel safaris 35
camping
Kalama Community
Wildlife Conservancy
278
Lake Elmenteita 99
Lake Magadi 89
Lake Nakuru National
Park 104
Maji Moto Group Ranch
120-1
Mara North Conservancy
121-3
Marsabit National Park
282
Masai Mara National
Reserve 116-19
Mathews Range 279
Mida Creek 248
Naboisho Conservancy
124
Olare-Orok Conservancy
125
Samburu National
Reserve 277
Shaba National Reserve
277
Shompole
Conservancy 90
camping safaris 22, 35-6
canoeing
Mida Creek 248
car travel 386-90
language 401
caracals 330, **330**
cattle 165, 365
caves 51
Cave of Skulls 203
Chyulu Hills National
Park 190-1
Mau Mau Cave 102
Mt Elgon National Park
144
Obsidian Cave 97
Shetani Caves 191
Shipton's Caves 172
Slave Caves 229
caving 190
cell phones 18, 378

cement factories 352
cemeteries
Baden-Powell's Grave
150
Central Highlands 51,
148-82, **149**
accommodation 148
climate 148
food 148
highlights 149
history 149-50
travel seasons 148
Central Island National
Park 294
Chaimu Crater 191
Chale Island 228
chang'a 324
cheetahs 20, 329, 358-9,
34, 329
Masai Mara National
Reserve 113
Naboisho Conservancy
124
children, travel with
46-9, **48**
chimpanzees
Ol Pejeta Conservancy
160
Chogoria 179-80
Chogoria Route 171
cholera 393
Christians 316
Chyulu Hills National Park
189-90
circumcision 140
climate 18, 24-5
climbing 41, 51, see also
hiking
Hell's Gate National
Park 98
Mt Kenya 167-8
Mt Longonot 89
coast 352
cocktails 324
coffee 323
coffee estates 69
Karunguru Coffee Estate
182
colobus monkeys 335,
334, see also
primates
Diani Beach 221
Kericho 135
Lake Elmenteita 99
Lake Naivasha 92
Loita Hills 121
Mt Elgon National Park
144
Ol Donyo Sabuk National
Park 181

Saiwa Swamp National
Park 147
colonialism 58, 207
conservancies &
conservation centres
360-1, 366
Borana Conservancy 165
Colobus Conservation
Centre 221
Il Ngwesi Group Ranch
165
Kalama Community
Wildlife Conservancy
278
Lamu Marine
Conservation Trust
266
Lekurruki Community
Ranch 166
Lewa Wildlife
Conservancy 162-5
Maa Trust 126
Maji Moto Group Ranch
120-1
Mara North Conservancy
121-3
Masai Mara Area Con-
servancies 123
Mbulia Conservancy 196
Mt Kenya Wildlife
Conservancy Animal
Orphanage 157
Mt Suswa
Conservancy 92
Mugie Conservancy 157
Naboisho Conservancy
123-4
Namunyak Wildlife
Conservancy 279
Ol Pejeta Conservancy
160-2
Olare-Orok Conservancy
124-5
Olderikesi Conservancy
125-6
Segera Ranch 160
Shompole
Conservancy 90
Siana & the
Southeastern
Conservancies 126-7
Soysambu
Conservancy 99
Tsavo Conservancy
199-200
West Gate Community
Conservancy 278-9
Wild Living 241
conservation 4, 123, 359-61
conservation projects 23
Amboseli 189
Big Life Foundation 189

East African Whale Shark
Trust 224
Elephant Research
Camp 186
Laikipia Wildlife Forum
154
Lion Guardians 189
Maasailand Preservation
Trust 189
Mwamba Field Study
Centre 243
Namunyak Wildlife
Conservancy 279
North Coast 241
Constant Gardner, The 74
consulates 373
Coriolis effect 157
costs 32-3, 369, 374
craft centres
Kazuri Beads & Pottery
Centre 65
Nanyuki Spinners &
Weavers 159
Shanzu Transitional
Workshop 236
credit cards 377
crime 371-2
crocodiles
Bamburi Beach 234
Mamba Village Crocodile
Farm 233
Masai Mara National
Reserve 114
Crying Stone of Ilesi 137
cultural centres
Bomas of Kenya 65
cultural safaris 36
culture 23, 315-16
currency 18
customs regulations 370
cycling 41, 385-6
Diani Beach 224
Hell's Gate National
Park 98
cycling tours
Ol Pejeta Conservancy
161

D
dangers, see safety
de Brazza's monkeys 335,
334
Mt Elgon National Park
16, 144
Saiwa Swamp National
Park 147
deforestation 355
democracy 296-7
dengue fever (break-bone
fever) 393

desertification 355
deserts 30, 348, 353
dhow trips 22, 224, **15**
Lamu Island 262, **44**
Mida Creek 248
dhows 265
Diani Beach 221-8, **223**
accommodation 224-6
activities 222-4
drinking & nightlife 227
festivals & events 224
food 226-7
information 227
sights 221-2
tours 224
travel to/from 227-8
diarrhoea 396
Dida Galgalu Desert 282
diphtheria 393
disabilities, travellers with 378-9
diving 22, 43
Diani Beach 223
Kilifi 240
Malindi 251
Wasini Island 230-1
Watamu 243
dog tracking 161
Donkey Sanctuary 257
Donovan, Alan 65
drinking water 396
drinks 323-4
driving, see car travel
drought 297
duikers
Arabuko Sokoke Forest Reserve 247
Mt Elgon National Park 144

E
East Africa Campaign 202
East African Safari Rally 25
Echo of the Elephants 186
ecological issues
Lake Baringo 109
Lake Victoria 129
Mara North Conservancy 122
economy 296
Egerton Castle 106
El Molo peoples 289, 314
Eldoret 140-2, **141**
electricity 373

Map Pages **000**
Photo Pages **000**

Elephant Cave 146
Elephant Research Camp 186
elephant shrews 52, 246
elephants 20, 339, 355-6, **9**, **11**, **48**, **327**, **338**
Amboseli National Park 9
Buffalo Springs National Reserve 275
Elkony Caves 146
Lewa Wildlife Conservancy 162
Masai Mara National Reserve 113
Mudanda Rock 198
Mugie Sanctuary 157
Naboisho Conservancy 124
Samburu National Reserve 275
Segera Ranch 160
Shompole Conservancy 90
Eliye Springs 293-4
Elsamere 92
Elsa's Grave 177
embassies 373
Embu 180-1, **180**
emergencies 19
language 400
endangered species 355-9
environment 351-61
environmental issues 297, 355-61
Lake Naivasha 95
equipment, trekking 43
Esoit Oloololo (Siria) Escarpment 114-16
etiquette 324, 373-4
events, see festivals & events
Ewaso Ngiro River 45, **39**, **349**
exchange rates 19, 377

F
fast food 325
Faza 268
female genital mutilation 316
Ferguson's Gulf 294
festivals & events 24-5, see also sporting events
Bukusu Circumcision Festival 140
East African Safari Rally 25
International Camel Derby 25

Kenya Fashion Week 69
Kenya Music Festival 25, 69
Lake Turkana Festival 24, 289
Lamu Cultural Festival 256
Lamu Painters' Festival 256
Lamu Yoga Festival 256
Lewa Safaricom Marathon 163
Maulid Festival 25, 256
Mombasa Carnival 25, 213
Mombasa Triathlon 213
Rhino Charge 25
Tusker Safari Sevens 25
field guides 354
films 296, 304, 320
first aid 392-3
fishing 43
Lamu Marine Conservation Trust 266
Shimoni 229
Wasini Island 231
Watamu 243
Flame Trees of Thika (Memories of an African Childhood), The 182
flamingos 50, 107
flower farming 95
flying lessons 41
flying safaris 36, 41
food 49, 321, see also individual locations
etiquette 324
language 325-6, 398-400
forests 352-3
fortresses
Lamu Fort 257
fossils 298-9
Funzi Island 228-9

G
Gabbra people 314
Galana River 197
Gallmann, Kuki 156
Gama, Vasco da 207, 250
gazelles 336, **337**
Buffalo Springs National Reserve 275
Solio Game Reserve 154
Gazi 228
Gede Ruins 249, 250, **28**
genets 343

geology
Marafa Depression 254
gerenuks 336, **336**
Buffalo Springs National Reserve 275
giardiasis 396
Gibe 3 hydroelectric dam 291
giraffes 61-3, 339, 358, **48**, **338**
Buffalo Springs National Reserve 275
Lake Nakuru National Park 102
Ruma National Park 131
Segera Ranch 160
Solio Game Reserve 154
gliding 41, see also individual locations
Gogo River Bird Sanctuary 62
Going Out 81
Grave of Denys Finch Hatton 86
Great Rift Valley 351, see also Southern Rift Valley
Great Rift Valley, The 92
Grevy's zebras 339, 357, **339**, see also zebras
Gusii people 311-12

H
habitat 327-50
Happy Valley 302
hartebeests
Mugie Sanctuary 157
Solio Game Reserve 154
Hatton, Denys Finch 86
He, Zhang 206
health 49, 392-6
insurance 392
planning 392
heat exhaustion 396
helicopter trips 154
Hell's Gate National Park 15, 97-8, **97**, **2**, **15**
hepatitis 393-4
High Altitude Training Centre 139
Highland Castle 172
hiking 21, 51
Archer's Post 274
Cherangani Hills 291
Chogoria 179
Koitoboss 144-5
Lirhanda Hill Lookout 138
Loroghi Hills Circuit 284

Mt Kenya 10
Mt Kenya National
  Park 169
Mt Koh 291
Mt Longonot 11
Mt Sekerr 291
Wei-wei Valley 291
hippos 340, **340**
  Bamburi Beach 234
  Lake Nakuru National
    Park 102
  Ol Pejeta Conservancy
    161
history 298-309
  British East Africa 301-3
  Independence 303-5
  Mombasa & the South
    Coast 205-6, 206-7
  Portugese arrival 300-1
  slavery 206, 300-1
  WWI 202
hitchhiking 390
HIV/AIDS 140, 315, 394
  Kiberia 74
hogs
  Mt Elgon National Park
    144
holidays 24-5
Homa Bay 130-1
horse riding 154
Hot Zone, The 146
House of Columns 251
Huxley, Elspeth 182
hyenas 343, **342**
  Solio Game Reserve 154

I
I Dreamed of Africa 156
Il Ngwesi Group Ranch 165
immigration 382
impalas
  Bamburi Beach 234
Indian people 315
infectious diseases 393-6
insurance 374-5
International Camel
  Derby 25
internet access 375
internet resources 19
  safaris 37
Isaaten Conservancy 126-7
Isiolo 271, 274, **274**
Islamic holidays 374
Islamic Party of Kenya 207
Island of War 207
Iten 139
itineraries 26-30, 34-5, **26**,
  27, **29**, **30**

ivory 356
Ivory-burning Site 61

J
jackals 343, **342**
  Masai Mara National
    Reserve 113
jewellery 320
juice 323
Jumba la Mtwana 236-7

K
Kakamega 137
Kakamega Forest 13, 137-
  40, **138**, **13**
Kalacha 290-1
Kalama Community Wildlife
  Conservancy 278
Kalenjin people 310
Kanderi Swamp 197
Kanyamaa Escarpment 131
Karen 78
Karen Blixen's House &
  Museum 64-5
Karura Falls Lookout 152
Kaya Kinondo 221
kayaking
  Watamu 244
Kenana Knitters 105
Kenya Fashion Week 69
Kenya Music Festival 25, 69
Kenya Wildlife Service
  (KWS) 359-60
Kenyan independence
  303-5
Kenyatta, Jomo 303-6
Kenyatta, President
  Uhuru 61
Kenyatta, Uhuru 307-9
Kericho 135-6, **136**
Kiambethu Tea Farm 86
Kibaki, Mwai 307-9
Kibera 74
Kifaru Ark 61, see also
  Nairobi National Park
Kikopey Nyama Choma
  Centre 96
Kikuyu people 310
Kilifi 240-2
Kilifi Creek 240
Kipepeo Butterfly Farm
  250
Kipungani 265
Kisii 134, **134**
Kisii people 311-12
Kisii soapstone 135
Kisite Marine National Park
  14, 230, **15**

Kisumu 127-30, **128**
  climate 110
  travel seasons 110
Kisumu Main Market 127
Kiswahili, *see* Swahili
Kitale 142-4, **143**
kitesurfing 45, 251
  Diani Beach 222
  Kipungani 265
  Malindi 251
Kiunga Marine National
  Reserve 269
Kiwayu Island 268-9
Komote 289
Kora National Park 177

L
Laikipia Plateau 13,
  154-66, **149**, **12**, see
  also Central Highlands
  accommodation 148
  conservation 156
  food 148
  highlights 149
Lake Nakuru National Park
  14, 102-5, **103**, **14**, **349**
Lake Turkana Festival
  24, 289
Lake Turkana Wind Power
  287
lakes 348, 353-4
  Lake Baringo 108-9
  Lake Bogoria 107-8
  Lake Elmenteit 98-100
  Lake Magadi 89
  Lake Naivasha 90,
    92-7, **93**
  Lake Nakuru 14, 102-5
  Lake Oloiden 94
  Lake Turkana 13, 288-
    94, **12**
  Lake Victoria 127-34
Lamu (island) 14, 52, 255-
  65, **255**
  climate 238
  food 238
  highlights 239
  travel seasons 238
Lamu Archipelago 255-69,
  239, **255**, **44**
  accommodation 238
  festivals & events 256
  getting to/from 256
Lamu Cultural Festival 256
Lamu Fort 257
Lamu Island 255-65
  festivals & events 256
  travel to/from 262

  travel within 262-3
Lamu Painters' Festival 256
Lamu (town) 256-63,
  258, **14**
  accommodation 257, 259
  food 259-60
  history 256
  information 261-2
  safety 261
  shopping 261
  sights 256-7
Lamu Yoga Festival 256
language 18, 300, 325-6,
  397-403
  courses 375
  glossary 402
Layeni 289
legal matters 376
Lekurruki Community
  Ranch 166
Leleshwa-Olarro
  Conservancy 126-7
leopards 20, 329, **328**
  Lake Nakuru National
    Park 102
Lewa Downs 163
Lewa Safaricom Marathon
  163
Lewa Wildlife Conservancy
  25, 162-5, **21**
LGBT+ travellers 375
lion tracking 161
lions 20, 116, 200, 329, 357,
  10, **328**, **350**, see also
  Big Five
  Lake Nakuru National
    Park 102
  Masai Mara National
    Reserve 113, 116
  Meru National Park
    177, 179
  Naboisho Conservancy
    124
  Ol Pejeta Conservancy
    161
  Samburu National
    Reserve 275
  Shompole
    Conservancy 90
  Solio Game Reserve 154
  Tsavo Conservancy
    199, 200
  Tsavo East National
    Park 197
  Tsavo National Park 10
liquor 324
literature, see books
local transport 390-1
lodges 22, 36, 164 see also
  individual locations

Lodwar 292-3
Loita Hills 121, 125
Longonot National Park 89-90
Loroghi Hills Circuit 284
Loyangalani 13, 288-90
Luhya people 311
Lunga Lunga 231
Luo people 311

M

Maa Trust 126
Maasai people 51, 116, 123, 312, 313, **5**
    Maa Trust 126
    Shrompole 90
Maasai homestays
    Masai Mara National Reserve 119
Maathai, Wangari 60
magazines 370
Maji Moto Group Ranch 120-1
malaria 394-5
Malindi 250-5, **252**
Malindi Marine National Park 250-1
Man-Eaters of Tsavo, The 199
Manda Island 266
maps 376
Mara Circuit 34
Mara North Conservancy 121-3
Mara River 113-14
Marafa Depression 254
Maralal 284-6, **285**
Maralal International Camel Derby 284-5
Mara Triangle 114-16
marathon running 25, 139
    Lewa Safaricom Marathon 163
Marburg virus 146
Marich 291-2
Marich Pass 291
marine parks 364
    Kisite Marine National Park 14, 230, **15**
    Kiunga Marine National Reserve 269
    Malindi Marine National Park 250-1
    Mombasa Marine National Park & Reserve 234-5

Watamu Marine National Park 243
markets
    City Market (Nairobi) 81
    Kibuye Market 130
    Kisumu Main Market 127
    Lamu Market 257
    Maasai Cattle Market 188
    Spice Market 209
    Tuesday Maasai Market 81
Marsabit 279-81, **281**
Marsabit National Park 281-2, **282**
Marsh Pride 116
Masai Mara National Reserve 9, 51, 112-20, **111**, **114**, **8**, **33**, **34**, **44**, **350**
    accommodation 116
    activities 116
    food 120
    information 120
    sights 113-17
    travel to/from 120
    travel within 120
masks 216
Matondoni 265
Matthews Range 279
Mau Mau rebellion 304
Maulid Festival 25, 256
Mbasa Island 132
Mbita 132-3
Mbulia Conservancy 196
measures 370
media 376
medical services 393
Meirelles, Fernando 74
Menengai Crater 102
meningococcal meningitis 395
Meru 176-7, **176**
Meru National Park 17, 177-9, **178**, **17**
Meru people 310-11
Merz, Anna 163
Mfangano Island 133-4
Mida Creek 247-8
migration
    animals 9, 51, 113
    birds 25, 196
Mijikenda 205
miraa 181
Mkwiro 230
Mnarani 240
mobile phones 18, 378
Moi, President Daniel arap 61, 306-7

Mombasa 52, 206-19, **205**, **208**, **210-11**, **232**
    accommodation 204, 213
    climate 204
    drinking & nightlife 216
    festivals & events 213
    food 204, 213-14
    highlights 205
    history 206-7
    information 217
    safety 217
    shopping 216-17
    tours 212
    travel seasons 204
    travel to/from 217
    travel within 218
Mombasa Carnival 25, 213
Mombasa Marine National Park & Reserve 234-5
Mombasa Republican Council 207
Mombasa Triathlon 213
money 18, 373, 376-7
    bargaining 370
    park entry fees 364
moneychangers 377
mongooses 343, **343**
monkeys, *see* primates
More Fire: How to Run the Kenyan Way 139
Mosque by the Sea 237
mosques
    Jamia Mosque 61
    Mandhry Mosque 209
    Mosque with the Two Mihrabs 267
mosquitoes 396
Moss, Dr Cynthia 186
motorcycle safaris 36
motorcycle travel 386-90
mountain biking 154, *see* cycling
mountaineering 41
mountains 348
Moyale 282-3, **283**
Mt Elgon 16, 144, **16**
Mt Elgon National Park 144-7, **145-6**
    birdwatching 144
Mt Kenya 10, 51, 157, **174**, **10**
Mt Kenya National Park 166-73, **170**, **174**, **21**
Mt Kenya Wildlife Conservancy Animal Orphanage 157
Mt Kulal 288
Mt Longonot 11, **11**

Mt Poi 279
Mt Susua 92
Mt Suswa Conservancy 92
Mtwapa 236-7
Mudanda Rock 198
museums & galleries 320
    Baden-Powell Museum 150
    Circle Art Gallery 60
    Elsamere 92
    Fort Jesus 207-9
    Gede Ruins 250
    Go-Down Arts Centre 60
    Karen Blixen's House & Museum 64-5
    Kitale Museum 143
    Kuona Trust Centre for the Visual Arts 60
    Lamu Museum 256
    Morani Information Centre 160-1
    Murals 100
    Railway Museum 60
    Taita Hills WWI Museum 201
    Tazama Art Gallery 60
    Treasures of Africa Museum 143
music 317-18
Muslims 316
Mwangi, Meja 319

N

Nabahani Ruins 267
Naboisho Conservancy 123-4
Nairobi 16, 50, 54-86, **55**, **56-7**, **62**, **66-7**, **72**, **2**, **16**
    accommodation 54, 69-75
    activities 68-9
    climate 54
    courses 69
    drinking & nightlife 78-80
    entertainment 80, 81
    festivals & events 69
    food 54, 75-8
    highlights 55
    history 55, 58-9
    information 81-4
    medical services 82-3
    safety 81-2
    scams 82
    shopping 80-1
    sights 59-65
    tours 69
    travel seasons 54

travel to/from 84-5
travel within 85-6
with children 47
Nairobi National Park 61,
65, **62**, **16**
Naivasha 90-1, **91**
Nakuru 100-2, **101**
Namanga 185
Namunyak Wildlife
Conservancy 279
Nanyuki 156-9, **158**
climate 148
travel seasons 148
Naro Moru 173-6
Naro Moru Route 169, 171
Narok 112
National Museum
(Nairobi) 59
national parks 27, 362-6
Aberdare National Park
152-4
Amboseli National Park
9, 185-7
Central Island National
Park 294
children 47
Chyulu Hills National
Park 189-90
Hell's Gate National Park
15, 97-8
Kisite Marine National
Park 14, 230
Kora National Park 177
Lake Nakuru National
Park 14, 102-5, **349**
Longonot National Park
89-90
Malindi Marine National
Park 250-1
Marsabit National Park
280, 281-2
Marsabit National
Reserve 280
Meru National Park 17,
177-9
Mombasa Marine
National Park &
Reserve 234-5
Mt Elgon National Park
144-7
Mt Kenya National Park
166-73, **170**
Nairobi National Park 61
Ndere Island National
Park 127
Ol Donyo Sabuk National
Park 181-2
Ruma National Park
131-2
Saiwa Swamp National
Park 147

Sibiloi National Park 292
South Island National
Park 288
Tsavo East National Park
197-9
Tsavo West National Park
10, 190-6
Watamu Marine National
Park 243
national reserves 362-
6, see also wildlife
reserves
Arabuko Sokoke Forest
Reserve 247
Kakamega Forest
Reserve 138
Lake Bogoria National
Reserve 107-8
Masai Mara National
Reserve 9, 51, 112-20,
111, **114**, **8**, **33**, **34**,
44, **350**
Samburu, Buffalo
Springs & Shaba
National Reserves
11, 275-8, **276**, **11**,
39, **349**
Shimba Hills National
Reserve 219-20
nature walks
Bamburi Forest Trails
235
Kakamega Forest Nature
Reserve 138-9
Lake Baringo 108
Masai Mara National
Reserve 116
Mida Creek 248
Nairobi Safari Walk 61
Ol Pejeta Conservancy
161
Ndere Island National
Park 127
Ndoto Mountains 279
newspapers 370
Ngangao Forest 203
Ngong Hills 86
Ngong Hills Racecourse 86
Ngulia Flyway 196
Ngulia Hills 191
Ngurunit 279
Njoro 105-6
North Coast 52, 238-269,
239
accommodation 238
climate 238
food 238
highlights 239
travel seasons 238
North Horr 290
Northern Circuit 34

Northern Kenya 52, 270-
94, **272-3**
accommodation 270
climate 270
food 270
highlights 272-3
travel seasons 270
Northern Migration 125
Nyahururu (Thomson's
Falls) 155-6, **155**
Nyali 231-4
Nyali Beach 232
nyama choma 77, 321
Nyeri 150-2

O
O'Connell, Brother Colm
139
Odinga, Raila 308-9
oil discovery 290
Ol Donyo Mara 287
Ol Donyo Nyiro 287
Ol Donyo Sabuk 181
Ol Donyo Sabuk National
Park 181-2
Ol Pejeta Conservancy
160-2
Olare-Orok Conservancy
124-5
Old Town (Mombasa) 207,
215, **215**
Olderikesi Conservancy
125-6
Olorgesailie Prehistoric
Site 89
Omani house 209
opening hours 19, 377
oryxes
Buffalo Springs National
Reserve 275
Solio Game Reserve 154
ostriches 347, **346**
Buffalo Springs National
Reserve 275
otters
Saiwa Swamp National
Park 147
Out of Africa 59, 64-5, 78,
86, 102
Out of Africa Lookout 102

P
paddle boarding
Mida Creek 248
Watamu 244
painting 320
Paradise Plains 113
parks & gardens

American Embassy
Memorial Garden 60
Arboretum 135
Uhuru Park 60
Parliament House 60-1
passports 382
Patas monkeys 160, 333,
333
Paté 268
Paté Island 266-8
phone codes 378
photography 377-8
plains zebras 339, **338-9**
planning 364, see also
individual regions
budgeting 18-19
calendar of events 24-5
children, travel with 46-9
internet resources 19
itineraries 26-30
Kenya basics 18-19
Kenya's regions 50-2
outdoor activities 40-4
safaris 31-9
travel seasons 18, 24-5
plastic bags 361
poaching 356
Ivory-burning Site 61
Laikipia 156
Lake Nakuru National
Park 106
Meru National Park 177
Point Lenana 169
politics 305-7, 314
Polo, Marco 206
population 297
Portuguese colonisation
205-6
postal services 378
primates
baboons 90, 92, 102,
144, 155, 219, 277,
333, **332**
colobus monkeys 92, 99,
121, 135, 144, 147, 181,
221, 335, **334**
chimpanzees 160
de Brazza's monkeys
16, 144, 147, 335, **334**,
335
Patas monkeys 160,
333, **333**
Sykes' monkeys 59, 138,
179, 181, 246
vervet monkeys 94, 135,
221, 333, **332**
private conservancies
see conservancies &
conservation centres
public holidays 374

R

rabies 395
radio 370
religion 297
Rendille people 314
renewable energy 361
restaurants 324, *see also* individual locations
Rhino Ridge 113
Rhino Valley 191
rhinoceroses 20, 24-5, 50, 340, 356-7, **14, 21, 341**
  Laikipia 154
  Lake Nakuru National Park 102
  Lewa Wildlife Conservancy 162, 163
  Meru National Park 177
  Ol Pejeta Conservancy 160
  Solio Game Reserve 154
Rift Valley 30
Rift Valley fever 395
rivers 348, 354
road accidents 373
Roaring Rocks 191
rock hyraxes 340, **341**
Rock Paintings 133
Rogo, Sheikh Ibrahim 207
Rojewero River 177
Rothschild's giraffes 358
rugby tournament 25
Ruma National Park 131-2
Running with the Kenyans 139
Rusinga Island 132-3

S

safaris 26, 31-9, 46
  Lewa Wildlife Conservancy 163
  Masai Mara National Reserve 116
  Meru National Park 178
  Mombasa 212
  Naboisho Conservancy 123-4
safety 370-3
  hitchhiking 390
  Laikipia 156
  Mugie Conservancy 157
sailing 45
  Kilifi 240

Map Pages **000**
Photo Pages **000**

Saiwa Swamp National Park 147
Samburu Area Conservancies 278-9
Samburu National Reserve 11, 275-8, **276, 11, 39, 349**
Samburu people 311
Saturday Nation 81
savannah 348, 351-2
scams 35, 372
scenic flights 41
school holidays 374
scorpions 396
sculpture 320
security 371
Segera Ranch 160
servals 330, **331**
Shaba National Reserve 275-8
Shanga 267
Shela 263-5
Sheldrick, David 63
Shimoni 229-30
Shompole Conservancy 90
Siana Conservancy 126-7
Sirimon Route 171
slavery 206, 300
smoking 370
snake bites 396
snakes
  Arabuko Sokoke Forest Reserve 247
  Bio-Ken Snake Farm & Laboratory 242
  South Island National Park 288
snorkelling 22, 25, 40, 43, 47
  Bamburi 234
  Diani Beach 222, 224
  Kiwayu Island 269
  Lamu Island 263
  Manda Toto Island 266
  Shimoni 229
  Tiwi Beach 220
  Wasini Island 230-1
  Watamu 243
Solio Game Reserve 154-5
Somalis 271
South Coast 52, 204-37, **205,** *see also* Mombasa
  accommodation 204
  climate 204
  food 204
  highlights 205
  travel seasons 204
South Horr 287

Southeastern Conservancies 126-7
Southeastern Kenya 51, 183-203, **184**
  accommodation 183
  climate 183
  food 183
  highlights 184
  travel seasons 183
Southern Rift Valley 50, 87-109, **88**
  accommodation 87
  climate 87
  food 87
  highlights 88
  travel seasons 87
souvenirs 216
spices 216
sporting events
  Tusker Safari Sevens 69
spotted hyenas 343, **342**
springs
  Eliye Springs 293-4
  Lake Bogoria 107
  Lake Magadi 89
  Maji Moto Group Ranch 120
  Mzima Springs 190
  Suam Hot Springs 146
Stoneham, Lieutenant Colonel 143
street children 371
street food 214
Swahili 29, 52, 205-6, 397-403
  glossary 402
  Mnarani 240
  time 400
Swahili architecture 251
  Paté Island 267
  Shanga 267
Swahili people 314
Swahili ruins 301
Sykes' monkeys 59, 138, 179, 181, 246

T

Taita Hills 202
Taita people 312
Takwa Ruins 266
taxes 378
tea 323
tea plantations
  Kiambethu Tea Farm 86
telephone services 18, 378
temples
  Jain Temple 209

Lord Shiva Temple 209
Swaminarayan Temple 212
terrorism 58, 373
  American Embassy Memorial Garden 60
textiles 320
Thika 182
Thimlich Ohinga Archaeological Site 131
Thiong'o, Ngũgĩ wa 316, 319
Thomson's Falls 155
Through Maasailand 146
time 18, 378
tipping 377
Tiwi Beach 220-1, **223**
toilets 378
Tom Mboya's Mausoleum 132
tourist information 378
tours 385
  Lamu 260
  Malindi 251
  Mida Creek 248
  Mombasa 212
  Mt Kenya National Park 169
tracks
  Loroghi Hills Circuit 284
  Southern Circuit 34
  Summit Circuit 171-2
traffic jams 191
transport
  language 401
travel to/from Kenya 382-5
travel within Kenya 385-91
trekking 41-2, *see also* hiking
  equipment 43
  Nanyuki 157
tribes 310-14, 315-16
Tsavo Conservancy
  lions 200
Tsavo East National Park 197-9, **192**
Tsavo River 194-5
Tsavo West National Park 10, 190-6, **192, 10, 28**
Tullow Oil 290
Turbi 283
Turkana people 313
turtles
  Lamu Marine Conservation Trust 266
  Watamu Marine National Park 243

Watamu Turtle Watch 242
Tusker Safari Sevens 25, 69
TV 370
typhoid 395

U
ugali 321
Umoja Village 274
Unesco World Heritage sites 353
Central Island National Park 294
Fort Jesus 207
Kaya Kinondo 222
Lamu Town 256-63
Lewa Wildlife Conservancy 163
Mt Kenya National Park 166-73
Sibiloi National Park 292
South Island National Park 288

V
vaccinations 392
Vasco da Gama Pillar 250
vegan travellers 325
vegetarian travellers 325
vervet monkeys 94, 135, 221, 333, **333**
visas 18, 284, 379-80
Voi 200-1
climate 183
travel seasons 183
volcanoes
Central Island National Park 294
Hell's Gate National Park 97-8
Menengai Crater 102
Mt Longonot 89
Mt Susua 92
Shetani Lava Flows 191
volunteering 380-1
Voorspuy, Tristan 156
Vuma Cliffs 240-2

W
Wainana, Binyavanga 319
walking, see hiking
walking tours 36

Gede Ruins 249
Lamu 260
war 297, 303-4
warthogs 340, **340**
Wasini Island 230-1
Watamu 17, 242-6, **244**, **17**
kitesurfing 243
Watamu Turtle Watch 242
water 323, 396
water sports
Wasini Island 230
Watamu 243-4
waterbucks 336, **337**
waterfalls
Chania Falls 182
Sheldrick Falls 219
Thika Falls 182
Thomson's Falls 155
weather 18, 24-5
weights 370
West Gate Community Conservancy 278-9
Western Highlands 134-47
Western Kenya 110-45, **111**
accommodation 110
climate seasons 110
food 110
highlights 111
travel seasons 110
Westlands 70, **72**
wetlands 30, 353-4
whitewater rafting 45
wild dogs 343, **342**
Laikipia 154
wildcats 330, **331**
wildebeests 336, **8**, **33**, **336-7**
Amboseli National Park 185
Masai Mara 112
Masai Mara National Reserve 113
wildlife 4, 9, 20-1, 23, 327-50
Laikipia 154
Maa Trust 126
Mt Kenya National Park 167
wildlife reserves 362-6, see also conservancies & conservation centres, conservation projects, zoos

Arabuko Sokoke Forest Reserve 247
Buffalo Springs National Reserve 275-8
Crater Lake Game Sanctuary 94
Crescent Island 92-4
David Sheldrick Wildlife Trust 63-4
Donkey Sanctuary 257
Giraffe Centre 61-3
Gogo River Bird Sanctuary 62
Haller Park 234
Kakamega Forest Reserve 138
Lumo Community Wildlife Sanctuary 202-3
Mara North Conservancy 121-3
Maralal National Sanctuary 284
Masai Mara National Reserve 112-20, **350**
Mombasa Marine National Park & Reserve 234-5
Mt Suswa Conservancy 92
Mugie Sanctuary 157
Ngulia Rhino Sanctuary 191-2
Rhino Sanctuary 178
Rukinga Wildlife Sanctuary 199-200
Samburu National Reserve 11, 275-8, **349**
Shaba National Reserve 275-8
Shimba Hills National Reserve 219-20
Shompole Conservancy 90
Shurr Community Conservancy 280
Soysambu Conservancy 99
Taita Hills Wildlife Sanctuary 201-2
Watamu Turtle Watch 242
wildlife watching 358
wind farms
Lake Turkana Wind Power 287

windsurfing 45
wine 323-4
women in Kenya 316
women travellers 381
Women Working Worldwide 95
wood carvings 216, 320
work 381
Wundanyi 203
WWI Battlefield Tours 202
WWII 303-4

Y
yellow fever 395
yoga
Lamu Yoga Festival 256
Watamu 244

Z
zebras 339, **28**, **31** see also Grevy's zebras, plains zebras
Buffalo Springs National Reserve 275
Laikipia 154
Masai Mara 112
Masai Mara National Reserve 113
Mugie Sanctuary 157
Segera Ranch 160
Zeitz Foundation 160
Zeitz, Jochen 160
zoos
Bio-Ken Snake Farm & Laboratory 242
Chimpanzee Sanctuary 160
Endangered Species Enclosure 160
Mamba Village Crocodile Farm 233
Mt Kenya Wildlife Conservancy Animal Orphanage 157
Nairobi Safari Walk 61
Snake Park 59

Map Legend

Sights

- Beach
- Bird Sanctuary
- Buddhist
- Castle/Palace
- Christian
- Confucian
- Hindu
- Islamic
- Jain
- Jewish
- Monument
- Museum/Gallery/Historic Building
- Ruin
- Shinto
- Sikh
- Taoist
- Winery/Vineyard
- Zoo/Wildlife Sanctuary
- Other Sight

Activities, Courses & Tours

- Bodysurfing
- Diving
- Canoeing/Kayaking
- Course/Tour
- Sento Hot Baths/Onsen
- Skiing
- Snorkelling
- Surfing
- Swimming/Pool
- Walking
- Windsurfing
- Other Activity

Sleeping

- Sleeping
- Camping
- Hut/Shelter

Eating

- Eating

Drinking & Nightlife

- Drinking & Nightlife
- Cafe

Entertainment

- Entertainment

Shopping

- Shopping

Information

- Bank
- Embassy/Consulate
- Hospital/Medical
- Internet
- Police
- Post Office
- Telephone
- Toilet
- Tourist Information
- Other Information

Geographic

- Beach
- Gate
- Hut/Shelter
- Lighthouse
- Lookout
- Mountain/Volcano
- Oasis
- Park
- Pass
- Picnic Area
- Waterfall

Population

- Capital (National)
- Capital (State/Province)
- City/Large Town
- Town/Village

Transport

- Airport
- Border crossing
- Bus
- Cable car/Funicular
- Cycling
- Ferry
- Metro station
- Monorail
- Parking
- Petrol station
- Subway station
- Taxi
- Train station/Railway
- Tram
- Underground station
- Other Transport

Routes

- Tollway
- Freeway
- Primary
- Secondary
- Tertiary
- Lane
- Unsealed road
- Road under construction
- Plaza/Mall
- Steps
- Tunnel
- Pedestrian overpass
- Walking Tour
- Walking Tour detour
- Path/Walking Trail

Boundaries

- International
- State/Province
- Disputed
- Regional/Suburb
- Marine Park
- Cliff
- Wall

Hydrography

- River, Creek
- Intermittent River
- Canal
- Water
- Dry/Salt/Intermittent Lake
- Reef

Areas

- Airport/Runway
- Beach/Desert
- Cemetery (Christian)
- Cemetery (Other)
- Glacier
- Mudflat
- Park/Forest
- Sight (Building)
- Sportsground
- Swamp/Mangrove

Note: Not all symbols displayed above appear on the maps in this book

OUR STORY

A beat-up old car, a few dollars in the pocket and a sense of adventure. In 1972 that's all Tony and Maureen Wheeler needed for the trip of a lifetime – across Europe and Asia overland to Australia. It took several months, and at the end – broke but inspired – they sat at their kitchen table writing and stapling together their first travel guide, *Across Asia on the Cheap*. Within a week they'd sold 1500 copies. Lonely Planet was born.

Today, Lonely Planet has offices in Franklin, London, Melbourne, Oakland, Dublin, Beijing and Delhi, with more than 600 staff and writers. We share Tony's belief that 'a great guidebook should do three things: inform, educate and amuse'.

OUR WRITERS

Anthony Ham

Nairobi, Southeastern Kenya, Southern Rift Valley, Western Kenya Anthony is a freelance writer and photographer who specialises in Spain, East and Southern Africa, the Arctic and the Middle East. In 2001, after years of wandering the world, Anthony finally found his spiritual home when he fell irretrievably in love with Madrid on his first visit to the city. Less than a year later, he arrived there on a one-way ticket, with not a word of Spanish and not knowing a single person in the city. When he finally left Madrid 10 years later, Anthony spoke Spanish with a Madrid accent, was married to a local and Madrid had become his second home. Now back in Australia, Anthony continues to travel the world in search of stories. Anthony also wrote the Plan, Understand and Survival Guide chapters for this book.

Shawn Duthie

Central Highlands & Laikipia, Northern Kenya Originally from Canada, Shawn has been travelling, studying and working around the world for the past 13 years. A love of travel merged with an interest in international politics, which led to several years of lecturing at the University of Cape Town and, now, as a freelance political risk consultant specialising in African countries. Shawn lives in South Africa and takes any excuse to travel around this amazing continent.

Anna Kaminski

South Coast, North Coast Originally from the Soviet Union, Anna grew up in Cambridge, UK. Her restless wanderings led her to settle briefly in Oaxaca and Bangkok and her flirtation with criminal law saw her volunteering as a lawyer's assistant in the courts, ghettos and prisons of Kingston, Jamaica. Anna has contributed to almost 30 Lonely Planet titles and has had her share of memorable experiences – from seeing the sun rise from the top of Borneo's Mt Kinabalu and riding all day on horseback to visit the Tsaatan reindeer herders on the border between Mongolia and Russia, to spending the night in a Latvian Soviet-era prison and attending a Vodou ritual in Haiti.

David Lukas

David wrote the Wildlife & Habitat chapter. He is a freelance naturalist who lives next to Yosemite National Park in California. He writes extensively about the world's wildlife, and has contributed to wildlife chapters for eight Lonely Planet guides on Africa, ranging from *Ethiopia* to *Africa*.

Published by Lonely Planet Global Limited
CRN 554153
10th edition – Jun 2018
ISBN 978 1 78657 563 0
© Lonely Planet 2018   Photographs © as indicated 2018
10 9 8 7 6 5 4 3 2 1
Printed in Singapore